NEWMAN AND HIS CONTEMPORARIES

The Young Newman (Courtesy of Birmingham Oratory)

NEWMAN AND HIS CONTEMPORARIES

EDWARD SHORT

t&t clark

Published by T&T Clark International
A Continuum Imprint
80 Maiden Lane, Suite 704, New York, NY 10038
The Tower Building, 11 York Road, London SE1 7NX

www.continuumbooks.com

British Library Cataloguing-in-Publication Data
A catalogue record for this book is available from the British Library

ISBN13: 978-0-567-02688-0 (Hardback)
ISBN13: 978-0-567-02689-7 (Paperback)

Library of Congress Cataloging-in-Publication Data
A catalog record for this book is available from the Library of Congress

Typeset by Fakenham Prepress Solutions, Fakenham, Norfolk NR21 8NN
Printed and bound in the United States of America

For My Mother

Table of Contents

"I have the responsibility of souls on me to the day of death ..."
John Henry Newman (14 June 1825)

"... It is my happiness in a matter of Christian duty ... to be guided simply by the decision and recommendation of the Holy See, the judge and finisher of all controversies ... My sole aspiration—and I cannot have a higher under the heavens—is to be the servant of the Vicar of Christ.... I have one resting point, just one, one plea which serves me in the stead of all direct argument whatever, which hardens me against censure, which encourages me against fear, and to which I shall ever come round, when I hear the question of the practicable and the expedient brought into discussion. After all, Peter has spoken ... Peter for eighteen hundred years has lived in the world ... If there ever was a power on earth who had an eye for the times, who has confined himself to the practicable, and has been happy in his anticipations ... such is the history of ages who sits on from generation to generation in the Chair of the Apostles as the Vicar of Christ and Doctor of his Church."
John Henry Newman, *Discourses on the Scope and Nature of University Education* (1852)

"... apparent opposites were in [Newman] blended. Thus, while his intellect was preeminently a logical one, and while it seemed to him impossible or immoral to discard the authority of logic, when plainly exercised within her legitimate domain, yet no one felt more deeply that both the heart and the moral sense possess their own secret tribunals in matters of reasoning as well as of sentiment... . The logical faculty was in his case most fortunately supplemented by an expansive imagination, which grasped thoughts immeasurably beyond the range of the mere logician... . Another most remarkable union in Newman of qualities commonly opposed to each other, was that of dauntless courage with profound thoughtfulness. The men of thought and study are often timid men ... indolent and averse to action ... In Newman there existed the rare union of the contemplative mind and the heroic soul."
Aubrey de Vere, *Recollections of Aubrey de Vere* (1897)

"I wonder, when the great day comes when all hearts are open, how many souls will have been moulded and saved through your words?"
Lady Herbert to John Henry Newman (30 June 1874)

Preface

In *The Roundabout Papers*, Thackeray's exuberant farewell to the periodical essay that he had done so much to enliven, he recalled how:

> Alexandre Dumas describes himself, when inventing the plan of a work, as lying silent on his back for two whole days on the deck of a yacht in a Mediterranean port. At the end of the two days he arose and called for dinner. In those two days he had built his plot. He had moulded a mighty clay, to be cast presently in perennial brass. The chapters, the characters, the incidents, the combinations were all arranged in the artist's brain ere he had set a pen to paper.[1]

Enviable Dumas! If I ever had such a thorough outline in mind it somehow went missing when I put pen to paper. Still, I have tried to be faithful to what prompted my undertaking this project in the first place, and that was to show Newman in relation to his contemporaries in order to show how much his personal influence meant to them, even to such contemporaries as Gladstone, Thackeray and Matthew Arnold, who had no intention of adopting his faith. Too many remain unfamiliar with Newman and I thought, in my missionary way, that if I could show how much he fascinated his own contemporaries, more of my contemporaries might be moved to see for themselves what a good and holy man he was, a man whose "gaiety of heart," as John Hungerford Pollen once wrote, "shed cheerfulness as a sunbeam sheds light."[2]

The criteria I followed in choosing my contemporaries were straightforward: I wanted contemporaries who were interested in Newman but also of interest in themselves. Of course, I left out hundreds who might have been covered in any book entitled *Newman and His Contemporaries*, but I had to keep within a reasonable word count and I could scarcely write about all of the contemporaries Newman influenced or by whom he was influenced. To write that book I would have needed several lifetimes. So I chose a limited number of well-known and not so well-known contemporaries, all of whom illustrate the vitality of Newman's influence.

Many assisted me with the genesis, research, writing and revising of this book. My father, John Francis Short, introduced me to the works of Cardinal Newman when I was a boy and always spoke of the gift of the Catholic Faith—what Newman called "the pearl of great price" —with useful lucidity. Father Ian Ker, the author of the definitive life and several other good books on Newman, generously read many of the chapters in draft and made comments that were as unsparing as they were helpful, though I cannot be sure that I have managed to amend all that he found amiss. Father Dermot Fenlon also read drafts of certain chapters and made many trenchant comments. Brother Lewis Berry carefully scanned the splendid photograph of Newman by the great photographer Herbert Rose Barraud (1845–1896) that adorns my cover. Henry Carrigan, Jr., now Senior Editor of Northwestern University Press, first contracted with me to write this book when he was North American Publisher at Continuum; I trust what I have done amuses him, if only from afar. Cynthia Read of Oxford University Press was full of support and good counsel. Brother Francis J. McGrath, FMS, the most recent editor of Newman's *Letters and Diaries*, as well as his uncollected sermons, gave me vital and generous assistance. Father George Rutler, Pastor of Church of Our Saviour in New York City, explained to me why Baron von Hügel always found Newman melancholy. Dr. Michael Alexander, the former head of the English Department at St. Andrews, read my chapter on Gladstone and made helpful suggestions. Paul Shrimpton of Magdalen College School, Oxford, gave me the benefit of his insights into book writing. Dr. Colin Barr, Professor of History at Ave Maria University, gave me advice that was at once scholarly and astute. Dr. Tracey Rowland, the author of two brilliant books on Pope Benedict XVI, dissuaded me from changing my name and joining the French Foreign Legion. D. J. Taylor, the biographer of Orwell, Thackeray and the Bright Young Things, advised me on Thackeray and the Garrick Club Affair. Dr. Craig Raine, Fellow of New College, Oxford, gave me kind words of support over that wonderful cider his College serves in their elegant silver drinking cups. Seth Lipsky, Editor-in-Chief of the irreplaceable *New York Sun* gave much good-hearted support. My dear friends, Jack and Nuala Scarisbrick, listened charitably to my hopes and fears with regard to this long-gestating book and gave reassuring counsel. Dr. Timothy Larsen of Wheaton College generously shared with me his lively views on Pusey's scholarly interest in the Bible, as well as an excellent essay on Huxley. Donal Fenlon, Librarian of the Royal Society of Antiquaries of Ireland gave me kind assistance. Christina Deane of the University of Virginia Library kindly scanned the *Vanity Fair* prints of Matthew Arnold, Henry Edward Manning and Pius IX included among my illustrations. The New York Public Library offered me efficient assistance with my research into the work of Richard Holt Hutton. Eileen Gunn, Chief Executive of the Royal Literary Fund in Johnson's Court, gave me kind and effective assistance with the application that Emily Bowles made to the Fund in her impecunious old age. Dr. Arnold Hunt, Curator of Historical Manuscripts at The British Library, generously supplied me with a copy of Miss Bowles's case file. The Dominican Sisters of Hawthorne gave me the grace of their prayers, as well as stalwart support. Father Aquinas Guilbeau, O.P. gave me the grace of his good company and prayers. Sister Helena Mayer, SHCJ, Archivist of the Society of the Holy Child Jesus, gave me indispensable help, as did Sister Elizabeth Mary Strub, SHCJ, who shared with me her work on Emily Bowles. Kim Levicki at Pro-Quest gave me free access to their *Spectator* archive, which was crucial for my chapter on Richard Holt Hutton. Philip Terzian, Literary Editor of *The Weekly Standard*, gave me generous and kind support, as did John Wilson of *Books & Culture* and Maria McFadden and Anne Conlon of the *Human Life Review*. James MacGuire of the Portsmouth Institute set me thinking about Newman and the Americans. Robert Crotty and the Guild of Catholic Lawyers showed friendly interest in my lucubrations, as did Frank Nugent of Hatchards. I should also like to express special thanks to Toby Short for his prayers and good wishes. Julieta Schiffino, who shares a birthday with Shakespeare cheered me on when I needed cheering. Stella and Heinz Becker kept me always in their prayers and good wishes, as did Cecilia Hernandez. I am also grateful to Barbara Weston for her generous support. Kim Storry of Fakenham Prepress Solutions in faraway Norfolk gave me admirably serene, efficient assistance. I am also grateful to her colleague David Defew, who kept the whole boiling on schedule. Tom Kraft, Anna Turton, Katie Gallof and Nicole Elliott at Continuum were also wonderfully helpful. Louise Dugdale did a brilliant job designing the book's cover. Nick Fawcett gave me the benefit of his excellent copy-editing skills. And Susan Tricklebank helped map out the index.

Lastly, I am grateful to my darling wife Karina, who came to share my love for the wonderful saint who inspired this book. Without her love and faith, her forbearance and encouragement, I should never have been able to begin or finish it. Despite this bountiful help, all errors in what follows, all solecisms and all stupidities, are mine and mine alone.

Edward Short
Astoria-Woodside-Astoria
2004–2010

Introduction

The literary critic and biographer Mona Wilson once began an introduction to a selection of Samuel Johnson's prose and poetry with a memorable disclaimer. "I shall say nothing of Johnson's life. No one should read even a selection from his writings who is not already familiar with the man. Boswell must come first. This is not to say that he is greater than his writings, or that they are only interesting because he wrote them, but they are the utterances of the whole man: no one else could have written them."[1] This is true of Newman as well. Before reading him, we need to know something of the man himself because his work is the unique expression of a figure of unusual integrity.

John Henry Newman was born on 21 February 1801 at 80 Old Bond Street in the City of London. A plaque hangs at the Visitor's Entrance to the London Stock Exchange marking the spot where his birthplace stood. A month and a half after his birth, Vice-Admiral Horatio Nelson won the battle of Copenhagen, the hardest fought of all his victories. Later, in 1805, Newman vividly recalled candles burning to celebrate Nelson's victory at Trafalgar. Newman's mother was of French Huguenot stock and his father was a banker in the City. He had two brothers and three sisters. As I show in a forthcoming book, *Newman and His Family*, it was by addressing his siblings' respective religious difficulties that Newman learned to address those of his contemporaries. In 1808 he attended Ealing School, where he was greatly influenced by the classical master, Walter Mayers (1790–1828), a moderate Evangelical who introduced him to the works of the great biblical commentator Thomas Scott (1747–1821), the deeply practical character of whose writings Newman would emulate in his own writings. Mayers also impressed on Newman one basal aspect of Christianity, and that was the primacy of dogma. "When I was fifteen (in the autumn of 1816)," Newman wrote in the *Apologia*, "a great change of thought took place in me. I fell under the influence of a definite Creed, and received into my intellect impressions of dogma, which, through God's mercy, have never been effaced or obscured. Above and beyond the conversations and sermons of the excellent man, the Rev. Walter Mayers, of Pembroke College, Oxford, who was the human means of this beginning of divine faith in me, was the effect of the books which he put into my hands, all of the school of Calvin."[2] In 1817, Newman entered Trinity College, where one of his tutors was the legendary Thomas Short (1789–1879), who lectured in Aristotle's Rhetoric. After he passed the age at which Aristotle says that man's powers are at their best, Short amused generations of undergraduates by observing, when he came to the relevant passage, "In those hot climes, you know, people came to their

1

acme much sooner than with us."[3] Despite Newman's poor showing in his final examination, Short was convinced that he could redeem himself and later recommended that he sit for the Oriel fellowship, to which he was duly elected in 1822. In 1825, Newman was ordained a priest. In 1828, he became Vicar of St. Mary's, Oxford where he gave the sermons that would stay with those who heard them for the rest of their lives. The discriminating Scot, J. C. Shairp, later the Oxford Professor of Poetry, who would become a good, if critical friend of Clough, left behind a vivid recollection of the sermons.

> Sunday after Sunday, month by month, year by year, they went on, each continuing and deepening the impression the last had made. As the afternoon service at St. Mary's interfered with the dinner-hour of the colleges, most men preferred a warm dinner without Newman's sermon to a cold one with it, so the audience was not crowded—the large church little more than half-filled .... About the service, the most remarkable thing was the beauty ... of Mr. Newman's voice, as he read the Lessons. It seemed to bring new meaning out of the familiar words .... Here was no vehemence, no declamation, no show of elaborated argument ... .[4]

This shunning of all declamatory effect was in keeping with Newman's humility. Although a brilliant man, he was never a pompous man. Nor was he intent on showing how clever he was. Some have suggested that he was egotistical, but the interest he took in himself was free of vainglory. Before converting, he wrote to his beloved Aunt Elizabeth, after visiting his grandmother's house in Fulham, where he had spent so many happy days as a child, "Alas my dear Aunt, I am but a sorry bargain, and perhaps if you knew all about me, you would hardly think me now worth claiming ..." By the same token, he was quick to point out, "Whatever good there is in me, I owe, under grace, to the time I spent in that house, and to you and my dear Grandmother, its inhabitants."[5] If Newman was an egotist, he was a peculiarly self-effacing one, knowing as he did that "where the thought of self obscures the thought of God, prayer and praise languish ..."[6]

As I show in my final chapter, Newman was intent on preserving as full a record of his life as possible to confute those who might try to misrepresent it. Then, again, the historian in him could not fail to see that there was a useful tale in his own persistent resolve to live the devout life, especially for the English people, who had all but lost the sense of what sanctity means. In this respect, it is amusing to read the testimonials of Oratorians in Newman's *Positio*, for nearly all of them remark the discomfiture that even the mention of sanctity caused parishioners and Oratorians alike.[7] The interest Newman took in his thoughts and feelings, his fortunes and misfortunes, was not egotistical but documentary. He might have been hesitant to draw parallels between his own life and the lives of the saints but they were unavoidable. In a memorandum regarding his *Lives of the English Saints*, he shed light on what he saw as the uses of documented sanctity. "The saints are the glad and complete specimen of the new creation which our Lord brought into the moral world, and as the

'the heavens declare the glory of God' as Creator, so are the Saints proper and true evidence of the God of Christianity, and tell out into all lands the power and grace of Him who made them." Moreover, Newman saw how documented sanctity could change hearts. "The exhibition of a person, his thoughts, his words, his acts, his trials, his features, his beginnings, his growth, his end, have a charm to every one; and where he is a Saint they have a divine influence and persuasion, a power of exercising and eliciting the latent elements of divine grace in individual readers, as no other reading can have." Indeed, Newman was convinced that "the Lives of the Saints are one of the main and special instruments, to which, under God, we may look for the conversion of our countrymen at this time."[8] That Newman did not consider himself a saint was emblematic of his humility; in one prayer he cries out, "O my God! what am I but a parcel of dead bones, a feeble, tottering, miserable being, compared with Thee!" Nonetheless, the sanctity he documented in his own long life speaks for itself.[9]

Shairp certainly understood why Newman's life merited close study—even by the man who lived it. "The look and bearing of the preacher were as of one who dwelt apart, who, though he knew his age well, did not live in it. From his seclusion of study, and abstinence, and prayer, from habitual dwelling in the unseen, he seemed to come forth that one day of the week to speak to others of the things he had seen and known."[10] This was an important point. One of the reasons why Newman fascinated his contemporaries is precisely because he did not share their worldly preoccupations. Yes, he paid attention to what was happening in England and in Europe: the journalism he wrote for various Tractarian and Catholic papers demonstrates what a well-informed, critical interest he took in political, social and imperial affairs. He was a dutiful and beloved parish priest who never neglected the souls under his charge. He had many friends and was himself a considerate, loyal friend. But he lived outside the world and only entered it to reaffirm the truths of religion. His sermons were the most immediate means with which he accomplished this, and for an introduction to his Anglican sermons, the literary critic Eric Griffiths is one of the best guides.

Newman had an acute suspicion of the workings of imagination in the religious life, of those who 'mix up the Holy Word of God with their own idle imaginings.' … He specifically mistrusts the power of imagination to doll up religious life and deliver it over as a toy for the delectation of a consumer who then 'appreciates' it rather than being judged by it. The sermons persistently warn against religious allure: 'Men admire religion, while they can gaze on it as a picture. They think it lovely in books;' 'Many a man likes to be religious in graceful language;' 'I am much opposed to certain *religious* novels … they lead men to cultivate the religious affections separate from religious practice;' 'It is beautiful in a picture to wash the disciples' feet; but the sands of the real desert have no lustre in them to compensate for the servile nature of the occupation.' The danger of whetting a taste for religion is that, once aroused, it leads people to consider religion as a matter of taste: they adopt the 'notion that, when they retire from the business of their temporal calling, then they may (in a quiet, unexceptionable way of course) consult their own tastes and likings.' Even the pious delight of his under-graduate audience, their very interest in him, might turn out in a parodic reversal of his hopes and intention to be complicit with that liberalism and doctrinal indifferentism against which he preached …[11]

In 1832, after completing his first book, *The Arians of the Fourth Century*, Newman toured the Mediterranean with his dear friend Hurrell Froude and his High Church father, Archdeacon Froude, visiting Gibraltar, Malta, the Ionian Islands, Sicily, Naples, and Rome, where he was impressed by the devoutness of the Roman Catholic faithful and the power of the Roman Catholic liturgy, though he continued to regard the Roman Catholic Church as "crafty," "polytheistic," "degrading," and "idolatrous."[12] Whether as an Anglican or a Catholic, Newman never minced his words.

For all of his Protestant prejudices, Newman found Rome fascinating. Many Victorian Anglicans left behind lively accounts of their first encounters with the eternal city. Dickens, after attending Mass in Rome, recalled how "Dotted here and there, were little knots of friars … in their coarse brown dresses and peaked hoods, making a strange contrast to the gaudy ecclesiastics of higher degree, and having their humility gratified to the utmost, by being shouldered about, and elbowed right and left, on all sides. Some of these had muddy sandals and umbrellas, and stained garments: having trudged in from the country. The faces of the greater part were as coarse and heavy as their dress; their dogged, stupid, monotonous stare at all the glory and splendour, having something in it, half miserable and half ridiculous." The Mass itself left less an impression on him. "There was certainly nothing solemn or effective in it; and certainly very much that was droll and tawdry," though he was, he admitted, moved by the "raising of the Host, when every man in the guard dropped on one knee instantly, and dashed his sword on the ground," which he considered had a "fine effect."[13] But no account of Rome was as rich and complex as Newman's. After attending his first Mass, he wrote to his mother, whose own Huguenot Protestantism was unshakable: "as I looked on, and saw … the Holy Sacrament offered up, and the blessing given, and recollected I was in church, I could only say in very perplexity my own words, 'How shall I name thee, Light of the wide west, or heinous error-seat?'"[14] In April 1833 when the Froudes left Rome for France, Newman decided to return to Sicily by himself, which, as he wrote, "filled me with inexpressible rapture, and to which (in spite of dirt and other inconveniences) I feel drawn as by a loadstone."[15] Here is one of those episodes in Newman's life which the biographer dismissive of hagiography will find problematic. Why was Newman so drawn to this place? Why did he insist on leaving the Froudes and going there alone? He says himself that he was "drawn by a strange love of Sicily to gaze upon its cities and its mountains."[16] But clearly there was something else that drove him to make this solitary, risky sojourn. It was not simply love of Sicily or love of beauty or a traveler's whim. Whether he realized it or not, Newman was a pilgrim in Italy, not a tourist. What are those lines by T. S. Eliot from *Four Quartets*?

In order to arrive at what you do not know
    You must go by a way which is the way of ignorance
In order to possess what you do not possess
    You must go by the way of dispossession
In order to arrive at what you are not
    You must go through the way in which you are not …[17]

At Leonforte, when Newman fell seriously ill with typhoid fever, he repeated aloud, "I have not sinned against light." Near death, he was convinced that he would be spared death. In the lucid intervals of fever he told himself not once but many times: "God has work for me."[18] Biography alone cannot make sense of these things. In a *Rambler* piece on the life of Saint John Chrysostom (1859), Newman wrote that what readers wanted was "to trace and study … the real, hidden but human life, or the *interior* of such glorious creations of God …"[19] To get at the essence of Newman's "real, hidden but human life" we must similarly avail ourselves of the resources of hagiography, without confusing hagiography with panegyric.

After recovering from fever, with the help of a loyal Neapolitan servant named Gennaro, who had been a sailor aboard the *Victory* at the Battle of Trafalgar, Newman sailed from Palermo to Marseille on an orange boat. While becalmed in the Straits of Bonifacio, he wrote the poem that expresses so movingly his trust in the Light that meant so much to him.

    LEAD, Kindly Light, amid th' encircling gloom,
      Lead Thou me on!
    The night is dark, and I am far from home—
      Lead Thou me on!
    Keep Thou my feet; I do not ask to see
    The distant scene,—one step enough for me.

When Newman arrived back in England in July of 1833, John Keble preached his famous assize sermon "On National Apostasy," which Newman always regarded as the start of the Oxford Movement. Advanced by a series of tracts, the Movement became known as Tractarianism. Newman, together with John Keble, Hurrell Froude and Edward Pusey, sought to reinvigorate the Church of England by returning it to its apostolic roots. In this regard, D. C. Somervell was right to recognize that "Its original appeal was the vocational pride of the clergy, and its principal adherents have always been found among the clergy and what are conveniently called the clerically-minded laity."[20] Froude called the Tractarians "ecclesiastical agitators."[21] One of the ironies of the Oxford Movement was that Newman was eventually condemned by precisely the same bishops whose episcopal authority he worked so brilliantly to advance. Eventually, in seeking to defend Anglicanism, Newman came to see that it was indefensible. In September, 1843, he resigned the living of St. Mary's and in October, 1845, he resigned his Oriel fellowship.

In converting to Roman Catholicism in 1845, Newman left behind not only Oriel and St. Mary's but an entire English way of life. In *Vanity Fair*, the profile of Newman accompanying Spy's caricature confirmed how "This secession came upon the Anglican Church as a crushing blow under which, as Mr. Disraeli said, 'it reeled and from which it has not recovered and never will,' while the Roman Catholics declared it to be, as it indeed it was, 'the most momentous conversion which has occurred since that of Queen Christina of Sweden.'"[22] In my chapters on Keble and Pusey, I look at how Newman's conversion affected his relations with these two prominent Anglo-Catholic figures. In my chapter on Thackeray, I discuss how one of Newman's favorite novelists became fascinated with Newman after attending his King William Street lectures in 1850, later published as *Lectures on Certain Difficulties felt by Anglicans in submitting to the Catholic Church*, which was largely composed with Keble and Pusey in mind.

After being ordained in Rome, Newman returned to England and founded the Birmingham Oratory, where he left behind Oxford's undergraduates to minister to a lively mix of Irish Catholics, Old Catholics, English converts and Anglicans doubtful of the legitimacy of the Church of England. In 1853 Newman founded the Catholic University in Dublin and in 1859 the Oratory School, where Hilaire Belloc spent his schooldays and Gerald Manley Hopkins was a master. In my chapter, "Newman and the Americans," I show how Newman's idea of university education may have stalled on the banks of the Liffey but revived in America, where it helped form and civilize the immigrant citizenry of that exuberant land. In 1864, Newman published his great autobiography, *Apologia Pro Vita Sua*, in response to Charles Kingsley claim in *Macmillan's Magazine* that, for Newman and the Catholic clergy, truth for its own sake need not and on the whole ought not to be a virtue. With the publication of the *Apologia*, the deep suspicion with which Protestant England had formerly regarded Newman changed to admiration, sympathy and affection.

Shortly before the publication of the *Apologia*, Newman began corresponding with Richard Holt Hutton, the editor of the *Spectator*. In my chapter on Hutton, I show how attuned he was to Newman's war against liberalism, which he saw, in part, as a war against the rising positivism of the nineteenth century. The critical evenhandedness that Hutton brought to his study of Newman is absent from the work of Frank Turner, the Yale professor of history, who follows the Victorian controversialist Walter Walsh (1847–1912), in seeing Newman as at once deluded and duplicitous: the usual straw man of No Popery polemics.[23] In his introduction to his edition of the *Apologia*, Prof. Turner asserts that "... Newman had great difficulty establishing a substantial link other than the term itself between what he designated as liberalism in the 1830s and 1840s and that of the 1860s." To try to substantiate this, Turner quotes another assertion, this time from Owen Chadwick: "The fact is, what Newman denounced as liberalism, no one else regarded as liberalism." This would have been news to Pusey, Keble, Hurrell Froude, James Mozley, Cardinal Manning, Bishop Ullathorne, Richard Church, Richard Holt Hutton and many other Anglicans and Catholics, who not only knew what Newman meant by liberalism but shared his apprehensions about it. Yet having made this unsubstantiated charge with respect to Newman's contemporaries, Prof. Turner turns to Newman's commentators and insists that "none of his well-informed commentators has been able to assign the concept substantial content or meaning because they have left it alienated from the historical and religious contexts ..."[24] This is another false assertion. If we revisit the work of Newman's "well-informed commentators," whether that of Richard Holt Hutton, Wilfrid Ward, Henry Tristram, Charles Stephen Dessain, Meriol Trevor or Ian Ker, we can see that all of them put Newman's fight against liberalism in historical and religious context. Indeed, they give it center stage. For Father Tristram, the "supreme mission" of Newman's life was "to stem, as far as it lay in his power, the tide of unbelief and to dissipate what seemed to him to be the 'terrible deceit of these latter days.'" Accordingly, in his own excellent anthology of Newman's work, published in 1948, he focused on Newman's "protracted struggle against the 'doctrine that there is no positive truth in religion,' or 'liberalism,' as [Newman] called it, which from tentative beginnings in his earlier years continued to gather strength during the course of his life, and has become the great menace of to-day."[25] To substantiate his point, Father Tristram quoted not an interested Puseyite like Owen Chadwick but the philosopher Alfred North Whitehead (1861–1947), who had no axes to grind in these matters.

> The witness of history and of common sense tells us that systematic formu-
> lations are potent engines of emphasis, of purification, and of stability.
> Christianity would long ago have sunk into a noxious superstition, apart
> from the Levantine and European intellectual movement, sustained from the
> very beginning until now. This movement is the effort of Reason to provide
> an accurate system of theology.... . Thus the attack of the liberal clergy and
> laymen, during the eighteenth and nineteenth centuries, upon systematic
> theology was entirely misconceived. They were throwing away the chief
> safeguard against the wild emotions of superstition.[26]

Here, in approving "the effort of Reason to provide an accurate system of theology," Whitehead might be describing the work of the early Church Fathers, which meant so much to Newman's religious development and, indeed, paved the way for his conversion. Prof. Turner exposes his own deep misunderstanding of Newman when he speaks of him as "a quasi schismatic priest and typical religious seeker."[27] Newman was not a religious seeker: he was a religious finder. As he told an unknown correspondent in 1874, "*Means* always cease when the *end* is obtained. You cease walking when you have got home — if you went on walking, you would get all wrong. *Inquiry* ends, when you at length *know* what you were inquiring about. When the water boils, you take the kettle off the fire; else, it would boil away. So it is with private judgment; till you have found the truth, it is the only way you have of arriving at it — but when you have got the truth, there is nothing to inquire about."[28] Prof. Turner is equally wrong to claim that Newman was "schismatic." On the contrary, whether as an Anglican or a Catholic, Newman never abandoned unity because he never abandoned truth. In 1879, when he received his red hat, he pointedly referred to the fight against liberalism as the fight for truth:

For thirty, forty, fifty years I have resisted to the best of my powers the spirit of liberalism in religion. Never did Holy Church need champions against it more sorely than now, when, alas! it is an error overspreading, as a snare, the whole earth … Liberalism in religion is the doctrine that there is no positive truth in religion, but that one creed is as good as another, and this is the teaching which is gaining substance and force daily. It is inconsistent with any recognition of any religion, as *true*. It teaches that all are to be tolerated, for all are matters of opinion. Revealed religion is not a truth, but a sentiment and a taste; not an objective fact, not miraculous; and it is the right of each individual to make it say just what strikes his fancy … . As to Religion, it is a private luxury, which a man may have if he will; but … which he must not obtrude upon others, or indulge in to their annoyance.[29]

Here Newman recognized how liberalism threatens not only the integrity but the objectivity of truth and, *pace* Prof. Turner, his fight against it in his own century continues to guide our fight against it in ours.

Newman demonstrated his controversial mettle by rebutting the leader of England's political liberals, William Ewart Gladstone, who charged that papal infallibility would undermine the loyalty of English Catholics. Newman responded with *A Letter to the Duke of Norfolk* (1875), which brilliantly parried Gladstone's wild thrusts. In my chapter on Gladstone, I give an account of the fraught relationship between Newman and the Prime Minister in order to put one of Newman's great works of controversy in context.

Newman was made a Cardinal by Pope Leo XIII in 1879. When the red hat was bestowed, the English, Irish, Scotch and American Residents in Rome issued a statement affirming that "We feel that in making you a Cardinal the Holy Father has not only given public testimony of his appreciation of your great merits and of the value of your admirable writings in defence of God and His Church, but has also conferred the greatest possible honour on all English-speaking Catholics who have long looked up to you as their spiritual father and their guide in the paths of holiness."[30] In his later years, Newman beheld the unfolding of what he called "the great *apostasia*" with prophetic clarity. "My own belief," he told one correspondent in 1864, "is, that, if there be a God, Catholicism is true; but this is the elementary, august, and sovereign truth, the denial of which is in progress. May He Himself give grace to those who shall be alive in that terrible day, to fight His battle well. All the forms of Protestantism, allow me to say, are but toys of children in the great battle between the Holy Catholic Roman Church and Antichrist."[31] Later, in 1873, speaking to seminarians at the opening of St. Bernard's Seminary, he was even more admonitory: "I will admit that there were certain specific dangers to Christians at certain other times, which do not exist in this time … Still I think that the trials which lie before us are such as would appal and make dizzy even such courageous hearts as St. Athanasius, St. Gregory I, or St. Gregory VII. And they would confess that dark as the prospect of their own day was to them severally, ours has a darkness different in kind from any that has been before it … Christianity has never yet had experience of a world simply irreligious."[32] That England should now be "the epicenter of the culture of death," as one rather Newmanian English Catholic recently described it, would dismay but not surprise Newman.[33]

Newman died on the evening of 11 August 1890. A good sense of the impact of his death on his contemporaries can be gleaned from the obituaries that appeared in contemporary newspapers: in an appendix to the 32nd volume of Newman's *Letters and Diaries*, they run to over sixty pages. For a sense of one aspect of his achievement, readers can turn to his books. Throughout his career, Newman remained extraordinarily prolific. Some of his more noteworthy books include *The Tamworth Reading Room* (1841); *Oxford University Sermons* (1843); *Essay on the Development of Christian Doctrine* (1845); *Loss and Gain* (1847); *Anglican Difficulties* (1850); *Lectures on the Present Position of Catholics* (1851); *Apologia Pro Vita Sua* (1864); *An Essay in Aid of a Grammar of Assent* (1870); *The Idea of a University* (1873); and *A Letter to the Duke of Norfolk* (1875). In addition to these, Newman also wrote splendid sermons and letters.

Since most of the contemporaries I chose to cover were Protestants, it might be useful to describe something of the Anglican ethos from which Newman bolted. In 1884, Newman had occasion to contrast the Anglican with the Catholic Church in England and, speaking of the former, he wrote: "think of the numbers, the wealth, the prestige, the popularity, the political weight of that communion; of the knowledge of the world, the learning, the traditions of its three centuries. Think of its place in English history, its biographies, ecclesiastical and lay, its noble buildings, memorials often of the Catholic past but in the occupation of Protestantism …" These were the many enticing emblems of the power of the Established Church on which Newman turned his back when he converted to Catholicism. In contrast, there were no plums associated with Catholicism in England. When he asked what Catholics had to show "in contra," Newman's answer was not entirely facetious: "the Gunpowder Plot and the blundering Stuarts!"[34]

Tract 90 (1841) is another good way into the Anglican world that Newman left because it famously precipitated what would become the crisis of Tractarianism. Newman wrote the tract to keep such young Rome-leaning Anglicans as William George Ward and Francis Oakeley within the Church of England by arguing that the 39 Articles, to which all dons, as well as Anglican clergymen were required to subscribe, "do not oppose catholic teaching; they but partially oppose Roman dogma."[35] In effect, he was arguing for the inclusiveness of the Articles, which Elizabeth I had originally framed, in part, to conciliate her more obdurately Catholic subjects. Yet this was not how the majority of Newman's co-religionists saw matters. For the bishops, as for most of the English, the Articles were unambiguously Protestant and Newman was guilty of trying to subvert them. Indeed, there were some who were convinced that Newman's object in interpreting the Articles thus was to Romanize the English Church and when that failed to abscond with as many converts as he could. Newman himself would always claim that he was baffled by the fierce indignation and indeed fury that Tract 90 set off: as he told Maria Giberne, a lifelong friend, in writing the Tract he was "aiming at no idea at all."[36]

The No Popery hysteria that gripped England after Tract 90 was mild compared to that which followed the reconstitution of the English hierarchy on Michaelmas Day, 1850, when Cardinal Wiseman spoke of how "Catholic England has been restored to its orbit in the ecclesiastical firmament from which its light has long vanished and begins anew its course of regularly adjusted action round the centre of unity, the source of jurisdiction ..."[37] In response, the English rabble, emboldened by Prime Minister Lord John Russell, burned Wiseman and the pope in effigy. This recrudescence of No Popery confirmed Newman's sense of how averse the English were to the very idea of Catholicism, which he first encountered among his own siblings. In the chapters that follow, I show how Newman took this aversion as the great given of his work. The English had been effectively turned against their traditional faith, and he dedicated a good deal of his energies to trying to make them understand what they and their Protestant forbears had repudiated. One way that "the ruling spirits of the English Reformation" had contrived "to make Protestantism live," Newman pointed out in *The Present Position of Catholics in England* (1851), was to embody it in the person of the Sovereign.

> English Protestantism is the religion of the throne: it is represented, realised, taught, transmitted in the succession of monarchs and an hereditary aristocracy. It is religion grafted upon loyalty; and its strength is not in argument, not in fact, not in the unanswerable controversialist, not in an apostolical succession, not in sanction of Scripture—but in a royal road to faith, in backing up a King whom men see, against a Pope whom they do not see. The devolution of its crown is the tradition of its creed; and to doubt its truth is to be disloyal towards its Sovereign. Kings are an Englishman's saints and doctors; he likes somebody or something at which he can cry "huzzah," and throw up his hat. Bluff King Hal, glorious Bess, the Royal Martyr, the Merry Monarch, the pious and immortal William, the good King George, royal personages very different from each other,—nevertheless, as being royal, none of them comes amiss, but they are all of them the objects of his devotion, and the resolution of his Christianity.[38]

This identification of Protestantism with the English throne—the cynosure of loyalty—helps account for the rancor set off by Tract 90, which was regarded as an attempt to undermine that loyalty. A public letter issued by the inhabitants of Blackburn to their Bishop, in the wake of Tract 90, gives a good account of the loathing Catholicism inspired in a people convinced that it was synonymous with treason:

> Adhering as we hope we ever shall do, to the principles [of the English Reformation], we can feel neither sympathy nor respect for any of those pioneers of Popery who are industriously labouring to undermine the walls

which they have been appointed to defend, and who seem resolved to reduce our country again to that yoke of bondage which our forefathers were unable to endure. We rejoice therefore … that we have amongst us a faithful watchman on one of the chief towers of our citadel, vigilant to detect, fearless to denounce, and equally zealous to counteract the insidious devices of traitors within our gates, or the open and more honest assaults of the enemy without.[39]

While many around him were succumbing to the general hysteria, Newman remained characteristically calm. After first becoming aware, in 1839, of his doubts about the legitimacy of the Church of England, he resolved to test his doubts before making any decisive move. He could counsel others against precipitancy because he had taken the same good counsel himself. As it happened, he waited for six long deliberative years. Apropos this period, he wrote in his *Apologia* that "A death-bed has scarcely a history; it is a tedious decline, with seasons of rallying and seasons of falling back; and since the end is foreseen, or what is called a matter of time, it has little interest for the reader, especially if he has a kind heart." Yet his letters of the period reveal another more complicated history: his gradual acceptance of a new, if quite uncertain, Catholic future.[40] His Anglican deathbed was also a Catholic cradle.

To understand how revolutionary converting to Roman Catholicism was in nineteenth-century England, one has to recognize that for the English it was not only spiritually misguided—Roman Catholicism being synonymous with corruption, superstition and backwardness—it was also profoundly un-English. Readers can see something of this in Arthur Hugh Clough's epistolary novel in verse, *Amours de Voyage*, and in Thackeray's response to Newman's lectures, *Anglican Difficulties*. The Irish might succumb to the despotism of priests but not free-born Englishmen. When it became clear that Newman would soon commit the unthinkable and convert, the ranks of the Anglo-Catholic faithful became aggrieved. As one Tractarian woman wrote to Jemima, "A sound from Littlemore and St. Mary's seems to reach us even here … but, when the voice ceases … we shall have sad thoughts … Such *was* our guide, but he has left us to seek his own path—our champion has deserted us—our watchman whose cry used to cheer us is heard no more."[41] In my chapters on Keble and Pusey I show how Newman tried to convince his old Anglican friends how Catholicism completed Tractarianism. Yet, after Newman's secession, many of the Tractarians he left behind—including Keble and Pusey—spent the rest of their lives trying to salvage the Tractarianism that his departure had so deeply undermined.

Still, throughout his last years as an Anglican, Newman was adamant about dissuading impetuous would-be converts from taking a step they might regret. "Converts to Rome," he insisted, must "not go out from St. Mary's parsonage."[42] The career of Richard Waldo Sibthorp became the great cautionary tale. A Fellow of Magdalen College, Sibthorp converted to Roman Catholicism in 1841 and was ordained a priest in 1842. Shortly thereafter, while staying on the Isle of Wight, he began to have second thoughts. In 1843, he converted back to

Anglicanism, claiming that it was the sea air that convinced him that Rome was, after all, πόρνη μεγαλη—the "great whore."[43]

Denounced by the Anglican episcopate, cut by friends, vilified in the public prints, Newman retreated to the lay community he had set up at Littlemore, only venturing out to give sermons at St. Mary's or to meet friends in Oxford. When he finally decided to convert on October 9th, 1845, he was received into the Church by the Passionist priest, Domenico Giovanni Luigi Barberi (1792–1849), a short, stocky, ebullient man who had worked with the English converts George Spencer and Ambrose de Phillipps De Lisle to pray for the conversion of England as early as 1828. When Barberi arrived on October 8th to receive Newman he was sopping wet from a five-hour coach journey from Aston, Staffordshire, where he had set up the first Passionist house in England. Later, he wrote back to his Superiors of his first encounter with Newman: "The door opened—and what a spectacle it was for me to see at my feet John Henry Newman begging me to hear his general confession and admit him into the bosom of the Catholic Church! And there by the fire he began his general confession with extraordinary humility and devotion."[44] That evening, Newman, Frederick Bowles and Richard Stanton made their profession of faith and Father Domenic gave them conditional baptism. The following morning, in the small Littlemore chapel, Father Dominic said mass on an altar improvised out of Henry Wilberforce's writing desk, and all three were given communion. Two years later, Newman wrote to Father Dominic from Rome: "I have thought of writing to you many times since I have been here, but am not sorry to have waited till I can tell you something about ourselves. We are to be Oratorians … How long we shall remain here I do not know – when we return, we shall set up, I suppose, in some large town, and try to convert that numerous class of youths who at present have a little education and no religion …"[45] Father Dominic's impression of the man whom he set on his Catholic way was of a characteristic acuity: "In my judgment he is one of the most humble and lovable men I have met in my life."[46]

Many other contemporaries from a wide range of backgrounds left behind striking impressions of Newman. After the publication of the *Apologia*, F. D. Maurice (1805–1872), the liberal theologian and founder of the Christian Socialist Movement, wrote to A. P. Stanley, Dr. Arnold's biographer: "I would have given much that Kingsley had not got into this dispute with Newman. In spite of all apparent evidence, I do believe that Newman loves truth in his heart of hearts, and more now than when he was an Anglican."[47] That Kingsley was one of the most prominent members of the Christian Socialist Movement gave this regret added point. Thomas Huxley (1825–1895), Darwin's disciple, regarded Newman as "one of the acutest and subtlest disputants who have ever championed Ecclesiasticism."[48] Edward Pusey, the learned Canon of Christ Church and later head of the die-hard Tractarians, wrote to Newman in July of 1839, after the death of his wife, of whom Newman had been very fond, "God bless and reward you for all your love and tender kindness to us … Your first visit was to me like that of an angel sent from God. It seems as though it had changed, in a degree, the character of my subsequent life … I pray that He may make you what, as you say, there are so few of, 'a great saint.'"[49] Edward Badeley, Q.C. the convert and lawyer to whom Newman turned for legal counsel during the Achilli trial, wrote to another of Newman's friends, James Hope-Scott, who converted after the Gorham Judgment:[50] "you will respect the high character of Dr. Newman, his genius, his learning, his piety, his zeal, the purity of his motives, the sanctity of his life."[51] An American from Virginia named William Ryan wrote to Newman in 1887: "Dr. Hage, the most eminent divine in the Southern Presbyterian Church, in referring to you recently, said he was catholic enough to wish the venerable English Cardinal well. Said he: 'I regard Cardinal Newman as one of the Saintliest men of the Nineteenth Century, and when I am sorry and depressed I read one of Dr. Newman's sermons for refreshment.'"[52] Of all the many laudatory letters Newman received in his long life, this might have pleased him the most.

The Anglo-Irish poet and convert Aubrey de Vere (1814–1902), whose friends included Wordsworth, Edward Fitzgerald and Alfred Tennyson, and whose father had been at Harrow with Byron and Peel, was equally struck by Newman. At their first meeting, Newman put de Vere in mind "of a high-bred young monk of the Middle Ages, whose asceticism cannot quite conceal his distinguished elegance."[53] De Vere, whom his niece Lady Shaw described as "a gentleman to his fingertips, courteous, kindly, and honourable," corresponded frequently with Newman and became one of his good friends.[54] In a letter to Sara Coleridge, who made a wonderful sketch of Newman, de Vere confirmed that "Newman is wholly free from temptation toward infidelity ... he antici-pates an unprecedented outburst of infidelity all over the world ... to withstand it he deems his special vocation ... There is occasionally an iron hardness in Newman; but in him, as in Dante ... an exquisite and surpassing sweetness."[55] Nothing in his long life pleased de Vere more than walking in his beloved Curragh Chase in Limerick, which gave his thinking a certain philosophical balance. When Huxley, Mill and Tyndall began publishing their attacks against what they claimed was the irrationality of the Christian faith, de Vere marveled at how his contemporaries could credit them: Comtists, after all, knew nothing of God—not even that He existed.[56] In recognition of de Vere's interest in Irish affairs—he worked heroically to save lives during the famine—Newman appointed him to the chair of Political and Social Science of the Catholic University in Dublin, though no Catholic Irish students would enroll in any of the proposed lectures of the Anglo-Irish convert.[57] After Lord Frederick Cavendish, the newly appointed Chief Secretary of Ireland, was hacked to death with surgical knives by Fenians in Phoenix Park, de Vere wrote a prescient pamphlet, *Constitutional and Unconstitutional Political Action* (1882), which, had it been read, might have spared the place that James Joyce called *Errorland* a century of additional violence.[58] De Vere's poetry is unreadable but his auto-biography and letters are full of interesting things. In one, this tall, spare, genial man wrote with moving simplicity of what prompted his conversion: "My convictions with respect to the claims of the Roman Catholic Church seemed to me to reach such a degree of certainty and moral urgency as left me no choice, as a conscientious man, desirous of being sincere with himself and with others, and of obeying the will of God."[59] Here was confirmation of precisely the religious certainty that Newman would defend in the *Grammar of Assent* (1870), which Gerard Manley Hopkins praised for its "justice and candour and gravity and rightness of mind …"[60] Unfortunately, when Hopkins offered to write a commentary of the *Grammar*, Newman turned him down, telling him: "I could not, as a matter of conscience, allow you to undertake a work which I could not but consider as at once onerous and unnecessary …"[61] Hopkins, who was fond of Duns Scotus's insights into the individuality of knowledge, might have written a lively commentary.

The man who inspired so much respect and affection was self-deprecatory, even dismissive about his writings. Apropos his brilliant sermon on religious development, which he would later expand into *An Essay on the Development of Christian Doctrine* (1845), he wrote to Pusey: "If any one values his luncheon on Thursday, he must not go to hear me at St. Mary's, for my sermon is of portentous length—and my only satisfaction is that, if any persons go out of curiosity, they will be punished."[62] About his *Fifteen Sermons Preached Before the University of Oxford* (1843), he was even more impatient: "I am publishing my University Sermons, which will be thought sad dull affairs—but having got through a subject I wish to get rid of it."[63] Later, when he sent Dean Church his *Grammar of Assent* (1870) he wrote hoping that it would not "bore him."[64] It is some proof of the abiding power of these and indeed most of his books that since their first publication they have never gone out of print. Yet for Newman, writing was never an end in itself.

William Clifford, the Bishop of Clifton, certainly recognized this when he preached at Newman's funeral mass.

> God in his tender mercy towards this land, chose him for a special work, and endowed him with gifts specially fitting him for that work … But the preaching and writings of Dr. Newman … are far from constituting the whole or even the greater part of what, at this time, he was doing for the Church of God. His kind and gentle nature, the sympathy he always felt towards those who were in anxiety and doubt, and the art he had of gaining their confidence and ministering to them comfort and advice, no less than the high esteem in which his learning was held, caused men of all classes and callings to have recourse to him in their difficulties, and he was most indefatigable in giving them his assistance both in person and by letter. There is scarcely an individual of any note who has been received into the Church in the last thirty years who has not in the course of his search after truth received assistance from Cardinal Newman. Many owe their conversion, under God, entirely to him.[65]

This was an assessment with which Cardinal Manning, who was not always uncritical of Newman, concurred: "beyond the power of all books has been the example of his humble and unworldly life: always the same, in union with God; and in manifold charity to all who sought him. He was the centre of innumerable souls, drawn to him as Teacher, Guide, and Comforter, through long years, and especially in the more than forty years of his Catholic life. To them he was as a spring of light and strength from a supernatural source."[66]

For all the immense influence he had on his contemporaries, Newman was uncomfortable with the very notion of influence. "I assure you," he wrote to one correspondent, "nothing has haunted me more continually for years than the idea that undergraduates are trusting me more than they should—and I have done many things by way of preventing it."[67] In another letter to John Keble, his confidante and fellow Tractarian, he wrote: "I am commonly very sluggish and think it a simple bore or nuisance to have to move or to witness movements ... as to influencing people, making points, advancing and so on, I do not think these are matters which engross or engage me or even interest me."[68] "Of all persons," he confessed to another correspondent, "*I* need guidance and comfort most."[69] Then, again, he was concerned that "... even those who think highly of me have the vaguest, most shadowy, fantastic notions attached to their idea of me; and feel a respect, not for me, but for some imagination of their own which bears my name."[70] He was never unaware of how influence can miscarry.

In light of this distrust of influence, the sway Newman held over others was all the more extraordinary. "When I was fifteen or sixteen," the Pre-Raphaelite painter Edward Burne-Jones (1833–1898) recalled, "Newman taught me so much ... things that will never be out of me ... In an age of materialism, he taught me to venture on the unseen, and this so early that it was well in me when life began, and I was equipped before I went to Oxford with a real good panoply and it has never failed me ... So he stands as a great image or symbol of a man ... who put all this world's life in one venture."[71] Matthew Arnold spoke for many of his agnostic contemporaries when he wrote to Newman in 1871: "We are all of us carried in ways not of our own making or choosing but nothing can ever do away the effects you have produced on me, for it consists in a general disposition of mind rather than in a particular set of ideas. In all the conflicts I have with modern Liberalism and Dissent, and with their pretensions and shortcomings, I recognize your work."[72] In the poetry of Arthur Hugh Clough, which delves unsparingly into the misgivings of unbelief, the appeal of Newman was ubiquitous. Clough might have tried to resist it but it was always there. Clough's friend, J. C. Shairp, who, as we have seen, left so vivid an account of what it was like to hear Newman's legendary sermons at St. Mary's, spoke for many of his contemporaries when he said that Newman was "a man in many ways the most remarkable that England has seen during this century, perhaps the most remarkable whom the English Church has produced in any century."[73]

What was it about the man that was so special? Frederic Rogers, a close friend, who later became Permanent Under Secretary for the Colonies, gave a good account of his personal appeal. "Newman seemed to have an intuitive perception of all that you thought and felt, so that he caught at once all that you meant or were driving at in a sentiment, a philosophical reflection, or a joke ... And so there was in talking with him that combination of liveliness and repose which constitutes ease; you seemed to be talking with a better kind of self, which was drawing you upwards. Newman's general characteristics—his genius, his depth of purpose; his hatred of pomp and affectation; his piercing insight into the workings of the human mind ... are all matters of history."[74] The decorative artist and convert John Hungerford Pollen (1820–1902) singled out Newman's charming attentiveness to the views of others: "Delightful it was ... to hear him draw out with the gentlest possible forceps, what each friend or professor had to say on his own particular theme ... He encouraged you to put your conclusions into terms; to see what they looked like from various sides ... but all this under the form of easy conversation."[75] Mark Pattison, the author of the classic *Memoirs of an Oxford Don* (1885), had been a thoroughgoing Tractarian from 1840 to 1842 but when Newman converted he repudiated the Movement, charging that "the 'Tracts' desolated Oxford life, and suspended, for an indefinite period, all science, humane letters, and the first strivings of intellectual freedom ..."[76] Yet not even Pattison could deny the power of Newman's influence. "Thin, pale, and with large lustrous eyes piercing through this veil of men and things, he hardly seemed made for this world. But his influence had in it something of magic. It was never possible to be a quarter-of-an-hour in his company without a warm feeling of being invited to take an onward step ... Newman always tried to reach the heart and understanding of those with whom he had to do."[77]

He was at his best with the bereaving. Having lost his beloved sister Mary when she was 19 and he was 27, and so many other dear friends and family, he could readily empathize with the bereft. John Bramston, an Anglican vicar, who had not seen Newman in years, wrote him in 1844 of "the deep affliction it has pleased God to visit me withal—My dearest wife breathed her last this morning at 2 o'clock ... Give me a line my dear friend and you may be blessed to support a tottering pilgrim in the narrow way."[78] Newman wrote back saying how vividly he remembered Bramston, who had gone out of his way 22 years before to put an awkward Newman at ease at a college party. "Time comes and goes, years pass," Newman wrote, "but kind deeds, warm affections, services of love, the religious ties which bind heart to heart, remain." He also remembered Bramston's wife. "In great truth I say that there is no one scarcely whom I have seen but once, whose memory has been so fixed in me as hers ..." As for counsel, Newman insisted that "I am not the person to teach or admonish you." Yet, doubtless remembering the loss of Mary, he told Bramston: "This sorrowful time will pass away—but you will not lose what for the moment you may seem to have lost irrevocably. You will have greater comfort in looking back upon the past than you can now believe possible ... for you are from henceforth by God's great mercy one of those who have their 'treasure in heaven.'"[79]

William Lockhart, who spent some time at Littlemore, and converted in 1842, put it best when he spoke of Newman's "simplicity, meekness and humility; God, not self, was the centre of all his thoughts ..." He was "a seer who saw God, and spoke that which he had seen."[80]

This was the sympathetic response to Newman. There were less than sympathetic responses. The autodidact Congregationalist and hero of the free churches, A. M. Fairbairn (1838–1912), launched a blistering attack on Newman in a lively book called *Catholicism Roman and Anglican* (1899), which is still worth reading, in which he depicted his Catholic adversary as not only out of step with the triumphant liberalism of his age but actually afraid of it. What is remarkable about Fairbairn is how he manages to encapsulate so many of the criticisms lodged against Newman in his own lifetime and indeed, in some quarters, still lodged against him. For example, Fairbairn took issue with Newman for being a reactionary and a crypto-skeptic—something of which many positivists and Protestants of various stripes accused him. For Fairbairn, Newman's "whole inner history" could be summed up by recognizing how "He not only doubted reason, but he mocked and scorned all who sought to enlist it in the services of religion. It was to him no witness or oracle of God, but simply a servant, whose duty was to obey, and whose only virtue was obedience."[81] And he sought to substantiate his claim by contrasting Newman's alleged resistance to reason with the presumed progress that the various rationalists of the age were making. Thus, for Fairbairn, "the formative period of Newman's life, 1826–1833, and the decade that followed, may be described as a period during which men were waiting for a relevant constructive interpretation of the Religion of Christ.

The revolutionary forces were spent, constructive forces were at work in every region of thought and life; and they needed but the electric touch of a great religious ideal to be unified and made ministrant to Religion. The old monarchical and oligarchical theories having perished, the Philosophical Radicals were seeking, with but poor success, a new basis for politics, that they might determine what was the chief good; and new-methods in legislation, that they might promote and secure the greatest happiness of the greatest number. John Stuart Mill had just escaped from the dogmatic Empiricism of his father; had been spiritually awakened by the poetry of Wordsworth and the philosophy of Coleridge; and was looking about for a faith by which to order his life. Charles Darwin was just beginning to watch the methods of nature and to learn how to interpret her; and while Newman was making verses and gathering impulses in the Mediterranean, he was away in the *Beagle* exploring many seas and lands. In the "loneliest nook in Britain," under the shadow of hills and within sight of moorlands consecrated by the heroism and martyrdoms of his Covenanting forefathers, Thomas Carlyle was doing his strenuous best to wed the thoughts that had come to him from German literature and philosophy, with the substance and spirit of his ancestral faith; the effort taking visible shape in the egoistic idealism of his *Sartor Resartus*, and leading him to look into man and his recent history with the eyes that were to see in the French Revolution the tragedy of retribution and righteousness. Transcendental Idealism was in full career in Germany; Hegel and Schleiermacher were lecturing in Berlin, the one applying his philosophy to the explication of religion and history, the other his criticism to the documents, facts, and doctrines of the Christian faith; while in Tubingen, Strauss was combining and developing the two, with results that were to break upon the alarmed world in a certain *Leben Jesu*. In France, Saint Simon had developed his *Nouveau Christianisme*, pleading that Religion might be more an energy directing "all social forces towards the moral and physical amelioration of the class which is at once the most numerous and the most poor": and Comte had begun the *Cours de Philosophie Positive*, explaining how the theological and metaphysical states had been passed, and the final and positive state had come; and what were the new ideas of Society, of God, and of Religion on which it was to rest.[82]

Here were the contemporaries whom Fairbairn considered the choice and master spirits of the age: Darwin, Carlyle, Hegel, Schleiermacher, Strauss, Saint Simon and Comte. Newman was not completely opposed to all of these figures. He had the odd good word for Carlyle. "I commend to your notice," he wrote to his sister Jemima in 1839, "if it comes in your way, Carlyle on the French Revolution—a queer, tiresome, obscure, profound, and original work. The writer has not very clear principles and views, I fear, but they are very deep."[83] And he had fun with Comte's lunatic metaphysics. "As time went on, I believe he considered religion necessary for the mind – but it was all subjective. I believe he instituted a worship, a rite, to the Aggregate of humanity, the Auto-Man. Religious books would be necessary on this score—and nothing could be better than those of the Middle Ages. He had a great admiration for the Medieval Church—it educated the world in the only possible way for his own truer and purer system …"[84] And he did not regard all of Darwin's theories as incompatible with Christianity: "We do not deny or circumscribe the Creator, because we hold he has created the self-acting originating human mind, which has almost a creative gift; much less then do we deny or circumscribe His power, if we hold that He gave matter such laws as by their blind instrumentality moulded and constructed through innumerable ages the world as we see it. If Mr Darwin in this or that point of his theory comes into collision with revealed truth, that is another matter – but I do not see that the principle of development, or what I have called construction, does."[85] For all of his readiness to see the good points in these men, Newman did not imagine them or their theories capable of saving the world, and it was for this that Fairbairn found him reprehensible:

> Everywhere the struggle was towards positive ideas, constructive ideals, such an interpretation of man's nature, history, and universe, as would tend to a more perfect organization of society and a better ordering of life. Newman's attitude was precisely the opposite. Change was in the air; he felt it, feared it, hated it. He idealized the past, he disliked the present, and he trembled for the future. His only hope was in a return to the past, and to a past which had never existed save in the imagination of the romancer. What he hated and resisted he did not take the trouble to understand …. . One seeks in vain in Newman's early writings—poems, essays, articles, pamphlets, tracts—for any sign or phrase indicative of real comprehension of the forces he opposed. He does not comprehend their real nature or drift; what reasons they have for their being, what good they have in them, what truth; what wrongs to redress, what rights to achieve: he only feels that they are inimical to his ideals. There is no evidence that he ever tried to place himself in the position of the philosophical radical, or the rational critic, or the constructive socialist, or the absolute idealist; and look at his and their

questions through their eyes and from their standpoint. He hated them and their works too utterly to attempt to do so—perhaps he was haunted by a great doubt as to what might happen if he did … . He emphasized the church idea, the historical continuity, sanctity, authority, rights, prerogatives and powers of the organized society or body which called itself here the Anglican, there the Catholic church. The more he claimed for the church, the more he had to claim; the more he set it in opposition to the movement and tendencies of living thought, the more absolute and divine he had to make its authority. The logic of the situation was inexorable,—if the church alone could save man from the spirit embodied in "Liberalism," then it must be a divine and infallible church, the vicar and voice of God on earth. But the logic of the situation was one, and the logic of history another and tragically different. In the past Catholic authority had bent like the rush in the river before the stream and tendency of thought; if it had had divine rights it had been without divine wisdom; men and countries it had owned, it had been unable to hold; and for centuries the noblest life, the best minds, the highest and purest literatures of Europe had stood outside its pale … . Newman went to Rome, and carried with him, or drew after him, men who accepted his principles; but the "Liberalism" he hated went its way, all the mightier and more victorious for the kind of barrier he had tried to build against it. He succeeded wonderfully in making Roman Catholics of Anglicans; but he failed in the apologetic that saves the infidel, and baptizes the spirit of a rational and revolutionary age into the faith of Christ.[86]

Here are charges against Newman that Owen Chadwick and the scurrilous Frank Turner would also bring, all combined into one compendious dossier. In this, Fairbairn's treatment of Newman resembles Noel Annan's treatment of Evelyn Waugh: for both Fairbairn and Annan, their Catholic subjects were "deviants" precisely because they dissented from the liberal consensus of their respective ages. This intolerance of dissent points up the sequacity that often defines rationalists.[87] "For intellectuals," as Paul Johnson observed, "far from being highly individualistic and non-conformist people, follow certain regular patterns of behavior. Taken as a group, they are ultra-conformist within the circles formed by those whose approval they seek and value. That is what makes them, *en masse*, so dangerous, for it enables them to create climates of opinion and prevailing orthodoxies, which often generate irrational and destructive courses of action."[88] In his bright books *Earthy Powers* and *Sacred Causes*, the wonderfully dissentient Michael Burleigh showed just how irrational and destructive those ideas would prove. What set Newman apart from the intellectuals of his age was not only his Roman Catholicism, with its healthy distrust of the remedies of men, but his own ingrained independence, his readiness to judge things for himself, not in accordance with the approved dicta of parties or cliques. Adhering to the reasonable authority of the Church of Rome freed him to exercise his private judgment critically on issues on which Fairbairn was content to follow the shibboleths of his "rational and revolutionary age."

Fairbairn's charges were also echoed by Frederick Meyrick (1827–1906), the High Church tutor, dean and bursar of Trinity College, Oxford, whose claim that "It is an entire mistake to suppose that the religious movement in Oxford of the last century owes its origin to Newman, or required his help for its success" provided Peter Nockles with his thesis for that slippery book, *The Oxford Movement in Context: Anglican High Churchmanship* 1760–1857 (1994).[89] For Meyrick, the Oxford Movement, "as a concerted movement, failed, and turned out a fiasco, because Newman led it. Keen as was his intellect, Newman was never guided by his reason, but always by his emotions; and a man so constituted cannot lead a host to victory, though he may stir up in them the enthusiasm which, if directed aright, insures success."[90]

My readers should keep these criticisms of Fairbairn and Meyrick in mind while looking at the chapters that follow to see if any of them survive scrutiny. Did Newman idolize the past? Did he resist change? Was he dismissive of the views of others? Did he fail to understand the nature of the liberalism he opposed? Was he secretly skeptical himself and therefore intent on discounting the skepticism of others? Did he offer himself up to the direction of emotion? Was his preoccupation with the Roman Church authoritarian? Did he disdain reason? Did he embrace the infallibility of the Roman Church to escape the implications of skepticism? These are objections that some still lodge against Newman, and we should look at the record of his life, as it is found in his books and letters, to see if they hold water.

In researching *Newman and His Contemporaries*, I discovered afresh what an important place Newman's letters hold in his work. Of course, he set great store by letters. As he told his sister Jemima, "A man's life is in his letters. Biographers varnish; they assign motives; they conjecture feelings; they interpret Lord Burleigh's nods; but contemporary letters are facts."[91] This is not entirely true. Some biographers varnish but so do letter writers, and in any case, letters, like any documents, require interpretation. Ian Ker draws deeply on the letters in his great intellectual biography but never without showing how they relate to Newman's books or his thought as a whole. In 1890, Anne Mozley published the letters of Newman's Anglican period with minimal editorial comment, precisely in accordance with Newman's own recommendations; but no one would now suggest that her two volumes adequately capture his Anglican career. The problem with Wilfrid Ward's otherwise admirable biography is that he began his account in 1845, blithely assuming that Mozley's two volumes already covered the earlier period of Newman's life. Consequently, his own account is unbalanced. Nevertheless, Newman was certainly right to insist on the testimonial force of letters for any biographer wishing to arrive at a fair estimate of his subject. His own letters furnish this testimony by showing how much his interest in his own life was bound up with his interest in the lives of his contemporaries. Accordingly, I have made Newman's letters my particular quarry. They are, after all, some of the best letters in the language. When all 33 volumes become more widely available in an affordable edition, more general readers will come to appreciate how wonderfully good they are. For my own purposes, the letters proved indispensable because they show like nothing else what animated Newman's life, which was not only love of God but love of neighbor—a love which won over even the captious Fairbairn, whose last letter to Newman was a letter of thanks: "Your Eminence I desire to thank you very cordially for your courtesy in sending me the paper on 'Scepticism used as a Preparation for Catholic Belief'. It will be my duty to weigh carefully its varied criticisms and elucidations and I gladly recognise its fair and judicial tone even where unable to admit the correctness of its views or the relevance of its arguments. I remain, Your Eminence Your very obedient Servant A. M. Fairbairn."[92] That the two men should have managed to finish their controversy on this amiable note pleased Newman. As he wrote to Richard Holt Hutton: "I have another great satisfaction. I sent Dr Fairbairn my new answer to him. He seems to have taken my act very kindly as 'courteous' – which was enough to enable me to write to thank him for his letter. And thus, although I suppose he will use his right to reply, I don't expect anything from him of an unpleasant character."[93] In his controversy with Fairbairn, where their first principles were so irreconcilably opposed, Newman might have cited that apothegm of his from the *Oxford Sermons*: "When men understand what each other mean, they see, for the most part that controversy is either superfluous or hopeless." In confronting his liberal critics, Newman would often encounter this unbridgeable divide. Yet he brought to controversy more than first principles, and in this he reminds us of something else he said in his *Oxford Sermons*:

> Men persuade themselves, with little difficulty, to scoff at principles, to ridicule books, to make sport of the names of good men; but they cannot bear their presence; it is holiness embodied in personal form, which they cannot steadily confront and bear down: so that the silent conduct of a conscientious man secures for him from beholders a feeling different in kind from any which is created by the mere versatile and garrulous Reason.[94]

Here is a good description of that personal influence which so many of Newman's contemporaries found so captivating. In the chapters that follow I trust I have done this aspect of my subject justice.

CHAPTER 1

John Keble and the Crisis of Tractarianism

"I fear so very much that all you who do not come forward will go back.
You cannot stand where you are."
John Henry Newman, *Loss and Gain* (1847)[1]

When we revisit the history of the Oxford Movement, whether in Newman's letters and writings, or those of other Tractarians and Anglicans, or the classic account that R. W. Church wrote, we naturally concentrate on Newman's long-gestating conversion. This is the event that gives all the other events their interest and point. Had Newman not converted, the Movement would have ended, not, as Church famously wrote, in "catastrophe," but in bathos. And yet Newman, for all his inexhaustible richness, never deliberated or acted in isolation.[2] He consulted others, especially those, whether living or dead, whose good judgment promised good counsel. This flowed naturally from his distrust of private judgment. If it was ill-advised to trust oneself in acquiring one's religious opinions, it was equally ill-advised to trust oneself in testing them. So Newman consulted St. Athanasius and St. Augustine, St. Cyprian and St. Austin; he reread the Caroline divines Bramhall, Bull, Wake, Stillingfleet, Taylor, and Laud; he corresponded with his old Oriel pupil, S. F. Wood; he corresponded with William Dodsworth and W. F. Hook; he kept Henry Edward Manning abreast of his evolving thoughts, and through Manning, Gladstone; he exchanged letters with a brilliant Irish priest and professor of philosophy at Maynooth, Dr. William Russell; he sparred with the future Cardinal Nicholas Wiseman on, among other matters, "idolatrous usages;" he read the Spiritual Exercises of St. Ignatius Loyola; he conferred with the Tractarian lawyers Edward Bellasis, Edward Badeley and James Hope; he confided in his sister Jemima.[3] But the person whose confidence and counsel he sought out most was John Keble. There were a number of reasons why Newman should have singled Keble out. He wrote to his good friend on 18 May 1843, when unsure whether he should retain or relinquish St. Mary's, "I feel it is almost ungenerous to entangle you in my troubles; at least it would be so, were it not a rule of the Gospel that Christians should not stand alone or depend on themselves. And if so, to whom can I go, (for surely I may speak without irreverence) but to you who have been an instrument of good to so many, myself inclusive? To whom is it natural for me to go but to you whom I have tried to follow so long and on so many occasions? To whom would Hurrell go, or wish me to go but to you? And doubt not that, if such is the will of Providence, you will in the main be able to do what is put on you."[4] There were other reasons why Newman sought out Keble, "that meek, patient, and affectionate soul."[5] Newman meant his "dearly, deeply beloved friend" to share his doubts about the Anglican Church so he could join him in discovering the one holy catholic and apostolic Church. Newman meant Keble to undergo the crisis of Tractarianism fully conscious of the stakes involved. If we grant that this reason, more than any other, underlay Newman's confidences, two things follow. First, the primary purpose of his correspondence with Keble was not introspection but apostolic counsel. Second, Keble's failure to convert, his decision to remain within the Anglican fold, had an immense impact on Newman's future life as a Catholic, for henceforth he would devote a good deal of that life to trying to persuade Keble and the Anglo-Catholic party to reconsider their attachment to the Established Church. In this respect, the correspondence can be read as a prelude to Newman's *Anglican Difficulties*, the lectures he delivered in 1850 to show his former co-religionists the true character of the Established Church in relation to the Movement of 1833. In a passage addressed to his former Tractarian friends and relations, Newman declared the primary object of his lectures with moving urgency.

> My dear brethren, there is but one thing which forces me to speak,—and it is my intimate sense that the Catholic Church is the one ark of salvation, and my love for your souls ... It is [the] keen feeling that my life is wearing away, which overcomes the lassitude which possesses me, and scatters the excuses, which I might plausibly urge to myself for not meddling with what I have left for ever, which subdues the recollection of past times, and which makes me do my best, with whatever success, to bring you to land from off your wreck, who have thrown yourselves from it upon the waves, or are clinging to the rigging, or are sitting in heaviness and despair upon its side.[6]

Here Newman fully involved himself in his critique of the Established Church and it is this personal witness that gives his correspondence with Keble in the pivotal period before his conversion its special character. Before revisiting those labyrinthine letters, I shall look at how both men viewed the various factors that gave rise to the Oxford Movement, as well as the *via media*, which Newman devised to try to find some happy medium between Rome and Augsburg. But first I should say something of Keble's life.

"From all I could hear," Tom Mozley wrote of Keble's youth, "he spent his earlier years in what may be called the sacred seclusion of old English family life, among people enjoying a perfect harmony of taste and opinion."[7] Mozley is not the most reliable of memoirists but here he hit on an essential truth about Keble. The world outside his own embattled High Church world—the world of liberals and rationalists, Evangelicals and Roman converts—shattered the "sacred seclusion" that he had known and enjoyed as a child and he would spend most of his subsequent life trying to recapture its lost harmony.

Keble was born at Fairford, Gloucestershire, on 25 April 1792. For over fifty years, his father, John (1745–1834) was vicar of Coln St. Aldwyn, three miles north of Fairford, a short ride on horseback but "in those days of muddy, unmade side-roads, a tiresome enough journey for any wheeled vehicle, especially in winter."[8] His mother, Sarah, the daughter of John Maule, incumbent of Ringwood in Hampshire, was of Scotch descent. John was the second child and eldest son of a family consisting of two sons and three daughters. "We are so united, so fond of home," Keble wrote to his friend John Coleridge, "and just separated enough to make us know and value each other's society."[9] From his father, Keble inherited the High Church Anglicanism that he never abandoned. His younger brother Tom, the vicar of Bisley, also kept alive the father's High Churchmanship, and in what became known as the Bisley school, which included Isaac Williams and George Prevost, he resisted the more radical, Rome-leaning aspects of Tractarianism. Charlotte Yonge, a close friend of Keble's, characterized him as "of the old reticent school, reverent and practical."[10] Whenever Keble met with religious points of view of which he approved he would say, "Yes, that is exactly what my father taught me."[11] In the preface to his *Sermons Academical and Occasional* (1848), Keble gave memorable expression to his ingrained conservatism when he remarked, "it is a sad truth, that no one of us is safe from being called on, at any moment, to exercise something like a judgment of his own, on matters which in better times would have been indisputably settled for him. If we are spared external persecution, and escape trials of our faith and courage, we are tempted perhaps more severely than the early Christians on the side of intellectual pride and willfulness. Our guide is comparatively out of sight, and we are the more tempted to be our own guides; and all thoughtful persons know how that must end."[12] In trying to make sense of why Keble resisted Rome, one can never underestimate his allegiance to the Church of England. As Dean Church pointed out, Keble "was a deeply convinced Churchman, finding his standard and pattern of doctrine and devotion in the sober earnestness and dignity of the Prayer Book.... And as his loyalty to the Church of England was profound and intense, all who had shared her fortunes, good or bad, or who professed to serve her, had a place in his affections; and any policy which threatened to injure or oppress her, and any principles which were hostile to her influence and teaching, roused his indignation and resistance."[13]

Little is known about the childhood Keble spent in Fairford. Surviving family letters attest to what Battiscombe calls the family's "Franciscan fondness for animals:" they kept not only tame hares and tame rooks but tame kestrels.[14] Moreover, all the men in the family, with the exception of the absent-minded John, were crack horsemen. Besides that, we know that Keble was so enchanted with the biblical scenes on the stained-glass windows in Fairford Church that he later replicated them in his own church at Hursley.

The gentleness and intransigence in Keble's character could only have been reinforced by his never having had to endure the barbarities of public school life; he was educated at home by his father. This gave him not only a shyness, but also a belief in the rightness of his own point of view that some found abrasive. Tom Mozley, who became an Oriel Fellow in 1829 and later married Newman's sister Harriett, complained that Keble "had not the qualities for controversy, or debate, which are necessary for any kind of public life. He very soon lost his temper in discussion. It is true there were one or two in our college who might have tried the temper of an angel, but there was really no getting on with Keble without entire agreement, that is submission."[15] The historian James Anthony Froude, Hurrell's brother, felt the same: "To his immediate friends he was genial, affectionate, and possibly instructive, but he had no faculty for winning the unconverted. If he was not bigoted, he was intensely prejudiced. If you did not agree with him there was something morally wrong with you ..."[16] Owen Chadwick qualifies this by pointing out that when admirers of *The Christian Year* met the author, "they found his person to conform perfectly to his book ... modest, quaint, unpretentious, quiet, even naïve." Those more familiar with Keble "saw his intolerance and some at least thought it too fierce. But they allowed their reverence to brush a kindly shadow over the warts. They accepted the limitations and enjoyed the man in despite."[17]

When Keble enrolled in his father's college, Corpus Christi, at the precocious age of 14, "a fresh, glad, bright, joyous boy," he was well-prepared and went on to have a brilliant university career, obtaining a double first when he was 18, an honor attained only once before, two years earlier, by the 20-year-old Robert Peel, the future Prime Minister.[18] (The next man to garner a double first would be Newman's brother Frank.) When Keble's beloved older sister Elizabeth heard of his academic accomplishments, she wrote to congratulate him, "It is indeed stupendous that such a young chap should be likely to make such a fuss and row in the world," though she was "monstrous glad" when he returned to Fairford at end of term.[19] Having her bright brother at home was better than hearing of his triumphs from afar.

One notable friend that Keble made at Oxford was Thomas Arnold, a contentious, radical, lively young man who later became the famous Headmaster of Rugby and the leader of Broad Church Anglicanism, with whom Keble broke over issues demonstrating that if there was a gentleness there was also a certain ruthlessness in his character. As Dean Church remarked, "to his attainments he joined a temper of singular sweetness and modesty, capable at the same time, when necessary, of austere strength and strictness of principle."[20] In 1811, Keble was elected to a Fellowship at Oriel College, where he joined Richard Whately, the university's premier logician, Edward Copleston, who became Provost, and John Davison, a taciturn Northcountryman, who shared Keble's conservative, High Church loyalties. Beginning in the 1820s, Oriel became home to the Noetics, who although initially committed to demonstrating the reasonableness of the Christian religion, later made common cause with the Whig-liberal governments of the 1830s and Broad-Churchmanship of the 1850s and 1860s. If Keble was not entirely comfortable with the liberal sympathies of the Noetics, he enjoyed the tutorial influence he exerted over Hurrell Froude, Robert

Wilberforce and Isaac Williams, all of whom would later become significant figures in the Oxford Movement.

In 1816, Keble was ordained and took temporary charge of the Eastleach and Burthorp parishes near his father's parish of Coln St. Aldwyn. Living out of Oxford always suited him: he relished returning to the country, as he said, to "give myself up entirely to my profession, my dear, delightful profession, which I grow fonder of every day."[21] By 1821, Keble was already contemplating retiring from the Oriel Senior Common Room. "My Donship begins to sit uneasy upon me," he confessed. "I know very well it is not the life for me, and I always feel more at home in my parish in two hours than in my College in two weeks." In the spring of 1823, Keble resigned his Oriel Fellowship to take up the curacy of Southrop, a few miles from Fairford. After this, Keble was rarely in Oxford. "Yet," as Tom Mozley recalled, "everybody who visited Oriel inquired after Keble, and expected to see him. It must be added that he was present in everybody's thoughts, as a glory to the college, a comfort and a stay, for the slightest word he dropped was all the more remembered from there being so little of it, and from it seeming to come from a different and holier sphere."[22]

Next to his father, the man who influenced Keble most was Hurrell Froude, "that infinitely attractive *enfant terrible*," as Ronald Knox wrote of him, "who so charmed and dazzled and shocked his contemporaries."[23] Like Keble, Froude grew up in a country parsonage; he was brought up to regard the English Church as "the one historic uninterrupted Church;" and he delighted in riding.[24] But there the similarities between the two ended, for Froude had nothing of Keble's deferential conservatism; he exulted in the paradoxical. The more reserved, circumspect Keble was drawn to Froude because, as he said, his "paradoxical way was one of his artifices for veiling deep earnestness and real meaning."[25] As Keble told Newman when they were at work together on the publication of Froude's *Remains*, "deep reverence will occasionally veil itself, as it were, for a moment even under the mask of its opposite, as earnest affection is sometimes known to do. Any expedient will be adopted by a person who enters with all his heart into this portion of the ancient Character, rather than he will contradict that Character altogether by a bare, unscrupulous, flaunting display of sacred things or good thoughts."[26] Froude himself recognized this quality in Hamlet. "When Hamlet is talking nonsense to the grave-diggers, or calls the Ghost 'old mole', we annex to his words a depth of feeling, which, so far from describing, he is endeavoring to conceal. Indeed this may be said of almost every word and action which is given to that most astonishing character."[27] This was precisely the sort of reserve that Keble divined in his sardonic young friend. For Froude's biographer, Piers Brendon, "It is a great tribute to Keble's perception that he alone first managed to pierce Froude's sparkling exterior, and come to an appreciation of his inner worth."[28] In his *Apologia*, Newman would fully corroborate Keble's estimation by recalling his dearest friend "as a man of high genius, brimful and overflowing with ideas and views," which, besides being strikingly original, "were too many and strong even for his bodily strength, and which crowded and jostled each other, in their effort after distinct shape and expression. And he had an intellect as critical and logical as it was speculative and bold."[29] In questioning the soundness of the Reformers of the English Reformation, in arguing that the sacramental tradition, not Erastianism, was the true source of ecclesiastical authority, and in holding that Roman Catholics were entitled to respect, not obloquy, Froude articulated some of the basal tenets of Tractarianism. Keble inspired Froude to approach the devout life with the practical assiduity it requires, and Froude inspired Keble to think beyond Tory High Churchmanship. "If a national Church means a Church without discipline," he wrote in one letter, "my argument for discipline is an argument against a national Church; and the best thing we can do is to unnationalize ours as soon as possible ... let us tell the truth and shame the devil; let us give up a national Church and have a real one."[30] Even more radically, he wrote: "I believe it to be the most indispensable of all the duties of external religion, that every one should receive the communion as often as he has opportunity ... the Church of England has gone so very wrong in this matter, that it is not right to keep things smooth any longer."[31] Froude's reforming influence can be seen clearly in Keble's assize sermon "On National Apostasy," though it is difficult to detect it in Keble's later acquiescence in precisely the Erastianism of which Froude was so trenchantly critical. What Froude's influence might have achieved if he had not succumbed to tuberculosis at the age of 35 has always inspired intriguing speculation.

In 1827, when the provostship of Oriel fell vacant, Froude zealously campaigned for Keble's election. Newman and Pusey plumped for Edward Hawkins because, as Mark Pattison later recalled, he "was superior to Keble in some of those more superficial qualities which recommend a man as a head of a college—in ready tact, in aptitude for the small details of administration, and strict attention to the enforcement of college rules ... when Hawkins, by Newman's support, obtained the prize, it was not denied that the college had made a proper choice."[32] Froude had felt otherwise, arguing that if Keble were made Provost he "would bring in with him quite a new world,"—one in which "donnishness and humbug would be no more in the College, nor pride of talent, nor an ignoble secular ambition."[33] Yet, his view might very well have changed in light of Newman's argument that "we are not electing an angel but a Provost."[34] In all events, Froude, unlike Isaac Williams, another Keble supporter, bore no grudges when Keble withdrew his candidacy. After the election, Froude was instrumental in bringing Newman and Keble closer together. Later, with his own death imminent, Froude would often say to family and friends, "Do you know the story of the murderer who had done one good thing in his life? Well, if I was ever asked what good deed I have ever done, I should say I had brought Keble and Newman to understand each other."[35]

In the same year as the election for provost, Keble published *The Christian Year* (1827), the single best-selling book of poetry in the nineteenth century; in 1873, when the book's copyright expired, 158 editions had been published with total sales of 379,000. The modest Keble found the popularity of the book embarrassing, though he was pleased to be able to use the proceeds to renovate his church at Hursley. Later, in 1831, when Keble became Oxford's Professor of Poetry, he spoke of poetry as "a kind of medicine divinely bestowed upon man, which gives healing relief to mental emotion, yet without detriment to modest reserve, and while giving scope to enthusiasm yet rules it out with order and due control." Reserve, for Keble, was an essential attribute of the good poet: "the more keenly a man pursues any desired object the less keen is he to discourse of it to all and sundry;" and to substantiate his contention, he cited the example of "our own Hebert, who hides the deep love of God which consumed him behind a cloud of precious conceits."[36] This conception of poetry as impersonal and indirect—what one might call expressive concealment—recalls that of another Anglo-Catholic poet, T. S. Eliot, who famously held that "Poetry is not a turning loose of emotion, but an escape from emotion; it is not the expression of personality but an escape from personality. But, of course, only those who have personality and emotion know what it means to want to escape these things."[37] Keble's poetry also recalls Eliot's in its allusiveness; the Bible, the Prayer Book, George Herbert, Wordsworth and the work of the Caroline divines all find echoes in his stanzas.[38] There was another resemblance: both poets were keenly aware of how form calls forth unforthcoming thought and feeling. The poet Anne Ridler, who was Eliot's secretary at Faber and Faber between 1935 and 1940, when he was managing director there, recalled Eliot "saying that sometimes for the release of the deepest and most secret feeling to use a very strict form is a help because you concentrate on the technical difficulties of mastering the form and allow the content of the poem a more unconscious and freer release."[39] For Keble, the demands of metrical composition enabled poets "to soothe and compose their deepest emotions without violating a true reserve." Eliot tried to benefit from the same metrical therapy in "The Waste Land" (1922). On Margate Sands, the disenchanted poet mesmerized a generation by confessing that he could connect nothing with nothing, though whether what he called his "grouse against life" gave him the solace he sought is doubtful. Keble's views on poetry paralleled his views on theological matters.[40] If there was no place in poetry for the explicit, neither was there any place in theology for certainty, which, citing the work of Bishop Butler, he would increasingly adjudge unwarrantable.

In 1829, Keble persuaded Newman and Froude to join him in contesting Robert Peel's re-election to the Oxford seat over his volte-face with respect to Catholic Emancipation and helped elect in his place the conservative High Church candidate Robert Inglis. Keble was also joined by Newman and Froude in his opposition to the first Reform Bill of 1832. In his assize sermon, "On National Apostasy," preached on 13 July 1833, Keble made his opposition to the depredations of the liberals more explicit still by taking the Whig government to task over its Irish Temporalities Bill, which reduced the number of bishoprics and reallocated resources within the Church of Ireland. For Keble, the Whig government of Earl Grey was arrogating to itself privileges that only the Anglican Church should possess, and he saw in their hostility to the established religion a wider, more insidious apostasy spreading through the nation, which he urged his compatriots to resist. Keble's sermon helped launch the Oxford Movement, which was founded to defend the integrity of the Anglican Church against what Newman, Keble, Froude and their fellow Tractarians considered the encroachments of liberal politicians. The Cambridge intellectual historian Basil Willey recognized that "the movement was only political and anti-liberal because it was primarily spiritual; its deepest concern was with the invisible world; not with politics … its driving power, a hunger and thirst after righteousness, an effort towards true sanctity."[41]

In 1831, Keble returned to Oxford to take up the Poetry Professorship, which he held for four years. While fulfilling the duties of the Poetry Chair and supporting the Tractarians with tracts and the prestige of his reputation, Keble continued to assist his ailing father with his parish work until his death in 1834. In 1836, he took over the living of Hursley in Hampshire. Charlotte Yonge described the dutiful solicitude with which Keble ministered to his parishioners. "The vicar was the personal minister to each individual in his flock— teaching in the school, catechizing in the church, most carefully preparing for Confirmation, watching over the homes, and, however otherwise busied, always at the beck and call of every one in the parish. To the old men and women of the workhouse he paid special attention, bringing them little dainties, trying to brighten their dull minds as a means of reaching their souls, and endeavouring to raise their spirits to higher things."[42] Keble himself was fond of saying that "nothing in the world is really important except in so far as it may be brought to bear upon religion and nothing in religion itself is important except as in so far as it may be brought to bear upon practice."[43] However, before and after Newman's conversion, Keble's sense of the relation between profession and practice encountered unforeseen difficulties.

In 1835 Keble married Charlotte Clarke, who, judging from the miniature that was painted of her in the year of her marriage, was a bright beauty. "The lady," Tom Mozley recalled in his memoir, "was a strikingly handsome, pleasing, and dignified woman." Frederick Faber's brother thought her *too* handsome, describing her as a "pretty, showy person."[44] Hurrell Froude weighed in with his accustomed bluntness: "I hear that K's ἀποστασία has been announced to the papers—I do verily believe that 9 tenths of the people who hear of it will be a little shocked."[45] Few of Keble's letters after his marriage failed to mention his wife's delicate health, though this did not prevent her teaching the village children, making improvements to the garden or dancing minuets with her husband at vicarage parties. After Hurrell Froude's death in 1836, Charlotte's heart went out to Newman. "I shall be very glad for poor Newman to have the comfort of John's being in Oxford," she wrote to Elizabeth Keble. "He seems very much to need it; and nobody, I suppose, can so entirely sympathize with him both in his distress for the loss, and also in the views and opinions which knit them all three together."[46] Battiscombe summed up Charlotte as "cultured, affectionate, attractive, with just sufficient poise and knowledge of the world to fill up what was lacking in her husband."[47] That she complemented Keble must have been comically obvious on his wedding day when he appeared late with a broken collar-bone, suffered the day before after falling from his horse. He often composed his verses while riding, which did not redound to his horsemanship.

Keble's marriage was happy. Whether at home in Hursley vicarage or wintering in Penzance, Torquay or Bournemouth, he delighted in the wife he called "my conscience, my memory, and my common-sense."[48] If the marriage began in some trepidation, it flowered in affection and respect. Even in the poetry of reticence there was a place for joy.

> The voice that breathed o'er Eden,
>   That earliest wedding-day
> The primal marriage blessing,
>   It hath not passed away.

In 1836, Keble broke with his friend Thomas Arnold over Melbourne's appointment of R. D. Hampden to the Divinity Chair. In *Oxford Malignants*, written in response to the Tractarians' opposition to Hampden, Arnold took off the gloves: "The attack on Doctor Hampden bears upon it the character not of error but of moral wickedness ... for such persecution, the plea of conscience is not admissible; it can only be a conscience so blinded by willful neglect of the highest truths, or so corrupted by the habitual indulgence of evil passions, that it rather aggravates than excuses the guilt of those whom it misleads."[49] Against this lively invective Keble held his ground. When John Coleridge wrote to tell him that he had visited Arnold at his home, Fox How, Keble wrote back a stinging reply: "I cannot but judge it unkind to our old friend and also hardly fair to others who want to be guided in forming a correct judgement of his opinions that after this treason to the Holy Catholic Church (I cannot call it less) of which he has been guilty, good churchmen should still think it right to carry themselves towards him as if he had not taken part, and a prominent part, with the prevailing form of Anti-Christianism. It is unkind to him as it makes him judge lightly of the amount of his own errors, unkind to others as encouraging them to sympathise with him, to say nothing of the graver questions as to whether it be not something like disloyal communication with our Master's enemies. I had therefore rather direct to you anywhere but at Arnold's, but I suppose the post-man will not be much corrupted by seeing your two names together on the direction, so I shall even venture. But unless the view which I take of the whole drift of Scripture and of Christian antiquity can be altogether shaken it is impossible for me to think any person voluntarily drawing closer his connection with a person under such circumstances is in a certain sense partaker of his misdeeds ... I do not know what friends are for if they are not to mention such things to one another."[50] Here was proof of how much what Keble called "the Holy Catholic Church" meant to him and also of how ready he was to shun those—even good friends—who assailed her doctrines. Apropos Newman's attack on Hampden's Bampton Lecture, Arnold wrote to one of his Rugby pupils, William Charles Lake, who would later become a Fellow of Balliol and write glowing reminiscences of Newman, "Hampden is a good man, and an able one; a lover of truth and fairness; and I should think that the wholesome air of such a man's lectures would tend to freshen men's faith, and assure them that it had a foundation to rest upon, when the infinite dishonesty and foolery of such divinity as I remember in the lecture-rooms and pulpits in times past, would be enough to drive a man of sound mind into any extravagance of unbelief."[51] What Arnold omitted to mention was that Hampden had written a pamphlet calling for the abolition of the 39 Articles and was as opposed by most Broad Churchmen for his liberal anti-dogmatical views as he was by the Tractarians, who recoiled from the prospect of opening Oxford's doors to dissenters and atheists. Frederic Rogers was an exception, arguing, "if Dissenting tradesmen begin to send their sons to Oxford, it might chance that the effect would be just that the Church would appropriate some of the best blood of Dissent, the very people who would otherwise be most effective against her."[52] Newman took an unalloyedly hostile view of the liberal divine. "As to Dr Hampden," he wrote to a friend, "your imagination, I am sure, cannot picture any thing a quarter so bad as he really is – I do think him worse than a Socinian – In the British Magazine of this month, you will see a Pamphlet called 'Elucidations etc' stitched in, which gives you some but a very faint notion of his opinions. There is no doctrine, however sacred, which he does not scoff at – and in his Moral Philosophy he adopts the lowest and most groveling utilitarianism as the basis of Morals – he considers it is a sacred duty to live to this world – and that religion by itself injuriously absorbs the mind. Whately, whatever his errors, is openhearted, generous, and careless of money – Blanco White is the same, though he has turned Socinian – Arnold is amiable and winning – but this man, judging by his writings, is the most lucre loving, earthly minded, unlovely person one ever set eyes on."[53]

After years of failing health, Hurrell Froude died in 1836 of tuberculosis, and two years later Keble and Newman published his controversial *Remains* in four volumes. In 1841, Newman shared Tract 90 with Keble, who saw no grounds for counseling against publication. From 1841 to 1843, after the outcry against the alleged Romanizing tendencies of Tract 90, Newman wrote Keble a series of letters seeking advice on his doubts about the Anglican Church. In the wake of Tract 90, Keble braced himself for what he knew would be open season on the Tractarians. In the summer of 1841, when Keble invited him to attend the laying of the foundation stone of St. Saviour's, Leeds, which Pusey, at the instigation of F. W. Hook, financed—it was intended to be a model urban Tractarian church—Keble declined. "I have no great appetite just at present to go where clergy meet, for I expect I shall get (to use a significant expression) *a monkey's allowance*. So I stay to be kicked at home, with full expectation of getting plenty more."[54]

Payback for the perceived transgressions of the Apostolical party took petty forms. Peter Young, Keble's curate, was denied ordination by the Bishop of Winchester because he cited Caroline divines in answer to questions about the Real Presence.[55] Keble's pupil Isaac Williams was passed over for the Poetry Professorship. "A system of espionage, whisperings, backbitings, and miserable tittle-tattle," Dean Church recalled in his history of the Oxford Movement, "sometimes of the most slanderous or the most ridiculous kind, was set going in Oxford. Never in Oxford, before or since, were busybodies more truculent or more unscrupulous. Difficulties arose between Heads of Colleges and their tutors. Candidates for fellowships were closely examined as to their opinions and their associates. Men applying for testimonials were cross-questioned on

No. 90, as to the infallibility of general councils, purgatory, the worship of images, the *Ora pro nobis*, and the intercession of the saints; the real critical questions upon which men's minds were working being absolutely uncomprehended and ignored ... It was enough to suppose that a Popish Conspiracy was being carried on."[56] Battiscombe accurately summed up the response Keble made to this campaign of covert persecution. "Keble had always admired the Non-Jurors for their fidelity to their oath, for their High Church principles, and for their total disregard of worldly profit. If they had faced the dreary prospect of living in an ecclesiastical no-man's-land he supposed that he could do likewise, and from now onwards their example was never far from his mind."[57] It was one of the ironies of Keble's life that in choosing to remain in the English Church—which he associated with all that he held most dear, his wife, his father, his family, his friends, the then unspoiled loveliness of the English countryside, and his beloved Hursley vicarage—he willy-nilly chose a place of exile in a mid-Victorian society intent on casting away all that constituted the "perfect harmony" of his High Church upbringing. He died on 29 March 1866.

The Personal Influence of John Keble

"It seems strange," the entry for Keble in the old *DNB* pointed out, "that so shy, homely, unambitious man, living so retired a life, should yet have been the prime factor in the great religious movement of his time. Newman emphatically asserts in his *Apologia* that Keble was the "true and primary author" of the Oxford Movement. The explanation must be sought in his character ..."[58] Newman wrote of his dear friend in the *Apologia*, recalling how: "Keble was a man who guided himself and formed his judgments, not by processes of reason, by inquiry or by argument, but, to use the word, in a broad sense, by authority. Conscience is an authority; the Bible is an authority; such is the Church; such is Antiquity; such are the words of the wise; such are hereditary lessons; such are ethical truths; such are historical memories, such are legal saws and state maxims; such are proverbs; such are sentiments, passages, and prepossessions. It seemed to me as if he ever felt happier, when he could use argument mainly as a means of recommending or explaining what had claims on his reception prior to proof."[59] This was a fair description of Keble's accustomed approach to argument. In his "Preface on the Present Position of English Churchmen" (1847), with which he opened *Sermons Academical and Occasional* (1848), he forgoes argument altogether:

> ... to a romantic imaginative mind at least, the Roman claims stand out in a very obvious manner, and the English deficiencies are quite confessed and palpable. "Yours," they will tell us, "undeniably is the poor, the homely, the unattractive side of the alternative. Who would not have God's Saints, and their miracles, disclosed to Him, rather than regard them as so many unrevealed mysteries? Who would not possess rather than want an entire

and definite system of doctrine, and poetical ritual, extending through all parts of life? Who, if he could help it, would acknowledge such as the Tudor monarchs and their favourites as framers in any sense of the religious system he lives under?" In these and many more instances, which Roman Catholics are never tired of alleging, let it be granted that we stand, *prima facie*, in a position more or less humiliating: I say, to acquiesce in it, because it is providentially our own position,— to be dutiful and loyal amid the full consciousness of it,—savours of the same kind of generous contentment, as the not being ashamed of lowly parentage, nor unloving towards a dull monotonous home.[60]

This was the "a poor thing but mine own" defense of Anglicanism. Battiscombe regrets that Keble did not mount the case for the legitimacy of the Anglo-Catholic version of Anglicanism more forcefully; Anglo-Catholic readers of his "Preface" can only be grateful that he kept his comments on the subject to a minimum. Newman captured the essence of Keble's position rather unsparingly in *Anglican Difficulties*, in which he has a suppositious Tractarian mount the case for stasis along the same lines to which Keble would resort. "The question is deeper than argument while it is very easy to be captious and irreverent. It is not to be handled by intellect or talent, or decided by logic." Anglo-Catholics unfortunately find themselves "in a very anomalous state of things, a state of transition; but they must submit for a time to be without a theory of the Church, without an intellectual basis on which to plant themselves. It would be an utter absurdity of them to leave the Establishment, merely because they do not at the moment see how to defend their staying in it. Such accidents will from time to time happen in large and complicated questions ..."[61] Still, the Anglo-Catholic party "have light enough to guide them practically—first, because even though they wished to move ever so much, they see no place to move into; and, next, because, however it comes to pass, however contrary it may be to all the rules of theology and the maxims of polemics, to Apostles, Saints, common-sense, and the simplest principles of reason,—though it ought not be so in the way of strict science,—still, so it is, they are, in matter of fact, abundantly blest where they are."[62] Here was parody of an unmerciful accuracy.

What Keble lacked in coherence, he made up for in personal influence. For W. J. Copeland, Newman's curate at Littlemore, who had made a long study of Tractarianism, without ever finishing his proposed history of the movement, "The secret of the influence exercised by Keble was a loving sympathy which seemed to be always endeavoring to do one good, unknown, as it were by oneself, and avoiding, above all, the least acknowledgement."[63] In the *Apologia*, Newman recalled meeting the man who would become one of his dearest friends with unforgettable vividness. "The first time that I was in a room with him was on occasion of my election to a fellowship at Oriel, when I was sent for into the Tower, to shake hands with the Provost and Fellows. How is that hour fixed in my memory after the changes of forty-two years, forty-two this very day on which I write! ... I bore it till Keble took my hand, and then felt so abashed and unworthy of the honour done me, that I seemed desirous of quite sinking into the ground."[64] Frederick Oakeley, who would become the most avid of the younger Rome-leaning Tractarians, along with his good friend, William George Ward, recalled Keble as someone who "who speaks the more forcibly in proportion as he speaks less often, and whose sayings so calm, deep, and comprehensive, strike on many ears in these tumultuous days with almost the force of oracular intimations."[65] This is certainly how Newman saw Keble. "His had been the first name which I had heard spoken of, with reverence rather than admiration, when I came up to Oxford," Newman remembered. "When one day I was walking in High Street with my dear earliest friend ... with what eagerness did he cry out, "There's Keble!" and with what awe did I look at him! Then at another time I heard a Master of Arts of my college give an account how he had just then had occasion to introduce himself on some business to Keble, and how gentle, courteous, and unaffected Keble had been, so as almost to put him out of countenance."[66]

After joining Keble on a reading party at Southrop in 1823, Hurrell Froude wrote to his father, "I think the more I see of him I get to like and admire him more; in everything but person and manner he seems so very like my mother." All who knew her confirmed that Margaret Froude exuded true sanctity. In his brilliant study of Froude, Piers Brendon writes of how "She imbued the good life with a heroic quality and identified self-denial and suffering with the chivalric privilege of the saint and the ascetic." By likening Keble to his mother, Froude could not have paid his friend and counselor a handsomer compliment. Moreover, as Brendon points out, "When Froude understood truths intellectually he only grasped them partially and passively; he needed the full-blooded example of a Margaret Froude or a Keble to provide the imaginative stimulus which made him accept these truths with his whole being and use them as a basis for action." Froude was unsparingly critical of most of the people he met, but he saw in Keble rare goodness, and understood that it was not the kind that would meet with much success in the world. "He is the sort of person that the generality will not approve of," he wrote to his father, "till they are prepared to venerate him."[67] Froude's father, for his part, after Froude's early death, acknowledged that Keble "was the most valued of my dear Hurrell's friends."[68]

Dean Church recognized how essential Froude was to the dissemination of Keble's influence. "Mr. Keble had not many friends and was no party chief. He was a brilliant university scholar overlaying the plain, unworldly country parson; an old-fashioned English Churchman, with great veneration for the Church and its bishops, and a great dislike of Rome, Dissent, and Methodism, but with a quick heart; with a frank, gay humility of soul, with great contempt of appearances, great enjoyment of nature, great unselfishness, strict and severe principles of morals and duty. What was it that turned him by degrees into so prominent and so influential a person? It was the result of his convictions and ideas, and still more of his character, on the energetic and fearless mind of a pupil and disciple, Richard Hurrell Froude ..."[69] As Church shows, Keble inspired Froude, and vice versa. "Keble attracted and moulded Froude: he impressed Froude with his strong Churchmanship, his severity and reality of life, his poetry and high standard of scholarly excellence. Froude learned from him to be anti-Erastian, anti-methodistical, anti-sentimental, and as strong in his hatred of the world, as contemptuous of popular approval as any Methodist ... But Froude, in accepting Keble's ideas, resolved to make them active, public, aggressive ..."[70] It is questionable, for example, whether Keble would have had the impetus to write his assize sermon, "On National Apostasy," without the inspiration of his younger, more incendiary friend.

Isaac Williams, the Welsh devotional poet, recalled his tutor and friend with equally glowing fondness. He had never met anyone like him. "It was to me quite strange and wonderful that one so distinguished should always ask one's opinion, as if he was younger than myself. And one so overflowing with real genuine love in thought, word, and action, was quite new to me, I could scarcely understand it. I had been used to much gentleness and kindness, which is so fascinating in good society, but this was always understood to be chiefly on the surface; but to find a person always endeavouring to do one good, as it were, unknown to one's self, and in secret, and even avoiding that his kindness should be felt and acknowledged as such, this opened upon me quite a new world."[71] Many who knew Keble would have seen their own experience in Williams' description of how this "new world" affected him. "Religion a reality, and a man wholly made up of love, with charms of conversation, thought, and kindness, beyond what one had experienced among boyish companions,—this broke in upon me all at once ..."[72]

Newman and Keble

Newman and Keble initially were shy of one another. Keble was High Church and Newman still had tinges of the Evangelical about him, which he only gradually outgrew. And there was an age difference of nine years. Nonetheless, the two had more in common than they might have recognized. Both were profoundly influenced by their fathers. Newman took from his father's life a profound distrust of worldly success and Keble took from his a yearning for the High Church that he had known as a child. Both came from large, close-knit families. Both were deeply changed by the death of a beloved sister— Newman losing his 19-year-old sister Mary when he was 27 and Keble losing his 18-year-old sister Sarah when he was 22. Both were fairly well-read and yet looked askance at the pretensions of learning undisciplined by faith. Both had a profound sense of place. Both were renowned for gentleness and courtesy, which never prevented their being ruthless when principle was at stake. Both had beautiful voices. Both were poets. Both delighted in women. Both were prescient about what would be the consequences of liberal reform. Both recognized the evils that would accompany the rise of the periodical press.[73]

Yet, important as these similarities were, nothing bound Newman and Keble together more than their religious vows. Newman wrote in his journal, "As the time approaches for my ordination, thank God, I feel more and more happy. Make me Thy instrument ... make use of me, when Thou wilt, and dash me to pieces when Thou wilt. Let me, living or dying, in fortune and misfortune, in joy and sadness, in health & Sickness, in honour and dishonour, be Thine."[74] On the day itself, Sunday, 13 June 1825, he wrote: "It is over. I am thine, O Lord; I seem quite dizzy, and cannot altogether believe and understand it ... Yet, Lord, I ask not for comfort in comparison of sanctification ... I feel as a man thrown suddenly into deep water." Then, the day after, the full import of his new life took hold: "I have the responsibility of souls on me to the day of my death."[75] Keble was no less serious about his vows. After his ordination, he wrote to his good friend John Coleridge: "Pray earnestly, my dear, my best friend, that He would give me His grace, that I may not be altogether unworthy of the sacred office on which I am, rashly I fear, even now entering; but that some souls hereafter may have cause to bless me. Pray that I may be freed from vanity, from discontent, from impure imaginations; that I may not grow weary, nor wander in heart from God's service; that I may not be judging others uncharitably, nor vainly dreaming how they will judge me, at the very moment that I seem most religiously and most charitably employed."[76] Newman took as his motto *cor ad cor loquitor*—"heart speaks to heart." What enabled the hearts of Newman and Keble to speak so clearly to one another, despite their many differences, was their shared commitment to their pastoral vows.

Newman made many friends at Oxford, most notably his oldest and, before Froude, his closest friend, John Bowden, the memory of whose "happy and cheerful deportment" he never forgot, as well as Frederic Rogers, with whom he would later have so painful a falling out.[77] But Keble linked Newman to something beyond Oxford: unaffected, personal sanctity, the manifest love of God, without which religion is hollow, "a mere system, a law, a name ..."[78] A sister of one of Keble's friends captured something of what Newman prized in Keble when she confided to her diary, "Without making any fuss about it, he seems so interested in every one, and has such a continual quiet cheerfulness about him ... But it is his religious character that has struck me more than anything else, as it is indeed that from which everything else proceeds. I never saw any one who made so little *display* of it ... he seems to me a union of Hooker and George Herbert—the *humility* of the one and and *love* of the other. In short, altogether he is a man whom the more you see of and know, the less you must think of yourself."[79] Then, again, Keble was Newman's link to Hurrell Froude, whose dissatisfaction with the Anglican Church influenced Keble so deeply. For Newman, Keble personified that hunger for catholicity, which Newman never stopped hoping would motivate like-minded Anglicans to repudiate their *de facto* Protestant church and embrace the "one true Fold of the Redeemer."[80]

Newman and Keble first joined forces over the controversy that arose in Oxford over Catholic Emancipation (1829). Many historians have tended to view the controversy merely in terms of Robert Peel's volte-face. A. J. P. Taylor, for example, acknowledged the principle at issue but only to call attention to Peel's duplicity. "Peel was for many years the outstanding spokesman of the Protestant cause. Emancipation, he argued, would destroy the historic constitution; it would threaten the security of the established Church; it would not satisfy the Irish. Faced with rebellion in Ireland, he turned round, jettisoned his previous arguments, and announced that emancipation was the only way to keep Ireland quiet. Both sets of arguments made sense but not in the same mouth."[81]

Keble and Newman opposed Catholic Emancipation not because they were wedded to the Established Church but because they saw it as strengthening the liberal assault on dogmatic Christianity. When Peel was turned out of his Oxford seat by Robert Inglis, the candidate for whom Newman and Keble had campaigned, Newman was exultant. "We have achieved a glorious Victory," he crowed. "We have proved the independence of the Church and of Oxford."[82] Some have suggested that this was proof of how much Newman had fallen under the High Church influence of Keble but he did not need Keble's influence to recognize that the dismantling of the old order would necessarily dismantle the old order's religion. Newman was very clear about this: "Emancipation is the symptom of a systematic hatred to our Church borne by Romanists, Sectarians, Liberals and Infidels. If it were not for the Revolution which one would think must attend it, I should say the Church must fall ..." This was a sweeping prediction, as Newman acknowledged in his postscript: "What glorious enunciations I have excathedrized at the end of my letter."[83] Yet scarcely four years later, after the passing of the First Reform Bill (1832), Wellington, an incisive critic of these events, would confirm the accuracy of Newman's predictions: "The revolution is made," he wrote, "power is transferred from one class of society, the gentlemen of England, professing the faith of the Church of England, to another class of society, the shopkeepers, being Dissenters from the Church, many of them Socinians, others atheists." In 1838, Wellington would confirm Newman's prescience even more starkly: "The real question that now divides the country and which truly divides the House of Commons is church or no church. People talk of the war in Spain, and the Canada question. But all that is of little moment. The real question is church or no church."[84] The historian Jonathan Clark also shows the extent to which Newman's reading of the likely impact of Catholic Emancipation on the religion of the English was borne out by subsequent events. "The Church's identification with the old order turned her into a scapegoat; far from radical opinion being assuaged, the very scale and profundity of the revolution of 1828–1832 meant that, for the Church, there was no forgiveness. Even the Whig Lord Melbourne soon declared: 'What all the wise men promised has not happened; and what all the damned fools said would happen has come to pass.'"[85]

Melbourne may have conceded that Newman saw things with more clarity than his clever Whig friends, but he still found his writings impenetrable. In a letter to Lord Holland, the Prime Minister confessed: "I hardly make out what Puseyism is. Either I am dull or its apostles are very obscure. I have got one of their Newman's publications with an appendix of four hundred and forty-four pages. I have read fifty-seven and cannot say I understand a sentence, or any idea whatever."[86] Yet Newman was equally critical of the defenders of the English Church. "The talent of the day is against the Church," he admitted to his Mother. "The Church party, (visibly at least, for there may be latent talent, and great times give birth to great men,) is poor in mental endowments. It has not activity, shrewdness, dexterity, eloquence, practical powers. On what then does it depend? on prejudice and bigotry."[87]

Keble's position on Catholic Emancipation has often been confused with that of High Church die-hards, but it was more nuanced than that. In his *Apologia*, Newman noted how in Keble the defenders "of the political doctrines of the great clerical interest though the country" might find "intellectual, as well as moral support" but they would find something else as well. Keble's "weak point, in their eyes, was his consistency; for he carried his love of authority and old times so far, as to be more than gentle towards the Catholic Religion, with which the Toryism of Oxford and of the Church of England had no sympathy. Accordingly, if my memory be correct, he never could get himself to throw his heart into the opposition made to Catholic Emancipation, strongly as he revolted from the politics and the instruments by means of which that Emancipation had been won. I fancy he would have had no difficulty in accepting Dr. Johnson's saying about 'the first Whig' …" [88] In fact, Keble's response to the revolutionary implications of Catholic Emancipation and the Reform Bill that followed it was at once pragmatic and far-sighted. He saw that the old order was being toppled, and if the religion of the old order was not to suffer the same fate it would need to distance itself from a liberal parliament that was hostile to any dogmatic Christianity. In this regard, Keble was always interested in the example of the disestablished American Episcopal Church, which held out the possibility that the new world might somehow salvage the old. "I had a pleasant letter this morning from a clergyman in the USA," he wrote to his friend John Cornish in the wake of the First Reform Bill. "The letter would much comfort me if I were inclined to despond about our Church, but I don't know how it is, I can't help hoping well for her. I would not be a party to separating her from the State but if Providence should so order it, and if we are to get sound *Discipline* by it, 'twill be a very great consolation. I only hope the clergy will stand firm and avoid all base compromise; what I fear most is our continuing in a kind of modified connection with the present republican State of England." In the same letter, Keble did not rule out pulling up stakes and seeking asylum elsewhere. "Will you join me in buying some land in New Brunswick, or somewhere, that we may have a place to fly to in the case of the worst? I am seriously thinking of it. I don't so much mean a place to fly to as a place where one might find bread and cheese if we could not pick it up here, for it seems to me as if one ought to be among the last to leave the wreck."[89] For those who had grown up under the shadow of the French Revolution such gibes were not entirely facetious.

Keble's understanding of the predicament into which liberal reform threw the Church of England can be seen in his assize sermon "On National Apostasy" (1833), which for Newman marked the beginning of the Oxford Movement. Dean Church captured the embattled climate out of which the sermon arose. "It became more and more plain that great changes were at hand, though not so plain what they would be. It seemed likely that power had come into the hands of men and parties hostile to the Church in their principles, and ready to use to its prejudice the advantages which its position as an establishment gave them; and the anticipation grew in Keble's mind, that in the struggles which seemed likely, not only for the legal rights but for the faith of the Church, the Church might have both to claim more, and to suffer more, at the hands of Government."[90] The questions and concerns Keble raised in the sermon would exercise the Tractarians from 1833 to 1845 and beyond. "What are the symptoms, by which one may judge most fairly, whether or no a nation, as such, is becoming alienated from God and Christ?" Keble asked at the beginning of the sermon. "And what are the particular duties of sincere Christians, whose lot is cast by Divine Providence in a time of such dire calamity?"[91] Here was the clarion call that unified the Tractarians.

Tract 90 and the Crisis of Tractarianism

The "glorious clamor," as Maria Giberne called it, that broke over Tract 90 forced Keble to recognize that the rift in the Anglican Church between those who read her articles in a Protestant and those who read them in a Catholic light could not widen indefinitely.[92] Sooner or later, Anglicans would have to decide whether they wished to subscribe to a Protestant or to a 'catholic' church, and if they chose the latter, they would have to decide whether the English Church truly met the criteria for catholicity. This was the crisis of Tractarianism. Newman wrote the Tract to convince Rome-leaning Tractarians like George Ward and Frederick Oakeley that the 39 Articles "Though the offspring of an uncatholic age ... are, through God's providence, to say the least, not uncatholic, and may be subscribed by those who aim at being Catholic in heart and doctrine." Newman stressed that "the Articles are evidently framed on the principle of leaving open large questions ... They state extremely broad truths, and are silent about their adjustment." Where Newman drew the Protestant ire of his Anglican compatriots was in contending that, "it is a duty which we owe both to the Catholic Church and to our own, to take our reformed confessions in the most Catholic sense which they will admit; we have no duty towards their framers."[93] To sidestep this duty would be to concede the definition of Anglican dogma to the Broad Church party, which, of course, was only interested in dissolving, not defining dogma. What baffled so many of Newman's contemporaries was his insistence on treating the 39 Articles as a living document, not as one buried in the past. And this was why it was so ironic of critics like F. D. Maurice to characterize Newman's interpretation of the Articles as "non-natural" because, on the contrary, Newman's interpretation was profoundly natural.[94] His understanding of how history plays out in the world of the present animates the Tract's entire argument. "The Protestant confession was drawn up with the purpose of including Catholics," he reminds his readers, "and Catholics now will not be excluded. What was an economy in the Reformers, is a protection to us. What would have been a perplexity to us then is a perplexity to Protestants now. We could not then have found fault with their words; they cannot now repudiate our meaning."[95]

In the most memorably acid passage of Tract 90, Newman wrote: "let the Church, our Mother, sit still; let her be content to be in bondage; let her work in chains; let her submit to her imperfections as a punishment; let her go on teaching with the stammering lips of ambiguous formularies, and inconsistent precedents, and principles but partially developed. We are not better than our fathers; let us bear to be what Hammond was, or Andrews, or Hooker; let us not faint under that body of death, which they bore about in patience; nor shrink from the penalty of sins, which they inherited from the age before them."[96] One reader of the Tract, Robert Belaney, a Cambridge M.A. who resigned his Anglican living in 1852 and later became a Catholic priest at Glasgow, wrote to Newman to assure him that his warning was welcome in at least one quarter. "I began to read the Tract with some alarm when I heard of the sensation it had made at Cambridge," Belaney wrote, "hardly believing that so much noise could have arisen without any cause ..." But he was surprised by how thoroughly he agreed with Newman. "I am rejoiced with the Tract. Its notoriety will give notoriety to others that have preceded it, and they will together, turn men to religious inquiry who had hitherto thought only of the subject as if it concerned them less than the state of the funds. You have, I think, broken the chain which bound the Christian community to a deadly and deadening system—a system as remote from that which has been preserved to us in the Liturgy, as truth is from its counterfeit."[97]

In 1841, Keble privately printed a letter to his friend John Coleridge setting out his view of the controversy, which was later published as "The Case of Catholic Subscription to the Thirty-Nine Articles Considered with Especial Reference to the Duties and Difficulties of English Catholics in the Present Crisis." Keble "saw nothing in the sense of what was said, which had not been taught at large long ago, without a shadow of scandal ..."[98] He was as surprised as Newman that the Tract should have caused such an uproar. For men like Keble and Newman (and for that matter, Gladstone), all steeped in history, the idea that the Articles could be given a Catholic reading was a commonplace.

In the national debate over Tract 90, Pusey and Keble stood by their belea-guered friend.[99] To the Bishop of London, apropos the suppression of Tract 90, Pusey pointed out on Newman's behalf: "Books have appeared, and are appearing continually, denying the doctrine of baptismal regeneration, terming the doctrine which our Church teaches a heresy, but no one interferes with or censures them."[100] Later, in 1865, Pusey after publishing his first *Eirenicon*, suggesting grounds for some rapprochement between the English and the Roman Church, reprinted Tract 90, convinced, as he told Keble, that "People are now prepared for it ... my historical preface will remove a good deal of prejudice ... Liddon [Pusey's biographer] agrees with me, that the ... slur on Tract XC is a great hindrance to the Catholic interpretation of the Articles."[101] At the time of the Tract's original publication, however, Keble, for all his attempts to remain upbeat, saw the storm over Tract 90 as an ominous sign of things to come. "My feeling about it is that if we are right in the main, their censure [that of the Heads of Houses] if carried will cause more good than harm, and the annoyance of it to oneself be no more than one deserves in many ways. But I hardly know how to reconcile to the notion of Oxford falling off from Catholicism so expressly. It will make one's life, what remains of it, much less poetical."[102] From this point on, as Church observed in his history of the Oxford Movement, and indeed as Newman so accurately predicted in his King William Street lectures, later published as *Lecturers on Certain Difficulties felt by Anglicans in Submitting to the Catholic Church* (1850), the Tractarian clergy were discredited men. "Oxford repudiated them. Their theories, their controversial successes, their learned arguments, their appeals to the imagination, all seemed to go down, and to be swept away like chaff, before the breath of straightforward common sense and honesty. Henceforth there was a badge affixed to them and all who belonged to them, a badge of suspicion and discredit, and even shame, which bade men beware of them, an overthrow under which it seemed wonderful that they could raise their heads or expect a hearing."[103]

Via Media

Since so much of the crucial correspondence between Newman and Keble from 1841 to 1845 turned on the via media, we should examine how both men regarded that elusive property.[104]

Newman's conversion to Rome cast a fair amount of what he did within the Oxford Movement in an ironic light but there were few more ironic things in that career than the letter he sent off to Charles Russell, an Irish Catholic priest and professor of Church History at Maynooth, in response to a letter in which the professor admitted: "Every day, every new event, increases the confidence with which I put up my humble prayers that I may be permitted to see it fully accomplished—to see your Church once again in her ancient and honourable position, to have the happiness of knowing that you and your devoted friends are ministering to the same altar to which my own life is vowed."[105] In response to Russell's moving letter, Newman defended the Anglican Church with arguments that he would later use to repudiate her.

> I do not look so despairingly at our Church as you do. While I think (of course) that she is a branch of the Church Catholic, I also have lately had my hopes increased as to the prospect of her improvement in doctrinal exactness, by the very events which seem to you to show that Catholic truth is but barely tolerated within her pale. I have every reason to be made sanguine by the disturbance which has followed Tract 90, which I never have been before … . My only anxiety is lest your branch of the Church should not meet us by those reforms which surely are necessary—It never

could be, that so large a portion of Christendom should have split off from the communion of Rome, and kept up a protest for 300 years for nothing. I think I never shall believe that so much piety and earnestness would be found among Protestants, if there were not some very grave errors on the side of Rome. To suppose the contrary is most unreal, and violates all one's notions of moral probabilities. All aberrations are founded on, and have their life in, some truth or other—and Protestantism, so widely spread and so long enduring, must have in it, and must be witness for, a great truth or much truth. That I am an advocate for Protestantism, you cannot suppose—but I am forced into a Via Media, short of Rome, as it is at present.[106]

In describing himself as "forced into a Via Media" Newman was only telling the abject truth. More than twenty years later, in his *Apologia*, he would recall the faltering progress of the theory that promised a happy medium "between the extremes of Romanism and popular Protestantism as preserved in the English Church." There, he cited his article, "The State of Religious Parties," from the April 1839 number of the *British Critic*, in which he had written that all who did not wish to be "democratic, or pantheistic, or popish," must "look out for *some* Via Media which will preserve us from what threatens, though it cannot restore the dead." These were typical of the terms in which Newman recommended his mediatorial theory—never as a perfect solution to his doubts about the catholicity of the English Church but as a *pis aller*. "The spirit of Luther is dead; but Hildebrand and Loyola are alive. Is it sensible, sober, judicious, to be so very angry with those writers of the day, who point to the fact, that our divines of the seventeenth century have occupied a ground which is the true and intelligible mean between extremes? Is it wise to quarrel with this ground, because it is not exactly what we should choose, had we the power of choice? Is it true moderation, instead of trying to fortify a middle doctrine, to fling stones at those who do? ... Would you rather have your sons and daughters members of the Church of England or of the Church of Rome?"[107]

Later, in a letter to Henry Wilberforce, written in January 1846, after he had converted, Newman admitted that his doubts about the via media had been fairly persistent. Responding to an article questioning his belief in the Anglican Church when still a Tractarian, Newman told Wilberforce that "in truth the writer confuses faith in the English Church, with faith in the particular theory on which it is to be supported and the particular body of evidence which forms its credentials. This theory is familiarly called the Via Media. Now in the year 1834 or 35 my belief even in this theory was so strong, that I recollect feeling an anxiety about the Abbé Jager, with whom I was controverting, lest my arguments were unsettling him and making him miserable. Those arguments were not mine, but the evolution of Laud's theory, Stillingfleet's etc which seemed to me clear, complete, and unanswerable. I do not think I had that unhesitating belief in it in 1836-7 when I published my Prophetical Office, or rather I should say that zeal for it – for I believed it fully or at least was not conscious I did not. It is difficult to say whether or not a flagging zeal involves an incipient doubt.... . I thought the theory true, but that all theories were doubtful and difficult, and all reasoning a weariness to the flesh."[108] Yet, in familiarizing himself with the patristic history on which the via media theory was largely based, Newman began to have more serious doubts. "As time went on and I read the Fathers more attentively, I found the Via Media less and less satisfactory. It broke down with me in 1839. So much on the theory of the Anglican Church – but as to the Church itself I implicitly believed in her divinity till a late date. I cannot tell when – I suppose till I gave up St Mary's"[109]

Even in 1834, in "Home Thoughts from Abroad," a dialogue between three friends about the nature of the Anglican Church and its relation to Rome, Newman had already given expression to a view of the acceptability of the via media that was highly skeptical.

> What is the ground of Andrewes and Laud, Stillingfleet and the rest, but a theory which has never been realized? I grant that the position they take in argument is most admirable, nearer much than the Romanist's to that of the primitive Church, and that they defend and develop their peculiar view most originally and satisfactorily; still, after all, it is a *theory*,—a fine-drawn theory, which has never been owned by any body of churchmen, never witnessed in operation in any system. The question is not, how to draw it out, but how to do it. Laud's attempt was so unsuccessful as to prove he was working upon a mere theory. The actual English Church has never adopted it: in spite of the learning of her divines, she has ranked herself among the Protestants, and the doctrine of the Via Media has slept in libraries ...[110]

This did not stop Newman from expounding the via media in 1837 in a book of the same title which he dedicated to Martin Routh (1755–1854), the legendary Magdalen don, who was as fond of his eighteenth-century wig as he was of all the traditions of his college. Once he became President of Magdalen, he married a woman 35 years younger, though she aged more rapidly than her long-lived husband. Tuckwell recalled this unique woman vividly: "With strongly marked features, a large mustache and a profusion of grey hair, she became a familiar sight, driven about Oxford by a hunchback named Cox in a little chaise drawn by a donkey. 'Woman,' the president would call to her as soon as he saw the chaise arriving, 'Woman, the ass is at the door.'"[111] In a letter to Routh, Newman reiterated his doubts about the soundness of the via media: "I cannot venture to hope that there is nothing in my volume of private and questionable opinion – but I have tried, as far as may be, to follow the line of doctrine marked out by our great divines, of whom perhaps I have chiefly followed Bramhall, then Laud, Hammond, Field, Stillingfleet, Beveridge and others of the same school."[112] To Manning he was even more candidly diffident. "My book, I expect, will be out next Wednesday. It is an anxious thing. I have to deal with facts so much more than in writing Sermons – and facts which touch people to the quick. With all my care I may have made some floors – and I am aware that I deserve no mercy from your Protestants – and if they read me, shall find none. Then again the Via Media is ever between the cross fires of Papists and Protestants." [113]

This enduring doubt about the only theory that enabled Newman to cling to some belief in the catholicity of the Anglican Church must be kept in mind when one revisits the series of letters that Newman wrote to Keble about whether he should retain St. Mary's because it refutes Church's suggestion that if the Heads of Houses had been less intemperate in their response to Tract 90 Newman might have remained faithful to the via media. All the evidence we have prior to 1841 shows that Newman would probably have repudiated the via media in any case, regardless of how the Heads of Houses responded. Church, however, was right about the fallout of Tract 90: "It was a favorite boast of Dean Stanley's in after-times that the intervention of the Liberals saved the Tractarians from complete disaster. It is quite true that the younger Liberals disapproved the continuance of harsh measures ... But the debt of the Tractarians to their Liberal friends in 1845 was not so great as Dean Stanley ... supposed to be the case ... . The Tractarians were saved by what they were and what they had done, and could do, themselves. But it is also true, that out of these feuds and discords, the Liberal party which was to be dominant in Oxford took its rise, soon to astonish old-fashioned Heads of Houses with new and deep forms of doubt more audacious than Tractarianism, and ultimately to overthrow not only the victorious authorities, but the ancient position of the Church, and to recast from top to bottom the institutions of the University." [114]

Keble's uneasiness with the via media of the Anglican Church was at once more guarded and less decisive. In a revelatory sermon entitled, "Endurance of Church Imperfections," preached before Oxford on the Feast of St. Andrew, 1841, he wrote, "When God seems to be breaking down what He hath built, and plucking up what He hath planted; when we know not how soon our house may be left unto us desolate; let us not then, of all times, be seeking great things for ourselves; neither in the way of temporal safety and ease, nor even in the way of spiritual assurance and comfort; but let us turn our thoughts more dutifully than ever to the plain straightforward keeping of the Commandments of God ... accounting it a great thing, if we do but probably see our way in the very next step we are to take, and if we have but a reasonable chance of being in God's Church now, and of pardon and peace when we come to the eternal world." [115] There is a distinct note of diffidence in this, as well as the suggestion that accepting uncertainty might be an exercise of humility, of spiritual mortification. "For surely to serve God loyally in doubt and anguish and perplexity concerning the faith, it is as great a trial of disinterestedness as to serve Him in the midst of outward and bodily discomforts." [116] And comparing the English to the Roman Church, with respect to what he calls "the great foundations of the faith," he writes of how "we are met in one place by startling indecision, in another by no less startling positiveness ..." [117] Speaking first of the Anglican Church, he remarks how "the discipline of the Church ... has vanished from among ourselves," and wonders "how much of grace and perfection is lost by the Church submitting for any length of time to this absence of discipline ..."[118] Making every allowance for the indecisiveness of the Anglican Church, Keble expressly warns his auditors not to seek any certainty elsewhere, which he regards as "a temptation which may and ought to be met practically by the like exercise of self-control as any other indulgence of natural feeling."[119] And, again, he counsels against succumbing to this temptation on the grounds that there is something pleasing to God in our abiding uncertainty. "Bear a part in the overwhelming trials of the Household of God, now seeming to be forsaken," Keble exhorts the faithful, elaborating on God's words to Baruch. "Teach yourself to acquiesce in what befalls you, by considering how strange it would seem, how unaccountable in the sight of Angels, were you to be exempt from fear and anguish, now when the windows from on high are opened and the foundations of the earth do shake. Rather learn to take with thankfulness your share of the perplexity, as a token of hope that you are yet in God's Household, since you are accounted worthy to be afflicted in her affliction." From this Keble derived guidance for the perplexed Anglican faithful that he would recommend in the years leading up to and after Newman's conversion. "If the whole Kingdom of God be indeed in the decayed condition, which so many appearances indicate; how dare any individual among us seek great things for himself, either in the way of certainty or sensible comfort ... ?" For Keble, certainty in religious matters had become tantamount to presumptuousness. "Who among us have led such lives, that we may safely trust our own impressions of having received full satisfaction, either in the judgment or in our feelings?"[120] Those who allow themselves to hunger for certainty are culpable of vainglory. "They have too much of a seeming Paradise in them, too little of the Cross." This is the "startling positiveness" that Keble sees in those impressed by the claims of Rome, while "a rightly disposed and considerate person ... would rather be startled and rendered suspicious by arguments and statements which sound entirely satisfactory ..." Moreover, this same "rightly disposed person" should "greatly mistrust the probable effect of any change, which is made not out of simple obedience and from a longing after abstract perfection."[121] This laid the ground for the argument for staying put, which Keble gamely mounted, though not without strenuous special pleading.

> If the Communion in which you are placed by God's Providence has *prima facie* the most evident notes of the Church, all except visible Communion with other parts of Christendom: if it appear to be linked by due succession with those who were sent out to preach among all nations, beginning at Jerusalem; if it acknowledge the same Scriptures, and interpret them by the same Creeds, as did the whole Church in her days of perfect union; if it seems also to possess the Holy Sacraments unmutilated in all things essential, or at least as completely so as those who invite you away from it: for surely the omission of the Cup in the Eucharist is in itself a greater liberty to take with the institution of Jesus Christ, than any deviation allowed by us from the services of the early Church—if your Church, moreover pray constantly for the actual Communion which it unhappily wants, and have never yet forfeited it, as the Donatists did, by pronouncing other Churches out of the

Body of Christ:—then continue in it, and do your best for it, by prayer, by good works, by patience, by self-denial, by humility ...[122]

This was the summons to stasis that Keble would make before and after Newman converted. But here he sought to strengthen his case by making the claim that "the mark of the Cross seems rather to belong to those who struggle on in a decayed and perhaps still decaying Church, bearing their burden as they may, than those who allow their imaginations to dwell on fancied improvements and blessings to be obtained on possible changes of Communion."[123] Moreover, he argued that "Even if it were granted, for argument's sake, that some other portion of the Church is abstractedly better than our own, has surer marks of life and reality in it: are we quite sure that men's passing over to it would not involve them in the moral guilt of schism, though wanting perhaps the formal nature of a schismatical act?"[124] Another consideration for Keble was that "the evils of our present religious condition be they what they may ... were none of our own choosing. We are not therefore, responsible for them, any further than. as each in his station may have neglected providential helps to discern and amend them. But the evils of a man's new profession, should he take on him to choose for himself, will be his by a very peculiar responsibility."[125] No one should be tempted to leave an unreal for a real Church because the latter may be as untenable as the former. "What if the practical corruptions, questionable theoretical claims, and preemptory anathemas of his new Communion, bring him back before long to as sorrowful a feeling as at first, of the decayed and disunited condition of the whole Church; aggravated by the consciousness, that at such a time he has been seeking great things for himself, and has little regarded the consequences to his brethren."[126] Here the reference to Newman's case could not be more pointed, though Keble must have regretted posing this question: "Is there one single instance, since the heat of the Reformation was over, of any person passing from the English to any other Church ... and afterwards becoming at all remarkable for sanctity?"[127]

These passages from Newman and Keble show that before their crucial correspondence, each was inclined to a fairly consequential position: Newman was rolling up the via media, breaking free of what he would later call "the paralogisms of our ecclesiastical and theological theory" while Keble was digging in.[128] Still, Newman knew intimately that there were grounds for Keble to reconsider his entrenched position; he was discovering them himself in the most searing way possible; and he was intent on sharing these grounds with his friend. The drama of their correspondence lies in seeing how Newman used his experience of conversion to try to bring Keble round to an equally decisive understanding of the implications of the crisis of Tractarianism.

Newman/Keble Correspondence 1841–1845

In the midst of the furor over Tract 90, Newman reached out to Keble for advice. "The Heads of Houses having censured the Tract as an evasion and thereby indirectly condemned the views of doctrine contained in it," Newman wrote to Keble, "the Bishop (even though he put it on the ground of peace etc) would virtually in the eyes of the world be censuring it." Newman was concerned not so much for himself as for those within the Tractarian fold who shared his Catholic reading of the articles. "I do not think I can acquiesce in such a proceeding by any active co-operation of mine … I am at this moment the representative of the interests of many who more or less think with me."[129] Keble wrote back: "Certainly I do not see how it is consistent silently to suppress the Tract and go on as if the point was given up, even at a Bishop's command. The least you can do must be to get leave to accompany the suppression with a public declaration that you do so and so for obedience' sake, not at all giving up the view. If the Bishop allows this, he permits his clergy to hold the view, as consistent with the literal and grammatical sense; which is a great point gained. If he does not allow it, I do not see, unwilling as I am to come to the conclusion, how you can retain St Mary's." He also clearly recognized that if Newman resigned St. Mary's, it would have implications for him. "And if you give it up on such a ground, I do not see how I and others in other dioceses can remain as we are without scandal. We must in some way or other declare our own sense of the Articles; by reprinting No. 90, or writing fresh Tracts, or by direct application to our Bishops. I for one feel I must do something, though I cannot clearly see as yet what that something would be. Otherwise we entangle ourselves in the snare of holding office and receiving church payments on an implied condition which we know in our hearts we are not fulfilling. In short there is no end to the serious results which such a step on the Bishop's part would have … If all the Bishops join, that is another thing: and will leave, I imagine, no choice, unless by respectful remonstrance we could induce them to mitigate their sentence. It is a sad case, but we ought to be thankful that we have Lay Communion to fall back upon."[130] That Keble was contemplating such a move, with whatever reservations, must have encouraged Newman to hope that his friend was not entirely opposed to conversion.

Newman bore up under the storm set off by Tract 90 with characteristic aplomb. Keble saw his friend at the very height of the storm and reported on how jaunty he found him. "I went out to Littlemore and saw him on Friday and he came in that evening and slept and I saw him yesterday morning. He looked a little wan, but had been very cheerful about it altogether …" Newman admitted that he might have been "rash" and would probably have to explain himself but he was not downhearted. Pusey noticed the same equanimity in their provocative friend: "The pseudo-traditional and vague ultra-Protestant interpretation of the Articles has received a blow from which it will not recover. People will abuse Tract 90, and adopt its main principles. It has been a harassing time for Newman, but all great good is purchased by suffering; and he is wonderfully calm …"[131]

"The apparent termination of the affair of Tract 90 left Newman 'without any harass or anxiety' on his mind," as Father Francis Bacchus observed in the Oratory's edition of *Correspondence of John Henry Newman with John Keble and others 1839–1845* (1917). "It was natural that he should feel an inward peace after the meekness with which he had borne the contumely ... [of] the University, and the arduous act of obedience which he had rendered to his Bishop. Then the doubt which had assailed him in the autumn of 1839 seems to have been almost quiescent. Nevertheless, he felt that retirement and self-effacement became him, and in consequence withdrew more and more to Littlemore, and occupied himself with his translations from St. Athanasius for the Library of the Fathers." That Newman was translating the works of St. Athanasius at this tumultuous period of his life had a certain appositeness, for the saint whom he considered a "great refuge" had been banished from Alexandria no less than three times for his own intransigent orthodoxy.[132] Newman was doubtless grateful for the opportunity to read more closely one of his favorite Fathers. But, as Father Bacchus dryly observed, Newman's "security did not last long."[133] On 5 October 1841, he wrote to Keble, apropos the Jerusalem Bishopric, "It really does seem to me as if the Bishops were doing their best to uncatholicize us, and whether they will succeed before a rescue comes, who can say?"[134] On October 10th, he wrote to his good friend, S. F. Wood, "There is not a single Anglican at Jerusalem, but we are to place a Bishop ... there, to collect a communion of Protestants, Jews, Druses, Monophysites, conforming under the influence of our war steamers, to counterbalance the Russian influence through Greeks, and the French through Latins."[135] On November 24th, Newman wrote to another good friend, James Hope, the barrister who made a fortune representing the railroads and later married the granddaughter of Walter Scott, "Nor do I see that anyone should be surprised at my resolving on such a course. I have been for a long while assuring persons that the English Church was a branch of the Catholic Church. If, then, a measure is in progress which in my judgment tends to cut from under me the very ground on which I have been writing and talking, and to prove all I hold a mere theory and illusion—a paper theology which facts contradict—who will not excuse it if I am deeply pained at such proceedings?"[136] Keble took a very much less critical view of the Bishopric.[137] Having nothing like the same personal stake in the formation of the via media as Newman had, he could look dispassionately at a scheme that made a mockery of Newman's "paper theology." Also, at this time, he had his hands full with the controversy surrounding the successor to Oxford's Poetry Chair. Isaac Williams was naturally Keble's preferred choice but he was being pointedly passed over because of his Tractarian sympathies, which Keble was right to see as an indirect attack on his own Tractarian affiliations. Nevertheless, as he wrote to his brother Tom, Keble grasped how the Jerusalem Bishopric was pushing his friend closer and closer to Rome. "It comes to this, that his sympathies are more that way (towards Rome) than any other among existing systems, but he is withheld by conscience from acting upon them. This is not a pleasant position, but is it either a very uncommon one, or, in this case, a peculiarly dangerous one? Is it not a great security that he is so fully aware as he seems to be of his danger?"[138]

Newman's awareness of his "danger" was acute enough. Yet his own sense of why he should resign his living at St. Mary's was straightforward. First, as he wrote to Keble in March 1843, he was not influencing his parishioners but rather "persons who are not given me in charge," undergraduates mostly, who attended his services and sermons "without, perhaps against, the wish of their proper guardians." Then, he was concerned that his sermons were not likely to reinforce his auditors in their Anglican faith. "What influence I exert is simply and exactly, be it more or less, in the direction of the Church of Rome—and that whether I will or no. What men learn from me, who learn anything, is to lean towards doctrines and practices which our Church does not sanction. There was a time when I tried to balance this by strong statements against Rome"—in February 1843, Newman had placed a formal retraction of his anti-Catholic statements in the *Oxford Conservative Journal* and the *Oxford University Herald*—"which I suppose to a certain extent effected my object. But now, when I feel I can do this no more, how greatly is the embarrassment of my position increased! I am in danger of acting as a traitor to that system, to which I must profess attachment or I should not have the opportunity of acting at all." The momentousness of what he was about in thus contemplating resigning St. Mary's was not lost on him: indeed it caused him to doubt whether he even knew what he was saying. "I am so bewildered," he wrote to Keble, "that I don't know right from wrong, and have no confidence of being real in any thing I think or say."[139]

Keble wrote back on 3 May 1843: "I have turned the subject of your connexion with St. Mary's every way in my mind as well as I can; and it seems to me that the time is come when there will be nothing wrong in your retiring, if your own feelings prompt you to do so, as of course they must on many accounts." Still, Keble urged his friend to try to keep hold of Littlemore: "the loss of your sermons from St. Mary's will be compensated by your labours in giving private advice and hearing confessions." Then he pointed to the silence that had met Newman's retraction of his anti-Catholic statements to reassure him that "people are restrained in this instance, themselves know not how, and it gives one good hope that you will be allowed to go on quietly in what you judge, on the whole, your duty." He followed this with an interesting admission: "I am not sure that I ought not to follow your example, committed as I am to the very same principles; only that I do not think so much of Bishops' words in their Charges as you do …" This was one of the grounds on which Keble would justify remaining within the Anglican Church: the fact that the Bishops had not *formally* censured Tract 90. However, whether Keble did in fact share the "very same principles" would be proven in the months ahead. He ended his discussion of the matter with a nice distinction: "without saying that it is your duty to retire, one may very well think that it is perfectly open for you to do so. Whichever way you resolve, I do not see that you can do very wrongly."[140] Such sympathy from Keble must have been doubly welcome at a time when Newman's loyalties could not have been more agonizingly torn.

In the meantime, the estrangement from old friends that would become Newman's lot in Protestant England after he converted had already begun. The breakdown of his relations with his good friend Frederic Rogers (1811–1889) was only one instance of many. While still at Eton, Rogers had chosen to go to Oriel expressly because of Newman's connection with the college. A lawyer, he later went on to become a colonial administrator. In 1831, he spent the long vacation with Newman and his family at Iffley. After taking a double first, he became a Fellow of Oriel from 1833 to 1845. From the first, Rogers was a staunch adherent of the Oxford Movement. He was also one of Newman's most trusted advisers. In 1860, he became Permanent Under Secretary of State for the Colonies and in 1871 he was raised to the peerage as Baron Blachford—the first civil servant to be so honored and one of the first to join the Privy Council. However, beginning in 1839, when Newman confided in him his doubts about the legitimacy of the Anglican Church, Rogers drew apart from his old friend and in April of 1843 he wrote to inform him that continued relations on their old footing would not now be possible.

> I do not like meeting you again without having said, once for all, what I hope you will not think hollow or false. I cannot disguise from myself how improbable—perhaps impossible—a recurrence to our former terms is. But I wish, before the time has past for such an acknowledgment, to have said how deeply and painfully I feel—and I may say have more or less felt for *years*—the greatness of what I am losing, and to thank you for all you have done and been to me ... I *do* feel most earnestly how much of anything which I may venture to be thankful for in what I am is of your forming— how more than kind—how tender you have always been to me, and how unlikely it is that I can ever again meet with anything approaching in value to the intimacy which you gave me ... I should have been pained at leaving all this unsaid.[141]

On 4 May 1843, Newman shared with Keble the sense of guilty tergiver-sation that was only one trial through which his conversion had to proceed. "I have enough consciousness in me of insincerity and double dealing, which I know you abhor, to doubt about the correctness of what I shall tell you of myself. I really cannot say whether I am stating my existing feelings, motives, and views fairly, and whether my memory will not play me false. I cannot hope but I shall seem inconsistent to you—and whether I am or have been I cannot say. I will but observe that it is very difficult to realize one's own views in certain cases, at the time of acting, which is implied in culpable inconsistency; and difficult again, when conscious of them, to discriminate between passing thoughts and permanent impressions, particularly when they are unwelcome. Some thoughts are like hideous dreams, and we wake from them, and think they will never return; and though they do return, we cannot be sure still that they are more than vague fancies; and till one is so sure they are not, as to be afraid of concealing within what is at variance with one's professions, one does not like, or rather it is wrong, to mention them to another."[142] In a second letter written on the same day Newman made good on this ominous preamble by announcing to his friend: "At present, I fear, as far as I can realize my own convictions, I consider the Roman Catholic Communion the Church of the

Apostles, and that what grace is among us (which, through God's mercy, is not little) is extraordinary, and from the overflowings of His Dispensation."[143]

When Keble received the letters, he took them unopened to an abandoned chalk-pit, "moved," as Battiscombe nicely put it, "by the animal instinct to hide which is common to all creatures in pain," and there, after a "grand swallow of pain," he read the long-dreaded and yet still unbelievable news that his friend was contemplating leaving the Church of England.[144] It is one of the great scenes in the Tractarian drama. A full ten days later, Keble finally managed to write back to his friend, meeting his anguished candor with ready empathy. "Believe me, my very dear Newman, that any thought of willful insincerity in you can find no place in my mind. You have been and are in a most difficult position, and I seem to myself in some degree able to enter into your difficulties: and, although one sees of course how an enemy might misrepresent your continuing in the English Priesthood with such an impression on your mind, I have no thought but of love and esteem and regard and gratitude for you in this as in everything ..." Still, Keble could not resist making a number of eleventh-hour appeals. Newman should recognize that leaving the English Church would bring him "in every respect nearer ... the temptation of going over." He should remember that "for what is wrong without our fault in the place where God's Providence has set us, we are not ourselves answerable, but we are for what may be wrong in the position we choose for ourselves." Then, again, Newman should ask himself whether his recent retraction of his anti-Catholic statements was unduly influencing him. "Do you not think it possible that you may have over-estimated the claims of Rome in your later studies from a kind of feeling that your earlier expressions had done her wrong?" Then, again, by leaving the English Church, Newman would "undo what little good may have been done of late"—a consideration that Jemima also urged her brother to bear in mind. But the most revelatory appeal Keble made was the one to which he would return on numerous occasions in the future. "As to the question itself I am really too ignorant of the parts of history to which you refer to say a word: but can it be that the evidence seems so overpowering as to amount to moral certainty? and if not, ought not but a small probability on the other side to weigh against it practically?"[145]

Here, Keble was calling on the English theologian Joseph Butler (1692–1752) to try to win back his friend's eroding loyalty. Butler, whom Newman considered "the greatest name in the Anglican Church," had a profound influence on the poet Coleridge, Hazlitt, Gladstone, Keble, F. D. Maurice and R. D. Hampden—to name only a few for whom the *Analogy of Religion* (1736) was a kind of theological *vade mecum*.[146] The trouble was that Keble's Butler had become something of an oracle of uncertainty, whereas Newman's remained rooted in probability, a touchstone of certitude. The cross purposes of the two men were evident in their respective readings of Butler. In 1884, Newman had occasion to contrast his own reading of Butler with that of Keble. "As to the question of probability," Newman wrote to W. S. Lilly, a convert who had been asking him questions about the *Grammar of Assent*, "I think you have said somewhere(?) that you follow Butler in considering probability to be the guide of life. This has a good sense and a bad. I think Anglicans, even Keble(?) mean by probability a mere practical probability i.e. what is safe to act upon, whether true or not;

whereas Catholics hold that it is a real speculative assent (or certitude) to a truth, to which I add speculative, true, but arising, not from demonstration, but from the result of a combination and joint force, equivalent to demonstration, of many separate probabilities, how many and how strong in order to such an equivalence, being left to the judgment, <an act of φρόνησις> which goes by rules to[o] subtle for analysis ..."[147] Newman might have also referred his correspondent to his *Apologia*, where he affirmed: "speaking historically of what I held in 1843–4, I say, that I believed in a God on a ground of probability, that I believed in Christianity on a probability, and that I believed in Catholicism on a probability, and that all three grounds of probability, distinct from each other of course in subject matter, were about the same kind of probability, a cumulative, a transcendent probability, but still probability; inasmuch as He who made us, has so willed that in mathematics indeed we should arrive at certitude by rigid demonstration, but in religious inquiry we should arrive at certitude by accumulated probabilities,—inasmuch as He who has willed, I say, that we should so act, and, as willing it, He co-operates with us in our acting, and thereby enables us to do that which He wills us to do, and bestows on us if our will does but co-operate with His, a certitude which rises higher than the logical force of our conclusions."[148] Later, in *The Grammar of Assent*, Newman would return to this theme of probability, but here it is sufficient to note that, unlike Keble, Newman understood the Bulterian axiom—"Probability is the guide of life"—as a warrant for belief, not skepticism.

Equipped with his own more dubious reading of Butler, Keble stressed how uncertain his own judgment had become. "I have one most earnest request to make of you, that you will not in the smallest degree depend on my advice or opinion in this matter ... It frightens me to think how rashly and with how small preparation I have been dealing with these great matters, and I have all manner of imaginations as to how my defects may have helped to unsettle people, and in particular to hinder you from finding peace."[149] This was no false modesty. For Keble, his inability to meet Newman's doubts with any counter-vailing reassurance left him wracked with guilt and he reproached himself for not being able to reconcile his friend to the Anglican fold, however fissiparous it had become.

On May 18th Newman again argued that retaining St. Mary's would be "an offence and a stumbling block."[150] The impossibility of his position could not have been more evident to him. "Persons are keen-sighted enough to make out what I think on certain points, and then they infer that such opinions are compatible with holding situations of trust in the Church. This is a very great evil in matter of fact. A number of younger men take the validity of their interpretation of the Articles etc. from me *on faith*. Is not my present position a cruelty to them, as well as a treachery to the Church?"[151] With such honorable qualms Keble could not take issue. "It seems to me that, supposing a person to have *no doubt at all* of the schismaticalness of the body he belongs to, (e.g. to be as sure of it as one is of Episcopacy) and that impression to continue after long, honest and self-denying endeavours to rid of it, accompanied of course by conscientiousness in other parts of duty ... he could not well go on exercising a trust committed to him by that body, every act of which would seem to imply that he does not consider itself in schism." [152] And, again, in advising his friend, Keble tried to imagine how he should act if wracked with the same doubts. "I feel that I should myself be quite unequal to it, and should perhaps be continually liable to be urged into some sudden step, by the sort of calls, often sudden ones, which the situation brings with it. You see therefore that on the whole my leaning is towards your retiring as quietly as you can ..." [153] That having been said, Keble hastened to assure his friend that he had no such doubts— or perhaps only tolerable doubts. For one, he did not credit "the *un-enacted* leanings and tendencies" of Bishops with regard to Tract 90. "Formal decisions are in my mind the providential indications for ordinary persons in such perplexities and until such are produced, against me, I shall, as at present advised, uphold No. 90 as sufficiently Anglican. It is true I have strong and evident temptations to deceive myself in this matter, more than you and others; and I do not pretend to say I am comfortable, what right have I to be so? but one can but do as seems best, and say God forgive me." [154] On June 3rd, Newman wrote to Keble to report that Pusey had been suspended for two years for preaching a sermon making reference to the Real Presence. Increasingly, the notion that Anglicanism could be understood in "Catholic" terms was wearing thin.

In July, Keble advised Newman, as he had advised Arnold when he came to him with his doubts, "to withdraw as much as possible for a while from theological study and correspondence, and be as entirely taken up as ever you can with parochial concerns"—though since he also knew that Newman would soon lose Littlemore as a result of resigning St. Mary's, this was not the most tactful advice. [155] In any case, Newman's response could not have given Keble much confidence in his ability to dispense useful counsel to his friend. "If I were to have any thing more directly practical it should be an hospital," Newman wrote. "I fear the more parochial duty I took, the more I should realise, and the greater temptation I should be under to give up, our present defective system, which seems to be without the capabilities of improvement." [156] In time, Keble's own experience would verify the accuracy of that shrewd assessment.

When it became clear that Newman's doubts would not be dispelled by parochial work or due deliberation, Keble resumed a tack that he had taken previously: he urged Newman to abide his doubts. Newman had sent Keble a sermon, "Outward and Inward Notes of the Church," (1841) in which he had suggested that where men found themselves in a Church without "Notes of the Kingdom" they might have no alternative but to seek for such Notes within themselves—a last resort, as Newman admitted in his *Apologia*, "abhorrent both to my nature and to my past professions." [157] Keble's response to this fairly desperate remedy was tell-tale: "I think that in what you say both of the inward and the outward Notes of that Kingdom, you imply an expectation of rather more certainty than we have a right to look for as to our position ..." [158] And it followed for Keble that if uncertainty was one's lot, then one should reconcile oneself to the Church in which one had been born: "I certainly should be glad to see recognized in this or some other part of your Sermons the duty of men's remaining where they are, not only as long as they have spiritual consolations, but even under any degree of distress and doubt." But this was precisely what Newman had been doing since 1839, with increasing untenability.

Keble's other conjecture confirmed suspicions that Newman was already considering. "Then ought not all people to suspect that it is at least as much their own fault as their Church's, if they do not find Christ's tokens there? And, if there be danger of evil spirits seducing us either way, is not the danger less on the side of patience and acquiescence? ..."[159] Reading this, Newman must have felt immured in an echo chamber. Still, for the benefit of Keble, Newman clarified his doubts, not about Rome but about Canterbury. "I suppose the Catholic theory is, that creeds, sacraments, succession, etc. are nothing without unity .... The only way I have ever attempted to answer this, is by arguing that we really were, or in one sense were, in unity with the rest of the Church—but, as you know, I never have been thoroughly satisfied with my arguments, and grew more and more to suspect them."[160] Keble's response showed how much the strain of keeping up with Newman was telling on him. "Your letters, as you may suppose, make me rather giddy ..."[161] The letter Newman wrote to the Bishop of Oxford on 7 September 1843 could only have intensified Keble's vertigo, for it was on that day that Newman asked his Lordship's permission to resign St. Mary's. On Christmas Eve, 1843, Newman wrote to Manning a letter which clearly showed that he was beginning to think of his Anglican work with a sort of retrospective defensiveness. "I own indeed to great presumption and recklessness in my work on ecclesiastical subjects," he wrote to then Archdeacon Manning, "yet still I have honestly trusted our Church and wished to defend her as she wishes to be defended. I wasn't surely wrong in defending her on that basis which our divines have ever built and on which alone they can pretend to build. And how could I forsee that when I examined that basis I should feel it to require a system different from hers and that the Fathers to which she led me would lead me from her?" Of course, this did not mean that in December 1843, Newman had already converted. "Surely I will remain where I am as long as I can. I think it is right to do. If my misgivings are from above, I shall be carried on in spite of my resistance."[162] But every day he was moving closer and closer to Rome. The end of Newman's ordeal was in sight, while Keble's had only begun.

On 22 January 1844, Keble admitted to his friend that "It is a long time since we had any communication, and something within me tells me, it is a heartless thing to let Christmas and New Year come and go, and not say one word to you, to whom under God one is indebted for so very much of the comfort and hope which they have been allowed to bring with them ... I think and think, it seems all to no purpose; for when I come to set it down, it will be only telling you over again what you have yourself told me and others. These, however, are some of my impressions:"[163] And here Keble made clear that Newman was not the only one suffering excruciating doubts.

First, I feel more strongly with every month's, week's, day's experience, the danger of tempting God, and the deep responsibility I should have to bear, were I to forsake this communion; and yet with the same lapse of time one seems to feel more and more the truth and beauty and majesty of so much which they have and we seem at least to have not ...[164]

This passage should be borne in mind when readers consider the extent of Keble's understanding of the claims of Rome, or, put another way, the extent to which his ignorance of those claims can be regarded as invincible. But it also exemplifies the states of mind that Newman described to James Hope in a letter of 2 November 1843. "I did not explain sufficiently the state of mind of those who are in danger," Newman wrote to Hope. "I only spoke of those who are convinced that our Church was external to the Church Catholic, though they felt it unsafe to trust their own private convictions. And you seemed to put the dilemma, 'Either men are in doubt or not: if in doubt, they ought to be quiet; if not in doubt, how is it that they stay with us?' But there are two other states of mind which might be mentioned. (1) Those who are unconsciously near Rome, and whose *despair* about our Church, if anyhow caused, would at once develop into a state of conscious approximation and *quasi*-resolution to go over. (2) Those who feel they can with a safe conscience remain with us, while they are allowed to testify in behalf of Catholicism, and to promote its interests; i.e., as if by such acts they are included, in the position of catechumens."[165] This is a fascinating letter because it describes at once the Keble who was "unconsciously near Rome." despairing of Anglicanism and ready to approach a "*quasi*-resolution to go over"—the Keble, in other words, to whom Newman was appealing in his pivotal correspondence between 1841 and 1844—and the Keble who eventually chose to remain within the English Church with the object of bringing it closer to what he regarded as its true catholic identity.

Still, what Newman did not mention in this otherwise acute analysis was the hurdle standing in the way of any Englishman contemplating conversion (which, in his own case, as he recognized, had been extremely difficult to scale) and that was anti-Romanism.[166] And it was this ingrained bias that convinced Anglicans that all arguments in favor of Rome must be not only delusions but satanic delusions. The "Evil One," Keble told Newman, might be endeavoring "to ruin the good work, supposing it begun, in the English Church, by laying hold of any undiscerned weakness or ill tendency in the agents to entice or drive them out of it. Such tendencies one can imagine in your case; among the rest a certain restlessness, a longing after something more, something analogous to a very exquisite ear in music, which would keep you, I should think, in spite of yourself, intellectually and morally dissatisfied, wherever you were ..."[167] Newman, in other words, might be contemplating leaving the English Church because the devil had set him to search for an ideal phantasmal Church—a charge which would be made by others interested in discrediting his conversion. In his historical jeu d'esprit *Let Dons Delight* (1939), Ronald Knox has a High Churchman admonish a Rome-leaning Tractarian with arguments that echo those of Keble and Gladstone. Anglicanism, Dr. Greene tells his fellow dons in 1838, "has come down to us in our history as a part of English life, as the religion of a nation, adapted to its temper and modeled by its history; it is from that that it derives its substance; it is the religion of Englishmen or it is nothing … We all know the dog in Aesop, who dropped his bone while he jumped after what was only a reflection in the water. So it is with you gentlemen; you neglect to preserve the Church of England as it is in fact, while you are running after an ideal church which is not there."[168]

Keble spoke for many when he shared with his friend the dismay his conversion would cause among those whom he had formerly led. "Another thought one has is of the utter confusion and perplexity, the astounding prostration of heart and mind, into which so many would be thrown, were their guide and comforter to forsake them all at once, in the very act, as it would seem to them, of giving them directions which they most needed. I really suppose that it would be to *thousands* quite an indescribable shock, a trial almost too hard to be borne, making them skeptical about everything and everybody …"[169] Indeed, in another letter, he spoke of Newman in terms reminiscent of those that Enobarbus used to describe Cleopatra. "Wherever I go, there is some one to whom you have been a channel of untold blessing. You must not be angry, for I feel as if I could not help saying it, and I am sure the very air of England around you would say the same."[170] Of course, this was not lost on Newman. Yet, in his clear-sighted way, he recognized that the unsettling of the faith of the English, such as it was, might not be a bad thing. "People are unsettled as it is," Newman wrote to Keble on 23 January 1844. "As years go on, they either will become settled, or they will be gradually more and more unsettled. If *my* thoughts had been led through the early Church to Rome, why should not others? We know nothing of the effects of one's own hypothetical acts. There have been events ten thousand times more unsettling than the change of individuals now. St. Paul must have unsettled all the good and conscientious people in the Jewish Church. Unsettling may be a blessing, even where minds are *not* already unsettled."[171] But then Newman confessed something to his old comrade in catholicity that must have given Keble a jolt. "One thing I will add—I sometimes have uncomfortable feelings as if I should not like to die in the English Church. It seems to me that, while Providence gives one time, it is even a call upon one to make use of it *in* deliberateness and waiting—but that, did He cut short one's hours of grace, this would be a call to make up one's mind in what seemed most probable."[172] Here was recognition of the force of probability that Keble would not find in Joseph Butler.

On 8 June 1844, Newman wrote Keble a long letter, sharing with his friend the graces that had seen him through previous trials. "When I was a boy of fifteen, and living a life of sin, with a very profane spirit, He mercifully touched my heart; and with innumerable sins, yet I have not forsaken Him from that time, nor He me. He has upheld me to this hour, and I have called myself His servant."[173] When suffering from severe fever in Sicily and feeling near death, he nonetheless kept crying out, "'I have not sinned against light.'"[174] Afterwards, he sat crying profusely on his bed; Gennaro, his faithful guide asked him what the matter was, and Newman "could but say to him … that I thought God had some work for me." That work became clear once he returned to England. Keble preached his Sermon on National Apostasy in July of 1833 and the

Oxford Movement was launched. Now, however, Newman was assailed with doubt. "I have thought much lately of the words in Bishop Andrewes' Morning Prayer—'Despise not the work of Thine own hands,'—he repeats it in various forms, as addressed to Each of the Persons of the Most Holy Trinity. May I not take comfort in this plea which they contain? 'Thine Hands have made me and fashioned me.' I look back to past years, or rather to all my years since I was a boy and I say, 'Is it come to this? Has God forgotten to be gracious? would He have led me on so far to cast me off? what have I done to be given over, if it be such, to a spirit of delusion? Where is my fault? which has been the false step, if such there be?'"[175]

By making his friend so privy to the doubts of conversion, Newman was preparing him for an understanding of how such doubts could be overcome. Certainly, in no other letters was Newman so intent on involving his correspondent in the lacerating doubts of conversion. In effect, Newman took up such doubts to show how they could be resolved: this is what gives his letters to Keble their apostolic power. "What then is the will of Providence about me?" Newman asks. "The time for argument is passed. I have been in one settled conviction for so long a time, which every thought seems to strengthen. When I fall in with friends who think differently, the temptation to remain quiet becomes stronger, very strong—but I really do not think my conviction is a bit shaken. So then I end as I began—Am I in delusion, given over to a lie? am I deceiving myself convinced when I am not? Does any subtle meaning or temptation, which I cannot detect, govern me, and bias my judgment? But is it possible that Divine Mercy should not wish me, if so, to discover and escape it? Has He led me thus far to destroy me in the wilderness?"[176]

Then, again, there were other reasons why one might put the thought of converting out of one's head, besides doubt as to the rightness of one's contemplated move. Keble, who was so attached to family and friends, to the parishioners of Hursley, to everything associated with home, would certainly have agreed with Newman when he observed how "all inducements and temptations are for remaining quiet, and against moving. The loss of friends what a great evil is this! The loss of position, of name, of esteem—such a stulti-fication of myself—such a triumph to others. It is no proud thing to unsay what I have said, to pull down what I have attempted to build up." In earlier letters, Newman had been rather far-sighted and dispassionate about the impact his conversion might have on others; but as he came closer and closer to taking the actual final step, his strong fellow feeling rose up and he admitted that "what quite pierces me" was "the disturbance of mind which a change would cause to so many—the casting adrift, to the loss both of religious stability and comfort—the temptation to which many would be exposed of scepticism, indifference, and even infidelity."[177]

Still, for Newman, despite these doubts, despite this uncertainty, the conviction was "growing more urgent and imperative continually, that the Roman Communion is the only true Church."[178] On June 11th, Keble responded to Newman's letter, which had come, he wrote, "not unexpected, yet very much like a clap of thunder," by returning to what he had said before but with renewed dismay: "What shall I and thousands more do? And where shall we go?" Keble's sense of being cut adrift was deepened by the posthumous publication of Thomas Arnold's papers. "You will readily understand what is the bitterest part of one's feelings in the whole matter, both in respect of Arnold and of your change—not that I mean to compare the two subjects in the least degree in point of distressfulness—but in both one has a sad depressing thought, that, if one were or had been other than one is, the anguish might have been averted or mitigated."[179] When it came to keeping Newman from bolting, Battiscombe agreed with Keble's rueful assessment: if Newman "were to be held to the Church of England it must be by being convinced of the intellectual soundness of her position, and it was just this that Keble could not do for him. As he admitted ... Keble had never 'got up' the controversy with Rome ... An unkind person might say that his reluctance to explore the position was due to an unformulated suspicion as to what such explanation might reveal, but the explanation is a highly improbable one. The truth of the matter was that Keble was too indolent to trouble his head with the study of a subject naturally distasteful to him."[180] Yet it is dubious whether Keble ever truly imagined that Newman was writing to him to elicit arguments for remaining within a fold that he had already largely made up his mind to leave. When he responded to Newman's long letter of June 8th, for example, Keble wrote: "So long as your letter may be considered as stating a case, I really hardly know what to say. I feel as if I had suggested on former occasions all that I could now say; but I still shrink from the thought of committing myself to Rome, as it is."[181] This clearly indicates that, for Keble, the object of Newman's letters was to persuade him to consider Rome, not to persuade him to mount convincing arguments in favor of Canterbury.

When Keble expressed regret for not mounting such arguments, he was throwing wool over his own and Newman's eyes. The only argument he was prepared to make was that there could be no certainty as to whether Canterbury or Rome represented the one true Church. "Do you not think it possible," he asked Newman, "that the *whole* Church may be so lowered by sin, as to hinder one's finding on earth anything which seems really to answer to the Church of the Scriptures?" When Keble suggested that Newman's own sermon put this idea into his head, Newman must have repented of the glib exasperation to which he had given expression in his sermon, "Outward and Inward Notes of the Church," especially when Keble followed this up by asking "will it not be well to prepare yourself for disappointment, lest you fall into something like scepticism?" The idea that one could escape skepticism by embracing doubt was not one that Newman would have found persuasive. But this was precisely what Keble was advocating. "You know I have always fancied that perhaps you were over sanguine in making things square, and did not allow enough for Bishop Butler's notion of doubt and intellectual difficulty being some men's intended element and appropriate trial."[182] Here, again, Keble sidestepped the crisis enjoined by Newman's epistolary witness by trotting out a highly dubious reading of Butler.[183]

Newman, for his part, rejected the notion that the object of religious inquiry should be doubt. When he read of his old Oriel colleague Blanco White (1775–1841) being praised for discrediting the Gospels along Straussian lines and embracing skepticism, he was incredulous. An apostate Catholic priest of Irish ancestry, White grew up in Seville before moving to London in 1810, where he was friends with Lord and Lady Holland and the tutor (briefly) of Henry Fox. Gravitating to Oxford in 1826, he became an honorary member of Oriel and a prominent member of the Noetics, before abandoning the Anglican Church for Unitarianism. During White's stint at Oriel, he and Newman were good friends, sharing a passion for Beethoven and often playing their violins together. They parted ways when Newman campaigned against Peel and Catholic Emancipation, which White considered untenably partisan. They were also on different sides of the Hampden controversy, White being rumored to have inspired Hampden's heretical Bampton Lectures.[184] When White's autobiography (1845) was posthumously published, Newman found its endorsement of doubt deeply disturbing. "Is this the *end* of Life? Can there be a greater paradox than this?" Those who hold such views, "really do think it is no harm whatever being an Atheist, so that you are sincerely so and do not cut people's throats and pick their pockets."[185] T. S. Eliot would similarly marvel at "those who would once have been considered intellectual vagrants," who "are now pious pilgrims, cheerfully plodding the road from nowhere to nowhere, trolling their hymns, satisfied that they may be 'on the march.'"[186] Nonetheless, it was a mark of Newman's fairness that although he thought White's infidelity deplorable he was quick to assure Gladstone that White himself "was a fastidiously honorable man, in word and deed."[187]

In his response to his friend's letter, Newman was too intent on commiserating with Keble over the posthumous publication of Arnold's papers to disabuse him of his own supposed appetite for doubt. "As to Arnold's 'Remains,'" he wrote, "I cannot put myself enough in your place to know the precise points which pain you so acutely—but for myself, there seems much to take comfort in as things are. I do not think the book will produce any great *effect* in a wrong direction. Of course there is a great deal in it to touch people—but there is so little *consistency* in his intellectual basis, that I cannot think he will affect readers permanently." As far as Newman could see, posterity would be grateful to Arnold for his school reforms and ignore the rest. Then Newman summed up his own thoughts about his occasional antagonist with amusing dispatch: "if it is right to speculate on such serious matters, there is something quite of comfort to be gathered from his removal from this scene of action, at the time it took place; as if so good a man should not be suffered to commit himself *cominus* against truths, which he so little understood."[188]

The same witty judiciousness that Newman applied to Dr. Arnold he applied to the via media that he had spent so much time defending. "The only feeling I am at all suspicious of," Newman wrote to Keble on 21 November 1844, "is ... a feeling of intellectual contempt for the paralogisms of our ecclesiastical and theological theory .... What I have asked myself is, 'Are you not perhaps *ashamed* to hold a system which is so inconsistent, so untenable?'" Such withering reassessments must have shaken Keble in his own attachment to the via media, but if, as was evidently the case, his attachment remained finally unshaken, he must have seen in Newman's letter an eerie echo of his own objections to moving. "I cannot deny I should be ashamed of having to profess it," Newman wrote of what he now considered an untenable system, "yet I think the feeling, whatever be its strength, is not at all able to do so great a thing as to make me tear myself from my friends, from their good opinion, from my reputation for consistency, from my habitual associations, from all that is naturally dear to me."[189] This was strange coming from Newman because, by November, 1844, the self-sacrifices he described were precisely those he was prepared to make to embrace the Catholic Church; it was Keble who was resisting Rome because it would tear him from friends, family, and everything that was dear to him. Newman made his own position clear when he reiterated what he had shared with his friend earlier, that "My sole ascertainable reason for moving is a feeling of indefinite risk to my soul in staying ... I don't think I could die in our Communion. Then the question comes upon one, is not death the test?"[190] This was hardly the sort of question he would put to himself if he were truly considering remaining within the Anglican Church. Newman raised these earlier apprehensions about losing family and friends, which he knew were uppermost in Keble's mind, to goad his friend into testing them against an infinitely more decisive test—the test of death. However one reads Newman's letters to Keble at this time, one cannot read them as mere introspective effusions from a divided soul. Even while working out his own difficult destiny, Newman continued to conduct his own indirect apostolate on behalf of Keble.

Nevertheless, the appeals in Newman's letters fell on deaf ears: Keble would not be budged. "I want very much to thank you for your two kind letters," he wrote on December 27th, "and for thinking so much of me in all your perplexities ... Certainly it is a sad unsettled world: the two lessons out of Isaiah for Christmas Eve struck me as a melancholy contrast between what this part of Christendom is and what it might be; but *is it better elsewhere?*"[191] Then, on 3 October 1845, Keble wrote to Newman to tell him "I feel as if I had something to say to you, although I don't know what it will be; but Charlotte's illness having for the present abated, I find that I am better able than I have been for near a fortnight past to think and speak coherently of other things, and what can I think of so much as you, dear friend, and the αγωνία which awaits us with regard to you ..." Obviously, Keble had been turning over in his own mind what Newman had said about death being the test as to whether one should move. This was accentuated by the fact that his brother Tom's life was "hanging by a thread." And "At such times," Keble wrote, "one seems in a way to see deeper into realities, and I must own to you that the impression on my own mind of the reality of things I have been brought up among, and of its being my own fault not theirs, whereinsoever I am found wanting,—this impression seems to deepen in me as Death draws nearer, and I find it harder and harder to imagine that persons such as I have seen and heard of lately should be permitted to live and die deceiving themselves in such a point, as whether they are aliens to the grace of God's Sacraments or no." So, Newman had his answer, though it was not the one he wished to hear. Instead, with redoubled insistence, Keble threw back at Newman precisely the argument of hearth and home, of "all bands of birth," as Lancelot Andrewes put it, that his friend had tried to expose as insufficient.[192] Speaking for his fellow Tractarians, or at least those prepared to remain loyal to the Church of England, Keble wrote: "everything has fallen out so as to foster the delusion, if delusion it be, that we are not quite aliens, not living among unrealities. Yet you have no doubt the other way." Again, Keble insisted, in these matters uncertainty ruled, and this argued against moving. "It is very mysterious, very bewildering indeed; but, being so, one's duty seems clearly pointed out: to abide where one is, till some call come upon one. If this were merely my own reason or feeling, I should mistrust it altogether, knowing, alas! that I am far indeed from the person to whom guidance is promised, but when I see the faith of others, such as I know them to be, and so very near to me as God has set them, I am sure that it would be a kind of impiety to dream of separating myself from them."[193]

The Scotsman J. C. Shairp, the friend of Arthur Hugh Clough and Matthew Arnold, responded similarly when he first encountered what was for him the Tractarians' strange new insistence on the sacraments and the apostolical succession. "Well," he recalled thinking, "if all you say be true, then I never can have known a Christian. For up to this time I have lived among people who were strangers to all these things." No arguments would budge this central objection. Speaking of his youthful self, Shairp recalled, "It would have taken something stronger to make him break faith with all that was most sacred in his early recollections. Beautiful examples of Presbyterian piety had stamped impressions on his memory not to be effaced by sacerdotal theories or subtleties of the schools."[194] If Shairp viewed the via media with the settled opposition of an adherent to the Kirk, Keble and most of the English looked even more askance at Roman Catholicism. For Keble, when an Englishman converted, he was willy-nilly "deciding on his own authority what are the limits of the Kingdom of Christ, what the evangelical terms of salvation. He is pronouncing not only on the truth, but on the importance also, of many and various propositions, which being in debate among those who call themselves Catholics, are settled under anathema by the Roman councils. He is consigning millions, who had no other thought than to live and die true subjects of the visible Catholic Church, to the comparatively forlorn hope of incurable ignorance and uncovenanted mercy."[195] This was similar to the feeling that Newman recognized in his sister Jemima's refusal to consider the claims of Rome. When he wrote to Lord Coleridge towards the end of his life that he could "quite understand … good people not becoming Catholics, from the *home* feeling which was so strong in Keble …," he got at something fundamental not only about Keble but about most of the Anglican English.[196] The campaign to brand the old faith foreign, mounted first by the Henrician and then the Elizabethan Reformation, had succeeded only too well; by the nineteenth century most English people regarded it as the antithesis of home. And yet Newman always looked forward to the time when these divisions would be obliterated. When Shairp died in 1887, Newman wrote to a mutual friend:

Neither my fingers nor my eyesight allow me to express in writing the debt of gratitude which I owe to the late Principal Shairp for the kindness with which he has so many times spoken of me in his publications, nor the deep sorrow with which I heard of his death ...

But passing by my personal feelings, I lament the Principal's loss to us on a more serious account. In this day of religious indifference and unbelief it has been long my hope and comfort to think that a silent and secret process is going on in the hearts of many, which, though it may not reach its limit and scope in this generation or the next, is a definite work of Divine Providence, in prospect of a state of religion such as the world has never yet seen; issuing, not indeed in a millennium, but in a public opinion strong enough for the vigorous spread and exaltation, and thereby the influence and prosperity of Divine Truth all over the world.[197]

In his correspondence with Keble, Newman assiduously sought to enlist Keble in this "silent and secret process," convinced, as Pusey was convinced, that "When all else had been said and done, people would wait and see what came from Hursley before they made up their minds as to the path of duty."[198]

In his response to Newman after he had converted, after "the thunderbolt," as he called it, had "actually fallen upon us, and you [had] actually taken the step which we greatly feared," Keble claimed to regret not being able to dissuade Newman from his move. "Besides the deep grief of losing you for a guide and helper, and scarce knowing which way to look, (though I trust, thanks (in good part), to your kindness in many ways I am not so wretched as I was), you may guess what uncomfortable feelings haunt me, as if I, more than any one else, was answerable for whatever of distress and scandal may occur. I keep on thinking, 'If I had been different, perhaps N. would have been guided to see things differently, and we might have been spared so many broken hearts and bewildered spirits.'"[199] This is a criticism that one hears echoed even by those sympathetic to Keble, convinced as they are that at the very least he should have argued the case for the catholicity of the Church of England by pointing to the catholicity of the Orthodox Church, though the odds of such an argument cutting any ice with Newman were slim. Whether Keble himself really imagined that he had the theological wherewithal to parry the objections to Anglicanism raised by Newman is dubious. After Pusey told him that "Reassurance from you encourages people better than anything else," Keble admitted: "I have thought a good deal whether there is anything I could say or do, painfully consciously as I am that I have all my life been going on authority in the points at issue between us and Rome, and now that authority fails me. And the persons whom you speak of as wanting to be reassured would be little helped, I fear, by being told that however they may doubt, they are to stay and work on as well as they can, and not to go until conviction quite forces them; which I am afraid is the most I could say at present." This was nothing if not honest, though to another correspondent Keble admitted the qualms this caused him: "it keeps occurring unpleasantly to me, that this is hardly consistent with the priest's office and especially so when, as sometimes happens, I am asked for advice; then indeed I have to think of the blind leading the blind."[200] It is more likely that he regretted not mounting a stronger case for Anglicanism—an Anglicanism which, he acknowledged, was as inconsistent and as uncatholic as Newman charged it with being—only because he knew that his co-religionists would find fault with him for not mounting such a case. In his response to Newman's conversion he was already preparing his response to his Anglican detractors. But in a subsequent letter to Newman, Keble struck a note of pitiable helplessness, suffused with love and gratitude, which more accurately reflected his true feelings towards his lost guide.

> My dearest Newman, you have been a kind and helpful friend to me in a way in which scarce any one else could have been, and you are so mixed up in my mind with old and dear and sacred thoughts, that I cannot well bear to part with you, most unworthy as I know myself to be; and yet I cannot go along with you. I must cling to the belief that we are not really parted—you have taught me so, and I scarce think you can unteach me—and having relieved my mind with this little word, I will only say God bless you and reward you a thousandfold all your help in every way to me unworthy, and to so many others. May you have peace where you are gone, and help us in some way to get peace; but somehow I scarce think it will be in the way of controversy. And so, with somewhat of a feeling as if the Spring had been taken out of my year, I am always, your affectionate and grateful J. Keble.[201]

Newman responded to his dear friend with one of the most moving letters he ever wrote:

> Littlemore. November 14, 1845

> May the Holy Trinity,
> Father, Son, and Spirit,
> return to you sevenfold, My dear Keble, all the good, of which you have been the instrument towards me, since I first knew you. To you I owe it, humanly speaking, that I am what and where I am. Others have helped me in various ways, but no one can I name but you, among those I ever knew, except one who is gone, who has had any part in setting my face in that special direction which has led me to my present inestimable gain.

> Do not let me pain you, My dear Keble, by saying this. Let me not seem rude. Let it be your comfort, when you are troubled, to think that there is one who feels that he owes all to you, and who, though, alas, now cut off from you, is a faithful assiduous friend unseen.

> Ever Yours very affectionately John H Newman[202]

Moving as this letter is, it is also perplexing. How Keble could have been instrumental in Newman's conversion at the same time that he insisted that there could be no grounds for considering Roman Catholicism the one holy catholic and apostolic Church needs explaining, especially since Keble repeatedly put the claims of hearth and home before objective truth. Beyond that, he doubted whether sinful divisive man could ascertain the claims of truth. Newman's fear that remaining within a communion hostile to true catholicity put one's soul in peril left him untroubled. Yet by taking up the objections to Rome that Keble countenanced and subjecting them to "the burden of long probationary deliberation," Newman demonstrated how negligible such objections were before the certainty that only the one true fold could bestow.[203] In trying to convert Keble, Newman converted himself.

CHAPTER 2

Staying Put: John Keble After 1845

In the correspondence between Newman and Keble in the crucial period between 1841 and 1845, Newman ostensibly turned to Keble to help him resist Rome, but as events unfolded he began to share doubts about Canterbury with Keble that he knew Keble shared, to prompt his friend to consider making the same move to Rome on which he was increasingly resolved himself. This effort to convert his friend did not end with Newman's conversion. Even after Keble effectively severed relations with his old friend, Newman continued to think kindly towards him. In 1847, when he was considering becoming an Oratorian, he wrote of St. Philip Neri, the founder of the Oratorian Order, to his sister Jemima, "This great Saint reminds me in so many ways of Keble, that I can fancy what Keble would have been, if God's will had been he should have been born in another place and age; he was formed on the same type of extreme hatred of humbug, playfulness, nay oddity, tender love for others, and severity, which are the lineaments of Keble."[1] Even earlier, in December of 1845, Newman wrote to his old friend Maria Giberne, who would become a Visitation nun in 1856, after living in Rome for ten years, first with the Colonna family and then the Borghese: "And now, My dear Miss G. that you have the power, pray begin your intercessions very earnestly (though I need not say it) for those dear friends of mine, or ours, who are still held back, or rather imprisoned in their old error, and that by their own good feelings and amiable affections. You have all the Saints of heaven to add [aid] you now, and especially that first and most glorious of Saints whose name you bear. First of all pray for dear Isaac Williams who is to appearance on his death bed. He has an abscess on his back, from which they augur the worst … And next do not forget the two Kebles, to one of whom we owe so much. And lastly let me name Pusey, whose conversion (of which there are no signs) would be followed by so many."[2] In this respect, Newman would be the figure who most fulfilled the role of Samuel that Keble had extolled in his sermon "On National Apostasy"—not only praying for the apostate but remonstrating with them for continuing to repudiate their ancient constitution. In this chapter, I shall look at how Keble squared his remaining within the Anglican Church from 1845 until his death at a time when its suppositious catholicity all but vanished.

In 1846, Keble sent Newman a copy of *Lyra Innocentium*, in the introductory verses of which, the poet prayed that he be given the guidance to guide others:

> And with no faint nor erring voice
>   May to the wanderer whisper, "Stay;
> God chooses for thee; seal his choice,
>   Nor from thy Mother's shadow stray;
> For sure thy Holy Mother's shade
>   Rests yet upon thine ancient home:
> No voice from Heaven has clearly said
>   'Let us depart;' then fear to roam."

Here was Keble's accustomed argument for staying put recast in verse. In his review of the book, Newman passed over this paean to stasis and described instead the tragic impasse in which so many Tractarians found themselves after 1845.

> When the opening heart and eager intellect find themselves led on by their teachers, as if by the hand, to the See of St. Peter, and then all of a sudden, without good reason assigned, are stopped in their course, bid stand still in some half position, on the middle of a steep, or in the depth of a forest, the natural reflection which such a command excites is, "This is a mockery; I have come here for nothing; if I do not go on, I must go back."[3]

Here was the impasse that fueled Keble's uncertainty, which he falsely ascribed to Joseph Butler. And Newman described it with deadly psychological precision: "A forlorn feeling comes over the mind, as if after all there was nothing real in orthodoxy—as if it were a matter of words, about which nothing is known, nothing can be proved—as if one opinion were as good as another." This despair of certainty in dogma did indeed overtake Keble. Still, in the same review, Newman reaffirmed the hope that never left him for as long as Keble lived. "As to the author personally, we cannot help cherishing one special trust, which we hope is not too sacred to put into words. If there be one writer in the Anglican Church who has discovered a deep, tender, loyal devotion to the Blessed Mary, it is the author of the Christian Year. The image of the Virgin and Child seems to be the one vision upon which both his heart and intellect have been formed; and those who knew Oxford twenty or thirty years ago, say that, while other college rooms were ornamented with pictures of Napoleon on horseback, or Apollo and the Graces, or Heads of Houses lounging in their easy chairs, there was one man, a young and rising one, in whose rooms, instead of these, might be seen the Madonna di Sisto or Domenichino's St. John—fit augury of him who was in the event to do so much for the revival of Catholicism. We will never give up the hope, the humble belief, that that sweet and gracious Lady will not forget her servant, but will recompense him, in royal wise, seven-fold, bringing him and his at length into the Church of the One Saviour, and into the communion of herself and all Saints whom He has redeemed."[4]

In the years after 1845, Keble joined with Pusey to try to rally the "Catholic" party within the Church of England, but with little success. Their rearguard action against the proponents of liberalism and rationalism was fairly futile: the Tractarian party had lost its combative confidence. Speaking of the remaining Tractarian faithful, Dean Church recalled, "We sat glumly at our breakfast tables every morning, and then some one came in with news of something disagreeable—some one gone, some one sure to go ... The only two 'facts' of the time were that Pusey and Keble did not move, and that James Mozley [the editor of *The Christian Remembrancer* and the chief publicist for Tractarianism after Newman's departure] showed that there was one strong mind and soul still left in Oxford. All the rest were the recurring tales, each more sickening than the other, of the 'goings over' ..."[5] Keble fell prey to subjective notions of truth, remarking to his good friend, the novelist Charlotte Yonge, "No doubt we could ask Roman Catholics many questions they could not answer; and they could ask us many we could not answer; we can only each go on our own way, holding on to the truth which we know we have."[6] Newman recognized that individuals apprehended the same truths differently but, as he wrote to his friend Richard Holt Hutton in 1864, he also recognized that, "minds being very various, the subjective acquiescence in a doctrine cannot be the invariable measure and test of its objective reality or its truth."[7]

The reversals suffered by the Tractarians were part and parcel of reversals suffered by religion generally after 1850. Rosemary Hill, A. W. Pugin's lively biographer, accurately observes of this shift: "The England of Prince Albert and the Great Exhibition did not feel the romantic pull of the olden times so strongly. The dream of 'reunion' with Rome that had faded through the 1840s now vanished. Between the Evangelical and High Church parts of the Established Church, a Liberal, Broad Church movement was emerging anxious that England, having escaped the Continental revolutions of 1848, should now avoid the reaction to those revolutions which had seen the Catholic Church reassert itself already in Belgium and Austria, as it would soon in France."[8] The Gorham Judgment (1850), which asserted Erastian over against papal aggression, was but a foretaste of the triumphant liberalism to come. Pusey made no bones about what he and Keble were up against: "the Low Church," he wrote, "mean a war of extermination against us. Every fresh attack hems us in, and increases our difficulties, and mows down those whom we can ill spare."[9] John Ruskin (1819–1900), so eccentric in many ways, was representative of one conventional strand within the Low Church when he wrote to a friend in May 1851: "You speak of the Flimsiness of your own faith. Mine, which was never strong, is being beaten into mere gold leaf, and flutters in weak rags from the letter of its old forms; but the only letters it can hold by at all are the very old Evangelical formulae. If only the Geologists would let me alone, I could do very well, but those dreadful Hammers! I hear the clink of them at the end of every cadence of the Bible verses—and on the other side, these unhappy, blinking Puseyisms; men trying to do right and losing their Humanity."[10]

Clinging to the Rigging

Once the case for the catholicity of the English Church became untenable, Keble's attempts to justify his refusal to convert were at once dogged and half-hearted. One sees this most arrestingly in his long sermon, "On Eucharistical Adoration" (1858), in which he asserted that English Churchmen "stand as orthodox Catholics upon a constant virtual appeal to the oecumenical voice of the Church, expressed by the four great Councils, and by general consent in all ages during which she continued undivided. And if that voice be disputed, is there any conceivable way of bringing the dispute to an issue, except only another true Oecumenical Council, when such by God's grace may be had?" That this was an unpersuasive justification for an English Church continually disputing its own identity was not lost on Keble, who, to his credit, conceded that "Many a devout and loving heart, I well know, will rise up against this case. To be on this conditional, temporary footing, will strike them as something so unsatisfactory, so miserably poor and meagre, so unlike the glorious vision which they have been used to gaze on of the one Catholic Apostolic Church." But rather than dispute with these skeptics, Keble agreed with them, admitting that the Anglican Church was "poor indeed" and "disappointing" but "not otherwise than as the aspect of Christianity itself in the world is poor and disappointing, compared with what we read of it in the Gospel." This was another prolegomenon to the argument for staying put, which Keble duly mounted. "Men will not escape from this state of decay by going elsewhere, though they may shut their eyes to the reality of it. Rather, whatever our position be in the Church, since God Almighty has assigned it to us for our trial, shall not we accept it and make the best of it, in humble confidence that according to our faith it will be to us?"[11] In another letter, he made the same case with a different appeal. "I do indeed feel that to turn one's back on a Communion while such a person as Pusey remains in it, would be a great responsibility."[12]

The responsibility to which Newman felt bound was to do what he could to convince Keble, however indirectly, that remaining in such an uncatholic communion would be a great irresponsibility. If, as Newman told his old friend Frederic Rogers, Lord Blachford, Keble was "the one Prophet and Preacher, as he may be called, of the spiritual miseries which now surround us," he can also be seen as one of the greatest casualties of those miseries.[13] Still, if Keble was difficult, Pusey could seem impossible. To Thomas Francis Knox, the grandson of the Earl of Ranfurly and the Earl of Kilmorey, who would later become the Superior of the London Oratory, after being received into the Church with Frederick Faber in 1845, Newman wrote in August 1846, "I was called to Pusey at Tenby the other day, as he wrote me word he was extremely ill ... I am made quite melancholy at the utter impossibility (humanly speaking) which appeared of his ever changing. He does not seem to have the elements, or the capacity to change; he has no doubts, no misgivings, no difficulties—It is a simple 'mystery' to him still, that I have made a change."[14]

After Newman's conversion, Keble spent the last twenty years of his life trying to convince himself that remaining within the decidedly uncatholic

English Church had not been a mistake. He began this enterprise with some flourish, famously asserting, in the teeth of the Gorham Judgment, that, "If the Church of England were to fail altogether yet it would be found in my parish."[15] Battiscombe gamely commends this "declaration of faith" by saying that it "might have been uttered by the North Country saint, Bernard Gilpin, or by any other of the many parish priests who, like Gilpin, stayed with their people through all the religious changes and chances of the reigns of Henry VIII, Mary, and Elizabeth I." What she omits to mention is that Gilpin flatly rejected transubstantiation and, during Elizabeth's reign, prided himself on working to separate recusants from their Catholic faith. "A mischief doth increase easily and spread and creep further in one day than good lessons in a whole month," Gilpin observed of the residual potency of the outlawed faith against which he so sedulously labored.[16] If this was the sort of English faith that Keble possessed, he was further away from Rome than Newman dared imagine.

As time passed, Keble found himself increasingly on the defensive about the tenability of Anglicanism. In 1846, Keble got word that George Ryder (1838–1905), who later become the Chairman of the Board of Customs, was contemplating going over. "If it is not too late," Keble wrote to his old pupil, "I beseech you by whatever is dear to you to reconsider what you are doing; have pity on the broken hearts and bewildered minds, which are more and more broken and bewildered by every step; and be quite sure—for how can anyone doubt it that reflects? –that it *must* come of some evil principle, when one is urged to do anything whatever without regard to consequences and so much the more, as one is responsible for others besides." Again, any argument in favor of Rome must be satanic delusion. Moreover, conceding that Rome was more coherent than Canterbury was no argument in Rome's favor: "I cannot see, supposing our Church ever so defective, how it follows that of course the Roman Catholic Church is right and yet according to the engagement you make in acceding to it, you must be prepared to die for the truth of each separate statement that it makes, as unreservedly as for the truth of the Incarnation." Moreover, for Keble, "the *onus probandi* lies on those who go, not those who stay, and therefore I hope to go quietly on—*comfortably i*s another thing, but one feels that one has been all one's life much more comfortable than one deserves."[17] The mixture here of funk and sanctimony was typical of Keble. Such considerations carried no weight with his aristocratic friend. Once Ryder went over, Keble closed his doors to him. "I could not have him to dine," he explained; "I should consider it scandalous in respect to the servants."[18] Such ostracism awaited all who converted in nineteenth-century England. As Battiscombe notes: Ryder's "decision cut him off not only from Keble and like-minded friends but also from his aristocratic relations. His daughter never forgot her bitter sensations when, as a small child, she passed the Ryder family mansions in Berkeley Square and realised that she and her mother could never enter those stately doors."[19]

Then Keble charged that Ryder, like Newman, was overly swayed by intel-lectual considerations. "In this case all is purely abstract and intellectual—the aim of development—political rather than religious." For Keble, "the word *intellectual*" was "a sort of mark set upon this Roman Catholic Movement, to warn English Catholics against it; and the kind of person whom I see everywhere being carried away by it are either of the sort to be dazzled by intellect themselves, or else in such relation to J.H.N. or some other person, that they are tempted to put faith in him individually." This was not true of Manning or Faber or Robert Wilberforce or many others who found their way to the faith largely without any direct help from Newman. Nonetheless, Keble had decided to dig in. "On one way or the other, every single instance has been such to drive me further and further away back from any tendency I might have had that way; and I hope I am sincere in thanking God that I am a much more contented Anglican now than I was a year ago." Here, the note of defensiveness had become pitiably shrill, and again, he called on Bishop Butler to fortify his doubt. "Will you forgive my saying that you yourself, my dear Ryder, betray to my mind the intellectual restlessness I complain of, where you complain in your letter that you cannot 'maintain the cause of the Church of England.'—and that you have 'found no sufficient answer to what the Roman Catholics urge.'" The second of those propositions was bad enough but it was the first that rankled Keble even more; why should Anglicans suddenly need to defend Anglicanism? "I am sure it is long since I dreamed of 'maintaining the cause' of all the truths I firmly believe, or of 'finding sufficient answers' to all objections. In such matters I should have made shipwreck long ago had I not accepted, and tried to act upon the theory of Bishop Butler—that theory which now seems to be so sadly despised and forsaken by so many of our friends."[20]

Writing in December 1845 to an Anglican who confessed himself similarly incapable of finding a "sufficient answer to what the Roman Catholics urge," Newman wrote: "there is no conviction such as to preclude all hesitation or delay in joining the Catholic Church; the test of our being called" was "not any great vividness of impression, but its continuance. I have generally said to persons, Fix a time, and observe whether your conviction lasts through it, and how it stands at the end of it." Of course, this was what Newman himself did from 1839 till his conversion in 1845. But then he made an observation that could very well have been prompted by the case of Keble: "And this, I suppose must be considered, – that, if a person be external to the aids and graces of the Church, he cannot have the true gift of faith, and can at best but rule his course by reason, which is an uncertain guide – and almost involves doubt as its attendant. Persons then, in waiting to be certain, may be waiting for that which from the nature of the case cannot be theirs." Of course it was ironic that Newman should characterize such cases as overly reliant on reason but it was doubly ironic that he should urge his correspondent to consult Butler: "On the whole I should say about such cases as yours, Wait till you have such a conviction as Bishop Butler would say is sufficient in a practical matter, recollecting that doubt is the condition of our nature, and that the merit of faith consists in making ventures."[21] Again, different interpretations of Butler caused Newman and Keble to see the crisis of Tractarianism differently.

Still, Keble had convinced himself that Newman and those influenced by Newman were the ones who were relying excessively on reason. When Robert

Wilberforce (1802–1857), the Oriel Fellow who wished to tutor along the same pastoral lines as Froude and Newman, prepared to convert in 1854, Keble lashed out at what he complained was his friend's overly rational approach to faith: Wilberforce, like Newman, went "on general or abstract principles, metaphysical, legal, or what not, instead of clinging to Scripture and to primitive antiquity." This contradicted Keble's own understanding of the role of unwritten tradition in the deposit of the faith, which he extolled in his sermon on tradition. To another correspondent he wrote: "Poor dear R.W.; I own I was surprised … for the last report I had heard was an improved one, and I had heard nothing for a long time … I dare say your account of it is the right one; but it disappoints and mortifies one to see one, who used to be so truthful and candid, lending himself at once to the violent contradictions of fact, and *petitiones principii*, which are quite necessary to every part almost of the Roman Theory."[22] Here it is interesting to note that, if, in his correspondence with Newman, Keble showed Rome a certain resolute neutrality, he relaxed this restraint with other correspondents. To Wilberforce himself, when his doubts about the Anglican Church first surfaced in 1851, Keble wrote: "Your kind letter did me good. It made me hope that you were consenting to measure things by the standard that God has appointed, and to bear the uncertainty where he leaves us uncertain rather than insist on being distinctly guided in everything by the present Church … Do you not think there is in this view a kind of lowliness more suitable to the Christian *ethos* than in the sort of claim to Inspiration (for it is really not less) that the opposite view implies?"[23] As far as Wilberforce could see, one did not require any special inspiration to recognize that the Act of Supremacy (1534) excommunicated the English Church. And Wilberforce was not motivated by pride when he resigned his living at Burton Agnes in Yorkshire, left England for Paris and entered the Roman Church on All Saint's Eve. Although an Anglican priest twice married and twice widowed, Wilberforce was given a special dispensation by the pope to enter Holy Orders. Wilberforce entered the same Accademia Ecclesiastica where Manning had received his instruction. David Newsome's claim that Wilberforce was an unhappy Catholic is not borne out by Wilberforce's correspondence.[24] On 9 April 1856, he wrote to Newman: "I went into Retreat at St. Eusebio the beginning of last month, and was amazingly impressed by the Exercises. Moreover, they chimed in remarkably with the tendency of my own mind. I felt a greater freedom than before in giving myself up to the service of the Church; and those usages, which I had before looked upon as an impediment, became a positive object of attraction. This is especially the case with Devotion to Our Blessed Lady, which I have come to regard as a reward to my faith in being a Catholic. I cannot say how this has arisen; it has been the result of meditating on the truths of the Gospel and of seeking guidance by prayer."[25] Wilberforce's conversion might have particularly stung Keble because it put him in mind of how his own living wife might be preventing him from taking the final step that Wilberforce took after his second wife's death.

Defensiveness bred incoherence in Keble. While ready enough to argue that Newman was to blame for encouraging Ryder and Wilberforce to see their faith in merely intellectual terms, Keble also held, in a letter to John Coleridge of October 1847 that "Newman went (unconsciously of course) rather from impulse than from reason, and that good treatment and sympathy would probably have kept him."[26] This was wrong: it was intellect that had kept Newman Anglican when his heart and conscience told him to convert. As he wrote to one correspondent: "It is sad to me, to think that you still remain uncertain and unsettled; and, while others have seized and are enjoying the high calling offered to them, you are, if you will allow me to say so, wasting precious years in vanity. Having myself been called to the Church late in life, when my best days were gone, I feel for those who persevere in losing what cannot be recalled. You say that, 'though you feel this' (the ground on which you rest your position,) 'in a dry argumentative way, you constantly feel your position to be most painful.' Others have had and have the same feeling. Is not this a reductio ad absurdum of that ground? Is it not the witness of heart and conscience, of the whole man, that that argument will not work, and therefore cannot be true, difficult as it may be to find what is the intellectual flaw in what seems so specious? It will serve as an excuse for the insincere, not as a stay for the earnest."[27] In the *Apologia*, Newman would express this truth even more powerfully: "For myself, it was not logic that carried me on; as well might one say that the quicksilver in the barometer changes the weather. It is the concrete being that reasons; pass a number of years, and I find my mind in a new place; how? the whole man moves; paper logic is but the record of it. All the logic in the world would not have made me move faster towards Rome than I did; as well might you say that I have arrived at the end of my journey, because I see the village church before me, as venture to assert that the miles, over which my soul had to pass before it got to Rome, could be annihilated, even though I had had some far clearer view than I then had, that Rome was my ultimate destination. Great acts take time."[28]

That Keble's last years were not altogether happy is clear from his letters. "I cannot give a good account of my parish," he wrote to Coleridge in 1862, "people are sadly disappointing, and neither 'true religion, nor useful learning' appears to me to flourish and abound. I often think that 'tempus abire tibi est,'—do think of it for me a little calmly, and—and yet I creep on from day to day, fancying that perhaps I may do better, and quite ashamed to think of the condition in which my successor would find things, if I were to make a vacancy at present. 'Too late, too late,' are the words that haunt me from morning to night; and sometimes I wish I had been at a public school, that I might be a man of business, and get on with things as I ought ..."[29] Coleridge tried to account for this dissatisfaction by remarking that Keble was given to bouts of depression but additional woes now fed his disenchantment: Charlotte was gravely ill; Hursley could no longer epitomize any living Church; Oxford was rife with the impious liberalism of Jowett and Pattison; and the apostasy about which he had warned his contemporaries in 1833 was everywhere gaining ground. Recoiling from what he could glimpse of the future, he turned more and more to the past.

Meeting in Old Age

On 4 August 1863, Keble wrote to Newman a letter after a silence of nearly twenty years. "It is a great thing, I know, for me to ask, after so many years, that you should look kindly upon what comes from me, for I cannot conceal it from myself, nor yet acknowledge it without a special sort of pang, that what I have heard occasionally from Crawley and Copeland of your feeling as to your friends' silence touches me perhaps as much as any, and it is one of the many things which now in my old age I wish otherwise." Newman could not have been unmoved by Keble's honesty. "I ought to have felt more than I did what a sore burden you were bearing for conscience's sake and that it was the duty of us all to diminish rather than aggravate it so far as other claims allowed ... I can but ask that if I had been towards you too much as if you have been dead, you will now be to me as if I were dying, which, of course, must early be my condition; for though (D.G.) wonderfully well, I am in my seventieth year. Do then, my dear friend, pardon me what has been wrong in this (I can see it in some measure but I dare say there is more which I do not see) and let me have the comfort of hoping that your recollection of me will not henceforth be embittered by anything more than is inseparable from our sad position, as I am sure your kindness to me has always been the same."[30]

Newman's response teemed not only with fond memories but large-hearted forgiveness. "Did you ever read Mrs Sheridan's Tale of Nourjahad? such I think is the name. I have not read it since a boy. I am like one of the seven sleepers awakened, when you so write to me, considering all my recollections of Hursley and of Bisley, which remain photographed on my mind, are of twenty-five years ago, or thirty. I cannot think of little Tom but as of the boy I carried pick a back, when he was tired in getting from the steep valley to the table land of Bisley. And I recollect your Father, and your dear Sister, and your wife, as you cannot recollect them – at least the latter two – for in my case their images are undimmed by the changes which years bring upon us all ..." When it came to Keble's silence Newman bore no grudges. "Never have I doubted for one moment your affection for me – never have I been hurt at your silence. I interpreted it easily – it was not the silence of men, nor the forgetfulness of men, who can recollect about me and talk about me enough, when there is something to be said to my disparagement. You are always with me a thought of reverence and love, and there is nothing I love better than you, and Isaac, and Copeland and many others I could name, except Him whom I ought to love best of all and supremely. May He Himself, who is the over abundant compensation for all losses, give me His own Presence – and then I shall want nothing and desiderate nothing – but none but He, can make up for the losses of those old familiar faces which haunt me continually."[31] The appositeness of the allusion to Lamb's poem could not have been lost on Keble, who probably knew the lines by heart: "I have a friend, a kinder friend has no man/Like an ingrate, I left my friend abruptly/Left him, to muse on the old familiar faces."

Four months after these exchanges, on 30 December 1863, Newman opened a parcel sent to him by an unknown correspondent and found a heavily marked review of volumes 7 and 8 of Anthony Froude's *History of England* signed by "C.K." One of the marked passages read:

> Truth for its own sake had never been a virtue with the Roman clergy. Father Newman informs us that it need not, and one the whole ought not to be; that cunning is the weapon which Heaven had given to the Saints wherewith to withstand the brute male force of the wicked world which marries and is given in marriage. Whether his notion is doctrinally correct or not, it is at least historically so.[32]

Here was the charge by Charles Kingsley that goaded Newman into writing his *Apologia Pro Vita Sua* (1864), in which he revisited the events leading up to his conversion to refute what Newman called Kingsley's "gratuitous slander."[33] That Newman frequently had Keble in his thoughts while at work on the book is evident from his correspondence. To William Copeland, Newman's old curate at Littlemore, who brought Keble, Rogers and Church back in touch with Newman after they had been out of touch for nearly twenty years, he wrote: "I am very low – it is one of the most terrible trials that I have had. And I have to write against time, and to refresh my memory against time. Longman seemed to think an answer ought not to be delayed, if there was to be any – and people won't read a fat book – so the only way was to begin at once, and write as I printed. I do trust I shall be carried through it, but at my age it is a perilous toil. There will be at least five parts. The one on which I need your assistance is the fourth. It will be most kind if Keble looks at it too. The single point is, Have I made mistakes of fact, over-stated things, etc? or again left out important things? or can some point be strengthened? What I shall ask Keble (as well as you) to look at, is my sketch from (say) 1833 to 1840 – but, mind, you will be disappointed – it is not a history of the movement but of me – it is an egotistical matter from beginning to end. It is to prove that I did not act dishonestly – I have doubts whether anyone could supply instead of me what I have to say – but, when you see it, you will see what a trial it is. In writing I kept bursting into tears ..."[34] On April 25th, Keble wrote to Newman: "I feel as if I ought to write you a long letter, but it must be only a few lines just now, to implore you not to be seriously worried by such trash as Mr Kingsley's .... We (if I may say) want you, dear J.H.N. – all Christendom wants you – to take your stand against the infidelity which seems to be so fast enveloping us all .... I wish, if it please God, we may meet before very long ..."[35] On April 27th, Newman responded: "Thank you for your affectionate letter. When you see part of my publication, you will wonder how I ever could get myself to write it. Well, I could not, except under some very great stimulus. I do not think I could write it, if I delayed it a month. And yet I have for years wished to write it as a duty. I don't know what people will think of me, or what will be the effect of it – but I wish to tell the truth, and to leave the matter in God's hands."[36]

This was to be Newman's own account of his conversion and he was writing it at breakneck speed. Proofs of Newman's genius abound in his life and work but none is quite as astonishing as the fact that he managed to compose the

Apologia in less than three months. "I am writing from morning to night, hardly having time for my meals," he wrote to Keble. "I write this during dinner time – This will go on for at least 3 weeks more ..." What is remarkable is that he knew that Keble would not take issue with his account of their pivotal relationship, which shows how confident he was in his own veracity. "I dare say, when it comes to the point, you will find nothing you have to say as to what I send you – but I am unwilling not to have eyes upon it of those who recollect the history. You will be startled at my mode of writing."[37] Keble could scarcely contain his delight with what Newman sent. On June 28th, he wrote: "My very dear Newman I will not wait any longer before thanking you with all my heart for your loving words to me and far too loving of me—If I wait till I write as I could wish, I should never write at all—for indeed dear friend the more and the more intently I look at this self drawn photograph (what a cruel strain it must have been to you) the more I love and admire the Artist—Whatever comes of controversial points, I see no end to the good which the whole Church, we may reasonably hope, may derive from such an example of love and candour under most trying circumstances."[38] If Newman regretted Keble's reference to what he called "the whole Church," he rejoiced in his old friend grasping at least one of the book's elemental objects: "You have said things," Keble told Newman, "which by the blessing of God will ... materially help us in our sad weary struggle against Unbelief."[39]

In September 1865, Newman shared with Keble his impression of Pusey's *Eirenicon* (1865), his belated response to Newman's *Lectures on Certain Difficulties felt by Anglicans in submitting to the Catholic Church* (1850), which set out to bring Anglicans and Roman Catholics closer by suggesting that what kept them apart was Rome's acquiescence in extravagant devotions to the Blessed Virgin—not an argument likely to win any support from Newman. "If Pusey is writing to hinder his own people from joining us, well and good," Newman wrote to Keble, "he has a right to write as he has done – but how can he fancy that to exaggerate, instead of smoothing contrarieties, is the way to make us listen to him? I wish I were not obliged to say that his mode of treating with us is rhetorical and unfair."[40] Later, in his *Letter to Pusey* (1866), Newman addressed Pusey directly, observing that: "There was one of old time who wreathed his sword in myrtle; excuse me—you discharge your olive-branch as if from a catapult."[41]

In the same month, Newman finally met Keble for the first and only time after he converted. The account Newman gave of their meeting is memorable. At first, after a fair amount of shilly-shally, Newman decided against going to see his old friend; Pusey, he knew, would be meeting with Keble at Hursley and he decided to put off his meeting until he could see Keble alone. But the account Newman gave to Ambrose St. John is better than any paraphrase, particularly the picture it paints of Pusey recoiling as Newman made his unexpected entrance.

I had forgotten the country and was not prepared for such beauty, in the shape of Woods. Keble was at the door, he did not know me, nor I him. How mysterious that first sight of friends is! for when I came to contemplate him, it was the old face and manner, but the first effect and impression was different. His wife had been taken ill again in the night, and at the first moment he, I think, and certainly I, wished myself away. Then he said, Have you missed my letters? meaning Pusey is here, and I wrote to stop your coming. He [[then]] said I must go and prepare Pusey. He did so, and then took me into the room [[where Pusey was]]. I went in rapidly, and it is strange how action overcomes pain. Pusey, as being passive, was evidently shrinking back into the corner of the room – as I should have done if he had rushed in upon me. He could not help contemplating the look of me narrowly and long – Ah, I thought, you are thinking how old I am grown, and I see myself in you – though you, I do think, are more altered than I am. Indeed, the alteration in him shocked me (I would not say this to every one) – it pained and grieved me. I should have known him any where – his face is not changed, but it is as if you looked at him through a prodigious magnifier. I recollect him short and small – with a round head – smallish features – flaxen curly hair – huddled up together from his shoulders downward – and walking fast. This was as a young man – but comparing him even when last I saw him [[in 1846]], when he was slow in his motions and staid in his figure, still there is a wonderful change. His head and his features are half as large again – his chest is very broad (don't say all this) – and he has, I think, a paunch – His voice is the same – were my eyes shut, I should not have been sensible of any lapse of time. As we three sat together at one table, I had as painful thoughts as I ever recollect, though it was a pain, not acute, but heavy. There were three old men, who had worked together vigorously in their prime. This is what they have come to – poor human nature – after 20 years they meet together round a table, but without a common cause, or free outspoken thoughts – but, though kind yet subdued, and antagonistic in their mode of speaking, and all of them with broken prospects.[42]

On February 3rd, Keble wrote Newman one of his most heartfelt letters: "that which I have daily and almost hourly feared for so many years is now, humanly speaking without doubt coming upon me. We came here [Bournemouth] for the second time after I saw you at Hursley; my wife had begun to look up a little and so she has once or twice for a day or two at a time since then: but on the whole it has been what G. Herbert calls a steady "undressing" – something or other which seemed to be a part of her laid by day after day – chess, the piano, drawing, writing, accounts – and now even reading a few verses is almost too much for her … . You never saw much of her dear Newman, so I ought not to run on about her …"[43] His old friend responded with affectionate solitude: "What am I to say to your most touching letter? I can do no more than think of you and her … You are under the severest trial which man can suffer; and I earnestly pray that you and she may be supplied in all your need, day by day, and have every grace necessary to bring you both to heaven … I can do no more than think of you and love you. I wish I could do more—but there is only One who is powerful, One who can will and do."[44] As it happened, this would be Newman's last letter to Keble, who died little over a month later.

Post-Mortems

Comments that Newman made about Keble after his death may have qualified the sympathetic esteem in which he held his elusive friend but they never diminished it. To Henry James Coleridge, John Coleridge's second son, who became a Jesuit, Newman wrote: "Keble had from youth a great drawing to Catholicism"—something "Pusey had never had," though he was quick to add that it was wrong to "infer from this that Keble was not in good faith ...".[45] To Pusey, he elaborated: "According to my own idea it was Jewel, as forced upon Keble's attention by Froude, whose writings first opened Keble's eyes to the unsatisfactory doctrine of the Reformers ... in contradistinction to the high Anglican school; and from that time Keble took a much higher line of theology, and hardly recollected himself what he held before, as is the case with men who have originally taken what they received, without question, and have not precisely examined its meaning, coherence, and grounds."[46] In a letter to H. A. Woodgate, Newman recalled: Keble "was most diffident of his own opinion, and with difficulty made up his mind. I recollect Rickards, a great judge of character, saying forty years ago, 'Don't you see K's special infirmity! indecision – You see it in the rolling of his eyes.' Hence you could not get his own opinion on an important point. It was the opinion of his brother, his sister, or his wife."[47] This estimate of Keble's thinking was far more critical than the one that found its way into the *Apologia*. Still, if Keble reluctantly acknowledged the short-comings of Jewel and the other Reformers, he never revised his view of the papacy. "The one doctrine dear Keble did not receive was that communion with the Holy See was necessary for being in the Church," Newman wrote to one correspondent. "The few hours that I saw him in September, it astonished me how far he seemed to go. I suppose he looked forward to Purgatory with real comfort, as a mode of honouring God."[48]

In 1875, Newman was asked to provide some introduction to a collection of Keble's essays and in response he wrote a letter full of suave evasion, which, in its way, achieved something of Keble's own accustomed reticence. "I wish it were easier for me than it is to comply with the request you have made me to give you my judgment upon Mr Keble's literary merits," he wrote to his correspondent. "Not that it would be any great effort to descant in a general way on his various endowments as an author, on his learning, his conscientiousness, his incessant and persevering industry, and the classical taste with which he writes; but praise of this kind, to which others besides him have a claim, would come very short of doing justice to him, or of satisfying you. Yet I should not succeed in the attempt to do more ... . As to Mr Keble, all I venture to say of him in this respect is this:– that his keen religious instincts, his unworldly spirit, his delicacy of mind, his tenderness of others, his playfulness, his loyalty to the Holy Fathers, and his Toryism in politics, are all ethical qualities, and by their prominence give a character of their own ..."[49] What this letter shows, if it shows anything, is how careful Newman was to eschew criticizing Keble in public, not only because he respected and loved his old friend but because he did not wish to offend those Anglicans who might still be brought round to making the move to Catholicism that Keble himself so spectacularly failed to make.

In 1878, Newman wrote to Edward Stuart Talbot, the first warden of Keble College, "I wonder whether you would care to have any letters of Keble which I find. The other day I came on a parcel of them belonging to the years 1830–1835. They have only this importance, but this they have, to refute the notion which the *Times* and others have put out, that Keble was diverted from his characteristic line and position in the Anglican Church, and made a tool of by others."[50] Another misconception that Newman helped Talbot dispel was the one that charged that Newman misled Keble. Isaac Williams, who, as a member of the more conservative High Church Bisley school, opposed Newman's influence on Keble and put it about that Keble actually regretted this influence. In his autobiography, Williams quoted Keble telling him, apropos the claims of Rome, "Now that I have thrown off Newman's yoke, these things appear quite different." Even more improbably, he quoted Keble telling him that the 1830s constituted "a sort of parenthesis in my life," and he was happy that he had now regained "my old views such as I had before." This sounds like Williams putting words in Keble's mouth, as does this: "Pusey and Newman were full of the wonderful progress and success of the Movement, whereas I had always been taught that the truth must be unpopular and despised, and to make confession for it was all one could do, but I see I was fully carried away by their sanguine views."[51] In no correspondence did Keble ever suggest that he considered Newman's influence "a yoke;" nor is it credible to suggest that Pusey and Newman were overly sanguine about the progress of the Tractarian Movement. And if Keble regarded the 1830s as a "parenthesis" in his life, during which he came to embrace the via media, where did this leave the "catholic" version of Anglicanism to which he remained so loyal?

When, in August 1878, Newman provided Talbot with a packet of Keble's letters, he included a memorandum, entitled "Notice to Letters of 1843–1845," which was as revelatory of Newman as it was of Keble. "In the Letters which follow I have made erasures, which may seem strange and arbitrary, unless I say something to account for them." This was particularly true in light of Newman's stated opposition to suppressing biographical information, but Keble posed a special case. "Let me observe then that dear John Keble's heart was too tender and his religious sense too keen, for him not to receive serious injury to his spirits and his mental equilibrium by the long succession of trials, in which his place in the Oxford Movement involved him." Newman usefully catalogued the trials in which Keble was forced to act in those pivotal years. "The affair of Number 90, Williams's failure in his contest for the Poetry Professorship, the Jerusalem Bishoprick, Young's rejection when offering himself for Orders, Pusey's censure by the six Doctors, the promotion of Thirlwall and others, my own religious unsettlement and that of so many others, the charges and hostile attitude of the Bishops, the publication of Arnold's Life and Letters, and the prospect of the future thus opened upon him, (not to dwell upon the serious illness of his wife and his brother) were too much for him, and threw him into what must be called a morbid state of mind, which showed itself to his intimate friends in the language of self accusation and even of self abhorrence." For Newman, "This heart-rending trial, of which perhaps I saw more than any one, is remarked upon by Sir John Coleridge in his Life of him … though he has not attempted any sufficient explanation of it." Neither Coleridge nor, it has to be said, any subsequent biographer has done justice to this aspect of Keble's life. Newman realized how central it was. "One of Keble's special imaginations at this time was, that in some way or other, directly or indirectly, positively or negatively, he was the cause of my own distrust of the Church of England, and in his letters to me he expressed in obiter dicta, in ejaculations, in single words and half sentences, in shocking language to one who knew and loved him so well as I did, his keen realization of these and other fancies, and the anguish which they caused him.

> To me nothing is more piercingly painful than the contrast between the cheerfulness and playfulness which runs through his early letters and the sadness of his later. This must remain any how; it is founded on the successive circumstances of his history; it is part of his life; nor could one expect it to be otherwise; but I could not be so cruel to that meek, patient, and affectionate soul, to that dearly, deeply beloved friend, as so leave to a future generation the exhibition of those imaginary thoughts about himself which tormented him, which grew out of grave troubles, which were very real, and which are sufficiently recorded for posterity when they are made, as in a notice like this, to suggest to a reader the weight of those troubles.[52]

Charlotte Keble

Newman fully recognized how much Keble relied on his wife in all his trials. To Jemima, he explained how, after meeting Keble, he agreed to meet his friend again when Charlotte Keble's health improved, "but she never got better, and [Keble] was obliged to give up the idea. The wonder is how he could ever bear so long the suffering which his wife has undergone. Spasmodic asthma is a fearful complaint to see. Mr. St. John has for years suffered from it, though he is better now—it is like seeing a person in a chronic condition of hanging or drowning."[53] To Henry Wilberforce, apropos Charlotte, Newman candidly speculated: "She suffered a great deal at last; so, Keble was spared a great deal. When I found she was surviving, it struck me (I trust it is really a charitable thought) that she was to be kept awhile to do penance for having kept Keble from being a Catholic."[54] This was the sort of matter-of-factness about the supernatural that gives so much of Newman's correspondence its power. Charlotte *was* an obstacle in the way of Keble's converting. If Keble had followed Newman into the Catholic Church he would have found himself without means of supporting himself and this would have created grave practical problems for his sickly wife. One need only recall the fury that Thomas Arnold's two conversions inspired in his wife, Julia (née Sorell) to appreciate what might have been Charlotte's point of view, or indeed that of any wife of an Anglican clergyman contemplating conversion. After Arnold's second conversion, Julia sent off a blistering letter to Newman on Guy Fawkes Day, 1876:

Sir,

You have now for the second time been the cause of my husband's becoming a member of the Church of Rome and from the bottom of my heart I curse you for it. You know well how very weak and unstable he is, and you also know that he has a wife and eight children. You know well that he did nothing for the Roman Catholic Church in the ten years he belonged to it before, and you know well that he will do nothing for it now, but the temptation of having one of his father's sons under your direction was too much for you, and for the second time you counselled him to ignore every social duty and become a pervert. He has brought utter ruin upon us all, but what is that to you? …[55]

Whether or not Charlotte's last illness was penitential, Newman realized that for both Charlotte and her husband the end was imminent. "I was prepared for dear Mr Keble's death," he told one correspondent, "from knowing how frail he was and how his wife's illness tried him. I last heard from him about two months ago – He then said she was slowly (using a word of George Herbert's) 'undressing–' she had been obliged to give up first her music, then her drawing, then her books – and so, she was stripping herself of every thing but her body – which God would take off from her in His own time. It was a sort of race between them which should die first."[56] Here was more matter-of-factness, which might very well offend some sensibilities. Keble, however, preferred having a spade called a spade. After all, the poem to which he alluded was Herbert's "Repentance," which opens with the lines:

> Lord, I confess my sinne is great;
> Great is my sinne. Oh! gently treat
> With thy quick flow'r, thy momentarie bloom;
> Whose life still pressing
> Is one undressing,
> A steadie aiming at a tombe.

Keble prepared himself for his own tombe with fitting humility. "He had borne up, in spite of his infirmities, longer than I had supposed possible," Newman told Emily Bowles. "He was seized with fainting fits. His friends took him from [Charlotte's] room. When he got into his own, he fancied it a Church. He knelt down, and said the Lord's Prayer. Then he began a Latin Hymn—they could not make out what. Those were his last words. Thus he ended with the prayer which he first said on his knees as a little child."[57]

Now that Pope Benedict XVI has offered Anglicans disaffected with the Church of England, including married Anglican priests, the opportunity to join the Catholic Church through the auspices of his Apostolic Constitution, the predicament that John Keble faced seems all the more poignant. It was with the case of Keble in mind that Newman wrote to Ambrose Phillipps De Lisle, who had written a pamphlet suggesting that some means be found of admitting Anglo-Catholic priests into Roman Catholic communion: "Nothing will rejoice me more than to find that the Holy See considers it safe and promising to sanction some such plan as the Pamphlet suggests. I give my best prayers, such as they are, that some means of drawing to us so many good people, who are now shivering at our gates, may be discovered."[58] Apropos these prayers, William Oddie speculates that, "Now, 140 years later, the Holy See has decided that such a scheme is indeed 'safe and promising;' and I do not think ... that it is entirely fanciful to believe that Newman's 'best prayers' may have had something to do with this result."[59]

The Mystery of Stasis

Nevertheless, Keble's case also calls to mind the mystery of stasis. In September of 1873, Newman wrote an extraordinary letter to a Miss Rowe, who had courageously but somewhat diffidently converted. "It is quite clear you have a great deal to learn about the Catholic Faith," he wrote to her, "or you would never have asked me the questions which I answered in my former letter. The prime, I may say the only reason for becoming a Catholic, is that the Roman Communion is the only True Church, the Ark of Salvation. This does not mean that no one is saved who is not within that Church, but that there is no other Communion or Polity which has the promises, and that those who are saved, though not in the One Church, are saved, not by virtue of 'the Law or Sect which they profess', as the 39 Articles say, but because they do not know better, and earnestly desire to know the truth, and in consequence are visited by a superabundant mercy of God which He has not promised and covenanted." Did this apply to Keble? For the purposes of his letter, Newman was prepared to suggest that it might. "I think I have heard the late Mr. Keble say, 'If the Roman Church is the True Church, really, I do not know it – really I do not see it.' There are numbers, I joyfully believe, in the Church of England," Newman reckoned, who were similarly situated—"aided by God's grace, and I trust in the event justified and saved, not, however, by virtue of the Church of England, which is a human work and a political institution, but by grace extending beyond the True Church, to 'the children of God who are scattered abroad.'" But no sooner did he allow for this superabundant grace than he reaffirmed distinctions that he might very well have put to Keble.

> You will see then that no Catholic can hold the Anglican Church to be a branch of the Catholic Church. If it is, a man may safely remain in it – if it is, ours is not the Catholic Church. You have left it, because you wished to pass from what was not the Church to what was.

The Church is a visible body – and a one body. It is not two bodies – to be a visible body, there must be a visible unity between its portions. Where is the visible unity between the Church of Rome and the Church of England? If indeed a man says there is an invisible unity between them, I deny it ... but if he tells me there is a visible unity between the two, (and a visible unity is necessary for a visible body, such as St. Paul speaks of) he is uttering the greatest paradox that ingenuity can invent and he refutes himself.[60]

Did Keble, in his heart of hearts, truly embrace this paradox? It is impossible to say. In 1873, in commending Miss Rowe for her heroic move, Newman called attention to the mystery of those who are not led forward, who choose stasis. "From what you tell me you have long meditated on the step you have taken, and have gradually been led forward. God has not failed to answer your prayers and efforts, and in His own way has made you a Catholic. It is strange and sad to think how many converts like you are solitary, – Doubtless it is intended to throw their thoughts directly on their Lord and Saviour, to increase their faith, and to try their constancy." No one would have brought home the strange sadness of this more than his dear friend John Keble. Still, Newman told Miss Rowe, "You have gained the 'Pearl of great price'. You must thank God, and pray and resolve that you never will let it go."[61]

Making sense of the relationship between Newman and Keble, or indeed the Tractarian Movement as a whole, without reference to that "pearl of great price" is not possible. In July of 1846, in a letter to Manuel Johnson, the genial Radcliffe Observer, at whose house he spent his last night at Oxford, Newman gave expression to the hope that animated all of his love for his former Tractarian friends—but for Keble most of all.

Mrs Bowden was received into the Church this morning. Alas, that what is such a source of joy to myself, should not be so to many I love! Yet I will not abandon the hope that one by one, if in no other way, we shall have that joy repeated in their case. And then the lingering, prolonged, repeated, wearing distress which they undergo in their successive losses, will be recompensed to themselves and to us by their regaining all at once all that has gone from them. And thus, my dear Johnson, the Catholic Church will be the true type of heaven to us all – for it will bring together in one all those who die off from the world, and you and I and all of us shall have that great delight of being, what we once were, brethren together in the house of prayer and praise, and one beyond separation – Oh might it be – ...[62]

For all his hope that he and his Tractarian friends and relations might some day be reunited, Newman nevertheless was adamant that searching for the one holy catholic and apostolic Church could not substitute for the Church itself. "We have found the Christ, we are not seeking," he insisted in one of his great Oxford sermons.[63] Keble argued that since searching for the true Church was necessarily an uncertain business, one should be content with the actual, if imperfect church in which one had been born. Here their differences culminated. And yet, in a letter to Father Coleridge, written in 1864, Newman saw his relationship with his old friend from one of those removes that only charity makes possible. Keble, he wrote, "considered that religious truth came to us as from the mouth of Our Lord—and what would be called doubt was an imperfect hearing as if one heard from a distance. And, as we were at this time of the world at a distance from Him, of course we heard indistinctly—and faith was not a clear and confident knowledge or certainty, but a sort of loving guess."[64] Newman could not have put a kinder construction on the irresolution that kept his friend from embracing "the truth and beauty and majesty," as Keble called them, of the Roman Church.[65] This was the indecision with which he responded to the crisis of Tractarianism and it haunts the Anglican church still.

CHAPTER 3

The Anglican Difficulties of Edward Pusey

"The course of everything is onwards, not backwards."
John Henry Newman to Isaac Williams[1]

Nearly two years after his secession from the English Church, Newman wrote to his good friend Mrs. Bowden from Rome, where he and Ambrose St. John were studying at the College of Propaganda: "The interest felt here about Dr Pusey has been very great ... People fancied he certainly was to come over ... and they were unwilling to think ... that so many prayers should be unavailing. He is indeed more extensively prayed for than any one man out of the Church ... Indeed it is very difficult to believe they will be in vain – yet humanly speaking, there is no hope."[2] Seventeen years later, in his *Apologia*, Newman would confirm the accuracy of his earlier assessment. "People are apt to say that he was once nearer to the Catholic Church than he is now; I pray God that he may be one day far nearer to the Catholic Church than he was then; for I believe that, in his reason and judgment, all the time I knew him, he never was near to it at all."[3] Nonetheless, throughout his Catholic career, Newman never gave up trying to help Pusey resolve his Anglican difficulties and always treated his conversion as though it were a distinct possibility. By revisiting their correspondence, we can see how their private exchanges complemented their public exchanges, including the lectures Newman delivered in Birmingham and later published as *Anglican Difficulties* (1850), Pusey's three volumes of *Eirenicon* (1866–1869), and Newman's *Letter to Pusey* (1866). Their letters also show how Newman's plans to establish an Oratory in Oxford complicated their differences, which reached an impasse in the First Vatican Council, though Pusey, like many others, misread the import of the Council. Finally, in the abiding solicitude that Newman showed Pusey, we can see not only his personal affection for a friend of over sixty years but his concern for the difficulties of all Anglicans stalled between disenchantment with Canterbury and distrust of Rome.

Edward Bouverie Pusey (1800–1882) was born at Pusey House in Berkshire on Friday, the 22nd of August, in the same year that Lewis Carroll was born, another Christ Church divine. Pusey's father was the Honorable Philip Bouverie, the youngest son of Jacob, first Viscount of Folkestone, who exchanged the name of Bouverie for Pusey when he succeeded to the Pusey estate in the historical Vale of the White Horse, near Faringdon in Berkshire. His mother was Lady Lucy, daughter of Robert, 4th Earl of Harborough and widow of Sir Thomas Cave, who died at the age of 26 after just two years of marriage. Before his sudden demise, Sir Thomas would often exclaim to his pretty young wife, with unearthly prescience, "This is too much happiness to last." Six years after he expired, Lady Lucy married Philip Pusey, who, at 51, was 24 years older than his bride. Pusey's father was an exacting, solemn, imperious man, whom Liddon describes as so set in his ways, after his exorbitant bachelorhood, that he would brook no opposition either from his wife or his children. By all accounts, he was a thoroughgoing martinet. He was also an ardent Tory who adorned the walls of his study with portraits of Pitt. He initially forbade his elder son Philip from marrying Lady Emily Herbert, because her father, Lord Carnarvon, was not only a Whig but fond of Queen Caroline. Nevertheless, Pusey's father was a dutiful landlord. He munificently subscribed to many London charities, reprobated atheists and scorned the undogmatical zeal of Evangelicals. He lavished alms not only on poor clergymen, poor cottagers and poor tradesmen but others only masquerading as poor. "His own simple integrity," Liddon observed, "made it difficult for him to suspect others of deception."[4] After the old man's death, Edward and Philip paid tribute to their father's openhandedness by inscribing on a window of Pusey parish church: "To the memory of Philip Pusey, Pious and Bounteous, A.D. 1828."[5] What no memorial could record was the long crippling shadow he would cast on his younger son.

"All that I know about religious truth," Pusey told Liddon, "I learned, at least in principle, from my mother, but then, behind my mother, though I did not know it at the time, was the Catholic Church," which is reminiscent of Humpty Dumpty telling Alice, "When *I* use a word ... it means just what I choose it to mean—neither more nor less."[6] If Pusey had ever told his Hanoverian mother that the religion he had learned at her knee had anything to do with the Catholic Church she would not have known what he was talking about. Nevertheless, it is true that Lady Lucy drilled Pusey in his catechism and set him a useful example of charity, self-sacrifice and duty. She was also remarkably keen on putting others first, even going so far as to insist that guests take her own room when they visited her in Grosvenor Square. In his God-fearing mother, Pusey saw another St. Monica.[7]

Together with piety and generosity, there was a strong strain of self-abnegation in Lady Lucy and a concomitant contempt for the comforts of life, which also informed Pusey's character. In old age, Newman recalled dining with his friend on Easter Day in 1837 "and bitterly complaining that we had only roast veal without a drop of melted butter or other sauce ..."[8] In such ostentatious austerity Lady Lucy reveled. As Liddon recalled, "She rarely or never would lean back in her chair, and she used to say that to stoop was the mark of a degenerate age."[9] That her son had a most pronounced stoop must have grieved the old woman.

The dour formality of both parents deepened Pusey's melancholy shyness. His best modern biographer David Forrester quotes something Pusey wrote after his father died to argue that the despotic rule of the father nearly broke the son. "What indeed the natural character was, I scarcely myself know, yet I feel myself now, as a branch which has been so long bowed down, that even when the weight which depressed it, has been removed, though it can partly, cannot wholly recover its original direction."[10] The sense of thwarted growth that Pusey suffered under his father's roof followed him to Mitcham in Surrey, where he prepared for Eton with, among other young aristocrats, the future Tory Prime Minister, Edward Stanley, the Earl of Derby. Throughout his education, whether at Mitcham, Eton or Christ Church, Pusey found himself surrounded by young aristocrats, who would later assume positions of power in the England emerging from the Napoleonic wars. When Newman nicknamed Pusey ὁ μέγας ('the great one'), it was with these connexions in mind. At Eton, the corporal punishment to which Pusey had been introduced at Mitcham was practiced with even greater ferocity by the notorious Dr. Keate. Lytton Strachey gives a vivid sketch of the sort of life Pusey encountered in the Eton of that day. "It was a system of anarchy tempered by despotism. Hundreds of boys, herded together in miscellaneous boarding-houses, or in that grim 'Long Chamber' at whose name in after years aged statesmen and warriors would turn pale, lived, badgered and over-awed by the furious incursions of an irascible little old man carrying a bundle of birch-twigs, a life in which licensed barbarism was mingled with a daily and hourly study of the niceties of Ovidian verse. It was a life of freedom and terror, of prosody and rebellion, of interminable floggings …"[11] Whether this regimen compounded the shyness that he had acquired at home is impossible to say; it certainly laid the groundwork for what would become his prodigious scholarship.

Before entering Oxford, Pusey spent 15 months under the instruction of Dr. Edward Maltby, Vicar of Buckden, near Huntingdon, where he prepared for Classical Honours at Oxford. It was Maltby, later appointed Bishop of Chichester and Bishop of Durham, who wrote to his close friend Lord John Russell in 1850 to denounce the re-establishment of the English Catholic hierarchy, which inspired Russell's vitriolic "Durham Letter." In that last paroxysm of No Popery the Prime Minister fulminated against the Tractarians for attempting to Romanize Great Britain. "There is a danger … which alarms me more than the aggression of a foreign sovereign," Russell wrote.

> Clergymen of our Church who have subscribed the Thirty-nine Articles and have acknowledged inexplicit terms the Queen's supremacy have been the most forward in leading their flocks, step by step, to the verge of a precipice. The honour paid to saints, the claim of infallibility for the Church, the superstitious use of the sign of the Cross, the muttering of the Liturgy so as to disguise the language in which it was written, the recommendation of auricular confession, and the administration of penance and absolution—all these things are pointed out by clergymen as worthy of adoption, and are now openly reprehended by the Bishop of London in his Charge of the clergy of his diocese … I have but little hope that the propounders of these innovations will desist from their insidious course; but I rely with confidence

on the people of England, and I will not bate a jot of heart or life so long as the glorious principles and the immortal martyrs of the Reformation shall be held in reverence by the great mass of the nation, which look with contempt on the mummeries of superstition, and with scorn at the laborious endeavors which are now being made to confine the intellect and enslave the soul.[12]

Pusey could never be accused of promulgating papal infallibility, though he was in favor of auricular confession, which did not endear him to his Victorian contemporaries. William Tuckwell, the famous memoirist of Tractarian Oxford, recalled how Pusey was fond "of groping into the spiritual interiors of those with whom he found himself alone ..." Indeed, for Tuckwell, Pusey's "habit of acting towards others as a confessor seemed to have generated a scientific pleasure in religious vivisection."[13] In his *Memoirs of an Oxford Don*, Mark Pattison complained that when he went to Pusey to confession, out of what he described as a "morbid state of conscience," Pusey "told a fact about myself, which he got from me on that occasion, to a friend of his, who employed it to annoy me."[14] This charge notwithstanding, the advice that Pusey gave Pattison about his religious doubts was sound. "I am persuaded that yours is only a temptation not uncommon in which everything of this world comes before the mind as real, everything spiritual as unreal ... What I wished to say to this is (1) that it is a known fact that Satan has power to vest doubts with the mind (2) that faith, being the gift of God, was upheld by him and so ... was not a question at all of argument, but of a moral probation."[15] The force and clarity of this may explain why so many Anglicans sought Pusey out for spiritual advice. Nonetheless, in 1873, when Pusey sought signatories for a Declaration on Confession, Dean Church turned him down. "I am most thankful," Church wrote to his friend, "to those, who, like yourself, have turned our attention to this great and once neglected remedy and medicine for many sinful souls. But, however inconsistent I may be called, I cannot go beyond liberty. I cannot seem to be on the side of those who, if not in formal statement, yet practically press for more."[16]

Doubtless because he was notoriously partial to confession, as well as the titular head of the Tractarians, Pusey bore much of the brunt when the storm broke over Wiseman's re-establishment of the Catholic hierarchy. As Liddon observes, "His letters at this time are full of expressions which show how thankful he would have been ... had it pleased God, to be allowed to lie down and die."[17] Nonetheless, when studying with Maltby at Buckden, Pusey had not yet acquired his later High Church views and agreed with much of his tutor's Whiggery, favoring, for example, both the repeal of the Test and Corporation Acts and Catholic Emancipation, though his view of Roman Catholicism was comically patronizing.

The Roman Catholics, though they have ... adulterated the Faith, have yet retained the foundations. I do not mean to deny the practical idolatry into which they have fallen, or that the good works of self-emaciation, hairshirts, flagellations, &c., have not had a merit ascribed to them which interfered with the merits of Christ: yet still, whatever they may have added, they did hold that acceptance was through Christ; and as to the mediation of the saints, it was, in *theory*, only the same as one asking a good man to pray for us ... Yet ... there have been hundreds of thousands of sincere men among the Roman Catholics ... and ... there are many at whose feet it would be happiness to think that we might sit in the kingdom of heaven. There may be much love where there is little knowledge ...[18]

Another important development occurred before Pusey entered Oxford: he fell in love. Maria Barker was a 17-year-old redhead whose uninhibited forthrightness appealed to Pusey's shy diffidence. Something of her personality can be gleaned from her letters. In one, after being scolded for mocking her mother's friends, she writes: "Not being ... at all solicitous for the favourable opinion of persons I never care to see again, I can always talk nonsense to anyone, and moreover can lead people to talk of that most interesting person *themselves*."[19] How she was initially attracted to Pusey is a puzzle; when they first met, she was enamored of such heroic figures as Edward the Confessor, Joan of Arc, Robert Bruce, and George Washington—not the sort of people who would remind one of the small, sedentary, burrowing Pusey. She was also infatuated with everything related to the Royal Navy, which prompted her would-be suitor to exclaim, perhaps not altogether truthfully, that one of his favorite biographies was Southey's *Life of Nelson*. One reason why Maria and Newman got along so well was that Newman shared her fondness for the exploits of soldiers and sailors.[20] Despite the fact that she found Pusey "gloomy," "grave," and "stuffy," Maria recognized something special about the brooding young man who lavished so much welcome attention on her: "You were the first person I ever knew," she told him, "to whom I fancied myself not incomprehensible."[21]

That Oxford did not know quite what to make of Maria is evident from Liddon's ambivalent description of her. "Besides the attraction of her good looks, Maria was undoubtedly accomplished; while her character although as yet unformed, combined with elements of impulsiveness and self-will, qualities of rare beauty; which Pusey believed himself to have discerned from the first and instinctively."[22] Besides this, Liddon said conspicuously little about the woman who meant so much to Pusey, perhaps because he regarded her eccentricities as unbecoming to his subject's dignity. In 1883, Newman responded to Liddon's queries by recalling, "She was a tall, handsome person. Before her marriage she had no interest in religion, but she must always have had qualities of goodness ... which only required to be drawn out by Grace. She was however at first, after their marriage, very odd, and I did not like to go to the house. Her oddities were the talk of Oxford: Whately, who was a rough, noisy talker, was open mouthed about it."[23] When Pusey's father got wind of his son's attachment to the unsuitable Miss Barker, he flatly forbade him to see her. It was only after an agonizing courtship of nine years—in which Pusey took to identifying himself with Byron—that he finally managed to secure his father's consent to the marriage. Afterwards, Pusey shared with his wife his prenuptial ordeal. "I scarce ventured to form a hope, believing myself to be to you an entire stranger

... Every word, silence, look, action was then of too anxious importance ever to be forgotten. I suppose never was mind so tortured to discover a meaning in what perhaps had none, or heart so racked till the first dawn of real hope beamed upon me ..."[24] To beguile this long period of lovesick suspense, Pusey began throwing himself into work with morbid abandon. If Byron sought to alleviate his troubles by bedding Italian countesses, Pusey sought to alleviate his by losing himself in relentless reading. "I have lived so retired," he later wrote to his wife, "that of me is known less than the little which it (the world) ordinarily knows of any one; it has only known that I have been at times intensely employed: it has given me the credit for being so always, and not knowing any of the mixed motives, anything of the distress of mind, which this study was partly intended to cure or at least stupefy ..."[25] A habit formed in maudlin youth became, with time, unbreakable, and for the rest of his life Pusey would read on average 16 hours a day.

At Oxford, Pusey entered the Christ Church that had been remade by Dean Cyril Jackson, who may have retired in 1809 but whose reforms were still having an impact in the 1820s. Colin Matthew points out that Jackson "made Christ Church an eighteenth-century forerunner of the French *écoles*: a college intimately linked with politics and administration, with the explicit purpose of creating a government elite of the highest quality. Liverpool, Canning, Peel and Gladstone were the greatest products of the Jacksonian tradition: but with them flowed a constant stream of civil and colonial servants, M.P.'s, lords lieutenant and viceroys. This then was the atmosphere in which the young Pusey found himself: Hanoverian, scholarly but worldly, politically moderately conservative, but flexible: above all, *practical*." If Pusey made himself an unobtrusive member of this finishing school for proconsuls—Matthew notes that "he was not known as an unusual undergraduate"—he was far too impractical to follow its prescriptions.[26] He renounced the pro-consular path for the more rarefied preoccupations of scholarship. Later, after sitting and winning a fellowship to Oriel, he immured himself in his studies and bid the pro-consular world pass.

Once at Oxford, Pusey came under the influence of Charles Lloyd, Regius Professor of Divinity, a short, rotund, prematurely bald, perspicacious man, whose lectures and articles influenced not only Pusey but Newman, the convert Francis Oakeley and other Tractarians.[27] (Frank Newman once remarked, apropos his brother and Lloyd: "I always thought it his calamity, that by the premature death of Lloyd ... my brother gained so very immature an influence in Oxford."[28]) At Oriel Lloyd lectured a handpicked number of fellows in his library, where, instead of standing behind a lectern, he strode back and forth peppering his auditors with questions, at the same time that he helped himself to liberal pinches of snuff. Despite his unusual methods, Lloyd had a serious object: he meant to encourage his fledgling parsons to trace their Anglicanism beyond Henry VIII and the Act of Supremacy to the Roman missals and the Breviary.[29] This solicitude for the professional knowledge of his charges led Lloyd to push for the establishment of theological colleges like those that would be set up at Durham University in 1832 and at Oxford later in the century. As Lloyd's biographer remarks: "Whereas a young barrister-to-be went to the Inns of Court and medical students trained in hospitals, there was no provision for divinity students to study theological, liturgical and pastoral matters in any strictly professional and technical way."[30] His concern for the professional standards of Anglican clergy led Lloyd to take an interest in the critical methods that were being pioneered by German theologians. That he had failed to master the language himself only made his interest greater. Nor was he discouraged by the neglect of German at Oxford, where the language was considered intellectually suspect. As one contemporary recalled, "knowledge of German subjected a divine to the same suspicion of heterodoxy which we know was attached some centuries back to the knowledge of Greek."[31] In the spring of 1825, Lloyd told Pusey, "I wish you would learn something about those German critics."[32] Pusey obliged by visiting the country not once but twice, learning the language, and writing *An Historical Enquiry into the Probable Cause of the Rationalist Character lately predominant in the Theology of Germany* (1828–1830), in which he charted the evolution of German rationalism. In an extraordinarily capable performance for so young a scholar, Pusey characterized Spener's Pietism as a reaction against the "dead orthodoxism" of Lutheranism, which emerged from the Reformation, and likened it to Schleiermacher's emphasis on intuition and feeling (*Anschauung und Gefühl*), which was a reaction against the rationalism of Kant and Fichte. By "orthodoxism," Pusey meant "a stiff and false orthodoxy ... an orthodoxy that clung to the mere letter of a certain sum of credenda without, or with very little reference to anything further."[33] In the lecture-rooms of Germany, Pusey was witnessing religious disputes that were not dissimilar from those that would soon embroil Oxford. He did not draw explicit parallels because, as Liddon explained, "It seemed to him that it would be immodest in a young man of twenty-eight, not yet in Holy Orders, to say in so many words that the attitude of the English High and dry Churchmen towards spiritual religion, and the attitude of English Evangelicals towards theological knowledge, were not without peril to the faith; and that the experience of Protestant Germany, in circumstances different yet analogous, might not be repeated at home."[34]

Pusey was not sanguine about the book's reception: "I do not expect very merciful handling .... The sentiments scattered up and down will fare still worse than the style; and I expect to be thought one-third mystic, one-third sceptic, and one-third (which will be thought the worst imputation of all) Methodist, though I am none of the three."[35] After the book's release, the High Churchman Hugh James Rose accused Pusey of succumbing to the very rationalism that Lloyd had sent him to Germany to reconnoiter by omitting to recognize that it was the unepiscopal, undogmatical character of German religion that made it vulnerable to rationalism. Pusey eventually took Rose's point, destroyed all the copies of his treatise that he could lay hands on and left instructions in his will that the book never be reprinted. He clearly saw, once he had fully digested what he had imbibed of the new skeptical criticism, that something of its muddled diffidence had undermined his own settled convictions. What he wrote to Maria, for example, on his return, flatly contradicted those convictions: "I cannot think that while our Saviour was upon earth, it could have been by any believed that He was 'God manifest in the Flesh;' it seems to me too tremendous to have been known, nor then useful: all the passages which bear upon this point, while He was upon earth, I consider as nothing more than the germ of the truth, not the truth itself, as preparation for the discovery, not the discovery."[36] Had this been the case, the Incarnation would have been an unaccountable failure. In 1862, Pusey looked back on the controversy with Rose with candid clear-sightedness. He admitted, apropos his treatise, that "I very likely expressed myself badly or vaguely" but reaffirmed that the only object he had in writing the book was to help Germany "throw off the slough of that stiff Lutheranism and contracted Pietism by a fresher, more living faith, the faith of the Creeds." He also admitted that he resented having rationalists claim that he was himself a rationalist. "I have seen it stated by Rationalizers that I was then rationalizing. The Cambridge Rationalist party took up my book against Rose. I may … have expressed myself vaguely, inaccurately. But, in God's mercy, none of the unbelief which I studied ever affected me as to any one article of faith. I was ordained soon after the publication of my first book, believing all which I had been taught—the Catholic faith."[37]

Apropos Pusey's repudiation of his treatise, Matthew was rueful: "Pusey stood … in about 1830, as a potentially powerful influence in the understanding in Britain of modern German scholarship, theology, and methodology: had he maintained his views and activities in these fields, it is not altogether fanciful to think that he could have developed into one of the seminal intellects of Victorian Britain."[38] The notion that Pusey failed to become one of the great Victorians because he did not enmesh himself sufficiently in German biblical criticism is risible. Pusey may not have been the most introspective of men but he recognized that in the case of Germany and its religious difficulties, his first impression had been the right one: "I can remember the room in Göttingen in which I was sitting when the real condition of religious thought in Germany flashed upon me. 'This will all come upon us in England; and how utterly unprepared for it we are!'"[39] Germany offered a warning, not a model.

In 1826, on his second trip to Germany, which Pusey made at Lloyd's urging, he undertook the study of the Hebrew cognates, Arabic, Syriac, and Chaldee. "I purpose," he wrote, "using … all the aids which I can find for the better understanding of the Old Testament, and contributing what I can myself from my knowledge of Eastern language allied to Hebrew."[40] For two years, he studied Arabic under Georg Freytag, the premier Arabist in Europe. In 1828, in recognition of Pusey's prodigious learning, the Duke of Wellington appointed him Regius Professor of Hebrew. Pusey's scholarly undertakings were far-ranging. He purchased important Hebrew manuscripts for the Bodleian, including the Oppenheimer collection, the greatest of the Hebrew collections in the library; together with his older brother Philip, he founded scholarships for the study of Hebrew; he founded a Theological Society for young fellows and supported other theological colleges, most munificently Salisbury Theological Study, to which he gave £2,500; and, for nearly six years, he worked to complete the catalogue of oriental manuscripts in the Bodleian Library begun by his predecessor. "The Catalogue," Freytag wrote Pusey, "will be an irrefragable proof for those who come after us, both of your talents and of your rare industry."[41]

Pusey also completed the monumental *Lectures on Daniel the Prophet*, which, despite its unfashionable conservatism, commanded widespread respect. As the Evangelical historian Timothy Larsen observes, "*Daniel the Prophet* was so formidable that, in Britain at least, it was unanswerable."[42] Most reviews of the book in British religious journals were laudatory. Prof. Larsen quotes the Old Testament scholar Rev. J. J. Stewart Perowne, who praised Pusey in the *Contemporary Review* for bringing to bear on his subject "a perfect encyclopedia of learning ... He has cast into his volume the labour of a lifetime. It is by far the most complete work which has yet appeared, no Continental writer having handled the subject with anything like the same fullness or breadth of treatment. In England we need scarcely say it is unrivalled. Few men amongst us could have produced such a book."[43] Since the Hebrew chair included the canonry of Christ Church, Pusey had to be ordained to the priesthood, and so nine days after his appointment, on Sunday 23 November 1828, at All Saints, Cuddesdon, Bishop Lloyd ordained him priest. It should be remembered, however, that, unlike Newman and Keble, Pusey never had the practical responsibility of caring for a parish, which had important implications for his understanding of the via media. It also deepened his constitutional vagueness, which was the aspect of the man that John Ruskin, who entered Christ Church in 1837, found most striking. In his autobiography, *Praeterita*, Ruskin recalled Pusey as "not in the least a picturesque or tremendous figure, but only a sickly and rather ill put together English clerical gentleman, who never looked one in the face, or appeared aware of the state of the weather."[44]

Shortly before and after his ordination, Pusey suffered terrible personal losses, which exacerbated his accustomed melancholy. In April 1828 his father died, and in May of the following year, Charles Lloyd went, after catching cold at an anniversary dinner of the Royal Academy in Somerset House. And then, as though to prove that sorrows come not single spies but in battalions, Pusey's infant daughter Katherine died. Newman had performed the child's baptism—"the only service which we dare perform with a rejoicing conscience and a secure mind"—and when he learned of the loss he sent Pusey a letter of condolence that his friend always prized. "Of course only parents can tell the sorrow of the loss of a child," Newman admitted, "but all persons can see the comfort contained in it—to know you have given eternal life and happiness to an immortal spirit ... You have done for her what you could—you have dedicated her to God, and He has taken the offering."[45] As the lives of the two men unfolded, the experience of loss would become a shared sorrow, though Newman never regarded his losses with Pusey's luxuriant self-reproach. "The impression has come gradually upon me," Pusey wrote to his wife on the third anniversary of his daughter's death, "that the loss of our dear Katherine was not merely a trial of my cheerful surrender of her ... but a chastisement of me."[46] Whether this was humility or persecution mania, Pusey rarely differentiated suffering from retribution.

Pusey's correspondence shows that in his relations with his family he replicated the despotic misrule that had characterized his father's household. For example, he made altogether too much of Maria's flippant doubts about Christianity, which might very well have been voiced simply to tease him. "It is fearful to think how near you were to the borders of entire unbelief," he wrote to her in one letter, after she had confessed, apropos the Epistle to the Romans, that "had that Epistle been given to me to read as a mere human production, I should have thought its author … either a fool or an hypocrite, either ignorant of what he was about, or willing to deceive with a shew of understanding what no one else could."[47] For Pusey, trifling irreverence was nascent apostasy. "There is probably scarcely any male mind," he informed his young wife, "which had got as far as you did, and to some of the principles in which you seem to have almost acquiesced, which would have stopped short of abandoning Christianity. Do not distress yourself about this; I mention it as proof of God's mercy to you, and in part to shew the danger of principles, not to blame; I should not *necessarily* by any means think any man the worse for having been not only on the verge, but within the prison of unbelief … The unbeliever is to me the object of deep compassion not of censure."[48] By turns unctuous and bullying, Pusey sought to convert Maria by silencing, rather than addressing her doubts. He also insisted that she practice his own austerities, particularly with respect to fasting, and this despite the fact that she was for most of their marriage gravely ill. She was even made to share his view of the necessity for corporeal punishment in the rearing of their three sickly children, Lucy, Philip and Mary. In all things, wife and children were enjoined to comply with Pusey's will. "I trust we shall continue to pray to be more completely like-minded," he wrote in one letter to Maria, with an odd, almost incantatory insistence. "I do not mean in this to allude to any special thing; only I should wish that we should be like-minded in all—nor as if you were to come to me in all things, but that we should be like-minded." If his father had run his household with what Liddon characterized as "military exactness," Pusey ran his as though it were a theocracy.[49]

No one can study Pusey's life without recognizing how adverse an influence his father had on him. From his father he inherited his imperiousness, his solipsism, his intransigence, and his need to overwork, which, in turn, explains why he fell so deeply in love with Maria, who offered him escape from the solitude to which his unhappy studies consigned him. Before he fell in love with Maria, he was "a reading automaton," a lonely, sad, introverted youth, who seemed tailor-made for Byron's cult of ennui.[50] Afterwards, he could scarcely imagine life without her: "Everything shews me more and more how great a treasure God has given me in you …"[51] Indeed, in one letter, he assured Maria that if he had "a window" in his breast, she would see, "what else you can never know, how deeply, fervently grateful and obliged is your Edward."[52] Together with this deep emotional attachment to Maria came premonitions of her loss. "I cannot picture to myself what would be my condition without you … kind as you are, beyond all human kindness to me, and deeply as I love you, we must not become so necessary to each other, as to 'sorrow without hope' were the other taken ... I fear I shall be plunging deeper and deeper, if I continue."[53]

Personal worry joined with worries over what the European revolutions of 1830 portended. As clearly as Keble and Newman, Pusey saw that the old order was collapsing. "A new order of things (whether we or our children shall see the development of it, or whether we, as is more probable, shall only witness its fearful preludes) but a new state of things must, I imagine come ..." In abandoning his youthful liberalism, Pusey pledged himself to the defense of an embattled Christianity, which he saw the Prime Minister Earl Grey and the Whigs betraying. Pusey's "apparent volte-face in political outlook is not surprising," Forrester remarks, "when one appreciates that his fear of an impending crisis was echoed in the writings and sermons of churchmen of all parties."[54] In taking the liberals of the Grey government to task for their misappropriation of church prerogatives, Pusey suggested ways that the Anglican clergy could wrest back these prerogatives to strengthen the National Church. In his pamphlet, *Cathedral Institutions* (1833), he argued that the National Church should return cathedrals to the purposes for which they had been originally founded by becoming once again centers of learning and clerical education. For Pusey, such training was vital if the Church was to withstand the coming assault. "Our next contest," he prophesied, "will be ... with a half-learned infidelity ... We shall not suffer much, probably from the shallowness of French, or from the speculations of the unsound part of German metaphysics: the one is too commonplace for us, and we are too much bent upon physical science and matters of sense to employ ourselves on the other. But the struggle will probably be with shallow views of the older Dispensation, shallow conceptions and criticisms of Divine truths, superficial carpings at the details of revelation, an arbitrary selection of such portion of its doctrines as may best admit of being transmuted into some corresponding doctrine of Deistical belief."[55] Much of the history of the Anglican Church in the last two centuries bears out Pusey's prediction. Newman approved of the pamphlet (despite its reference to Calvin as a saint) because it argued for the indispensability of Tradition. "As to Scripture being practically sufficient for making the Christian," he wrote to Pusey before he set sail for the Mediterranean with Hurrell Froude in December 1832, "it seems to me a mere dream—nor do I find it anywhere said so in Scripture—nor can I infer logically that what is *the* sole oracle of *doctrine* is therefore also of *practice* and *discipline*."[56]

It was, in part, to reinvigorate practice and discipline that Newman and Froude founded the Oxford Movement on their return from the Mediterranean. Keble's preaching of his sermon "On National Apostasy" (1833) at the same time that Pusey published his *Cathedral Institutions*, demonstrates the accord to which these highly different men made their different ways, though for Pusey it was "The Christian Year" (1827), not the sermon on apostasy, which first "turned the tide," as Newman expressed it, "and brought the talent of the University round to the side of the old theology and against what was familiarly called 'march-of-mind.'" Pusey entirely agreed with Newman that "In and from Keble the mental activity of Oxford took that contrary direction which issued in what was called Tractarianism."[57] In an earlier letter to Maria, Pusey had told her that "I always loved J.K. for his connection with Fairford, but all he has said and done and written makes me esteem him more."[58] When Pusey decided to throw in his lot with the Tractarians, and issued Tract 18 on 21 December 1833, it was fitting that his theme should be fasting. "I feel some hope," Pusey wrote to his brother apropos the Tract, "that, by God's blessing, it may have some tendency to promote a more humble, submissive, acquiescing frame of mind towards God, in these days of tumult, self-confidence, and excitement."[59] Pusey called his readers attention to the example of the early Christians.

> Their whole life was a Fast, a death to this world, a realizing of things invisible. It was when dangers began to mitigate, when Christianity became (as far as the world was concerned) an easy profession, it was then that the peril increased, lest their first simplicity should he corrupted, their first love grow cold! Then those who had spiritual authority in the Church increased the stated Fasts, in order to recall that holy earnestness of life, which the recentness of their redemption, and the constant sense of their SAVIOUR'S presence, had before inspired. Fasts were not merely the voluntary discipline of men, whose conversation was in heaven; they were adopted and enlarged in periods of ease, of temptation, of luxury, of self-satisfaction, of growing corruption.[60]

Pusey's own growing austerities would always keep pace with the growing corruption of the Anglican Church. Nevertheless, after the publication of the Tract, Pusey was surprised that some found his treatment of the subject objectionable. "I was not prepared for people questioning, even in the abstract, the duty of fasting," he wrote Newman. "I thought serious-minded persons at least supposed they practiced fasting in some way or other. I assumed the duty to be acknowledged, and thought it only undervalued."[61] Pusey would encounter similar opposition when he attempted to affirm his understanding of the Real Presence, which was an eccentric amalgam of Protestant and Catholic views.

For Newman, Pusey's decision to join the Tractarians was cause for celebration. "His great learning, his immense diligence, his scholar-like mind, his simple devotion to the cause of religion, overcame me, and great of course was my joy, when, in the last days of 1833, he showed a disposition to make common cause with us ... Without him we should have had little chance, especially at the early date of 1834, of making any serious resistance to the Liberal aggression. But Dr. Pusey was a Professor and Canon of Christ Church; he had a vast influence in consequence of his deep religious seriousness, the munificence of his charities, his Professorship, his family connexions, and his easy relations with University authorities ... He was able to give a name, a form, and a personality, to what was without him a sort of mob ..."[62] If Pusey had misgivings about taking up with this mob, they were dispelled by Thomas Arnold, the Broad Church Headmaster of Rugby, who wrote, in response to Tract 18, "you are lending your co-operation to a party second to none in the tendency of their principles to overthrow the Gospel." Here was criticism from one of the most notable of the march-of-mind men, the shallowness of which proved Pusey's point: Anglican divines were in need of better training. "Your own tract is perfectly free from their intolerance as well as from their folly," Arnold assured Pusey, "yet I cannot sympathize with its object, which has always appeared to me to belong to the Antiquarianism of Christianity,—not to its profitable history ..." Critics frequently claimed that in embracing the doctrinal concerns of the Fathers the Tractarians were embracing antiquarianism. One reason why Pusey launched the Library of the Fathers was to prove such critics wrong. If readers could see what the Fathers wrote, they would see that the concerns of the Fathers were theirs. Arnold, however, refused to concede that there was anything the early Church could teach nineteenth-century Christians. "The history and writings of the early ages of the Church have their use,—but it is an indirect not a direct one,—like the use of some of the historical parts of the Old Testament; that is, it will not furnish examples or precedents to be applied in the lump to present things." Forrester rightly points out that it is questionable how familiar Pusey was with the Fathers when he first joined the Tractarians; so much of his time was taken up with the Bodleian catalogue and with his duties as Professor of Hebrew, not to mention his wife and four children; but he certainly knew enough about the Fathers to know that Arnold knew less.[63] When the Headmaster of Rugby wrote that he was "amazed at some apparent efforts in this Protestant Church to set up the idol of Tradition: that is, to render Gibbon's conclusion against Christianity valid by taking like him the Fathers and the second and subsequent periods of the Christian History as a fair specimen of the Apostles and of the true doctrines of Christ," Pusey must have felt his concern for the training of Anglican clergy richly vindicated. Liddon observed that "It was not likely that Pusey would be influenced by such criticisms."[64] Arnold's fulminations opened Pusey's eyes to aspects of liberalism—particularly its designs on the National Church—of which he had not been adequately aware. "The system pursued in Oxford seems to be a revival of the Nonjurors," Arnold contended, "a party far too mischievous and too foolish ever to be revived with success. But it may be revived enough to do harm,—to cause the ruin of the Church of England first, and so far as human folly and corruption can, to obstruct the progress of the Church of Christ."[65] Since Pusey had immense respect for Keble precisely because he had acquainted him with the Nonjurors, the high-churchmen of the seventeenth century who remained loyal to the Stuarts, Arnold's comments only confirmed his growing antipathy to liberalism. "It was at Fairford," Pusey wrote to Keble in 1837, "many years ago when I was thoughtlessly, or rather, I must say, confidently, taking for granted that the Stuarts were rightly dethroned, that I heard for the first time a hint to the contrary from you. Your seriousness was an unintended reproof to my petulant expression about it, and so it stuck by me."[66]

In 1836, in Tracts 67–69 on baptism, Pusey corroborated the aspect in Keble that Newman singled out for praise: his grasp of what Newman called "the Sacramental system; that is, the doctrine that material phenomena are both the types and the instruments of real things unseen—a doctrine which embraces in its fullness, not only what Anglicans, as well as Catholics believe about Sacraments properly so called; but also the article of 'the Communion of Saints;' and likewise the Mysteries of the faith."[67] After the loss of his daughter and wife, Pusey had a deep personal need to embrace the Communion of the Saints. He also had a direct personal motive for affirming the sacrament of baptism. "A pupil of mine," he recalled, "was on the verge of leaving the Church for Dissent, and on the ground that the Church taught Baptismal Regeneration in the Prayer-book. So I set myself to show what the teaching of Scripture of Holy Baptism was."[68] This was a task for which the biblical scholar in Pusey was peculiarly suited, and he went about it with gusto.

One critical reader, H. V. Elliott, distilled the essence of the Broad Church opposition to the tract: "My great fear ... is lest you should introduce an extreme value of forms and rites, to the detriment of spiritual worship, and ultimately of real holiness: lest you should exalt the Church to a par with, or above, the Word of God; and bring religion to be so much identified with the outward reception of the Sacraments as to disparage that private and secret walk with God, without which the Sacraments themselves will lose their power."[69] For Pusey, those who rejected the doctrine of baptismal regeneration, far from engaging in any "private and secret walk with God," "entered into a most perilous path, which ... must end in the rejection of all Scripture truth."[70] Newman recognized that the Anglican Church's predominantly negative attitude towards baptismal regeneration was indicative of a general antipathy to the sacramental. In 1834, he wrote his friend John Bowden: "The Evangelicals, taking advantage of the distracted state of the Church, are making a push to get their way in it – and the Bishop of London ... [is] temporizing, conceding ½ way, and so making matters clear for their ultimate triumph. The organs of the innovators profess they account the doctrine of baptismal regeneration *heretical*."[71] To another correspondent, he wrote: "My friend Bowden tells me his wife has just heard a sermon in Petersham Church in which it was positively asserted, that Baptismal Regeneration was an invention of our Bishops of the last Century. The unsettled opinions of the Clergy in our own parts is what has led Pusey to write his Tract. I suppose we must expect to be taken with the controversy as with a snare – it will blaze up all round us before we know where we are. Indeed in all matters the state of the Church is most deplorable – scarce one man in ten thousand knowing any one reason for any one part of our doctrine or discipline, and relinquishing the most sacred things carelessly from not knowing their value."[72] For Newman, Anglicans had been misguided by "certain celebrated Protestant teachers, Puritan or Latitudinarian, and have suffered in consequence. Hence, we have almost embraced the doctrine that God conveys grace only through the instrumentality of the mental energies, that is, through faith, prayer, active spiritual contemplation, or (what is commonly called) communion with God, in contradiction to the primitive view according to which the Church and her Sacraments are the ordained and direct visible means of conveying to the soul what is in itself supernatural and unseen." Moreover, Newman recognized that Pusey was taking up the subject of baptism to expose "a modern system of theology of extensive popularity and great speciousness" that tended to deny the validity of all the sacraments.[73] One of the chief architects of that modern theology, Frederick Denison Maurice, confided in his son how he took Pusey's Tract "with him on a walk … and how as he went along it became more and more clear to him that it represented everything that he did not think and did not believe, till at last he sat down on a gate, in what were then the open fields of Clapham, and made up his mind that it represented the parting point between him and the Oxford school. He always spoke of it with a kind of shudder, as it were, of an escape from a charmed dungeon. 'They never have allowed any one who has once come within their meshes to escape,' was often his last sentence on the subject."[74] This would confirm the view that Newman eventually took of the relation between Tractarianism and the Established Church, to which he gave trenchant expression in *Anglican Difficulties*. Tractarianism could not thrive within an Established Church that was so fundamentally at odds with the sacramental.

The description of baptismal regeneration that Pusey included in Tract 67 shows how essential it was to his Tractarian faith.

> "Baptismal regeneration," he wrote, "as connected with the Incarnation of our Blessed Lord, gives a depth to our Christian existence, an actualness to our union with Christ, a reality to our sonship to God, an interest in the presence of our Lord's glorified Body at God's right hand, a joyousness amid the subduing of the flesh, an overwhelmingness to the dignity conferred on human nature, a solemnity to the communion of saints who are the fullness of Him Who filleth all in all, a substantiality to the indwelling of Christ, that to those who retain this truth the school which abandoned it must needs appear to have sold its birthright."[75]

The person who first persuaded Newman of these truths was John Bird Sumner (1780–1862), whose *Apostolical Preaching considered in an Examination of St. Paul's Epistles* (1815) made a great impression on him. In 1873, when a correspondent asked Newman advice about baptism, 40 years after he had first read Sumner's book, he wrote: "I think Sumner's Apostolical Preaching might be of use to you. It is a very good book. When its author wrote it, he was a mild high churchman, according to the character of his day. He wrote it against 'Evangelical' Preaching, and there can be no doubt that, when he wrote it, he did profess Baptismal Regeneration. His book would be of use to you as showing you the ground work on which that doctrine is commonly held— and the place it holds in the system of Christian teaching. It is one doctrine out of many, one out of a consistent whole. It is implied, it is required by the whole. Sumner's book sets before you that whole."[76] After becoming Archbishop of Canterbury in 1848, Sumner repudiated baptismal regeneration by acquiescing in the Gorham Judgment, which ruled "that a clergyman of the Church of England need not believe in baptismal regeneration." If the head of the Anglican Church could connive in such a ruling, the Tractarian contention that the Anglican Church was "catholic" could carry no conviction. Nevertheless, latter-day apologists for Sumner's acquiescence bring an amusing ingenuity to their defense of the Archbishop. For Peter Nockles, when Sumner denied the heretical import of Gorham's rejection of baptismal regeneration he "protested his own consistency"—surely a nuanced way to account for the abandonment of settled conviction.[77] Nigel Scotland, in his entry on Sumner in the *Oxford Dictionary of National Biography*, claims that in deserting the doctrine, the Archbishop showed "diplomacy and *savoir-faire*." Owen Chadwick tries to put as good a face as possible on the proceedings by remarking that "Even Archbishop Sumner agreed with Blomfield that the judicial committee was unsatisfactory as a judge of unsound doctrine."[78]

Pusey, on the contrary, insisted that the doctrine of baptismal regeneration must be upheld. In 1850, together with 14 others, he signed resolutions stating that if the Church of England accepted the Gorham Judgment, the Church "forfeits ... the office and authority to witness and teach," and "becomes formally separated from the Catholic body, and can no more assure to its members the grace of the Sacraments and the Remission of Sins." After Sumner upheld the Gorham Judgment, six of the signatories seceded from the Anglican Church, including Henry Edward Manning, Robert Wilberforce, William Dodsworth, Henry Wilberforce, Edward Badeley and James Hope. Pusey and Keble conspicuously chose not to follow them.[79] Later, in a letter to his old friend Lord Blachford, Newman recalled this lamentable failure: "Pusey must be ever in the recollection that the Gorham judgment stands good in law and usage, which 20 years ago he protested would, if successful, unchurch the English Church. But I quite enter into your feeling about the old jog trot curriculum."[80]

Pusey never lived down this failure to stick to his convictions over the Gorham Judgment. Even Liddon acknowledged the indefensible position in which this failure put his hero, and did not omit from his otherwise laudatory life the public letter from the quietly heroic William Dodsworth (1798–1861), a rich Yorkshire timber merchant's son and Cambridge graduate, who began his career as an Evangelical before joining the Tractarians. In the wake of the Gorham Judgment, despite being married, he resigned his living at Christ Church, Albany Street, to convert to Catholicism on 1 January 1851. In his letter decrying Pusey's capitulation, he addressed Pusey directly:

I must add one word on the grief and surprise which it has occasioned me, and many others besides me, that *you* should have taken this line in our present difficulties. You have been one of the foremost to lead us on to a higher appreciation of that 'Church system,' of which sacramental grace is the very life and soul. Both by precept and example you have been amongst the most earnest to maintain Catholic principles. By your constant and common practice of administering the sacrament of penance; by encouraging everywhere, if not enjoining, auricular confession, and giving special priestly absolution; by teaching the propitiatory sacrifice of the Holy Eucharist, as applicatory of the one sacrifice on the cross, and by adoration of Christ Really Present on the altar under the form of bread and wine; by your introduction of Roman Catholic books 'adapted to the use of our Church;' by encouraging the use of rosaries and crucifixes, and special devotions to our Lord ... by advocating counsels of perfection, and seeking to restore, with more or less fullness, the conventual or monastic life;—I say, by the teaching and practice, of which this enumeration is a sufficient type and indication, you have done much to revive amongst us the system which may be pre-eminently called 'SACRAMENTAL.' And yet now, when, by God's mercy to us, a great opportunity has occurred, of asserting and enforcing the very keystone of this system, and apart from which the whole must crumble away—forgive me for speaking so plainly—you seem to shrink from the front rank. You seem ready to hide yourself ... behind ambiguous statements which can be subscribed in different senses.[81]

The Gorham Judgment was not the only difficulty that Pusey encountered in the practice of his Tractarian faith. In 1843, his sermon "The Holy Eucharist a Comfort to the Penitent" also came under attack from university authorities. "In candor and fairness," the Vice-Chancellor wrote Pusey, "I think it right to confess that its general scope and certain particular passages have awakened in my mind painful doubts with regard to its strict conformity to the doctrines of the reformed Church of England."[82] Pusey's response was less indignant than incredulous: "I felt so entirely sure that I heartily concur with the doctrine of the Church of England, I have so often and decidedly expressed my rejection of the doctrine of Transubstantiation, and the Canon of the Council of Trent upon it, that, neither before nor after preaching my sermon, had I the slightest thought any could arraign it as contrary to the doctrines of our Church ..." His inquisitors might have thought differently when Pusey proceeded to explain what he meant by the bread and wine: "I believe that after Consecration the Holy Elements are in their natural substances bread and wine, and yet are *also* the Body and Blood of Christ."[83] In a letter to Newman, Pusey wrote: "I have asked the Vice-Chancellor for two or three days that I might put references to my sermon. I thought this best, that they might not be exposed unconsciously to condemn e.g. St. Cyril of Alexandria when they thought they were only condemning me." When the Vice-Chancellor and six others withdrew to consider the contents of the sermon further, Pusey wrote his mother, "It seems as if something very momentous was going on, but that I had nothing to do but to wait for it, and pray and abide, as I trust, under the shadow of His wings, and be at rest."[84] Edward Hawkins, the Provost of Oriel, who had instigated the proceedings, concluded his condemnation, in which five of his colleagues joined, by observing that, although Pusey "did not design to oppose the doctrine of the Church of England," he was "led into erroneous views and expressions, partly by a pious desire to magnify the grace of God in the Holy Eucharist, and partly by an indiscreet adoption ... of the highly figurative, mystical, and incautious language of certain of the old Fathers."[85] That not only Hawkins but five other dons objected to this language puts the judgment of mid-nineteenth-century Oxford in an arrestingly unflattering light.

Rather than confront Pusey himself, Hawkins delegated Richard Jelf, a close friend of the accused and then canon of Christ Church, who dutifully presented Pusey with a document requesting that he recant the sermon's alleged heterodox content, particularly "the idea of any carnal or corporeal presence of Christ in the holy Eucharist."[86] Pusey duly signed the document, even though he regarded its condemnation as "unstatutable and unjust."[87] In return for this sworn confession, he was suspended from preaching for two years and told to keep mum about the matter—or, as Liddon neatly put it, "He was obliged to be silent about his own enforced silence."[88] Once word leaked out about what had taken place, Frederick Faber, then Fellow of Magdalen, wrote the Vice-Chancellor to explain that "the silence of the gentlemen who examined the sermon is very perplexing to us who may have to preach at some time or other before the University. We have no means of knowing what is held to be heretical doctrine respecting the Eucharist ... and consequently cannot avoid the danger which Dr. Pusey has incurred."[89] Newman and Keble advised Pusey to publish the sermon with a catena of Anglican authorities; Pusey took both their advice and published it in June of 1843. After he finally read the sermon, Keble told Pusey: "I am really quite at a loss to imagine how they can justify their sentence without condemning almost all the writers in your Catena, and certainly all the Fathers."[90] Gladstone wrote from Carlton House Terrace echoing Keble: "I am quite at a loss to account to myself for steps which seem so groundless. However unwarranted, they must be deeply painful to one whose feelings have ever been kept so much in harmony as yours with the actual Church of England ..."[91]

Here was the heart of the matter: what did constitute the teaching of the Church of England? For Liddon, "A narrow and ignorant view of the Anglican Formularies, not as they were meant to be, but as two or three generations—partly careless, partly bigoted, partly untheological—had taken them to be, was to be stereotyped and thrust on all the Church, clergy and laity alike. It made men despair of Anglicanism, or realize what they had to expect if they remained true to their Church awaiting its deliverance. If Pusey, with his learning, piety and position could be treated in this way, what were others to expect?"[92] Newman's response to the summary judgment was clear-sighted: the condemnation of Pusey's sermon was "the first formal University act against us ... It seems very impolitic in the House of Heads—for if there is a Puseyite who will rouse the sympathies of the people, it is Pusey. All sorts of people admire and respect him. On the other hand I am not without anxiety as to the effect upon him personally. I could fancy it making him retire into himself, and breaking his spirit both morally and spiritually."[93] For himself, as he told Henry Wilberforce, "I have neither time nor will to meddle with these dirty matters," though he was very much concerned that Pusey's explanations after the fact would only make matters worse.[94] "Better say nothing," he wisely counseled his voluble friend, "than not speak clearly ..."[95]

If Newman was prepared to give Pusey moral support in his wrangles with Oxford's anti-Tractarian authorities, he was also unstinting in practical help. In this regard, Newman's solicitude for the physical well-being of Pusey and his wife was characteristic. In August 1838, when Maria Pusey's long-suffering health had taken a turn for the worse, Newman counseled Pusey to go South for the winter months. "I am concerned you do not give an improved account of Mrs Pusey. Are you quite sure that the South might not be expedient for her? If you went to Malta, you could have all your books with you – a steamer carries any quantity of luggage. In the winter you would have hardly any fellow passengers to incommode you – and would hardly lose a day's work. When there, you would be settled quite as much as in England. You would find probably Rose there – and you might instil good principles into Queen Adelaide, who deserves them. I am quite sure that in point of usefulness, you would lose no time at all. They have a superb library attached to St John's Church – and I doubt not the MSS are well worth inspecting. They come from Vienna."[96] Pusey was game but his doctor advised against it, telling him that his wife had only months to live. When Newman heard the news, he offered ready support: "You know, should you like me to walk with you in the morning, there is no reason why I should not come to you at six as well as at any other times. You have but to send me a note overnight ... Pray tell dear Mrs. Pusey that I am continually thinking of her, and pray (what I doubt not) that you may have grace so to part from each other that you may meet again in peace."[97] Pusey wrote Newman back: "Anything from you must always be soothing ... My six o'clock walk is at an end, for from four or five or seven in the morning is now her time of greatest suffering ... I am afraid of misleading you, as if I felt better than I do; yet I wish this to be a season of penitence."[98] To Pusey's tendency to see all misfortune as retributive, Newman countered with more balanced advice: "I hardly know how to answer your note ... But it seems to me you must not suffer yourself to suppose that any punishment is meant in what is now to be. Why should it? I mean, really it is nothing out of God's usual dealing. The young and strong fall all around us. How many whom we love are taken out of our sight by sudden death, however healthy—Whether slowly or suddenly, it comes on those in whose case we do not expect it. I do not think you must look on it as 'some strange thing.' Pray do not."[99] When Maria's state worsened, Lady Lucy left Grosvenor Place to be with her son in Christ Church. On the morning of Trinity Sunday, Newman wrote to his friend to assure him that prayers were being said by all his friends. "This, you will see, requires no answer. I have nothing to say—only I wish you to remember that many persons are thinking of you and making mention of you, where you wish to be mentioned. Do not fear you will not be strengthened according to your day. He is nearest, when He seems furthest away. I heard from Keble a day or two since, and he wished me to tell you they were thinking of you at Hursley. This is a day especially sacred to peace—the day of the Eternal Trinity, who were all blessed from eternity in themselves, and in the thought of whom the mind sees the end of its labours, the end of its birth, temptations, struggles, and sacrifices, its daily dyings and resurrections."[100]

When the end came, Lady Lucy sent for Newman. Shortly afterwards, Pusey wrote to Keble: "God has been very merciful to me in this dispensation, and carried me on, step by step, in a way I dared not hope. He sent Newman to me (whom I saw at my mother's wish against my inclination) in the first hour of sorrow; and it was like the visit of an angel. I hope to go on my way 'lonely, not forlorn' ..."[101] Later, Pusey thanked Newman directly, "God bless and reward you for all your tender kindness towards us."[102] On 1 June 1839, Maria was buried in the nave of Christ Church Cathedral, a day Pusey would never forget. Years afterwards, whenever he crossed the quadrangle to the cathedral, Pusey would always keep his eyes on the pavement, rather than risk seeing again, if only in his mind's eye, the shroud on his wife's coffin as he followed it to her grave.[103] On her tombstone, Pusey considered inscribing the line, "Requiem aeternam dona eis, Domine, et Lux perpetua eis," though taking anything from the Breviary caused him concern: he did not wish to be thought condoning "the modern corruptions of Rome."[104] It was only after Newman told him that he had nothing to worry about that he went ahead with the incision. Nevertheless, here was pitiable proof that even in moments of the most shattering bereavement Pusey continued to agonize over his Anglican difficulties.

It was after his wife's death that the image of the mature Pusey—unsociable, donnish, ponderous, grim—took permanent shape. As the biographer of Dean Church observed, "Any taste which Pusey might have had for the sights of this world was sternly put aside with other gentlemanly amenities after his wife's death."[105] In his reminiscences of the Canon of Christ Church, Tuckwell recalled: "In those days he was a Veiled Prophet, always a recluse, and after his wife's death ... invisible except when preaching ... I can see him passing to the pulpit through crowds ... the pale, ascetic, furrowed face, clouded and dusky always as with suggestions of a blunt or half-used razor, the bowed, grizzled head, the drop into the pulpit out of sight until the hymn was over, then the harsh unmodulated voice, the high-pitched devotional patristicism, the dogmas, obvious or novel, not so much ambassadorial as from a man inhabiting his message; now and then the search-light thrown with startling vividness on the secrets hidden in many a hearer's heart. Some came once from mere curiosity, and not again, some felt repulsion, some went away alarmed, impressed, transformed."[106] Later, after becoming friendly with him, Tuckwell noted, "Two things impressed me when I first saw him close: his exceeding slovenliness of person; buttonless boots, necktie limp ... unbrushed coat collar ... and the almost artificial sweetness of his smile contrasting as it did with the somber gloom of his face when in repose." Newman would write to the convert T. W. Allies at the height of his controversy with Pusey, "It is harsh to call any mistakes of his, untruthfulness. I think they arise from the same slovenly habit which some people would recognise in his dress, his beard, etc."[107] What Tuckwell and most others at Oxford could not see beneath the dour public persona was Pusey's lacerating self-recrimination, which he attempted to describe to Keble: "My dear wife's illness first brought to me, what has since been deepened by the review of my past life, how, amid special mercies and guardianship of God, I am scarred all over and seamed with sin, so that I am a monster to myself: I loathe myself, I can feel of myself only like one covered with leprosy from head to foot: guarded as I have been there is no one with whom I do not compare myself, and find myself worse than they."[108] With thoughts like these preoccupying his mind, it is no wonder he neglected his appearance.

If 1839 was a turning point in Pusey's life, it was even more so in Newman's, when, in the course of studying early Church history, he discovered that there were grounds for doubting the legitimacy of the Anglican Church. For the next six years, he subjected his doubts to careful re-examination. However, no sooner did his doubts about the illegitimacy of Canterbury become confirmed than his doubts about the legitimacy of Rome intensified. If Newman was slow to convert, it was only because he feared that his developing convictions about the claims of Rome might be delusive. As he wrote to Manning, "What keeps me yet [within the Anglican fold] is what has kept me long—a fear that I am under a delusion ..." He was understandably leery of a Roman Church about which he knew so little: "I was scarcely ever for an hour in the same room with a Roman Catholic in my life," he admitted.[109] Indeed, as late as December of 1844, he confided to his dear friend John Keble: "No one could have a more unfavorable view than I have of the present state of the Roman Catholics—so much so that any who joined them would be like the Cistercians at Fountains, living under trees till their house was built ..."[110] Despite these doubts, Newman's Catholic faith was becoming stronger day by day. During the long period in which he feared that his doubts might be the result of sinfulness—a fear Anglicans inclined to Rome were encouraged to feel by an Establishment Church naturally hostile to Rome—he undertook St. Ignatius's Spiritual Exercises, which, he told Keble, he found of "extreme utility." For Newman, Loyola "and his followers after him, seem to have reduced the business of self discipline to a science—and since our Enemy's warfare upon us proceeds doubtless on system, every one, I suppose, must make a counter system for himself, or take one which experience has warranted."[111] Undertaking the Spiritual Exercises finally proved to Newman that his growing confidence in the truth of Catholicism was not delusive. When the Bishop of Oxford ordered Newman to cease publication of the Tracts in response to the furor over the presumed heterodoxy of Tract 90, Pusey was confident that Newman would abide the episcopal condemnation, just as he had abided the condemnation he had received over his sermon on the Eucharist. As late as 1844, Pusey sent Newman a birthday note telling his friend that, "If such as I might express anything in sending what is solemn, it would be the hope that in all the sorrows and anxieties whereby you are to be perfected, you may be bathed and refreshed by that Sudor Sanguineus, and that as each pang comes over you ... you will commit our Church to Him, who endured It for us."[112] Newman wrote back that Pusey was under "a false impression from which I can relieve you. I am in no perplexity or anxiety at present. I fear that I must say that for four years and a half I have had a conviction, weaker or stronger, but on the whole constantly growing, and at present very strong, that we are not part of the Church. I am too much accustomed to this idea to feel pain at it ... Alas! I fear I have removed pain from your mind in one way, only to give a greater pain in another. And yet is it possible you can be quite unprepared for this avowal? It was the Monophysite and Donatist controversies which in 1839 led me to this clear and distinct judgement."[113] It was possible:

Pusey would not hear what Newman was telling him and chose instead to imagine that his friend was simply over-reacting. "I have such conviction that you are under God's guidance, that I look on cheerfully still, that all will be right,—I mean for our poor Church and you ... Indeed, of late, I have wished to know nothing, lest my very knowing it should be hurtful. I have the same confidence in you as ever."[114] Nevertheless, Newman again sought to disabuse his friend. "I think you do not put yourself enough into my position, and consider how a person would view things, and at the end of near five years. I suppose it is possible for a Church to have some profound wound, which, till healed, infallibly impeded the exercise of its powers and made attempts to act futile. How should we feel, e.g., if we saw a man with a broken leg attempting to walk?"[115] Keble, at least, knew what was coming. "I myself for some time," he wrote Pusey, "have hardly dared to expect any other event than you now fear ... Yet when one does a little realize it, it seems a depth of disappointment beyond imagination. But surely there are those to whom there will be light in the darkness."[116]

In the midst of this gathering darkness, Pusey lost his eldest daughter Lucy, whose sickly constitution finally gave way after a severe attack of whooping cough. As Liddon avows, "Lucy was more to Pusey than his other children, more, perhaps than any other person in the world."[117] She sympathized with his religious interests, read Newman's sermons after she had been confirmed, and even resolved to devote herself to the religious life to look after the sick and poor. "She was the one being," Pusey told Newman, "around whom my thoughts of the future here had wound."[118] To his son, Philip, he confided, "I cannot tell you how her simplicity and devotion and love wound round my heart, and how I loved her ..."[119] Lucy reminded Pusey not only of his departed wife but of Newman. In a letter to his friend, written in the throes of his impending loss, Pusey related how his daughter had told him, 'Now I am so near death, it seems that my love of God is not what is should be,'" which prompted her distraught father to tell Newman "She is a child of your writings."[120] Newman, whose loss of his sister Mary brought home to him death's full, life-illuminating significance, wrote Pusey back a letter showing how shared grief united the two men, even at a time when their ecclesiological views were increasingly at odds. "You may fancy what heart ache your note of to-day has given me. Yet all is well, as you better than I can say. What would you do more than is granted you as regards dear Lucy? She was given you to be made an heir of heaven." Indeed, for Newman, Lucy, like Mary, must be accounted a saint, who required of Pusey nothing less than self-sacrificial love. "Have you not been allowed to perform that part towards her? You have done your work—what remains but to present it finished to Him Who put it upon you? You are presenting it to Him, you are allowed to do so, in the way most acceptable to Him, as a holy blameless sacrifice, not a sacrifice which the world sullied, but as if a baptismal offering, perfected by long though kind and gentle sufferings. How fitly do her so touching words which you repeat to me accord with such thoughts as these! 'Love' which she asks for, is of course, the grace which will complete the whole. Do you not bear in mind the opinion of theologians that it is the grace which supplies all things, supersedes all things, and is all in all?"[121] Later, in 1879, doubtless recalling these vital letters from Newman, Pusey would ask an Anglican colleague, who had falsely suggested that Pusey had tried to dissuade Newman from accepting the Cardinal's hat: "Why do people gossip about such a sacred thing as a love of above half a century?"[122]

The dejection into which Lucy's death threw Pusey was aggravated by concerns about the deteriorating state of the Anglican Church. "It is not that I mistrust God's goodness," he wrote to Newman, "but man's, our own, prayer-lessness. I hear of continual prayer among the Roman Catholics; there may be such among ourselves; but there is much want of love and disunited prayer."[123] In August 1844, while traveling down to Oxford from London, Newman heard of Pusey's deepening gloom from a mutual friend and tried to buck him up by suggesting that Rome might not be the unalloyed evil Pusey imagined. "Will you, please, think of this—that whatever be the event of things, (of which we know nothing, and whether good or bad we may know nothing) yet nothing can hinder the *fact* that it has pleased God to work, and to be working, through you more good than can be told. Is it a good that souls should be made more serious? that they should be turned towards themselves and towards repentance [sic]? that they should spend their substance, not on themselves, but in the service of religion? that they should have truer views of the creed? more reverence, more faith, more love? Now, has not Divine Mercy made you the means of all this in a way far beyond your own expectation? ... Is it not a hundred times more certain that these things are good than that joining the Church of Rome is evil? Is it not wrong to be downhearted?"[124] If Newman's main purpose in this heartfelt letter was to suggest to Pusey that Rome might be a welcome alternative to an English Church fraught with "disunited prayer," it was not a purpose Pusey acknowledged. Instead, like Keble, he insisted on regarding continued membership in the Anglican fold as a kind of necessary mortification for unexpiated sin. "Jeremiah was allowed to weep for his people, and Ezekiel to sit astonished seven days, and St. Paul to have great heaviness of heart for his kinsmen according to the flesh; and so, now that the work which God seemed to have in store for our Church seems threatened, I, a sinner, may have sorrow for what my own sins may, to an extent I know not of, have caused."[125] As for the likelihood that Newman himself would ever contemplate secession, Pusey was categorical: "write or speak or act as I may, I do not believe that it can ever be; it goes against my whole nature to believe it. I cannot think that we should be so utterly deserted as that it should be permitted."[126] Newman was at a loss. "What am I to say but I am one who, even five years ago, had a strong conviction, from reading the history of the early ages, that we are not part of the Church?" In August 1844, Newman might not have been fully convinced of the rightness of Rome but he was convinced of the wrongness of Canterbury. "For a long, long time my constant question has been, 'Is it a dream? Is it a delusion?' and the wish to have decisive proof on this point has made me satisfied to wait—it makes me satisfied to wait still—but, should such as I be suddenly brought down to the brink of life, then, when God allows no longer time for delib-eration, I suppose he would feel he must act, as is on the whole safest, under circumstances." Newman could not have been more explicit, and yet, recognizing the sort of stubborn denial he was up against, he ended the letter with an obviously weary plea: "And now, my dear P do take in the whole of the case, nor shut your eyes, as you do so continually, and God bless all things to you, as I am sure He will and does."[127] Pusey's reply could have inspired no confidence in Newman that he was getting through to his obdurate correspondent. "I do not shut my eyes now; I feel everything I do is hollow, and dread its cracking. But though I feel in a vessel threatened with shipwreck, I trust that our Lord is still in her, and that, however periled, she will not perish."[128] Pusey, at any rate, would muddle through. When, in early 1845, Convocation threatened to condemn Tract 90, Pusey wrote to Newman, "Recollect that I am committed to Tract 90 as well as you," which elicited from Newman a response that showed that he was not in need of reassurances. "Long indeed have I been looking for external circumstances to determine my course, and I do not wish this daylight to be withdrawn. Moreover, I have had to take so lukewarm a part about Ward that I am really glad and relieved to find myself at last in the scrape."[129] As it happened, the censure against Newman was vetoed, though indignation over the anti-Tractarian Heads of Houses who threatened the censure was considerable. "Sorrow for Oxford and the Church is even at this moment the strongest feeling in my breast," Gladstone told Pusey, "yet indignation at this proposal to treat Mr. Newman worse than a dog really makes me mistrust my judgment, as I suppose one should always do when any proposal seeming to present an aspect of incredible wickedness is advanced."[130] Newman looked on the proceedings with indifference. "The matter now going on has not given me a moment's pain, nay or interest," he told one correspondent.[131] He was coming to final terms with the radical realization, which had first dawned on him six years before that "the Church of England is in schism" and, in comparison, the threats of Oxford dons seemed trumpery things.[132]

In February 1845, Newman wrote to Pusey, "My dear P, please do not disguise the fact from yourself that ... I am as much gone over as if I *were already gone*. It is a matter of time only."[133] The Fathers of the ancient Church proved decisive: "this line of reading and no other," he told Keble, "has led me Romewards."[134] Levi Silliman Ives, the only American Episcopal bishop to convert as a result of the Oxford Movement, also credited the early Fathers with sealing his conversion. That the Fathers should have proven to Newman the untenably schismatic character of the Anglican Church could not have been easy for Pusey to accept. This may explain the odd surprise he affected at Newman's secession, despite the innumerable indications he had been given that his friend's conversion was indeed imminent.

If Keble responded to the crisis of Tractarianism with agonizing indecisiveness, Pusey responded as though there really had been no crisis. Newman went over to Rome, Pusey claimed, out of over-sensitive pique. "It is an exceeding mystery that such confidence as he had once in our Church should have gone," Pusey wrote in a long letter to the *English Churchman* after Newman's secession. "Even amidst our present sorrows it goes to the heart to look at that former self, and think how devotedly he worked for our Church;

how he strove to build her up. It looks as if some good purpose for our Church had failed; that an instrument raised up for her had not been employed as God willed and so is withdrawn. There is a jar somewhere. One cannot trust oneself to think, whether his keen sensitiveness to ill was not fitted for these troubled times. What, to such dulled minds as my own, seemed as a matter of course, as something of necessity to be gone through and endured, was to his ... 'like the piercing of a sword.'"[135] Newman, from his standpoint, confessed that he and Pusey were at cross purposes well before 1845. "I had from the first," he wrote in the *Apologia*, "a great difficulty in making Dr. Pusey understand such differences of opinion as existed between himself and me. When there was a proposal about the end of 1838 for a subscription for a Cranmer Memorial, he wished us both to subscribe together to it. I could not, of course, and wished him to subscribe by himself. That he would not do; he could not bear the thought of our appearing to the world in separate positions, in a matter of importance. And, as time went on, he would not take any hints, which I gave him, on the subject of my growing inclination to Rome." In his resolute assumption that Newman was somehow at one with his own adherence to the English Church, Pusey behaved with something of his father's accustomed imperiousness. In the *Apologia*, Newman catalogued the long history of Pusey's quixotic denial of facts. "A common friend of ours broke it all to him in 1841, as far as matters had gone at that time, and showed him clearly the logical conclusions which must lie in propositions to which I had committed myself; but somehow or other in a little while, his mind fell back into its former happy state, and he could not bring himself to believe that he and I should not go on pleasantly together to the end. But that affectionate dream needs must have been broken at last; and two years afterwards, that friend ... set himself, as I have said, to break it. Upon that, I too begged Dr. Pusey to tell in private to any one he would, that I thought in the event I should leave the Church of England. However, he would not do so; and at the end of 1844 had almost relapsed into his former thoughts about me, if I may judge from a letter of his which I have found. Nay, at the Commemoration of 1845, a few months before I left the Anglican Church, I think he said about me to a friend, "I trust after all we shall keep him."[136] When Manning shared with Pusey letters Newman had written to him in 1843 clearly preparing him for his conversion, Pusey would not credit them and, later, wrote Gladstone: "Knowing Newman intimately, I do not think that the portentous expression in his letters (forwarded to me by Manning) have a necessary or immediate bearing upon certain steps of outward conduct."[137] This tendency to ignore evidence contrary to his own wishes or prejudices can also be seen in Pusey's reading of the Fathers, whose affirmations of papal primacy, the honors due to the Mother of God, and the nature of the Real Presence he simply passed over.[138]

On 9 October 1845, Father Dominic, the Passionist came to Littlemore to take him away for good into the Roman Catholic Church. Liddon's comment on the momentous day is worth quoting: "The period of hesitation and suspense, within which Pusey had never quite ceased to hope, and certainly had never ceased to pray, was at an end. The dreaded event had come at last; Newman was lost to the English Church."[139] If Pusey never ceased to hope and pray that Newman would somehow remain within the Anglican communion of his birth, Newman, for his part, once he converted, never ceased to hope and pray that Pusey would join what he called "the One Fold of the Redeemer," though he was never unmindful of the many hindrances that stood in the way.[140] Indeed, in this regard, Newman might have agreed with the Bishop of London, who, on hearing of Newman's secession, consoled himself with the thought that if the English Church retained "only ten" communicants, Canon Pusey would be one of them.[141]

If Newman's relations with Keble broke down altogether after Newman's conversion, only resuming 20 years later, when a mutual friend suggested they meet, his relations with Pusey never broke off, though they became distinctly strained. On his 47th birthday, Newman wrote to Pusey, "Would I could say something which would sound less cold … but really I dare not. I could not without saying something which would seem rude. Alas! I have no alternative between silence and saying what would pain."[142] Nevertheless, he did manage to write to Pusey with some candor, as was evident in one of the first letters he wrote as a Catholic, when he was still at Maryvale, Oscott. "I cannot conceive, and will not, that the subject of so many prayers as are now offered for you, beginning at Rome, and reaching to Constantinople and England, should ultimately remain where you are. This, my dearest Pusey, is an earnest which satisfies me about the future, though I don't tell others so – nor am I anxious or impatient at the delay, for God has His own good time for everything—." But, by the same token, Newman was concerned about reports he was hearing of the unwarranted authority Pusey was arrogating to himself. "What does make me anxious, is, whenever I hear that, in spite of your evident approximation in doctrine and view to the Roman system, you are acting in hostility against it, and keeping souls in a system which you cannot bring out into words, as I consider, or rest upon any authority besides your own."[143] This was frank, but not as frank as a letter he did not send, in which he returned to the ticklish subject of Pusey's trying to dissuade Anglo-Catholics from converting. "I will say at once then, that it has affected me very much to hear that you are taking the salvation of others upon yourself. You say to them 'Remain in the English Church – I will be answerable for you.' O my dear P. who gave you authority, who taught you thus to speak? – where is such a responsibility contemplated in the Anglican formularies? What precedent is there for it? The awe and terror which this step has excited has been one cause of people's praying for you at this moment so earnestly."[144] Even though unsent, this letter is important, because it shows the extent to which Newman regarded Pusey as the *de facto* leader of the Tractarian party and, as such, accountable for the considerable sway he exercised over Anglo-Catholics. The saintly Keble might have been more beloved but Pusey was the acknowledged arbiter of the party's patchwork theology. In April 1841, Mrs. Brookfield, Thackeray's friend, acknowledged this by drolly confiding to her diary: "To day I am going to dine with some ultra-ultra-ultra evangelicals of aunts, who believe Pusey to be the Pope in disguise and Newman the head of the Jesuits."[145]

When Mrs. Bowden eventually chose to follow Newman and convert to Rome, Pusey sent Newman a letter which reaffirmed his allegiance to Canterbury, after sending one to Mrs. Bowden in which he wrote as though she had *not* converted, telling her at the same time that it remained "a mystery" why Newman had made his own move.[146] Again, Pusey ignored whatever contravened his wishes. Moreover, what is remarkable about this letter is how much it defines the position that he would maintain for the rest of his long life. "I could hardly write anything which would not pain you," he confessed to Newman. "For you have one wish for me; and I am no nearer that than heretofore. I cannot unmake myself; I cannot see otherwise than I have seen these many years ... I am no nearer to thinking that the English Church is no true part of the Church, or that inter-communion with Rome is essential, or that the present claims of Rome are Divine. I earnestly desire the restoration of unity, but I cannot throw myself into the practical Roman system, nor renounce what I believe our gracious Lord acknowledges. And so I must go on, with joy at the signs of deepening life among us, and distress at our losses, and amazement that Almighty God vouchsafes to employ me for anything, and thinking it less than I ought to expect when everything is brought to a contrary issue from what I desire."[147] Here was the reasoning with which Pusey reconciled himself to remaining within the Anglican Church, to which he would return again and again until his death in 1882. It was with this in mind that Newman wrote in the *Apologia*, "When I became a Catholic, I was often asked, 'What of Dr. Pusey?' When I said that I did not see symptoms of his doing as I had done, I was sometimes thought uncharitable. If confidence in his position is, (as it is) a first essential in the leader of a party, this Dr. Pusey possessed pre-eminently. The most remarkable instance of this was his statement, in one of his subsequent defenses of the Movement, when moreover it had advanced a considerable way in the direction of Rome that among its more hopeful peculiarities was its 'stationariness.'"[148] This was an astute observation on Newman's part because if one took away the odd Roman trappings from Pusey's Tractarianism, what Newman called its "mimic Catholicism"[149]—the auricular confession, the sisterhoods, the training of Anglican monks at St. Saviour's Leeds—it was not much different from the Anglicanism that the Provost of Oriel, Edward Copleston, described when he claimed that, "The scheme of revelation we think is closed, and we expect no new light on earth to break in upon us ... We hold it our especial duty ... to keep strict watch round that sacred citadel, to deliver out in due measure and season the stores it contains, to make our countrymen look to it as a tower of strength ..."[150]

In their uneasy relationship after Newman's conversion, Pusey, as we have seen, in the long letter that he submitted to the *English Churchman*, attributed Newman's conversion to "over-sensitiveness." Newman's riposte appeared five years later in the lectures he gave at the Oratory Church in King William Street in May and June 1850, which he later published as *Lectures on Certain Difficulties felt by Anglicans in submitting to the Catholic Church*. Owen Chadwick claimed that Newman had made a hash of the lectures by "writing long hours and too late at night" and that publishing them was "to his discredit."

Moreover, "It was the only book by Newman which many Anglicans found it impossible to forgive." That Liddon made no mention of Pusey's response to the book in his exhaustively documented biography might say something about the silent fury it inspired. In the course of the lectures Newman reintroduced all the arguments that he had once advanced so ingeniously to defend the via media, and demolished them one by one. Pusey and the remaining Tractarian faithful, who had latterly looked to Newman as their most eloquent champion, now watched aghast as he swung the wrecking ball. For Chadwick, unseemly vindictiveness was to blame: Newman, "suffering … from the disease of being a new convert," delivered his lectures with one object in mind: "burning what once he had adored," though as John Griffin persuasively shows, Newman was a good deal more sparing in his critique than he might have been.[151] In composing the lectures, he was motivated not by mockery or polemical advantage but concern for the well-being of his former companions.

The lectures, which are still too little known, are divided into two parts. In the first five lectures Newman showed how the Rome-leaning principles of the Movement of 1833 did not spring from nor could remake the Established Church. The Movement and the Establishment, Newman argued, "were in simple antagonism from the first, although neither party knew it; they were logical contradictories … what was the life of the one was the death of the other."[152] For Richard Hutton, the literary critic and editor of the *Spectator*, who was a good friend of Walter Bagehot and Arthur Hugh Clough, "here was a great subject with which Newman was perfectly intimate, giving the fullest scope to his powers of orderly and beautiful exposition, and opening a far greater range to his singular genius for gentle and delicate irony than anything which he had previously written."[153] In the remaining five lectures, Newman defended the Roman Church against its Protestant critics. Thus, in the first group he showed why the Tractarians could not flourish in the Established Church, and in the second, why their logical home was the Catholic Church. What is striking about the lectures is their infectious exuberance. Written at white heat in a matter of weeks, they have something of the same effervescence as *Loss and Gain*, Newman's charming Tractarian novel. Still, he was anxious about their reception. "I am perplexed," he wrote to Faber, "either some of them will be most impressively dull—or they will be too much on the other tack; and I am frightened at the chance of being satirical etc. before the Blessed Sacrament."[154] As it happened, Newman delivered the lectures in the lower chapel, where, as he proceeded, "The Fathers of the Oratory were heard to titter, the Romish ladies to giggle, while a scarcely suppressed laughter arose from the *heretical* Protestants." Eye-witness accounts verify the accustomed directness of Newman's speaking style. "His delivery is simple, earnest, untheatrical and devoid of impassioned gesture or exciting declamation," wrote one listener.[155] Hutton was also in attendance and noted the power of Newman's voice, despite its simplicity. "Never did a voice seem better adapted to persuade without irritating. Singularly sweet, perfectly free from any dictatorial tone, and yet rich in all the cadences proper to the expressions of pathos, of wonder, and of ridicule, there was still nothing in it that anyone could properly describe as insinuating, for its simplicity, and frankness, and freedom from the half-smothered notes which express indirect purpose, was as remarkable as its sweetness ..."[156] Since many of Newman's jokes were at his own expense—having written himself most of the Tractarian writing from which he quoted—he could hardly be accused of mean-spiritedness. Like Fielding, he meant to laugh the Tractarians out of their follies and in this high-spirited, satirical exercise he did not spare himself.

The first issue he took up was whether the Fathers could be legitimately cited as an authority for Tractarianism. Speaking of the early Christians whose writings had successively established Catholic orthodoxy against the challenges of various heresies, Newman wrote: "There was no mistaking that the principles professed, and doctrines taught by those holy men, were utterly anti-Protestant ..." As for the Tractarians, "being satisfied of this, which was their principal consideration, it did not occur to them accurately to determine the range and bounds of the teaching of the early Church, or to reflect that, perhaps, they had as yet a clearer view of what it did not sanction, than of what it did."[157] Nonetheless, Pusey founded the Library of the Fathers with the express purpose of showing that the patristic authority for Tractarianism was self-evident, "rescuing the faith," as Newman put it, "from private teaching on the one hand and private judgment on the other."[158] But then the true import of the Fathers began to dawn on them—or, at least some of them. And here Newman could not resist a certain *schadenfreude*. "Judge then of their dismay, when, according to the Arabian tale, on their striking their anchors into the supposed soil, lighting their fires on it, and fixing in it the poles of their tents, suddenly their island began to move, to heave, to splash, to frisk to and fro, to dive and at last to swim away, spouting out inhospitable jets of water upon the credulous mariners who had made it their home."[159] Once they turned their minds "to the doctrinal controversies of the early Church, they saw distinctly that in the reasonings of the Fathers, elicited by means of them, and in the decisions of authority, in which they issued ... at least the rudiments, the anticipation, the justification of what they had been accustomed to consider the corruptions of Rome. And if only one, or a few of them, were visited with this conviction, still even one was sufficient, of course, to destroy that cardinal point of their whole system, the objective perspicuity and distinctness of the teaching of the Fathers."[160] To make matters worse, the Anglican episcopacy proceeded to turn on the Tractarians—the same Tractarians who had never wavered in their support of the ungainsayable authority of the episcopate. As Newman remarked, "the authorities in question gladly availed themselves of the power conferred on them by the movement against the movement itself. They fearlessly handselled their Apostolic weapons upon the Apostolical party. One after another, in long succession, they took up their song and their parable against it. It was a solemn war-dance, which they executed round victims, who by their very principles were bound hand and foot, and could only eye with disgust and perplexity this most unaccountable movement, on the part of their 'holy Fathers, the representatives of the Apostles, and the Angels of the Churches.' It was the beginning of the end."[161]

That Pusey had been one of the most celebrated victims of this "solemn war-dance," having been suspended from preaching for two years because he dared to suggest that the Eucharist might have something to do with the Real Presence, makes Liddon's silence on the matter all the more remarkable. But the testimony of the Fathers and the betrayal of the Anglican hierarchy left the Tractarians in an increasingly difficult position. "Their initial principle, their basis, external authority, was cut from under them; they had 'set their fortunes on a cast;' they had lost; henceforward they had nothing left for them but to shut up their school, and retire into the country. Nothing else was left for them, unless, indeed, they took up some other theory, unless they changed their ground, unless they ceased to be what they were, and became what they were not; unless they belied their own principles, and strangely forgot their own luminous and most keen convictions; unless they vindicated the right of private judgment, took up some fancy-religion, retailed the Fathers, and jobbed theology. They had but a choice between doing nothing at all, and looking out for truth and peace elsewhere."[162] This was calling a spade a spade, though for Liddon the lesson of the Fathers *vis-à-vis* the Tractarians could not have been more different. "The Fathers are to be studied," he wrote in the first volume of his biography, "not with the object of discovering in them some new truth, but in order the better to appreciate the treasures of doctrine and devotion which are offered us by the Church of England."[163] Like his hero, Liddon simply ignored whatever he was unprepared to acknowledge.

Newman's critique of Tractarianism was made all the more persuasive by his willingness to criticize his own Tractarian writings, especially his sermon "Grounds for Steadfastness in our Religious Profession (1841)," about which he wrote: "No one can read the series of arguments [set forth in the sermon] … without being struck by the author's clear avowal of *doubt*, in spite of his own reasonings, on the serious subject which is engaging his attention. He longed to have faith in the National Church and he could not."[164] Pusey had explicitly claimed in his letter to the *English Churchman* that Newman had left the National Church because, as he wrote, "his keen sensitiveness to ill was not fitted for these troubled times. What, to such dulled minds as my own, seemed as a matter of course, to be gone through and endured, was to his … 'like the piercing of a sword.'"[165] Sensitiveness, Newman demonstrated, had nothing to do with the matter. Speaking again of his sermon, Newman wrote: "one inward evidence at least Catholics have, which [he himself] had not,—certainty. I do not say, of course, that what seems like certainty is a sufficient evidence to an individual that he has found the truth, for he may mistake obstinacy or blindness for certainty; but, at any rate, the *absence* of certainty is a proof that a person has not yet found it, and at least a Catholic knows well, even if he cannot urge it in argument, that the Church is able to communicate to him that gift."[166]

Newman appreciated that the Tractarians could counter by arguing that they had "clear evidence of the influences of grace" in their hearts. "More than this," he wrote, "you tell me of the peace, and joy, and strength which you have experienced in your own ordinances. You tell me, that when you began to go weekly to communion, you found yourselves wonderfully advanced in purity.

You tell me that you went to confession, and you never will believe that the hand of God was not over you at the moment when you received absolution. You were ordained, and a fragrance breathed around you; you hung over the dead and you all but saw the happy spirit of the departed."[167] Newman could readily concede all of this because he had vivid memories of experiencing the same Tractarian graces himself. "Can I wipe out from my memory, or wish to wipe out, those happy Sunday mornings, light or dark, year after year, when I celebrated your communion-rite, in my own church of St. Mary's; and in the pleasantness and joy of it heard nothing of the strife of tongues which surrounded its walls? When, too, shall I not feel the soothing recollection of those dear years which I spent in retirement, in preparation for my deliverance from Egypt, asking for light, and by degrees gaining it, with less of temptation in my heart, and sin on my conscience, than ever before? O my dear brethren, my Anglican friends! I easily give you credit for what I have experienced myself."[168] But Newman was careful to show that if the subjective experience of grace was to be considered the test of religious truth, "I must allow to others what I allow to you ... Are you willing to place yourselves on the same footing with Wesleyans? yet what is the difference? or rather, have they not more remarkable phenomena in their history, symptomatic of the presence of grace among them, than you can show in yours? Which, then, is the right explanation of your feelings and your experience,—mine, which I have extracted from received Catholic teaching; or yours, which is an expedient for the occasion, and cannot be made to tell for your own Apostolical authority without telling for those who are rebels against it?"[169]

This was a nice question, which the Tractarians never answered. "I give you credit for what you are, grave, serious, earnest, modest, steady, self-denying, consistent; you have the praise of such virtues," Newman wrote, "and you have a clear perception of many of the truths, or of portions of the truths, of Revelation. In these points you surpass the Wesleyans; but if I wished to find what was striking, extraordinary, suggestive of Catholic heroism—of St. Martin, St. Francis, or St. Ignatius—I should betake myself far sooner to them than to you."[170] If some were concerned that such reasoning would unsettle the faith of the Tractarians—as so many did fear—Newman insisted that his intentions were entirely constructive. "I wish to deprive you of your undue confidence in self; I wish to dislodge you from that centre in which you sit so self-possessed and self-satisfied. Your fault has been to be satisfied with but a half evidence of your safety; you have been too well contented with remaining where you found yourselves ... Learn to fear for your souls. It is something, indeed, to be peaceful within, but it is not everything."[171]

Still, Newman assured them that the gains they had achieved as Tractarians should encourage them to follow the logic of those gains. "It is scarcely possible to fancy that an event so distinctive in its character as the rise of the so-called Anglo-Catholic party in the course of the last twenty years, should have no scope in the designs of Divine Providence. From beginnings so small, from elements of thought so fortuitous, with prospects so unpromising, that in its germ it was looked upon with contempt, if it was ever thought of at all, it suddenly became a power in the National Church, and an object of alarm to her rulers and friends."[172] Newman had no interest in denying the extent of the work that he had helped to accomplish. "In a very few years a school of opinion was formed … and it extended into every part of the country. If, turning from the contemplation of it from within, we inquire what the world thought of it, we have still more to raise our wonder; for not to mention the excitement it caused in England, the movement and its party-names were known to the police of Italy and the back-woodsmen of America." The many Americans who followed the progress of the Oxford Movement might have bristled at being referred to as "back-woodsmen" but they could hardly dispute the accuracy of Newman's point: the Movement had extended far beyond Oxford. "And so it proceeded, getting stronger and stronger every year, till it has come into collision with the Nation, and that Church of the Nation, which it began by professing especially to serve; and now its upholders and disciples have to look about, and ask themselves where they are, and which way they are to go, and whither they are bound."[173] Newman's solicitude for the Anglo-Catholic party of the nineteenth century prefigures Benedict XVI's offer of reunification to Anglo-Catholics in the twenty-first century. This also gives the lie to the contention that Newman's intent in the lectures was merely destructive. On the contrary, he was always prepared to recognize what was good about the Movement of 1833: he only meant to stress that its good was unfinished. "Providence does nothing in vain; so much earnestness, zeal, toil, thought, religiousness, success, as has a place in the history of that movement, must surely have a place also in His scheme, and in His dealings towards His Church in this country, if we could discern what that place was. He has excited aspirations, matured good thoughts, and prospered pious undertakings arising out of them: not for nothing surely—then for what? Wherefore?"[174] Not, Newman was convinced, to have the Tractarians delude themselves into imagining that they could find a home within the National Church.

> If, however, as I trust is the case, God has not in vain unrolled the pages of antiquity before your eyes, but has stamped them upon your hearts; if He has put into your minds the perception of the truth which, once given, can scarcely be lost, once possessed, will ever be recognized; if you have by His grace been favoured in any measure with the supernatural gift of faith, then, my brethren, I think too well of you, I hope too much of you, to fancy that you can be untrue to convictions so special and so commanding. No; you are under a destiny, the destiny of truth—truth is your master, not you the master of truth—you must go whither it leads. You can have no trust in the Establishment or its Sacraments and ordinances. You must leave it, you must secede; you must turn your back upon, you must renounce, what has—not suddenly become, but has now been proved to you to have ever been—an imposture. You must take up your cross and you must go hence.[175]

Considering the beauty of Newman's voice, to which so many attested, it must have been moving hearing him deliver these powerful words.[176]

Under no circumstances, Newman urged, should the Tractarians consider themselves a party within the National Church and attempt to proceed as they had proceeded in the past. "No, my brethren, it is impossible, you cannot recall the past; you cannot surround yourselves with circumstances which have simply ceased to be. In the beginning of the movement you disowned private judgment, but now, if you would remain a party, you must, with whatever inconsistency, profess it."[177] Here, Newman was directing his comments squarely at Pusey, who, again and again, after Newman's conversion, sought to re-establish the Movement on its old footing, the footing it had enjoyed before the storm over Tract 90, before the Jerusalem Bishopric, before the Gorham Judgment.

If Newman advised the Tractarians against trying to present themselves as a party within the National Church, he was even more adamant about dissuading them from trying to present themselves as a branch of the Catholic Church, which, then as now, was a term fraught with contradiction.[178] This was an important passage of the lectures because, 15 years later, when Pusey wrote his *Eirenicon*, he would again urge that the Anglican Church be considered a branch of what he called "Christ's One Holy Catholic Church."[179] Addressing the Tractarians directly, Newman pointed out:

> By a Branch Church is meant, I suppose, if we interpret the metaphor, a Church which is separate from its stem; and if we ask what is meant by the stem, I suppose it means the 'Universal Church,' as you are accustomed to call it. The Catholic Church, indeed, as understood by Catholics, is one kingdom or society, divisible into parts, each of which is in inter-communion with each other and with the whole, as the members of a human body. This Catholic Church, as I suppose you would maintain, has ceased to exist, or at least is in *deliquium*, for you will not give the name to us, nor do you take it yourselves, and scarcely ever use the phrase at all, except in the Creed; but a 'Universal Church' you think there really is, and you mean by it the whole body of professing Christians all over the world, whatever their faith, origin, and traditions, provided they lay claim to an Apostolical Succession, and this whole is divisible into portions or branches, each of them independent of the whole, discordant one with another in doctrine and in ritual, destitute of mutual intercommunion, and more frequently in actual warfare, portion with portion, than in a state of neutrality. Such is pretty nearly what you mean by a Branch ...[180]

Having defined the term, Newman proceeded to show how "a Branch Church ... is virtually synonymous with a National; for though it may be in fact and at present but one out of many communions in a nation, it is intended, by its very mission, as preacher and evangelist, to spread through the nation; nor has it done its duty till it has so spread, for it must be supposed to have the promise of success as well as the mission."[181] In other words, the Tractarians could not have a Branch Church and, at the same time, imagine that they had any genuine autonomy. As a National Church, subservient to the State, their Branch Church could never be anything but an Erastian Church. In an ideal world Newman recognized that the Church, if allowed autonomy, might actually support and complement the State. "I repeat," Newman argued, "the great principles of the State are those of the Church, and, if the State would but keep within its own province, it would find the Church its truest ally and best benefactor. She upholds obedience to the magistrate; she recognises his office as from God; she is the preacher of peace, the sanction of law, the first element of order, and the safeguard of morality, and that without possible vacillation or failure; she may be fully trusted; she is a sure friend, for she is indefectible and undying." But Newman appreciated that in practice the State always wielded the upper hand because "it is not enough for the State that things should be done, unless it has the doing of them itself; it abhors a double jurisdiction, and what it calls a divided allegiance; *aut Cæsar aut nullus*, is its motto, nor does it willingly accept of any compromise. All power is founded, as it is often said, on public opinion; for the State to allow the existence of a collateral and rival authority, is to weaken its own ..."[182] For the Tractarians to imagine that they could maintain some anti-Erastian autonomy as a branch church was delusive.

Having described the Erastian perils that confront the branch church, Newman was careful to describe what would result if the Anglo-Catholics ever made peace with the Established Church, a warning as timely today as it was in the mid-nineteenth century. They would end up instructing their faithful that "one man's opinion is as good as another's; that Fathers and Schoolmen, and the greater number of Anglican divines, are puzzled-headed or dishonest; that heretics have at least this good about them, that they are in earnest, and do not take doctrines for granted; that religion is simple, and theologians have made it hard; that controversy is on the whole a logomachy; that we must worship in spirit and in truth; that we ought to love truth; that few people love truth for its own sake; that we ought to be candid and dispassionate, to avoid extremes, to eschew party spirit, to take a rational satisfaction in contemplating the works of nature, and not to speculate about 'secret things;' that our Lord came to teach us all this, and to gain us immortality by His death, and the promise of spiritual assistance, and that this is pretty nearly the whole of theology; and that at least all is in the Bible, where every one may read it for himself ..."[183]

Here was precisely the easy-going, undogmatical, liberal faith of the Established Church, in which Pusey and Keble sought to insinuate their Anglo-Catholic party. But what this had to do with the true Church mystified Newman. "I cannot believe that Bishops, and clergymen, and councils, and convocations have been divinely sent into the world, simply or mainly to broach opinions, to discuss theories, to talk literature, to display the results of their own speculations on the text of Scripture, to create a brilliant, ephemeral, ever-varying theology, to say in one generation what the next will unsay; else, why were not our debating clubs and our scientific societies ennobled with a divine charter also? God surely did not create the visible Church for the protection of private judgment: private judgment is quite able to take care of itself."[184]

Here, one might say, the Roman Catholic Newman, and not Pusey, was acting as the Tractarians' true leader, by urging them to look more critically at their piecemeal, idiosyncratic, contentious Christianity. In essence, Newman was encouraging the Tractarians to apprehend their predicament with the same clear-sighted seriousness with which he apprehended his own predicament when he was Vicar of St. Mary's and faced with the same crisis of Tractarianism.

In this respect, what inspired the lectures was not score-settling or polemical one-upmanship but love. "The time is coming, or is come, when you must act in some way or other for yourselves, unless you would drift to some form of infidelity, or give up principle altogether, or believe or not believe by accident. The *onus probandi* will be on your side then. Now you are content to be negative and fragmentary in doctrine; you aim at nothing higher than smart articles in newspapers and magazines, at clever hits, spirited attacks, raillery, satire, skirmishing on posts of your own selecting; fastening on weak points, or what you think so, in Dissenters or Catholics; inventing ingenious retorts, evading dangerous questions; parading this or that isolated doctrine as essential, and praising this or that Catholic practice or Catholic saint, to make up for abuse, and to show your impartiality; and taking all along a high, eclectic, patronising, indifferent tone; this has been for some time past your line, and it will not suffice; it excites no respect, it creates no confidence, it inspires no hope."[185] This was an unsparing portrait of precisely the religious no-man's-land that Newman himself had inhabited after he recognized the fundamental defects of the National Church and before he embraced "the one and only fold of the Redeemer."[186]

The final advice he gave his old comrades-in-arms could not have been more momentous. They had a choice to make but it was a choice they could only make after they had defined what they truly believed. The response to the crisis of Tractarianism that Pusey had given in *The English Churchman* was glib and evasive. In *Anglican Difficulties*, Newman was forcing him and his Tractarian colleagues to come down to brass tacks and make a decision. "And when, at length, you have one and all agreed upon your creed, and developed it doctrinally, morally, and polemically, then find for it some safe foundation, deeper and firmer than private judgment, which may ensure its transmission and continuance to generations to come. And, when you have done all this, then, last of all, persuade others and yourselves, that the foundation you have formed is surer and more trustworthy than that of Erastianism, on the one hand, and of immemorial and uninterrupted tradition, that is, of Catholicism, on the other."[187]

Richard Hutton considered *Lectures on Certain Difficulties felt by Anglicans* "the first book of Newman's generally read amongst Protestants, in which the measure of his literary power was adequately taken."[188] The Unitarian *Christian Reformer* saw the piece less as a work of literary art than as a warning. Corroborating what Newman had to say about the Erastian cast of the Anglican Church, the paper observed that "the head of the English Church has lately avowed his rejection of the doctrine of apostolic succession; and Arnold, following therein Hooker, Burke, and other high authorities, affirms the identity of Church and State. The Anti-State-Church Association are little aware that they are opposing the only body which can effectually repel a Church of mere priests, and that the abolition of the State Church would be the triumph of priestcraft; that the doctrines of Newman, could they ever prevail, would lead to the most frightful spiritual tyranny that the world was ever cursed by ... There are statements in this volume concerning Catholicism which we should have rejected as calumnious and grossly exaggerating from the pen of a Protestant."[189] The Tory *Quarterly Review* agreed that "Romanism is essentially despotic;" indeed, the independence that Newman was proposing from Erastianism would logically prove this.[190] Of course, dissenters were also opposed to the Established Church and as independents they "should see nothing to censure, but rather much with which to sympathize" in Newman's "bold assertion of ecclesiastical freedom," if only they could be sure "that the spiritual corporations, which lay such stern claim to this freedom, should cede to others what they thus demand for themselves." But on this score they were skeptical. "The power, which not only claims independence, but which claims that independence on the ground of its being the one infallible authority on all matters of religion, carries in its very nature all the seeds of the worst tyranny."[191] On Newman's relationship to his Tractarian audience, the reviewer was a good deal more perceptive. "The measure of failure, which has ... driven him elsewhere in search of greater liberty and a more genial home, has taught his old companions in arms some lessons of caution, and without producing much change in their opinions, has reconciled them to a change of policy. The resolve of not a few among them is to be less bold, less obtrusive, to work, and wait, and hope."[192]

Indeed, in this regard, they might very well have concurred with G.K. Chesterton, who once observed of Newman: "The quality of his logic is that of a long but passionate patience, which waits until he has fixed all corners of an iron trap."[193] Yet as Newman wrote to Mrs. Froude, it was clear that the challenges had caused others to reconsider their allegiance to an Erastian, Protestant, and increasingly undogmatical Church. "Now as to Keble and Pusey, perhaps it is more wonderful that a person of my age (when I left them) should have embraced a new religion, than that they should not have done the same ... Yet my anticipation, as W.F. [William Froude] has recorded it, has been remarkably fulfilled. One after another, moving not as a party, but one by one, unwillingly, because they could not help it, men of mature age, from 40 to past 50, in all professions and states, numbers have done what I have done ... such as Manning, R. Wilberforce, H. Wilberforce, Allies, Dodsworth, Hope Scott, Badeley, Bellasis, Bowyer, Monsell, Sir John Simeon, Dr Duke, Biddulph Phillips, Dean Madavori, Bishop Ives, the de Veres, H. Bowden, Mrs Bowden, Lady Lothian, Lady G. Fullerton, Lord H. Kerr, etc ... . It is surely much easier to account for Keble and Pusey not moving, Catholicism being true, than for all these persons moving, Catholicism being not true."[194]

In the wake of Newman's secession, Pusey committed himself to the same enterprise as Keble, trying to divest the National Church of its inalienably Protestant pedigree. In a letter to Mrs. Froude in March 1863, Newman observed: Pusey "has been pledging himself to all people deeply, that the Church of England has a vital power in it, able to cast out all disease from its system." Yet, as Newman reminded his correspondent, "for the last 12 years there has been a determinate action, going on within [the English Church], towards the destruction of what it retains of the Catholic Creed." And yet, despite these undeniable signs of the Protestant cast of the National Church, Newman realized that there were other factors keeping Pusey within the Anglican pale. More than theological considerations contributed to Pusey's decision to stay put. "Twenty years ago I used to say that, if Pusey once despaired of the English Church, he would die. He was near death (apparently) about the year 1832, and his weakness of body showed itself in a deep despondency about the state of religion. The Tract movement set him up again, as if a new life were breathed into him. When he was condemned by the 5 Doctors in 1843, I feared the life would go out of him – but he was too sanguine to be touched by it – and the same dream of hope has sustained him on till now. The chance is that, in spite of the annoyance of the moment, hope will still tell a flattering tale – but my fear is, that, if he did get disgusted with the Church of England, it would end, not in his looking towards Rome, but in his death."[195]

In November 1864, Newman wrote to tell Pusey that there was a possibility that he might set up an Oratory in Oxford. "Two or three things have combined – first, our youths are beginning to go to Oxford, and the Colleges are admitting them – secondly the late Mr A Smith suddenly offers me land – thirdly my diocesan puts, to my surprise, the Oxford Mission into my hands." Having explained to Pusey the factors that prompted his considering the Oxford Oratory, Newman hastened to assure his friend that his object was in no way polemical. "My late declaration of principles is a sufficient pledge, to all who are anxious on the point, that I have no hostile feeling towards the Anglican Communion – and nothing but love for Oxford. Nor would I be a party to any measures different from those which follow from those principles. I have no plans, nor, I may say, expectations. I am too old to be able to speculate on the future – and, if I found an Oratory at Oxford, it may be as much as Providence means me to do." Then, again, he was frank with Pusey about the reluctance with which he regarded the project. Indeed, for Newman, merely "to see Oxford, would be to me inexpressibly painful, as the coming to life again of men who have been apparently drowned"—not a choice of metaphor likely to flatter his old friend.[196] The proposed Oratory alarmed Pusey. "The establishment of a mission of yours ... must in its own nature be aggressive, even against your will (for there are so few of your own young men here) ... We should have all the anti-Roman controversy, which, as you said, strikes at you through sides, and the ultra Protestant spirits awakened. At least, this seems to me the necessary consequence, its further consequences none can tell; but ... any weakening of the so-called High Church would be very fatal to the English Church, and, if corrupted, the English Church would be a terrible instrument for evil. You, I know, are alive to all the struggles which have been going on, especially as to our Prayer-book. While that remains the High Church party must exist. If it should be changed, I do not see what would resist rationalism. I suppose many have thought so before, but I have long thought this the final struggle in the Church of England."[197] Newman was indeed alive to these struggles and he sympathized with Pusey and the Tractarians. In 1863, he had written to a correspondent, "As to Pusey, I have little opportunity in the case of any of my Oxford friends of showing my affection for them in word or in deed—but of them, and especially of him, I should have only kind words, personally, to utter, whenever I spoke at all. And I feel for them very much now, facing, as they do, so terrible a billow of laxity and scepticism in faith."[198] Matthew Arnold had seen something of this billow in 1854 at Balliol, where he had been an undergraduate 13 years before: "I am much struck with the apathy and poorness of the people here, as they now strike me, and their petty pottering habits … Animation and interest and the power of work seem so sadly wanting in them … the place, in losing Newman and his followers, has lost its religious movement, which after all kept it from stagnating, and has not yet as far as I see, got anything better."[199] Yet, at the same time, Newman could not help but notice that Pusey and the Tractarians continued to throw their lot in with an Established Church that had no place for them, which was a danger against which he had warned them in his King William Street lectures over ten years before.

Pusey, for his part, after he learned that Newman had been dissuaded from establishing his proposed Oxford Oratory, commiserated with him in language that is still echoed by some who are intent on distorting Newman's Catholic career. "It is a strange lot, but a great token of God's love, that you should be hidden and misunderstood now, as you were when here." Since historians estimate that after Newman became a Catholic he personally converted at least a thousand people, it is hard to imagine how he could have managed this if at the same time he was either hidden or misunderstood.

In the same letter objecting to the proposed Oxford Oratory, Pusey also confessed to Newman, apropos his *Apologia*, which had recently been published, "I began a letter to you when I had read the early part of the Apologia. I could not read on, for it seemed like parting over again." This was in sharp contrast to Keble's response to the book, which he lost no time in sharing with Newman: "The more intently I look at this self drawn photograph (what a cruel strain it must have been to you), the more I love and admire the Artist—Whatever comes of controversial points, I see no end to the good which the whole Church, we may reasonably hope, may derive from such an example of love and candour …"[200] Pusey only read the bits about himself. "One thing I wished to ask you," he wrote Newman with the unabashed egotism that was so much a part of his make-up: "what was the exact meaning of your prayer, that I might be 'nearer the Catholic Church before I die.' Does it mean that I should not only be nearer but in the Roman Communion? My confession of faith in 1848 when you so lovingly came to me at Tenby, had it pleased God that I should die, would have been, 'I believe explicitly all which I know God to have revealed to his Church, and implicitly any thing which He has revealed, though I do not know it.'"[201]

This letter suggested to Newman that Pusey was not as settled in his religious views as he might imagine, and, in response, Newman showed the extent to which he still hoped his Tractarian friend might reconsider those views: "As to my meaning in the passage to which you allude, I think that the only body, which has promises attached to it, is the Catholic Church – and if I think the Anglican Communion, as such, is not included in the Catholic Church, I think it has not any divine promise or power. Then I believe too *Extra Ecclesiam nulla salus*, and, as I think the head and heart of that Ecclesia is Rome, I think that to be in communion with Rome is to be united to the Church of the promises, of grace and of salvation."[202]

Here, again, despite the unlikelihood of Pusey's converting, Newman never ceased sharing with him the promise of the Roman Church. And here, too, one can see the characteristic tact that Newman brought to addressing Pusey's Anglican difficulties. The manner in which he chose to proselytize was always disarmingly direct. "As to individual proselytism," he wrote his friend, "you must recollect that we only feel and do what you feel and do towards Dissenters. By what right have you converted from Dissent, as you say, 32 out of 40 Bishops of the Anglo-American Church? By the same right we have converted a number of men who are now among our Priests – You write to the Wesleyans and try to co-operate with them; but I am sure you would make a Wesleyan, whom you met with, a good Anglican, if you could. I am not aware that Manning and Ward convert individuals, any more than I should, in order to weaken the Anglican Church, but from love to the soul of the individual converted, as you would feel love for the Wesleyan."[203]

Manning, being Manning, was blunter. In *The Workings of the Holy Spirit in the Church of England: A Letter to E.B. Pusey* (1864), he rejected Pusey's claim that the English Church was "the great bulwark against infidelity in this land" by arguing that, far from being a part of the Catholic Church, the English Church was no Church at all "in any divine and true sense," though he did allow that this did not nullify "the workings of the Spirit of God or the operations of grace in it."[204] At the same time, he conceded that most of the English were not culpable for their ignorance of the truth "because in these three hundred years the Catholic Church has been so swept off the face of England that nine or ten generations of men have lived and died without the Faith being so much as proposed to them, or the Church ever visible to them." In this category, Manning placed "children, the poor, and the unlearned," all of whom "were born into a state of privation. They knew no better. No choice was before them. They made no perverse act of the will in remaining where they were born." But it was different, Manning insisted, for the educated—"I cannot class them under the above enumeration of those who are inculpably out of the truth. I leave them, therefore, to the only judge of all men." Nonetheless, whether learned or unlearned, Anglicans must recognize that the English Church was tottering, a fact which inspired no gloating from Manning. For him, "the troubles of the Anglican Church" only inspired "a sincere desire that God may use these things to open the eyes of men to see the untenableness of their position; coupled with a very sincere sorrow at the havoc which the advance of unbelief is making among the truths which yet linger in the Church of England."[205] Moreover, he confessed, "I regard the present downward course of the Church of England and Christianity of England with great sorrow and fear. And I am all the more alarmed because, of those who are involved in it, so many not only refuse to acknowledge the fact, but treat us who give warning of the danger as enemies and accusers."[206] In denying that the Anglican Church was a "bulwark against unbelief," Manning gave precisely the concrete reasons for his beliefs that Newman had encouraged his former Tractarian friends to give for theirs, which, alas, they never gave. Nevertheless, it is clear that in taking issue with Pusey's claim, Manning was also taking issue with Newman, who had recently characterized the Anglican Church as "a serviceable breakwater against doctrinal errors more fundamental than its own."[207] Accordingly, Manning argued that the National Church could not be regarded as any bulwark against unbelief because the Reformation out of which it was created was the "true and original source of the present spiritual anarchy of England." He showed how "all forms of Christianity lying round about" the Catholic Church "were but fragments more or less mutilated," which placed Anglicans on the same par as Dissenters. He argued that if the Anglican Church "sustains a belief in two Sacraments, it formally propagates unbelief in five; if it recognises an undefined presence of Christ in the Sacrament, it formally imposes on its people a disbelief in Transubstantiation and the Sacrifice of the altar; if it teaches that there is a Church on earth, it formally denies its indissoluble unity, its visible Head, and its perpetual Divine voice." He put a very fundamental question: "What is the ultimate guarantee of the Divine revelation but the Divine authority of the Church? Deny this, and we descend at once to human teachers." And here the Ultramontane in Manning could not resist observing that "The perpetual and ever-present assistance of the Holy Ghost, whereby the Church in every age is not only preserved from error, but enabled at all times to declare the truth, that is, the infallibility of the living Church at this hour—this truth the Anglican Church ... denies. But this is the formal antagonist of infidelity, because it is the evidence on which God wills that we should believe all that His veracity reveals." There were no emollients in any of that, nor in this: "If the Catholic faith be the perfect revelation of Christianity, the Anglican Reformation is a cloud of heresies; if the Catholic Church be the organ of the Holy Ghost, the Anglican Church is not only no part of the Church, but no Church of Divine foundation. It is a human institution, sustained, as it was founded, by a human authority; without priesthood, without sacraments, without absolution, without the Real Presence of Jesus upon its altars. I know these truths are hard. It seems heartless, cruel, unfilial, unbrotherly, ungrateful so to speak of all beautiful fragments of Christianity which mark the face of England, from its thousand towns to its village greens, so dear even to us who believe it be both in heresy and in schism."[208] This was indeed hard, but, as Manning admitted, he only brought himself to write it because "in these late years" he was "on the frontier which divides us;" and "people have come to me with their anxieties and their doubts. What would you have done in my place?"[209] Although frequently faulted for advocating a gratuitously bellicose Catholicism, Manning, for all his tactlessness, was nonetheless a truth teller. If Pusey saw Tractarianism as a means of improving the *esprit de corps* of the Anglican clergy, Manning was intent on showing him that that clergy, from its corrupt Erastian inception, was not valid. Nothing that Newman ever said to Pusey was quite as hard-hitting as this.

Now, for three hundred years the Anglican clergy have been trained, ordained, and bound by subscriptions to deny not only many Christian truths, but the Divine authority of the ἡ ἀεί ἐκκλησία, the living Church of every age. The barrier against infidelity is the Divine voice which generates faith. But this the Anglican clergy are bound to deny. And this denial opens a flood-gate in the bulwark, through which the whole stream of unbelief at once finds way. Seventeen or eighteen thousand men, educated with all the advantages of the English schools and Universities, endowed with large corporate revenues, and distributed all over England, maintain a perpetual protest, not only against the Catholic Church, but against the belief that there is any Divine voice immutably and infallibly guiding the Church at this hour in its declaration of the Christian revelation to man. How can this regarded as "the great bulwark in God's hand against infidelity"?[210]

Pusey's initial response to Manning's letter was one of weary resignation. "They tell me that I should in some way write an answer to Manning's letter, because he has addressed it to me. I wish that I could have been left quiet to what is my work." In his formal response, which he published as his *Eirenicon*, Pusey sought to accomplish three things: to defend himself against Manning; to find a means of reconciling the 39 Articles to the Canons of Trent; and to establish which practices the Roman Church considered *de fide*, or, in effect, a finite list of Catholic doctrines. "Our difficulties are mostly in the practical system rather than in the *letter* of the Council of Trent. If Rome could authenticate all which she allows individuals to say in explanation—I mean, if a Council of the Roman Church would say, 'Such and such things are *not de fide*,' as well as what is *de fide*—the greatest difficulty in the way of the reunion of the two churches would, I think, be gone ... My letter is, in fact, a reawakening of Tract XC, which, though its principles have sunk deep, is not much known by the rising generation."[211]

That Pusey chose to respond to Manning with what he called a "reawakening of Tract XC" showed the extent to which he was stranded in the Tractarian past, a no-man's-land between Canterbury and Rome—acquiescence in the Gorham Judgment had left him no alternative. Still, he had to respond to Manning with something and so he chose to "rehabilitate Tract XC, because," as he told William Copeland "an exposition of this sort, as being true, is essential to our position. The beginning is only the old story which has been told so often:—Tract XC over again, which made me ask dearest N. to let me republish Tract XC."[212] For years Copeland had been planning to write a history of the Tractarians, but towards the end of his life he had only dictated a few chapters before paralysis overtook him.[213] Nevertheless, Pusey expected great things from their collaboration. "What a mass of facts you have, of which I know nothing! I shall be so glad to see your History. What I am doing is very simple, like an old world, long hid by a cloud, and the cloud parting ..." What is striking is that Copeland—a scholar of considerable attainments—fully entered into Pusey's project. "Great care and accuracy indeed will be needed in touching the old *vexata quaestio*," he told Pusey. "Now more than ever, [Keble's] lines are realised ..."

> Round about the battle lowers
> And mines are hid beneath our towers.[214]

As far as Newman was concerned, if Pusey wished to rehash Tract 90, he would willy-nilly have to rehash the untenability of the via media. For Newman, the Tract's purpose "was simply that of justifying myself and others in subscribing to the Thirty-nine Articles, while professing many tenets which had popularly been considered distinctive of the Roman faith." But Pusey now wished to use the Tract to justify his own subscription to the Articles. In response to Pusey's request for a list of what the Church considered *de fide*, Newman wrote back: "You indeed want the Church to decide what is *de fide* and what is not – but, *pace tuâ*, this seems unreasonable. It is to determine the work of all Councils till the end of time ... No one on earth can draw the line between what is *de fide* or what is not, for it would be prophesying of questions which have [not] yet turned up."[215]

In his long review of the book, Richard Church noted the same tendency that surfaced in so many of Pusey's undertakings—the tendency to ignore embarrassing realities. "Where a man's main basis is charitable hope and presumed goodwill," Church wrote, "he is apt to take the things which he sees for more than they are worth, and to shut his eyes to those which stand in the way of what he knows to be desirable and right ... The test of a practical issue being far off, there is the temptation to go on arranging things as we think best, without fairly asking ourselves—what am I really aiming at? What is it that I expect or ask for? What am I coming to? When Dr. Pusey talks seriously of the Roman Church 'giving explanations,' or of the Thirty-nine Articles and the Decrees of Trent passing away and being merged in the decisions of an English General Council, we are tempted to ask—Is he talking of the world as we know it?"[216] Then, again, Church recognized that there was something else about Pusey that aggravated the air of unreality that permeates so much of the *Eirenicon*. "If Dr. Pusey had more sense of the ludicrous he would see that most people on all sides require an effort to keep their gravity when they are asked to think of the Roman Church 'making explanations.' The instinctive and only natural attitude of the Roman mind is to expect unconditional submission from those who are clearly wrong to those who are clearly right."[217] *Quite so*, one can imagine Manning responding.

Of Pusey's bellicose ecumenism Newman wrote to Keble: "I really marvel that he should have dreamed of calling it an Irenicon ... If Pusey is writing to hinder his own people from joining us, well and good, he has a right to write as he has done – but how can he fancy that to exaggerate, instead of smoothing contrarieties, is the way to make us listen to him?" Pusey had made extravagant devotions to the Blessed Virgin a central part of his objections to Roman Catholicism, but Newman recognized the bad faith in such charges. "I never can deny my belief that the Blessed Virgin prays efficaciously for the Church," Newman confessed, "and for individual souls in and out of it. Nor can I deny that to be devout to her is a duty following on this doctrine – but I never will say, even though St Bernardine said it, that no one is saved who is not devout to her." Pusey confused devotion with doctrine. "Suarez teaches dogma, and dogma is fixed. St. Bernadine is devotional, and devotion is free."[218] Simply because effusive Catholics made extravagant claims about the Blessed

Virgin did not invalidate the Church's doctrines pertaining to the Mother of God. In an incisive essay on the controversy between Pusey and Newman, Roderick Strange remarks that, in response to Pusey's *Eirenicon*, Newman was "appealing for a higher standard of scholarship," which is true, but he was also appealing for a higher standard of honesty. Nevertheless, Father Strange is certainly right to remind readers that there is a cautionary tale in the controversy between Newman and Pusey: "It warns us that Agreed Statements ... will count for nothing, *even combined with love, sympathy, and friendship*, unless there exists among us deeply-felt, unequivocal trust."[219]

That Pusey never responded to the King William Street lectures, never read the *Apologia*, never read Bishop Ullathorne's response to the *Eirenicon*, and only responded to bits and pieces of Newman's response in his *Letter to Pusey*, demonstrates how heedless he could be of the views of others, a trait which, as we have seen, he shared with his father. If a certain high-handedness and self-absorption prevented Pusey from condescending to win the trust of those with whose points of view he differed, this was not the case with Newman. One can read *Letter to Pusey* and get a perfectly reliable sense of Pusey's point of view. Indeed, Newman mounts Pusey's case better than Pusey. Speaking of the claims made by the devotional writers quoted by Pusey, Newman wrote: "Sentiments such as these I freely surrender to your animadversion; I never knew of them till I read your book, nor, as I think, do the vast majority of English Catholics know them. They seem to me like a bad dream. I could not have conceived them to be said ... but I will say plainly that I had rather believe (which is impossible) that there is no God at all, than that Mary is greater than God. I will have nothing to do with statements, which can only be explained, by being explained away. I should not repeat them myself; but I am looking at them, not as spoken by the tongues of Angels, but according to that literal sense which they bear in the mouths of English men and English women. And, as spoken by man to man, in England, in the nineteenth century, I consider them calculated to prejudice inquirers, to frighten the unlearned, to unsettle consciences, to provoke blasphemy, and to work the loss of souls."[220] Nothing in Pusey's tract puts the case against rogue devotion more succinctly than that.

Dean Church gave Newman high marks for taking Pusey's point. "It is something that a great writer, of whose genius and religious feeling Englishmen will one day be even prouder than they are now, should disconnect himself from the extreme follies of his party, and attempt to represent what is the nobler and more elevated side of the system to which he has attached himself."[221] However, for Newman, Pusey was not so much objecting to the real Church, as to a caricature of his own polemical manufacture. "Certain I am," he told Keble, "that, as an Irenicum, it can only raise a smile – and I wish that were all it would raise. The first duty of charity is to try to enter into the mind and feelings of others. This is what I love so much in you, my dear Keble; but I much desiderate it in this new book of Pusey's – and I deplore the absence of it there ..."[222] Nonetheless, Keble took Pusey's part. As he told Newman, Pusey was "just amplifying and carrying out the idea in Number 90, on which his whole book is grounded ... God forbid that you, my dear N. should be the person to cut away the ground from under our feet, and that with such very severe words and thoughts towards one whom you know and love so well."[223] Here, not for the first time, Newman saw the force of Tractarian solidarity.

Throughout Pusey's eirenical enterprises, Newman was adamant that Pusey must not be given the impression that the Roman Church would retreat from its doctrines regarding papal primacy or the Blessed Virgin, though, even in this regard, he was remarkably conciliatory. As Newman told Father Coleridge, a Jesuit convert disinclined to conciliate Pusey at all, "Of course I take a different view of Pusey from what you do – but for argument's sake I will allow that, as you say, he shuffles desperately – also, I take the very ground that you do, viz that his word is taken as law by numbers, when it should not be. Also, of course I think and desire, that for the sake of those numbers, and moreover (which it strikes me you do not so much consider) for the sake of himself, what he says incorrectly, should be set right, and brought home to him as requiring such right-setting."[224] This was characteristic of the personal concern that Newman showed Pusey, despite his often scabrous peace-making.

In preparing to compose his response to the *Eirenicon*, which would be published as *Letter to Pusey*, Newman recognized that if he was to win a sympathetic hearing, he would need to marshal his own controversial armory with tact and care. "I do not call exposing a man's mistakes 'speaking against him' – nor do I suppose any one would. But if, instead of exposing those errors in detail, and as matters of fact, in simple grave language, a controversialist began by saying 'This man is absurd – he shuffles – he misrepresents – he is keeping men from the truth' – every word of it might be true, but I should say he was calling names, and indulging in abuse. For by abuse I mean accusation without proof – or condemnation before proof – and such a process of putting the cart before the horse defeats itself, and has no tendency to convince and persuade those whom it concerns." That Newman had been treated so unfairly by other controversialists made him doubly aware of what fair controversy required. "If there is one thing more than another likely to shock and alienate those whom we wish to convert," Newman told his good friend Father Coleridge, "it is to ridicule their objects of worship. It is wounding them in their most sacred point." Here, Newman was clearly moving away from the exuberant raillery that was so much a part of his King William Street lectures. "They may have a false conscience, but, if they are obeying it, it is laughing at them for being religious." Then, again, Newman was especially intent on treating the Tractarians indulgently because he could enter into their Tractarian convictions. "I can recollect myself firmly believing that what your friend calls a piece of a quartern loaf, was, not only that, but the body of Christ – and, to my own consciousness, I as truly believed it and as simply adored it, as I do now the Blessed Sacrament on Catholic Altars. And what I did then, I know many Anglicans do now."[225] For himself, Newman wrote to Anne Mozley: "I never have minded my friends writing against me – what I have complained of is their imputing motives, or bringing in other personalities ... Pusey pained me, for in print he attributed my conversion to 'oversensitiveness –' this is what in another connexion I have called 'poisoning the wells.'"[226] By contrast, Newman showed how criticisms could be leveled and disagreements articulated without *ad hominem* vitriol.[227] In this, he always exemplified his own definition of a gentleman: "He may be right or wrong in his opinion, but he is too clear-headed to be unjust; he is as simple as he is forcible, and as brief as he is decisive."[228] Newman's public and private responses to Pusey and his Anglican difficulties are distinguished not only by fairness and clarity but by generosity. At the same time, Newman was forthright about the import of Pusey's reckless misrepresentations. "Bear with me, my dear Friend, if I end with an expostulation," he wrote, referring to Pusey's treatment of the Blessed Virgin, but "is it not the effect of what you have said to expose her to scorn and obloquy, who is dearer to us than any other creature? Have you even hinted that our love for her is anything else than an abuse? Have you thrown her one kind word yourself all through your book? I trust so, but I have not lighted upon one."[229] As he observed in the introductory remarks of the book, "There was one of old time who wreathed his sword in myrtle; excuse me—you discharge your olive-branch as if from a catapult."[230]

One of the governing convictions of Newman's response to the Eirenicon was that neither Pusey nor the Anglo-Catholic party as a whole could begin to reconcile Anglicans to the Roman Church until they appreciated that the Universal Church was a living Church, with all that life connotes. This was an important principle to share with Pusey precisely because of his tendency to involve the Faith in an alien "stationariness." But Newman wished to share the same principle with his ultramontane friends, who were, in their way, just as inclined as Pusey to embrace delusive fixity. Speaking of the devotion to the Blessed Mother, Newman wrote:

> It is impossible, I say, in a doctrine like this, to draw the line cleanly between truth and error, right and wrong. This is ever the case in concrete matters, which have life. Life in this world is motion, and involves a continual process of change. Living things grow into their perfection, into their decline, into their death. No rule of art will suffice to stop the operation of this natural law, whether in the material world or in the human mind. We can indeed encounter disorders, when they occur, by external antagonism and remedies; but we cannot eradicate the process itself, out of which they arise. Life has the same right to decay, as it has to wax strong.[231]

For Dean Church, "the substance of Dr. Pusey's charges remains after all unanswered, and there is no getting over them while they remain. They are of that broad, palpable kind against which refinements of argumentative apology play in vain."[232] Whether, in meeting Pusey's objections, Newman was engaged in vain "argumentative apology," readers can judge for themselves. Certainly, he did not limit himself to dry discussions of what was *de fide* and what *de jure*. In delving into the springs of religious devotion, Newman spoke from the heart. "Religion acts on the affections," he reminded his readers. "And of all passions love is the most unmanageable; nay more, I would not give much for that love which is never extravagant, which always observes the proprieties, and can move about in perfect good taste, under all emergencies. What mother, what husband or wife, what youth or maiden in love, but says a thousand foolish things, in the way of endearment, which the speaker would be sorry for strangers to hear; yet they are not on that account unwelcome to the parties to whom they are addressed ... . So it is with devotional feelings ... What is abstractedly extravagant may in particular persons be becoming and beautiful ... When it is formalized into meditations or exercises, it is as repulsive as love-letters in a police report. Moreover, even holy minds readily adopt and become familiar with language which they would never have originated themselves, when it proceeds from a writer who has the same objects of devotion as they have ..."[233]

Here, again, Newman was directing his comments as much to Manning, Ward, and the Ultramontanes of *The Dublin Review* as to Pusey and the Tractarians. Perhaps predictably, the "bumptious Romans," as Edward Caswall nicely referred to Manning and his friends, rose to the bait.[234] "Whether he likes it or not," Manning wrote of Newman in reply, "he has become the centre of those who hold low views of the Holy See, are anti-Roman, cold and silent, to say no more, about the Temporal Power, national, English, critical of Catholic devotions, and always on the lower side. I see danger of a Cisalpine Club rising again, but I see much danger of an English Catholicism of which Newman is the highest type. It is the old Anglican, patristic, literary, Oxford tone transplanted into the Church. It takes the line of deprecating exaggerations, foreign devotions, Ultramontanism, anti-national sympathies. In one word, it is worldly Catholicism, and it will have the worldly on its side, and will deceive many." To defend the Church against these literary dangers, Manning looked to a quarter that tended to be overlooked: "The thing which will save us from low views about the Mother of God and the Vicar of our Lord is the million Irish in England ..."[235]

Apropos Manning's letter, David Newsome, in his lively dual biography, *The Convert Cardinals: Newman and Manning* (1993) makes an important, if arguable point.

> This is an uncomfortable letter to read, but it expresses precisely the difference of stance between the two men. The one word that jars is 'worldly.' If Manning meant by that 'unspiritual,' he could hardly have been wider of the mark. But this was not his meaning. On the many occasions on which he used this word, the meaning consistently attached to it is a readiness to tone down the doctrine of the Church for pragmatic reasons, a disposition to compromise or dilute what the Church actually teaches in order to render it more serviceable in its ministering to the world ... Manning never doubted Newman's spirituality; what he disliked was his disposition to pander to the English anti-Roman spirit. This did not, however, deter him from making reconciliatory gestures. He refused to show offence over Newman's riposte to Pusey. In fact, he wrote to thank him for 'doing, so much more fully, that, which I was going to attempt.[236]

While this might be an accurate account of what Manning meant by charging Newman with being 'worldly,' it underestimates the extent to which Newman's tact served his apostolate to the Tractarians. Moreover, such tact did not require Newman to dilute or compromise Church doctrine. Many of the works Newman wrote as a Catholic were written, directly or indirectly, to appeal to the Tractarians and certainly there is no dilution or compromise of doctrine in *Loss and Gain*, the different volumes of Catholic sermons, the Catholic essays, *Anglican Difficulties*, *Lectures on the Present Position of Catholics in England*, the *Idea of a University*, the *Apologia*, the *Letter to Pusey*, the *Grammar of Assent* or the *Letter to the Duke of Norfolk*. For Manning to have suggested otherwise was mischievous.

What is most striking about the *Letter to Pusey* is how much of it is a reaffirmation of principles first enunciated in Newman's King William Street lectures. In both compositions, Newman grounded his case for Catholicism in the Fathers and urged Pusey and the Tractarians against trying to imagine themselves a branch church. "The difference between the passages in ... Anglican Difficulties and Letter to Dr. Pusey is not greater than that which strikes a stranger between photographs of the full face and the side face of the same person," Newman himself noted in a memorandum.[237]

> They are different aspects of the same object. The grace of God is good without mixture of evil; but it operates upon an imperfect and corrupt subject matter, the human heart; and, while its manifestations are one and the same in every people, at the same time those manifestations are not simply good, but good and bad mixed, good viewed as coming from divine grace, not simply good, but partly extravagant and perverse as being distorted and, as it were, refracted, by the human medium, in which that grace is received.

Although both *Anglican Difficulties* and the *Letter to Pusey* are full of good things, no one can entirely appreciate the solicitude Newman showed Pusey without reading his correspondence. In response to Pusey's objections to indulgences, which he shared with Protestants on the Continent, who were deeply, indeed barbarously mistaken about the practice, Newman posed a useful question: "are there any grounds, theological, of historical fact, or in reason, of sufficient strength to hinder men from giving credit to the word of the Church which is 'the pillar and ground of the Truth?' I know of none."[238] Apropos Mary, the Queen of Purgatory, regarding which Pusey was deeply undecided, Newman wrote: "I believe this is the whole of it. The Blessed Virgin is the great pattern of prayers, especially intercessory. And in this age especially she (and the Saints too and the Church too) is the witness against the prevailing theories, such as Mr. Buckle's that all things go on by fixed laws which cannot be broken; thus introducing a practical atheism. If she is the Intercessor, and the effectual intercessor, she is so as regards earth, as regards Purgatory, as regards the whole created Universe."[239] In another letter, in response to a query from Pusey about transubstantiation, Newman was happy to rely on Trent, which, he recognized, guards the mystery of the Eucharist: "to tell the truth, I cannot get beyond the words of the Tridentine Canon, that the substance of the bread is changed into the Substance of the Body of Christ, and that the species remain – and I do not think we know any thing more, nor can answer any questions safely."[240]

When the First Vatican Council (1870) declared the doctrine of papal infallibility, Pusey's eirenical enterprises, such as they were, closed shop. Despite his usually robust appetite for theological discussion—his correspondence with Newman is full of long queries on transubstantiation—he would not dispute the infallible, even though it is clear that he misunderstood the import of the definition of the doctrine, which was not as sweeping as so many feared. Newman thought the defining of the doctrine inopportune not only because it might appear to favor Manning and the Ultramontanes but also because it might alienate the Anglo-Catholic party. At the same time, he opposed the timing of the definition because, as he told the Ultramontane Herbert Vaughan, "I am not partial to what you call 'movements'— In the Catholic Church I consider *rest* to be the better thing"[241] Definitions of papal infallibility, he feared, even if doctrinally sound, might cause confusion and, inadvertently, unsettle the faithful. Newman was also annoyed to find that Ultramontanes were citing his *Essay on Development* to defend their own radical definition. In his excellent exposition of Newman's inopportunism, Ian Ker quotes something Newman said before the infallibility issue arose to show how opponents often cited his work to misrepresent his thinking, which dogged Newman in his own time and continues to dog his legacy in ours.[242] In 1862, to his dear, if volatile friend Mary Holmes, the governess, Newman confided: "through my life, those persons who have done me harm by their tongues, have been by me myself put into those very positions and situations from which they have been able to use their tongues against me."[243] Nonetheless, when the infallibility definition was finally settled, it was more astringent than the Ultramontanes would have wished and was hardly calculated to alarm fair-minded Tractarians. The Council merely declared that "it is to be a divine revelation that when the Roman pontiff speaks *ex cathedra*—that is, when he using his office as shepherd and teacher of all Christians, in virtue of his apostolic authority, defines a doctrine of faith or morals to be held by the whole Church—he, by the divine assistance promised him in blessed Peter, possesses that infallibility with which the divine Redeemer was pleased to invest his Church in the definition of doctrine on faith and morals, and that, therefore, such definitions of the Roman pontiff are irreformable in their own nature and not because of the consent of the Church." Still, the definition was too much for Pusey. Early in his eirenical endeavors, he had been surprised to hear from Newman how indeterminable the living faith was. Now, he was given proof of that reality in terms that his prejudices against the very notion of infallibility were calculated to reject.

Nevertheless, if Pusey's efforts at reconciling himself and his co-religionists to Rome were unsuccessful, they were far from futile. As Church recognized, they did result in Anglicans seeing how willing Catholics were to address their objections. And for Church this meant that "though there is always risk in dwelling on what is impracticable, we should not like to say that the consideration of this great question was useless, even when for the present it seems to lead to nothing. In our narrow grooves of sect and party and communion, it is wholesome to be taken out into a larger range of thought, a wider view of possibilities, a more extended circle of sympathies. A more disheartening subject of contemplation than that of Christian unity it is not easy to conceive; but a man can hardly think about it seriously without learning to be more forbearing, more distrustful of loud assertions and narrow claims, more capable of entering into the ideas of others ..." And here Church paid an indirect compliment to Newman and his measured approach to Edward Pusey and his Anglican difficulties, "for though we cannot believe that there is anything to be done or hoped for at the present moment, it is well to notice that discontent with the narrow views inherited from ancient quarrels and a disposition to take a larger and more generous view of the divisions of Christendom are not only found among Protestants. In spite of the general and tyrannous pressure of opinion, there are Roman Catholics writers both in England and in Germany who can discuss the great question with a frankness, a modesty, a boldness, which would do honour to any controversialist ... Where there is manifestly moderation, self-restraint, honesty, and a desire to be accurate and to be fair, it is injurious to our own character as candid men not to see in them a promising sign for the future. These things take a long time to produce their effects in making people understand one another; but they will do so in the end."[244] No one now can read these words without hearing in them an augury of the generous offer Pope Benedict XVI has made to our own Anglo-Catholics avid for unity.

The night before Pusey died, Newman wrote to a correspondent: "Today is the anniversary of the death of two most intimate friends of mine, very dear ones, John Bowden and Charles Marriott; it will be strange if I have to add to them Edward Pusey. I said Mass for him this morning. I have known him for sixty years; and he has ever been the same, subduing me by his many high virtues, and, amid severe trials of friendship, the most faithful of friends."[245] Dean Church similarly observed of the old Tractarian leader, that "no man was more variously judged, more sternly condemned, more tenderly loved."[246] No sterner judgment was made than that of Frederick York Powell, the Regius Professor of Modern History at Oxford, who wrote a friend after Pusey's death, "I dare say he has done some good but I feel to him as I do towards those poor Jesuit fathers that suffered in Elizabeth's reign. They are to be respected, pitied, and condemned, as fighters against the light. When a man can't be at ease without a priest to bolster up his debility or nullity of conscience, it is time he went into a convent and stayed there. He isn't fit for the wholesome workaday life, and his influence can't be good. It is a pity to see Liddon and such fine fellows warped by this miserable little man's teachings."[247] This "wholesome workaday" understanding of the "light" would loom large in the life of another significant contemporary of Newman's: William Froude.

Thomas Huxley (1825–1895), one of the great proponents of this new light, who famously told Bishop Samuel Wilberforce that he would rather be descended from an ape than a bishop, looked back on what Newman had done for the Anglo-Catholic party that Pusey inherited and saw an ambiguous legacy. "Dr. Newman made his choice and passed over to the Roman Church half a century ago," Huxley wrote in a piece called "Agnosticism: A Rejoinder"

(1899). "Some of those who were essentially in harmony with his views preceded, and many followed him. But many remained: and, as the quondam Puseyite and present Ritualistic party, they are continuing that work of sapping and mining the Protestantism of the Anglican Church which he and his friends so ably commenced. At the present time, they have no little claim to be considered victorious all along the line. I am old enough to recollect the small beginnings of the Tractarian party, and I am amazed when I consider the present position of their heirs. Their little leaven has leavened, if not the whole, yet a very large lump of the Anglican Church; which is now pretty much of a preparatory school for Papistry." Here, Huxley was at once right and wrong. Yes, the crisis of Tractarianism had forced the Anglo-Catholic party to make a choice between Rome and Agnosticism but, no, Pusey and the Tractarians had not been successful in "sapping and mining the Protestantism of the Anglican Church," which proved more durable than either Pusey, Newman or Huxley himself would have thought possible. Still Huxley was right about the most important aspect of Newman's Anglican legacy: Newman "believed that his arguments led either Romeward, or to what ecclesiastics call 'Infidelity,' and I call Agnosticism. I believe that he was quite right in this conviction, but while he chooses the one alternative, I choose the other …"[248]

In 1879, on Guy Fawkes Day, Newman wrote to his friend, the Anglican clergyman Octavius Ogle, "I was delighted to see your nieces – but when I had parted from their sweet faces, it came upon me, alas, alas, how rudely I had treated your wife, in not asking whether she was at home, when I found [you] were not. But old age is full of absurdities – and just as I tumble down steps, so I am apt to commit all manner of mistakes, especially when I go from home and am thrown into circumstances out of the common."[249] To which Ogle replied: "It is quite a natural outcome of your goodness that you should so kindly think of my wife and trouble yourself to write about her." And then he added something which encapsulates not only Newman's long relationship with Pusey but with many Anglicans: "I wonder if you know how much you are loved by England. I wonder if any man, at least of our time, was ever so loved by England – by all religiously minded England. And even the enemies of faith are softened by their feeling for you. And I wonder whether this extraordinary and unparalleled love might not be – was not meant to be – utilized, as one means to draw together into one fold all Englishmen who believe. I can conceive no more powerful nor truer ειρηνικον. But I suppose we shall go on loving you and you will go on being loved by us, and nothing will come of it on earth. But 'God fulfils Himself in many ways.' Meanwhile I shall always hope that my dear love for you may be a hallowing influence in all I say and think and do."[250]

Pusey echoed these sentiments when he wrote to an Anglican priest in 1879, "You may assure your friends that nothing either has or can come between my deep love for John Henry Newman."[251] Newman, for his part, summed up his relationship with Pusey and his Anglican difficulties in a postscript to another Anglican priest: "I love Pusey, but that does not suffice for communion."[252] Despite all of Newman's good efforts, Pusey went to his grave preferring his own "mimic Catholicism" to the real thing.[253] Newman had to content himself with less celebrated scalps. In 1866, the convert Thomas Allies wrote him, "There is residing close by me now a Mr Dewar who has just resigned a living in Lincolnshire, and become a Catholic with his wife and family. He tells me that your Letter to Dr Pusey was the first thing to do away with his difficulties as to the worship of our Blessed Lady."[254]

CHAPTER 4

The Certainty of Vocation: Newman and the Froudes

"*We can believe what we choose*. We are answerable for what we choose to believe."

> John Henry Newman to Mrs. William Froude (27 June 1848)

"Here we find ourselves in this world, with an instinct telling us that it is our duty to serve God, yet without the means of doing so as certain as the instinct is certain. As in the natural order of things a man would starve, if he did not find the means of living, so in like manner it is incumbent on us to look out for, to labour for, and so to gain the spiritual means, by which our souls may live—and this is the very end of our lives."

> John Henry Newman to Louisa Simeon (24 May 1869)

In his sermon, "God's Will the End of Life" (1849), Newman gave eloquent expression to his understanding of the primacy of vocation at a time when his own vocation had been profoundly renewed.

> Everyone who breathes, high and low, educated and ignorant, young and old, man and woman, has a mission, has a work. We are not sent into this world for nothing; we are not born at random; we are not here, that we may go to bed at night, and get up in the morning, toil for our bread, eat and drink, laugh and joke, sin when we have a mind, and reform when we are tired of sinning, rear a family and die. God sees every one of us; He creates every soul … for a purpose. He needs, He deigns to need, every one of us. He has an end for each of us; we are all equal in His sight, and we are placed in our different ranks and stations, not to get what we can out of them for ourselves, but to labor in them for Him. As Christ has His work, we too have ours; as He rejoiced to do His work, we must rejoice in ours also.[1]

This sense of vocation was uppermost in his thoughts when he was preparing to leave Littlemore, three months after he was received into the Catholic Church. On Christmas Eve 1845, he wrote to his dear friend Catherine

Froude, "You may think what a pain it is to quit this neighborhood. I am now beginning my thirtieth year since my matriculation. Thus I have spent nearly two thirds of my life here ... Yet I have no position in this place and no calling. I have no better reason for staying than at any place along the road, beyond the fact that I am here. It comes upon us all that life is short, and that one must not stay all the day idle, when there is one that hires us, and work to be done."[2] In the long correspondence that Newman conducted with Catherine and her husband William Froude, he would return to this theme of vocation again and again. From the first, Newman saw in Catherine a woman with his own unbiddable respect for truth, who was ready to sacrifice even family ties to co-operate with God's grace. As it happened, all but one of her four children eventually followed her into the Catholic Church. The one portrait we have of her, which hangs in Newman's bedroom at the Birmingham Oratory, captures an elegant, intelligent, handsome woman, who, as she looks up from the book she is reading, turns to the viewer an amused expression: sitting for her portrait clearly appealed to her sense of the absurd. There was also an admirable humility about her: she characterized herself in one letter to Newman as "an ignorant, weak-minded person," and yet one "with the most fervent wish to know and believe the Truth."[3] It is clear from the letters that Newman sent her and from her surviving responses that she was someone whom Newman found deeply sympathetic. In William, he saw not only a talented engineer but a loving father and devoted husband, a kind, fair-minded, conscientious man, who was nonetheless convinced, as he told Newman, that "all the really high cast minds, which are engaged in the advancement of science and also pursue it in that really philosophical spirit which alone serves to consolidate the advances made, all treat their own conclusions with a scepticism as profound, and as corroding as that with which they treat Theology." William had in mind such men as T. H. Huxley, Frederic Harrison, Herbert Spencer, John Morley, James Fitzjames Stephen and his brother, Leslie Stephen. Huxley epitomized the thought of these men when he wrote that, for "the improver of natural knowledge ... scepticism is the highest of duties; blind faith the one unpardonable sin."[4] One reason why Newman was intent on sharing his sense of vocation with William was that he saw him as representative of those "engaged in the advancement of science," who, then as now, regarded faith as an untenable because unscientific prejudice. Newman might not have entirely agreed with William in considering these men "high cast minds"—in one letter to his friend, he admitted, "I have long thought your great men in science to be open to the charge of superciliousness"[5]—but he knew their influence, and he wished to parry their arguments.[6] In 1849, in his sermon "Faith and Doubt," Newman summarized the cult of skepticism to which William and so many others subscribed. For these men, "it is a fault ever to make up our mind once for all on any religious subject whatever ..." Indeed, "however sacred a doctrine may be, and however evident to us—let us say, for instance, the divinity of our Lord, or the existence of God—we ought always to reserve to ourselves the liberty of doubting about it." For Newman, "so extravagant a position ... confutes itself ..."[7] Yet for over thirty years, Newman vigorously debated the matter with William, trying to make him see that thoroughgoing skepticism is as unsustainable in religion as it is in any other arena. Newman's biographer Ian Ker captured the essence of what Newman meant when he pointed out how "Newman's treatment of doubt anticipates Wittgenstein's fundamental insight into the absurdity of universal skepticism, since to doubt everything is to nullify the language of doubt itself."[8] Accordingly, Newman rejected Descartes' metaphysics by arguing that it was credulity, not doubt, that enabled us to advance in knowledge.

By the same token, Newman never discounted genuine scientific inquiry: it was only skepticism masquerading as science that met with his disapproval. In a lively memoir, Sir Rowland Blennerhassett, a Kerry born liberal Catholic who was friendly with Lord Acton and Ignaz Döllinger, opposed Parnell's Home Rule nationalism, and took a deep interest in Irish education and land law, recalled conversations he had had with Newman at the Oratory in 1860:

> I remember distinctly getting at once the impression from my very first conversation with Newman that the opinion then very commonly held as to his position on the intellect of the modern world was quite erroneous, and I was confirmed in this view some little time afterwards. He spoke to me about Mr. Darwin's 'Origin of Species.' I saw clearly from the tone of his observations that both Roman Catholics and Anglicans were equally wrong in their views of his attitude to free scientific inquiry. Nothing could be more mistaken than to imagine that he looked at it askance, or felt any alarm whatever as to its ultimate effects on Christian faith. That was certainly not perceived by the world at large in 1860. Even men who knew him fairly well were quite mistaken about him. They imagined he closed his mind to the teachings of science and that he clung to the Church of Rome out of fear of free inquiry. I am afraid that even at the present moment there are some who ought to know better who still misunderstand him in this respect. They mistake the critical faculty which made it impossible for him to accept as gospel scientific propositions which may be true but are still unproven for a cowardly and untruthful state of mind which must culminate in hopeless obscurantism.[9]

Another reason why Newman showed William and his doubts such solicitude was to return his loyalty: "I never forget the aid William afforded me when I was lowest, at the time of the Achilli matter," he told Catherine in 1873.[10] Joyce Sugg, in her engaging book, *Ever Yours Affly: John Henry Newman and his Female Circle*, points out that William "was one of the multitude of friends who contributed to Newman's heavy expenses and to the fine imposed on him."[11] And yet perhaps the most fundamental reason why Newman corresponded with William at such length and over so many years about such a deeply personal matter was that he loved the man and would not abandon him to his sophistical doubts. "Whatever pain it is to me to think of our actual differences of opinion," he told his intransigent friend on Christmas Eve, 1859, "I feel no separation from you in my heart, and, please God, never shall."[12]

Charles Stephen Dessain, the great founding editor of Newman's letters and diaries, said that the "fundamental interest of Newman's life" was "his devotion to the cause of Revealed Religion."[13] In this chapter, I shall show how Newman shared this lifelong vocation with Catherine and William Froude by sharing with them his insights into such matters as faith and reason, certitude and assent, the vitality of grace, the life of prayer, and, not least, the difficulties felt by Anglicans in trying to submit to the Catholic Church. I shall also show how these insights informed the writing of *An Essay in Aid of a Grammar of Assent* (1870), which, in exemplifying Newman's personal approach to philosophy, reaffirmed that "It is in the experience of daily life that the power of religion is learnt."[14] Before looking at Newman's correspondence with his two friends, I shall briefly place Catherine and William in some biographical context.

Catherine Froude née Holdsworth (1810–1878) was the daughter of Arthur Howe Holdsworth (1780–1860), who was educated at Eton, elected M.P. for the rotten borough of Dartmouth between 1802 and 1820, and Governor of Dartmouth College from 1807 until his death. She met Newman in 1836 at Dartington in Devon, where Archdeacon Froude was rector, and began corresponding with him in 1838. A good sense of her witty, playful, searching intelligence can be gleaned from Newman's letters and diaries. In one letter, Hurrell Froude told Newman that Catherine had heard—"as proof of unfeeling bigotry in you"—that he had refused to see his brother Frank on his return from Persia. He also told his friend that she "was sapping hard at your Arians,"—that is to say, *The Arians of the Fourth Century* (1833), Newman's first book, which first exhibited Newman's abiding interest in the development of dogma and put Catherine on the road to conversion. Her friendship with Newman was very close. "Dear Fr Newman," she wrote in 1862, after she had known him for nearly thirty years, "You are dearer to me than anyone in the world, after my husband and children and my dear sister. – What would I give to be able to help you!"[15]

William Froude (1810–1879), whom Catherine married in 1839, was the brother not only of Newman's close friend Hurrell but also of Anthony, whose history of Tudor England expressly refuted the Tractarian critique of the English Reformation. "In his History," J. W. Burrow wrote in his lively book on Victorian historiography, Anthony "was to defend the Dissolution, applaud the Reformers, and damn Queen Mary of Scots and all 'sentimental' Catholic versions of English history. Froude, in fact, came to hold a stance unprecedented in English historiography: friendly to Puritanism and to strong monarchy, hostile to the monasteries and by no means tender to early capitalism. It is perhaps no wonder that [J. R.] Green described his *History* as disfigured ... by paradox."[16] Since Hurrell and indeed Archdeacon Froude also thought in paradoxical terms—Hurrell was fond of telling the Fellows of Oriel's Senior Common Room that "The cultivation of right principles has a tendency to make men dull and stupid"— Anthony was upholding a family tradition, though his entirely favorable view of Henry VIII and his Reformation could not have been more different from that of his Tractarian brother, who particularly condemned the Reformers' Erastianism.[17] In 1892, Anthony was appointed

Regius Professor of Modern History at Oxford, a post he assumed after the death of E. A. Freeman, his most relentless critic.[18] If Hurrell and Anthony were alike in taking their opposite positions with a certain flippant élan, William was at once more methodical and more eccentric. At Oriel, Thomas Mozley remembered William as the college chemist. "His rooms on the floor over Newman's were easily distinguishable to visitors entering the college, by the stains of sulphuric acid ... extending from the window sills to the ground. The Provost must sometimes have had to explain this appearance to his inquiring guests ..." Mozley also recalled William making laughing-gas in his rooms, which caused "one of the sweetest tempered men I ever knew" to put up his fists and make "menacing gestures at the company" and another to imagine himself "a regiment of cavalry performing rapid evolutions." Then William asked Mozley to help him navigate a small boat he had refurbished. He "took a small Oxford sailing boat, strengthened its frame, decked it fore and aft, and himself made a pump with which he could discharge the water as fast as a waterman standing in the river could throw it in with a bucket. He gave much study and pains to the work, putting it to severe tests. His intention was to sail down the Thames and the Channel, up the Dart, and surprise his father at Dartington." But alas Mozley knew nothing of navigation and the voyage was scrapped, though it says something for William's pertinacity that the boat did eventually makes its way to Dartington.[19] Nonetheless, for all his quirkiness, Froude was undoubtedly clever. After briefly falling under Newman's sway at Oriel, where he received a First in Mathematics, William went on to become a brilliant railway and naval engineer, whose work on the rolling of ships still guides shipbuilders. At Chelston Cross, his whimsical country house in Torquay, he built a splendid flying staircase starting from the balcony round the hall and extending to the floor above. The Admiralty also furnished him with a large covered experimental tank, where William performed his meticulous nautical tests. As both a railway and a naval engineer, William worked under the greatest of all Victorian engineers, Isambard Kingdom Brunel (1806–1859), about whom Samuel Smiles wrote: "He was the very Napoleon of engineers, thinking more of glory than of profit, and of victory than of dividends. He would do everything on the most splendid scale, and was alike ambitious of making the best possible steam-ship and the best possible railway."[20] According to his biographer, Brunel's "conventional religious belief" was "weakened by the natural scepticism of a ruthlessly logical and inquiring mind."[21] And yet if Brunel had not tempered his skepticism with faith, and very staunch faith at that, it is questionable how many of his engineering projects would have succeeded. As Smiles attests, "it is impossible to doubt the good faith of the engineer; if shareholders suffered, he suffered with them. The public at least have certainly no ground of complaint; for it is unquestionable that both railway traveling and steam navigation were greatly advanced by the speculative ability of Mr. Brunel ..."[22]

If the skepticism of his scientific colleagues disposed William to agnosticism, the goodness of individual Catholics disposed Catherine to Catholicism. In April 1854, William wrote to Newman: "I must say something in reply to your kind letter about Kate ... I fully believe that as far as reasonable or reasoning conviction goes, her judgment is against Catholicism – as far as feeling goes it is in its favour – the feeling being partly what might be called fascination occasioned by the magnitude and endurance of the system, and what appears to her the adaptations of its ceremonial to her own peculiar turn of mind – and partly her entire love and admiration for the few Catholics she has known – a love and admiration which goes entirely beyond that which she feels for any other persons whatever." This might seem a predictable response on the part of a husband who thought the Catholic Church founded on unverifiable assertion: his wife was being swayed by personal affection, not conviction. And yet William was honest enough to acknowledge that this affection could not be discounted. "My conversations with her, have led me to see that I had if anything underrated the force of this fascination, and it would not surprise me if it were some day or other wholly to outweigh all opposing influences of whatever kind." Indeed, William recognized that he might not be able to meet this fascination with any counter arguments, "at least of a nature commensurable with the force of those springs which push her forward." This doubtless encouraged Newman to believe that William might yet see the cogency of the Catholic faith, though in another passage of the same letter he could only have been reminded of how his own conversion estranged him from friends and family. "You will readily understand I am sure," Froude told Newman, "that it is with no very cheerful feelings that I contemplate as almost a probable result a change which though it could not impair affection, would in its very nature make an end of that full community of thought and judgment in which affection has had such scope. I cannot trust myself to think or speak of it."[23]

Froude had cause to be concerned: Catherine *was* changing, even though the change was gradual. In November 1843, she wrote to Newman: "Mr. Roger's suspicion that you might be approximating towards Rome, were the first hint I had had—and I will own it was a great blow and shake altogether." Here, Catherine was no different from most of his Tractarian friends, who were bewildered by his abandonment of the Anglo-Catholic via media. And yet, unlike many in the Tractarian camp, what Catherine saw in his turn to Rome was not inconsistency or betrayal but vocation. Despite the fact that Newman's case for the catholicity of the English Church "had," as she said, "rooted itself in my mind," she also confessed that his abandonment of that case prompted her to ask fundamental questions about herself and indeed about Newman. "When I had this shake, what was I to do?—being as I said before, quite unable to *guide myself* ..." Earlier in the letter, she gratefully acknowledged that "Private judgment was never a besetting sin of mine ..." On the contrary, she was "most thankful" that she had found in Newman "a Guide on whom I might lean ... most truly, a 'light to my paths,'" ever since she began reading his wonderful sermons in 1834. "So," she confided in her friend, "I thought over the matter again and again in my own head—and it came upon me, that even if you did in the end leave the Church I might be quite sure you would not do so without a *call* so to do, and surely after the life you have led, you are not likely to mistake a call,—and then I thought over what would be my objections to Romanism, in the event of the necessity of a change—and they appeared to me to have unaccountably dwindled away during the last four or five years,—though I had not been conscious of it …" Newman's call had sown the seeds of her own call, though, having shared with Newman these insights into the slow, surprising progress of her faith, Catherine hastened to admit that, when it came to her own vocation, "I could not contemplate the possibility of such a change without extreme pain,—and I know, I have no call, no inclination for it *yet*, though, how far I might be affected by such a movement on the part of others I do not know …"[24] Newman doubtless saw a most promising sympathy in that electric *yet*.

In December 1843, two months after he had resigned his living at St. Mary's, Newman replied to Catherine's letter with moving candor. "I keep saying to myself continually, 'I did not make my circumstances.' Not that I can doubt that much that is wrong and earthly mixes up in every thing I do, or that my present state of perplexity is a punishment on me for sins committed; yet after all surely on the supposition that people are born under a defective religious system … what can their course be, if they act religiously but first to defend it, and, as time goes on, to mistrust it? Surely I cannot blame myself, whatever my present opinion may be, in having done all I could first to maintain myself and others where we are providentially placed,—yet this is the circumstance which, I suppose, has given you the most distress … to have given yourself to a view of theology such as is drawn out in my Lectures on Romanism, and then to begin to suspect, or at least to be told by the person who wrote them that it is not trustworthy."[25] Recognizing that he had been "born under a defective religious system" helped Newman give Catherine the steadying counsel she needed. "So far at least results from what has passed," Newman wrote to her, "that it is a duty to be very slow in taking up and acting upon any new belief. Granting that there is this great distinction in the two judgments, that the former was biased (properly so) by a deference to a system in which one found oneself, and the latter is unwillingly forced upon the mind, still there is the greatest reason for dreading lest one should be the sport of mere argumentative demonstration."[26] Here Newman was doing for Catherine what he had done for Keble: sharing with her his doubts so she could learn from them and, in the process, resolve her own doubts. And that last insight would inform a good deal of what Newman would say to William about the limits of reason in ascertaining dogmatic truth. Still, what was perhaps most persuasive about this letter was its honesty. Newman made no bones about the fact that in pursuing the Anglo-Catholic via media he had pursued what he wished to be the truth, not the truth itself. Indeed, his own nagging misgivings would not let him confuse the two. "From beginning to end … I was under the great apprehension lest the view should prove a mere paper view, a fine theory, which would not work, which would not move. I felt strongly the objection that it has never been carried into effect, and in the opening sentences of the last Lecture I speak in the language of despondency."[27] In that passage of the *Lectures on the Prophetical Office of the Church* (1837), Newman described the exhaustion he felt after putting Anglicanism to the test. "When the excitement of the inquiry has subsided, and weariness has succeeded," he wondered whether "what has been said is but a dream, the wanton exercise, rather than the practical conclusion of the intellect." And he followed this revelatory use of the passive with a kind of Johnsonian gravity. "Such is the feeling of minds unversed in the disappointments of the world, incredulous how much it has of promise, how little of substance; what intricacy and confusion beset the most certain truths; how much must be taken on trust, in order to be possessed; how little can be realized except by an effort of the will; how great a part of enjoyment lies in resignation."[28] Newman often resorted to rhetoric as to a tonic and here was no exception: "Religion seems ever expiring, schisms dominant, the light of Truth dim, its adherents scattered. The cause of Christ is ever in its last agony, as though it were but a question of time whether it fails finally this day or another."[29] For Newman, as for St. Augustine and Chesterton, both of whom shared Newman's genius for autobiography, rhetoric was also proof of conviction.[30] "St. Augustine," Henry Chadwick recognized, "is a man who describes important events in his life by using a high style; that is his way of saying that they are important."[31] If Newman's letter was a sincere apology, it was also a summons to courage, which is always useful in a crisis. "I feel I owe you some amends …," Newman wrote to Catherine, "for having led you to take up what now you find I question myself." No matter, he assured his friend: "to overcome impediments is a token of power."[32]

On the night before he decided to convert, after he had overcome his own impediments, Newman wrote to Catherine from Littlemore, "Father Dominic the Passionist … sleeps here tonight as a guest of my friend Dalgairns whom he received ten days ago. He does not know of my intention, but I shall ask him to do the same charitable work for me … He was at Littlemore for half an hour on St. John Baptist's day last year, when I saw him. As I had all but finished my book … and friends objected to my driving my change into the Advent or Christmas seasons, when they did not wish to be unsettled, I made up my mind to be received at once. And since I had all along been forced to act by my own judgement, I was not sorry for what seemed an external call to which I could show obedience."[33] Newman shared with his friends his sense of the primacy of vocation four months later when, looking back on his Anglican career, he observed, "Nay even my responsibilities at St. Mary's, as one who had the cure of souls, have always all along weighed most oppressively on me and do still. Alas, I will not speak against my circumstances, when my own personal fault is so great—Yet how dreadful is a cure of souls in the English Church, an engagement, with no means to carry it into effect …"[34]

Such pastoral futility did not afflict the Catholic Newman. He was always ready to share what he recognized as the prize of vocation. "Oh that I were near to you," he wrote to the Froudes in June 1848, "and could have a talk with you!—but then I should need great grace to know what to say to you—This is one thing that keeps me silent—it is, dear friends, because I don't know what to say to you. If I had more faith, I should doubtless know well enough; I should then say, 'Come to the Church, and you will find all you seek.' I have myself found all I seek—'I have all and abound'—my every want has been supplied—and so it has in all persons, whom I know at all well, who have become Catholics …" But Newman wished to impress upon them "two propositions": "that [it] is the duty of those who feel themselves called towards the Church to obey it" and "that they must expect trial, when in it, and think it only so much gain when they have it not ..."[35] Of course, for Newman, "this world is a world of trouble," but his friends should not let that sway them. "You must come to the Church not to avoid [the world], but to save your soul." Having said this, Newman was at pains to make clear that "Catholicism is a different religion from Anglicanism—You must come to learn that religion which the Apostles introduced and which was in the world long before the Reformation was dreamed of—but a religion not so easy and natural to you, or congenial, because you have been bred up in another from your youth." Speaking of that "different religion," Samuel Johnson once told Boswell that "A good man, of a timorous disposition, in great doubt of his acceptance with God, and pretty credulous, might be glad to be of a church where there are so many helps to get to Heaven ..."[36] Newman, with his eminently practical approach to Catholicism, could not resist itemizing for the Froudes these "many helps to get to Heaven." "You will then have the blessedness of seeing God face to face. You will have the blessedness of finding, when you enter a Church, a Treasure Unutterable – the Presence of the Eternal Word Incarnate – the Wisdom of the Father who, even when He had done His work, would not leave us, but rejoices still to humble Himself by abiding in mean places on earth for our sakes, while He reigns not the less on the right hand of God. To know too that you are in the Communion of Saints – to know that you have cast your lot among all those Blessed Servants of God who are the choice fruit of His Passion – that you have their intercessions on high ... and above all the Glorious Mother of God ... And to feel yourself surrounded by all holy arms and defences – with the sacraments week by week, with the Priest's benediction, with crucifixes and rosaries which have been blessed, with holy water, with places or with acts to which Indulgences have been attached, and the 'whole armour of God' – and to know that, when you die, you will not be forgotten, that you will be sent out of the world with the holy unction upon you, and will be followed with masses and prayers; – to know in short that the Atonement of Christ is not a thing at a distance, or like the sun standing over against us and separated off from us, but that we are surrounded by an atmosphere and are in a medium, through which his warmth and light flow in upon us on every side, what can one ask, what can one desire, more than this?"[37] At the same time, Newman understood that the Catholic Church could never be incorruptible. "Rome," he wrote to Mrs. Froude on St. Stephen's Day, 1854, "ever shows a recollection of its pagan greatness ... The Roman population seems to me like the ruins of the old city and the malaria which lives among them, and I never should be surprised at an outburst of Paganism. The church has ever been seated upon those ruins, and thus upon the cinders of a volcano."[38] In this, Newman followed Chesterton, who once observed, "When Christ at a symbolic moment was establishing His great society, He chose for its corner-stone neither the brilliant Paul nor the mystic John, but a shuffler, a snob, a coward—in a word, a man. And upon this rock He has built his Church, and the gates of Hell have not prevailed against it. All the empires and the kingdoms have failed, because of this continual weakness, that they were founded by strong men and upon strong men. But this one thing, the historic Christian Church, was founded on a weak man, and for that reason it is indestructible. For no chain is stronger than its weakest link."[39]

Anglicans considering converting to Rome will find in Newman's letters to Mrs. Froude useful counsel. In March 1854, when Newman was in Dublin, he wrote to ask his friend, "My dear Mrs. Froude, do you pray for 'effectual grace?' Suppose I come to a high wall – I cannot jump it – such are the moral obstacles which keep us from the Church. We see the Heavenly City before us, we go on and on along the road, till a wall simply crosses it. Human effort cannot clear it – there is no scaling, no vaulting over. Grace enables us to cross it – and that grace is called effectual grace. Our first grace is sufficient to enable us to pray for that second effectual grace – and God gives grace for grace."[40] In a long letter delving into the question of certainty, Newman advised Mrs. Froude, apropos her husband and his resolute skepticism, "I do not see that I am bound to believe W.F.'s statement of the unsatisfactoriness of religious inquiry, and the necessity of an everlasting suspense, until I am sure that he contemplates the probability of that being true, which is not improbable in itself, and which all those who have attained certainty say is true ..." Then, to make his apostolate to the Froudes as real and as practical as possible, Newman wrote them a prayer:

O my God, I confess that Thou canst enlighten my darkness—I confess that Thou only canst. I wish my darkness to be enlightened. I do not know whether Thou wilt; but Thou canst, and that I wish, are sufficient reasons for me to ask, what Thou at least has not forbidden my asking. I hereby promise Thee, that, by Thy grace which I am seeking, I will embrace whatever I at length feel certain is the truth, if ever I come to be certain. And by Thy grace I will guard against all self deceit which may lead to take what nature would have, rather than what reason approves.[41]

When Catherine finally converted on 19 February 1857, she wrote to Newman: "I cannot say how grateful I feel to God, for having helped me and supported me so wonderfully." Nevertheless, speaking of William, she admitted: "my heart aches for him; for he is miserable at the idea of our virtual separation—and he has nothing to fall back on, whereas I could not be unhappy if I tried, even with all my sorrow for him. I can only regret that I delayed so long,—for in spite of all my perplexities and difficulties, I feel that I might have done this before, had it not been for my own fault;—and what years of life I should have gained. However, it is no use to regret the past." She was particularly grateful to Newman for his tact. "I must tell you again how from my heart I thank you for what you have done to help me. – Other Catholics always seemed 'making a case' when they said things to me,—you always contrived to say exactly what suited my mind."[42] This was not only a handsome but an accurate compliment, for Newman never did "make a case." In his correspondence with Catherine, as in his *Grammar of Assent*, he proceeded from the conviction that, in matters of faith, there was no case to make. As he told Catherine as early as 1844, "The great remedy of all uneasiness is to feel that we are in God's hands, and to entertain an earnest desire to do His will."[43] In 1848, he landed on the definition of faith to which he would adhere ever after: "Faith then is not a conclusion from premises, but the result of an act of the will, following upon a conviction that to believe is a duty."[44] Then, again, in a letter of 1851, he told Catherine, "I disapprove the plan of thinking that everything must be level to reason when you are called to a system of faith. The single question is, 'have I reason enough to resolve to place faith?'"[45]

In concluding her letter to Newman, Catherine wrote: "I know you will not now leave off your kind thoughts for me,—but will pray that I may have prudence and courage to go through all that is before me." In his response, Newman was careful not to make light of the difficulties that lay ahead for a wife who had decided to convert without her husband. "You may fancy what joy your letter gave me. You will be sustained by the blessings and the graces which will surround you in the great trials which you may undergo. But every thing will be made light to you—and you must gain your husband by your prayers."[46]

If the assent to Catholic truth that he found in Catherine was a source of deep joy to Newman, the impediments he encountered in trying to share his faith with William were a source of continual frustration. "It quite put me out, when William was here, to think how little I could explain myself to him," he wrote to Catherine in 1843. "In truth, it is hardly possible to do so in a little while. Every thing I said seemed to be shot out like bullets, round and hard and sudden—Arguments grow out of the mind, but when you see friends but seldom, there is a necessary abuse of a certain medium of communication which is the very life of conversation and discussion—I could only lament it ..." Later, in his sermon, "Faith and Doubt," preached in September 1849, Newman doubtless recalled his exchanges with William when he observed how "conviction is a state of mind, and it is something beyond and distinct from the mere arguments of which it is the result; it does not vary with their strength or their number." Requiring ever more arguments might simply be a kind of spiritual procrastination. And here he might have been indirectly addressing not only William but Catherine as well. "As regards the Catholic Church: men are convinced in very various ways,—what convinces one, does not convince another; but this is an accident; the time comes anyhow, sooner or later, when a man ought to be convinced, and is convinced, and then he is bound not to wait for any more arguments, though more arguments be producible." For Newman this was not the counsel of precipitancy. "Knowing the temptations which the evil one ever throws in our way," he recognized that the "point of conversion" might pass and the would-be convert lose "his chance of conversion." And once past, the chance might never return, for "God has not chosen every one to salvation: it is a rare gift to be a Catholic; it may be offered to us once in our lives and never again ..." Here was a summons to seize the day which one would not find in Lovelace or Herrick. "If we have not seized on the 'accepted time,' nor know 'in our day the things which are for our peace,' oh the misery for us! What shall we be able to say when death comes, and we are not converted, and it is directly and immediately our own doing that we are not?"[47] The keeper of anniversaries in Newman could never forget this grave hazard. In 1854, while he was staying in Harcourt Street in Dublin, Newman wrote to Catherine, "I did not forget you and William on the 28th [Hurrell Foude had died on 28 February 1836], when my intention at Mass was the repose of the souls of Hurrell, Mr S. [Samuel] Wood, and my dear friend John Bowden, who, all three (humanly speaking) would have been Catholics, had they lived till now."[48]

At the same time, Newman could never discount the revulsion Catholicism inspired in the English. "I grieve to hear you confirm," he wrote to Catherine in the same letter, "what I have long felt the mysterious antipathy of our population to Catholicism ... I don't suppose that Hurrell or I had ever any real idea of the English population being influenced by Church principles ... but certainly every event since 1833 has gone to show those, who would be Catholics, that they must come out of their own people as Abraham or St Paul."[49] Newman's failure to gain fair consideration for the Catholic Faith from his siblings, from Keble and Pusey, and from so many others within the Anglo-Catholic camp, also contributed to this realization. And that he once shared this "mysterious antipathy" sharpened it still more. In 1844, in attempting to explain to Catherine what held him back from embracing what Vincent of Lérin called the "high gifts and the strong claims of the Church of Rome," Newman confessed that, "Nothing ... but a strong positive difficulty or repulsion has kept me from surrendering my heart to the authority of the Church of Rome; a repulsive principle, not growing out of Catholic, Anglican, or Primitive doctrine, in the way in which I viewed that doctrine, but something antagonistic ... To be violent against Rome was to be dutiful to England, as well as a measure of necessity for the English theory"—that is to say, the via media, in which Newman invested so much theoretical ingenuity.[50]

That Newman managed to come out of his own people and embrace Catholicism, despite his prejudices against Rome, would always impress upon him the force of grace. This is why he never gave up trying to help Pusey and Keble resolve their difficulties in submitting to the Catholic faith, and why he devoted so much careful thought and attention to Catherine and William. If he could disabuse himself of such prejudices, so could they. Moreover, the transformative power of grace always reminded him of what he might have been had he not co-operated with the grace that came his way. In 1840, he furnished a preface to a life of the Anglican divine George Bull (1634–1710), in writing which he might have said to himself, "There for the grace of God go I ..." Of Bull, the bishop of St. David's, whose learned defense of Nicene Anglicanism won his works a prominent place in Pusey's Library of Anglo-Catholic Theology, Newman wrote: "He is the firm uncompromising disciple of the ancient Fathers, yet the inveterate enemy of Rome: the champion of the faith both against Unitarian error and the licentiousness of Luther ... Such a mould of mind and character, whether in every point we adopt it for ourselves or not, we must confess to be eminently national; and to assimilate itself, more than any other, to the historical and doctrinal vicissitudes, and the complicated conditions of the Anglican Church."[51] Then, again, Newman could not resist wondering what might have happened if Keble had succeeded Edward Copleston as Provost of Oriel in January 1828. "I for one should probably be Tutor of Oriel to this day," he told Catherine in 1844. "I should have gone on with Mathematics which I was bent on doing ... I should have gone on with Niebuhr and Aristotle."[52]

Considering how easily he might have been deflected from his own true course, Newman could not but rejoice in the guidance of grace. Here was the joy of the man who had not let "the point of conversion" pass him by.

> O my dear brethren, what joy and what thankfulness should be ours, that God has brought us into the Church of His Son! What gift is equal to it in the whole world in its preciousness and in its rarity? In this country in particular, where heresy ranges far and wide, where uncultivated nature has so undisputed a field all her own, where grace is given to great numbers only to be profaned and quenched, where baptisms only remain in their impress and character, and faith is ridiculed for its very firmness, for us to find ourselves here in the region of light, in the home of peace, in the presence of Saints, to find ourselves where we can use every faculty of the mind and affection of the heart in its perfection, because in its appointed place and office, to find ourselves in the possession of certainty, consistency, stability, on the highest and holiest subjects of human thought, to have hope here and heaven hereafter, to be on the Mount with Christ, while the poor world is guessing and quarrelling at its foot, who among us shall not wonder at his own blessedness? who shall not be awe-struck at the inscrutable grace of God, which has brought himself, not others where he stands? ..."[53]

This recalls the experience of St. Augustine, whose reading finally transported him beyond reading: "I had no wish to read more, nor was there need. At once a light of serenity flooded into my heart and all the darkness of doubt was dispelled."[54]

Some have unfavorably compared Newman's Catholic sermons, which he preached in Alcester Street in Birmingham in 1849 in what he described as "a gloomy gin distillery" and later collected in *Discourses Addressed to Mixed Congregations* (1849), with those he preached as an Anglican in his *Parochial and Plain Sermons* (1834–1843).[55] Ian Ker speaks of them as "Italianate."[56] Yet Richard Holt Hutton, the discriminating editor of *The Spectator*, rightly perceived that "though they have not ... the delicate charm ... I might almost say the shy passion of the Oxford sermons, they represent the full-blown blossom of his genius, while the former show it only in bud."[57] They also contain rehearsals of positions he would later take up more fully in *A Grammar of Assent*, as here, in the sermon, "Faith and Private Judgment:" "In the ordinary course of this world we account things true either because we see them, or because we can perceive that they follow and are deducible from what we do see; that is, we gain truth by sight or by reason, not by faith. You will say indeed, that we accept a number of things which we cannot prove or see, on the word of others; certainly, but then we accept what they say only as the word of man; and we have not commonly that absolute and unreserved confidence in them, which nothing can shake. We know that man is open to mistake, and we are always glad to find some confirmation of what he says, from other quarters, in any important matter; or we receive his information with negligence and unconcern, as something of little consequence, as a matter of opinion; or, if we act upon it, it is as a matter of prudence, thinking it best and safest to do so. We take his word for what it is worth, and we use it either according to our necessity, or its probability ... This is very different from Divine faith; he who believes that God is true, and that this is His word, which He has committed to man, has no doubt at all. He is as certain that the doctrine taught is true, as that God is true; and he is certain, *because* God is true, *because* God has spoken, not because he sees its truth or can prove its truth. That is, faith has two peculiar-ities;—it is most certain, decided, positive, immovable in its assent, and it gives this assent not because it sees with eye, or sees with the reason, but because it receives the tidings from one who comes from God."[58] Here is another passage from a Catholic sermon, "Faith and Doubt," which would also find its way into the *Grammar*, which makes the point above from a different angle. Throughout his life, Newman listened to Protestants disparaging Catholics for adhering to an infallible faith; but Newman followed St. Augustine in recognizing that one could not have light that was still dark.

> When, then, Protestants quarrel with us for saying that those who join us must give up all ideas of ever doubting the Church in time to come, they do nothing else but quarrel with us for insisting on the necessity of faith in her. Let them speak plainly; our offence is that of demanding faith in the Holy Catholic Church; it is this, and nothing else. I must insist upon this: faith implies a confidence in a man's mind, that the thing believed is really true; but, if it is once true, it never can be false. If it is true that God became man, what is the meaning of my anticipating a time when perhaps I shall not believe that God became man? this is nothing short of anticipating a time when I shall disbelieve a truth. And if I bargain to be allowed in time to come not to believe, or to doubt, that God became man, I am but asking to be allowed to doubt or disbelieve what I hold to be an eternal truth. I do not see the privilege of such a permission at all, or the meaning of wishing to secure it:—if at present I have no doubt whatever about it, then I am but asking leave to fall into error; if at present I have doubts about it, then I do not believe it at present, that is, I have not faith. But I cannot both really believe it now, and yet look forward to a time when perhaps I shall not believe it; to make provision for future doubt, is to doubt at present. It proves I am not in a fit state to become a Catholic now. I may love by halves, I may obey by halves; I cannot believe by halves: either I have faith, or I have it not.[59]

In coming out from his own people and embracing the Catholic Faith Newman recognized that he might be responsible for unsettling those whom he had formerly led. "The pain I suffer from the thought of the distress I am causing," he confided in Mrs. Froude, "cannot be described—and the loss of kind opinion on the part of those I desire to be well with. The unsettling of so many peaceable, innocent minds is a most overpowering thought, and at this moment my heart literally aches and has for days. I am conscious of no motive but that of obeying some urgent imperative call of duty ..."[60] Again, it was vocation that drove him. And yet, as we have seen, he saw such unsettling, in some respects, as not only unavoidable but salutary. As he wrote to Mrs. Froude in April 1844, "So far from my change of opinion having any fair tendency to unsettle persons as to truth and falsehood as objective realities, it should be considered whether such change is not necessary, *should* truth be a real objective thing, and made to confront a person who has been brought up in a system *short of* truth. Surely the *continuance* of a person who wishes to go right in a wrong system, and not his giving it up, would be that which militated against the objectiveness of Truth—leading to the suspicion that one thing and another were equally pleasing to our Maker, where men were sincere." Speaking of his change of allegiance, Newman admitted to Mrs. Froude that he had been unsettled himself, unsure whether, in what he described as his "long continued inward secret ordeal," he was in possession of the truth or doubt, or, worse, delusion.[61] But what finally convinced him that he was indeed in possession of the truth was a renewal of vocation, for "if the doubt comes from Him, He will repeat the suggestion. He will call us again as He called Samuel; He will make our way clear to us. Fancies, excitements, feelings go and never return—truth comes again and is importunate."[62]

In "Faith in Private Judgment," he also described another kind of doubt, which he regarded as characteristically Protestant. To describe this doubt he asked: "What is faith?" And he defined it as an "assenting to a doctrine as true, which we do not see, which we cannot prove, because God says it is true, who cannot lie. And further than this, since God says it is true, not with His own voice, but by the voice of His messengers, it is assenting to what man says, not simply viewed as a man, but to what he is commissioned to declare, as a messenger, prophet, or ambassador from God." Now, for Newman, "Such is the only rational, consistent account of faith; but ... Protestants ... laugh at the very notion of it. They laugh at the notion itself of men pinning their faith ... upon Pope or Council; they think it simply superstitious and narrow-minded, to profess to believe just what the Church believes, and to assent to whatever she will say in time to come on matters of doctrine. That is, they laugh at the bare notion of doing what Christians undeniably did in the time of the Apostles. Observe, they do not merely ask whether the Catholic Church has a claim to teach, has authority, has the gifts;—this is a reasonable question;—no, they think that the very state of mind which such a claim involves in those who admit it, namely, the disposition to accept without reserve or question, that *this* is slavish. They call it priestcraft to insist on this surrender of the reason, and superstition to make it. That is, they quarrel with the very state of mind which all Christians had in the age of the Apostles ..." Here Newman rejected the Protestant claim that it was Protestants who upheld the faith of the primitive Church by showing that they had no faith in the sense in which the Apostles understood the term. On the contrary, they reserved the right to judge for themselves; they recognized no authority; they prided themselves on their private judgment. And if Protestants were transported back into the primitive Church, their prejudices would not have credited what the Apostles had to say. For Newman, "those who thus boast of not being led blindfold, of judging for themselves, of believing just as much and just as little as they please, of hating dictation, and so forth, would have found it an extreme difficulty to hang on the lips of the Apostles ..." They "would have simply resisted the sacrifice of their own liberty of thought, would have thought life eternal too dearly purchased at such a price, and would have died in their unbelief. And they would have defended themselves on the plea that it was absurd and childish to ask them to believe without proof, to bid them give up their education, and their intelligence, and their science ..." And this, as Newman argued, in spite of "those difficulties which reason and sense find in the Christian doctrine, in spite of its mysteriousness, its obscurity, its strangeness, its unacceptableness, its severity ..." Protestants, with their skeptical principles, would never "surrender themselves to the teaching of a few unlettered Galilæans, or a learned indeed but fanatical Pharisee." They would have insisted on their Protestant prerogatives and shown Paul and the Apostles the door. And, for Newman, if "This is what they would have said then; ... is it wonderful they do not become Catholics now? The simple account of their remaining as they are, is, that they lack one thing,—they have not faith; it is a state of mind, it is a virtue, which they do not recognise to be praiseworthy, which they do not aim at possessing."[63]

Newman would make a similar point to Mrs. Froude: "holding as I do, that there is really no medium between scepticism and Catholicism, the very fact that so few of those who had before been influenced by me, have become Catholic, is almost a proof, after all allowances for deference to individual Anglicans, for attachment to what they have been brought up in, for confusion of mind, for desire to act deliberately and other operating causes, that a number of so called Anglo Catholics who still profess to believe secretly doubt."[64] At the same time, Newman told Mrs. Froude, "If you saw more of me, you would not fancy I entertain such hard thoughts about people out of the Church, as you seem to do." Moreover, he hastened to assure his friend, Catholics distinguished "between formal and material error."[65] Still, that there was no medium between skepticism and Catholicism was one of Newman's long-standing convictions, to which he gave memorable expression in a wonderfully inspired passage from *The Tamworth Reading Room* (1841): "Life is not long enough for a religion of inferences," he wrote; "we shall never have done beginning, if we determine to begin with proof. We shall ever be laying our foundations; we shall turn theology into evidences, and divines into textuaries. We shall never get at our first principles. Resolve to believe nothing, and you must prove your proofs and analyze your elements, sinking farther and farther, and finding 'in the lowest depth a lower deep,' till you come to the broad bosom of scepticism. I would rather be bound to defend the reasonableness of assuming that Christianity is true, than to demonstrate a moral governance from the physical world. Life is for action. If we insist on proofs for every thing, we shall never come to action: to act you must assume, and that assumption is faith."[66]

William always bristled whenever Newman told him that he would eventually see the unsustainability of doubt. As fond as he was of Newman, William felt no affinity whatever with his friend's Catholic certitude. "No one, I think, who has ever enjoyed the privilege of affectionate intercourse with you can fail to experience acute pain on coming to feel that he has become practically severed from you," he told Newman, "in whatever way the severance has arisen – Rogers has always said that it was, to him, 'like losing a limb' and I know of no expression which has so accurately described my own feeling." This admission was prompted by Newman telling William, after he had received his son Hurrell (Newman's grandson) into the Church: "As to yourself, I do not believe, and never will believe, that in the bottom of your mind you really hold what you think you hold, or that you master your own thought. I think that some day or other you will allow the truth of what I say."[67] In a long letter William tried to disabuse his friend of this sanguine assessment. "It may indeed be as you tell me that I 'do not really hold what I seem to hold' and 'do not master my own views' –. But to me it seems as if, different as are many of my opinions ... from those you would teach me, there is, underlying all such differences, and irrespective of them or undercutting them, a source of disagreement between us indefinitely stronger than them, seated in the very principle of 'thinking' and of 'concluding' and in the very nature of 'thoughts' and of conclusions – and pervading the laws, which govern the various states of mind included in the various senses of the term 'belief,' and which fix the duties attached to them." None of this would have come as a surprise to Newman: he already knew the extent of William's sprawling skepticism; but he must have been surprised to hear William's account of its genesis. "My convictions so to call them," he declared, "are the growth of a life. I seem to hold them, or to be held by them, very completely, and to see my way through them, as clearly as I can see my way through anything – they first were reared I am confident under the mental training I received from my Brother Hurrell and I am persuaded they have since been legitimately developed." That William credited Hurrell with inculcating this skeptical temper in his brother must have struck Newman as a cruel irony; Hurrell, after all, had been so instrumental in turning Newman to Rome. Indeed, William was convinced that if Hurrell had lived, he would have come round to his own radically skeptical views. For William, Hurrell's "mind was, as he himself felt, in many respects in a state of transition, and it is at least possible that he would have arrived at the same conclusions as those at which I have arrived, and there are many reasons which incline me to think he would have done so. But the consciousness that this surmise may be an error, does not at all shake my confidence that the principles of thought by which I am guided are not merely those which the experience of life has fully verified to me, but are also those which he was the first to develop in my mind."[68]

Anthony would not have agreed. "My brother was young, gifted, brilliant, and enthusiastic. No man is ever good for much who has not been carried off his feet by enthusiasm between twenty and thirty; but it needs to be bridled and bitted, and my brother did not live to be taught the difference between fact and speculation. Taught it he would have been, if time had been allowed him. No one ever recognized facts more loyally than he when once he saw them. This I am sure of, that when the intricacies of the situation pressed upon him, when it became clear to him that if his conception of the Church, and of its rights and position, was true at all, it was not true of the Church of England, in which he was born, and that he must renounce his theory as visionary or join another communion, he would not have 'minimised' the Roman doctrines that they might be more easy for him to swallow, or have explained away propositions till they meant anything or nothing. Whether he would have swallowed them or not I cannot say; I was not eighteen when he died, and I do not so much as form an opinion about it; but his course, whatever it was, would have been direct and straightforward; he was a man far more than a theologian; and if he had gone, he would have gone with his whole heart and conscience, unassisted by subtleties and nice distinctions ... ." Anthony rarely allowed sincerity to spoil the fun of his paradoxical irreverence but here he spoke from the heart with a brother's affection of a brother's sincerity.[69]

Anthony may have been convinced that Hurrell "had the contempt of an intellectual aristocrat for private judgement," but William saw him as the progenitor of his own doctrinaire doubt.[70] "I have no skill of saying much in few words," Newman's prolix friend admitted, "and the profusion of words into which I run my thoughts tends oftener to mystify than to explain. But I will at least endeavour to convey to you as distinctly as I can that rule or principle of thought which ... seems to hold my mind in the most complete antagonism to Catholicism," and with that William shared with his friend his manifesto of universal doubt:

> More strongly than I believe anything else I believe this. That on no subject whatever, – distinctly not in the region of the ordinary facts with which our daily experience is conversant – distinctly not in the domain of history or politics, and yet again a fortiori, not in that of Theology, is my mind, (or as far as I can tell the mind of any human being,) capable of arriving at an absolutely certain conclusion. That though of course some conclusions are far more certain than others, there is an element of uncertainty in all. That though any probability however faint, may in its place make it a duty to act as if the conclusion to which it points were absolutely certain, yet that even the highest attainable probability does not justify the mind in discarding the residuum of doubt; and that the attempt (by any other means than a reiterated and (if so be) improved examination of all the bases of the whole probability) to enhance or intensify the sense of the preponderance of the probabilities in either scale, is distinctly an immoral use of faculties. And then, whereas on concluding that it is one's duty to act on such and such a degree of probability, (whether great or small) the mind is very strongly drawn and inclined, to overrate the degree of probability in reference to which we proceed to act, this inclination is a temptation to be resisted, not an intimation to be relied on.[71]

Wishing, perhaps, to appear even-handed, William acknowledged that there might be some valuable aspects of faith. "I do not overlook the view that 'Spiritual insight is granted as the reward of Faith,'" though even here he was dubious. "I feel it to be one in the highest degree improbable, if the merit of the Faith be measured as Theologians seem to measure it, directly, as the positiveness of the Belief and inversely as the strength of the evidence. Thus measured, 'Faith' seems to be but another word for 'prejudice' – i.e as the formation of a judgement irrespective of, or out of proportion to the evidence on which it rests – and I regard it as … an immoral use of the faculties – While on the other hand the only pattern of Faith which I can conceive to be meritorious, is the temper which, while it realises as carefully as possible the exact degree of doubtfulness which attaches to its conclusions, acts nevertheless confidently on the best and wisest conclusions it can form – in confidence that the best and wisest use of every faculty we possess must be that use which will be most pleasing to Him by whom those faculties, whether perfect or imperfect, have been given us 'to be exercised therewith'." And here he claimed that it was precisely this enlightened skepticism that made the Victorians' various mechanical accomplishments possible. "It is but of late years that this temper has been thoroughly appreciated in the pursuit of scientific truth and in the cultivation of the mechanical arts," though, for William, this "thorough appreciation" was "confined to the higher class of minds …" Nevertheless, "if year by year, Physical science and the mechanical arts have … made progress with increasing rapidity … it is only by virtue of the wider and freer scope of action which this principle has conquered for itself in those districts of thought. The principle is making some progress even in Politics. By and Bye I hope it will master men's minds in the province of Religion." This, in sum, was William's metaphysic of skepticism: "Our 'doubts' in fact, appear to me as sacred, and I think deserve to be cherished as sacredly as our beliefs; and our 'will' has no function in reference to the formation or maintenance of our 'Belief', but that of insisting that all probabilities on either side shall be honestly regarded, and weighed, and borne in mind."[72]

Newman's response was as fair-minded as it was candid. "Your letter of this morning has been a very great comfort to me. The greatest evils in the intercourse of friends is ignorance about each other's feelings." That having been said, Newman assured his skeptical friend that "The line you draw out in your letter is familiar to me … not that you do not bring it out more clearly than I perhaps have done to myself … Still, I have long meditated on its subject. I think it a fallacy, but I don't think it easy to show it to be so. It is one of various points which I have steadily set before me, as requiring an answer, and an answer from me … I am saying all of this to show how little I can mean to be disrespectful to your view on the subject, and how little I should dream of putting it down in a few magisterial words. At the same time I do with all my heart, and what is more to the purpose, with all my reason think it a sophism; but you will perfectly understand that a sophism may require an effort of almost genius to overset … In truth, I think there is a far deeper philosophy on the subject than yours, if I could develop it."[73] After encouraging him to "work out this question … which you more than anybody else" are "competent to examine fully," Froude asked him "whether when you say that you feel the view which I endeavored to express is a sophism, you mean that it is so in reference to the pursuit of truth generally or only in reference to the pursuit of Religious truth."[74]

Here was one of the main questions that Newman would set himself to answer in *Aid to a Grammar of Assent*, and in responding to William's letter, he laid out some of the lines of argument that he would pursue in depth in that extraordinary book. First, Newman assured his friend that "I do not mean that there is any thing sophistical in the principles on which non-religious truth is pursued at present, but that theologians ... all affirm that Christianity is proved by the same rigorous scientific processes by which it is proved that we have an Indian Empire or that the earth goes round the sun." Second, "the scientific proof of Christianity is not the popular, practical, personal evidence on which a given individual believes in it ..." And, for Newman, "there is a popular and personal way of arriving at certainty in Christianity as logical as that which is arrived at by scientific methods in subjects non-religious ..." Then, too, Newman doubtless startled his scientific friend when he observed that, "when all scientific proof, even for the existence of India, is examined microscopically, there will be found hiatuses in the logical sequence, so considerable, as to lead to the question, 'Are there no broad first principles of knowledge which will protect us from scepticism as to all reasoning on things external to us, both scientific and popular?'"[75] If William imagined that skepticism would somehow spare his own cherished first principles, he was mistaken.

An Essay in Aid of a Grammar of Assent is a demanding book. When Mrs. Froude confessed that she was "reading the Grammar through again, (for the 6th or 7th time) by way of light and airy reading," Newman thanked her for "the compliment you pay my crabbed assent."[76] To another old friend, Maria Giberne, he wrote in February 1870, a month before the *Grammar* was published: "I have now done my last work. I use the word 'work' in its true sense – for some books are not work, but this book has been a real hard work. I have done five constructive works in my life, and this is the hardest, though all have been hard – my Prophetical Office, which has come to pieces – my Essay on Justification, which stands pretty well – and three Catholic – Development of doctrine – University Education, and the last which I have called an Essay in aid of a Grammar of Assent."[77] To James Hope-Scott, the Catholic lawyer and munificent philanthropist whose own faith Newman found so exemplary, he described the writing of the book as "like tunneling through a mountain— I have begun it, and it is almost too much for my strength ... Perhaps the tunnel will break in, when I get fairly into my work. When I have done it, if I am to do it, and done my letters of past years, then I shall say, Nunc dimittis."[78] Yet readers should not be put off by the air of difficulty that has always surrounded the book. Yes, it is demanding but it is also immensely rewarding. If one approaches it as a record of Newman's attempts to share with the Froudes—and by extension, all readers, Christian and non-Christian—his sense of vocation, it becomes a good deal more accessible. Indeed, in discussing the role of personal testimony in the apprehension of truth, Newman addresses each reader *cor ad cor*:

> In religious inquiry each of us can speak only for himself, and for himself he has a right to speak. His own experiences are enough for himself, but he cannot speak for others: he cannot lay down the law; he can only bring his own experiences to the common stock of psychological facts. He knows

what has satisfied and satisfies himself; if it satisfies him, it is likely to satisfy others; if, as he believes and is sure, it is true, it will approve itself to others also, for there is but one truth. And doubtless he does find in fact, that, allowing for the difference of minds and of modes of speech, what convinces him, does convince others also. There will be very many exceptions, but these will admit of explanation. Great numbers of men refuse to inquire at all; they put the subject of religion aside altogether; others are not serious enough to care about questions of truth and duty and to entertain them; and to numbers, from their temper of mind, or the absence of doubt, or a dormant intellect, it does not occur to inquire why or what they believe; many, though they tried, would not be able to do so in any satisfactory way. This being the case, it causes no uneasiness to any one who honestly attempts to set down his own view of the Evidences of Religion, that at first sight he seems to be but one among many who are all in opposition to each other. But, however that may be, he brings together his reasons, and relies on them, because they are his own, and this is his primary evidence; and he has a second ground of evidence, in the testimony of those who agree with him. But his best evidence is the former, which is derived from his own thoughts; and it is that which the world has a right to demand of him; and therefore his true sobriety and modesty consists, not in claiming for his conclusions an acceptance or a scientific approval which is not to be found anywhere, but in stating what are personally his own grounds for his belief in Natural and Revealed Religion,—grounds which he holds to be so sufficient, that he thinks that others do hold them implicitly or in substance, or would hold them, if they inquired fairly, or will hold if they listen to him, or do not hold from impediments, invincible or not as it may be, into which he has no call to inquire.[79]

This echoes something Newman had told Catherine Holdsworth thirty years before: "The only safety many people find against Catholic truth is not inquiring, but that cannot last in the 19th century."[80]

Despite the refreshing personal testimony that Newman brings to his book, he never confuses personal testimony with subjectivism. Indeed, as the great Thomist Etienne Gilson pointed out, Newman gives his readers no warrant to "present the *Grammar of Assent* as exalting the inner faith of the believer at the expense of the objective truth of dogma," which, for Gilson, would be "about the worst misrepresentation of Newman's thought that it is possible to imagine."[81] On the contrary, "far from doing away with systematic theology, the doctrine of Newman presupposes its necessity. His own problem is not to pursue the definition, organization, and systemization of theological truth, but … to study the birth, the life … of real assent in the minds of concrete and existing men."[82]

The birth of that assent, for Newman, is made possible by conscience, about which he writes with moving eloquence. "Half the world would be puzzled to know what was meant by the moral sense; but every one knows what is meant by a good or bad conscience. Conscience is ever forcing on us by threats and by promises that we must follow the right and avoid the wrong; so far it is one and the same in the mind of every one, whatever be its particular errors in particular minds as to the acts which it orders to be done or to be avoided ..." For Newman, "conscience ... is concerned with persons primarily, and with actions mainly as viewed in their doers, or rather with self alone and one's own actions, and with others only indirectly and as if in association with self." Nevertheless, it "does not repose on itself, but vaguely reaches forward to something beyond self, and dimly discerns a sanction higher than self for its decisions, as is evidenced in that keen sense of obligation and responsibility which informs them. And hence it is that we are accustomed to speak of conscience as a voice ... and moreover a voice ... imperative and constraining, like no other dictate in the whole of our experience."[83]

Newman begins with conscience because, as he says, "what I am directly aiming at, is to explain how we gain an image of God and give a real assent to the proposition that He exists. And next, in order to do this, of course I must start from some first principle;—and that first principle, which I assume and shall not attempt to prove, is ... that we have by nature a conscience." And then he demonstrates how "Conscience has an intimate bearing on our affections and emotions, leading us to reverence and awe, hope and fear, especially fear ... No fear is felt by any one who recognizes that his conduct has not been beautiful, though he may be mortified at himself, if perhaps he has thereby forfeited some advantage; but, if he has been betrayed into any kind of immorality, he has a lively sense of responsibility and guilt, though the act be no offence against society,—of distress and apprehension, even though it may be of present service to him,—of compunction and regret, though in itself it be most pleasurable,—of confusion of face, though it may have no witnesses. These various perturbations of mind which are characteristic of a bad conscience, and may be very considerable,—self-reproach, poignant shame, haunting remorse, chill dismay at the prospect of the future,—and their contraries, when the conscience is good, as real though less forcible, self-approval, inward peace, lightness of heart, and the like,—these emotions constitute a specific difference between conscience and our other intellectual senses,—common sense, good sense, sense of expedience, taste, sense of honour, and the like ..."[84] Then, again, as Newman shows, conscience "always involves the recognition of a living object, towards which it is directed ... If, as is the case, we feel responsibility, are ashamed, are frightened, at transgressing the voice of conscience, this implies that there is One to whom we are responsible, before whom we are ashamed, whose claims upon us we fear." To make this matter of personal responsibility more vivid still, Newman connects it to personal terms to which most of us can readily relate. "If, on doing wrong, we feel the same tearful, broken-hearted sorrow which overwhelms us on hurting a mother; if, on doing right, we enjoy the same sunny serenity of mind, the same soothing, satisfactory delight which follows on our receiving praise from a father, we certainly have within us the image of some person, to whom our love and veneration look, in whose smile we find our happiness, for whom we yearn, towards whom we direct our pleadings, in whose anger we are troubled and waste away. These feelings in us are such as require for their exciting cause an intelligent being: we are not affectionate towards a stone, nor do we feel shame before a horse or a dog; we have no remorse or compunction on breaking mere human law: yet, so it is, conscience excites all these painful emotions, confusion, foreboding, self-condemnation; and on the other hand it sheds upon us a deep peace, a sense of security, a resignation, and a hope, which there is no sensible, no earthly object to elicit."[85]

Sir Anthony Kenny in his *Philosophy in the Modern World* (2007) responds to this passage by remarking, "It is difficult for members of a post-Freudian generation to read this passage without acute discomfort ... The feelings that [Newman] describes may indeed be appropriate only if there is a Father in heaven. But no feelings can guarantee their own appropriateness in the absence of reason."[86] Kenny's objection is useful because it exhibits the very pert, unfeeling, arid intellectualism against which so much of the *Grammar* is written. To return to Newman after Kenny's commentary is to leave the fashionable shadows for an ancient sunlight.

"The wicked flees, when no one pursueth;" then why does he flee? whence his terror? Who is it that he sees in solitude, in darkness, in the hidden chambers of his heart? If the cause of these emotions does not belong to this visible world, the Object to which his perception is directed must be Supernatural and Divine; and thus the phenomena of Conscience, as a dictate, avail to impress the imagination with the picture of a Supreme Governor, a Judge, holy, just, powerful, all-seeing, retributive, and is the creative principle of religion, as the Moral Sense is the principle of ethics.[87]

Moreover, for Newman, Protestantism is the "religion of civilization" precisely because it rejects conscience, which it sees as primitive and barbaric, and "since this civilization itself is not a development of man's whole nature, but mainly of the intellect, recognizing indeed the moral sense, but ignoring the conscience, no wonder that the religion in which it issues has no sympathy either with the hopes and fears of the awakened soul, or with those frightful presentiments which are expressed in the worship and traditions of the heathen."[88] Newman makes a similar point in one of his *Oxford Sermons*, where he says of St. Paul, "even in the case of the heathen, the Apostle was anxious to pay due respect to the truths which they already admitted, and to show that the Gospel was rather the purification, explanation, development, and completion of those scattered verities of Paganism than their abrogation."[89] Looking from conscience to the world, Newman saw another confirmation of the existence of God, though one fraught with an inquisitorial mystery. "What strikes the mind so forcibly and so painfully is His absence (if I may so speak) from His own world. It is a silence that speaks. It is as if others had got possession of His work. Why does not He, our Maker and Ruler, give us some immediate knowledge of Himself? Why does He not write His Moral Nature in large letters upon the face of history, and bring the blind, tumultuous rush of its events into a celestial, hierarchical order? Why does He not grant us in the structure of society at least so much of a revelation of Himself as the religions of the heathen attempt to supply? Why from the beginning of time has no one uniform steady light guided all families of the earth, and all individual men, how to please Him? Why is it possible without absurdity to deny His will, His attributes, His existence? Why does He not walk with us one by one, as He is said to have walked with His chosen men of old time? We both see and know each other; why, if we cannot have the sight of Him, have we not at least the knowledge? On the contrary, He is specially 'a Hidden God;' and with our best efforts we can only glean from the surface of the world some faint and fragmentary views of Him. I see only a choice of alternatives in explanation of so critical a fact:—either there is no Creator, or He has disowned His creatures. Are then the dim shadows of His Presence in the affairs of men but a fancy of our own, or, on the other hand, has He hid His face and the light of His countenance, because we have in some special way dishonoured Him? My true informant, my burdened conscience, gives me at once the true answer to each of these antagonist questions:—it pronounces without any misgiving that God exists:—and it pronounces quite as surely that I am alienated from Him; that 'His hand is not shortened, but that our iniquities have divided between us and our God.' Thus it solves the world's mystery, and sees in that mystery only a confirmation of its own original teaching."[90]

Such teaching, however true, is not complete. "Natural Religion is based upon the sense of sin; it recognizes the disease, but it cannot find, it does but look out for the remedy. That remedy, both for guilt and for moral impotence, is found in the central doctrine of Revelation, the Mediation of Christ." Although it comes at the very end of the book, Newman's account of the rise of Christianity is masterly. "Thus it is that Christianity is the fulfilment of the promise made to Abraham, and of the Mosaic revelations; this is how it has been able from the first to occupy the world and gain a hold on every class of human society to which its preachers reached; this is why the Roman power and the multitude of religions which it embraced could not stand against it; this is the secret of its sustained energy, and its never-flagging martyrdoms; this is how at present it is so mysteriously potent, in spite of the new and fearful adversaries which beset its path."[91] Here was a radiant rebuttal of the claims of Gibbon, though no mention of it will be found in the commentary on Gibbon of John Pocock, J. W. Burrow or Patricia Craddock. For Newman, the rise of Christianity was not a tale of fanaticism or credulity or even virtue.[92] Rather, its power rose from that "gift of staunching and healing the one deep wound of human nature, which avails more for its success than a full encyclopedia of scientific knowledge and a whole library of controversy, and therefore it must last while human nature lasts. It is a living truth which never can grow old."[93] Here Newman directly refuted the charge, brought by so many of his agnostic and Protestant critics, that in embracing Roman Catholicism he was embracing the superannuated or the reactionary. For Newman, there was nothing fusty about the one holy catholic and apostolic Church. "Some persons speak of it as if it were a thing of history, with only indirect bearings upon modern times. I cannot allow that it is a mere historical religion. Certainly it has its foundations in past and glorious memories, but its power is in the present. It is no dreary matter of antiquarianism; we do not contemplate it in conclusions drawn from dumb documents and dead events, but by faith exercised in ever-living objects, and by the appropriation and use of ever-recurring gifts."[94] And, here, Newman substantiated his point by citing the example of Holy Mass, "which He who once died for us upon the Cross, brings back and perpetuates, by His literal presence in it, that one and the same sacrifice which cannot be repeated. Next, there is the actual entrance of Himself, soul and body, and divinity, into the soul and body of every worshipper who comes to Him for the gift, a privilege more intimate than if we lived with Him during His long-past sojourn upon earth. And then, moreover, there is His personal abidance in our churches, raising earthly service into a foretaste of heaven. Such is the profession of Christianity, and, I repeat, its very divination of our needs is in itself a proof that it is really the supply of them."[95]

The *Grammar of Assent* was, on the whole, well received. Newman was particularly pleased with a review that the leading Tractarian writer James Mozley wrote for the *Quarterly Review*, in which he treated Newman's Essay "as what it really and in substance is, a defence, and powerful defence, of a common Christianity, which has filled up a vacant place in Christian apologetics ..."[96] Others took issue with the book, including F. D. Maurice writing in the *Contemporary Review* and the high court judge and journalist James Fitzjames Stephen writing in *Fraser's Magazine*. Maurice used his review to tout his own anti-theological Christianity: "The revelation of Christ brings to me evidence that it was not the work of priests and doctors of the law, seeing that priests and doctors were the great enemies of it ... Priests and doctors speak of a God whose purpose is to destroy the great majority of His creatures; Christ reveals to us a God of salvation; His Apostles testify of a day when all shall be gathered up in Him. Dr. Newman speaks of 'Christianity' doing this and that. If Christianity is not the revelation of Christ the Son of God, I cannot see what it has done but mischief."[97] Stephen, who turned to journalism to take his mind off what he regarded as the "buffoonery" of circuit life, saw Newman's text as little more than an endorsement of exploded Popery.[98] "When the Church was in the plenitude of its power," he told his readers, it taught that "the Supreme God was ... a Being who looked approvingly on an *auto-da-fé*, who could be bribed to remit the penalties of sin by masses purchased with money, who, though all-wise and all-good, could be turned aside from His purpose by entreaties or remonstrances of the saints. The same notion is still evidently held by Father Newman ..." Stephen's response to one passage in the book is worth quoting at length, especially since William Froude thought so highly of him (Stephen was one of those whom he regarded as a "high cast mind"). The passage from Newman is the one where he illustrates what he means by the "indefectability" of certitude.

Let us suppose we are told on an unimpeachable authority, that a man whom we saw die is now alive again and at his work, as it was his wont to be; let us suppose we actually see him and converse with him; what will become of our certitude of his death? I do not think we should give it up;

how could we, when we actually saw him die? At first, indeed, we should be thrown into an astonishment and confusion so great, that the world would seem to reel round us, and we should be ready to give up the use of our senses and of our memory, of our reflective powers, and of our reason, and even to deny our power of thinking, and our existence itself. Such confidence have we in the doctrine that when life goes it never returns. Nor would our bewilderment be less, when the first blow was over; but our reason would rally, and with our reason our certitude would come back to us. Whatever came of it, we should never cease to know and to confess to ourselves both of the contrary facts, that we saw him die, and that after dying we saw him alive again. The overpowering strangeness of our experience would have no power to shake our certitude in the facts which created it.[99]

In response, Stephen gave witty vent to his impatience with the miraculous: "No better illustration could have been given of the difference between what is called in commendation 'a believing mind,' and a mind trained to careful and precise observation. In such a case as Father Newman supposes, a jury of modern physicians would indisputably conclude that the man had never been really dead, that the symptoms had been mistaken, and the phenomena of catalepsy had been confounded with the phenomena of death. If catalepsy was impossible, if the man had appeared, for instance, to lose his head on the scaffold, they would assume that there had been a substitution of persons, or that the observers had been taken in by some skilful optical trick. Father Newman, may, perhaps, go further and suppose that they had themselves seen the man tied to a gun and blown to pieces beyond possibility of deception. But a man of science would reply that such a case could not occur. That men once dead do not return to life again has been revealed by an experience too uniform to allow its opposite to be entertained even as a hypothesis."[100] This is wonderfully funny but it also proves Newman's point that there is no happy medium between scepticism and Catholicism.

Etienne Gilson put the author of the *Grammar* in useful perspective: "Newman did not write as a disciple of the scholastic masters whose works illustrated the thirteenth century; he wrote in the free style of a twelfth-century master, full of classical erudition and fond of good language, but, at the same time, a man of his own epoch ... When Newman entered the Catholic Church, he brought with him a more purely patristic intellectual formation than would have been the case if, born in the Church, he had received in it his early theological formation. The Church alone has authority to say what place John Henry Cardinal Newman will later occupy in the memory of the faithful, but it is not too early to say that, owing to him, the great theological style of the Fathers has been worthily revived in the nineteenth century."[101]

In the several passages quoted here from the *Grammar of Assent*, readers can see the extraordinary perspicuity with which Newman takes up the themes of Natural Religion and Revealed Religion. But he also stresses again and again that, by their very nature, there can be no scientific proof of the truth of these matters. "In thus speaking of Natural Religion as in one sense a matter of private judgment, and that with a view of proceeding from it to the proof of Christianity, I seem to give up the intention of demonstrating either. Certainly I do; not that I deny that demonstration is possible. Truth certainly, as such, rests upon grounds intrinsically and objectively and abstractedly demonstrative, but it does not follow from this that the arguments producible in its favour are unanswerable and irresistible. These latter epithets are relative, and bear upon matters of fact; arguments in themselves ought to do, what perhaps in the particular case they cannot do. The fact of revelation is in itself demonstrably true, but it is not therefore true irresistibly; else, how comes it to be resisted? There is a vast distance between what it is in itself, and what it is to us. Light is a quality of matter, as truth is of Christianity; but light is not recognized by the blind, and there are those who do not recognize truth, from the fault, not of truth, but of themselves. I cannot convert men, when I ask for assumptions which they refuse to grant to me; and without assumptions no one can prove anything about anything." Indeed, in this respect, as Frederick Copleston remarked in his history of philosophy, "unbelief or scepticism is in the same boat as faith," and to illustrate his point he quoted from Newman's University Sermons: "Unbelief ... considers itself especially rational, or critical of evidence; but it criticizes the evidence of Religion, only because it does not like it, and really goes upon presumptions and prejudices as much as Faith does, only presumptions of an opposite nature ... It considers a religious system so improbable, that it will not listen to the evidence of it; or, if it listens, it employs itself in doing what a believer could do, if he chose, quite as well, what he is quite as well aware can be done; viz., in showing that the evidence might be more complete and unexceptionable than it is." For Copleston, "Sceptics do not really decide according to the evidence; for they make up their minds first and then admit or reject evidence according to their initial assumption."[102]

To say that one cannot mount irresistible arguments for the existence of God is not to say that one cannot know certitude, which Newman defines as "the perception of a truth with the perception that it is a truth." And here he was directly addressing the vexed matter with which he debated William Froude for so many years. "We may indeed say, if we please, that a man ought not to have so supreme a conviction in a given case, or in any case whatever; and that he is therefore wrong in treating opinions which he does not himself hold, with this even involuntary contempt;—certainly, we have a right to say so, if we will; but if, in matter of fact, a man has such a conviction, if he is sure that Ireland is to the West of England, or that the Pope is the Vicar of Christ, nothing is left to him, if he would be consistent, but to carry his conviction out into this magisterial intolerance of any contrary assertion; and if he were in his own mind tolerant, I do not say patient (for patience and gentleness are moral duties, but I mean intellectually tolerant), of objections as objections, he would virtually be giving countenance to the views which those objections represented. I say I certainly should be very intolerant of such a notion as that I shall one day be Emperor of the French; I should think it too absurd even to be ridiculous, and that I must be mad before I could entertain it. And did a man try to persuade me that treachery, cruelty, or ingratitude was as praiseworthy as honesty and temperance, and that a man who lived the life of a knave and died the death of a brute had nothing to fear from future retribution, I should think there was no call on me to listen to his arguments, except with the hope of converting him, though he called me a bigot and a coward for refusing to inquire into his speculations. And if, in a matter in which my temporal interests were concerned, he attempted to reconcile me to fraudulent acts by what he called philosophical views, I should say to him, 'Retro Satana,' and that, not from any suspicion of his ability to reverse immutable principles, but from a consciousness of my own moral changeableness, and a fear, on that account, that I might not be intellectually true to the truth. This, then, from the nature of the case, is a main characteristic of certitude in any matter, to be confident indeed that that certitude will last, but to be confident of this also, that, if it did fail, nevertheless, the thing itself, whatever it is, of which we are certain, will remain just as it is, true and irreversible."[103]

William found the *Grammar of Assent* unpersuasive. Writing to Newman in 1871, Catherine summed up the quixotic skepticism that prevented her husband from assenting to the truths of Christianity: "I believe from what you have said when we have talked on the subject, that you do understand him certainly. It seems to me that Wm is so utterly removed from the common run of Sceptics; and his mistakes appear to me to proceed in great measure from crankiness, and a sort of over-scrupulousness." This has the ring of truth, for certainly William was free of the peevishness that distinguished so many Victorian agnostics from Mark Pattison to Leslie Stephen. As his biographer, David K. Brown attests, William "was a very lovable man, admired by Admirals and dockyard mateys alike."[104] In 1863, Newman confirmed this assessment in a letter to Sister Mary Gabriel Du Boulay: "I am engaged just now in receiving one of the Froudes – a boy of 16 who arrived here yesterday from school. My dear friend, his Father, who is not a Catholic has seen his children one after another, (this is the fourth) received into the Church: and he has borne it so gently, so meekly, so tenderly, (though it has given him a sense of desolation most cruel to bear) that I do trust God's mercy has the same gift in store for himself. Please give him your prayers, and ask your Sisters to do the like. It is the infallibility of the Church which is his stumbling stone. He would confess that her authority is probable, – but he cannot receive her absolute infallibility, and since she claims (as he thinks) what she has not, therefore the claim itself is a proof against her. What a good Catholic he would make, if the grace of God touched his heart! Get our Lady to ask for him – what a joyful day it would be![105] That Catherine never despaired of her husband's eventual conversion is clear from a letter she wrote to Newman in July 1876 in which she thanked him for a recent visit he had made to Chelston Cross: "I have been intending day after day to write to you: – but somehow, whenever I have thought of your stay here, I have felt ready to cry. – It was such a delight, – and it passed so quickly – as all happy times do; – and it leaves the sort of ache on my mind in thinking that I did not enjoy it half enough, – and that also is what happy times do. – I think when a longer time has passed, I shall enjoy more to look back upon it; – to the drives,

– and the talks in the hall, – and the great pleasure it gave us all to see that you seemed to enjoy it. – I cannot tell you all that my dear husband has said since, of his love for you, and admiration of you, – that too makes me inclined to cry, – for I want, – what I cannot have, and the very sweetness and affection he shows us all makes me feel the separation more keenly. But somehow I cannot believe that any one so good can be out of God's favour: – and so I hope and hope."[106] After Catherine's death in July 1878, William sought to beguile his bereavement on a cruise and suddenly died himself at Simonstown, South Africa. Newman was composing a long letter to him on the very themes that he had addressed so painstakingly in the *Grammar*—certitude and assent—when he heard the news. The Devonshire Association recalled William glowingly. "He would bring the same intense, yet almost playful attention to the construction of a toy as to the analysis of the curves of an ironclad or the behavior of an Atlantic wave. With such a character, he brought brightness wherever he went. His voice had an almost pathetic tone, the outcomes of a sympathetic heart. And one in any trouble, not knowing who or what he was, must have thought his life was spent in tender concern for others which springs from forgetfulness of self, and sense of the mystery of human life."[107] Shortly before her own death, Catherine confirmed something of that mystery when she remarked of her obdurate, talented, heart-broken husband: "It is always extraordinary to me (seeing what excellent sense and judgment he has on most subjects) that in talking of Catholic matters, he does talk such nonsense. Such as 'there can be nothing in the system of spiritual direction unless every director is infallible,' as if one ought never to go to a doctor unless the doctor is infallible ...'"[108] This was doubtless true, though Newman never allowed such nonsense to prevent him from sharing with William the certitude of his own vocation and indeed his own love. As Newman wrote to his friend in his last letter, which, alas, William never received: "the Moral Governor of the world extends a supernatural aid to the efforts of nature to find religious truth, which He does not accord to inquirers in the theory of Natural Science. That φρόνησις which in every branch of inquiry is required for obtaining knowledge, is guided and enlightened by Him to right conclusions in religion, as it is not prospered supernaturally in the arts and sciences. And the conditions of obtaining this aid are faith, dependence on him and a spirit and habit of prayer."[109]

Three years before Froude's death, Newman put the matter even more bluntly to Edmond G. Holmes, a young man who took a First in Classics at St. John's and later went on to become an Inspector of Schools. Holmes had sent Newman a paper taking issue with the rationalism of Herbert Spencer and John Stuart Mill, and Newman wrote back to him that while his correspondent "must make allowance for an old man, who finds it very difficult to screw up his mind to a metaphysical argument ... I can truly say that I warmly sympathise and concur with you in the substance of your argument, and am rejoiced to have evidence in it that there are those in the rising generation who will in their day make a successful stand against the tyranny under which we at present lie of a 'science falsely so called,' which is so shallow, so audacious, so arrogant, and so widely accepted."[110]

CHAPTER 5

A Better Country: Newman's Idea of Public Life

"Life passes, riches fly away, popularity is fickle, the senses decay, the world changes, friends die. One alone is constant; One alone is true to us: One alone can be true; One alone can be all things to us; One alone can supply our needs; One alone can train us up to our perfections; One alone can give meaning to our complex and intricate nature; One alone can give us a tune and harmony; One alone can form and possess us."

John Henry Newman, "The Thought of God and the Stay of the Soul" (1839)

In "Who's To Blame?" (1855), written in response to the public outcry against the Crimean War, Newman captured perfectly the predicament of ministers first goaded into war and then blamed once the campaign turned sour. No campaign—or only the Sicilian Expedition of the Peloponnesian War—ever turned sour in quite so calamitous a way as the siege of Sebastopol. It cost the British more than 21,000 lives and did nothing to protect the Holy Places for which it was initially launched. "Cholera and drunkenness, courts martial and floggings" is the way Christopher Hibbert summed it up.[1] Yet while Newman thought it "a piece of simple Johnbullism," he refused to scapegoat either the cabinet or Whitehall.[2] He had been made a scapegoat too frequently himself to wish to scapegoat others. Instead, in a passage of exuberant irony, he came to the defense of John's Bull's "workhouse apprentices:"

England, surely, is the paradise of little men, and the purgatory of great ones. May I never be a Minister of State or a Field-Marshal! I'd be an individual, self-respecting Briton, in my own private castle, with the *Times* to see the world by, and pen and paper to scribble off withal to some public print, and set the world right. Public men are only my *employés*; I use them as I think fit, and turn them off without warning. Aberdeen, Gladstone, Sidney Herbert, Newcastle, what are they muttering about services and ingratitude? were they not paid? … can they be profitable to me their lord and master? … having no tenderness or respect for their persons, their antecedents, or their age … I

164

think it becoming and generous,—during, not after their work … to institute a formal process of inquiry into their demerits, not secret, not indulgent to their sense of honour, but in the hearing of all Europe, and amid the scorn of the world,—hitting down, knocking over, my workhouse apprentices, in order that they may get up again, and do my matters for me better.[3]

Newman's empathy for public men came to the fore most admirably after Gladstone was blamed for the death of General Gordon in January 1885—a death he felt deeply. "Though I know no one in the Soudan, and scarcely any of their relatives, I am in real distress at the thought of what those relatives are suffering. Neither the Crimea nor the Indian Mutiny has come home to me, I don't know why, as this has. Perhaps it is because the misfortune is so wanton, and on that ground makes one so indignant. Five successful engagements, won at a cruel price, but all for nothing."[4] His registration of the tragedy was only sharpened when he learned that Gordon had read and reread his poem "The Dream of Gerontius" (1865) throughout the siege of Khartoum. Of course, what Newman was feeling about the losses in the Sudan was shared by many in England. In March 1885, Henry James gave a vivid description of the fallout of Gordon's death in London:

The ministry is still in office, but hanging only by a hair, Gladstone is ill and bewildered, the mess in the Soudan unspeakable, London full of wailing widows and weeping mothers, the hostility of Bismarck extreme, the danger of complications with Russia imminent, the Irish in the House of Commons more disagreeable than ever, the dynamiters more active, the income tax threatening to rise to its maximum, the general muddle, in short, of the densest and darkest … Gladstone hates foreign relations and has tried to shirk them all, and is paying his penalty in the bitter censure of his own party as well as the execration of the other. It is a pitiful end of a great career. The people that abuse him most are the good old Liberals …[5]

Newman shared James's concern for "the poor fellows in the Soudan" but he refused to scapegoat Gladstone. "I think that all praise is due to Gladstone for being so exemplary both personally and publicly as Prime Minister," he wrote, "and I am unspeakably shocked and indignant to be told … of his private character having been the butt of slander."[6] The magnanimity of this has to be seen in light of the fact that only ten years before Gladstone had publicly accused Newman and indeed all English Catholics not only of disloyalty but intellectual and moral subservience. Another example of Newman's empathy for public men can be seen from *The Rambler* of September 1859. A correspondent had written in accusing France and her "impious apostles" of trying to attack the Pope's temporal power. Newman responded back: "I [am] far too cautious … to take Louis Napoleon's part; but it is another thing to indulge in invectives, nay slanderous invectives, against him. Public men have characters, as other men; and their characters are dear to them. We should do as we would be done by. We may fairly criticize what they have done; we cannot fairly impute what they have not done as yet, and what they disown."[7]

Newman's refusal to impute bad motives to public men grew out of his recognition that this was precisely what English Protestants had been doing to Catholics for centuries. In that witty anatomy of Protestant prejudice, *The Present Position of Catholics in England* (1851)—a book as indispensable to understanding the English as Astolphe de Custine's *Letters from Russia* (1843) is to understanding the Russians —Newman showed with what methodical thoroughness "the fathers and patrons of the English Reformation ... fastened on ... Catholics first the imputation, [and] then the repute of ignorance, bigotry, and superstition." Long before Herbert Butterfield exposed the fallacies of the Whig version of history or G. R. Elton showed how Thomas Cromwell had used English law to outlaw English Catholicism or Eamon Duffy proved how resented that outlawing was by a people fond enough of their traditional Catholic faith, Newman showed "what had to be done in order to perpetuate Protestantism" in England.[8]

> Convoke the legislature, pass some sweeping ecclesiastical enactments, exalt the Crown above the Law and the Gospel, down with the Cross and up with the lion and the dog, toss all priests out of the country as traitors; let Protestantism be the passport to office and authority, force the King to be a Protestant, make his Court Protestant, bind Houses of Parliament to be Protestant, clap a Protestant oath upon judges, barristers-at-law, officers in army and navy, members of the universities, national clergy; establish this stringent Tradition in every function and department of the State, surround it with the luster of rank, wealth, station, name, and talent; and this people, so careless of abstract truth, so apathetic to historical fact, so contemptuous of foreign ideas, will *ex animo* swear to the truth of a religion which indulges their natural turn of mind, and involves no severe thought or tedious application.[9]

The respect Newman showed public men—even those whose policies he opposed—was usually reciprocated. In a general preface to his political novels, Disraeli blamed the failure of Young England not on the misrepresentations of his Liberal opponents nor on the short-sightedness of the British electorate but on "the secession of Dr. Newman", which, he thought, "dealt a blow to the Church of England under which it still reels."[10] Newman's *Plain and Parochial Sermons* (1834–1843) inspired "supreme admiration" in Robert Cecil, Lord Salisbury. "For a conservative-minded young man with a feeling for history", his biographer Andrew Roberts pointed out, "Tractarianism was an intoxicating force, preaching a traditional creed with clarity and conviction and it was to provide the main spiritual and intellectual influence on Cecil's life."[11] Rosebery, Gladstone's protégé, revered Newman. Recalling a meeting with him at Norfolk House in 1880, when Newman was 79, he wrote: "He is much younger looking than his photographs, less wrinkled, has a deliciously soft voice and manner ... He said he was very gratified to me for the anxiety to see him ... I told him I had always had the *Apologia* in my room, at which he used even stronger expressions of courtly but genuine surprise."[12] Later, when Newman's body was laid out on the high altar of the Oratory Church in Birmingham, Rosebery wrote in his Journal, "This was the end of the young Calvinist, the Oxford don, the austere vicar of St. Mary's. It seemed as if a whole cycle of human thought and life were concentrated in that august repose. That was my overwhelming thought. Kindly light had led and guided Newman to this strange, brilliant end ..."[13] For Newman's influence at Oxford, Gladstone thought "there is no parallel in the academical history of Europe, unless you go back to the twelfth century or the University of Paris." That influence had played a considerable part in causing first his sister Helen and then his two dearest friends, Henry Manning and James Hope-Scott, to convert—or, to come "unfixed", as he liked to put it—but he could never discount it.[14] In a letter to Dean Church, Newman wrote, apropos the Liberal Prime Minister, "Gladstone is making up for the late savageness towards us, by eating up the Turks. Certainly I rejoice at it, though I doubt the prudence of a statesman committing himself to such a fancy as a sudden expulsion of the Turks from Europe. They were long in getting into Europe, and their expulsion must be gradual, except that in this time of the world things move much faster than they did centuries ago. As to G. I suppose he has given up party politics, and thinks he has a right to indulge himself in what is called sentiment. For myself, not being a politician I don't know enough, to be so terrified at Russia, as both Whigs and Tories are."[15] The only major Victorian Prime Minister who remained immune to Newman's spell was Palmerston, which was perhaps not surprising, since it was Palmerston, as Secretary for Foreign Affairs, who first received the ineffable Dr. Achilli into England, the Dominican apostate whose successful libel action set Newman back £12,000 in court costs.

Newman had not always shown magnanimity towards ministers of state. In 1829, he called Sir Robert Peel a "Rat" for abandoning his opposition to Catholic Emancipation and led the campaign at Oxford to unseat him as "unworthy to represent a religious, straightforward, unpolitical body, whose interests ... he had betrayed." When Peel's loss to Sir Robert Inglis was announced, Newman was exultant: "We have achieved a glorious Victory," he crowed. "We have proved the independence of the Church and of Oxford."[16] A few weeks before the Whigs pushed through the first Reform Bill, Newman was gloomy about what the consequences would be for the Established Church: "I dread above all things the pollution of such men as Lord Brougham affecting to lay a finger hand upon it. This vile Ministry. I cannot speak of them with patience." Afterwards, he was no less resigned: "As to the ministry, their conduct is so atrocious that it is almost out of the world's proceedings that they should escape without punishment."[17] A year later, in sunny Italy, he was still stewing: "I have (alas) experienced none of that largeness and expansion of mind, which one of my friends privately told me I should get from traveling—I cannot boast of any greater gift of philosophic coolness than before, and on reading the papers of the beginning and middle of February, hate the Whigs ... more bitterly than ever."[18]

Cardinal Manning called Newman a "great hater."[19] Newman hated Peel and Brougham because they were usurping the prerogatives of the Anglican Church and attempting to replace religion with rationalism, God's laws with political expedients. Of course, it was a futile fight. Newman was attempting to eradicate Erastianism from a Church Erastian to its very roots. Yet his quarrel with liberal reform extended beyond his solicitude for the autonomy of the English Church. In 1832, he wrote to S. F. Wood, his Oriel friend who later became a barrister: "I am willing to grant for argument's sake all that any sensible well-judging man may believe on the questions of reform but still ... the difference between this and that system is as *nothing* compared with the human will ... till the will be changed from evil to good, the difference of the results between two given systems will be imperceptible."[20] Or, as Johnson told Boswell: "Sir, most political schemes of human improvement are very laughable things."[21]

Newman might have deplored what he called the "gross, carnal, unbelieving world" but he recognized its power.[22] "Many persons openly defend the aim at rising in the world, and speak in applause of an honourable ambition as if the prizes of this world were from heaven," he wrote, "and the steps of this world's ladder were the ascent of Angels ... Others, again, consider that their duty lies simply in this,—in making money for their families ... Faith, hope, love, devotion, are mere names; some visible idol is taken as the substitute for God."[23] Newman could be full of eloquent contempt for such worldly enterprise:

> What have we, private Christians, to do with hopes and fears of earth, with schemes of change, the pursuit of novelties, or the dreams of reforms? The world is passing like a shadow: the day of Christ is hastening like a shadow: the day of Christ is hastening on. It is our wisdom, surely, to use what has been provided for us, instead of lusting after what we have not, asking flesh to eat, and gazing wistfully on Egypt, or on the heathen around us. Faith has no leisure to act the busy politician, to bring the world's language into the sacred fold, or to use the world's jealousies in a divine polity, to demand rights, to flatter the many, or to court the powerful. What is faith's highest wish and best enjoyment? A dying saint shall answer ...[24]

In the *Apologia Pro Vita Sua* (1864), looking back on his Tractarian polemics, Newman admitted to giving vent to a good deal of "fierceness" and "sport".[25] As a Catholic, he would treat his predominantly Protestant audiences to even more barbed provocation. Flannery O'Connor once said that to drive home realities to an audience resistant to them, the Catholic novelist had to be prepared to use strong methods. "When you can assume that your audience holds the same beliefs as you do, you can relax a little and use more ordinary means of talking to it; when you have to assume that it does not, then you have to make your vision apparent by shock—to the hard of hearing you shout, and for the almost-blind you draw large and startling figures."[26] In his sermon "The Religion of the Day" (1832), Newman let rip: "I do not shrink from uttering my firm conviction that it would be a gain to the country were it vastly more superstitious, more bigoted, more gloomy, more fierce in its religion than at present it shows itself to be."[27] In *Difficulties of Anglicans* (1850), he made a distinction fundamental to his whole reading of public life: the Church "aims at realities, the world at decencies." "Worship of comfort, decency, and social order" motivates the world, the Church "regards this world, and all that is in it, as mere shadows, as dust and ashes, compared to the value of one single soul." It follows, then, for the Church, that "unless she can, in her own way, do good to souls, it is no use her doing anything; she holds that it were better for sun and moon to drop from heaven, for the earth to fail, and for all the many millions who are upon it to die of starvation in extremest agony, so far as temporal affliction goes, than that one soul, I will not say, should be lost, but should commit one single venial sin …"[28] One can only imagine how that went down with his Anglican audience.

Battening as it did on periodicals for which it was axiomatic that the Catholic Church was backward, repressive, superstitious and corrupt, such an audience would have found Newman unsympathetic in any case. Newman responded by charging that these periodicals flattered the Englishman's intellectual pride, his conviction that since 'an Englishman's house is his castle' … it followed that "he himself is the ultimate sanction and appellate authority of all he holds" and that those holding contrary views—namely, Roman Catholics—were "irrational and ludicrous." In one of his sermons, Newman called attention to the routine distortion of religion even in publications favorable to religion:

> Look round upon … our periodical publications: is it not too plain to need a word of proof, that religion is in the main honoured because it tends to make this life happier, and is expedient for the preservation of our persons, property, advantages, and position in the world? … whether we will believe it or no, the truth remains, that the strength of the Church … does not lie in earthly law, or human countenance, or civil station, but in her proper gifts; in those great gifts which our Lord pronounced to be beatitudes. Blessed are the poor in spirit, the mourners, the meek, the thirsters after righteousness, the merciful, the pure in heart, the peacemakers, the persecuted.[29]

The idea of religion as little more than an engine of philanthropy is now widely embraced but Newman rejected it as an idolatry set up to gratify moral vanity. For him, the point of religion was not to make us happier, healthier, richer or more philanthropic but to bind us to the will of God.

In the *Apologia* Newman listed propositions of the liberal faith that he had "denounced and abjured" as leader of the Oxford Movement. One of them was "Virtue is the child of knowledge, and vice of ignorance. Therefore, e.g. education, periodical literature, railroad traveling, ventilation, drainage, and the arts of life, when fully carried out, serve to make a population moral and happy."[30] In *The Tamworth Reading Room* (1841), Newman exposed what he thought the folly of this proposition in an attack on Sir Robert Peel's scheme for endowing a library for the working classes from which books of divinity would be excluded. The series of letters first appeared in *The Times* and reaffirms his conviction that religion alone makes moral reform possible by reforming the will. "The problem for statesmen of this age is how to educate the masses, and literature and science cannot give the solution … You do not get rid of vice by human expedients ... If virtue be a mastery over mind, if its end be action, if its perfection be inward order, harmony, and peace, we must seek it in graver and holier places than libraries and reading rooms."[31] In *The Idea of a University* (1873), for which *The Tamworth Reading Room* can be seen as a trial run, he put the case more powerfully still: "Quarry the granite rock with razors, or moor the vessel with a thread of silk; then may you hope with such keen and delicate instruments as human knowledge and human reason to contend against those giants, the passion and the pride of man."[32]

Newman may have disputed the moral efficacy of education but never its utility. Too often educators dismiss Newman's ideas on education as impracticable. On finishing reading *The Idea of a University*, Roy Jenkins, the former Oxford Chancellor, confessed that the book left him "dazzled but intellectually unsatisfied. Newman had mostly held me spellbound in the grip of his prose, but he had convinced me neither that he had a practical plan for an Irish university in the 1850s or that he had left guidelines of great relevance for a university of any nationality or any or no faith today."[33] Yet the Catholic gentleman that Newman wished to form is as needed today as he was in the 1850s and anything but impractical. "The man who has learned to think and to reason and to compare and to discriminate and to analyze, who has refined his taste, and formed his judgment, and sharpened his mental vision, will not indeed at once be a lawyer, or a pleader, or an orator, or a statesman, or a physician, or a good landlord, or a man of business, or a soldier, or an engineer, or a chemist, or a geologist ... but he will be placed in the sciences or callings I have referred to, or any other for which he has a taste or special talent, with an ease, a grace, a versatility, and a success, to which another is a stranger ... In this sense ... mental culture is emphatically *useful*."[34]

All too often, Newman felt, liberal periodicals, which had another idea of utility in mind, were corrupting this mental culture. The politician and law reformer Henry Brougham, whom Newman took to task in *The Tamworth Reading Room*, was a frequent contributor to the liberal *Edinburgh Review* and one of the founders of that 'godless place in Gower Street,' London University. Sidney Smith, a friend of Brougham's, was another contributor to the *Edinburgh Review*, and no fan of the Oxford Movement. In a letter to Lady Davy he wrote: "I have not yet discovered of what I am to die, but I rather believe I shall be burnt alive by the Puseyites. Nothing so remarkable in England as the progress of these foolish people. I have no conception what they mean, if it be not to revive every absurd ceremony, and every antiquated folly ..."[35] Yet Newman was himself a journalist and worked to balance both the liberal and the conservative points of view that he encountered in the public square.

In a *Rambler* article on "Policy of English Catholics towards Political Parties," published in 1859, he wrote: "It is an absurdity to talk of an alliance of Catholics with Conservatives, or Whigs, or Liberals, or Progressists; unless, and so long as, any one of these parties takes upon itself the championship of Catholic grievances, and the other parties combine to perpetuate them." Class was another factor. "The Wesleyans, the Quakers, the Unitarians, for the most part belong to one class in society; it is natural that their political, social, and secular interests should be the same. It is not so with Catholics ... [The Catholic Church] has specimens of every class in the community, of high and low, rich and poor, learned and unlearned. The children of Whigs and Tories, the families of high-church dignitaries, the heirs of great territorial possessions, professional men, high-born ladies, agriculture, trade, manufactures, the shop-keepers of towns, mechanics, peasants, the poor, the indigent—they all meet together in our religious pale." Nowhere is this more vividly illustrated than in Newman's letters.

Many of the least discriminating of Newman's commentators continue to claim him for the liberal or the conservative camp. Ian Ker, in his many books on Newman, including his great biography, demonstrates that Newman is both liberal and conservative, and neither. In *Newman and the Fullness of Christianity* (1993), he remarks how "The theological office of the Church ... may find itself in opposition to both the ... political and pastoral offices. And Newman does not hesitate to say that at times it will have to give way ... If a deference to theological inquiry is the essence of a liberal Christian, then to that extant Newman is a liberal. But where he is not a liberal is in asserting that the theological is not the only office of the Church and that at times it has to play a subordinate office. Newman eludes the usual categories of liberal and conservative."[36]

In the *Apologia*, Newman defined the tenets of liberalism to which he objected: "that truth and falsehood in religion are but matter of opinion; that one doctrine is as good as another; that the Governor of the world does not intend that we should gain the truth; that there is no truth; that we are not more acceptable to God by believing this than by believing that; that no one is answerable for his opinions; that they are a matter of necessity or accident; that it is enough if we sincerely hold what we profess; that our merit lies in seeking, not in possessing; that is a duty to follow what seems to us true, without fear lest it should not be true; that it may be a gain to succeed, and can be no harm to fail; that we may take up and lay down opinions at pleasure; that belief belongs to the mere intellect, not to the heart also; that we may safely trust to ourselves in matters of Faith, and need no other guide ..."[37]

Although no Tory, Newman thought alliances between Catholics and the Conservative party a good thing if they served Catholic interests. In the *Rambler* in July 1859, he acknowledged the cynical incredulity that met one such alliance under Lord Derby's administration: "Nothing is so little tolerated by the public as the pretence that any one acts on so impossible a motive as pure philanthropy." Cardinal Wiseman canvassed Derby to provide Catholic chaplains for Catholics in workhouses and jails. When Derby agreed, Wiseman gave him his support. (Wiseman reviewed Mayhew's *London Labour and London Poor* when it first came out in 1851 and was well informed about the plight of London's poor.)[38] Newman wrote a memorable poem for prisoners, which shows his characteristic sympathy for the outcast.

> Help, Lord, the souls which Thou hast made,
>   The souls to Thee so dear,
> In prison for the debt unpaid
>   Of sins committed here.

> Oh, by their patience of delay,
>   Their hope amid their pain,
> Their sacred zeal to burn away
>   Disfigurement and stain;
> Oh, by their fire of love, not less
>   In keenness than the flame,
> Oh, by their very helplessness,
>   Oh, by Thy own great Name,
> Good Jesu, help! Sweet Jesu, aid
>   The souls to Thee most dear
> In prison, for their debt unpaid
>   Of sins committed here.[39]

Yet, while Newman was prepared to support the Tories when they were willing to advance the purposes of the Church, he was always leery of conservatism. While he recognized that "The Roman Pontiffs owe their exaltation to the secular power and have a great stake in its stability and prosperity ... [and] cannot bear anarchy ... think revolution an evil ... pray for the peace of the world and the prosperity of all Christian States, and ... effectively support the cause of order and good government," he also saw that "the Pope never is, and cannot be" conservative in the party sense of the word, for that "means a man who is at the top of the tree, and knows it, and means never to come down, whatever it may cost him to keep his place there. It means a man who upholds government and society and the existing state of things ... not because it is good and desirable, because it is established, because it is a benefit to the population, because it is full of promise for the future,—but rather because he himself is well off in consequence of it, and because to take care of number one is his main political principle. It means a man who defends religion, not for religion's sake, but for the sake of its accidents and externals; and in this sense Conservative a Pope can never be, without a simple betrayal of the dispensation committed to him."[40] The Conservative politician who profited most from defending religion "for the sake of its accidents and externals" was Disraeli, whom Newman rarely supported, though he must often have preferred Disraeli's "suet pudding legislation," as one Conservative MP characterized it, to Gladstone's wild liberalism—"it was flat, insipid, dull but ... very wise and very wholesome."[41]

In weighing in on the Gladstone and Disraeli question that has set so many undergraduates scribbling over the years, Newman revealed his fundamental skepticism about the claims of political liberals and conservatives alike: "I confess I am much perplexed between Mr. Disraeli and Mr. Gladstone. Gladstone is a man of personal religion, and has been so from a boy; Disraeli is a man of the world, a politician, and in thought and in belief as much a Jew as he is Christian. On the other hand he is the representative of all the old traditions which Tories used to cherish and the Pope at this time represents [this was written in April 1872], while Gladstone is the leader of a mixed multitude, who profess a Babel of religions or none at all. I never can feel respect for Mr. Disraeli's self—I never can hold fellowship with Gladstone's tail."[42] At the same time, it was characteristic of Newman to admit to his old friend, Frederic Rogers, later Lord Blachford, "If I was brought into the House of Lords, I should have just the same hang dog look as Disraeli. It is a comfort to have discovered a point of sympathy with a man I do not like."[43] Nevertheless, in the wake of Disraeli's triumph at the Congress of Berlin in June 1878, which countered the gains Russia made at the end of the Russo-Turkish War with the treaty of San Stefano and inspired Bismarck's famous remark *Der alte Jude, das ist der Mann*, Newman applauded Disraeli's repulse of panslavism, despite the fact that both Dean Church and Lord Blachford deplored it. "As to Disraeli's fine work," Newman wrote to Blachford, "I confess I am much dazzled with it, and wish it well. It is a grand idea ... hugging from love the Turk to death, instead of the Russian bear, which, as a poem or romance, finds a weak part in my imagination. And then it opens such a view of England, great in the deeds of their forefathers, showing that they are not degenerate sons, but rising with the occasion in fulfilment of the 'Tu ne cede malis, sed contra audentior ito.' And then it is so laughably clever a move, in a grave diplomatic congress – and then it opens such wonderful views of the future, that I am overcome by it. Nor do I see the hypocrisy you speak of."[44]

The Latin motto here—'Do not give into evil but proceed ever more boldly against it'—is from Virgil (*Aeneid*, VI, 95). It is also the motto of the Ludwig von Mises Institute, which was founded in 1982 "to undermine statism in all its forms," a mission which would have met with Newman's wholehearted approval. In 1834, he wrote an open letter to the *British Magazine* on the topic of centralization—statism in embryo—and in the letter he remarked how "It must be evident to any one who looks ever so little into the political transactions of the day, that the principle of centralization is steadily working its way into the various departments of our national system." While Newman conceded that the principle was not entirely unwelcome in all cases, he recognized how "it seems to have been a characteristic of the British constitution hitherto ... to view the principle with jealousy, as hostile in its tendency to the liberty of the subject ..." For proof of this, Newman asked his readers to consider "the story of the foreigner's surprise on finding Waterloo Bridge was built, not by the government, but by individuals" or the fact "that our received English dictionary is the work of an individual ... or that our theatres and travelling are left to private speculation; or that our magistrates are unpaid; or that our East India empire was acquired by a mercantile company. On the other hand, the late numerous Commissions, the Education Board in Ireland, the Metropolitan Police, the Poor Law Amendment Bill, are all evidence of the growing popularity of the centralizing system." For Newman, this new appetite for centralization "has been the means of throwing us into the strange inconsistency of advocating a principle almost of tyranny, in the management of hitherto private matters, at the very time we were exulting in the triumph of a great Reform measure, which was to supersede the necessity of a government, and to make the House of Commons, and so the people, their own rulers. But in truth the inconsistency is but apparent; the destruction of local influences which centralization involves, and the disorganization of the parliament, as the

seat and instrument of the administration, alike tending to the aggrandizement
of the executive, as the main-spring of all national power, and virtually identical
with the government."[45] Here was a prescient response to the creeping centralization that would eventually culminate in the British nanny state.

If Newman declined to march under the banner of party, he was never shy
of holding politicians to account for policies he found reprehensible. Indeed, on
whether priests should feel free to criticize public men, he could not have been
more forthright:

> It is sometimes said ... that a clergyman should have nothing to do with
> politics. This is true, if it be meant that he ... should not side with a political
> party as such, should not be ambitious of popular applause, or the favour
> of great men, should not take pleasure and lose time in business of this
> world, should not be covetous. But if it means that he should not express
> an opinion and exert an influence one way rather than another, it is plainly
> unscriptural ... *If*, indeed, this world's concerns could be altogether disjoined
> from those of Christ's Kingdom, then indeed all Christians (laymen as well
> as clergy) should abstain from the thought of temporal affairs, and let the
> worthless world pass down the stream of events till it perishes; but if (as is
> the case) what happens in *nations* must affect the cause of *religion* in those
> nations, since the Church may be seduced and corrupted by the world, and
> in the world there are myriads of souls to be converted and saved, and since
> a Christian nation is bound to become part of the Church, therefore it is our
> duty to stand as a beacon on a hill, to cry aloud and spare not, to lift up our
> voice like a trumpet, and show the people their transgression, and the house
> of Jacob their sins.[46]

In his *Letter to His Grace the Duke of Norfolk* (1875), Newman proved
his readiness to take Gladstone to task for his misrepresentations of papal
infallibility and the loyalty of English Catholics. In *The Vatican Decrees in
their Bearing on Civil Allegiance: An Expostulation* (1874), Gladstone, under
the mischievous tutelage of Dollinger and Acton, had impugned the loyalty
of English Catholics and claimed, apropos the Church, that "no one can
become her convert without renouncing his moral and mental freedom."[47] The
pamphlet sold 150,000 copies. Newman disposed of Gladstone's calumnies
with remarkable forbearance. It is true that he was more interested in repudiating Ultramontanism than remonstrating with Gladstone but nevertheless
he showed admirable restraint. William Ullathorne, Newman's bishop in
Birmingham, was considerably less restrained in his response. "It is something
new and strange to maintain that the Church has no right to expostulate
with the world at large, whilst the world at large has a right to expostulate
with the Church," this forthright Yorkshireman wrote. "The title itself of the
Expostulation involves a false assumption, and expresses the fundamental error
of the book. *The Vatican Decrees* have no *bearing on civil allegiance* ..."[48]

The tendency of public men to oversimplify complex issues, as Gladstone
certainly did in his inflammatory pamphlet, was as common in Newman's day

as it is in our own. In the *Grammar of Assent* (1870), Newman wrote of the similar tendency to think in stereotypes in a way that recalls his own fuzzy notions of the Catholic Church before he converted: "I suppose most men will recollect in their past years how many mistakes they have made about persons, parties, local occurrences, nations and the like, of which at the time they had no actual knowledge of their own: how ashamed or how amused they have become since ... they came into possession of the real facts concerning them ... Thus, we must have cold and selfish Scots, crafty Italians, vulgar Americans, and Frenchmen, half tiger, half monkey ... Those who are old enough to recollect the wars with Napoleon, know what eccentric notions were popularly entertained about them in England; how it was even a surprise to find some military man, who was a prisoner of war, to be tall and stout, because it was the received idea that all Frenchmen were undersized and lived on frogs."[49] After converting, Newman found the real Church a revelation. "I gazed at her ... as a great objective fact. I looked ... at her rites, her ceremonial, and her precepts; and I said, 'This *is* a religion' ..."[50] Later, he told his friend James Hope-Scott: "I have not had a single doubt, or temptation to doubt, ever since I became a Catholic ... My great temptation is to be at *peace* ..."[51]

Newman's idea of public life is of a powerful simplicity. If public life is not rooted in love of God, in service to God, it is rooted in idolatry, and where the visible idol replaces the unseen God, falsehood, heartbreak and unreality follow. This is the essential truth of Newman's animadversions on public life. It is an uncompromising truth, though not a particularly novel one. Even Matthew Arnold, the inspector of schools, realized that:

> the world, which seems
> To lie before us like a land of dreams,
> So various, so beautiful, so new,
> Hath really neither joy, nor love, nor light,
> Nor certitude, nor peace, nor help for pain ...[52]

Newman could have been addressing Arnold directly—or anyone in public life—when he said: "The world ... praises public men, if they are useful to itself, but simply ridicules inquiry into their motives ... All public men it considers to be pretty much the same at bottom; but what matter is that ... if they do its work? It offers high pay, and it expects faithful service; but, as to its agents, overseers, men of business, operatives, journeymen, figure-servants, and labourers, what they are personally, what are their principles and aims, what their creed, what their conversation; where they live, how they spend their leisure time, whither they are going, how they die—I am stating a simple matter of fact, I am not here praising or blaming, I am but contrasting,—I say, all questions implying the existence of the soul, are as much beyond the circuit of the world's imagination, as they are intimately and primarily present to the apprehension of the Church."[53]

For Newman, people in public life were not abstractions, not "workhouse apprentices" but children of God with immortal souls. And as such, they were accountable; they faced a reckoning. "Observe in the parable," Newman reminded his Birmingham parishioners, "the Master of the Vineyard did but one thing ... He did but ask *what had they done*. He did not ask what their opinion was about science, or about art, or about the means of wealth, or about public affairs ... They were not required to know how many kinds of vines there were in the world, and what countries vines could grow in, and where they could not. They were not called upon to give their opinion what soils were best for the vines. They were not examined in the minerals, or the shrubs ... this was the sole question—whether they had *worked* in the vineyard."[54]

The words of St. John haunt nearly everything Newman wrote about what ought to be the relation between religion and public life: "The world passeth away; and the lust thereof, but he that doeth the will of God abideth for ever." That it is possible to be in the world but not of the world is one of Newman's great themes. He means always to persuade his audience that the will of God can be done, indeed must be done in public life. This is not to say that he shared Gladstone's "great object" of "religionizing the State."[55] On the contrary, he approved of the separation of Church and State. Towards the end of his life, in an address to the Catholic Union of Great Britain, he said: "I think the best favour which Sovereigns, Parliaments, municipalities, and other political powers can do us is to let us alone." But he was adamant that public men cannot leave their religion behind them when they enter public life. There is not one vineyard for religion and another for public life. In this, he follows St. Francis de Sales, who held passionately that "It is a mistake, a heresy, to want to exclude devoutness of life from among soldiers, from shops and offices, from royal courts, from the homes of the married." It may be true that "to touch politics is to touch pitch."[56] It may be true that a life of money-getting distracts us from religion, "from the constant whirl of business."[57] It is impossible "to recount the manifold and complex corruption which man has introduced into the world ..."[58] Yet "the abuse of good things is no argument against the things themselves."[59] Indeed, "things that do not admit of abuse have very little life in them."[60] In his moving funeral oration for his friend Hope-Scott, whom Newman extolled as a model of Catholic public life, he recalled that "He was one of those rare men who do not merely give a tithe of their increase to their God; he was a fount of generosity ever flowing." His building of churches, his acts of kindness to poor converts, single women, and sick priests proved that he was indeed "the steward of Him who had given what he gave away ... the steward of One to whom he must give account. He had deep within him that gift which St. Paul and St. John speak of, when they enlarge upon the characteristics of faith. It was the gift of faith, of a living, loving faith, such as 'overcomes the world' by seeking a 'better country, that is a heavenly.' This it was that kept him so 'unspotted from the world' in the midst of worldly engagements ..."[61] Living, loving faith amidst worldly engagements: this was Newman's idea of public life.

CHAPTER 6

Newman and the Female Faithful

If Newman's correspondence is the record of an immense epistolary apostolate that spanned nearly seventy years, the pastoral letters he sent to his female correspondents are some of the best he ever wrote. The women to whom he wrote are not, on the whole, household names. Most of them do not have entries in the *Oxford Dictionary of National Biography* or even its Catholic equivalents, the biographical dictionaries of Gillow or Boase. Some, like Geraldine Penrose Fitzgerald, Lady Chatterton and Lady Georgiana Fullerton, were authors, but even these are largely forgotten and their writings only remembered for their historical interest. (Fitzgerald inspired an amusing response from Newman when she sent him one of her books: "I have begun your story," he told her, "and it reads very well, with more ease and flow than your earlier Tales. But I dread what is to come. Old men do not like tragedy or sensation."[1]) Those who were well known in their own day because of their rank, such as the convert peeresses Lady Lothian and the Duchess of Norfolk, are now only known to the historian or the devoté of Burke's Peerage. Newman's first circle of female correspondents left few memorials; the only reason why Mary Holmes, the governess, or Elizabeth Bowden, the wife of Newman's closest friend at Oxford, or Maria Giberne, an old family friend who would go on to become a Visitationist nun, are known to posterity is because Newman befriended them.[2] And yet his friendships with these and other women were some of the deepest he formed, and his letters to them and theirs to him document how deeply they shared the faith for which they sacrificed so much. In the chapter that follows, I shall look at this rich correspondence to show how sympathetic Newman was to the unique difficulties that Catholic women faced in Protestant England. I shall also show how some of his correspondence sheds light on his published writings. And, lastly, I shall show how his affinity with women often brought out the best in him.

Something of Newman's understanding of women stemmed from his early childhood. With no members of his family was he closer than with his mother and sisters. In a letter to his mother, written when he was 21, he gave heartfelt expression to this special bond.

> I am indeed encompassed with blessings for which I never can be properly thankful, but the greatest of them is so dear and united a home. If your fear

is, lest my jesting letters to Harriett should unconsciously be written half in earnest, I can only protest, that however other places may agree with me, I am not in my own proper element when I am away from you and my sisters. Land animals may plunge into the water and swim about in it, but they cannot live in it; and, even for the short space they were in it, they must still drink in the air.[3]

As a result of the female nurturing he had received as a child, Newman would always prize the sympathy and support he received from women, whether cradle Catholics, converts, nuns, or those in-between women, whom he called "nunnish ladies."[4] Isaac Williams once observed that Newman "never seemed to me so saintlike and high in his character as when he was with his mothers and sisters ..."[5] In 1844, a couple of months before he resigned his Oriel fellowship, he wrote to his Aunt Elizabeth of his grandmother's house in Fulham where he had spent so many memorable days in his childhood: "Whatever good there is in me, I owe, under grace, to the time I spent in that house, and to you and my Grandmother, its inhabitants."[6] To Sister Mary Gabriel du Boulay (1826–1906), whom he received into the Church in 1850, prior to her joining the Dominican Nuns at Stone in Staffordshire, he confided the trials he had undergone in writing the *Apologia*. "I have done a book of 562 pages, all at a heat; but with so much suffering, such profuse crying, such long spells of work, sometimes 16 hours, once 22 hours at once, that it is a prodigious awful marvel that I have got through it ... you must go on praying that I may not feel the bad effects of such a strain on me afterwards."[7] It is clear from his correspondence that women put him at ease in ways that men did not, which gave his pastoral letters to women an extraordinary candor and depth. It is also striking how often he chose to confide in his female correspondents about matters that concerned him most. In 1863, at what was perhaps the nadir of his personal life, when he felt misunderstood not only in England but also in Rome, when he might have said with Charlotte Bronte's Mr. Rochester, "fortune has knocked me about ... she has even kneaded me with her knuckles, and now I flatter myself I am hard and tough as an India rubber ball,"[8] he wrote to Emily Bowles:

This age of the Church is peculiar – in former times, primitive and medieval, there was not the extreme centralization which now is in use. If a private theologian said any thing free, another answered him. If the controversy grew, then it went to a Bishop, a theological faculty, or to some foreign University. The Holy See was but the court of ultimate appeal. Now, if I, as a private priest, put any thing into print, Propaganda answers me at once. How can I fight with such a chain on my arm? It is like the Persians driven on to fight under the lash. There was true private judgment in the primitive and medieval schools – there are no schools now, no private judgment (in the religious sense of the phrase), no freedom, that is, of opinion. That is, no exercise of the intellect. No, the system goes on by the tradition of the intellect of former times. This is a way of things which, in God's own time, will work its own cure, of necessity; nor need we fret under a state of things, much as we may feel it, which is incomparably less painful than the state of the Church before Hildebrand, and again in the fifteenth century.[9]

Newman wrote this, in part, in response to Miss Bowles's urging him to play some greater part in the life of the Church in London. Whenever prodded in this way, Newman demurred, knowing that he could be more effective by remaining at his desk in Edgbaston. He also felt called on by his patron to resist involving himself unduly in public affairs. "We are not better than our Fathers …" he wrote to her. "The Cardinal Vicar called Philip, to his face and in public, an ambitious party man, and suspended his faculties. It is by bearing these things that we gain merit …" When Newman ended by noting, "I never wrote such a letter to any one yet, and I shall think twice before I send you the whole of it," he confirmed the extent to which he chose to take Miss Bowles into his confidence. A week later, he confided in her how he saw his life as a Catholic at a time when even the newspapers were speculating that he might be contemplating returning to Protestantism, a rumor which prompted him to write to the Editor of the *Morning Advertiser*: "I have not, and never have had, any desire or intention whatever of leaving the Church of Rome, or of becoming a Protestant again …"[10] His letter to Miss Bowles is also of interest because it serves as something of a prelude to his autobiography: six months later, he would be embroiled in the Kingsley controversy and preparing to write the *Apologia*.

> Sometimes I seem to myself inconsistent, in professing to love retirement, yet seeming impatient at doing so little; yet I trust I am not so in any very serious way. In my letter to the Bishop of Oxford, on occasion of Number 90, I said that I had come forward, because no one else had done so, and that I rejoiced to return to that privacy which I valued more than any thing else. When I became a Catholic, I considered I never should even write again, except on definite unexciting subjects, such as history and philosophy and criticism; and, if on controversial subjects, still not on theology proper. And when I came here, where I have been for 14 years, I deliberately gave myself to a life of obscurity, which in my heart I love best. And so it has been, and so it is now, that the routine work of each day is in fact more than enough for my thoughts and my time. I have no leisure. I have had to superintend two successive enlargements of our Church, to get the Library in order, to devote a good deal of pains to our music, and a great deal more to our accounts. Then, there was my Dublin engagement, and now there is the School …[11]

Newman was not complaining of the way his Catholic life had unfolded. "I am not only content, but really pleased that so things are." Still, being so capable a man, he would always have concerns as to whether he was using his talents properly. "First, lest my being where I am is my own doing in any measure, for then I say, 'Perhaps I am hiding my talent in a napkin.' Next, people say to me, 'why are you not doing more? how much you could do!' and then, since I think I could do a great deal, if I were let to do it, I become uneasy. And lastly, willing as I am to observe St Philip's dear rule that 'we should despise being despised,' yet when I find that scorn and contempt become the means of *my Oratory being injured*, as they have before now, then I get impatient." Aware that he was speaking with unusual candor, he signed off: "Now observe, the letter of which I send you ... is a freer one *than I ever wrote to any one before.*"[12]

Emily Bowles (1818–1904), or Miss Bowles as Newman always called her, was the devout, outspoken, ardent sister of Frederick Bowles, the Tractarian convert with whom Newman was received into the Church and who joined the Oratory for a time before moving on to the Isle of Wight and Harrow. Miss Bowles's family was well-to-do and came from Abingdon in Berkshire, where they lived next to the Eystons, an old recusant family, who were descendants of Sir Thomas More. Miss Bowles first met Newman in 1840 when she was 22 and he was 39. A fine-boned, petite, vivacious woman with piercing eyes, she was received into the Catholic Church in Rome in 1843. When they first met, Newman must have seen in her something of his own independence of mind. Appropriately enough, it was another independent figure, Cardinal Charles Acton (1803–1847), the doyen of the English College, who received her into the Church, after his mother took her under her wing.

Miss Bowles was not only a devout but a sociable woman. In one letter, she described for Newman an evening party she attended at 72 Eaton Place, the home of the liberal politician and convert, Sir John Simeon, a good friend of Newman's and a staunch supporter of the Oratory School:

> I was there last night, to a great assembly to meet Tennyson – whom I was very glad to see and know. Otherwise it was painful. Mr Lecky was there whose "Morals" [*History of European Morals* (1869)] you have no doubt seen – and who is certainly a remarkable man – 25 – and looking like a lank-gawky, dreamy boy. He was introduced to me – but he came in late – and I did not say much. He said he was tired of hearing and reading strictures on his book. He is very interesting to me – pure minded and good evidently – having no belief – no ground of standing – no certainty of comparing – seeking God and finding Him only in glimpses – says conscience is the only guide – and wrongdoing only hindering self progress. I felt the greatest pain to see that soul – on the threshold of life – with a ship freighted out with such gifts – without compass or rudder. There were two girls friends of his, who say they would give the world to believe there was anything beyond this life – but have no belief ... . And poor Louy [Louisa Simeon, Sir John's daughter, with whom Newman also corresponded] – looking so bright and noble – in the midst of all this throng of half-unbelieving protestants half unCatholic Catholics. Surely Sir John is not wise to drift into this seething mass of doubtful society – and take this child with him?[13]

Here one gets a good glimpse into Miss Bowles's delight in people, her eye for social comedy, her deep but never sanctimonious faith, and her critical acumen. W. E. H. Lecky (1838–1903), the brilliant historian of eighteenth-century Ireland, never did feel comfortable in society and his lack of faith trapped him in a Victorian skepticism he never transcended.[14] And she was right about Tennyson: his table-talk was full of charm. Recalling his peculiarly rhapsodic juvenilia, Tennyson told one dinner companion: "At about twelve and onwards I wrote an epic of six thousand lines à la Walter Scott—full of battles, dealing too with sea and mountain scenery—with Scott's regularity of octo-syllables and his occasional varieties. Though the performance was very likely worth nothing I never felt myself more truly inspired. I wrote as much as seventy lines at one time, and used to go shouting them about the fields in the dark."[15] One can easily imagine the lover of poetry in Miss Bowles delighting in such reminiscences. When she first read Newman's verses, they struck her as "startling oracles or newly discovered inscriptions in a strange character," utterly different from what she described as the "running water" of Keble's verses.[16] Like many young English Protestant women inclined to Rome, she was also deeply moved by Emily Agnew's *Geraldine: A Tale of Conscience* (1837), which vividly described the heroine embarking on the religious life:

> Amongst her numerous sister-novices, Geraldine found exemplified the effects of the admirable instructions they received from the spiritual lectures and exhortations of mother Juliana … . In all the novices, was marked the endeavour to guard those doors by which the interior life is molested; no one relating, or willingly hearing, news of the world she had left; and no one being occupied with any soul but her own; each being responsible, under God, to her mistress alone; and bound to give each other the edification only of silent example. Thus, in holy silence and peace, each soul was hidden with Christ; or, as it is of novices we spoke, it was her prayer and aim to be thus hidden: for … during the noviciate the greatest warfare takes place between nature and grace … The sensibilities and little artifices of self-love—the desire that the poor should recognise, and feel grateful, to one's individual self—the wish to relate with credit to one's self, at the recreation, some interesting scene—chagrin at being no longer sent to the places where one had become so useful, and so popular,—all this had passed; for the true spouse of Christ had long realized the truth that "all that is not God is nothing!" and insensible to the popular voice of praise or blame, to the gratitude or ingratitude of the object relieved, to the interior satisfaction or difficulty experienced in the path of duty, walks simply with her God, disregarding everything that would lift the idol self on the altar raised in her heart to Him alone.[17]

For a well-to-do Anglican woman, brought up on the decorous pieties of what Thackeray once called "Church of Englandism," this was a religion from a different world and Miss Bowles was deeply drawn to it. That she emulated Geraldine by joining a convent and ministering to female prisoners shows what a direct personal impact the book had on her. *Geraldine* may also have influenced Newman. He reviewed the book for the *British Critic* and although he noted its amateurism and theological errors, he also praised its characters for being "amusingly drawn."

> There is a religious indifferentist, with a sufficient insight into the absurdities of the popular ways of thought, a hankering after Catholicity, and a

kindness towards the imaginative parts of Romanism; a Whig lord enduring Protestantism and Romanism, yet attached to neither; a High-Church Oxford divine; a Reformation-Society Protestant; a pert young lady inclined to the Presbyterian persuasion; and a parish clergyman of the modern school, amiable, active, uxorious and absurd.[18]

It is difficult reading this without wondering whether Newman wrote *Loss and Gain*, in part, as a kind of Oxonian *Geraldine*, one which would "recommend the Roman Catholic religion to the English Protestant" but in a more substantial, truer, wittier way. It is also worth pointing out that when Newman wrote his review in July 1837, he was still committed to promulgating the via media. Consequently, the pro-Roman moral of *Geraldine* was not one for which he could muster much sympathy. "It is impatience and a sinful impatience," he declared, "to go out of the English Church for what every believing mind may find in it." And here he made the argument for staying put that Keble and Pusey would make repeatedly after Newman abandoned the Church of England. "The capabilities of our actual state, in the hands of any individual who is moved to use them, are so great, that, putting duty out of the question, it is great inconsiderateness to require more than is given us ... We have the high doctrines of the Sacraments, Apostolical Succession, Confession, Absolution, Penance, Fasts, Festivals, the daily Service, all recognized as existing ordinances; what do we want but the will to bring into existence what the Prayer Book contains ..."[19]

When Miss Bowles met Newman at Littlemore, which Matthew Arnold described as "a mean house such as Paul might have lived in when he was tent-making at Ephesus," she recalled how "One face, grand, reticent, powerful both in speaking and at rest, and slightly forbidding ... detached itself from the rest and remained for ever stamped on my mind."[20] She also recalled "the awful sense of the Invisible Presence which he [Newman] brought among us." With these exalted notions in her head, she was taken aback when the Vicar of St. Mary's turned to her and asked, "Will you have some cold chicken?" Invariably, Newman's unaffected simplicity baffled his more romantic admirers. Later, in the 1860s, Miss Bowles returned to Littlemore and reported back to Newman: "The trees have grown up, now making the churchyard a shady grove—and there I stood in your place—calling up all the words I had heard— the voice that had shown me the way of salvation .... The bells seemed to bring you constantly before me ..."[21] And yet she also recalled that when she and the Catholic Eystons saw him that day they were convinced that he would never become a Catholic himself. Doubtless Miss Bowles had read Newman's review of *Geraldine* in the *British Critic* and recalled his claiming that it would be "nothing but sinful impatience to go out of the English Church for what every believing mind may find in it." Moreover, on that day in Littlemore in 1840, Newman did not appear preoccupied or distraught. Over twenty years later, when she read his account of his true condition at that time in the *Apologia*, she was amazed to learn of "what anguish and travail of the soul lay hidden ... beneath that calm face and voice of utter serenity."[22]

After converting, Miss Bowles joined Cornelia Connelly's Society of the Holy Child and accompanied her to the opening of the Society's first Convent at Derby. Later she was sent to Liverpool as superior to found a convent and school. There she purchased property for the Society without Connelly's approval with money borrowed from her brothers, which drove the Society into serious debt. Consequently, Connolly and Bowles fell out and never reconciled. Once Bishop Goss of Liverpool relieved Miss Bowles of her vows, she left the Society. Joyce Sugg, in her excellent book, *Ever Yours Affly: John Henry Newman and his Female Circle*, demonstrates that in the bitter financial row that followed, Miss Bowles was clearly in the wrong, though it has to be said that she did pay for her poor judgment by losing her own patrimony as well.[23] After leaving Connelly's new order, Emily returned to London, where she set herself up in lodgings in Mayfair at No. 2 South Street, not far from Farm Street, "in those reduced circumstances of the Victorian age," as Meriol Trevor noted, "which admitted of her keeping a servant."[24] When Newman came to visit in 1865, she sat him down in her drawing room, which, as she recalled, "he seemed to fill with his sweet dignity, the singular charm of his majestic simplicity and the magic of his voice."[25]

Another frequent visitor to Miss Bowles's South Street lodgings was Lady Georgiana Fullerton, the author of two of the most celebrated religious novels in nineteenth-century England, *Ellen Middleton* (1844), which dramatized the need for confession, and *Grantley Manor* (1847), a more explicitly Catholic book, which treated of a secret Protestant–Catholic marriage. Lady Georgiana Leveson-Gower, the daughter of the 1st Earl Granville, and Lady Harriet Leveson-Gower, second daughter of William Cavendish, fifth duke of Devonshire, was born at the very pinnacle of the aristocracy at Tixall Hall in Staffordshire. Her grandmother, after whom she was named, was that beautiful Georgiana, Duchess of Devonshire, the friend of Fox, Sheridan and Marie Antoinette, of whom Gainsborough and Sir Joshua Reynolds painted so many magnificent portraits. It is strange to think of the devout Lady Georgiana descended from this other Georgiana, who was so insatiably fond of drink, cards and party politics. Yet the passion and the dedication that the one gave to the gaming table, the other gave to the care of Christ's poor. Lady Georgiana's father also had something of the eighteenth-century Duchess in his make-up. The intimate friend of Canning, he served as ambassador at Paris from 1834 to 1843 but was so addicted to whist that he actually lost £23,000 at a sitting at Crockford's.[26] Nevertheless, he doted on his daughter and did not neglect her education. She was taught piano by Liszt and given enough French lessons to make her completely fluent in the language, which doubtless endeared her to Becky Sharp's creator.[27] She also recalled sitting on the knee of George III. Yet despite her impeccably patrician upbringing, she was a simple woman who lived her life with dutiful simplicity. In 1833, she married Alexander George Fullerton, an officer in the Irish Guards from Ballintoy Castle, Antrim. For the first eight years of their marriage they lived in Paris in the home of Earl Granville. In 1843, Fullerton converted to Rome and three years later his wife followed, after receiving instruction from that extraordinary Jesuit, Father Brownbill, who received so many of Newman's friends into the Church, including Maria Giberne, Sir John Simeon, Mr. and Mrs. George Ward, Catherine Anne Bathurst, Mr. and Mrs. Richard Simpson, Mrs. Henry Wilberforce and the Marchioness of Lothian.[28] The death of Lady Georgina's only son in 1854 at the age of 21 devastated her and her husband, and for the rest of her life she was in mourning.

When Lady Georgiana wrote to Newman in 1853 expressing interest in writing a historical novel set in the time of the early Church, Newman suggested an impressive reading list—including Bingham's Antiquities, Tillemont's books and Fleury's Ecclesiastical History—before observing, "Your difficulty will be character. This is the position in which you excel, and on which your works have hitherto turned—and female character. Now I do not know what work would help you to understanding the Roman female character. I suppose it was absolutely different in kind from the Protestant or English. I suppose a genuine Roman woman had very little education. The known historical specimens, on the other hand, were often monsters. I doubt whether any of them, heathen or Christian, had that peculiar refinement or feeling and complexity of motive and passion, which you delight to draw."[29] As it happened, Lady Georgiana never pursued the novel, though she might have had fun disabusing Newman of his one-dimensional notions of Roman matrons.

About her first novel, *Ellen Middleton*, Gladstone wrote a long, revelatory piece in *The English Review*, in which he concluded that "the eternal march of the Divine law of retribution forms the fundamental harmony of the book," after advising his readers: "Let us not conceal it from ourselves, that men cannot live for generations, and almost for centuries, deprived of any other spiritual discipline than such as each person, unaided by the external forces of the Church and the testimony of general practice, may have the desire and the grace to exercise over himself, without being the worse for it," a startling concession from a man who otherwise abominated the Catholic sacrament of confession.[30] One can see his tortured refusal to credit the clear logic of the novel in an amusingly defensive passage:

> ... this reminds us of a frivolous objection: it has been somewhere surmised, as of most other things in this day of reckless fancies, that if the representations of this book be just, we ought to return to the Church of Rome. No! but if they be just, then indeed we ought to return to the Church of England. We ought to remember her solemn admonitions of repentance; her constant witness in favour of holy discipline for the souls of her children; the heavy responsibility of self-examination and self-judgment which she throws upon them, the means of authoritative support, of consolation ever divine, though ministered through the weakness and foolishness of a fleshly organ, to which she habitually points the way as their meet refuge, if they shall not of themselves suffice to the discharge of that awful duty. Yes, we have, as a nation and as individuals, a long and weary path to traverse before we attain to the level of that practice which the injunctions of our own yet living and speaking mother require. When we have reached it, we may find that we have passed by the point to which belongs the system of auricular confession ...[31]

In a letter to Edward Pusey, Newman made reference to Gladstone's review, remarking of the novel's moral, which he saw as "the expedience of Confession," that the then President of the Board of Trade "seems to think it had better be begun," and not by Priests but by individual Anglicans, "by way of accustoming people to the *thing itself*. Yet so very awful a thing, as it is to many persons, requires that support from sacred and sacramental sanctions which a Priestly ordinance alone can give. Confession cannot well be disjoined from absolution."[32] After he converted, Newman took a very practical view of confession. When Henry Wilberforce's newly converted wife confided to him that she was unsure of how to approach the sacrament, Newman wrote back to her: "Do not trouble yourself over much about your confession. God asks what you can do and nothing more. Let your one thought be that of His tender mercy and love of you. Say every day a prayer to each of the Five Wounds – before the Crucifix, if you have one. If you have no prayer, say with the thought of each wound before you, one Our Father, Hail Mary, and Glory. And at some other time of the day make Acts of Faith, Hope, Love, and Contrition, as you find them in any Catholic Book."[33] Even as an Anglican, Newman recognized the indispensability of confession to the pastoral charge, writing in one of his letters: "I cannot understand how a clergyman can be answerable to souls, if souls are not submitted to him. There is *no real* cure of *souls* in our Church."[34]

In his monograph, *The Mind of Gladstone* (2004), the historian David Bebbington misrepresents Gladstone's ambivalent response to the novel by claiming that he found the characters "unamiable."[35] This is not true. In the pertinent passage, Gladstone remarks: "Again; it has been said that the characters of the book are unamiable: that Edward is too stern and hard; that Alice is too still; that Ellen repels more than she attracts. But it is no reproach to the painter, if, instead of daubing his canvas with masses of colour, cold and warm, in violent contrast, he follows nature in the inexplicable blending of her myriad shades."[36] By misrepresenting Gladstone's review of a novel that spoke so directly to the Liberal politician's sense of guilt—which his scrupulous diary exhibited on nearly every page and which his Anglican faith could do nothing to resolve—Bebbington hardly does justice to the mind of his subject. Nevertheless, Lady Georgiana was thrilled to have her first novel reviewed by so prominent a politician, however impelled he might have been to deny its true import.

After converting to Rome in 1849, Lady Georgiana would often visit Miss Bowles in South Street on her way to the Jesuit Church in Farm Street. After her death, Miss Bowles wrote a touching memorial of her friend for the *Dublin Review*. Turning over the pages of Mme. Craven's biography of Lady Georgiana, Miss Bowles wrote, "we live once more in that gracious presence, we note the peculiar radiance of the smile, the brightening of the eyes, the rich harmony of the low-pitched voice, so full of refinement and of power. We see her again, in her poor mourning garb, bent and feeble, making her way with a stick down South Street to the long-frequented church, in which we shall presently find her kneeling, rapt in prayer. Following her at a little distance, through Farm Street Mews, we wonder again, as we have many times wondered, whether the rude crowd of grooms gathered at their noisy work did not recognize in that poorly clad woman as she passed some higher angelic presence, that brought with it healing and a blessing. To us it ever truly verified the words, *Christianus alter Christus est.* May she plead for us in her Eternal Home!"[37] Hilaire Belloc's mother also vividly recalled Lady Georgiana. "Of her manifold charities one knows not how to speak. She was the kindest and the most industrious of women. The charge of orphans, sick people, and schools was a daily matter of course to her ... . And so, year by year, Lady Georgiana Fullerton's life went on, until the time came when she was attacked by a painful disease, and the black gown hung in long thin folds on a wasted figure, which recalled some early Italian picture in the severe grace of old age. On her deathbed she asked that the curtain covering her son's portrait should be withdrawn, saying that she had the courage to look at it now. Another time, when Father Gallwey was reading the Scriptures to her, he saw her eyes fill at an allusion to the death of a child; an involuntary revelation of the pain silently endured for thirty years. Please God they are now together, the mother and the son; and of her it may most emphatically be said: 'Blessed are the dead who die in the Lord!'"[38]

Interestingly enough, South Street had another resident (at No. 15) when Miss Bowles and Lady Georgiana were working together to relieve the sufferings of the London poor: Catherine Walters (1839–1920), otherwise known as Skittles, who was the last of the great Victorian courtesans, the friend and confidante of Gladstone, Lord Hartington and Edward, Prince of Wales. It is tempting to imagine what this lively woman would have made of the Tamworth Reading Room, the utilitarian library which Sir Robert Peel proposed in order to wean the British public off religion and offer them instead the edifying substitutes of education and knowledge, especially since the library also proposed something else, which, as Newman observed, "is not a little curious ..." While "all *'virtuous* women' may be members of the Library ... a very emphatic silence is maintained about women not virtuous. What does this mean? Does it mean to exclude them, while bad *men* are admitted? Is this accident, or design, sinister and insidious, against a portion of the community?" If, as Sir Robert maintained, the point of the library was "to *make* its members virtuous ... to 'exalt the *moral dignity* of their nature' ... to provide 'charms and temptations' to allure them from sensuality and riot," why should he exclude *unvirtuous* women? After all, "To whom but to the vicious ought Sir Robert to discourse about 'opportunities,' and 'access,' and 'moral improvement' ... ?" Indeed, "who else would prove a fitter experiment, and a more glorious triumph, of scientific influences? And yet he shuts out all but the well-educated and virtuous. Alas, that bigotry should have left the mark of its hoof on the great 'fundamental principle of the Tamworth Institution'!"[39] In Newman's witty skewering of Peel's empty moralism, Skittles would have seen the hypocrisy of an entire society held up to righteous derision.

In order to understand the work that Lady Georgiana, Miss Bowles and so many other Catholic converts did to alleviate the miseries of the London poor (Lady Georgiana, for example, at great personal expense, established the Sisters of Saint Vincent de Paul in England), it is necessary to grasp what an entirely different species the poor appeared to their better-off contemporaries. When Henry James was living in Piccadilly in the 1870s, he encountered the poor during Easter week. "From Good Friday to Easter Monday, inclusive, they were very much *en evidence,*" he wrote, "and it was an excellent occasion for getting an impression of the British populace. Gentility had retired to the background, and in the West End all the blinds were lowered; the streets were void of carriages, and well-dressed pedestrians were rare; but the 'masses' were all abroad and making the most of their holiday, and I strolled about and watched them at their gambols." After giving it as his opinion that the English upper classes were, on the whole, the handsomest and the best-dressed people in Europe, the aesthete in James turned his attention to the poor and found that, "They are as ill-dressed as their betters are well-dressed, and their garments have that sooty-looking surface which has nothing in common with some of the more romantic forms of poverty. It is the hard prose of misery—an ugly and hopeless imitation of respectable attire. This is especially noticeable in the battered and bedraggled bonnets of the women, which look as if their husbands had stamped on them in hobnailed boots, as a hint of what is in store for their wearers. Then it is not too much to say that two-thirds of the London faces, among the 'masses,' bear in some degree or other the traces of alcoholic action. The proportion of flushed, empurpled, eruptive countenances is very striking; and the ugliness of the sight is not diminished by the fact that many of the faces thus disfigured were evidently meant to please. A very large allowance is to be made, too, for the people who bear the distinctive stamp of that physical and mental degradation which comes from the slums and purlieus of this dusky Babylon—the pallid, stunted, misbegotten, and in every way miserable figures. These people swarm in every London crowd, and I know of none in any other place that suggest an equal degree of misery." Later, in December, James recalled a scene which seemed to sum up the condition of the poor when the city "was livid with sleet and fog, and against this dismal background was offered me the vision of a horrible old woman in a smoky bonnet, lying prone in a puddle of whisky! She seemed to assume a kind of symbolic significance ..."[40]

Newman was deeply appreciative of the works of mercy that Miss Bowles and her titled friends performed on behalf of the London poor and in one letter he sent her money with rather precise instructions: "I inclose a post office order for £5. If you think Miss S. ought to have £2, be so good as to ask her to accept it, according to her letter. As to the rest, I wish it to go in a special kind of charity, viz in the instrumenta, as I may call them, and operative methods, of your own good works – that is, not in meat and drink, and physic, or clothing of the needy, but (if you will not be angry with me) in your charitable cabs, charitable umbrellas, charitable boots, and all the wear and tear of a charitable person who without such wear and tear cannot do her charity."[41] The records Miss Bowles and Lady Georgiana Fullerton left of the charitable work they performed among the poor are scrappy but if one consults Mayhew it seems likely that they were not met with total hostility.[42] As one former costermonger told Mayhew, "I'm satisfied if the costermongers had to profess themselves of some religion tomorrow, they would become Roman Catholics, every one of them. This is the reason: London costers live very often in the same courts and streets as the Irish and if the Irish are sick, be sure there comes to them the priest, the Sisters of Charity—they are *good* women—and some other ladies. Many a man not a Catholic, has rotted and died without any good person near him. Why, I lived in Lambeth, and there wasn't one coster in one hundred, I'm satisfied, knew so much as the rector's name ..."[43]

Despite her charitable work, Miss Bowles also found time to become an accomplished author. She was a frequent contributor to *The Month* and wrote a well-received biography of St. Jane de Chantal and a novel, *In the Camargne* (1873), which is set in the region in France where St. Mary Magdalene is thought to be buried. Apropos the novel, the reviewer in *The Month* remarked: "Of course there is a love story, in which an English painter with a hollow heart wins the love of a 'daughter of the soil,' and nearly breaks it by his desertion ... We think the authoress is a little hard upon men in general, but that we imagine to be one of the newly-acquired 'rights of women' ..."[44] About the helpful comments that Newman made on the book, Miss Bowles later wrote, "It has always seemed to me that the minute pains taken in criticizing that small book was one of the greatest of his many extraordinary acts of kindness."[45] On Newman's seventieth birthday, as a token of her affection, Miss Bowles sent him a bottle of Chartreuse, which would have amused Saki, who observed in *Reginald* (1904): "People may say what they like about the decay of Christianity; the religious system that produced green Chartreuse can never really die."[46]

Friendly with Lord Acton, Cardinal Wiseman, George Ward, Father Henry Coleridge, S.J. and Bishop Ullathorne, Miss Bowles often relayed to Newman the gossip of Catholic London, even though it often annoyed him, especially the bits about himself. "When will you learn to know me as I am," he wrote to W.G. Ward in 1863, "and not in the haze of London rumours and gossip?"[47] When the Ultramontanes were agitating for an unlimited definition of papal infallibility, Miss Bowles, like many English Catholics, feared the worst and kept Newman abreast of what their fellow Catholics felt about the impending definition. In 1867, Newman sought to put the growing controversy in some perspective. "It is because you are out of health, that you have these nervous feelings about the future of the Church," he told her. "Exert a little faith – God will provide – there is a Power in it stronger than Popes, Councils and Theologians – and that is the Divine Promise, which controls against their will and intention every human authority."[48] In September 1869, Miss Bowles traveled to Birmingham to discuss the matter with Newman in person, telling him that if the papal extremists got their way, she could not be sure what her response might be. When Newman reminded her that "God *cannot* leave His Church," Miss Bowles pertly replied, "No, but I may cease to believe in it as His Church—I may leave it." "You will not," Newman replied: "We all must go through that gate of obedience, simply as obedience. And mind, if the dogma is declared, you will find that it will not make the slightest difference to you."[49] To Lady Simeon, he was equally insistent on a point that some still attempt to dispute. "I say with Cardinal Bellarmine whether the Pope be infallible or not in any pronouncement, anyhow he is to be obeyed. No good can come from disobedience, his facts and his warnings may be all wrong; his deliberations may have been biassed – he may have been misled, imperiousness and craft, tyranny and cruelty, may be patent on the conduct of his advisers and instruments, but when he speaks formally and authoritatively he speaks as our Lord would have him speak, and all those imperfections and sins of individuals are overruled for that result which our Lord intends (just as the acts of the wicked and of enemies to the Church are overruled) and therefore the Pope's word stands, and a blessing goes with obedience to it, and no blessing with disobedience."[50]

In 1875, Newman sent Miss Bowles a copy of his *Letter to the Duke of Norfolk*, in which he exposed the groundlessness of Gladstone's charges against the loyalty of English Catholics. After reading it through, Miss Bowles was pleased to see how it clarified the doctrine of infallibility for English Protestants. For herself, she freely admitted to "the burthen dragging down her love and loyalty," which the threats of the Ultramontanes only aggravated, "but your dear noble fearless Letter has unloosed it and thrown it over for ever."[51] She also assured Newman that "Whole bodies of Catholics of old traditions have rejoiced at your Letter – I mean such as the various families of Eystons and their relations who for centuries have given priests and martyrs and sufferers to the Church."[52]

Newman confided in Miss Bowles not only because he trusted her but because she was forthright: she spoke her mind. He was similarly appreciative of the rebarbative George Ward, the Ultramontane editor of the *Dublin Review*, "for his own absolute straightforwardness."[53] In one instance Miss Bowles gave him some particularly blunt advice. "You act *too perfectly*, as if dealing with Angels. Then, if others do not act as Angels … you are deeply wounded and grieved—suffering with intense sensitiveness not only the fault but the surprise." One can credit what Bishop Ullathorne's biographer once said of Newman— that, given the often unfair opposition he faced, "he must needs have been not merely uncommonly thick-skinned, but even rhinoceros-hided"—without entirely discounting Miss Bowles's point.[54] Her friend was often heedless of the guile of others. And yet Newman himself put the matter in a different light altogether, which showed how indifferent he was, like Geraldine's "true spouse of Christ," to "the popular voice of praise or blame."

> As to defending myself, you may make yourself quite sure I never will, unless it is a simple duty. Such is a charge against my religious faith – such against my veracity – such any charge in which the cause of religion is involved. But, did I go out and battle commonly, I should lose my time, my peace, my strength, and only show a detestable sensitiveness. I consider that Time is the great remedy and Avenger of all wrongs, as far as this world goes. If only we are patient, God works for us – He works for those who do not work for themselves. Of course an inward brooding over injuries is not patience, but a recollecting with a view to the future is prudence.[55]

If Miss Bowles felt free to speak her mind in her letters to Newman about aspects of the Church that annoyed her, Newman did not hesitate to do the same in his letters to her. Perhaps the best example of this is from a letter he sent to her in 1863, when he was still under a cloud in Rome for composing that deeply misunderstood article "On Consulting the Faithful in Matters of Doctrine," which appeared in the *Rambler* in 1859. "This country is under Propaganda," he wrote to Miss Bowles, "and Propaganda is too shallow to have the wish to use such as me. It is rather afraid of such. If I know myself, no one can have been more loyal to the Holy See than I am. I love the Pope personally into the bargain. But Propaganda is a quasi-military power, extraordinary, for missionary countries, rough and ready. It does not understand an intellectual movement. It likes quick results – scalps from beaten foes by the hundred."[56]

In 1876, Miss decided to come to Newman's aid and take Mrs. Wooten's place as Dame of the Oratory School, which must have been a trial for a woman who had lived so independently in London for so many years. Before she made her offer, Newman tried to warn her off: "It must be recollected that whoever comes will have to rough it at first, that is, she will be confronted with 50 or 60 new faces of boys of various ages ..."[57] Then, again, there was something else that Newman felt his faithful friend should consider. "If I understand you, you would not dream of so great a change in your life except for me, and you seem almost to wonder that I do not (as you think) see this. But I do, and take it very seriously, and am led to fear that no blessing will come upon me, if I thus wantonly misuse your feelings towards me." Still, Miss Bowles was undaunted and after she took the post, she stayed on for five years, though she lacked Mrs. Wooten's maternal warmth. Many of the Old Boys remembered her as a strict, forbidding figure.[58] When she retired in 1881, Newman sent her off in style in his own carriage accompanied by Father Neville. Later, when Miss Bowles became hard up, Newman wrote a letter on her behalf to the Secretary of the Royal Literary Fund in his wonderfully elegant hand: "Cardinal Newman presents his compliments to Mr. Blewitt ... and begs to say that he believes the circumstances of her case as stated by her, to be quite exact, and that after a brave struggle for more than 20 years to supply the fortune which without imprudence she had lost, she is now obliged to have recourse to the aid of friends."[59] Since she would live for another 25 years, Emily's old age was pinched. Nonetheless, she must have been pleased that her grant to the Royal Literary Fund—which eventually made her a grant of £30—was supported not only by Newman but by Hallam Tennyson, the poet's son.

In 1867, when the *Pall Mall Gazette* declared that the "actual Roman system" was "attractive only to women and to men of inferior intelligence and education," the paper was giving voice to a common British prejudice.[60] Yet Newman would have seen a kernel of truth in this, for Catholics were poorly educated, and the reason, as far as he could see, was plain: "There are those who wish Catholic women, not nuns, to have no higher pursuit than that of dress, and Catholic youths to be shielded from no sin so carefully as from intellectual curiosity."[61] Hence, the campaign, led by Cardinal Manning, to dissuade Catholic youths from going to Oxford or Cambridge. Nevertheless, with the passage of time, Newman saw that the Church's own internal divisions on mixed education were merely a part of a much deeper problem. In January

1873, he wrote to Canon Walker, "As to the prospects of the world, I agree with you they are very bad. It looks as if a great and almost fiery trial of souls, especially as regards faith, is destined for the next generation. I look at our poor boys here with anxiety and compassion, feeling what sophistries and temptations of the intellect and social perplexities may be in store for them in middle life. Will not the same fanaticism which resolves to have all the primary schools throughout the country in its hands, agitate for some means of exerting a control and introducing a teaching of its own into all the higher schools, some twenty years hence? Religion is in process of exclusion from the education of high and low, and what will be the issue of this tyranny?"[62]

Miss Bowles was certainly not one of those Catholics who imagined Catholic women should concern themselves only with dress, nor did three of her close friends, all converts. The Duchess Dowager of Norfolk, after the loss of her husband "never laid aside her widow's weeds" and Lady Georgiana Fullerton never "put off her mourning for her son."[63] Of Lady Georgiana, Bessie Belloc wrote: "In her younger days she must inevitably have been accustomed to the finest dresses ever made or worn, living, as she did, in the house of an ambassador of the first rank. She now never wore any costume but the black dress and shawl and plain cap, which might have suggested austerity but for the bright, merry eyes," which were "infinitely touching to those who knew the agony she had passed through."[64] In this, neither Lady Georgiana nor the Duchess of Norfolk could have said with William Allingham

> No funeral gloom, my dears, when I am gone
> Corpse-gazing, tears, black raiment, graveyard grimness ...

Yet for Miss Bowles, on the matter of dress, a third friend was even more remarkable. "Lady Lothian alone, with her admirable regard for her family of daughters and a married son, set her own wishes aside, and resumed the dress befitting her rank and the society in which she moved, with the dignity of one equally indifferent to velvets and jewels or shabby crepe and bombazine."[65] To be indifferent to good clothes when wearing "shabby crepe and bombazine" was one thing but to be indifferent to it when set out in the dress befitting a marchioness was quite another. At a time when the inspired couturier Charles Worth (1825–1895) was making dresses of brilliantly colored taffeta and gossamer tulle for a clientele that included Empress Eugénie of France, the queen of Sweden, and Pauline, Princess von Metternich, such indifference was indeed heroic.[66] No one could accuse the Marchioness of Lothian of being sybaritic.

Cecil Chetwynd Kerr, Marchioness of Lothian [née Lady Cecil Chetwynd-Talbot] was born in 1801 at Ingestre Hall, Staffordshire, the daughter of Charles Chetwynd-Talbot, 2nd Earl Talbot of Hensol and his wife, Frances Thomasine, daughter of Charles Lambart of Beau Parc, County Meath. Her father paid close attention to her education and, before she came out, had her studying Latin and reading Blackstone's Commentaries. As for her religious upbringing, it was moderately High Church. After marrying John William

Robert Kerr, 7th Marquess of Lothian, she took up residence in Scotland at Newbattle Abbey, Midlothian, where she and her husband had five sons and two daughters. Then, in 1841, tragedy struck when the marquess suddenly died on his estate at Blickling, Norfolk. Even before this terrible loss, Lady Lothian was one of Scotland's most ardent and generous supporters of Tractarianism. After her loss, her devotion deepened. She gave much of her time and largesse to building and endowing the Neo-Gothic church at Jedburgh for the Scottish Episcopal Church, which had been built in accordance with specifications set out by the Camden Ecclesiological Society. At the consecration of the church, she was joined by John Keble and W. F. Hook.

After Newman's secession and, then, the Gorham Judgment, in which Privy Councilors ruled that baptism need not be thought a sacrament, the marchioness began to have grave doubts about the legitimacy of the Anglican Church. Once Henry Manning converted in 1851, she confided to a correspondent, "I am very unhappy. I feel as if I were trifling with the concerns of eternity out of sheer cowardice, catching at every straw as an excuse for waiting."[67] Finally, in June of 1851, she embraced the Church of Rome. In December of the same year she visited Newman at the Birmingham Oratory and described to her brother how impressive she found him: "He was most kind. I was nervous, but without cause, for he is so full of sympathy and Christian love that he is the last person one need be afraid of. That which struck me most was his childlike sympathy and humility, and next to that, the vivid clearness with which he gives an opinion. He is a very striking looking person. His saying of Mass is most striking. I do not know what makes the difference, but one is conscious of a difference. It appeared to me very unearthly."[68] The "unearthly" quality that Lady Lothian saw in Newman was one that Newman saw in his dear friend Hurrell Froude, about whom he told Maria Giberne after Froude's death: "As to dear Froude, I cannot speak of him consistently with my own deep feelings about him, though they are all bright and pleasant. It is a loss such as I never can have again. I love to think and muse upon one who had the most angelic mind of any person I ever fell in with -- the most unearthly, the most gifted. I have no painful thoughts in speaking of him, though I cannot trust myself to speak of him to many, but I feel the longer I live, the more I shall miss him. You will do me a most exceeding kindness in giving me your sketch of him."[69]

Once converted, the marchioness saw to it that her younger children were received as well, though her eldest son, William, the eighth marquess, who later became admiral of the fleet and senior naval lord, remained Episcopalian. As a Catholic, Lady Lothian aided female prisoners and the poor in Edinburgh and established the Refugee Benevolent Fund in London. The marchioness was joined in her charitable works by her friends, Lady Londonderry, the great beauty, and Charlotte, Duchess of Buccleuch, both of whom followed her into the Church. When Lady Lothian's youngest son John, not yet 14, died at Ushaw College of pneumonia in January of 1855, while Lady Lothian was in Rome, Newman wrote her a moving letter of condolence: "I have heard that dear John has been thought too good for this world by Him who so lovingly brought him near Himself a year ago. Ever since I heard of his illness I have been thinking of him. I saw him last year at Ushaw, and was so struck by him that I talked of him to others for some time after. He came into my room of his own accord, and made friends with me in an instant. For him, how can I but rejoice that he should be taken out of this dark world in the freshness and bloom of his innocence and piety. But it comes over me most keenly that if once seeing him made me love him so much, what must it have been to you? And oh! how sad in a human light that you and his sisters should have been so far away – and poor Ralph in bed and unable to go to him!" Lord Ralph Kerr, John's elder brother, was ill with pleurisy at the Birmingham Oratory.[70] Later, in 1873, when she praised his eulogy for their dear departed mutual friend, James Hope-Scott, he wrote: "Who could know Mr Hope Scott without loving him! Whatever I said in my Sermon, however poor, would raise remembrances and affectionate thoughts in the minds of my hearers, better than any words of mine."[71] Newman's Oratory accounts show with what consistent generosity Lady Lothian and Hope-Scott supported both the Oratory Church and School.

Of the many people who converted to the ancient faith in England in the nineteenth century, Lady Lothian was not untypical. She was ready to make enormous sacrifices for the faith, even though these meant estrangement from family and dear friends. She gave unstintingly of her time and money to Christ's poor. She was at once deeply English and yet deeply devout. And she was familiar enough with the history of her country to know that the Protestant version of its history was profoundly false, though in this she had unusual advantages. Not all girls, certainly not aristocratic girls, grew up reading Blackstone.

Oddly enough, Newman blamed the Italians for the neglect of Catholic education, contending that such neglect had something to do with the fact that they enjoyed a "monopoly of the magisterium," though, in the *Apologia*, he also noted that "certainly, if there is one consideration more than another which should make us English grateful to Pius the Ninth, it is that, by giving us a Church of our own, he has prepared the way for our own habits of mind, our own manner of reasoning, our own tastes, and our own virtues, finding a place and thereby a sanctification, in the Catholic Church."[72]

In Newman's correspondence, we can see how he helped the English take hold of this Church of their own by helping the female faithful grapple with their difficulties. In 1866, one year after she converted, the prolific popular novelist Lady Chatterton (1806–1876), began to have very serious doubts. One of the reasons why she doubted her new faith was that she had come from a strong High Church background: her father was the Reverend Lascelles Iremonger, Prebendary of Winchester, and like most Britons she found the doctrines of Catholicism hard to credit, especially those regarding the Real Presence and the Blessed Virgin. "These are trials," Newman wrote to her, "which God puts upon us, and we cannot at our will put them aside. You have been so kind as to state fully your difficulties, and to say that you do not wish for an answer. Nor could I, without writing a volume, go through them all. Nor do I think, any more than you do, that it would fulfil any good purpose to attempt an elaborate answer to them. To make you happy, as a Catholic, is the work of God alone; if you put yourself into His hands, and ask for His grace perseveringly, He will gradually remove all your doubts and perplexities; of this I am most confident."[73] This resembled the advice that he gave to Lady Herbert of Lea when her son took it into his head to reject Christianity root and branch: "You know, it frequently happens that medical men say of a patient—'Leave him alone—give him no physic—let nature act' ... The best hope of his changing lies in his having no one to combat with him. Especially no one whom he loves or knows about. There is no *substance* in his scepticism, and this is most likely to come home upon him, if silence is offered to this restless activity of mind ..."[74] Still, if he would not refute Lady Chatterton, he would tell her what she was renouncing:

> To me it is wonderful that you should speak as you do. Why, what exercise of devotion is there, which equals that of going before the Blessed Sacrament, before our Lord Jesus really present, though unseen? To kneel before Him, to put oneself into His hands, to ask His grace, and to rejoice in the hope of seeing Him in heaven! In the Catholic Church alone is the great gift to be found. You may go through the length and breadth of England, and see beautiful prospects enough, such as you speak of, the work of the God of nature, but there is no benediction from earth or sky which falls upon us like that which comes to us from the Blessed Sacrament, which is Himself.[75]

Later, when Lady Chatterton complained of Newman's occasional asperity, her bishop William Ullathorne wrote: "I know Dr Newman's vigorous way. Depend upon it, my dear friend, it was from no want of sympathy, but from strong sympathy restrained, that he wrote. He wished to give you an electric shock, to startle you out of security, and to urge the exercises of faith as the means of entering into faith. Surgical operations are painful even though they come from a loving hand. Prayer, and prayer with the heart open, and as near to God as it can come, is the way to win the grace and gift of faith."[76] Lady Chatterton confirmed the soundness of this counsel when she wrote to Newman in September 1875: "Dear Doctor Newman,—When I sent you a little printed paper of my 'Confessions,' two years ago, you expressed great sorrow, and that it pained you to read it. You will see, from what I now send you, that I have, thank God, been able gradually to see that I was wrong. It has been a long process, and has caused me many most painfully sleepless nights and suffering days; but I know you will be kindly glad of the result."[77] Newman's response was exultant: "My Dear Lady Chatterton,—You will easily understand how I rejoiced to read your letter this morning. You will be rewarded abundantly, do not doubt it, for the pain, anxiety and weariness you have gone through in arriving at the safe ground and sure home of peace where you now are. I congratulate, with all my heart, the dear friends who surround you upon so happy a termination of their own anxieties and prayers. May God keep you ever in the narrow way and shield you from all those temptations and trials by which so many earnest souls are wrecked. This is the sincere prayer of yours most truly, John H. Newman."[78]

Between 1868 and 1875, Bishop Ullathorne wrote Lady Chatterton a series of letters about the Catholic faith that are some of the most powerful he ever wrote. In one, he counseled his doubt-ridden friend, who feared that she might be fonder of her friends than God: "When the love of God is supreme in us, then every other love partakes in this Divine love, becomes exalted, purified, and sanctified. For this is the grandeur of divine charity, that it draws all loves into the divine love, and regulates them all ... for this is the grand double law of Catholic charity, that whilst we love God, and are subject to God, we likewise love God in our neighbor and are subject to God in being humble to our neighbor. We love in them what is of God, and are subject to them in what is of God; and all this is referred to God, and not merely to the creature as such. Thus we learn to see God's side, which is the beautiful side in all persons."[79] In this passage, Ullathorne might have been describing the relationship that Newman had with all of his contemporaries.

Unlike some of the other women covered in this chapter, Lady Chatterton can be vividly known from her memoirs, which show that she was disposed to asking religious questions from an early age: "I remember that one governess considered me unteachable, because I could not say the second psalm by heart, and especially the verse, 'Why do the heathen so furiously rage?' which she used to repeat over and over again to me in the vain endeavour to beat it into my head. The fact is, I was wondering all the time why the heathen did so furiously rage, and who they could be; so that the more my mind was made to dwell on the words, the more puzzled I became, and the less I remembered my lesson." Later, after marrying, she spent a good deal of time in London society. "As we advance in life," she noted in one journal entry, "time flies so fast that it seems composed of nothing but Mondays. During the season in London, perpetual tumult and bustle, scarcely possible to gain a quiet half-hour, and then the rest of the time moving about from one country house to another. Delightful for the moment, but impressing upon one the perpetual change of all things—the perpetual passing away." In this fleeting world, she met some of the liveliest people of the age and always came away with amusing recollections of them. One was Walter Savage Landor, the poet and witty prose stylist, whose *Imaginary Conversations* are now so unjustly forgotten. "I sat next to Landor, without knowing who he was," she recalled. "I have seldom seen the expression of a highly cultivated mind and courteous genius so beautifully stamped on any countenance as on the Landor of those days."[80] After expressing admiration for his writing, she recalled him doubting whether anything he wrote would survive: "I shall never be much read —still less remembered. I have filed away my mind by too much reading. Shakespeare would never have become such an immortal author if he had been a great reader, and Milton would have produced a greater poem if his head had not been so full of reading. He has confused us with his variety."[81] She also met other lions. "I sat next to Macaulay," she jotted down in one journal entry, "who gave us a most interesting dissertation on painting, and related in short the history and vicissitudes of many of the most celebrated pictures in different countries. Sidney Smith waited in vain for what he called some of Macaulay's 'brilliant flashes of silence.' On Saturday we met Carlyle and Dickens at his house." When her first novel appeared, which was published anonymously, she made a point of bringing it up in conversation and "derived much amusement from hearing people talk about it and ask if I had read it. Of course I heard it abused as well as praised. I do not remember being much annoyed or pained by anything I heard; but I enjoyed the praise it received intensely, and the first bit of commendation that the *Quarterly Review* gave me kept me awake all night with joy."[82] When Queen Victoria ascended the throne, Lady Chatterton made this shrewd entry in her journal. "I am sure that the circumstance of a young girl coming now to the British throne has, at least, retarded the fall of the kingdom of England and legitimacy for a hundred years, and has tended to check the progress of revolution all over the world. I felt convinced of this when I heard yesterday at Lady Shelley's some old hardened politicians talking with tears in their eyes of the delight and admiration the first sight of their young Queen in the Council Chamber had caused."[83] Her faith also enlivened her journal. "We cannot love God, we cannot think with pleasure on Him during long sleepless nights, unless we have endeavoured to keep His commandments. To obey is, at first, a strong exercise of faith, as well as of self-control. By 'at first' I mean before our hearts are imbued with love of God ... We must all without exception submit to become children.... . no doubt, it is hard ... to acquire (I will not say to retain it, if they have it) that child-like Faith in things unseen, to become blind that [we] may see clearly, to obey that [we] may be free."[84] Reading these journal entries, it is easy to see why Bishop Ullathorne and, indeed, Newman became so fond of Lady Chatterton: she was an intelligent, charming, discerning woman.

After returning to the faith in the 1870s, Lady Chatterton, together with her second husband, Edward Heneage Dering, an officer in the Coldstream Guards, helped restore Baddesley Clinton, the moated manor house of grey sandstone in what was once the Forest of Arden in Warwickshire. In the 1590s, Catholic priests were hidden there in ingenious priest-holes. In the nineteenth century, under the direction of Marmion Ferrers and his wife Rebecca Dulcibella, the house became the center of a rather antiquarian, if passionate Catholicism, which was reflected in the Jacobean black velvet favored by the Ferrers. Despite her good works and popular writings, Lady Chatterton did not escape the mockery of gossips. After the death of her first husband, the Irish baronet Sir William Chatterton, the loss of whose rents during the potato famine sent him to an early grave, Lady Chatterton remarried. When Edward Dering, twenty years her junior, called on Lady Chatterton to pay court to her niece, the elder lady did not hear him correctly and thought he was paying court to her. He was too gallant to undeceive her and so they were married.[85]

As it happened, the marriage was happy. Dering was not only a devoted but a grateful husband, who appreciated how his wife's hard-won faith strengthened his own. Shortly before her death, he recalled: "In 1874–5 I could perceive a change in her feelings towards the Church. Her mind began to find repose in the contemplation of it. Her sympathies were attracted. She prayed continually for guidance, and in the month of April, 1874, wrote a few lines on a scrap of paper which I value more than anything and everything I possess, or might possess in this world. The lines were written in pencil one morning when about to attend the Communion Service in a Protestant church. They are as follows:

Keep me steadfast if I'm right,
If I'm wrong, God give me light,
Let me feel Thy presence near,
Give me Faith to banish Fear!"[86]

In 1866, when Lady Chatterton confessed to Newman her difficulties with what she regarded as the foreignness of the Catholic faith, Newman responded with a letter of characteristic acuteness, in which he addressed the same 'home thoughts' that prevented so many Anglicans from even contemplating, much less acceding to, the claims of Rome. "Every society has its own ways; it is not wonderful then, that the Catholic Church has its own way of praying, its own ceremonies, and the like. These are strange and perhaps at first unwelcome to those who come to them from elsewhere, just as foreign manners are unpleasant to those who never travelled. We all like home best, because we understand the ways of home. Abraham doubtless found his life in Canaan not so pleasant to him, as his native Mesopotamia. We ever must sacrifice something, to gain great blessings. If the Catholic Church is from God, to belong to her is a make-up for many losses. We must beg of God to change our tastes and habits, and to make us love for His sake what by nature we do not love."[87] And he followed this up with an appeal that could not have been more direct. "At this sacred season then, my dear Lady Chatterton, I appeal to you by the love of Christ, and beg of you, to resolve to take on you His easy yoke. Do not attempt to live without any yoke at all; take on you the yoke of Christ. Submit your reason and your will to Him, as He speaks to you in His Church. In addressing you, I feel I am not addressing a common person, but one who can distinguish great things from little, and who will not, on seriously weighing the matter, put details and minutiae before the great matters of the law. St Paul says that the Church is the pillar and ground of the Truth. He says that there is One Body as there is One Faith. Our Lord has built His Church on Peter. These are great facts -- they keep their ground against small objections, however many the latter may be. I cannot call your objections great ones; nor would you, if you saw them from the proper stand-point." And he signed off with a benediction, which Lady Chatterton must have recalled in the years ahead. "May God bless you, and give you grace, and lead you on, and may you bear patiently this time of darkness, till the True Light shines upon you."[88]

There were other female correspondents whose difficulties Newman addressed. To Elizabeth ('Isy') Froude (1840–1931), William and Catherine's daughter, who converted when she was 19 (largely as the result of Newman's influence) and would go on to marry Baron von Hügel, Newman wrote: "I am not at all surprised that you should be tried in the way you describe," after she wrote to him of her doubts. "If you were older, your trials would be of a different kind. The wise man says, 'If thou wouldest serve the Lord, prepare thy soul for temptation.' What you must do, is to beg our dear Lord to give you what you need. Recollect the man who cried out to Him 'I do believe, Lord – help my unbelief.'"[89] To Louisa Simeon (1843–1895), the convert Sir John Simeon's daughter, who had begun to have doubts about the faith in 1869 when she was 26, he wrote: "It often strikes me how very different my own generation is from the present. We were gradually brought into the Church – we fought our way – all difficulties of whatever kind met us – were examined and overcome – and we became Catholics as the last step of a long course, with little difficulty because it was only the last difficulty of a series. But you find yourself a Catholic suddenly, so to say, just as you are plunging into a world of opinion and into a conflict of intellectual elements all new to you ..."[90] Nevertheless, no sooner did he draw this contrast than he discounted it. For Newman, taking hold of the reality of the faith was a difficult business in any generation. "You must begin all thought about religion by mastering what is the fact, that any how the question has an inherent, irradicable [sic] difficulty in it. As in tuning a piano, you may throw the fault here or there, but no theory can any one take up without that difficulty remaining. It will come up in one shape or other. If we say, 'Well, I will not believe any thing,' there is a difficulty in believing nothing, an intellectual difficulty. There is a difficulty in doubting; a difficulty in determining there is no truth; in saying that there is a truth, but that no one can find it out; in saying that all religious opinions are true, or one as good as another; a difficulty in saying there is no God; that there is a God but that He has not revealed Himself except in the way of nature; and there is doubtless a difficulty in Christianity. The question is, whether on the whole our reason does not tell us that it is a duty to accept the arguments commonly urged for its truth as sufficient, and a duty in consequence to believe heartily in Scripture and the Church."[91]

Then, again, there were many practical difficulties for those who wished to embrace the Catholic faith in Protestant England. In 1873, Mrs. William Robinson Clark, wife of the Vicar of St Mary Magdalen, Taunton, who was also Rural Dean and a Prebendary of Wells, wrote to Newman of her reluctance to share her strong leanings towards Rome with her husband, whom she understandably feared would not credit them. After assuring her that he was saying Masses for her—"which is a greater service to you than my writing many forms of prayer"—Newman acknowledged that her predicament was indeed a "most painful trial" and "that there are others who have to undergo it ... does not make it less." Doubtless, he recalled the difficulty Catherine Froude faced when she was embracing a faith that she knew her husband William would probably never share. He might even have recalled the torments through which Julia Arnold (née Sorrell) put her husband Thomas Arnold, Matthew's younger brother, whom Newman tapped to teach English at the Catholic Univeristy in Dublin, when she learned that he had decided to convert. On the day that Arnold was received in Van Diemen's Land, Julia, who came from the same French Huguenot tradition as Newman's mother, threw a brick through the window of the Pro-Cathedral.[92] Newman wrote to Maria Giberne of Arnold and his wife: "He is a very good amiable fellow, but weak and henpecked. His wife is a Xantippe. From Australia, before he was received there, she sent me two abusive letters, and vowed he never should be a Catholic ... When I gave him a professorship at Dublin, she was still unmitigated – and when he came to Edgbaston, she used to nag, nag, nag him, till he almost lost his senses."[93] For Newman, Julia must have seemed a fair example of the female *unfaithful*. Then, again, he certainly would have recalled how his own conversion estranged him from his siblings, not to mention his many Oxford friends and colleagues. Keble would not speak to him for twenty years after his conversion, nor would Frederic Rogers. With such painful memories in mind, Newman admitted to Mrs. Clark, "I wish it were as easy to relieve you as it is easy to feel for you." Nevertheless, the advice he gave her was uncompromising. "You say 'Thank God, I have no longer any doubt about the Catholic Faith, I firmly believe Jesus Christ founded one Church, and that the head of the Church is the Pope.' Then you are bound to be received into that Church without delay." And what is more, "you must tell your husband. It does not answer to conceal from him so great an act. He has a right to claim it from you. It is the way for him to trust you—but if you act without telling him, he will think you dishonest … . I know I call you to an heroic act in bidding you be a Catholic—but God can be a stay and guide to you, and a Fount of peace and joy, though no human help can avail." Yet he sought to impress upon her that her difficulty was not insuperable. "You have a great trial before you, and on you; but even though it were that 'fiery trial,' of which St. Peter speaks, God can deliver you from it or preserve you in it."[94] By the same token, he was impelled to counsel catechumens like Mrs. Clark that "one cannot be a catechumen for ever," despite the fact that she had been advised by Newman's friend Henry James Coleridge, the Jesuit, to wait two years before making up her mind. Newman advised against waiting because, as he said: "You cannot be at peace till you are a Catholic …"[95] Still, Mrs. Clark said nothing to her husband, and when it became clear that she would not make this delicate avowal herself, Newman made it for her. His letter to the vicar of Taunton is a model of tact:

Reverend Sir,
I have great difficulty in writing to you, yet I feel I ought to do so.
I know I shall pain you most deeply, and may seem intrusive, but I cannot help that.
Now for perhaps two years, perhaps more, Mrs. Clark from time to time has written to me on the Subject of Religion. I have urged her on several occasions to let you know, she wrote to me and from her keen feeling of the distress it would cause you, she has put off doing so.
Some months ago on her way from Liverpool she called on me and she fully determined to tell you on getting home but I understand she did not.
It is almost rude in me to say how grave a trial I feel this must be to you but I do not like you to think, as you otherwise may that I am unfeeling.
I write because you ought to know that Mrs. Clark has seen me – also because I do not see more than one termination to her present state of (I may say) anguish. I have never till now been able to say to her 'You ought to join the Catholic Church.' I did not know enough about her state of mind. She's not sure she might not after becoming a Catholic change her mind and go back after a while, but I don't think that now. I think she is really drawn by

the highest motives to be a Catholic and that she would be faithful to the religion she chose.

With much respect and begging your forgiveness, if I have erred in judgment in what I have said or in writing at all, I am ...[96]

The Vicar's response was, in its way, even more tactful, even though it gave short shrift to his wife's difficulties.

Vicarage, Taunton June 10, 1877

My dear Sir

I thank you most sincerely for your kind letter. I had often wished to have one from you; but I little thought it would come in this way.

It was quite natural that my wife should apply to you, and I could have wished nothing better than that she should have your answers to her difficulties, if she had been straight-forward in the matter.

I need not say how great a trouble it is to me. But it is the greatest to know that she has been led to this by no real intellectual or spiritual difficulties. She imagines that she has long had doubts about the English Church. This is an entire delusion – she has simply 'drifted'; and I doubt whether she grasps, at this moment, one of the real difficulties of the question.

But I need not trouble you with my troubles. What even now she will do I cannot tell. She never had much power of thought and her memory and other intellectual powers have been weakened by illness, so that she is – or seems to be – of one mind today, of another tomorrow.

But I leave it all in the hands of One who orders all things well; and I want only to say to you that I have no complaint to make of yourself, and that I thank you most sincerely for your letter.

Perhaps – when these earthly shadows have passed away – we may meet where I can without reserve have you as a teacher; for then the veil will be removed from the one or the other; but even here I can say how truly I am yours respectfully

W. R. Clark[97]

What is striking here is how dismissive the Vicar was of his wife's hard-earned convictions. As far as he could see, she had been led to Roman Catholicism "by no real intellectual or spiritual difficulties:" she was simply delusive. Yet, far from being the response of a merely flippant husband, this was the inveterate response of an entire Anglican society to anyone who chose Rome over Canterbury. Even Newman, when he was contemplating conversion, feared that he might be in the grip of delusion.[98] Ten days after converting, on October 19, 1845, Newman wrote Edward Badeley (1803–1868), his legal adviser and friend: "Six years ago the Catholicity of the Church of Rome broke on my mind suddenly and clearly. I have never shaken off the impression, though for a long while I dreaded to allow it, lest it should be a delusion. Nay the dread of delusion has kept me where I was till the last month."[99] The convert

Thomas Francis Knox (1822–1882), who was one of the more learned of the English Oratorians and briefly served as Superior of the London Oratory, took his revenge against the Anglican impudence of regarding conversions to Rome as Satanic delusions by telling Pusey that the English Church itself was "a delusion of Satan."[100]

Mrs. Clark was not alone in her reluctance to tell an immovably Protestant spouse about a change of religion that could only make for unpleasant division. The Earl of Dunraven (1841–1926), the Tory politician and yachtsman, who had been born at Adare Manor in County Limerick and later reported on the Franco-Prussian war for the *Daily Telegraph*, after traveling to America to engage in big game hunting with Buffalo Bill Cody, wrote Newman in 1854, after he had requested his public support of the Catholic University in Dublin: "… it appears to me simply to amount to a public declaration of Catholicism: and as I most solemnly, in the sight of God believe that my doing so would cause my wife's death: I cannot, and will not do it." Of course, this did not mean that he despaired of converting completely; only that he needed more time. Again, he wrote to Newman: "I know she has been making efforts to look the thing in the face, and prays to have strength to do God's will: I also feel latterly I have felt more earnestly my own desire to place myself unreservedly under His guidance in the matter; and more at present I cannot do—Oh pray forgive me if I have written any thing amiss."[101] Lord Dunraven's wife was Florence Elizabeth (1841–1916), second daughter of Lord Charles Lennox Kerr. After her husband converted in 1855, she bowed to the inevitable but remained staunchly Protestant herself. On the peculiar difficulties of converting without one's spouse, Lord Dunraven and Mrs. Clark could have exchanged lively notes.

After Mrs. Clark was received into the Church in October of 1877, Newman praised the courage she showed in going through with her conversion under such painful circumstances. "It is such trial as yours which makes one feel what it was that the early martyrs suffered. I have not forgotten you in my prayers, and I earnestly hope and trust and am sure that a portion of that special comfort from the Paraclete which was given to them will be given to you …"[102] The heroics of daily life meant a good deal to Newman.[103]

He wrote many of his letters to the female faithful to convince them that quotidian perfection was possible if they persevered.[104] As he told his dear friend Maria Giberne, when she was finding it difficult to persevere in her new life as a Visitationist nun, "Though I am not a religious, I can easily understand the temptation which may come upon even the most holy souls, or rather especially upon holy souls, to think they have made a mistake in taking vows of perfection. But the thought must not distress you. Only consider what troubles of mind would have come on you, had you not become a nun. Ah, you would have said, I was called, and I did not respond etc etc."[105] At the same time, when he was not yet fifty, he explained to Mary Holmes, the governess, with whom he would correspond off and on for over thirty years, why perseverance was so necessary.

As time goes on you will know yourself better and better. Time does that for us, not only by the increase of experience, but by the withdrawal of those natural assistances to devotion and selfsurrender which youth furnishes. When the spirits are high and the mind fervent, though we may have waywardnesses and perversenesses which we have not afterwards, yet we have something to battle against them. But when men get old, as I do, then they see how little grace is in them, and how much what seemed grace was but nature. Then the soul is left to lassitude, torpor, dejection, and coldness which is its real state, with no natural impulses affections or imaginations to rouse it, and things which in youth seemed easy then become difficult. Then it finds how little self command it has, and how little it can throw off the tempter when he comes behind and places it in a certain direction or position, or throws it down, or places his foot upon it. Then it understands at length its own nothingness, and that it has less grace than it had but it has nothing but grace to aid it. It is the sign of a saint to grow; common minds, even though they are in the grace of God, dwindle, (i.e. seem to do so) as time goes on. The energy of grace alone can make a soul strong in age.[106]

Nine years later, Newman would make an entry in his journal that made clear just how necessary it was to renew "the energy of grace:"

O my God, not as a matter of sentiment, nor as a matter of literary exhibition, do I put this down. O rid me of this frightful *cowardice*, for this is at the bottom of all my ills. When I was young, I was bold, because I was ignorant—now I have lost my boldness, because I have … advanced in experience. I am able to count the cost, better than I did, of being brave for Thy sake, and therefore I shrink from sacrifices. Here is a second reason, over and above the deadness of my soul, why I have so little faith or love in me.[107]

One thing that distinguished the counselor in Newman was that he never gave advice, however demanding, that he was not prepared to take himself. When he was awaiting the impending verdict of the Achilli trial, in which he was forced to defend himself against the libel charge of a defrocked Italian Dominican, a pathological rapist, whom the Evangelical Alliance had brought over to England in 1850 to defame the Roman Church in a series of popular lectures, Newman wrote to Sister Mary Agnes Philip Moore, "My only pain is that of reading the too kind letters of my friends—and that I assure you is real pain. Last November when I had before me a boundless ocean of expense, responsibility, and trouble, and in February again, when the horizon was indefinitely removed from me, then I felt pain—but I have no pain at all now. When November comes, for what I know, I may have pain for a day or two, but I cannot tell. I am sure so many prayers ought to make me better, and I am sensible they do not—and this is pain—but it is not the trial and its consequences that pain me. For twenty years I have been writing in verse and prose about suffering for the Truth's sake, and I have no right to complain, if, after having almost courted the world's injustice, I suffer it."[108] Here was perseverance *ex corde*.

Newman was also good about counseling his female correspondents in another kind of perseverance: learning to exercise the patience necessary to know when they were *unready* for conversion. In 1878, when Stella Austin, a writer of children's stories, shared with Newman her difficulties about Catholicism—which included her doubts about transubstantiation—Newman was careful to remind her that "no one ought to join the Church till he *is* convinced—and your business is to pray to God to enlighten you, to give you honesty in inquiry, to go right on, not swerving from unpleasant conclusions, and to make you brave, when conviction comes. He will be with you, don't doubt Him. That you may do His will and so save your soul is the sincere prayer of Yours very truly John H. Newman."[109] Miss Austen converted in 1885. When Lucy Agnes Vaughan Phillips—the sister of Charles John Vaughan, Headmaster of Harrow School, and the wife of George Peregrine Phillips, an Evangelical clergyman, who died in 1837, at the age of 35—visited Newman in 1851 and shared with him her interest in converting, he wrote her a letter setting out both the claims and the obligations of Catholicism, which were clearly meant to dissuade her from taking any ill-considered steps.

> It is quite true that the Catholic Church claims your absolute submission to her in matters of faith – Unless you believe her doctrines as the word of God revealed to you through her, you can gain no good by professing to be a Catholic – you are not one really. At the same time she does not ask your confidence without giving reasons for claiming it – and one mode of proving her divine authority among others, certainly is that which it has occurred to you to adopt – viz to see whether certain of her doctrines are not like truth, or reasonable, or scriptural, or conformable to the state of the world. You certainly may gain a ground for believing her, through the vraisemblance of her doctrines – but you cannot fully prove them – you can only see their excellence to a certain point – else, what the need of a revelation? a revelation implies the grant of something which could not otherwise be known. If then you have chosen this way of approaching the Church, you must think it enough to prove her doctrines to a certain point – and then your argument will be this, 'Since I have been able to prove the Catholic doctrines so far, I will take the whole on faith –' just as you trust an informant who has in other matters already shown he has a claim to be trusted.

And then he made reference to the "notes of the Church" that animated so much of his *Essay on the Development of Christian Doctrine* (1845): "The more obvious reasons for believing the Church to come from God are its great notes, as they are called—such as its antiquity, universality, its unchangeableness through so many revolutions and controversies, its adaptation to our wants. The more you think on these subjects, the more, under God's grace, will you be led to see that the Catholic Church is God's guide to you."[110] As it happened, Mrs. Phillips proved an apt catechumen. In August 1851, she finally converted with her children (a boy and two girls) and when her brothers threatened to bring the children up Protestant, she absconded with them to the Continent. Having made her point, she returned to England, where she formed a small hospital in

Edgbaston, near the Oratory. One of her friends was the sister of A. P. Stanley, Arnold's biographer, Mary Stanley, who wrote to her when she was serving as a nurse in the Crimea: "Will you tell Dr. Newman when next you see him how much I hope soon to make his acquaintance for his first Volume of sermons were the first sermons I ever read with any pleasure; and the one on 'Obedience the best remedy for religious perplexity' has been my stay in many troubles."[111] Doubtless, she found great practical counsel in Newman's assurance that, "To all those who are perplexed in any way soever, who wish for light but cannot find it, one precept must be given,—*obey*." Indeed, for Newman, by resolving "to obey God, in the ordinary businesses of life, we are at once interested by realities which withdraw our minds from vague fears and uncertain indefinite surmises about the future." Certainly he had taken this advice himself when he was faced with very harrowing "indefinite surmises" before the Achilli trial.[112]

After publishing his *Grammar of Assent* in 1870, Newman was gratified to hear that his frequent correspondent, the governess Miss Holmes, had read the book. "It will please me much," he wrote, "if you say of the last 100 pages what you say for the chapter on certitude – for they were written especially for those who can't go into questions of the inspiration of Scripture, authenticity of books, passages in the Fathers etc etc ... ." Indeed, Newman had written his highly unconventional treatise "especially for such ladies as are bullied by infidels and do not know how to answer them ..." He "wanted to show that, keeping to broad facts of history, which every one knows and no one can doubt, there is evidence and reason enough for an honest inquirer to believe in revelation."[113] A solitary woman who never stayed long with any of the families that engaged her, Miss Holmes sought Newman out in 1840 after reading his sermons and converted in 1844. Although initially opposed to her converting, convinced that she was relying more on impulse than settled conviction, Newman soon came to see her Catholic faith as the still center in her otherwise itinerant, precarious life. If he warmed to her intelligence, he worried about her restlessness. When she found employment with the Blounts in Mapledurham, Oxfordshire, in 1864, Newman wrote to her: "I write you a line to congratulate you on your having got to Mapledurham. Now don't leave it, please. Don't be angry, if I say that you like strangers at first, but you tire of them, when they become acquaintances. No one, but yourself, can know the penances which you undergo in any family, be it ever so near perfection – much more in families which are not perfect – but you can't tell how it distresses me when I see one like yourself, who deserve so much better things, tossing on the waves – and this distress both makes me pleased, as now, that you have come into port again, and desirous that in port you should continue."[114] In the case of the *Grammar of Assent*, she apparently had no trouble grasping Newman's argument with respect to certainty, which baffled many of his more learned friends, including John Dalgairns (1818–1876), the Oratorian who would later become the Superior of the London Oratory, and T. W. Allies (1813–1903), an Old Etonian and former Fellow of Wadham College whom Newman appointed Lecturer of History at the Catholic University.[115] Newman also admired her pluck, even though some of her letters must have tried his patience. In one she wrote: "Your letter today has revealed to me that I have been making an idol of you, and henceforward I shall pray to have strength to do without you. You write to tell me, *you have nothing to say to me.* Ah, Mr. Newman, this is more like a Brutus than a Christian Father. I had presentiment that your letter would be painful, and I don't think any thing ever hurt me more."[116] Newman's response was full of forbearing charm. "My dear Miss Holmes, rouse yourself to better thoughts—resign yourself to things as they are ... Exert that strong sense and vigor of mind with which you are so largely gifted. Aim at subduing yourself, and ruling your feelings, and attaining equanimity. All this will seem very cold to you, but in Lent one may bear it."[117]

Newman could not abide being idolized. "I am *not* venerable, and nothing can make me so," he told Miss Holmes on another occasion. "Do not suffer any illusive notions about me ..."[118] At the same time, he was annoyed when he got wind of the idolatrous attention that Pusey was being paid, which the Canon of Christ Church did not discourage, especially in his female acolytes. One of these was Catherine Ward (1813–1897), whose life would crisscross with those of other contemporaries dear to Newman. The third daughter of Seth Stephen Ward of Camberwell, Catherine lived at Norland House, Clifton, with the family of her brother-in-law, Samuel Wayte, whose son, Samuel William, was a Fellow, later President, of Trinity College, Oxford, where Newman was an undergraduate from 1817 to 1820 and later received an honorary degree in 1877. In 1839 she had begun reading his sermons, and in 1845 she put herself under the spiritual direction of Edward Pusey, who, after Newman's secession from the Anglican Church in 1845, was the *de facto* leader of the Tractarian party within the Established Church. In 1848, Catherine wrote lengthy letters to Newman describing her tumultuous religious history and explaining how she was drawn to Catholicism after listening to Pusey describe his Anglo-Catholic pastiche of Catholicism—what Newman called his "mimic Catholicism."[119] In 1849, a year after Newman's extensive correspondence with her began, she converted to Rome. After converting, she sent altar hangings for Newman's first church in Alcester Street. In 1857, she married George Tylee (1807–1865), a retired Major-General, who had become a Catholic in 1847, after being influenced by his Cambridge friend, John Joseph Gordon (1811–1853), one of Newman's most trusted and beloved Oratorians, who, like so many of his dearest friends, died young. After George Tylee's death in Rome, Catherine lived on at Clifton, where she died in 1897.

In her first letter to Newman, Catherine described how she had begun to doubt Anglicanism, despite the instruction she was taking from Pusey. As her trust in the Church of England fell, her interest in Catholicism rose. "One great truth which draws me to her," she said, apropos the Roman Church, "is that wonderful Sacramental system, so lost, confused, almost vilified in the Church of England and tho' Dr. Pusey and others hold it, and give me leave to hold it, yet it is in such an isolated manner that I cannot feel it as a truth of the Church but only as held by individuals—in fact the Church of England as Dr. Pusey holds it, seems more like an Ideal Church, than real one."[120] Newman wrote her back a series of letters, which, taken together, are a kind of dress rehearsal for those sections in his King William Street lectures, later published as *Anglican*

Difficulties (1850), where he pointed out the incoherence of Puseyite Anglo-Catholicism. Specifically, he argued that "the Anglican Church cannot take support from the high religious excellence of individuals who are found in her" because "the direction of their holy feelings, views, and works is, not towards that Church, but away from it, and bears testimony consequently, not to it, but against it; whereas the whole company of Catholic Saints ... are the natural fulfilment of the idea, the due exemplification of the teaching, of the Catholic Church. Who will say that fasting, devotion, and the like are in any sense the fruit of the historical, real, tangible Church of England? Is not the idea of an Anglican Bishop or clergyman, that of a gentleman, a scholar, a good father of a family, a well conducted, kindhearted, religiously minded man, and little more?"[121] This was a point which many of his female friends were in a unique position to verify because in their charitable work they could see that the Anglican Church meant nothing to the lower orders, a fact for which there is ample corroboration in Henry Mayhew's study of the London poor. Speaking of the religion of the costermongers, for example, he wrote: "An intelligent and trustworthy man, until very recently actively engaged in costermongering, computed that not three in one hundred costermongers had ever been in the interior of a church, or any place of worship, or knew what was meant by Christianity."[122] For Newman, the fact that most clergymen of the Church of England tended to be removed from the poor put them beyond the pale of sanctity.[123] "Take a really true specimen of an Anglican, a fair specimen; e.g. ... the Bishop of London or Dr Hook; they are not the tenth, the twentieth, the infinitesmal part of a Saint; you could not multiply them up until they became saints; they tend to something different; their perfection is something different." Nor was Pusey representative of anything saintly within the Church of England. For Newman, it was self-evident that "no one would call [Pusey] a specimen of the Church of England; he is undeniably foreign, outlandish; whereas everyone would call St Carlo or St Francis de Sales, a specimen of the Catholic Church; I mean a specimen of its teaching, its profession, its aim. Is Dr Pusey more like a Monk or a Dignitary? is he of the Anglican type? How then can such as he be witnesses for the sanctity and divine life of the Anglican Church? As well might you say that the Irish character was cool, self possessed, patient, and unimaginative, because the Duke of Wellington is an Irishman."[124]

Newman, on the other hand, was revered by the Birmingham poor, who, according to an article in the *Daily Mail* felt a "great personal attachment" to him, arising "from the knowledge of his simple and sanctified life and his kindly love for the poor," an attachment which "was illustrated by their great anxiety to secure a seat in the church whenever of late years some great occasion had given rise to his Eminence being present."[125]

For Newman, to see the deficiencies of Anglo-Catholicism, one had only to take into account its chief architect. "Dear Dr Pusey does not witness by his virtues for his Church, he witnesses for himself, he witnesses for his own opinions," he told Catherine. Of course, Pusey and the remaining Tractarian faithful denied this. "But since he himself would shrink from such a conclusion, since he refers us to his Church and considers that he puts forth its doctrine not his own, I want to know what single individual that ever belonged to the Anglican Church does he follow. Not Laud, for Laud on the scaffold avowed himself an honest Protestant; not Hooker, for he gives up the Real Presence; not Taylor, for he blames both the Athanasian and Nicene Creeds; not Bull, for he considers that Transubstantiation 'bids defiance to all the reason and sense of mankind;' not Ussher, for he was a Calvinist; not Jewell, for he gave up the Priesthood; nor the Articles, for Dr P. puts an interpretation on them; nor the Prayer Book, for he believes about twice as much as the Prayer Book contains. Who before him ever joined the circle of Roman doctrine to the Anglican ritual and polity?" Here was that rhetorical panache that Newman's opponents found so tiresome and so unanswerable. Nevertheless, Newman wished to reassure his correspondent that he did "enter into and sympathize" with her "severe struggle of thought and feeling;" and he would remember her in his daily Mass, and, as he said, "earnestly trust you will soon be brought out of your difficulties …"[126] When, subsequently, she wrote regarding Our Lady, Newman wrote back in his helpful way, "As to her being the sole hope of sinners, this, I conceive, is literally true, in the sense in which such words are commonly used—Thus the sole cause of salvation is God, the sole cause is Christ, the sole cause is a certain illness or accident, the sole cause is baptism, the sole cause is faith … In like manner our Lady has a delegated omnipotence in her own sphere, i.e., of intercession …"[127] In a later letter, he returned to this basal reality: "devotion to the Blessed Virgin is the ordinary way to heaven, and the absence of it is at least a bad symptom of the state of our faith."[128]

In one of her letters, Catherine echoed one of the most persistent objections of the English to the Roman Church when she observed that "Infidelity prevails more where Roman Catholic religion prevails …" Newman was inclined to agree, though he recognized that verifying such things was not easy. "If I were to judge antecedently, I should grant this; for where there is the greatest light, shadows are strongest. He who can reject the Truth, not unnaturally is punished with fanatical hatred of it. And again, there is nothing else to go to then; Protestantism does not exist, or is despised as a half way house, and a sort of hypocrisy. But I am very doubtful about the fact; for really it seems to me as if the greater portion of the thinking class (par excellence) in England at present are very near professed infidels."[129]

When Catherine wrote to say that she had read Newman's *Essay on the Development of Doctrine* (1845), but was unsure as to why the Roman Church alone should possess what he called "the notes of the Church," he wrote back: "The Notes of the Church do not depend on the particular doctrine of this or that divine, but are such as … approve themselves to the mass of mankind, as being involved in the notion of a revelation. It is nothing to the purpose then that this communion or that says that itself has the Notes of the Church; or that the divines of this or that say so; for the fact is to be decided, not by any such private judgment, but by the consent of the world."[130] Here was another affirmation of Augustine's great maxim, which was so instrumental in Newman's conversion: 'Securus judicat orbis terrarum'—'The universal Church is in its judgments secure of its truth.'[131] "If Anglicans say that they have catholicity, that does not decide the question, any more than their saying that they are in the Church. Nor does it decide it, on the other hand, for a Roman Catholic to say that his communion has the Notes, or that his communion is the Church. The appeal and the decision lie with the bulk of mankind. Take then the Roman Church, and take the Anglican in a large town; let each call itself the Church, and just see what the people say to it. They may prefer the Anglican, as more Scriptural, as not being corrupt ... but they will all say, or will show they feel, that the Roman Church, whether corrupted, whether perverted, (which is a question of opinion) yet in matter of fact is the continuation of that old Church, called Catholic, which has been in the world from time immemorial, which has been in the world so long that you cannot say when it was not in the world, to which you can assign no date short of the Apostles."[132] This readiness to concede the corruptions of the Church was typical of a man who had not converted to Rome because he imagined the Church, in its human aspects, incorruptible. "There are now, as at all times," he told Catherine, "a thousand disorders within and without the Church –her head is in exile – her subject countries in political strife – her members full of imperfection – but there is that in her which is what she peculiarly promises, which no other body promises, and in which she does not deceive; she can present a Creed, she alone can do what a Messenger from heaven ought to do; and her children feel this and are satisfied. If you join the Catholic Church for fine services, for splendid temples, for outward show or appearance of any kind, if it were in you an indulgence of sentiment or imagination, you might in this event be disappointed; – you cannot be disappointed in seeking in it those great attributes which our reason tells us belong to the oracle of heaven and the Vicar of Christ."[133]

During the course of their correspondence, Catherine questioned the miracles of the Church. Newman was adamant that when it came to these and other objections, inquiry could be prolonged indefinitely, which prompted him to ask his correspondent: "And are you not in the way to be one of those who ever seek and therefore never find?" Here, he might have been thinking of his brother Frank, who succumbed to lifelong seeking, with calamitous consequences for his Christian faith. "Alas," Newman assured Mrs. Ward, "I can believe how wayward the mind may be under the fearful pressure of perplexities in faith, but how many there are in the Anglican Church who would leap for joy to attain that intellectual conviction which you have possessed ..." Moreover, he was adamant that it was wrongheaded to treat the truths of faith as though they were abstruse propositions, which somehow required ingenious unriddling. "As to the question of inquiring about religion, surely religion is not like the 'philosophy of Plato and Aristotle,' for the learned only," he insisted. "What a condemnation of any man's religious system, for him to allow that it is like a heathen science. To the poor is the Gospel preached. Accordingly the notes of the Church are simple and easy, and obvious to all capacities."[134]

This was a theme to which he would return twenty years later in an important letter to Louisa Simeon, which Newman sent in June of 1869 when Louisa was 26 and full of doubts about a faith that her smart young Protestant friends could only see as outmoded and irrational.

Another thought which I wish to put before you is, whether our nature does not tell us that there is something which has more intimate relations with the question of religion than intellectual exercises have, and that is our conscience. We have the idea of duty – duty suggests something or some one to which it is to be referred, to which we are responsible. That something that has dues upon us is to us God. I will not assume it is a personal God, or that it is more than a law (though of course I hold that it is the Living Seeing God) but still the idea of duty, and the terrible anguish of conscience, and the irrepressible distress and confusion of face which the transgression of what we believe to be our duty, cause us, all this is an intimation, a clear evidence, that there is something nearer to religion than intellect; and that, if there is a way of finding religious truth, it lies, not in exercises of the intellect, but close on the side of duty, of conscience, in the observance of the moral law.[135]

By the same token, Newman was quick to point out that "You must not suppose that I am denying the intellect its real place in the discovery of truth; but it must ever be borne in mind that its exercise mainly consists in reasoning,—that is, in comparing things, classifying them, and inferring. It ever needs points to start from, first principles, and these it does not provide – but it can no more move one step without these starting points, than a stick, which supports a man, can move without the man's action …" Here was an argument that he mounted many times, most notably in his *Oxford University Sermons* (1843) and, then, again, in *An Essay in Aid of a Grammar of Assent* (1870). For Newman, if the intellect could not provide the first principles of religion, "we have to ascertain the starting points for arriving at religious truth. The intellect will be useful in gaining them and after gaining them – but to attempt to see them by means of the intellect is like attempting by the intellect to see the physical facts which are the basis of physical exercises of the intellect, a method of proceeding which was the very mistake of the Aristotelians of the middle age, who, instead of what Bacon calls 'interrogating nature' for facts, reasoned out every thing by syllogisms. To gain religious starting points, we must in a parallel way, interrogate our hearts, and (since it is a personal, individual matter,) our own hearts, – interrogate our own consciences, interrogate, I will say, the God who dwells there." Here is an excellent example of that inspired counsel that is so characteristic of his letters to the female faithful. And, like all of his writing, it is splendidly practical. Newman never wrote to have his readers merely ponder possibilities: he wrote to encourage them to act. So, in his letter to Louisa, he ended by telling her, "I think you must ask the God of Conscience to enable you to do your duty in this matter. I think you should, with prayer to Him for help, meditate upon the Gospels, and on St Paul's second Epistle to the Corinthians … and this with an earnest desire to know the truth and a sincere intention of following it."[136]

Something about the doubts and difficulties of the young always appealed to Newman. Perhaps because he could sympathize with their disillusionment in confronting what James Joyce once called "that battered cabman's face, the world."[137] John Hungerford Pollen, who became Newman's Professor of Fine Arts at the Catholic University in Dublin recalled: "The late Cardinal's sympathy with the young was a feature of his character ... He felt for their generosity, their hopefulness, the trials, the struggles, the disappointments that might be in store for them in the unknown future."[138] When the eldest daughter of his closest undergraduate friend, Mary Anne Frances Bowden was unsure of what path she should take, Newman wrote her one of his most moving letters.

The Oratory Birmingham June 5 1866

My dear Child,

Fanny [Frances Jane Bowden] told me about you, as doubtless she has told you. I will not forget the Masses – they will help you, and you must simply put yourself into God's hands. As I understood F. you have no call on you to do any thing, or to decide on doing any thing, at this moment. Do you know, though this is of course a trial, yet I have ever felt it a great mercy. One of the greatest of trials is, to have it cast upon one to make up one's mind, – on some grave question, with great consequences spreading into the future, – and to be in doubt what one ought to do. You have not this trial – it is also a trial to wait and do nothing but how great a mercy is it not to have responsibility! Put your self then, my dear Child, into the hands of your loving Father and Redeemer, who knows and loves you better than you know or love yourself. He has appointed every action of your life. He created you, sustains you, and has marked down the very way and hour when He will take you to Himself. He knows all your thoughts, and feels for you in all your sadness more than any creature can feel, and accepts and makes note of your prayers even before you make them. He will never fail you – and He will give you what is best for you. And though He tries you, and seems to withdraw Himself from you, and afflicts you, still trust in Him, for at length you will see how good and gracious He is, and how well he will provide for you. Be courageous and generous, and give Him your heart, and you will never repent of the sacrifice

Ever Yours affectionately in Xt John H Newman[139]

This understanding of the daily choice implicit in Christianity was something Newman's bishop, William Ullathorne, also appreciated. "There is no master so large-minded, so generous, so well acquainted with you and your requirements as God," wrote this shrewd, good-hearted, reverant Yorkshireman, who had played so heroic a part in converting the convicts of New South Wales; "no father so loving and bountiful; no friend so free from all jealousy; none who so completely loves you for your greater good. While there is no tyrant so narrow-minded, so proudhearted, so exacting, so suspicious, so utterly bent on keeping you to your own littleness, as the one who we all know so well, of whose tyranny we have had such bitter experience, and who goes by the name of Myself. Yet God or yourself you must choose as your master."[140]

In impressing upon Mary Anne how vital it was for the individual Christian to form a personal relationship with God, without which no love of God was possible, Newman was echoing sentiments to which he gave powerful expression in one of his best sermons, "Love, the One Thing Needful," which he composed in February 1839. There he enjoined his readers to cherish "a constant sense of the love of your Lord and Saviour in dying on the cross for you," because "where hearts are in their degree renewed after Christ's image, there, under His grace, gratitude to Him will increase our love of Him ..." And since "Christ showed his love in deed, not in word," we should be "touched by the Thought of His cross far more by bearing it after him, than by glowing accounts of it." And here he advised his readers to make their meditations "simple and severe."

> Think of the Cross when you rise and when you lie down, when you go out and when you come in, when you eat and when you walk and when you converse, when you buy and when you sell, when you labour and when you rest, consecrating and sealing all your doings with this one mental action, the thought of the Crucified.[141]

Then, he exhorted his readers to "dwell often upon those His manifold mercies to us and to our brethren, which are the consequences of His coming upon earth; His adorable counsels ... the wonders of His grace towards us, from our infancy until now; the gifts He has given us, the aid He has vouchsafed; the answers He has accorded to our prayers ..." These personal mercies would put us in mind of more extensive mercies and lead us to "meditate upon ... His faithfulness to His promises, and the mysterious mode of their fulfillment; how He has ever led His people forward safely and prosperously ... amid so many enemies; what unexpected events have worked His purposes; how evil has been changed into good; how his Saints have been brought on to their perfection in the darkest times."[142] Here, he might have been directly invoking many of the women who would join him in making the love of God manifest, even though, when he wrote this, he had scarcely met them.

> It is by such deeds and such thoughts that our services, our repentings, our prayers, our intercourse with men, will become instinct with the spirit of love. Then we do everything thankfully and joyfully, when we are temples of Christ, with His Image set up in us. Then it is that we mix with the world without loving it, for our affections are given to another. We can bear to look on the world's beauty, for we have no heart for it. We are not disturbed at its frowns, for we live not in its smiles. We rejoice in the House of Prayer, because He is there "whom our soul loveth." We can condescend to the poor and lowly, for they are the presence of Him who is Invisible. We are patient in bereavement, adversity, or pain, for they are Christ's tokens.[143]

In the wonderful correspondence between Newman and his women friends— which if culled from the letters as a whole would capture the very essence of the man—we can see what a Christ-like affection Newman felt for those good, devoted, brave women, who meant so much to the Church, in its uncertain Second Spring. Newman's affection for them was an affection they entirely reciprocated. As Joyce Sugg remarks, "His women friends thought the world of him, were delighted when he was made a cardinal and at his death they would instantly have acclaimed him a saint if their opinion had been asked."[144] After Newman's death in 1890, Miss Bowles actually referred to him as their "lost Saint."[145] Forty years before, Newman had written to a Miss Munro, who was received into the Church by Cardinal Wiseman, "I have nothing of a Saint about me as every one knows, and it is a severe (and salutary) mortification to be thought next door to one. I may have a high view of many things ... but this is very different from *being* what I admire."[146] The female faithful would have begged to differ.

CHAPTER 7

Newman and Gladstone

Gladstone and Newman—unlike that other famous pair, Gladstone and Disraeli—had much in common. Their letters and diaries illuminate much about the religious character of one of the most religious societies that England ever produced. Even the Fabian historian Sir Robert Ensor, writing in the mid-1930s, conceded, in a typically backhanded way, that "No one will ever understand Victorian England who does not appreciate that among highly civilized, in contradistinction to more primitive, countries it was one of the most religious that the world has known."[1] When it became clear that that society was giving way to what Newman described as the "great apostasia," both Newman and Gladstone became trenchant critics of the rise of unbelief. Both were biblio-philes.[2] Both were redoubtable leaders. In March 1877, when he had just completed *The American*, Henry James wrote to his brother William describing a dinner he had attended with Gladstone, Lord Houghton, Dr. Schliemann ("the excavator of old Mycenae"), and Tennyson (who talked of nothing but port wine and tobacco): "I was glad of a chance to feel the 'personality' of a great political leader … That of Gladstone is fascinating—his urbanity extreme—his eye that of a man of genius—& his apparent self surrender to what he is talking of, without a flaw. He made a great impression on me—greater than any I have seen here."[3]

Newman never felt at ease hobnobbing with the famous or powerful.[4] He certainly never attended celebrity dinners, though Gladstone tried for years to get him to attend celebrity breakfasts. One of the most amusing aspects of their correspondence is how frequently Gladstone tried to get Newman to play the ecclesiastical lion and the inveteracy with which he politely declined. That was a role he conceded to Manning. Yet, for all his distaste for the trappings of leadership, Newman led a revival of religious life in England that inspired the hearts and minds of nearly everyone who came into contact with him. Indeed, it is still in progress. As the future Archbishop of Canterbury, Edward White Benson, wrote, after hearing Newman preach at St. Chad's in 1848, "Surely, if there is a man whom God has raised up in his generation with more than common power to glorify His name, this man is he."[5]

A good portion of the power of both men came from their voices. Gladstone was one of the few great orators never left speaking to green benches and red boxes.[6] And by all accounts he was even more impressive in the open air. T. P. O'Connor described him at 76 so enthralling a crowd in Liverpool that it was almost like "the trailing of a miraculous saint among masses of idolaters."[7] Newman was no orator and certainly never meant to inspire idolatry but nearly every one who ever met him or heard him preach remarked on the beauty of his voice. The Irish poet Aubrey de Vere recalled it as "so distinct that you could count each vowel and consonant in every word."[8] Sir John Coleridge, one of the judges at the Achilli trial, recalled it as "a sweet musical, almost unearthly voice … so unlike any other we had heard."[9]

Both men mulled over major projects for decades before bringing them to fruition. It was a conversation with the French historian Guizot in 1845 that first inspired Gladstone to try to improve conditions in Ireland.[10] Over thirty years later, after Gladstone had disestablished the Church of Ireland (1869) and passed the first Land Act (1870), he wrote to the French historian to thank him for his fertile suggestion.

> It is very unlikely that you shall remember a visit I paid you, I think at Passy in the autumn of 1845, with a message from Lord Aberdeen about international copyright. The Maynooth Act had just been passed. Its author, I think, meant it to be final. I had myself regarded it as *seminal*. And you in congratulating me upon it, as I well remember, said we should have the sympathies of Europe in the work of giving Ireland justice—a remark which evidently included more than the measure just passed, and which I have ever after saved and pondered. It helped me on towards what has since been done.[11]

Similarly, it was in an epistolary debate with his brother Charles in the spring and summer of 1825 that Newman began delving into the relation between faith and reason that he would return to fifty years later in *An Essay in Aid of a Grammar of Assent* (1870). Of course, that brilliant book was based on years of counseling the believing and the unbelieving. Yet in the letters he wrote to his brother when he was 24, Newman got at the root of apostasy. "A dislike of the contents of Scripture is at the bottom of unbelief; and since those contents must be rejected by fair means or foul, it is plain that in order to do this the evidences must in some sort be attacked …"[12]

Perhaps the greatest bond that Gladstone and Newman shared was their debt to Oxford, to what Newman recalled as "its splendour and its sweetness."[13] G. M. Young said that Gladstone remained a Christ Church man of the 1830s all his days.[14] Translating Aristotle at the feet of Mr. Biscoe, his classical tutor, made an indelible impression, which one can see "in those analytic and deductive memoranda which the poor Queen had to have translated before she could make head or tail of them."[15] When the Vice-Chancellor of Oxford sent him a card on his deathbed, acknowledging the years of service he had given as the university's MP, Gladstone dictated his response to his youngest daughter: "There is no expression of Christian sympathy that I value more than that of the ancient university of Oxford, the God-fearing, God-sustaining university of Oxford … My most earnest prayers are hers to the uttermost and to the last."[16]

The impact Oxford had on Newman was equally profound—it taught him to think, it made him a Catholic. Twenty years after deciding to leave the place to join what he called the "One True Fold"[17] he could still confide in a friend: "You can't tell how very much down I am at the thought of going to Oxford … the very seeing Oxford again, since I am not one with it, would be a cruel thing—it is like the dead coming to the dead. O dear, dear, how I dread it."[18] When he finally returned to accept his honorary Trinity fellowship in February 1878, he met his old tutor, Thomas Short, now 89, lunching on lamb chops, and found his old rooms occupied by a young man who had theatrical pin-ups on the walls. The diplomat James Bryce heard an after-dinner speech Newman gave during his visit and recalled "the aged face worn deep with the lines of thought, struggle and sorrow. The story of a momentous period in the history of the University and of religion in England seemed to be written there."[19]

Another story of that "momentous period" that has not been given the attention it deserves is the long association of Gladstone and Newman, particularly why Newman was so indulgent towards Gladstone, a man who struck many of his contemporaries—Disraeli and Queen Victoria come most readily to mind but there were many others—as hypocritical, self-righteous, reckless, erratic, even unbalanced. "I sometimes think him rather mad," Victoria's secretary, Henry Ponsonby, once said, "earnestly mad, and taking up a view with an intensity which scarcely allows him to suppose there can be any truth on the other side."[20] Salisbury saw Gladstone's self-righteousness as impervious to doubt: "The process of self-deceit goes on in his mind without the faintest self-consciousness or self-suspicion. The result is that it goes on without check or stint."[21] One of Gladstone's college tutors told William Allingham, the Irish poet and diarist, that when he complemented old Mr. Gladstone on his son's academic success, the old man looked grave and replied: "I have no doubt of William's ability; I wish I were equally sure of his stability."[22] Newman, by contrast, went out of his way to defend Gladstone, to make excuses for him when his enemies or even his own Party were intent on scapegoating him, to attribute only the best motives to his often dubious positions. He saw more in the man than the sanctimony and instability that so many others saw.

Gladstone's view of Newman would always be complex, but no reading of the development of that view can be complete without starting with some account of how he responded to Newman's conversion.

When Gladstone read Tract 90 in February 1841, he saw nothing objectionable about it. By the end of that rancorous year, however, he could only marvel at the division that was rending the Church of England. "God help this labouring Church, and send us no more of such disastrous years. Tract 90 … the Jerusalem Bishopric, Sibthorp's sad defection, and Oxford at deadly strife with herself upon the question of whether a connection with the Tracts is or is not a disqualification for holding a Poetry Professorship! Hitherto the sacred principle of communion had bound us all together, and had even gathered strength amidst the agitation and conflict of private opinions, but these shocks sadly strain the vessel."[23] When Gladstone learned of Newman's growing doubts about the English Church in the years following Tract 90 from his good friend Henry Manning, who shared with him Newman's candid letters on Anglicanism, Gladstone responded with "a heavy heart."[24] After September 1843, when Newman resigned the living of St. Mary's, Gladstone's concern took a critical turn. "I am persuaded that this powerful man has suffered and is suffering much … from exclusiveness of mental habit, and from affections partly wounded through cruelty, partly overwrought into morbid action from gloating as it were continually and immediately upon the most absorbing and exciting subjects."[25] This described what Gladstone himself was undergoing, not the calm deliberate judicious scrutiny to which Newman was subjecting his convictions. Still, for Gladstone, it was one thing for impulsive young Oxford men to defect to Rome after the outcry against Tract 90, but now that Newman himself seemed to be inclining in that direction, he was aghast. When Manning showed Gladstone the letter that Newman had written him on 25 October 1843, Gladstone could scarcely take it in. "I am so bewildered and overthrown I am wholly unfit … I cannot make this letter hang together." Newman had written to Manning with unambiguous finality, "I must tell you then frankly, lest I combat arguments which to me, alas, are shadows, that it is from no disappointment, irritation, or impatience, that I have … resigned St. Mary's—but because I think the Church of Rome the Catholic Church, and ours not a part of the Catholic Church, because not in communion with Rome, and feel that I could not honestly be a teacher in it any longer."[26] For Gladstone, Newman's potential defection was bad enough but what made it worse was to hear the erstwhile champion of Catholic Anglicanism repudiating the claim of the English Church to any part in the Catholic Church. On October 28th, Gladstone wrote back to Manning: "Alas! alas! for your letter and enclosures of this morning! My first thought is, 'I stagger to and fro like a drunken man, and am at my wit's end'." Nevertheless, Gladstone held out hope that all might not be lost: "even out of the enormity of the mischief arises some gleam of consolation …. I cling to the hope that what he terms his conviction is not a conclusion finally seated in his mind, but one which he sees advancing upon him without the means of resistance or escape."[27] By 1843, Newman might no longer be the reliable hammer of Rome that he had been in the early Tracts, where even Gladstone found him "too free in the epithets of protest and censure," but he was still an immense credit to the English Church, whose defection would be an incomparable loss.[28] Indeed, for Gladstone, Newman's wavering put the whole nation on tenterhooks; it was nothing less than "the greatest crisis & sharpest that the Church has known since the Reformation.—for such I do, for one, feel would be the crisis of the apostasy of a man whose intellectual stature is among the very first of his age, and who has indisputably headed the most powerful movement and the nearest to the seat of life that the Church has known, at least for two centuries."[29] With so much in the balance, some providential change of mind, some miraculous change of heart might still reclaim him. The very fact that Newman had been entertaining his doubts about the Catholic legitimacy of the English Church since 1839 might still work against Rome. Perhaps he was deliberately holding out for some reassurance from the Anglican Church. "He has waited probably in the hope of its being changed—perhaps he might wait still—& God's inexhaustible mercy may overflow upon him & us."[30] Gladstone would have been more hopeful still if he had known that Newman himself had questioned whether he might be under some delusion in suspecting Rome to be the one true Church. In all events, Gladstone was not prepared to concede defeat. "What is wanted," he wrote to Manning in December 1843, "is that cords of silk should one by one be thrown over him to bind him to the Church. Every manifestation of sympathy and confidence in him, as a man, must have some small effect."[31] When Newman discontinued his work on the Lives of the English Saints—in response to criticism that he and his collaborators were depicting the saints in ways that were too Romish—he wrote to James Hope, who was also a good friend of Gladstone's: "I am glad that Gladstone is pleased with what I did. I did all I could under my then engagements and promises. Had such opinions as his and Pusey's happened to come sooner, I should have given up the whole plan. At the same time I do not think I have more than thrown it back, and *when* it revives, of course it will be in less safe hands than mine. Also, G. ought to be aware, as I daresay he is, that a series of thwartings such as I have experienced ... but realizes, verifies, substantizes, a φαντασία [impression] of the English Church very unfavourable to her Catholicity." This was the ungainsayable logic that Gladstone would never concede. Newman could put himself in Gladstone's shoes because he, too, had tried to resist making concessions to the same remorseless logic of the inalienably Protestant Established Church but, as he told Hope, his resistance had given out. "If a person is deeply convinced in his reason that her claims to Catholicity are untenable, but fears to trust his reason, such events, when they come upon him again and again, seem to do just what is wanting: [they] corroborate his reason ... They force upon his imagination and familiarize his moral perception with the conclusions of his intellect. Propositions become facts."[32]

Comically, it was at Baden-Baden that Gladstone finally got word that his hopes for Newman's return to the Anglican fold were futile. On 29 October 1845, Newman met with the Passionist Father Dominic Barberi and was received into the Roman Catholic Church. Gladstone's response could hardly conceal how much he and so many others prized their "front rank man:" "The Church of England, being a reality, is not dependent on this or that individual, the immediate duty is, when one secedes, simply to think of the supplying his place, as a rear rank man steps forward when his front rank man falls in battle."[33]

What made Newman's secession personally unsettling to Gladstone was that it rejected so thoroughly the Catholic claims of the Anglican Church to which he was so passionately attached. On 31 January 1842, he wrote a long letter to *The Times* in which he held forth on what he meant by the Catholic core of the national Church.

It is one of the conspicuous benefits of the Catholic principle, that as it teaches men they are knit together by the sacred bond of communion in the body of the Saviour, and not by the unsure coincidence of the operations of their own weak judgments upon high and sacred truth, it can no longer remain a question of private inclination or choice founded thereon, whether to adhere to a given form of religion or to leave it. If such a body be bound within that sacred bond—that is, if it be Catholic—it is a duty to remain in it; if the silver cord be broken, it is a duty to depart. It is their business to be, not where they will, or where they like, or where they choose, but where they have the assured promise of the Spirit. But when the character of Catholicity is erased, the Church leaves them, and not they the Church ... Upon that word, that one word Catholic, they have concentrated their single hope and desire, their entire and undivided affections. Not because it is in opposition to the spirit of our reformed religion: on the contrary, they harmonize together. Not because it is in substation for the originality and intrinsically higher, but now neutralized, if not profaned, designation of Christian, but because, ennobled and consecrated in the struggles of sixteen hundred years, it has become inseparably associated with the idea of the everlasting Gospel as a permanent and substantive revelation from God, and is the only epithet which can now be said to constitute a fit and a full exponent of that idea. It alone is the fence which infidelity has never overleapt, the weapon it has never dared to handle. Without its bulwark lie the varying and uncertain forms of human waywardness: within it is the City of God.[34]

Ten years before, John Bowden, Newman's closest friend at Oxford, had made Gladstone's point even more boldly: "Our great error has been that we have forgotten ourselves, or at least forgotten to teach others, that we, Churchmen, are the Catholics of England; and, unless we can wrest the monopoly of the term from the Papists, we do nothing. We must disabuse our fellow churchmen of the idea that we belong to a Church, comparatively new, which, some 300 years ago, supplanted the old Catholic Church of these realms. Let us then bear, by all means, our Catholic title on our front ..."[35] Whether Newman, with his far greater familiarity with the patristic tradition and with the works of the Anglican divines of the seventeenth century, ever entirely persuaded himself that this was indeed the case is dubious. In any case, once Newman denied the Catholicity of the Anglican faith, Gladstone recognized that he was denying his own faith altogether. To understand where Gladstone got what he liked to call his own English Catholic faith we need to revisit his long political career, as well as his personal life.

Of all nineteenth-century public men, none plunged into the business of public life more voraciously than Gladstone and yet, by all accounts, he disliked public life. His grand nephew George Lyttleton calculated that during his sixty years in the House of Commons, during which he led four governments as Prime Minister, he planned to resign eighteen times. The son of a Liverpool merchant who made a pile trading sugar from the West Indies, Gladstone went first to Eton and then to Christ Church, the *alma mater* of such political luminaries as Canning, Peel, Salisbury, Dalhousie and Minto, as well as such religious leaders as John Penn, John Wesley, and Newman's good friend and associate, Edward Bouverie Pusey. Yet the sense of destiny that Gladstone brought to his political career can be traced not so much to his patrician education as to an encounter he had in the summer of 1817 when he was eight-and-a-half. While out walking with a schoolfellow a mile or so from his home, he met a madman with an axe and had it not been for an intervening passer-by, Gladstone might very well have been hacked to death.[36] The experience left him convinced that he had been spared to perform a special work, one ordained by God. In later life, he would become fascinated with axes, even collecting them.[37] His gratitude to the man who saved his life inspired his first recorded writing, a poem of thanksgiving:

> Oh! Lord how good wert thou in saving
>   A poor frail creature like me
> When death over my head was waving
>   Then in the Grave I should be.
>
> I am devoted to thy service
>   In spite of those wicked ones
> And 'tis with thy help O Lord
>   That I resist their temptations.
>
> Oh! Lord I pray thee bless the Man
>   The man that was so brave
> Oh! Lord I pray thee bless the Man
>   That Saved me from the Grave.[38]

Gladstone remained in politics for as long as he did largely out of a quixotic sense of duty. Duty to the royal family, duty to the nation's finances, duty to the lower orders, duty to Ireland, duty to the Liberal Party, duty to the Bulgarians, duty to the Armenians. (The undergraduate F. E. Smith spoke in the Oxford Union against his Armenian agitation on the grounds that "A man with a family has no right to become a knight-errant."[39]) In a letter to his father, the 21-year-old Gladstone confided his doubts about his "future destiny"—he was torn between the Church and politics—but said he was inclined to ministerial office because "Nothing could compete with the grandeur of its end or of its means, the restoration of man to that image of his Maker which is now throughout the world so lamentably defaced ... Spreading religion has a claim infinitely transcending all others in dignity, in solemnity, and in usefulness."[40] Four days later, Gladstone wrote in his diary: "On Monday when I was in Oxford and saw the people parading with flags and bands of music my first impulse was to laugh, my second to cry: and I thought how strangely men had missed the purpose of their being."[41] Ambivalence about public life would follow Gladstone to the grave. And yet in all his political schemes he retained an almost pastoral solicitude for what he called "the moral wilderness of the world."[42]

Later, in 1839, he told his wife-to-be Catherine Glynne that he would have preferred being a clergyman but had decided instead to make politics Christian. That remarkable woman agreed to be engaged to him then and there—at a garden party given by Lady Shelley at Lonsdale House, Parson's

Green. Indeed, she confided to her religiose suitor that she had copied out extracts from his book in order to learn them by heart.[43] The aristocratic connections that Catherine brought to the marriage, including the Hawarden estates, sweetened the considerable means Gladstone's father provided his son (including pocket money for "Linen, Books, Carriages, Plate &c") and paved the way for Gladstone's unprecedented political influence, which, as Colin Matthew remarked, made him "the arbitrator and mediator between the aristocracy and the middle class."[44] The deep attachment that large numbers of aristocratic and middle-class Catholics felt to Newman, as well as middle-class Anglicans, gave him a comparable influence, though the extent to which he understood and appealed to the lower orders is still not sufficiently recognized.

Most political marriages are complicated things—commingling the private and the public, passion and policy—but the Gladstone marriage was complicated still further by the tenacious sense of honor that bound husband and wife. In July 1851, Gladstone wrote to his wife: "When you say I do not know half the evil of your life, you say that which I believe in almost every case is true between one human being and another; but it sets me thinking how little you know the evil of mine of which at the last day I shall have a strange tale to tell."[45] Disraeli was famously funny about Gladstone being "inebriated with the exuberance of his own verbosity," but he could be concision itself when he spoke from the heart.[46]

"Politics," Gladstone wrote to his friend Manning in 1835, "would be an utter blank to me were I to make the discovery that we were mistaken in their association with religion."[47] This was an ironic remark coming from a man who would later connive at both the Jerusalem Bishopric[48] and the Gorham Judgment,[49] both of which proved that in the Church of England there was a very close association indeed between politics and religion, though not the sort that the author of *The State in its Relations with the Church* (1838) had in mind. In that book, Gladstone argued that the State should take an active role in reaffirming the established religion, as "that form of belief which it conceives to contain the largest portion of the elements of truth with the smallest admixture of error," without, however, encroaching on what he believed should be the English Church's spiritual autonomy. *The Times* described the book as full of "popish biases" and "contaminated" with the "new-fangled Oxford bigotries" being spread by "certain stupid and perfidious pamphlets entitled 'Tracts of the Times.'"[50] (Newman's response to this was amusing: "Gladstone's book has come out," he wrote to Charles Marriott, "and the Times denounces it as Puseyism. I suppose his avowals are magnificent. But the papers are now all up in arms as if against Popery. The Jesuits are scaring every one out of his life, and pushing us all 'from our stools.'"[51]) Yet for all his admiration of Newman's criticisms of evangelicalism in his *Parochial and Plain Sermons*, Gladstone never entirely embraced Tractarianism: it was too Roman.[52] In his lifelong insistence that the State advance the interests of religion, Gladstone had more in common with the "two-bottle orthodox," as conservative High Churchmen were called, than with the Tractarians.

Gladstone only attended one of the legendary four o'clock sermons at St. Mary's that gave the principles of the Oxford Movement their most eloquent definition: the third of the *Oxford University Sermons*, "Evangelical Sanctity the Completion of Natural Virtue" (1831), which he thought contained "much singular, not to say objectionable matter, if one may so speak of so good a man."[53] What Gladstone probably disliked about the sermon was that it took a dubious view of the moral efficacy of religion, about which Gladstone always tended to be sanguine. In one passage, Newman wrote:

> It is indeed by no means clear that Christianity has at any time been of any great spiritual advantage to the world at large. The general temper of mankind, taking man individually, is what it ever was, restless and discontented, or sensual, or unbelieving. In barbarous times, indeed, the influence of the Church was successful in effecting far greater social order and external decency of conduct than are known in heathen countries; and at all times it will abash and check excesses which conscience itself condemns. But it has ever been a restraint on the world rather than a guide to personal virtue and perfection of a large scale; its fruits are negative. True it is, that in the more advanced periods of society a greater influence and probity of conduct and courtesy of manners will prevail; but these, though they have sometimes been accounted illustrations of the peculiar Christian character, have in fact no necessary connexion with it. For why should they not be referred to that mere advancement of civilization and education of the intellect, which is surely competent to produce them? Morals may be cultivated as a science; it furnishes a subject-matter on which reason may exercise itself to any extent whatever, with little more than the mere external assistance of conscience and Scripture.[54]

These were distinctions that Gladstone never made in his own view of established religion, which, as he saw it, must have as one of its defining principles the amelioration of the nation's morals. In Newman's sharply distinguishing between religion and morality, and, worse, claiming that religion was only negligibly effective in reforming morals, Gladstone saw unwarranted pessimism. For Newman, on the contrary, to blur religion and morals was to confuse religion with ethics, to make it a kind of "moralism." Tracey Rowland, in her excellent book, *Ratzinger's Faith* (2008), nicely defines this as "the Kantian rationalist tendency to reduce Christianity to the dimensions of an ethical framework, or to equate faith with obeying a law."[55]

In his edition of Gladstone's *Correspondence on Church and Religion* (1910), D. C. Lathbury quoted from Richard Church's wonderful description of Newman's sermons to give his reader a sense of how special they were:[56] "Plain, direct, unornamented, clothed in English that was only pure and lucid, free from any faults of taste, strong in their flexibility and perfect command both of language and thought, they were the expression of a piercing and large insight into character and conscience and motives, of a sympathy at once most tender and most stern with the tempted and the wavering, of an absolute and burning faith in God and His counsels, in His love, in His judgments, in the awful glory of His generosity and His magnificence. They made men speak of the things which the preacher spoke of, and not of the sermon or the preacher."[57] Gladstone, Lathbury confirms, had no part "in this strenuous and passionate life. Even his friendship with James Hope does not seem to have led him to read the early 'Tracts for the Times,' with their brief, direct, stimulating appeals to the consciences of Churchmen. His knowledge of the Movement hardly began till it had passed its first triumphant stage and entered upon a period of reverses and, what was worse, of doubt and hesitation."[58] In a memorandum dated 7 December 1893, Gladstone confirmed Lathbury's point: "In the year 1841 or 1842, under a variety of combined influences, my mind attained a certain fixity of state in a new development. I had been gradually carried away from the moorings of an education, Evangelical in the party sense, to what I believe history would warrant me in calling a Catholic position, in the acceptance of the visible historical Church and the commission it received from our Saviour to take charge, in a visible form, of His work on earth. I do not mean to touch upon the varied stages of this long journey ... I shall only say that the Oxford Tracts had little to do with it: nothing to do with it at all ... except to say that it was ... due to them that Catholicism, so to speak, was in the air ..."[59] So to treat Gladstone as an honorary Tractarian is inaccurate. It is true that he did not openly oppose the Movement but neither did he march under its banner.

Once the ideal religious state set out in his book came to nothing, politics might have become something of a blank to Gladstone, but it was a blank into which he poured furious activity and in which he tried to establish a new religion, a new faith. In 1850 he had gone to Naples and there he saw how the Neapolitan government was persecuting the liberal minister Carlo Poerio and his followers for their support of the constitution of 1848. Gladstone attended Poerio's trial and was present when the government sentenced him to 24 years' hard labor in chains. He even managed to gain admittance to the dungeon where Poerio and thousands of other hapless political prisoners were being left to languish. There Gladstone discovered a truth about European conservatism that he never forgot. As he wrote to Lord Aberdeen, the Foreign Secretary: "It is the wholesale persecution of virtue ... It is the awful profanation of public religion ... It is the perfect prostitution of the judicial office ... It is the savage and cowardly system of moral as well as physical torture ... This is the negation of God erected into a system of government."[60] After this epiphany, Gladstonian liberalism was born. What it was exactly is not easy to say. John Vincent said that "it was an intelligent way of making the best of a weak international position. Disraeli's foreign policy pretended the weak position did not exist. For the illusion of morality it substituted the illusion of strength."[61] G. M. Young said it consisted of "a horror of all coercive powers, great or small—Empires, Papacies, Parliaments, Sultans, Colonial Offices, Trade Unions—which do not rest their authority on consent, habitual or expressed ..."[62] For Matthew it was "fiscal probity." David Bebbington saw it as having been less liberal than communitarian, embodying Gladstone's conviction that "Sectional selfishness, at whatever level, must give way to the common good."[63] Whatever definition one attaches to Gladstonian liberalism, it is clear that it made Gladstone peculiarly susceptible to what Newman called "smelling out Powder Plots,"[64] particularly plots laid by what Gladstone regarded as a tyrannical Papacy intent on stealing away the hearts and minds of Catholic and even Protestant Europe as it had stolen away his sister Helen and his close friends Henry Manning and James Hope.

However one views Gladstone's "rescue work" on behalf of London's prostitutes—and I am inclined to agree with Colin Matthew that, whatever else it was, it was not ignoble—he often seemed to prefer the company of pretty young trollops to his aging wife. Gladstone's love for his wife was strong but restive. This is important to keep in mind because when he confided to a friend about the intensity of his sense of political vocation, to what he called his "master-pursuit," he referred to its object rather tellingly as "My country-wife, i.e., the country as my wife ..."[65] From this, Matthew argues, rightly, that Gladstone's religion was "intricately and essentially linked to his sense of organic nationality."[66] F. D. Maurice put the nationalist case for Anglicanism in terms that Gladstone would hardly have disputed. "If our Church is both Catholic and Protestant, our Nation is wholly Protestant. In so far as we are a nation, united together under one king, we do by the very law of our existence protest against any power which assumes control over our kings, and denies their direct responsibility to God ... The nations were brought into their distinct life by the church ... they cannot retain their distinct life without the church ... conversely, the universal body sinks into a contradiction, when it refuses to recognize the personality of each national body ... We are not striving to make ourselves a Protestant nation ... we have been so implicitly at all times ..."[67] Like Maurice, Gladstone found Rome unacceptable not because it was not the true Catholic Church—though, of course, he never thought it was—but because it was not the true English Church. Duff Cooper once said that for the English there are only two religions: Roman Catholicism, which is wrong, and all the others, which don't matter.[68] Most of Gladstone's various articles on religion can be seen as an attempt to get his countrymen to agree that at least one of those other religions did matter.

The woman to whom Gladstone confided his remark about his "country-wife" was Mrs. Laura Thistlethwayte, suitably enough for the Gladstonian ηθος a former courtesan and an Irishwoman, whom he had met one afternoon in 1864 while riding in Rotten Row. When Lord Carnarvon got wind of their friendship, he had no doubt as to its import: "Gladstone seems to be going out of his mind ... He goes to dinner with her and she in return in her preachments to her congregation exhorts them to put up their prayers on behalf of Mr. G's reform bill."[69] Lord Stanley was equally astonished by the Liberal leader's new association. "Strange story of Gladstone frequenting the company of a Mrs. Thistlethwaite, a kept woman in her youth, who induced a foolish person with a large fortune to marry her. She has since ... taken to religion, and preaches or lectures. This, with her beauty, is the attraction to G., and it is characteristic of him to be indifferent to scandal. But I can scarcely believe the report that he is going to pass a week with her and her husband at their country house—she not being visited, or received in society."[70] Two days later, he records in his diary: "Malmesbury called ... and confirmed the story of Gladstone's going to visit the Thistlethwaites! A strange world!"[71] For Gladstone, Mrs. Thistlethwayte was an irresistible amalgam, combining as she did the allure of the pretty young prostitutes he met on his rescue missions, with his own passionate religiosity. As he confided in his Diary, "Duty and evil temptation are there before me, on the right & left. But I firmly believe in her words 'holy' and 'pure,' & in her cleaving to God."[72] Whether duty altogether prevailed as their relationship progressed is not clear from another entry: "It is difficult to repel, nay to check or to dissuade, the attachment of a remarkable, a signal soul, clad in a beautiful body."[73] What appears adulterous might have been innocent. Certainly the appearance of impropriety never ruffled Gladstone. When a Scot tried to blackmail him for talking to a prostitute after he submitted his 1853 budget, Gladstone nonchalantly turned the blackguard's letter over to the police. "These talkings of mine are certainly not within the rules of worldly prudence," he admitted, but he would not stop them to avoid threats of blackmail or obviate malicious gossip.[74] To those who tattled about his relationship with Mrs. Thistlethwayte he showed the same imperturbable indifference.

Mrs. Thistlethwayte is important because it was to her that Gladstone revealed the extent to which politics consumed him. In a typical letter he wrote: "My profession involves me in a life of constant mental and moral excess. I must before long endeavor to escape from it ... And what must be my destiny and duty, when that day arrives? Surely to try to recover & retain the balance of my mind: to awaken and cherish in myself the life of faith, of 'the substance of things hoped for and the evidence of things unseen': to unwind and detach that multitude of ties and interests which now bind me to the world I live in: to do something, if it be permitted me, for the glory of God ..."[75] These profoundly introspective letters are interesting when one recalls that what Gladstone most objected to about the Roman Church was auricular confession, which he considered 'priest-craft.' Queen Victoria shared his horror of confession, telling Dean Stanley in a memorandum of 1873, "A complete Reformation is what we want. But if that is impossible, the Archbishop should have the power given him, by Parliament, to stop all these Ritualistic practices, dressings, bowings, etc., and everything of that kind, and above all, all attempts at confession."[76] The essayist William Hazlitt might have been radical in some respects, but in his views on confession he was thoroughly conventional. "The contrariety and warfare of different faculties and dispositions within us has not only given birth to the Manichean and Gnostic heresies, and to other superstitions of the East, but will account for many of the mummeries and dogmas both of Popery and Calvinism—confession, absolution, justification by faith, etc; which, in the hopelessness of attaining perfection, and our dissatisfaction with ourselves for falling short of it, are all substitutes for actual virtue, and an attempt to throw the burden of a task, to which we are unequal or only half disposed, on the merits of others, or on outward forms, ceremonies, and professions of faith."[77] It was this widespread revulsion from confession that gave Lady Georgiana Fullerton's fictional treatment of the subject in *Ellen Middleton* (1844) such a fascination for Newman's contemporaries. Newman, for his part, even as an Anglican, held firmly that "Confession is the life of the Parochial charge, without it all is hollow."[78]

In another letter to Mrs. Thistlethwayte, Gladstone wrote: "If I were to send you the *counterpart* of what you have sent me [she had sent him an unfinished autobiography which he found 'like a story from the Arabian nights'], I should certainly repel you. But to do it would be beyond my power. I must in honesty say to you, probe me deeper; I will conceal nothing, falsify nothing consciously, but ... *make sure* that you know me. Do not take me upon trust ... I am a strange mixture of art and nature."[79] This was shrewd self-analysis. Gladstone was an unusual mélange of guilelessness and calculation. Whenever his defenders and detractors made their respective cases for or against him, they did so by citing one or the other of these qualities. Agatha Ramm, for example, the editor of the political correspondence between Gladstone and Granville, attributed Gladstone's political success to three things: his oratory, his manipulation of public opinion, and what she called his "most advantageous appearance of unworldliness."[80]

In his sermon "The Danger of Accomplishments" (1835), Newman roundly declared that "all formal and intentional expression of religious emotions, all studied passionate discourse, [is] <u>dissipation</u> ... a drain and waste of our religious and moral strength."[81] This could apply to a good deal of what Gladstone wrote and uttered over the years, especially when spurred on by what his wife feared might degenerate into religious mania, but it does not apply to the passage above, or many others, in which Gladstone captured that sense of desolation that strikes so many public men when they recognize how public life banishes them from their true country. Indeed, the spiritual poverty of public life was one of Gladstone's great themes. Again, in another diary entry he says: "I feel like a man with a burden under which he must fall if he looks to the right or left, or fails from any cause to concentrate his mind and muscle upon his progress step by step. This absorption, this excess ... is the fault of public life, with its insatiable demands which do not leave the smallest stock of moral energy unexhausted and available for other purposes ... Swimming for his life, a man does not see much of the country through which the river winds ..."[82]

After the Gorham Judgment, which caused Manning and Hope to defect, Gladstone did not want to see that country. When the Judgment was imminent, he wrote: "If Mr. Gorham be carried through ... I say not only is there no doctrine of Baptismal Regeneration ... but there is no doctrine at all."[83] In 1847, when the liberal Rev. G. C. Gorham was presented a vicarage in Exeter, Henry Phillpotts refused to install him because he refused to accept baptismal regeneration. Gorham appealed to the Judicial Committee of the Privy Council, and in 1850 they overruled Phillpotts. Just how hard this hit Gladstone is evident from a letter he wrote to Lord Lyttleton: "The case of the Church of England at this moment is a very dismal one, and almost leaves men to choose between a broken heart and no heart at all."[84] When Manning wrote to Hope and said he was shocked by the Erastianism[85] of the Judgment, Hope wrote back: "If you have not hitherto read Erastianism in the history of the Church of England since the Reformation, then I fear you and I have much to discuss before we can meet on common ground."[86] It was the Tractarians' refusal to concede the

Erastianism of the English Church that gave their movement so much of its passionate unreality. The Gorham Judgment proved that liberal politicians, not bishops, would be the final arbiters of what constituted Anglican doctrine. In the wake of the Judgment, Robert Wilberforce, the second son of the philanthropist, suggested to Manning that they find a colonial bishop and set up their own Free Church. "No," replied Manning. "Three hundred years ago we left a good ship for a boat; I am not going to leave the boat for a tub."[87]

In writing to Manning when he was on the brink of conversion, Gladstone made lightly veiled references to Newman that crackle with resentment, which show the rage he was storing up that would explode in the *Expostulation* (1875). "If you go over, I should earnestly pray that you might not be as others who have gone before you but might carry with you a larger heart and mind, able to raise and keep you above that slavery to a system, that exaggeration of its forms, that disposition to rivet every shackle tighter and to stretch every breach wider, which makes me mournfully feel that the men who have gone from the Church of England after being reared in her and by her, are far more keen and ... far more cruel than the mass of whom they joined."[88] Much is made of Newman's prose style but Gladstone could also write. He was one of those good, sloppy writers, rather like the Melville of *Moby Dick*. When his passions were aroused, he wrote with real power. His writing might be prolix, rambling, convoluted and overwrought but it captures perfectly his messy grandeur. The actress Ellen Terry, who first met Gladstone at the salon surrounding the painter G. F. Watts at Little Holland House in the early 1860s, recalled something of this grandeur when she wrote of the liberal politician, "Like a volcano at rest, his face was pale and calm, but the calm was the calm of the grey crust of Etna. You looked into the piercing dark eyes, and caught a glimpse of the red-hot crater beneath the crust."[89]

Another cause for the anger behind the *Expostulation* came from a prediction that Gladstone made to Manning in January 1851, four months before Manning converted. "Some things I have learned in Italy [he was writing from Naples] that I did not know before, one in particular. The temporal power of the Pope, that great, wonderful, and ancient creation, is *gone*; the problem has been worked out, the ground is mined, the train is laid, a foreign force, in its nature transitory, alone stays the hand of those who would complete the process by applying the match ... When that event comes it will bring about a great shifting of parts ... God grant it may be for good. I desire it because I see plainly that justice requires it, and God is the God of justice. Not out of malice to the Popedom: for I cannot at this moment dare to answer with a confident affirmative the question, a very solemn one: 'Ten, twenty, fifty years hence, will there be any other body in Western Christendom witnessing for fixed dogmatic truth?' With all my soul, I wish it well ..."[90] Here Gladstone gloated over the imminent demise of the Pope's temporal power. When that was dynamited, Popedom, as he called it, would be considerably weakened, as would "fixed dogmatic truth." Gladstone treated this as unavoidable: the justice of God. But twenty years later, events proved his bold prediction wrong: "Popedom" was thriving and with the advocacy of his old friend, Manning, which only added to his fury.

Of all the political projects that would consume Gladstone after the Gorham Judgment, none demanded more of his energies than trying to bring some solution to the religious, agrarian and political problems that made Ireland a byword for English misrule. G. M. Young might dismiss Gladstone's Irish efforts as "that heroic squandering of heroic endowments on a problem which (we may now say) the intellectual equipment of the age was not capable of solving,"[91] but there was as much practicality as heroism in Gladstone's vision of Irish Home Rule. Margot Asquith recalled the Grand Old Man telling her when she was a girl: "We are bound to lose Ireland in consequence of years of cruelty, stupidity and misgovernment but I would rather lose her as a friend than as a foe."[92] Roy Jenkins, in his wonderfully sprawling biography, sees Gladstone's Irish campaign in still more pedestrian terms: for Gladstone, the "cheese-paring" Chancellor of the Exchequer, Ireland was a "potentially dangerous source of demands upon the Treasury," and he was determined to see to it that the Irish were not allowed "to plunder the public purse."[93] Better, in other words, that they be their own rather than England's beggars.

Newman agreed that some form of Home Rule might be in order but he was leery of Gladstone's Irish policy. In 1868, he wrote: "Had I my way I should prefer Disraeli's mode of settling the Irish question to Gladstone's (if Disraeli was in earnest)—and so I think would most men, but ... I am a Gladstonite." Disraeli's policy was to endow the Church of Ireland and the Catholic Church concurrently and sit back and watch Ireland destroy the Liberal Party, which, of course, eventually, it did, though too late for Disraeli, who died in 1881, "almost incidentally," as John Vincent says, "after going out on a cold night."[94] In the same year, Newman wrote: "Gladstone the other day at Leeds complained of the little support given him by the middle class and gentry in Ireland. I think it was at the time of the Fenian rising that the Times had an article to the same effect. (Gladstone seemed to think them cowards; no, they are patriots.)"[95] Elsewhere, he wrote: "I wish with all my heart that the cruel injustices which have been inflicted on the Irish people should be utterly removed—but I don't think they go the best way to bring this about."[96] The Irish may now look askance at the Catholic faith of their fathers but Newman had seen enough of the country and its people to recognize that the nineteenth-century Irish owed a great debt to their priests. Newman's good friend, John Hungerford Pollen, who helped him design the University Church on St. Stephen's Green and spent a good deal of time with him in Dublin, observed that "Father Newman enjoyed a wide popularity among the priests of Ireland. In them he saw the courage, the constancy of a whole nation of confessors for the Faith; a nation to whom a debt of justice was due; a debt of which he desired earnestly to discharge his share."[97] Newman's work for the Catholic University in Dublin was often thwarted by those convinced that he did not understand Ireland. Yet he was at once more knowledgeable and more sympathetic to the Irish than many realized. To Gerard Manley Hopkins, he wrote: "If I were an Irishman, I should be (in heart) a rebel ... the Irish character and tastes [are] very different from the English."[98]

In *Modern Ireland 1600–1972*, Roy Foster claims that "'Fenianism,' in its generalized sense, responded to the well-meaning abstractions of armchair nationalists like Cardinal Newman ..."[99] What "well-meaning abstractions" Foster had in mind is unclear. Nothing abstract prompted Newman to cross St. George's Channel 56 times in the service of the Catholic University.[100] Newman's grasp of Irish affairs was much sounder and more realistic than Foster acknowledges. "This Fenianism," Newman told his friend Maria Giberne, "is a wide spreading conspiracy against British Rule – backed up by the United States, especially the Irish there. Considering our treatment of Ireland, it is not at all wonderful."[101] To another correspondent he wrote, "Governments ... if they are bad, unjust, or slovenly and do-nothing, naturally give scope and vigour to secret societies. Hence the Ribbon men, Whiteboys, Fenians etc etc of Ireland ..."[102] For Newman, Fenianism was a deplorable, if understandable, outcrop of misrule. He also recognized that it was less an Irish than an American movement, kept alive more by Irish-American sentimentality than incompetence at Westminster. Lastly, for Foster to claim that Newman's work in Ireland was that of "an armchair nationalist" fails to acknowledge the true practical character of that work. The principles that Newman set forth in his *Discourses on the Scope and Nature of University Education* (1852), and, later, in *The Idea of a University* (1873), were drawn up to revive university education, not armchair nationalism.

It is just as well that the topic of Gladstone never came up in the letters that passed between Newman and Hopkins, because the Jesuit poet detested the Grand Old Man—or, as the wags in the music halls called him, the "MOG," the Murderer of Gordon. In one letter, Hopkins wrote: "the duty of keeping this fatal and baleful influence, spirit or personality or whatever he is to be called out of political power is a duty paramount to that of forwarding any particular measure of Irish or other politics ..."[103]

Gladstone, for all his readiness to champion Irish home rule, never understood the Irish. The historian James Anthony Froude, who lived in Killarney, Kenmare and Kerry for extensive periods of his long life, and was friendly not only with landowners but with peasants, stated categorically that "Mr. Gladstone does not know Ireland well, nor its history well."[104] In *Gladstone and the Irish Nation*, the historian John Lawrence Hamilton argued that: "From his first contact with Irish politics [Gladstone] had sought to create in Ireland the conditions under which the Irish people could find a field for a self-respecting patriotism."[105] This is unpersuasive: if the Irish had not learned patriotism from Swift, Grattan, Wolfe Tone and Parnell, they were not likely to learn it from William Ewart Gladstone. Froude may have been wildly biased in some of his views on Ireland, even going so far as to claim (teasingly) that Cromwellian Ireland had been a golden age; but he was objective enough when it came to seeing the fundamental flaw of Gladstone's policies towards that unfortunate country.[106] "We have flattered ourselves that we were bestowing on Ireland the choicest of blessings," Froude wrote, "forgetting willfully that free institutions require the willing and loyal cooperation of those who are to enjoy and use them; that the freedom which the Irish desired was freedom from the English connnexion; and that every privilege which we conferred, every relief we conceded, would be received without gratitude, and would be employed only as an instrument to make our position in the country untenable." This was surely the more accurate view. England would not cure the evils of plantation with the half measures of paternalism. Nor could Gladstone claim any special insight into those evils. His attitude to Ireland resembled that of the Anglo-Irish diarist William Allingham, who once admitted: "I love Ireland: were she only not Catholic!"[107]

Ireland is central to any consideration of Gladstone and Newman because Gladstone's failed Irish University Bill in 1873 led directly to his attack on English Catholics in *The Vatican Decrees: An Expostulation* (1874). After disestablishing the Irish Church and getting the Land Bill passed, Gladstone's next priority was to reform Ireland's educational system. "We are pledged to redress the R.C. grievance," Gladstone announced in September 1872 to Earl Spencer, the Irish Lord Lieutenant, "which is held to consist in this, that an R.C. educated in a college or place where his religion is taught cannot by virtue of that education obtain a degree in Ireland. Beyond this, I think we desire that a portion of the public endowments should be thrown open, under the auspices of a neutral University, to the whole people of Ireland."[108] Subsequently, in a long speech that held the House of Commons "in a mesmeric trance,"[109] Gladstone proposed a scheme that would give the Catholics of Ireland access to non-denominational university education. According to F. S. L. Lyons, the great Irish historian, he "attempted to create a genuinely national and non-sectarian university by abolishing the Queen's University and one of its constituent colleges (Galway) and by bringing together within a single framework Trinity, the Catholic University, Belfast, Cork and Magee. With the massive insensitivity which that most subtle of men could sometimes muster, he thus succeeded in a single stroke in alienating every section of Irish opinion ..."[110] Worse, Gladstone proposed that his non-denominational university system should have no chairs for theology, philosophy or modern history. Roy Jenkins found the speech "a wonderful example of Gladstone's expository style, compelling, daring (there are a lot of attacks on venerable institutions and practices), with the figures never boring because, if not exactly made up for the purpose, they are selectively presented so as at once to surprise the listener and carry him along with the argument."[111] Yet even Jenkins realized that for all its ingenuity the speech had an irremediable flaw: it advocated something only Gladstone wanted.[112] Gladstone's Cabinet did not want the scheme because it saw no benefits accruing from increasing the number of university-educated Catholics. The Irish Catholic hierarchy did not want it because they were opposed to non-denominational education of any stripe, Gladstonian or otherwise. Gladstone, for his part, might have argued that the future of Ireland depended on the "moral and intellectual culture of her people" but by recommending the proscriptions of his "gagging clauses," which would prevent the study of precisely those subjects that nourish culture, Gladstone was essentially suggesting that "moral and intellectual culture" in English Ireland was impossible.[113] The speech exposed the gaping contradictions inherent in Gladstone's proposed educational reforms. No wonder the House broke out in laughter when they heard the clauses.

Newman saw the breathtaking incoherence of the bill from the start and never doubted that the bishops would reject it. His own view of the matter was rooted in his pastoral understanding of the teaching office: "It is simply unnatural to educate young men without encouraging thought on the subject which more than any other must interest ardent and able minds."[114] On the eve of the vote, sensing defeat, Gladstone wrote to Manning: "I shall fight to the last against all comers, but much against my inclination which is marvelously attuned by the vision of my liberty dawning like a sunrise from beyond the hills. For when this offer has been made, and every effort of patience employed to render it a reality, my contract with the country is fulfilled, and I am free to take my own course."[115] (Once again he yearned to retire.) The bill was defeated 284 votes to 287. For Newman, the results confirmed that Cardinal Cullen "could not accept the Bill without an enormous scandal. For near thirty years the Church has been protesting against mixed education, and resisting the schemes of Ministers which looked that way ..."[116] What surprised Newman was "how Gladstone could have fancied he could."[117]

When Gladstone surrendered the reins of power to Disraeli, Mrs. Gladstone asked her son Herbert, with blithe bigotry: "Is it not disgusting, after all Papa's labour and patriotism and years of work to think of him handling over his nest-egg to that Jew?'[118] Once free of the reins of power, Gladstone read Trollope's *Eustace Diamonds*, visited Christie's to see Lady Charlotte Schreiber's superb china collection, and even passed up opportunities to answer Disraeli in the Commons.[119] He seemed a changed man. "The future of politics hardly exists for me," he told Manning, "unless some new phase arise and ... a special call ... appear: to such a call, please God I will answer; if there be a breath in my body."[120]

The new call came over the Public Worship Regulation Bill (1873), which Disraeli introduced expressly to entrap his overzealous opponent. In vehemently opposing a bill that outlawed the ritualism of High Church and Anglo-Catholic clergy, Gladstone took the bait hook, line and sinker. He recognized the trap Disraeli was laying for him but could not resist walking into it. As he said to Granville, "in Disraeli I have nothing to complain of. It was quite plain that he meant business, namely my political extinction, and thought that Ritualism offered a fine opportunity ..."[121] Indeed, it did. Again, Gladstone had seriously miscalculated the pulse of his Party. Forster, Lowe, Goschen and especially Harcourt voted their Protestant prejudice—their contempt for the "Mass in Masquerade." Yet, in this instance, Gladstone was very much Disraeli's "paladin of principle, the very abstraction of chivalry."[122] He would not betray the Anglo-Catholic party. But once again his own Liberal Party branded him as someone who could not "interest himself ... in matters (even when they are great matters) in which he is not carried away by some too strong attraction."[123]

His political woes were compounded by personal upsets. In August, he learned that Lord Ripon, his long-standing political ally, who had been Lord President of the Council in his first ministry (1868–1873), was preparing to convert. "May he pause," was Gladstone's stunned reaction.[124] After successfully urging Newman's claim to the cardinalate in 1878, Ripon wrote to the aging convert for whom he had such immense respect: 'Those who like myself owe to your teaching, more than any other earthly cause, the blessing of being members of the Catholic Church, must rejoice with a very keen joy at this recognition on the part of the Holy See of your eminent services to the Church and to so many individual souls."[125] The *Saturday Review* treated Ripon's conversion as the *ipso facto* end of a distinguished political career, only adding that "Even if every article of the modern Romish Creed were indisputably true, a patriotic statesman ought still to regard the national interests as paramount to the policy of the Church."[126] *The Times* agreed: "A statesman who becomes a convert to Roman Catholicism forfeits at once the confidence of the English people."[127] However, when Gladstone became Prime Minister again in 1880, he appointed Lord Ripon Viceroy of India, where he introduced local self-government, improved Indian education, and lifted his predecessor Lord Lytton's censorship of the press. The Anglo-Indians loathed him.[128] When he tried to pass a bill that would allow Indian judges to try Europeans, they were furious because, as they saw it, Indian magistrates would try to stop them "beating their own niggers."[129] In his religious development—beginning as an Evangelical, finding common cause with F. D. Maurice's Christian Socialists, and even acting as Grand Master of the Freemasons before converting to Rome and building up the Catholic Union of Great Britain—Ripon had charted a course not unlike that of Newman's early mentor, Thomas Scott, who "followed truth wherever it led him."[130]

After learning of Ripon's defection, Gladstone went to visit Döllinger in Munich and found the excommunicated theologian as bitter as ever against the Ultramontanes, the faction within the Roman Church that wished to increase the power of the papal curia.[131] In fact the two men ran into Döllinger's excommunicator in the street, which must have made for an awkward encounter. Then it was on to Cologne to see Helen, his sister, whose conversion to Catholicism was a continual affront to Gladstone, though at this meeting he must have viewed her addiction to laudanum as the more alarming affliction. Despite these upsets or perhaps because of them, Gladstone vowed to fight back. As so many of his parliamentary opponents found to their chagrin, he was "terrible on the rebound." And so he proved in October of 1873, when he sent off to the *Contemporary Review* an article entitled "Ritualism and Ritual" (1874) which would supply the main charges of the *Expostulation*. Referring to what he claimed were the designs of Rome to "Romanise" the English people and their Church, he said: "Rome has substituted for the proud boast of *semper eadem* a policy of violence and change of faith; ... she has refurbished and paraded anew every rusty tool she was fondly thought to have disused ... no one can become her convert without renouncing his moral and mental freedom and placing his civil loyalty and duty at the mercy of another; and ... she has equally repudiated modern thought and ancient history."[132] That Gladstone could write that last sentence after advocating the "gagging clauses" of his University Bill illustrates how oblivious he could be to his own inconsistencies. The fact that he made no mention of the Catholic Irish in his charges against the moral and mental freedom, not to mention the civil loyalty of Catholics only made those inconsistencies more glaring.

Queen Victoria saw not only inconsistency but treachery in Gladstone's appearing to defend Roman Catholicism in the debate over the Public

Worship Regulation Bill and then attacking Roman Catholics themselves in his "Ritualism and Ritual" in his *Contemporary Review* article along the grossest No Popery lines.[133] Most of her inner circle also saw duplicity in Gladstone's apparent inconsistency. John Brown, her Scottish confidant, told Ponsonby that he was convinced that Gladstone was a Roman. When Ripon poped, Dr. Jenner, the Queen's physician, agreed: "Ripon was a friend of Gladstone's and that is enough." Disraeli told Ponsonby that Ripon would only be the first to go. Speaking of Gladstone's liberal cabinet, he remarked, "Ah! Yes, they will all go sooner or later!" According to Victoria's biographer, Elizabeth Longford, the rumors following Gladstone's volte-face and Ripon's defection gave birth to an even stranger rumor: "Queen Victoria toyed with the idea that Gladstone was a secret papist."[134]

After Newman read the *Contemporary Review* piece, he wrote Lord Emly a letter that rehearsed many of the points that would feature in his *Letter to the Duke of Norfolk*: the decrees did not augment the Pope's power; his infallibility pertained only to "general propositions on religion and morals ... not on matters of expedience;" and if the Pope influenced Catholic voters this was no different from the influence special interests routinely exerted.[135] There was an Anglican interest and a publican interest and a railway interest: why should Gladstone object to there being a Catholic interest? Moreover the decrees had no bearing on civil allegiance: that "remained what it was in Elizabeth's reign, when her Catholic subjects, with great zeal took part in the defense of their country against an Armada blessed by the Pope."[136] To his friend Lord Blachford he wrote: "Gladstone has offended us ... very deeply. It seems strikingly rude to Lord Ripon, and I hope it will have the effect of making some Catholic or other speak out. Gladstone's excuse is, I suppose, the extravagance of Archbishop Manning in his 'Caesarism', and he will do us a service, if he gives us an opportunity of speaking. [Manning's article, "Caesarism and Ultramontanism" (1874), took an ultramontane view of Church and State relations.] We can speak against Gladstone, while it would not be decent to speak against Manning. The difficulty is, *who* ought to speak."[137]

At first, William Monsell, Lord Emly, seemed the right man for the job. An Irish Catholic Unionist educated at Winchester and Oriel, who became M.P. for Limerick in 1837, Monsell converted in 1850 after the Gorham Judgment and held various offices in Liberal governments, including the postmaster general-ship from 1871 to 1873 in Gladstone's first government. He was created Lord Emly in 1874. A close friend of Newman's during the founding of the Catholic University, he also gave him good counsel during the Achilli affair and lent him the use of his house after that long ordeal was over. The two men did not altogether agree on all matters; Emly was a member of the liberal Catholic set headed up by Lord Acton and Richard Simpson and partial to the liberal Catholicism of Montalembert; but there was nothing anti-papal in his thinking as there was in that of some of his fellow liberals. In a letter to Monsell, written in January of 1863, Newman spelled out what he found objectionable about Simpson, a man whom he otherwise found likable.

I believe the very passages of Simpson, which our Bishop censured, were specified by Propaganda. Moreover, I think I am right in saying that the Acts of Propaganda are the Pope's in an intimate manner; a privilege which the other Sacred Congregations do not share. Therefore it gives great weight to the words of the Bishop of Birmingham, that the substance of them has the direct sanction of the Holy See. Nor have I any difficulty in receiving them as such. It has ever, I believe, been the course of proceedings at Rome, to meet rude actions by a rude retort; and, when speculators are fast or flippant, to be rough and ready in dealing with them; the point in question being, not the logical rights and wrongs of the matter, but the existing treatise or document in concreto. The Pope is not a philosopher, but a ruler. 'He strangles, while they prate.' I am disposed to think then that Simpson has no cause to complain, though he has been hardly treated. Why did he begin? why did he fling about ill sounding words on sacred and delicate subjects? I should address him in the words of the Apostle 'Quare non magis injuriam accipitis? quare non magis fraudem patimini?' I think he might have written a better pamphlet.[138]

Newman would not have shared so candid an assessment of Simpson's indiscretion if he doubted Monsell's own discretion.

As Gladstone's close associate for many years, Monsell knew that the Liberal leader's own personal experience must disprove his charges. "Ask yourself ... not to speak of myself who have been in close political connection with you for 27 years ... [whether] Dr. Newman, Lord O'Hagan, Aubrey de Vere or Lord Kenmare" had ever been mentally or morally enslaved or disloyal."[139] Gladstone conceded that the aspersions he cast on the loyalty of Catholics were unjust, but only after the controversy had run its course.[140]

Newman's editorial advice to Emly was revealing: he must remember "that really you will be answering, not Gladstone, but Archbishop Manning ... He ought to be answered and this is the opportunity—and you, as not being under his jurisdiction, have a great advantage, which an English Catholic has not ..."[141] Gladstone had "written so roughly of Catholic statesmen ... to bring them out, and get if possible, a disavowal of what he has said of their captivity." The tone of sympathy here is undeniable. Newman might have deplored Gladstone's heavy-handed tactics. He might have exposed his ignorance of the technical language in which so many of the decrees were couched.[142] He might have questioned his sense of fair play in attacking so vulnerable a minority as English Catholics.[143] But he was not unsympathetic to what he considered the well-deserved black eye that Gladstone had given the Ultramontanes. What Newman was saying to Emly was that since Gladstone's *Expostulation* had been particularly aimed at Manning and the Ultramontanes, it was necessary that any response to Gladstone's charges include a response to Manning and the Ultramontanes as well. So when Emly took off the gloves and said what must have been on many Irish minds: "It is a serious thing to declare war against the Irish people,"[144] Newman's response was to counsel restraint: "I think *you* had better wait before you publish. It can't be pleasant to a man like Gladstone to receive such private letters as you have sent, and we may damage the natural course of things by pressing him."[145] This was characteristic of the exceedingly considerate treatment Newman showed Gladstone throughout the controversy. Disraeli might have been convinced that Gladstone was not a gentleman but no one could say that about Newman.[146] Indeed, one of the best descriptions of how the two controversialists conducted themselves in the debate can be found in *The Idea of a University* (1873), which Newman had first published over twenty years before. In describing how the gentleman should conduct himself in controversy, Newman described how he actually responded to Gladstone's attacks, while "blundering discourtesy" fairly characterized his opponent's behaviour.

[The gentleman] is never mean or little in his disputes; never takes unfair advantage; never mistakes personalities or sharp sayings for arguments, or insinuates evil which he dare not say out. From a long-sighted prudence, he observes the maxim of the ancient sage that we should ever conduct ourselves towards our enemy as if he were one day to be our friend. He has too much good sense to be affronted at insults; he is too well employed to remember injuries and too indolent to bear malice. He is patient, forbearing and resigned, on philosophical principles ... If he engages in controversy of any kind, his disciplined intellect preserves him from the blundering discourtesy of better, though less educated minds; who like blunt weapons tear and hack instead of cutting clean, who re-state the point in argument, waste their strength on trifles, misconceive their adversary and leave the question more involved than they find it ...[147]

Newman often deprecated his political sense but he was accurate enough about the timing of Gladstone's attack. "When the University Bill was thrown out in 1873, *The Times* gave a hint that, since there was need of a cry, perhaps a party might be formed on the 'No Popery.' And I don't think they have forgotten it ... The unanimity of the House against the unhappy Ritualists seemed to me ... the very first step of a move against *us* and an omen of its success. Since then, Lord Ripon's conversion must have sunk deeply into the Protestant mind, though there is an affectation of making light of it."[148] The stinging rebuke the Liberals dealt their leader had its intended effect: if it was No Popery they wanted, Gladstone would give them No Popery.

Newman, for his part, was amused to see that Gladstone's *Expostulation* had done nothing to muzzle W. G. Ward, the Ultramontane firebrand, who was as minatory as ever. "The Pope, in virtue of his ecclesiastical office," he pronounced in *The Dublin Review*, "has the power of deposing any sovereign, whose government he may consider injurious to the spiritual welfare of that country." And furthermore, the Pope's temporal power "is the very bulwark and citadel of Catholic order, liberty and progress."[149] If Newman was prepared to be magnanimous towards Gladstone, he was patience personified with Ward. In 1875, he wrote to a correspondent: "you can tell me nothing more extravagant about his view of me than I know already. He has told friends that I am in material heresy, that he would rather not have men made Catholics than have them converted by me, and that he accounts it the best deed of his life that he hindered my going to Oxford by the letters he sent to Rome etc. He is so above board, and outspoken, that he is quite charming. It is the whisperers, and I have long suffered from them, whom (as Dickens says) I 'object to' ..."[150] Gladstone also had a soft spot for Ward, about whom he said: "I believe more perhaps than most men in the capacity of the human mind for self-delusion, and I thought Mr. Ward infatuated without being dishonest."[151]

Once Gladstone's pamphlet was published, Newman expressed shock and dismay. To Dean Church, he wrote: "I grieve indeed that he should have so committed himself—I mean by charging people quite as free in mind as he is, of being moral and mental slaves. I never thought I should be writing against Gladstone!"[152] To another: "As to Mr. Gladstone's letter I think it is quite shocking. I should not have thought it possible that a statesman could be so onesided."[153]

Newman was months writing and rewriting his rebuttal. Anxious to meet the high expectations raised by his promised response, he dreaded falling short. "Unless I really succeed, I shall do the Catholic cause harm. A failure would be really deplorable—Protestants would say, Now we know all that can be said— and we see how little that is."[154] He certainly did not want to come to the sort of controversial grief that Sir Thomas Browne had in mind when he spoke of those who: "from ... an inconsiderate zeal unto truth have too rashly charged the troops of error, and remain as the trophies unto the enemies of truth."[155] Then, too, he was concerned that he "might get into great embarrassment, if the Pope knew."[156] In 1873, Newman still worried that he might wind up in the Vatican dog house. And there was always the added difficulty that Gladstone was "so rambling and slovenly" that one could not "follow him with any logical exactness."[157] Then, at the very height of his anxiety, Baron Friedrich von Hügel wrote from the Grand Hotel in Cannes expressing "how deeply, profoundly indebted" he was to Newman's books and how grateful he was to Gladstone for forcing him to write another—praise which must have struck Newman as a cruel joke as he forged ahead with what he considered a "very wearisome occupation for an old man."[158] It was, he said, "the toughest job I ever had."[159]

Then, too, Newman was never eager to embroil himself in controversy. Although he made mincemeat of Henry Brougham in *The Tamworth Reading Room* (1841) and made Charles Kingsley regret that he ever impugned his veracity in *Apologia Pro Vita Sua* (1864), Newman disliked controversy. "I have great confidence in the maxim, *Magna est veritas et prævalebit*," he told one correspondent in 1841. "Controversy does but delay the sure victory of truth by making people angry ... Controversy too is a waste of time—one has other things to do." That last consideration must have told heavily on him. One can imagine Newman recalling his letter of 1841 and being tempted to disengage. "Truth can fight its own battle. It has a reality in it, which shivers to pieces swords of earth. As far as we are not on the side of truth, we shall shiver to bits, and I am willing it should be so." But, then, there is something in the same letter that might very well have recalled him to the pressing issue at hand. "The only cause of the prevalence of fallacies for the last 300 years has been the strong arm of the civil power countenancing them."[160] In refuting Gladstone, Newman could at least make some honorable stand against that "prevalence of fallacies."

Even if Newman's rebuttal had somehow fallen flat, the dedication of his work to Henry Fitzalan-Howard, the 15th Duke of Norfolk (1847–1917) would have been confutation enough of Gladstone's charge that Catholics could not be loyal Englishmen. After attending Newman's Oratory School, the Duke went abroad and lived for some time in the house of his uncle Lord Lyons in Constantinople. On returning home, from 1895 to 1900, he joined Lord Salisbury's government as postmaster-general. Then, at the age of 52, he decided to go off and fight in the South African War, which caused Salisbury to quip, "We shall have old Cross going next," referring to his 77-year-old Lord Privy Seal.[161] After returning home, Norfolk sat on many royal commissions. In the House of Lords he was a great advocate for education. He was one of the co-founders of the University of Sheffield and its first chancellor; the parks he donated to Sheffield totaled 160 acres. In 1887, he was sent by Queen Victoria as special envoy to Pope Leo XIII. He had an exacting, scholarly, imaginative understanding of royal ceremony, as his conduct of the coronations of Edward VII (1902) and George V (1911) demonstrated. The old *Dictionary of National Biography* summed up his career with old-fashioned sententiousness, which nicely conveys the true distinction of the man: "He earned the respect and esteem which are due to strong patriotism, to sober judgement, to unassuming dignity, and to strong moral and religious conviction."[162] There was nothing disloyal about the impeccably Catholic Norfolk.

When the ordeal of refuting Gladstone was nearly over, Newman wrote a charming letter to Charles Russell, the Professor of Philosophy at Maynooth, who had helped him understand the claims of Rome when he was on his Anglican deathbed, thanking him for his "great kindness" in wishing him well with the work. "I am like a man who has gone up in a balloon," Newman told Russell, "and has a chance of all sorts of adventures, from gas escapes, from currents of air, from intanglements in forests, from the wide sea, and does not feel himself safe till he gets back to his fireside. At present as I am descending, I am in the most critical point of my expedition. All I can say is that I have acted for the best, and have done my best, and must now leave the success of it to a higher power."[163]

When the *Letter to the Duke of Norfolk* appeared, Gladstone wrote to Newman to say that it exhibited not only "severe self control" but "a genial and gentle manner"; Newman had been "able to invest ... these painful subjects with something of a golden glow ..." Lord Acton, whose assessments of Newman were always tinged with a certain condescension, thought it: "admirable in its strength, strange in its weakness, incomparable in its speculation, tame and emasculated in action."[164] John Pope Hennessy wrote from the Stafford Club: "Your letter to the Duke of Norfolk is the only thing we can talk about in this club at present; and indeed in other clubs and in society generally it seems to be one of the two absorbing topics of the moment ...

I never remember so unanimous an expression of Catholic opinion on any question of the kind before."[165] Thomas Cookson, Provost of the Liverpool Chapter, acknowledged the sureness with which Newman had hit one of his main targets when he thanked him "for the service you have done to the Catholics of this country by your much desired and crushing, yet persuasive, answer to Mr. Gladstone's Expostulation .... I hope the reproach will not be fruitless, which you have given to some among ourselves whose language on Papal claims is usually high-flown, and not always accurate, and as a matter of course confirms the opinion of the governing class and of Protestants generally that they encroach upon civil rights."[166] Perhaps the most gratifying response came from an Irish Jesuit, Father James Jones, who wrote "I am sure you will bear with me when I say that your name was dear to me even before you became a Catholic, and that this feeling has been increased by every work that has since come from your hand, and by none more than this last ... I cannot help saying that I sympathize very much in your aversion to extravagance and intolerance in matters where the Church has left us free to form our own judgment .... I would gladly speak of that great theological light I have obtained in each section of your letter, and of the encouragement to thorough loyalty to the Church and the Pope that breathes in every page of it ..."[167] In writing back to him, Newman confessed: "Great as the weariness of writing has been, my anxiety has been quite as great a trial. I have never considered theology my line or my forte, and have not written on it except when obliged. Under these circumstances you may think how exceedingly gratified I have been to receive your letter. It is a great thing to have cause to believe, that on the whole I have been prospered in what I have written. Please sometimes say a prayer for an old man ..."[168]

Newman's response to Gladstone encapsulated all the undiminished regard he felt for his unscrupulous accuser: "It has been a great grief to me to have had to write against one, whose career I have followed from first to last with so much (I may say) loyal interest and admiration. I had known about you from others, and had looked at you with kindly curiosity, before you came up to Christ Church, and, from the time that you were launched into public life, you have retained a hold on my thoughts and on my gratitude ..." And he concluded by saying "I do not think I ever can be sorry for what I have done, but I never can cease to be sorry for the necessity of doing it."[169] Something of the truth of this letter can be seen in a letter he wrote over thirty-five years before to his friend Maria Giberne after Gladstone's sensational book on Church and State appeared: "When the Isis flows back, and St. Mary's spire turns into a railroad train, he will begin to waver and repent of his book."[170] (Gladstone reminded Newman of railway trains, rather as George Bernard Shaw reminded Yeats of sewing machines.) Apropos the radical new political order that was taking shape, after Gladstone's Irish University Bill was defeated, Newman wrote: "Everything is breaking up and the rudiments of a new formation are only seen by Him who has allowed such a disorganization to come to pass. It is not Gladstone's fault—he has done all he could—but he might as soon be expected by eloquence or skill to change the course of a railway train, as to change the direction or slacken the speed of the movements which are bringing in a new world."[171]

Gladstone and Newman were never more than associates. "I was not a friend of his," Gladstone told Acton after his death, "but only an acquaintance treated with extraordinary kindness ..."[172] They met no more than a dozen times over 65 years. Yet there was a deep bond between them. What forged the bond is not easy to say. They both saw themselves as working to advance the cause of faith—"the great and sacred cause,"[173] as Gladstone called it—though in later life Newman would tell Lady Simeon and a number of other correspondents that Gladstone had publicly vowed "to give the few remaining years of his life to preparing for eternity, but in no long time we find him setting out on his Scottish (Midlothian) expedition, and ever since he has been in the hands of the enemies of all religion. Alas, Alas ..."[174] To Lord Blachford, Newman was categorical: the Party that Gladstone had joined is "as openly unbelieving and as consciously uniting politics and infidelity as Gambetta's."[175]

When Gladstone embraced the radicals in his Party, Newman was more pained than angry. To one correspondent he wrote: "I grieve for Gladstone with a tenderness which I do not recognize in you. (He has never prospered in any true sense of the word, since 1874 he attacked wantonly the Holy Roman Church and the Holy See in the person of Pius ix.)"[176] "Tenderness" sounds an odd word to describe a relationship that had such little personal contact, but somehow it fits. "I cling to the hope of yet seeing you some day or other by some happy turn of fortune," Gladstone wrote to Newman in November of 1882.[177] One of Newman's last letters to Gladstone returned this note of fondness. Gladstone was staying in Edgbaston in November of 1888 and wrote to Father Neville asking if Newman could receive him. Newman wrote back: "It is a great kindness and compliment asking to see me. I have known and admired you so long. But I can't write nor talk nor walk and hope you will take my blessing which I give from my heart."[178]

Still, Gladstone's fondness for Newman was never unalloyed. In 1890, he wrote to Acton: "Ever since he published his University Sermons in 1843 I have thought him unsafe in philosophy ..."[179] To Richard Holt Hutton in the same year he said that Newman might have "done an incomparable and immeasurable work for the Church of England" but he "never placed the English Church upon its historical ground. I doubt if he was even tolerably acquainted with the history of the sixteenth century ..."[180] Gladstone pinched this charge from his good friend, Johann Joseph Ignaz von Döllinger (1799–1890), the liberal apostate who said about the author of *A Letter to the Duke of Norfolk*: "Whole stretches of Church history and the history of European culture are unknown to him, as the darkest Africa. There is no way of explaining his naïve and daring assertions."[181] Yet Gladstone attacked more than Newman's learning. "He was trained (as I was) in the Evangelical School, which is beyond all others ... the school of private judgment. By private judgment he excogitated the scheme of doctrine and thought which he taught in his Anglican works. By private judgment he grew sore with the manifold abuses and defects of the English Church; but then, also by private judgment, he measured the corruptions of the Roman, and recoiled from them. It is wonderful, and shows the loyalty of his affection, that, leaving nothing but rags and shreds to hang on by, he remained in the English Church until 1845."[182] This was the flagrant table-turning of a seasoned House of Commons man. It nicely illustrates what T. H. Huxley referred to as Gladstone's mastery of "the great art of offensive misrepresentation."[183] (Echoes of this willful misrepresentation can be found in M. G. Brock likening Newman to Wycliffe[184] or Frank Turner calling him "the first great, and perhaps most enduring, Victorian skeptic."[185]) Gladstone knew full well that Newman had always counseled against errant private judgment. "On certain questions, in certain emergencies," Newman argued in one letter, though one could quote hundreds of other similar passages, "I would rather consult half a dozen men, than go by the opinion of any one … It never can be right for a man always to go by his own judgment, relying simply on what seems to himself the right thing to do."[186] In charging Newman with having recourse to private judgment in converting to Catholicism, Gladstone sought not only to defend his own recourse to private judgement but to imply that Newman was never as Roman as he wished to appear.

In response to a pamphlet by the High Churchman Frederick Meyrick entitled *Does Dr. Newman deserve Mr. Gladstone's Praises?* (1875), Gladstone gave what was perhaps his most considered assessment of Newman's character:

I have, without doubt, spoken freely and largely of his merits, but indirectly and with reserve of his defects. To this I was moved by recollection of much kindness; by my belief in his truthfulness of intention; by my admiration of the disinterestedness which has marked his life, his content in an outward obscurity, his superiority to vulgar ambitions. I was sure, too, that he had, in dealing with me, repressed thoughts and words of wrath; and finally, as I was at this time in much correspondence with thorough-paced Vaticanists, I saw him shine morally in the contrast with them. Besides a want of robustness of character, I have ventured to glance at an obliquity of intellect. The first he has shown by shrinking from the bold action to which his insight, and many of his avowals, should have led him, and also in his adopting for some time after his secession too much of the ordinary tone of the Romish controversialist. The latter defect of his mind is too traceable in all his works, and the effect is, for practical purposes, you might as well argue with a Jesuit. His mind seems to be nearly the opposite of Bishop Butler's, whom, nevertheless, he sincerely, but I should say ignorantly, worships, as the Athenians worshipped the unknown God. He constantly reminds me of a very different man, Lord Westbury, in this great point, that he is befooled by the subtlety of his own intellect. I always felt that Westbury, when he was wrong, lost the chance that we ordinary mortals possess of getting right, because we feel a greater difficulty in sustaining untrue propositions; but in Westbury it was the same thing, in point of difficulty, to sustain a sound or unsound argument. So it is with Dr. Newman. But I must not pursue further this very curious subject.[187]

Newman would have been amused to know that he put Gladstone in mind of Richard Bethell, 1st Baron Westbury (1800–1873), one of Victorian England's most brilliant legal minds. After establishing an equity practice that brought in an income of over £20,000 a year, Bethell rose to the peak of his profession with what seemed effortless inevitability. In 1851, he was elected MP for Alyesbury; in the same year, he was appointed vice-chancellor of the duchy of Lancaster; in 1852, he became solicitor-general; in 1853, he received a knighthood; in 1856, he became attorney-general. It is true that he was passed over for Lord Chancellor in 1859 when Lord Campbell—the presiding judge at Newman's Achilli trial—was given the nod. But, in 1861, Campbell obligingly died and Bethell succeeded him. Once installed, he took the title of Baron Westbury of Westbury in the county of Wiltshire. In addition to his ambition and his brains, Bethell was notable for distrusting the common law system, convinced that the law of precedent was too unsystematic. He also became famous for ruling in the proceedings arising out of the publication of *Essays and Reviews* (1860), one of the authors of which had contended that there was no Hell. When Westbury found for the appellants in the case, contemporary wags suggested that his epitaph ought to be that "he took away from orthodox members of the Church of England their last hope of everlasting damnation."[188] In his witty entry for Westbury in the *Oxford Dictionary of National Biography*, R. C. J. Cocks sums up Westbury's life deftly: "Looking back on his career, late Victorians were surely right in seeing him as someone afflicted with both an overwhelming belief in his own intellectual superiority and an emotional need to prove this ability at every possible point, often at the cost of others. What made him so striking was the extent to which the quality of his mind often justified his own view of his talents."[189] However amusing it is to think of Westbury and Newman in the same light, it is difficult to see much resemblance in the two men. Gladstone's contention that Newman, like Westbury, could not somehow admit when he was wrong was an odd claim. If that were true, how could Gladstone account for Newman's conversion?

Gladstone availed himself of another opportunity to take a swipe at Newman in a piece called "The Place of Heresy and Schism in The Modern Christian Church," (1894), in which he defined his view of conscience:

> The Christian Church, no longer entitled to speak with an undivided and universal authority, and thus to take her place among the paramount facts of life, is not thereby invaded in her inner citadel. That citadel is, and ever was, the private conscience within this sacred precinct, that matured the forces which by a long incubation grew to such a volume of strength, as legitimately to obtain the mastery of the world. It would be a fatal error to allow the voice of that conscience to be put down by another voice, which proceeds not from within, but from without, the sanctuary. The private conscience is indeed for a man, as Cardinal Newman has well said, the viceregent of God.[190]

Had Gladstone published this during Newman's life, he would have received a sharp rebuke from the man whose understanding of conscience he so deliberately distorted. Gladstone, of course, was making reference to Newman's inveterately misinterpreted sally in *A Letter to the Duke of Norfolk*, where he observed: "If I am obliged to bring into after-dinner toasts (which indeed does not seem quite the thing) I shall drink—to the Pope, if you please—still, to Conscience, first, and to the Pope afterwards."[191] Newman never claimed that the Roman Catholic Church "put down" the dictates of conscience. On the contrary, for Newman, conscience corroborates the authority of the Roman Church, embodied as that is in the Magisterium.

> Thus viewing [the Pope's] position, we shall find that it is by the universal sense of right and wrong, the consciousness of transgression, the pangs of guilt, and the dread of retribution, as first principles, deeply lodged in the hearts of men, thus and only thus, that he has gained his footing in the world and achieved his success. It is his claim to come from the Divine Lawgiver, in order to elicit, protect, and enforce those truths which the Lawgiver has sown in our very nature—it is this and this only—that is the explanation of his length of life more than antediluvian. The championship of the Moral Law and of conscience is his *raison d'être*.[192]

Newman recognized that there could conceivably be occasions when the dictates of individual conscience might collide with the injunctions of a pope— he cites, for example, the rather droll hypothetical of a pope requiring the faithful to abjure wine—but he also recognized that only spiritual arrogance and pride could suggest that such occasions were likely to be frequent.

> Unless a man is able to say to himself, as in the Presence of God, that he must not, and dare not, act upon papal injunction, he is bound to obey it, and would commit a great sin disobeying it. *Prima facie* it is his bounden duty, even from a sentiment of loyalty, to believe the Pope right and to act accordingly. He must vanquish that mean, ungenerous, selfish, vulgar spirit of his nature, which, at the very first rumour of a command, places itself in opposition to the Superior who gives it, asks itself whether he is not exceeding his right, and rejoices, in a moral and practical matter to commence with scepticism. He must have no willful determination to exercise a right of thinking, saying, doing just what he pleases, the question of truth and falsehood, right and wrong, the duty if possible of obedience, the love of speaking as his Head speaks, and of standing in all cases on his Head's side, being simply discarded. If this necessary rule were observed, collisions between the Pope's authority and the authority of conscience would be very rare.[193]

Pope Benedict XVI's reading of Newman's statement in the *Letter to the Duke of Norfolk* about after-dinner toasts is worth noting here because he reads Newman with discerning sympathy. As Dr. Rowland points out, the after-dinner remark "is usually interpreted to mean that [Newman] put the authority of his own conscience above that of the pope's. Ratzinger offers a completely different interpretation. He says that Newman intended this to be a clear confession of his faith in the papacy … he meant it to be an interpretation of the papacy as an office which guarantees, rather than opposes, the primacy of conscience. In other words, Newman was making the point, which Ratzinger himself made prior to assuming the Office of Peter, that the pope cannot do whatever he likes, that the exercise of his prerogative powers are circumscribed by both Scripture and Tradition, that is, by the very data upon which a well-formed conscience relies."[194]

What is remarkable about Gladstone and Newman is that their very differences bound them together. Gladstone longed to be free of what he considered the slavery of politics so he could devote himself to God. In Newman, he saw a man who had made that devotion his life's work, his master-pursuit. The thought that he might have done the same if he had not stood for Newark all those many years ago made Newman a lifelong fascination. For Newman's influence at Oxford, Gladstone thought, "there is no parallel in the academical history of Europe, unless you go back to the twelfth century or the University of Paris."[195] That influence had played a considerable part in causing first his sister Helen and then his two dearest friends, Henry Manning and James Hope-Scott, to defect to Rome—or, to come 'unfixed', as he liked to put it—but, much as he agreed with Dean Church in seeing his influence as a "catastrophe", he could never discount it. And while it would be risible to suggest that Newman ever had any hankerings to enter politics, it is clear from his writings that he had great respect for public men and for the genuine good that public life could accomplish. In his funeral oration for Hope-Scott, he wrote: "We owe very much to those who devote themselves to public life, whether in the direct service of the State or in the prosecution of great national or social undertakings. They live laborious days, of which we individually reap the benefit." In Gladstone he saw possibilities for a renewed Christian public life that were not far short of the possibilities Gladstone himself saw. While the realism of his Catholic faith would never tempt Newman to share what Matthew refers to as Gladstone's "dream of a moral state married to a cleansed church together countering 'the moral movement … of the day … away from religion and towards infidelity,'"[196] he did see a place in the State for avowed men of religion working to advance the cause of religion, however Sisyphean that advance might prove. If Anglicanism could be made to serve as a bulwark against the rising tide of unbelief, there was no reason why Gladstone could not be similarly useful. Newman followed Gladstone's career with such closeness and such interest not because it was Gladstone's career—about Gladstone himself he once said, "Somehow there is great earnestness, but a want of amiableness about him"[197]—but because it was the career of a man of genuine faith grappling with what Newman once called the "gross, carnal, unbelieving world."[198]

Biographers from John Morley and Philip Magnus to Colin Matthew and Richard Shannon have charted Gladstone's political course from stern, unbending Tory to Grand Old Man of the Liberal Party. Yet when it came to the Church of Rome, which he likened to "an Asian monarchy: nothing but one giddy height of despotism and one dead level of religious subservience,"

Gladstone never outgrew the bigotry of his boyhood.[199] Much is made of Bishop Butler's influence on his religious thinking[200] and of the religious interest he took in Homer[201] but no one had more lasting influence than his first tutor, the Rev. Mr. Rawson, "a good man," as Gladstone recalled in an autobiographical fragment, "of high No Popery opinions."[202] Newman's religious development was infinitely richer. Yet he shared Gladstone's respect for liberty. At the end of his life, Gladstone would say: "I was brought up to distrust and dislike liberty, I learned to believe in it."[203] Newman could have said the same, though the liberty that most interested him was the liberty of a responsible laity taking a responsible part in the life of what he once pointedly called the "Catholic Roman Church."[204]

CHAPTER 8

Newman, Thackeray and Vanity Fair

This was the greatness of Thackeray, the man whom sentimentalists without hearts or stomachs have conceived as a mere satirist ... he felt, perhaps, more fully ... than any other Englishman the immeasurable and almost unbearable emotion that is involved in the mere fact of human life. Dickens, with his indestructible vanity and boyishness, is always looking forward. Thackeray is always looking back in life. And no man will ever properly comprehend him until he has reached for a moment that state of the soul in which melancholy is the greatest of all the joys.

> G. K. Chesterton, *Thackeray* (1903)

In "What Then Does Dr. Newman Mean?" Charles Kingsley quoted a passage from Newman's *Anglican Difficulties* to substantiate his charge that "Truth, for its own sake is no virtue in his eyes, and he teaches that it need not be." The passage was one of those gleeful grenades that Newman could not resist tossing at the Protestant Establishment now and again:

Take a mere beggar-woman, lazy, ragged, and filthy, and not over-scrupulous of truth—(I do not say she had arrived at perfection)—but if she is chaste, and sober, and cheerful, and goes to her religious duties (and I am supposing not at all an impossible case), she will, in the eyes of the Church, have a prospect of heaven, which is quite closed and refused to the State's pattern-man, the just, the upright, the generous, the honourable, the conscientious, if he be all this, not from a supernatural power—(I do not determine whether this is likely to be the fact, but I am contrasting views and principles)—not from a supernatural power, but from mere natural virtue.

From Kingsley's response, it was clear that the distinction between grace and natural virtue that Newman meant to make was not one his English Protestant audience was likely to appreciate. "He has taught the whole Celtic Irish population, that as long as they are chaste ... and sober ... and 'go to their religious duties' ... they may look down upon the Protestant gentry who send over millions to feed them in famine; who found hospitals and charities to which they are admitted freely; who try to introduce among them capital, industry, civilization, and, above

Newman at St. Mary's (Courtesy of Magdalen College)

Littlemore (Courtesy of Birmingham Oratory)

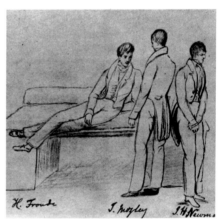

Newman with Thomas Mozley and Hurrell Froude (Courtesy of Birmingham Oratory)

Oriel College (Courtesy of Birmingham Oratory)

Richard Waldo Sibthorp – Prodigal Anglican

John Keble – Apostle of Uncertainty

Charlotte Keble – Kept Her Husband
Shivering at the Gate

Brougham, Russell and Grey – Liberal
Triumvirate

Wellington and Peel – Saw the Old Order
Toppled

Edward Bouverie Pusey – Canon of Christ
Church

Martin Routh of Magdalen with
Celebrated Wig

Joseph Blanco White – Fiddler from Seville

Frederick York Powell – No Puseyite
(*Vanity Fair*)

William Froude – Stalwart Sceptic

Catherine Froude – One of Newman's
Dearest Friends

Isambard Kingdom Brunel – William
Froude's Mentor

James A. Froude – Historian of Paradoxical
Whiggery

Benjamin Disraeli – Newman Pitied His
Hang-Dog Look

Earl of Rosebery – Marveled at Newman's
Incomparable End (*Vanity Fair*)

Frederick Rogers, Later Lord Blachford –
Proconsular Tractarian

Newman Reading *Ecce Homo* (1865)
(Courtesy of Birmingham Oratory)

Emily Bowles (Courtesy of Birmingham Oratory)

Lady Chatterton (photograph of painting at Baddesley Clinton)

Lady Georgiana Fullerton

The Duchess of Devonshire – Lady Georgiana Fullerton's Grandmother (Gainsborough)

Marchioness of Lothian – Dedicated Her Life to Caring for Christ's Poor

Julia Sorrell – Newman's 'Xantiappe'

Gladstone with Axe (Courtesy of Getty
Photos)

15th Duke of Norfolk (*Vanity Fair*)

Lord Ripon, Viceroy of India, Converted
in 1874

Newman 1873–4 Sketch by Lady Coleridge

William Makepeace Thackeray in 1848 – The Year Newman Founded the Birmingham Oratory and Thackeray published *Vanity Fair*

Isabella Shawe – Thackeray's Irish Wife

Mrs. Shawe – Thackeray's Mother-in-Law

Statue of William III in Dublin

Charles Kingsley – Muscular Christian

G. K. Chesterton – Funny Christian

Edmund Yates – Bounder

Garrick Club

Cardinal Wiseman

Cardinal Manning

Catholic University Church, Dublin

Catholic University, Dublin – Newman's
Oxford on the Liffey

Orestes Brownson – Convert from Vermont
by GPA Healy 1863 (Courtesy of Museum
of Fine Arts, Boston)

Richard Holt Hutton – Newman's Finest
Contemporary Critic

Newman in the 1860's (Courtesy of
Birmingham Oratory)

Frederick Denison Maurice – Broad
Church Mandarin

Newman at His Desk (Courtesy of
Birmingham Oratory)

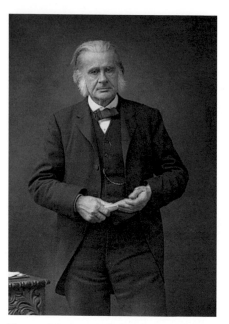

Thomas Huxley – Paladin of the Positivists

Thomas Carlyle – Newman Enjoyed His
French Revolution (1837)

William Ullathorne – Heroic Bishop of
Birmingham

John Ruskin – Knew His Bible by Heart

Pius IX – Newman Credited Him with
Giving the English a Church of Their Own

Leo XIII – Made Newman a Cardinal in
1877

Henry James – Mayfair Neighbor of
Convert Peeresses

Max Beerbohm – Understood How the
Dull Envy the Brilliant

Matthew Arnold – Hollow Man

Gerard Manley Hopkins – Enjoyed Newman's Prose

Thomas Arnold – Converted Twice

Rugby School Street Entrance – Scene of Clough's Boyhood Triumphs

Arthur Hugh Clough – Poet of Dilemma

Dr. Arnold of Rugby – Reviled the Oxford Malignants

Mark Pattison – Peevish Apostate

Aubrey de Vere – Newman's Anglo-Irish Friend from Limerick

Lord Tennyson – Emily Bowles's Friend

Newman in 1844 – On his Anglican Deathbed (Portrait by Richmond)

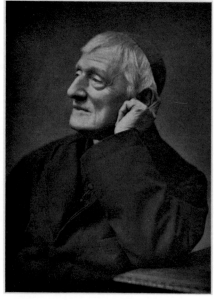

Dean Church – Historian of the Oxford Movement

Cardinal Newman (Courtesy of Birmingham Oratory)

all, that habit of speaking the truth, for want of which they are what they are and are likely to remain such, as long as they have Dr. Newman for their teacher ..." Indeed, for Kingsley, "if the Roman Catholic hierarchy in these realms had any sense of their own interests" ... they would have sent Newman not to the Catholic University in Dublin, but to "their furthest mission among savages of the South Seas."[1] After Newman published his *Apologia*, Kingsley sent off a defiant letter to Alexander Macmillan, in whose magazine his initial charge against Newman's veracity appeared: "I have determined to take no notice whatever of Dr Newman's apology. I have nothing to retract, apologize for, explain. Deliberately, after 20 years of thought, I struck as hard as I could. Deliberately I shall strike again ... though not one literary man in England approved. I know too well of what I am talking." As for the *Apologia* itself, "I cannot trust – I can only smile at – the autobiography of a man who (beginning with Newman's light, learning, and genius,) ends in believing ... in the Infallibility of the Church, and in the Immaculate Conception. If I am to bandy words, it must be with sane persons." Nor was he impressed by public opinion siding with Newman. "The world seems inclined to patronize Dr Newman and the Cafards just now, because having no faith of its own, it is awed by the seeming strength of fanaticism. I know them too well either to patronize or to fear them." And he closed with an interesting comment. "I wish poor dear Thackeray had been alive. He knew what I know, and would have taken a tone about this matter ... He was too true a liberal to pat lies and bigotry on the back."[2]

What Thackeray would have made of the *Apologia* and indeed of the controversy that brought it into being is an interesting question. Thackeray paid a fair amount of attention to Newman before his sudden death at the age of 52 in December 1863—the very month that Kingsley's calumny appeared. He attended Newman's King William Street lectures in 1850 and followed the Achilli trial, telling Lady Georgiana Fullerton, the Catholic convert and novelist, that Achilli was "a rascal hypocrite no doubt; but; as the law is, the verdict was right—though I think the judge's behaviour in the trial was most unfair and unworthy."[3] Newman, for his part, also followed Thackeray's career. *Vanity Fair* was published in book form in 1848, the year Newman founded the Birmingham Oratory. He also must have seen a good deal of Thackeray's fiction corroborating his own view of nineteenth-century English society. The Oratorian Ignatius Ryder told Thackeray's biographer Gordon Ray that "Newman was fond of Thackeray, reading faithfully everything that he wrote down to the last unfinished work."[4] When Thackeray died, Newman wrote a heartfelt letter lamenting his death. So Kingsley was right: Thackeray would probably have had a decided view of the row between him and Newman, but in order to see what that view might have been, we shall need to revisit Thackeray's life and work and, especially, his correspondence.

William Makepeace Thackeray (1811–1863) was born in Calcutta, the only child of Richmond Thackeray, an official of the East India Company, and his wife Anne Becher, the second daughter of another East India Company employee and his wife Harriet, a high-toned old Evangelical lady. In 1812, Richmond invited Captain Carmichael-Smyth to dinner, without knowing that this dashing Bengal Engineer, the younger son of a good Scottish family, was his wife's former lover, whom she had planned to marry before going out to India but presumed dead—a coincidence which the novelist in Thackeray must have seen as an unmistakable omen of his future profession. Duly, after his father's death in 1815, as if in accordance with the most hackneyed romantic fiction, Thackeray's mother married the captain and from 1838 until 1861 the reunited lovers lived in Paris. Many keys to Thackeray's religious views can be found in his copious correspondence with his mother, who shared her own mother's devotion to a fierce Evangelical faith. Thackeray would begin distancing himself from this faith as a young man at Cambridge but it would nonetheless color all of his later views on religion, including his view of Newman's Catholicism.

Educated at Charterhouse and Cambridge, where he left in 1830 without a degree, Thackeray entered the Middle Temple in 1831, but after coming of age he gave up the law for journalism. At Cambridge, he befriended the future translator of the Rubáiyát of Omar Khayyám, Edward Fitzgerald, a scoffing, idle, charming young man, whose Anglo-Irish eccentricities appealed to the bohemian in Thackeray. It was also Fitzgerald who turned him against the Bible Christianity that his mother had sought to instill in him. In the last year of his life, when his daughter Anne asked which of his friends he had cared for most, Thackeray replied "Old Fitz," before adding, "We shall be very good friends in hell together."[5] In 1830, after leaving Cambridge, Thackeray went to Weimar, where he met Goethe. Interestingly enough, he was in Germany only a few years after Pusey, and he reported back to his mother how "The doctrine here is not so strict as in England—many of the dogmas by which we hold are here disregarded as allegories or parables—or I fear by most people as fictions altogether"—the very concern that prompted the Regius Professor of Divinity at Christ Church, Charles Lloyd, to send Pusey there.[6] In 1833, Thackeray bought *The National Standard*, for which he was at once proprietor, contributor and illustrator. After the paper folded, he went to study art in Paris, where, at a masked ball, he met the enterprising adventuress on whom he would base his most brilliant heroine, Becky Sharp. On a subsequent trip to the city, in a boarding house in the Rue Ponthieu, Faubourg-St-Honoré, he met a 17-year-old Irish girl from Cork named Isabella Shawe, "a simple, girlish girl," as one of his friends recalled, with whom the novelist fell in love at the proverbial first sight.[7] In 1836, after an intensely epistolary courtship in which Thackeray played Pygmalion to Isabella's Galatea, they were married in the British Embassy. D. J. Taylor nicely describes the character of their love (from Thackeray's standpoint) as "a kind of *grand passion* hedged about with sentimental whimsy, in which the desired object [was] regarded as a wayward schoolgirl."[8] After returning to London, Thackeray and Isabella set up house in 18 Albion Street. For four years, they were happily married, with three daughters on whom they doted, and this despite the meddling of Mrs. Shawe, Thackeray's noisome mother-in-law, of whom he drew one of his funniest caricatures. Then in September 1840, while on shipboard with her husband from London to Cork, Isabella leaped overboard and was only rescued after she had been in the water for twenty minutes. Several additional suicide attempts followed. When it became clear that no cure for her madness would be forthcoming, Thackeray became a haunted man. "Has it never occurred to you," he asked one of his American friends, "how awful a thing the recovery of lost reason must be, without the consciousness of the lapse of time? She finds the lover of her youth a grey-haired old man, and her infants young men and women. Is it not sad to think of this?"[9] With these thoughts ravaging his mind, he rediscovered the Christian faith of his childhood. Amelia Sedley does the same in *Vanity Fair*, after her father goes bankrupt. Thackeray describes how "She went and knelt down by the bedside; and there this wounded and timorous, but gentle and loving soul, sought for consolation, where as yet, it must be owned, our little girl had but seldom looked for it. Love had been her faith hitherto; and the sad, bleeding disappointed heart began to feel the want of another consoler."[10] A month after Thackeray's wife made her suicidal leap from the steamer's water-closet, Thackeray also shared with his mother how he had sought consolation from the same neglected source: "God was so wonderfully gracious to me. Indeed I have a thankful spirit to him, & see good in the midst of all this misfortune …"[11] Eventually Thackeray had no alternative but to send Isabella to live with a nurse in Camberwell, though she outlived him by thirty years. Later, he would tell a friend, "Though my marriage was a wreck, I would do it over again, for behold love is the crown and completion of all earthly good."[12] One reason why he gave himself up so intently to journalism was to escape the guilt he felt for his wife's derangement, which appears to have developed from post-natal depression. Another reason was to pay his abounding debts.[13] Before marrying, Thackeray lost the bulk of his fortune when his Indian bank failed; he was also an extravagant gambler. To keep his creditors at bay, he became a consummate literary journalist, contributing regularly to *Punch*, *Fraser's Magazine*, the *Morning Chronicle*, the *New Monthly Magazine* and *The Times*. The number of first-rate comic pieces that he had to show for this prolific journalism is impressive, including *The Yellowplush Correspondence* (1837), *A Shabby Genteel Story* (1840), *The Great Hoggarty Diamond* (1841) and *The Book of Snobs* (1842). For George Orwell, what was admirable about Thackeray's work leading up to and including *Vanity Fair* was how well it captured the "atmosphere of surfeit" that hovered around this rackety, grasping, desolate world, "an atmosphere compounded of oysters, brown stout, brandy and water, turtle soup, roast sirloin, haunch of venison, Madeira and cigar smoke …"[14] *Vanity Fair* (1847–1848), his first major success and the culmination of all that he had done as a comic journalist, is an unsparing portrait of the fallen world from a man who knew the follies and the sorrows he described inside out.[15] In this respect, it exemplified the truthful record of sinful man that Newman thought secular literature should exemplify. The book's psychological insight also met with Newman's approval, since this was something at which he excelled as well.[16] Nowhere else does one get a better sense of the frenzied insecurity that characterized early nineteenth-century England, or its ruthlessness. "In this vast town one has not the time to go and seek one's friends," the narrator observes; "if they drop out of the rank they disappear, and we march on without them. Who is ever missed in Vanity Fair?"[17] And yet Thackeray showed his characters remarkable sympathy, which was a mark of the fellow feeling that suffused his psychological insight. In 1998, Andrew Davies brilliantly adapted the novel to the screen in a six-episode BBC production, in which he captured the thwarted love that gives so much of the book's comedy its pathos.

Thackeray followed the success of *Vanity Fair* with several other novels, which, taken together, chart what John Carey persuasively characterizes as a "history of capitulation," in which Thackeray succumbed to the very snobbery that he had written his early journalism and *Vanity Fair* to mock. "The novels after *Vanity Fair*," Carey argues, "are full of people not only of a higher class but nicer—noble fellows, angelic ladies. It is a condition of their insipidity."[18] *The History of Pendennis* (1848–1850) and *The History of Henry Esmond* (1852) have an interest, above and beyond their aesthetic flaws, because of their autobiographical import and the light they shed on Thackeray's thinking; but *The Newcomes* (1853–1855) and *The Virginians* (1857–1859) are painfully dull reads.[19] Before his death, Thackeray was at work on *Denis Duval*, an historical novel which, coincidentally, was set in Rye among England's French Huguenots, who doubtless reminded Newman of the Huguenots of his mother's family, the Fourdriniers, who were famous French paper-makers.

After Isabella lost her reason, Thackeray became infatuated with Jane Octavia Brookfield, a literary hostess, whose father had been the friend of Coleridge and Lamb. Since she was also the wife of one of his old Cambridge friends, Thackeray had to content himself with entering into a strenuously chaste *ménage a trois*. "However much I may love her & bless her and admire her, I can't forgive her for doing her duty," he confessed after putting a stop to what he referred to as his "uncouth raptures."[20] When Thackeray learned that his devotion to this handsome, intelligent, trifling woman had never been in the least reciprocated, he saw his sentimental adoration come to smash, though the experience proved useful for his fiction—and for his wonderfully funny pastiche, "The Sorrows of Werther."[21] In summing up William Dobbins' similarly abject devotion to Amelia Sedley, who throughout *Vanity Fair* remains devoted to the memory of her deceased husband, George Osborne, whom Becky Sharp calls "that selfish humbug, that low-bred Cockney dandy, that padded booby," the narrator echoes what Thackeray felt *vis-à-vis* Mrs. Brookfield: "He had placed himself at her feet so long that the poor little woman had been accustomed to trample upon him. She didn't wish to marry him, but she wished to keep him. She wished to give him nothing, but he should give her all. It is a bargain not unfrequently levied in love."[22] Fortunately, Thackeray did not live to see the Brookfield–Thackeray triangle reproduced in two of Mrs. Brookfield's vapid novels, *Only George* (1866) and *Not Too Late* (1868). On 23 December 1863 he returned home from dining, had a stroke and dropped dead.

Years of stalwart drinking hastened his end. In addition to having matutinal brandies and soda to rouse his appetite, he would have three or four glasses of wine with lunch, and then two bottles of wine with dinner, in addition to various drams and punches after dinner. William Allingham (1824–1889), the Anglo-Irish diarist who captured the table-talk of so many eminent Victorians, from Carlyle and Tennyson to Ruskin and Browning, described the novelist's delight in the rituals of the table. "Thackeray took me to dine with him at the

Palais Royal. He noticed with quiet enjoyment every little incident—beginning with the flourish with which our waiter set down the dishes of Ostend oysters. After tasting his wine Thackeray said, looking at me solemnly, through his large spectacles, 'One's first glass of wine in the day is a great event.'"[23] During the course of his adult life, he told one friend, he had imbibed enough to float a 74-gun battleship. In *Vanity Fair* good drink jokes abound: "Had he drunk a dozen bottles of claret," the narrator observes of James Crawley, "the old spinster could have pardoned him. Mr. Fox and Mr. Sheridan drank claret. Gentlemen drank claret. But eighteen glasses of gin consumed among boxers in an ignoble pot-house—it was an odious crime and not to be pardoned readily."[24] Newman could also be witty on the subject of drink. The response he made to his brother Frank on one occasion has become justly renowned. Attending a temperance rally where Manning shared the platform with Protestants "filled me with enthusiasm and joy," Frank recalled, "but I was merely a type of the thousands who listened in deep rapt silence to his magnificent speech." For Frank, something had to be done to address "the sights that make the streets on Saturday evenings in England [such] a degrading scene." Newman, however, would not be dragooned into this crusade against the bibulous poor and sent off one of his more memorable rebuffs: "As to what you tell me of Archbishop Manning, I have heard that some also of our Irish bishops think that too many drink-shops are licensed. As for me, I do not know whether we have too many or too few." Frank affected to find the reply callous. "The more I dwelt on this icy message, the less it seemed worthy, not only of a Christian, but of one who cared for human sin and human misery."[25] But there was more self-congratulatory posturing than conviction in Frank's indignation. Simply because Newman declined to harangue the crapulent did not make him indifferent to sin and misery. He tackled such things in the confessional, not on temperance platforms.

Thackeray and Newman had a number of things in common. They were on the receiving end of grievous personal loss. Thackeray, of course, lost his wife to madness and Newman lost scores of friends and loved ones to early death, including John Bowden, his closest friend at Trinity, and Hurrell Froude, his closest friend at Oriel. Both Thackeray and Newman were fond of women, whom they often made their confidantes—Thackeray, Mrs. Brookfield and his mother, and Newman, Mrs. Froude, Emily Bowles and Mrs. Bowden. Both men had a good sense of the ridiculous. They were keen social commentators. They both had decided views of Lord Brougham, the oleaginous Whig politico against whose Tamworth Reading Room Newman wrote with such witty polemical zest. For Thackeray, Brougham was "the best and wickedest old fellow" he had ever met, "enormously good fun," and "boiling over with humour & mischief."[26] Newman could never see him as anything but the "great sophist."[27] If their preferences as regards public men differed, Thackeray and Newman had distinct literary similarities. They were inspired satirists. They were inspired letter-writers. They both wrote an elegant, conversational English which owed as much to Addison as to Swift, whom Newman considered "the most native and natural of our writers."[28] They were gregarious men who had a wide circle of friends and acquaintances. They took as critical an interest in truth as they did in humbug. They paid lifelong mind to Vanity Fair.

They were also good travel writers. Thackeray could be wonderfully funny on America. In 1856, he wrote one of his friends, during a punishing, if lucrative lecture tour of the country: "Over a thousand miles of railroad I have not seen a beautiful prospect—only swamp, sand, pines, wood cabins or villages and negroes reposing here and there—on the Alabama river a view about as mournful as if it was a tributary to the Styx, on this Mississippi the same dreariness on a wider scale, in the taverns dirt stenches dreadful swearing in the bars gongs banging night & day to plentiful filthy meals, every mans & womans knife in the mouth or the dish alternately—I was drawing a picture for home & only made men performing this feat, but looking down the table at dinner to day every single woman was occupied so—and when we had done there came a giantess (we are both going to perform at the same fair no doubt) to eat alone—and when I looked down she had her knife down *her* great throat. I can hardly bear it."[29] Newman was equally vivid in the accounts he sent home of his travels. From Deal, where he had gone on holiday in 1862, he wrote William Neville: "Three days I have fed on an expensive old tough gander — never making a meal. Yesterday I attempted veal cutlets — they were made up of stringy, gristly, and sinewy meat, parts not quite done. I am now wild how to get a dinner. I am told there is an Hotel here better than the Clarendon, which was hardly better than a pothouse. My first entrance into the Coffee Room was attended by the simultaneous exit from it of two girls running, apparently from a young gentleman who was over his wine and walnuts. I shall go and try the Royal Hotel, though with sad trepidation. Another scheme I have is to go over to Ramsgate. It is a nice morning, and a return ticket is only 3 shillings. I can look about for lodgings. You see, I had laid in a stock of wine, and I did not know what to do with it. Else, I should have gone off to an Hotel at Ramsgate or Dover for the week till Austin came. Now I have been drinking it against time. I hope I shall not make myself drunk. Why has not one a bag like the Camel to keep wine in? — then, it would be laying in a stock for next week."[30]

Thackeray and Newman had a mutual friend in Mary Holmes, the governess, who first corresponded with Newman in the 1830s after reading his sermons but confessed to being disappointed when they finally met: Newman was too young and too unromantic. Thackeray first began corresponding with Miss Holmes after his wife went mad—he needed someone to teach his daughters their music lessons—but after finding her a sympathetic correspondent, he was disappointed to find that she was a small, unsightly woman in person, with red hair and a red nose. Miss Holmes also corresponded with Anthony Trollope, who wrote to her niece after her death: "I found her letters to be full of piety, good sense, and of most excellent literary criticism .... She was an honest, religious, and a high-minded lady, and I feel that her death has robbed me of a friend ..."[31] When Newman learned of Thackeray's sudden death, he wrote to Miss Holmes: "I ... write ... to express the piercing sorrow that I feel at Thackeray's death. You know I never saw him – but you have interested me in him – and one saw in his books the workings of his mind – and he has died with such awful suddenness.

A new work of his had been advertised – and I had looked forward with pleasure to reading it – and now the drama of his life is closed, and he himself is the greatest instance of the text, of which he was so full, Vanitas vanitatum, omnia vanitas. I wonder whether he has known his own decay – for a decay I think there has been. I thought his last novel betrayed lassitude and exhaustion of mind – and he has lain by apparently for a year. His last (fugitive) pieces in the Cornhill have been almost sermons – one should be very glad to know that he had presentiments of what was to come.

And he ended his letter with a *cri de coeur* that shows what an impact Thackeray's work had on him. "What a world this is – how wretched they are, who take it for their portion. Poor Thackeray – it seems but the other day since we became Catholics – now all his renown has been since that – he has made his name, has been made much of, has been fêted, and has gone out, all since 1846 or 1847, all since I went to Propaganda and came back a Philippine."[32]

Thackeray would have greatly enjoyed the fact that Newman saw a frazzled preacher in his last things. In his *Roundabout* essay, "De Finibus," Thackeray confessed, "Among the sins of commission which novel-writers not seldom perpetuate, is the sin of grandiloquence, or tall-talking, against which, for my part, I will offer up a special *libera me*. This is the sin of schoolmasters, governesses, critics, sermoners, and instructors of young or old people. Maybe (for I am making a clean breast, and liberating my soul), perhaps of all the novel-spinners now extant, the present speaker is the most addicted to preaching."[33] It is noteworthy that G. K. Chesterton also recognized this aspect of the novelist, confirming that "Thackeray, from the beginning of his life until the end, consistently and seriously preached a gospel. His gospel, like all deep and genuine ones, may be hard to sum up in a phrase, but if we wished to sum it up we could hardly express it better than by saying that it was the philosophy of the beauty and glory of fools."[34] Certainly this would apply to William Dobbin, Amelia Sedley, Joseph Sedley, Rawdon Crawley, even to Becky Sharp, if we agree that her cleverness ultimately proved a very beautiful, even a glorious foolishness. After all, she brings together Dobbin and Amelia. But Chesterton's paradoxical wit divined something even deeper in Thackeray's preaching. "He believed as profoundly as St. Paul that in the ultimate realm of essential values God made the foolish things of the earth to confound the wise. He looked out with lucent and terrible eyes upon the world with all its pageants and achievements; he saw men of action, he saw men of genius, he saw heroes; and amid men of action, men of genius, and heroes he saw with absolute sincerity only one thing worth being—a gentleman. And when we understand what he meant by that phrase, the absolute sufficiency of a limpid kindliness, of an obvious and dignified humility, of a softness for noble memories and a readiness for any minute self-sacrifice, we may, without any affected paradox, but rather with serious respect, sum up Thackeray's view of life by saying that amid all the heroes and geniuses he saw only one thing worth being—a fool."[35]

Newman took a similar position with respect to the Oratory. As he told his fellow Oratorian, John Dalgairns, "We must be content to be despised in (what the Protestant version calls) 'our day of small things.'"[36] To Ambrose St. John,

with whom he studied for the Catholic priesthood in Rome, he explained what
he meant more fully.

> I said not so long ago in Chapter, what I deeply feel, that no Oratory, which
> is likely to be in England, can so exactly fulfil the maxim of St Philip of
> 'amare nesciri.' It is our great privilege, that we can work in many ways here,
> and get no credit at all for it; and that, first, because we are not seen, and
> next because those, to whom we minister, are persons of low estate, of whom
> the world thinks little. And as to contempt, recollect, my dear Fathers, that
> St Philip, as Fr Bacci tells us, 'took great pleasure in being lightly esteemed,
> nay, even in being actually despised, and regarded as a man of no worth;
> and he was always saying to his spiritual children, 'Throw yourselves into
> God's hands, and be sure, that, if He wants any thing of you, He will make
> you good in all that He wishes to use you for.' Again 'As a crowning maxim,
> he laid it down as a rule, that to obtain the gift of humility perfectly, four
> things were necessary, spernere mundum, spernere nullum, spernere se
> ipsum, spernere se sperni.' 'He scarcely ever had this sentence of St Bernard
> out of his mouth, "to despise the world, to despise no one, to despise self, to
> despise being despised."'[37]

Another thing the two men shared was a rather generous view of Charles
Kingsley, the acolyte of Carlyle and Maurice, whose exaltation of the natural man
made him a fierce foe of everything Catholic. While seeing his "grave and gratuitous slander" as that of "a furious foolish fellow," Newman bore Kingsley no
grudges.[38] In the preface to the *Apologia*, he made it clear that, "I am in warfare
with him, but I wish him no ill; it is very difficult to get up resentment towards
persons whom one has never seen."[39] When the controversy had run its course,
he told one correspondent, "I should not have singled out Mr Kingsley for public
notice unless I thought it really worth while to deal a blow against a virulent
blasphemer of the Catholic Church." After Kingsley's death, Newman was sorry
that they had never had a chance to meet. He was convinced that Kingsley had
done him a favor by attacking him: it gave him an opportunity to clear his name
and defend the Catholic faith. Indeed, Newman went further: "by his passionate
attack on me [he] became one of my best friends, whom I always wished to shake
hands with when living, and towards whose memory I have much tenderness."[40]
He even said a "Mass for his soul on the news of his death."[41]

After Thackeray met Kingsley, he wrote of him as "a fine honest goahead
fellow, who charges a subject heartily impetuously with the greatest courage
and simplicity, but with narrow eyes (his are extraordinary brave blue &
honest) and with little knowledge of the world I think. But he's superior to us
worldlings in many ways, and I wish I had some of his honest pluck."[42] Despite
this favorable impression, Thackeray was not entirely impressed with Kingsley's
fiction. He recognized the provocative power of *Yeast* (1848), Kingsley's
fictional ragbag into which he threw his views on everything from the rustic
poor, Roman Catholicism, Tractarianism, non-conformity, and the game laws to
celibacy, sex, marriage, banking, sanitary reform, and the irrepressible Irish. But

Thackeray found *Alton Locke* (1850), Kingsley's chartist novel, an unreadable bore. Indeed, the condition-of-England novel, whether Disraeli's *Sybil* (1845) or Mrs. Gaskell's *Mary Barton* (1848) struck him as conventional as any other genre of fiction—and as little faithful to the reality of life.[43] What set *Vanity Fair* (1847) apart was Thackeray's witty defiance of convention, though he could never resist lampooning the conventions he eschewed. Early on in the novel, he makes his readers aware of how aware he is of these literary protocols in an amusing aside.

> We might have treated this subject in the genteel, or in the romantic, or in the facetious manner. Suppose we had laid the scene in Grosvenor-square, with the very same adventures—would not some people have listened? Suppose we had shown how Lord Joseph Sedley fell in love, and the Marquis of Osborne became attached to Lady Amelia, with the full consent of the Duke, her noble father; or instead of the supremely genteel, suppose we had resorted to the entirely low, and described what was going on in Mr. Sedley's kitchen;— how black Sambo was in love with the cook, (as indeed he was), and how he fought a battle with the coachman in her behalf; how the knife-boy was caught stealing a cold shoulder of mutton, and Miss Sedley's new *femme de chambre* refused to go to bed without a wax candle; such incidents might be made to provoke much delightful laughter, and be supposed to represent scenes of 'life.'

In *Vanity Fair*, Thackeray confounded expectations by abandoning the approved fictional conventions and offering instead what the poet Delmore Schwartz called the "scrimmage of appetite"—which exemplifies Newman's understanding of the inalienably secular nature of literature.[44] "Man's work will savour of man," Newman wrote in one of his discourses on university education, "in his elements and powers excellent and admirable, but prone to disorder and excess, to error and to sin. Such too will be his literature; it will have the beauty and the fierceness, the sweetness and the rankness, of the natural man ..."[45]

One can see Thackeray also confounding conventional expectations in his travel writing. *The Irish Sketch Book* (1843) is full of surprisingly favorable accounts of Irish priests. For Thackeray, Bishop Doyle, the founding pastor of Carlow Cathedral, "has the place of honour within it; nor, perhaps, did any Christian pastor ever merit the affection of his flock more, than that great and high-minded man. He was the best champion that the Catholic Church and cause ever had in Ireland: in learning and admirable kindness and virtue, the best example to the clergy of his religion; and if the country is now filled with schools, where the humblest peasant in it can have the benefit of a liberal and wholesome education, it owes this great boon mainly to his noble exertions and to the spirit which they awakened."[46] This echoes Newman's views. Writing to Miss Holmes in 1854 after he had been in Ireland off and on for three years to set up the Catholic University, Newman gave it as his decided opinion that "the Irish Priesthood is a nobly devoted body of men. You must not judge of them by the newspapers. I admire them exceedingly. Many of them are persons of cultivated minds generally. Those I have met about the country are zealous, hardworking men. You, who are getting so philosophically liberal about Italian architecture and Italian ways, will soon understand that, being intended for the people, they are taken from the people. There are but few in the upper classes Catholic in Ireland, and if the Bishops looked out for parish priests among the upper classes, even if they could get them, they would not suit the classes for whom they have to work. They are commonly taken out of the families of small farmers, they have strong constitutions, they know the habits of the people, and are fully trusted by them."[47] Nearly thirty years later, when Newman received the red hat, George Butler, Bishop of Limerick, wrote to congratulate him: "I do not know that any event in the Ecclesiastical world ever gave me more real joy than your elevation to the Cardinalate. I have been desiring it, and speaking of it as a thing that ought to be – and now that it is come I have a right to rejoice. It is strongly in my mind ... that amongst your many claims to favour and honor at the hands of the Church, what you did for Ireland in connexion with the Catholic University was not, and could not have been forgotten by our Holy Father. You laboured hard and suffered much, and made many sacrifices in our Cause whilst you were with us; and you did this because you loved our Nation, and you wished to give effect, as no one else could with equal power, to the behests of the Holy Father in our regard. It is most pleasant to me to think that Leo XIIIth, who loves us too, has remembered this ..."[48]

When it came to the Catholic priesthood, both Newman and Thackeray had been born into a world steeped in No Popery, but it is remarkable that when they saw real priests, not caricatures, they tended to be full of admiration.[49] This was the sort of thing that Thackeray prided himself on in his best work—stripping away convention and uncovering the truth beneath. Many good critics, from Gordon Ray to John Carey to D. J. Taylor, have touched on how irksome Thackeray found the taboos of nineteenth-century English fiction. "There are things we do and know perfectly well in Vanity Fair, though we never speak of them," the narrator of the novel observes: "as the Ahrimanians worship the devil, but don't mention him: and a polite public will no more bear to read an authentic description of vice than a truly refined English or American female will permit the word breeches to be pronounced in her chaste hearing. And yet, madam, both are walking the world before our faces every day, without much shocking us. If you were to blush every time they went by, what complexions you would have!"[50] Nevertheless, for all his willingness to have his fiction honor the truth of experience, it is remarkable how seldom he managed this when he was considering Catholics and Catholicism. In choosing to perpetuate the slurs of No Popery, he often chose caricature over reality, though there were revealing exceptions to this rule, when he seemed to recognize that the conventions of No Popery were as falsifying as the conventions of fiction. And his tour of Ireland, where he had the occasion to meet Catholic clergy face to face, was one of those exceptions.

To understand how Thackeray and Newman viewed the world, it is necessary to look a little more closely at their formative years. At Charterhouse, Thackeray was met with a kind of mob rule inescapable at a public school where the boys were often left to themselves. In his excellent biography of the novelist, D. J. Taylor gives a vivid picture of Carthusian school life beyond the classroom. "What the boys did outside school hours was largely ignored. Extra-curricular activities consequently ranged from bringing in pornographic books and planning excursions to watch public hangings at nearby Newgate to wandering around Holywell Street, where the local prostitutes stood soliciting custom. Even the most innocent activities took place against a distant clamour of moaning animals—the beasts of Smithfield being herded up for slaughter."[51] This may have been good fodder for the future novelist but scarred the intelligent, gentle boy. Once he escaped to Cambridge, Thackeray wrote to his mother, "I have not that gratitude and affection for that respectable seminary near Smithfield, which I am told good scholars always have for their place of education. I cannot think that school to be a good one, when as a child I was lulled into indolence & when I grew older and & could think for myself was abused into sulkiness and bullied into despair."[52] Later, in *The Irish Sketch Book*, he said of Eton what he could have said of Charterhouse: "There are at this present writing five hundred boys at Eton, kicked, and licked, and bullied, by another hundred—scrubbing shoes, running errands, making false concords, and ... putting their posteriors on a block for Dr. Hawtrey to lash at; and still calling it education. They are proud of it—good heavens!—absolutely vain of it; as what dull barbarians are not proud of their dulness and barbarism? They call it the good old English system."[53] Nevertheless, like so many Old Boys, Thackeray looked back on his schooldays with unabashed nostalgia, feeling for the ignominies of school life the same reminiscential tenderness that old soldiers often feel for war. Thackeray, for example, had his nose broken by a bully named Venables, which disfigured him for life, and yet repeatedly throughout his later writing he revisits the episode as though it had been all good fun. Nevertheless, however wistful Thackeray might have become about a place that was more brutalizing than nurturing, it gave him the sense of mission that made him a writer.

I have long gone about with a conviction on my mind that I had a work to do—a Work, if you like, with a great W; a Purpose to fulfil; a chasm to leap into, like Curtius, horse and foot; a Great Social Evil to Discover and to Remedy. That Conviction Has Pursued me for Years. It has Dogged me in the Busy Street; Seated Itself By Me in The Lonely Study; Jogged My Elbow as it Lifted the Wine-cup at The Festive Board; Pursued me through the Maze of Rotten Row; Followed me in Far Lands. On Brighton's Shingly Beach, or Margate's Sand, the Voice Outpiped the Roaring of the Sea; it Nestles in my Nightcap, and It Whispers, 'Wake, Slumberer, thy Work Is Not Yet Done.' Last Year, By Moonlight, in the Colosseum, the Little Sedulous Voice Came To Me and Said, 'Smith, or Jones' (The Writer's Name is Neither Here nor There), 'Smith or Jones, my fine fellow, this is all very well, but you ought to be at home writing your great work on SNOBS.[54]

Here was the sense of purpose that animates all of Thackeray's best work and it was Charterhouse that gave it to him. It was also Charterhouse that left him with a view of the world that was keenly ambivalent. Walter Bagehot once wrote, apropos this aspect of Thackeray: "Hazlitt used to say of himself … that he could not enjoy the society in a drawing room for thinking of the opinion which the footman formed of his odd appearance as he went upstairs. Thackeray had too healthy and stable a nature to be thrown so wholly off his balance; but the footman's view of life was never out of his head … just so this most impressible, susceptible genius could not help half accepting, half believing the common … view of life, although he perfectly knew in his inner mind and deeper nature that this apparent and superficial view of life was misleading, inadequate and deceptive."[55] At the same time, Thackeray's highly satirical view of the world convinced him that it was presumptuous of men to bother "the Awful Divinity … with their private concerns." For Thackeray, the idea of a personal God taking a personal interest in each of his creatures seemed faintly ridiculous. On the contrary, he saw in God a kind of impersonality: "In health, disease, birth, life, death, here, hereafter, I am His subject & creature. He lifts me up and sets me down … so He orders my beard to grow."[56] For one contemporary critic, "His fatalism is connected with a strong sense of the powerlessness of the human will. He is a profound sceptic. Not a sceptic in religious conviction, or one who ignores devotional feeling—far from it; but a sceptic of principles, of human will, of the power in man to ascertain his duties or direct his aims. He believes in God *out of the world*."[57]

In contrast, Newman's faith was profoundly personal, originating, as it did, "in the thought of two and two only absolute and luminously self-evident beings, myself and my Creator."[58] After a childhood in which, as he says, "I used to wish the Arabian Tales were true: my imagination ran on unknown influences, on magical powers, and talismans …," he was converted by the Rev. Walter Mayers, of Pembroke College, Oxford, his Evangelical classical master at Ealing School, whom he recognized as "the human means of divine faith in me."[59] Mayers put into his hands the book that made such a deep impression on Samuel Johnson, William Law's *Serious Call to a Devout and Holy Life*, as well as Philip Doddridge's *Rise and Progress of Religion in the Soul*, which converted William Wilberforce. Ealing also enabled Newman to pursue his delight in Latin verse and the English prose of Johnson and Gibbon. And yet, like Thackeray, Newman left school with a deep distrust of the world, caused, not by the snobbery of schoolboys but by his father's financial reverses, which ended in bankruptcy. Newman was also prone, as he said, from an early age, to a "mistrust of the reality of material phenomena."[60] Indeed, as a child, he confessed, "I thought life might be a dream, or I an Angel, and all this world a deception, my fellow angels by a playful device concealing themselves from me, and deceiving me with the semblance of a material world."[61] One salutary result of his conversion was that he was disabused of this notion, though he always tended to regard the unseen, supernatural world as more real than the seen, physical world, a tendency which would only deepen with the death of his beloved sister, Mary. "The world of spirits … though unseen, is present; present, not future, not distant. It is not above the sky, it is not beyond the grave; it is now and here; the kingdom of God is among us."[62]

In *Vanity Fair*, bankruptcy banishes old Mr. Sedley and his wife to the Fulham Road, "where the houses look like baby-houses; where the people, looking out of the first-floor windows, must infallibly, as you think, sit with their feet in the parlours; where the shrubs in the little gardens in front bloom with a perennial display of little children's pinafores ... whence you hear the sound of jingling spinets and women singing; where little porter pots hang on the railings sunning themselves; whither of evenings you see City clerks padding wearily ..." Only the prospect of death invokes the "kingdom of God ... among us."

> Suppose you are particularly rich and well-to-do and say on that last day, "I am very rich; I am tolerably well known; I have lived all my life in the best society, and thank Heaven, come of a most respectable family. I have served my King and country with honour. I was in Parliament for several years, where, I may say, my speeches were listened to and pretty well received. I don't owe any man a shilling: on the contrary, I lent my old college friend, Jack Lazarus, fifty pounds, for which my executors will not press him. I leave my daughters with ten thousand pounds apiece—very good portions for girls; I bequeath my plate and furniture, my house in Baker Street, with a handsome jointure, to my widow for her life; and my landed property, besides money in the funds, and my cellar of well-selected wine in Baker Street, to my son. I leave twenty pound a year to my valet; and I defy any man after I have gone to find anything against my character." Or suppose, on the other hand, your swan sings quite a different sort of dirge and you say, "I am a poor blighted, disappointed old fellow, and have made an utter failure through life. I was not endowed either with brains or with good fortune, and confess that I have committed a hundred mistakes and blunders. I own to having forgotten my duty many a time. I can't pay what I owe. On my last bed I lie utterly helpless and humble, and I pray forgiveness for my weakness and throw myself, with a contrite heart, at the feet of the Divine Mercy." Which of these two speeches, think you, would be the best oration for your own funeral? Old Sedley made the last; and in that humble frame of mind, and holding by the hand of his daughter, life and disappointment and vanity sank away from under him.[63]

Newman's sense of the fallen world as a place at profound odds with his Christian faith was strong before he converted to Catholicism, but after his conversion it became even stronger. Nowhere did he give this more dramatic expression than in the same lecture in which he cited the pious beggar-woman, which was expressly written to expose the Pharisaical streak in English Protestantism. If the English looked down their noses at pious beggary, and congratulated themselves on being free of improvidence and superstition, Newman knew that they would not take kindly to being told that the ragged devout might be nearer God's grace than "Polished, delicate-minded ladies, with little of temptation around them, and no self-denial to practise, in spite of their refinement and taste ..."[64] For Newman, these eminently respectable ladies, "if they be nothing more, are objects of less interest to [the Church], than many a poor outcast who sins, repents, and is with difficulty kept just within the territory of grace … . My brethren, you may think it impolitic in me thus candidly to state what may be so strange in the eyes of the world;—but not so, my dear brethren, just the contrary … . The Church aims at realities, the world at decencies …"[65]

With Newman, this critical view of the English would culminate in an understanding of history that radically differed from the Whig version of history, according to which all events in English history could be shown to be an ushering in and vindication of the triumphant Whig oligarchy. "The total result of this method," as Herbert Butterfield wrote in his classic book *The Whig Interpretation of History* (1931), "is to impose a certain form upon the present—all demonstrating throughout the ages the workings of an obvious principle of progress, of which the Protestants and whigs have been the perennial allies while Catholics and tories have perpetually formed obstruction. A caricature of this result is to be seen in a popular view that is still not quite eradicated"—in Newman's nineteenth century John Lingard and William Cobbett had only just begun to eradicate it—"the view that the Middle Ages represented a period of darkness when man was kept tongue-tied by authority—a period against which the Renaissance was the reaction and the Reformation the great rebellion."[66] Macaulay was the great champion of this point of view, seeing in post-Reformation England "the history of physical, of moral, and of intellectual improvement."[67]

Newman's view of English history could not have been more different: he saw a people, who, after a thousand years, "grew tired of the heavenly stranger who sojourned among them;" a people who "had had enough of blessings and absolutions, enough of the intercession of saints, enough of the grace of the sacraments, enough of the prospect of the next life. They thought it best to secure this life in the first place, because they were in possession of it, and then to go on to the next, if time and means allowed. And they saw that to labour for the next world was possibly to lose this; whereas, to labour for this world might be, for what they knew, the way to labour for the next also. Anyhow, they would pursue a temporal end, and they would account any one their enemy who stood in the way of their pursuing it. It was a madness; but madmen are strong, and madmen are clever …"[68] For Newman, this worldly madness was of a piece with England's new "temporal end."

> And so with the sword and the halter, and by mutilation and fine and imprisonment, they cut off, or frightened away from the land, as Israel did in the time of old, the ministers of the Most High, and their ministrations: they 'altogether broke the yoke, and burst the bonds.' 'They beat one, and killed another, and another they stoned,' and at length they altogether cast out the Heir from His vineyard, and killed Him, 'that the inheritance might be theirs.' And as for the remnant of His servants whom they left, they drove them into corners and holes of the earth, and there they bade them die out; and then they rejoiced and sent gifts either to other, and made merry, because they had rid themselves of those 'who had tormented them that

dwelt upon the earth.' And so they turned to enjoy this world, and to gain for themselves a name among men, and it was given unto them according to their wish. They preferred the heathen virtues of their original nature, to the robe of grace which God had given them: they fell back, with closed affections, and haughty reserve, and dreariness within, upon their worldly integrity, honour, energy, prudence, and perseverance; they made the most of the natural man, and they 'received their reward.' Forthwith they began to rise to a station higher than the heathen Roman, and have, in three centuries, attained a wider range of sovereignty; and now they look down in contempt on what they were, and upon the Religion which reclaimed them from paganism.[69]

In *Vanity Fair*, the Thackerayan narrator reports on how the English are faring in their pursuit of this "temporal end." Old Mr. Osborne is a fair specimen. "He firmly believed that everything he did was right, that he ought on all occasions to have his own way—and like the sting of the wasp or serpent his hatred rushed out armed and poisonous against anything like opposition. He was proud of his hatred as of everything else. Always to be right, always to trample forward, and never to doubt, are not these the great qualities with which dullness takes the lead in the world?"[70] By the same token, the narrator is careful not to be unduly censorious. Speaking of the presumed sins of the book's heroine, Becky Sharp, he remarks: "I protest it is quite shameful in the world to abuse a simple creature, as people of her time abuse Becky, and I warn the public against believing one-tenth of the stories against her.

If every person is to be banished from society who runs into debt and cannot pay—if we are to be peering into everybody's private life, speculating upon their income, and cutting them if we don't approve of their expenditure—why, what a howling wilderness and intolerable dwelling Vanity Fair would be! Every man's hand would be against his neighbour in this case, my dear sir, and the benefits of civilization would be done away with. We should be quarrelling, abusing, avoiding one another. Our houses would become caverns, and we should go in rags because we cared for nobody. Rents would go down. Parties wouldn't be given any more. All the tradesmen of the town would be bankrupt. Wine, wax-lights, comestibles, rouge, crinoline-petticoats, diamonds, wigs, Louis-Quatorze gimcracks, and old china, park hacks, and splendid high-stepping carriage horses—all the delights of life, I say,—would go to the deuce, if people did but act upon their silly principles and avoid those whom they dislike and abuse. Whereas, by a little charity and mutual forbearance, things are made to go on pleasantly enough: we may abuse a man as much as we like, and call him the greatest rascal unhanged—but do we wish to hang him therefore? No. We shake hands when we meet. If his cook is good we forgive him and go and dine with him, and we expect he will do the same by us. Thus trade flourishes—civilization advances; peace is kept; new dresses are wanted for new assemblies every week; and the last year's vintage of Lafitte will remunerate the honest proprietor who reared it.[71]

Together with this sensible counsel, the reader encounters something else in the book: a deep appreciation for the bond between mother and child, which shows that if religion *per se* is largely absent among the denizens of Vanity Fair, the religious impulse is not. "How his mother nursed him, and dressed him, and lived upon him;" the narrator observes of Amelia Sedley and her newborn, "how she drove away all nurses, and would scarce allow any hand but her own to touch him; how she considered that the greatest favour she could confer upon his godfather, Major Dobbin, was to allow the Major occasionally to dandle him, need not be told here. This child was her being. Her existence was a maternal caress. She enveloped the feeble and unconscious creature with love and worship. It was her life which the baby drank in from her bosom. Of nights, and when alone, she had stealthy and intense raptures of motherly love, such as God's marvellous care has awarded to the female instinct—joys how far higher and lower than reason—blind beautiful devotions which only women's hearts know."[72] When Lady Jane meets Rawdy, Becky's boy, she also affirms the power of maternal love, but from a different perspective: "Oh, thou poor lonely little benighted boy! Mother is the name for God in the lips and hearts of little children; and here was one who was worshipping a stone!"[73] (As Carey shrewdly observes, the little rich girls of Chiswick Hall, to whom Becky was obliged to teach music and French, robbed her of any maternal instinct she might have had.[74]) In these passages, Newman might have seen Thackeray nearing the Nativity and the Incarnation—even though his tendency to sentimentalize maternity often blinded him to the true import of these Christian realities.[75]

Notwithstanding the Christian undertones of *Vanity Fair*, Thackeray did not share Newman's Catholic reading of English history. In *Henry Esmond*, he endorsed the Whig view of history, even if in a sardonic, backhanded way.[76] Nevertheless, he did share Newman's recognition of the presence of the past. For Thackeray, the collapse of the old order was prefigured in the factions of the eighteenth century, in much the same way that Newman saw the heresies of the fourth prefiguring the heresies of the nineteenth century. In *Henry Esmond*, Thackeray considered these factions from the standpoint of the American colonies.

> A strange series of compromises is that English History; compromise of principle, compromise of party, compromise of worship! ... The Tory and High Church patriots were ready to die in defence of a Papist family that had sold us to France; the great Whig nobles, the sturdy republican recusants who had cut off Charles Stuart's head for treason, were fain to accept a king whose title came to him through a royal grandmother, whose own royal grandmother's head had fallen under Queen Bess's hatchet. And our proud English nobles sent to a petty German town for a monarch to come and reign in London and our prelates kissed the ugly hands of his Dutch mistresses, and thought it no dishonor. In England you can but belong to one party or t'other, and you take the house you live in with all its encumbrances, its retainers, its antique discomforts, and ruins even; you patch

up, but you never build up anew. Will we of the new world submit much longer, even nominally, to this ancient British superstition? There are signs of the times which make me think that ere long we shall care as little about King George here, and peers temporal and peers spiritual, as we do for King Canute or the Druids.[77]

Here Thackeray speaks of the incoherence of the Protestant Establishment with a lucidity that recalls that memorable passage in *Anglican Difficulties*, where Newman tells the Tractarians to look at what they are defending clearly, without romantic self-deception. "For this is the truth: the Establishment, whatever it be in the eyes of men, whatever its temporal greatness and its secular prospects, in the eyes of faith is a mere wreck. We must not indulge our imagination, we must not dream: we must look at things as they are; we must not confound the past with the present, or what is substantive with what is the accident of a period. Ridding our minds of these illusions, we shall see that the Established Church has no claims whatever on us, whether in memory or in hope; that they only have claims upon our commiseration and our charity whom she holds in bondage, separated from that faith and that Church in which alone is salvation. If I can do aught towards breaking their chains, and bringing them into the Truth, it will be an act of love towards their souls, and of piety towards God."[78]

Thackeray was a lackluster advocate of the Protestant Establishment because he was never comfortable with what he saw as the humbug at the heart of the Church of England. (Newman wrote to the Liberal politician William Monsell of what he thought Thackeray's "utter contempt of Protestantism."[79]) This was why Thackeray found the poet Arthur Hugh Clough sympathetic. After Clough resigned his Oriel fellowship, in February 1849, Provost Edward Hawkins, who had received Newman's resignation four years before, wrote to him, "Will you excuse my telling you that I have been reading your poem 'The Bothie, etc.', and cannot but say that what I was told of it was true, that there are parts of it rather indelicate; and I very much regretted to find that there were frequent allusions to Scripture, or rather parodies of Scripture, which you should not have put forth. You will never be secure from misbelief, if you allow yourself liberties of this kind."[80] Here was a humbug on which the satirist in Thackeray could not have improved. For Thackeray, Clough was admirable precisely because he "he gave up his Fellowship and university prospects on religious scruples. He is one of those thinking men, who I daresay will begin to speak out before many years are over, and protest against Gothic Xtianity."[81] Yet if Thackeray shared Clough's dismissive view of the Church of England, he also shared his paralyzing skepticism. Speaking of the symptoms of this pre-eminently modern malady, Walter Bagehot wrote: "If you offer them any known religion, they 'won't have that;' if you offer them no religion, they will not have that either; if you ask them to accept a new and as yet unrecognised religion, they altogether refuse to do so. They seem not only to believe in an 'unknown God,' but in a God whom no man can ever know."[82] In quoting from Clough's poetry to describe what he called his friend's "essential religion," Bagehot could have been describing something of Thackeray's as well:

O thou that in our bosom's shrine
Dost dwell, because unknown divine!
I thought to speak, I thought to say,
'The light is here,' 'behold the way,'
'The voice was thus,' and 'thus the word,'
And 'thus I saw,' and 'that I heard,'—
But from the lips but half essayed
The imperfect utterance fell unmade.

O thou in that mysterious shrine
Enthroned, as we must say, divine!
I will not frame one thought of what
Thou mayest either be or not.
I will not prate of 'thus' and 'so,'
And be profane with 'yes' and 'no.'
Enough that in our soul and heart
Thou, whatsoe'er thou may'st be, art.

Nevertheless, if Thackeray was skeptical, he was also shrewd: he had no illusions about the pretensions of his increasingly unbelieving contemporaries, and this was an aspect of his fiction that doubtless appealed to Newman. If Thackeray could not testify to the reality of belief, he could testify to the unreality of unbelief—another theme which exercised Clough.[83] "Search, search within your own waistcoats, dear brethren," Thackeray exhorts his readers, in his best parsonical manner, "you know in your hearts, which of your ordinaire qualities you would pass off, and fain consider as first-rate port." In an essay called "Small-Beer Chronicle" from his *Roundabout Papers* (1860–1863), which Carey unjustly dismisses as so much "banter and garrulity," Thackeray shows how military heroes now absorbed the nation's esteem.[84]

Some years ago a famous and witty French critic was in London, with whom I walked the streets. I am ashamed to say that I informed him (being in hopes that he was about to write some papers regarding the manners and customs of this country) that all the statues he saw represented the Duke of Wellington. That on the arch opposite Apsley House? the Duke in a cloak, and cocked hat, on horseback. That behind Apsley House in an airy fig-leaf costume? the Duke again. That in Cockspur Street? the Duke with a pigtail—and so on. I showed him an army of Dukes. There are many bronze heroes who after a few years look already as foolish, awkward, and out of place as a man, say at Shoolbred's or Swan and Edgar's. For example, those three Grenadiers in Pall Mall, who have been up only a few months, don't you pity those unhappy household troops, who have to stand frowning and looking fierce there; and think they would like to step down and go to barracks? That they fought very bravely there is no doubt; but so did the Russians fight very bravely; and the French fight very bravely; and so did Colonel Jones and the 99th, and Colonel Brown and the 100th; and I say again that ordinaire should not give itself port airs, and that an honest ordinaire would blush to be found swaggering so.[85]

Even allowing for Thackeray's bias against Wellington—he could never forgive the man for claiming that Charterhouse was "the best school of them all"—this was a fair, if mocking, characterization of Britain's growing idolatry of its great men, an idolatry that Newman also observed, though he always admired the bravery of soldiers. "A Protestant blames Catholics for showing honour to images; yet he does it himself," Newman remarked in *The Present Position of Catholics*. Indeed, "after preaching against the Catholic who crowns an image of the Madonna, he complacently goes his way, and sets light to a straw effigy of Guy Fawkes. But this is not all; Protestants actually set up images to represent their heroes, and they show them honour without any misgiving. The very flower and cream of Protestantism used to glory in the statue of King William on College Green, Dublin; and, though I cannot make any reference in print, I recollect well what a shriek they raised some years ago, when the figure was unhorsed. Some profane person one night applied gunpowder, and blew the king right out of his saddle; and he was found by those who took interest in him, like Dagon, on the ground. You might have thought the poor senseless block had life, to see the way people took on about it, and how they spoke of his face, and his arms, and his legs; yet those same Protestants, I say ... would call me one of the monsters described in the Apocalypse, did I but honour my living Lord as they their dead king."[86]

Newman saw his contemporaries' self-satisfaction as more than merely comical; he saw it as an expression of their worship of self. In a brilliant sermon entitled "The Religion of the Pharisee, The Religion of Mankind," which Newman delivered in the University Church, Dublin in 1856, he anticipated Charles Kingsley's response to his distinction between natural virtue and God's grace and saw it stemming from what he nicely called "Pharisaical excellence."

I know men profess a great deal, and boast that they are Christians, and speak of Christianity as being a religion of the heart; but, when we put aside words and professions, and try to discover what their religion is, we shall find, I fear, that the great mass of men in fact get rid of all religion that is inward; that they lay no stress on acts of faith, hope, and charity, on simplicity of intention, purity of motive, or mortification of the thoughts; that they confine themselves to two or three virtues, superficially practised; that they know not the words contrition, penance, and pardon; and that they think and argue that, after all, if a man does his duty in the world, according to his vocation, he cannot fail to go to heaven, however little he may do besides, nay, however much, in other matters, he may do that is undeniably unlawful. Thus a soldier's duty is loyalty, obedience, and valour, and he may let other matters take their chance; a trader's duty is honesty; an artisan's duty is industry and contentment; of a gentleman are required veracity, courteousness, and self-respect; of a public man, high-principled ambition; of a woman, the domestic virtues;

of a minister of religion, decorum, benevolence, and some activity. Now, all these are instances of mere Pharisaical excellence; because there is no apprehension of Almighty God, no insight into His claims on us, no sense of the creature's shortcomings, no self-condemnation, confession, and deprecation, nothing of those deep and sacred feelings which ever characterize the religion of a Christian, and more and more, not less and less, as he mounts up from mere ordinary obedience to the perfection of a saint.[87]

When Thackeray attended Newman's lectures in King William Street, he must have listened to the passage about the pious beggar-woman with particular interest because it echoed something from his own work. In *The Irish Sketchbook*, Thackeray had also spoken of the piety of a beggar-woman, which he actually encountered outside the Cathedral of Carlow. "There is a convent by the side of the cathedral," he recalled, "and, of course, a parcel of beggars all about ... profuse in their prayers and invocations of the Lord, and whining flatteries of the persons whom they address. One wretched, old, tottering hag began whining the Lord's prayer as a proof of her sincerity, and blundered in the very midst of it, and left us thoroughly disgusted after the very first sentence."[88] This was hardly sympathetic to the devotions of an old and doubtless confused woman, but still it was responsive to experience. Thackeray's response to Newman's passage about *his* beggar woman had no basis in experience and relied instead on caricature.

A man who admits that a lousy lying beggarwoman who goes to confess and says her prayers is more likely of salvation than a good wise honest humble conscientious man earnestly trying to fulfill his duty: a man who glories in asserting that every scoundrel who has been executed at Rome goes straightway and secure with the sacerdotal passport to Heaven, while his denouncer very likely goes to the Devil, ought *to be let go on*. The more he preaches in this way, the better for the Truth: the more he shows what the figure is under those fine copes and embroideries and behind all that chandlery and artificial flower-show, the better for the people who are now attracted by the splendour and the ceremonial and the sweet-chanted litanies and the charms of the orator's rhetoric. Put out the lights and lock up the incense pots. Stop the organ and take off the priest's fine clothes—and when we come to Mr. Newman's naked beau ideal, it seems to me we get a creature so hideous degraded and despicable, that the public scorn will scout him out of the world again.[89]

Thackeray's letter is as revealing for what it says as for whom it was written. Robert Montgomery (1807–1855) the recipient, was in many respects a rather Thackerayan character. Born in Bath, the illegitimate son of the resident clown at the Bath Theatre, who also appeared on the stage of the Haymarket and the English Opera at the Lyceum, Montgomery realized, at an early age, that he should have to make his way in the world on his wits. In this, he was rather similar to Becky Sharp. After meeting with early success with a book of poems entitled *Poetical Trifles* (1825), he wrote three more full-length books of verse, *The Omnipotence of the Deity*, *A Universal Prayer* and *Death: A Vision of Heaven*, all of which were extravagantly praised by Southey and Crabbe. Once he became famous, he tried to highlight what many saw as his physical resemblance to Lord Byron. Montgomery also produced numerous works of sermons and theology. In the pulpit, he could be memorably droll, once likening dead humanity to a "decayed Stilton cheese" which would only be restored to its proper ripeness by trumpeting angels at the Last Day.[90] In his own lifetime Montgomery commanded a huge audience. *The Omnipresence of the Deity* alone went into 28 editions. At a time when so much Evangelical belief was being eroded by an industrializing culture hostile to Christianity, Montgomery's poems offered consolation amidst growing apostasy.

That the author of *Vanity Fair* went out of his way to concur with this versifying preacher is revealing. In sending off his letter, Thackeray was defending something of the undogmatical faith that his mother had taught him when he was a child, a faith to which he resorted, fleetingly, after his wife lost her mind and, then again, when he was gravely ill with gastric fever in 1849. Indeed, his mother might have been one of the many readers who sent Montgomery's verses into so many popular editions. Thackeray was also showing support for the Broad Church, though that heterogeneous communion could only have welcomed seeing the newly converted Newman taking the Tractarians to task for unreality and imposture. Nonetheless, to another correspondent, Thackeray described his sense of kinship in terms that were almost tribal. "Newman," Thackeray complained, "is obliged to condemn the best and purest of all of us, his own mother, friends, brethren,—everybody.—Will we subscribe to that? Will we let that Lie go unquestioned among us?"[91] Here was the nationalist defense of Anglicanism—Anglicanism as inseparable from Englishry, from family, from friends, from home—which Gladstone, Keble, Pusey, and so many other Anglicans mounted to parry what they considered Newman's foreign Romanizing.

In his sermons, Newman warned against making the sentiments of men the measure of faith, insisting that "such is the religion of the natural man in every age and place;—often very beautiful on the surface, but worthless in God's sight; good, as far as it goes, but worthless and hopeless, because it does not go further, because it is based on self-sufficiency, and results in self-satisfaction."

I grant, it may be beautiful to look at, as in the instance of the young ruler whom our Lord looked at and loved, yet sent away sad; it may have all the delicacy, the amiableness, the tenderness, the religious sentiment, the kindness, which is actually seen in many a father of a family, many a mother, many a daughter, in the length and breadth of these kingdoms, in a refined and polished age like this; but still it is rejected by the heart-searching God, because all such persons walk by their own light, not by the True Light of men, because self is their supreme teacher, and because they pace round and round in the small circle of their own thoughts and of their own judgments, careless to know what God says to them, and fearless of being condemned by Him, if only they stand approved in their own sight. And thus they incur the force of those terrible words, spoken not to a Jewish Ruler, nor to a heathen philosopher, but to a fallen Christian community, to the Christian Pharisees of Laodicea,—'Because thou sayest I am rich, and made wealthy, and have need of nothing; and knowest not that thou art wretched, and miserable, and poor, and blind, and naked; I counsel thee to buy of Me gold fire-tried, that thou mayest be made rich, and be clothed in white garments, that thy shame may not appear, and anoint thine eyes with eye-salve, that thou mayest see. Such as I love, I rebuke and chastise; be zealous, therefore, and do penance.'[92]

Months after writing to Montgomery about the King William Street lectures, Thackeray gave proof of the ambivalence that always characterized his response to Catholicism. "After making a great noise myself," Thackeray wrote to the diarist Allingham, "I begin to wonder why we have made so much to-do about the Cardinal [Cardinal Wiseman, whose reconstitution of the English hierarchy instigated the period known as Papal Aggression]. Why shouldn't he come and set up a winking Virgin in the Strand? The claims of the Bishop of Oxford ... are not much less preposterous: and Dr. Pusey says 'quite right, it's not Popery the parsons have to fear but universal Protestantism.'—Is it coming?—it must, to get rid of these Papists—the old sixteenth century Protestantism can fight them: they've the best of that battle."[93] By the same token, Thackeray was a conventional enough Englishman to revile monasticism. Speaking of the *Imitation of Christ* of St. Thomas À Kempis, he observed: "The scheme of that book carried out would make the world the most wretched useless dreary doting place of sojourn—there would be no manhood no love no tender ties of mother & child no use of intellect no trade or science—a set of selfish beings crawling about avoiding one another, and howling a perpetual *misere*."[94]

Then, again, two years after attending the King William Street lectures, Thackeray read Newman's Anglican letters and wrote to Mary Holmes, the governess, "I am sure Newman's is a great honest heart ... [his] letters read very honest—better than that poor Bulwer with his bosh. It is very difficult for literary men to keep their honesty. We are actors more or less all of us ..." Newman would have agreed but not in the theatrical sense. He would certainly have agreed with the novelist that literary men "get to be public personages *malgré lui nous*."[95] Newman may not have been as reluctant a saint as some have claimed—his understanding of sanctity, after all, was eminently practical, even humdrum—but he was always a reluctant public man.[96]

However ambivalent about the world, which he both courted and scorned, Thackeray never imagined himself immune from its follies. To the journalist Robert Bell, who had taken exception to what he thought the satirical severity of *Vanity Fair*, Thackeray explained that his object in the book was "to indicate, in cheerful terms, that we are for the most part an abominably foolish and selfish people 'desperately wicked' and all eager for vanities ... Good God don't I see (in that may-be cracked and warped looking glass in which I am always looking) my own weaknesses lusts follies shortcomings? ... We must lift up our voices about these and howl to a congregation of fools ... You have all of you taken my misanthropy to task—I wish I could myself: but take the world by a certain standard ... and who dares talk of having any virtue at all."[97]

The significance of Thackeray's including himself in the brunt of his satire was not lost on Chesterton. "The one supreme and even sacred quality in Thackeray's work," Chesterton wrote, "is that he felt the weakness of all flesh. Wherever he sneers it is at his own potential self. When he rebukes, it is self-rebuke; when he indulges, he knows it is self-indulgence ... . Here then was his special contribution to that chaos of morality which the nineteenth century muddled through: he stood for the remains of Christian humility, as Dickens stood for the remains of Christian charity."[98]

If Victorian critics like Bell found Thackeray too misanthropic, more modern critics tended to find him too forgiving. "Every novelist has a knack for doing some one stunt," T. S. Eliot wrote to a correspondent in 1918. "Thackeray could do the *Yellowplush Papers* and the Steyne part of *Vanity Fair*, but he had a picture of himself as a kindly satirist. Not at all, he hadn't brains enough, nor courage enough to find out really what he could do well, which was high society sordidness, and do it."[99] This shows how little Eliot understood the charity behind Thackeray's satire, which is not the same thing as kindliness. Charles Kingsley was no more perceptive. When he took exception to what he thought Sir Pitt Crawley's improbable coarseness, Thackeray replied that he was "almost the only exact portrait in the whole book."[100] Knowing what a hodge-podge he himself was of virtue and vice, generosity and meanness, pride and humility, good sense and folly, refinement and baseness, Thackeray never portrayed his characters without similar contradictions.

Thackeray's brilliant portrait of Sir Pitt Crawley shows the extent to which he shared Newman's fascination with that once elaborate thing, the English gentleman. In *Vanity Fair*, he reported on the fortunes of the English gentleman abroad. "The respect in those happy days of 1817–18 was very great for the wealth and honour of Britons. They had not then learned, as I am told, to haggle for bargains with the pertinacity which now distinguishes them. The great cities of Europe had not been as yet open to the enterprise of our rascals. And whereas, there is now hardly a town of France or Italy in which you shall not see some noble countryman of our own, with that happy swagger and insolence of demeanour with we carry everywhere, swindling inn-landlords, passing ficti-tious cheques upon credulous bankers, robbing coach-makers of their carriages, goldsmiths of their trinkets, easy travelers of their money at cards,—even public libraries of their books:—thirty years ago you needed but to be a Milor Anglais, travelling in a private carriage, and credit was at your hand wherever you chose to seek it, and gentlemen, instead of cheating, were cheated."[101] In the *Idea of a University*, Newman also broke with convention on the subject by arguing how the gentleman might "have a cultivated intellect, a delicate taste, a candid, equitable dispassionate mind, a noble and courteous bearing in the conduct of life ..." but these things were "no guarantee for sanctity, or even for conscientiousness:" they could just as easily "attach to the man of the world, the profligate, the heartless."[102] And the moral for Newman was inescapable: "Taken by themselves," these attributes "do but seem to be what they are not;

they look like virtue at a distance, but they are detected by close observers, and on the long run; and hence it is that they are popularly accused of pretence and hypocrisy, not, I repeat, from their own fault, but because their professors and their admirers persist in taking them for what they are not, and are officious in arrogating for them a praise to which they have no claim. Quarry the granite rock with razors, or moor the vessel with a thread of silk; then may you hope with such keen and delicate instruments as human knowledge and human reason to contend against those giants, the passion and the pride of man."[103]

None of Newman's contemporaries brought to life this passion and pride more brilliantly than Thackeray. In *Vanity Fair*, when Mr. Osborne learns that the son he has disinherited has been killed at Waterloo, we see these two giants in all their fury.

> The gloom-stricken old father was still more borne down by his fate and sorrow. He strove to think that a judgment was on the boy for his disobedience. He dared not own that the severity of the sentence frightened him, and that its fulfillment had come too soon upon his curses. Sometimes a shuddering terror struck him, as if he had been the author of the doom which he had called down on his son. There was a chance before of reconciliation. The boy's wife might have died; or he might have come back and said, Father I have sinned. But there was no hope now. He stood on the other side of the gulf impassable, haunting his parent with sad eyes. He remembered them once before so in a fever, when every one thought the lad was dying, and he lay on his bed speechless, and gazing with a dreadful gloom. Good God! how the father clung to the doctor then, and with what a sickening anxiety he followed him: what a weight of grief was off his mind when, after the crisis of the fever, the lad recovered, and looked at his father once more with eyes that recognised him. But now there was no help or cure, or chance of reconcilement: above all, there were no humble words to soothe vanity outraged and furious, or bring to its natural flow the poisoned, angry blood. And it is hard to say which pang it was that tore the proud father's heart most keenly—that his son should have gone out of the reach of his forgiveness, or that the apology which his own pride expected should have escaped him.[104]

In *The History of Pendennis* (1848–1850), Thackeray turned away from such home truths, convinced that they would not endear him to the upper-class readership he meant to buy his books. Instead, he gave his readers more palatable fare: the coming of age of a would-be litterateur who only incidentally resembled himself as a young man.[105] In this ramshackle *Bildungsroman*, Arthur Pendennis is young Thackeray considerably sanitized and expurgated. And almost as if to justify his abandonment of his former truth telling, Thackeray boldly cited the example of Newman and his brother Frank to illustrate what he now claimed was the elusiveness of truth.

> "The truth, friend!" Arthur said imperturbably; "where is the truth? Show it me." That is the question between us. I see it on both sides. I see it on

the Conservative side of the House, and amongst the Radicals, and even on the Ministerial benches. I see it in this man who worships by Act of Parliament, and is rewarded with a silk apron and five thousand a year; in that man, who driven fatally by the remorseless logic of his creed, gives up everything, friends, fame, dearest ties, closest vanities, the respect of an army of churchmen, the recognised position of a leader, and passes over, truth-impelled, to the enemy, in whose ranks he is ready to serve henceforth as a nameless private soldier:—I see the truth in that man, as I do in his brother, whose logic drives him to quite a different conclusion, and who, after having passed a life in vain endeavours to reconcile an irreconcilable book, flings it at last down in despair, and declares, with tearful eyes, and hands up to Heaven, his revolt and recantation. If the truth is with all these, why should I take side with any one of them?[106]

This deeply autobiographical passage shows that if Thackeray had a good deal of respect for Newman, he also found the assaults on the Old Testament that Frank Newman made in his various books compelling. About Frank's book, *The Soul: Her Sorrows and her Aspirations* (1849), he was effusive. "There speaks a very pious loving humble soul ... with an ascetical continence too—and a beautiful love and reverence –I'm a publican and sinner; but I believe those men [Arthur Hugh Clough and Frank Newman] are on the true track."[107] Nevertheless, by having Pen claim that both the orthodoxy of John Henry Newman and the heterodoxy of Frank Newman could simultaneously lay claim to truth, Thackeray, in effect, was attempting to justify his own growing skepticism. Indeed, in Thackeray's table-talk, jotted down by Charles Bray, the friend of George Eliot, Thackeray claimed that Newman himself was prey to skepticism, which he converted to Roman Catholicism to repel—a charge that A. M. Fairbairn would level in the *Contemporary Review* twenty years later in May 1885. Thackeray, according to this account: "Talked of Newman. Called him a saint, in a way that was a blessing to hear, so heartily and truly did he utter it. Said that somewhere in his heart he (Newman) was a sceptic, but he had shut it down and locked it up as with Solomon's Seal, and went on really believing in the Catholic faith."[108]

Thackeray's ambivalence towards Newman and his faith has to be seen in the context of his more general ambivalence towards religion as a whole, which was aggravated by his lifelong opposition to his mother's Bible religion. In *Pendennis*, the literary hero articulates an approach to Truth that, at first, seems thoroughly conventional and conformist. "Some are called upon to preach: let them preach. Of these preachers there are somewhat too many, methinks, who fancy they have the gift. But we cannot all be parsons in church ... I will take off my hat in the place, and say my prayers there too, and shake hands with the clergyman as he steps on the grass outside." This was the latitudinarianism at the heart of so much Broad Church Christianity. But then Thackeray has Pen point out that the religious conventions to which he is willing to submit are not quite what they might be. "Don't I know that [the clergyman] being there is a compromise, and that he stands before me an Act of Parliament? That the church he occupies was built for other worship? That the Methodist chapel is next door; and that Bunyan the tinker is bawling out the tidings of damnation on the common hard by? Yes, I am a Sadducee; and I take things as I find them, and the world, and the Acts of Parliament of the world, as they are ..."[109] The Church of England might be imperfect but, for Thackeray, it was better than the alternatives, even if it was only kept together by opposition to what Soapy Sam Wilberforce called "the accursed abominations of the Papacy."[110] And yet it is impossible to read Thackeray's fiction without seeing how deeply torn he was about England's exile from Rome. In *The Newcomes* (1853), for example, he has Clive Newcome, whom he based on the Victorian painter Frederic Leighton (1830–96), describe the gulf between the Protestant English and the Roman Church with great poignancy. "There must be moments, in Rome especially, when every man of friendly heart, who writes himself English and Protestant, must feel a pang at thinking that he and his countrymen are insulated from European Christendom. An ocean separates us. From one shore or the other one can see the neighbour cliffs on clear days: one must wish sometimes that there were no stormy gulf between us ... Of the beautiful parts of the great Mother Church I believe among us many people have no idea; we think of lazy friars, of pining cloistered virgins, of ignorant peasants worshipping wood and stones, bought and sold indulgences, absolutions, and the like common-places of Protestant satire." And in this category, Thackeray was clearly including himself. Yet, like Macaulay, he also admired the staying power of the ancient faith. Beholding St. Peter's in Rome, Clive Newcome is enraptured: "Lo! yonder inscription, which blazes round the dome of the temple, so great and glorious it looks like heaven almost, and as if the words were written in stars, it proclaims to all the world that this is Peter, and on this rock the Church shall be built, against which Hell shall not prevail. Under the bronze canopy his throne is lit with lights that have been burning before it for ages. Round this stupendous chamber are ranged the grandees of his court. Faith seems to be realized in their marble figures. Some of them were alive but yesterday; others, to be as blessed as they, walk the world even now doubtless; and the commissioners of heaven, here holding their court a hundred years hence, shall authoritatively announce their beatification. The signs of their power shall not be wanting. They heal the sick, open the eyes of the blind, cause the lame to walk to-day as they did eighteen centuries ago." Here, Thackeray had Clive echo that famous passage in Macaulay's review of Ranke's *History of the Popes*, in which the Whig historian wrote of the perdurability of the Church with undisguised admiration: "She saw the commencement of all the governments and of all the ecclesiastical establishments that now exist in the world; and we feel no assurance that she is not destined to see the end of them all. She was great and respected before the Saxon had set foot on Britain, before the Frank had passed the Rhine, when Grecian eloquence still flourished at Antioch, when idols were still worshipped in the temple of Mecca. And she may still exist in undiminished vigour when some traveler from New Zealand shall, in the midst of a vast solitude, take his stand on a broken arch of London Bridge to sketch the ruins of St. Paul's." Yet Thackeray has Clive end his paean to Rome on a note that is almost rueful.

"Come, friend, let us acknowledge this, and go and kiss the toe of St. Peter. Alas! there's the Channel always between us ... So, you see, at those grand ceremonies which the Roman Church exhibits at Christmas, I looked on as a Protestant. Holy Father on his throne or in his palanquin, cardinals with their tails and their train-bearers, mitred bishops and abbots, regiments of friars and clergy, relics exposed for adoration, columns draped, altars illuminated, incense smoking, organs pealing, and boxes of piping soprani, Swiss guards with slashed breeches and fringed halberts—between us and all this splendour of old-world ceremony, there's an ocean flowing ..."[111]

Despite his fascination with Catholicism, Thackeray wished to be at once the level-headed man of the world for whom religion was a harmless convention and the "truth-impelled" bohemian for whom it was an unknowable mystery. Bagehot recognized that in failing to become either, Thackeray found his fictional niche: "He is great in minute anatomy. The subsoil of life—not the very surface, but just the next layer, which one little painful scratch will bring up—this is his region, and it is an immense one."[112] And in this very immensity, Thackeray found a terrible solitude, one might almost say desolation, as he showed in *Pendennis*:

Thus, oh friendly readers, we see how every man in the world, has his own private griefs and business, by which he is more cast down or occupied than by the affairs or sorrows of any other person. While Mrs. Pendennis is disquieting herself about losing her son, and that anxious hold she has had of him, as long as he has remained in the mother's nest, whence he is about to take flight into the great world beyond—while the Major's great soul chafes and frets, inwardly vexed as he thinks what great parties are going on in London, and that he might be sunning himself in the glances of Dukes and Duchesses, but for those cursed affairs which keep him in a wretched little country hole—while Pen is tossing between his passion and a more agreeable sensation, unacknowledged yet, but swaying him considerably, namely, his longing to see the world—Mr. Smirke has a private care watching at his bed-side, and sitting behind him on his pony; and is no more satisfied than the rest of us. How lonely we are in the world! how selfish and secret, everybody! You and your wife have pressed the same pillow for forty years and fancy yourselves united. — Psha, does she cry out when you have the gout, or do you lie awake when she has the tooth-ache? Your artless daughter, seemingly all innocence and devoted to her mamma and her piano-lesson, is thinking of neither, but of the young Lieutenant with whom she danced at the last ball—the honest frank boy just returned from school is secretly speculating upon the money you will give him, and the debts he owes the tart-man. The old grandmother crooning in the corner and bound to another world within a few months, has some business or cares which are quite private and her own—very likely she is thinking of fifty years back, and that night when she made such an impression, and danced a cotillion with the Captain before your father proposed for her: or, what a silly little over-rated creature your wife is, and how absurdly you are infatuated about

her—and, as for your wife—O philosophic reader, answer and say, — Do
you tell *her* all? Ah, sir—a distinct universe walks about under your hat and
under mine—all things in nature are different to each—the woman we look
at has not, the same features, the dish we eat from has not the same taste to
the one and the other—you and I are but a pair of infinite isolations, with
some fellow-islands a little more or less near to us.[113]

This should be contrasted with something Newman wrote to Miss Holmes
after she shared with him some of her family history. "You were right in
thinking that your family reminiscences would interest me," he wrote. "I think
nothing more interesting, and it is strange to think how evanescent, how apparently barren and result-less, are the ten thousand little details and complications
of daily life and family history. Is there any record of them preserved any where,
any more than of the fall of the leaves in Autumn? or are they themselves some
reflexion, as in an earthly mirror, of some greater truths above? So I think of
musical sounds and their combinations – they are momentary – but is it not
some momentary opening and closing of the Veil which hangs between the
worlds of spirit and sense?"[114] Here, Newman acknowledges the grounds for
skepticism that Thackeray saw, but only to show how the reality of the unseen
proves them specious.

Four years after writing this, in 1854, Thackeray was in Rome revisiting
questions broached by Newman in his William Street lectures. "The most
interesting man I have met with here is a convert, Mr. Pollen, whom Doyle
sent with a letter ...[115] I try and understand from him what can be the secret
of the religion for which he has given up rank chances and all good things of
this life."[116] It is unfortunate that this meeting went nowhere because Pollen
could have explained a good deal to Thackeray not only about Catholicism
but about Newman, whose true practical qualities he recognized more clearly
than many of his contemporaries. Educated at Eton and Christ Church, John
Hungerford Pollen (1820–1902) was the nephew of Charles Robert Cockerell,
the Professor of Architecture at the Royal Academy and architect of the
Ashmolean Museum, against whom Pugin railed with such mad venom. For
the disciple of true Gothic, the Ashmolean was an "unsightly pile of pagan
details."[117] In 1842, Pollen became a Fellow of Merton College, the ceiling of
which he adorned with figures boldly modeled after his family and friends. In
1846, after traveling throughout the Middle East, he was ordained priest. In
1847, he traveled to France, Italy and Germany to study church architecture.
On his return he joined Edward Pusey and Charles Marriot at the Tractarian
seminary of St. Saviour's, Leeds, where he became pro-vicar, while maintaining
his fellowship at Merton.[118] After the Bishop of Ripon protested against the
Tractarians praying to the saints, Pollen's Tractarian friends began trooping off
to Rome. He did not join their ranks until 1852, after a solitary tour of Ireland.
Resigning his fellowship at Merton, he went to Rome, where he met Thackeray.
In 1854, Newman offered Pollen the professorship of fine arts at the Catholic
University and he gladly accepted. Later he designed the University Church,
St. Stephen's Green, in the then-rarely-deployed Byzantine style, because, as he

told Newman, the British Isles had had enough of Pugin's Gothic. Newman agreed. "If Mr. Pugin persists ... in loading with bad names the admirers of Italian architecture," Newman told Ambrose Philipps de Lisle (1809–1878), the indefatigable ecumenist, "he is going the very way to increase their number. He will not be put down without authority which is infallible. And if we go to authority, I suppose Popes have given a greater sanction to Italian than to Gothic." Newman had very decided views on architecture, telling Lady Shrewsbury in 1848, before he set to building the Birmingham Oratory, "... the Gothic aisle is unsuited to an Oratorian Church ... I for one was converted to the Church, not by the medieval age, but by the primitive centuries—and it is natural that I should wish to renew the ecclesiastical structures of St. Ambrose and St. Leo. If the Catholic Church is large enough for different vocations and different orders ... it is large enough, without mutual jealousies, for different styles of architecture. If I can admire the Cisterian architecture, others ought to allow themselves to admire the Gregorian and the Oratorian."[119] In later life, Pollen worked with and befriended the Pre-Raphaelite painters Millais, Rossetti and Edward Burne-Jones. At the Tate one can see Pollen's beautiful daughter Anne (he eventually had ten children) in the girl in Burne-Jones's King Cophetua and the Beggar Maid. In 1863, at Thackeray's recommendation, Pollen was made the assistant keeper of the South Kensington Museum, later the Victoria & Albert, which might have been something of an act of atonement on Thackeray's part for his claiming in *The Paris Sketch Book* (1840), that Catholic art was an "absurd humbug."[120] Apropos William Thomas Roden's portrait of Newman, Pollen made some acute observations about caricature and reality, which might have profited both the satirist and the would-be Christian in Thackeray.

I want to relieve my mind of one or two reflections which crossed it on seeing the very clever picture of Fr Newman by Mr Roden. I think it shows great talent and but for certain accidental features I should ... be able to speak highly of it to Watts, Leighton and other painters who will be interested in hearing that some measure of justice has been given to any portrait of such a personage. The curious feature in it that continues to strike my remembrance is the expression not of seriousness but despair particularly expressed by some uncertain movements between those of tears and laughter (hysteria in fact) about the lines of the mouth. Now as I have long known and observed that organ I am well acquainted with the peculiar firmness, occasionally perhaps the sternness of its expression ... How comes it so changed and enfeebled in this otherwise serious portrait? It would seem as if the original were represented as despairing of some great issue, the salvation of the Catholics, e.g. (since he is a priest) or of the Protestants he once belonged to. But would such a man as we know him to be be ever in such a plight? ... Strong men have to undergo sorrow often and the person represented in the portrait has had an ample share of it and gone through great adversities. But would it not be a libel on any religion to represent the presence or remembrance of these things as causing despair? or a feeble inability to accept with confidence the dispensations of Providence. I should be surprised if a great painter represented the prophet and King David with any intimation of feebleness even under the tremendous inflictions we know of from history. A weak or a lugubrious look in a man who can give a rash opponent such sore bones when he leasts expects it and whose characteristic is a brightness and elasticity that "answers the whip" at all times seems to the artist world a needless element of failure.[121]

Newman bristled whenever attempts were made to caricature him as over-sensitive—this, after all, was what Pusey did after Newman converted. When an unknown female correspondent asked after the Roden portrait, Newman replied: "My dear Madam, If you saw me and talked with me you never would consider me sad or distressed – though the advance of years and the loss of friends of course have a depressing effect on mind and body. My painter, a man of genius, made, like men of genius, a great mistake. He acted on a theory. He caught at some passage of my Apologia, in which I speak of my sorrow at my loss of my Oxford friends and determined to represent me as mourning for them. My friends here were very much hurt at his acting on such a view, and from the first up to this time are not reconciled to what they consider a mistake."[122]

In addressing the misconceptions about Newman that found their way into Roden's portrait, Pollen recalled the larger misconceptions that Newman wrote the *Apologia* to expose. After Kingsley attempted to make his caricatures representative of the real man, Newman, as he said, "recognised what I had to do, though I shrank from both the task and the exposure which it would entail. I must, I said, give the true key to my whole life; I must show what I am, that it may be seen what I am not, and that the phantom may be extinguished which gibbers instead of me. I wish to be known as a living man, and not as a scarecrow which is dressed up in my clothes."[123] And in attempting to get his own portrait right, Newman knew that he would come in for criticism. "I may be accused of laying stress on little things, of being beside the mark, of going into impertinent or ridiculous details, of sounding my own praise, of giving scandal; but this is a case above all others, in which I am bound to follow my own lights and to speak out my own heart. It is not at all pleasant for me to be egotistical; nor to be criticized for being so. It is not pleasant to reveal to high and low, young and old, what has gone on within me from my early years. It is not pleasant to be giving to every shallow or flippant disputant the advantage over me of knowing my most private thoughts, I might even say the intercourse between myself and my Maker. But I do not like to be called to my face a liar and a knave; nor should I be doing my duty to my faith or to my name, if I were to suffer it. I know I have done nothing to deserve such an insult, and if I prove this, as I hope to do, I must not care for such incidental annoyances as are involved in the process."[124]

Thackeray also came in for a fair amount of misrepresentation. John Blackwood, the proprietor of *Blackwood's Magazine*, rejected a profile of the novelist after his death because, as he said, it was not true to the Thackeray he knew. "I do not much care for the stories you give," he told the author. Thackeray, he said, "used to tell such stories in a pitying half-mocking way in which it was impossible to say how much was sincerity and how much sham. But when he dropped that vein, and spoke with real feeling of men and things that he liked, the breadth and force of his character came out, and there was no mistake about his sincerity. None of the numerous sketches I have read give to me any real picture of the man with his fun and mixture of bitterness with warm good feeling."[125]

Still, the upshot of Thackeray's meeting with Pollen was to confirm him in his accustomed skepticism. "I have made an acquaintance with a convert, an Oxford man whom I like and who interests me," he wrote of Pollen to another correspondent. "And I am trying to pick my Oxford man's brains, & see from his point of view. But it isn't mine: and old Popery and old Protestantism seem to me as dead the one as the other. Wiseman I have heard and think him a tawdry Italian quack."[126] It is interesting that Thackeray should have used *quack* to describe Wiseman, because it is the same word that he used to describe the author of *Vanity Fair*.[127] Moreover, Thackeray was not the only English novelist of the time who took a dim view of Wiseman and the renewed English Catholicism he championed. Charlotte Bronte (1816–1855) also came away with an unflattering impression of the Anglo-Irish divine. "He has not merely a double but a treble and quadruple chin," she recalled, and has "a very large mouth with oily lips, and looks as if he would relish a good dinner with a bottle of wine after it.

> He came swimming into the room smiling, simpering, and bowing like a fat old lady, and sat down very demure in his chair, and looked the picture of a sleek hypocrite … The Cardinal spoke in a smooth whining manner, just like a canting Methodist preacher. The audience seemed to look up to him like a god. A spirit of the hottest zeal pervaded the whole meeting … All the speeches turned on the necessity of straining every nerve to make converts to popery. It is in such a scene that one feels what the Catholics are doing. Most persevering and enthusiastic are they in their work! Let Protestants look to it.[128]

Stock No Popery prejudices of this sort, together with disgust for his mother's rabid Bible religion always prevented Thackeray from embracing any definite Christianity. Apropos Pollen, he wrote to one correspondent: "I try and understand from him what can be the secret of the religion for which he has given up rank chances and all good things of this life." But Thackeray had to confess that he was still "so far off believing it," that he feared that when "poor Pollen … finds that I am only looking at it artistically as at Paganism Mahotmetanism or any other ism [he] will withdraw from me in sorrow, and … our pleasant acquaintance won't come to much."[129] Here Thackeray's faith stalled, and although there were times when he wished to advance beyond his tepid skepticism, he never managed it. Consequently, his settled view of Newman's lectures—and of the Roman Catholicism they recommended—was the view he had first articulated on coming away from them: "It is either Rome or Babylon, and for me it is Babylon," which was not so much a rejection of the Catholic polemicist in Newman as it was an acceptance of the natural man in Thackeray.[130] And yet, that Babylon *was* Rome according to traditional No Popery gives Thackeray's statement an unintended ambiguity, which is somehow fitting for this most ambivalent of would-be believers.

Which leads us to our overwhelming question: would Thackeray have taken Kingsley's part in the controversy over Kingsley's calumny in *Macmillan's Magazine?*[131] Before answering the question, it is necessary to revisit the genesis of the Garrick Club affair. It grew out of the rivalry between Thackeray and Dickens. Ever since Thackeray was a young man he had kept an envying eye on the spectacular rise of Dickens. In 1836 he offered to illustrate the *Pickwick Papers* and he even went twenty miles out of his way to visit Yarmouth to see the coastline associated with the Peggottys.[132] Over the course of their careers, both men drank in the same clubs and dined in the same private houses, literary lions only too aware of each other's literary power. Thackeray might have been more admiring of Dickens' talents than Dickens was of his, but he was still convinced that the more popular novelist was too sentimental for his own good. Dickens, for his part, disapproved of what he regarded as Thackeray's worldly cynicism and his want of fellow feeling. Then, again, there was class antagonism between the two men. Thackeray saw the Dickens family at the pier at Ramsgate once and noted how "embarrassingly coarse vulgar and happy" they looked.[133] Dickens felt Thackeray went to undignified lengths to ingratiate himself with the upper classes that he had satirized in his youth. He particularly disapproved of Thackeray trying to make them paying customers by appearing to share their philistinism. In his obituary of the novelist, whom he otherwise thought "a man of genius," Dickens wrote: "I thought that he too much feigned a want of earnestness, and that he made a pretense of under-valuing his art, which was not good for the art that he held in trust," He was galled to hear other obituaries referring to Thackeray as a "gentleman," as though the other novelists of Victoria's reign "were of the tinker tribe."[134] If Thackeray found fault with Dickens because he was an artist but not a gentleman, Dickens found fault with Thackeray because he was an artist *and* a gentleman. Dickens had something of the same contempt for Thackeray's social pretensions that G. M. Young had. "The Railway is the great Victorian symbol," Young wrote in an essay on Thackeray, "and I often picture the people of that age as a railway crowd, all pushing, scrambling, and shoving—backwards or forwards—at once. And what a journey lies before them, what mountains those tunnels will pierce, what valleys those airy viaducts will span, what novelties, what adventures, what delight! And among them I see a passenger whose joy is darkened by one anxiety—he is not quite sure if his ticket entitles him to travel first class."[135]

This rivalry between Dickens and Thackeray was the backdrop for the fracas that would erupt between the two men in 1858. It was immediately triggered by Dickens' falling out with his wife of over twenty years, Catherine, and his taking up with a young actress by the name of Ellen Ternan. This betrayal of the marital vow reached Thackeray's ears in May 1858. "To think of that poor matron after 22 years going away out of her house! O dear me it's a fatal story for our trade."[136] When someone at the Garrick Club suggested that Dickens had left his wife for someone other than the actress, Thackeray corrected the man. Dickens, getting wind of the remark, concluded that Thackeray was spreading malicious gossip, even though Thackeray's comment was clearly not malicious. In fact, Thackeray was studiedly neutral about the affair. Nevertheless, in the summer of 1858, in a paper called *Household Words*, Dickens published a full article on the affair, blaming his abandoned wife and attempting to justify himself. At the same time, a man signing himself "Lounger in the Clubs" wrote a profile on Thackeray for a little-known paper called *Town Talk*, in which, after giving an overview of Thackeray's career, he gratuitously slandered the novelist, much as Kingsley had gratuitously slandered Newman, by charging that Thackeray was not only an overpaid but a hypocritical lecturer. Apropos Thackeray's American lectures, which were based on his *English Humourists of the Eighteenth Century*, the writer wrote: "The prices were extravagant, the lecturer's admiration of birth and position was extravagant, the success was extravagant. No one succeeds better than Mr. Thackeray in cutting his coat according to his cloth. Here he flattered the aristocracy, but when he crossed the Atlantic, George Washington became the idol of his worship, the 'Four Georges' the object of his bitterest attack ..." Moreover, the writer of the piece added, there was a want of charity in what Thackeray wrote, "which is not to be balanced by the most brilliant sarcasm or the most perfect knowledge of the human heart"—a criticism which had a distinctly Dickensian ring about it. When it was revealed that the writer of the piece was Edmund Yates, a 27-year-old journalist who was a member of the Garrick Club, of which Thackeray and Dickens were also members, Thackeray took exception not so much because the piece was slanderous as because it was based on conversations overheard at the Club.

Yates was a colorful character. The son of theatrical parents, who secured him a position in the Post Office to keep him off the stage, he became head of the Missing Letter department before pursuing a career on Fleet Street. An unsavory scamp, he made society scandal his stock-in-trade and almost single-handedly invented the modern gossip-column.[137] When Thackeray saw Yates's piece on him, he sensed that it was not a solo performance. As D. J. Taylor points out in his account of the affair: "The appearance of a hostile article on the same day as Dickens' defense of his conduct in *Household Words* may have been simply coincidence, but it seemed to Thackeray—almost certainly correctly—that Dickens was using Yates as a cat's paw to punish him for taking sides in the dispute about his private life"—even though, as Taylor shows, Thackeray did not take sides.[138] For Thackeray, Dickens' part in the slanderous attack was the result of "pent up animosities and long cherished hatred."[139] Within a day of the offending article appearing, Thackeray wrote the vituperative young hack a letter nicely articulating the code of clubland honor that he had so blatantly violated.

We meet at a Club where, before you were born, I believe, I & other gentlemen have been in the habit of talking, without any idea that our conversation would supply paragraphs for professional vendors of 'Literary Talk,' and I don't remember that out of that Club I ever exchanged 6 words with you. Allow me to inform you that the talk wh. you may have heard there is not intended for newspaper remark, & to beg, as I have a right to do, that you will refrain from printing comments upon my private conversation, that you will forgo discussion however blundering on my private affairs; & that you will henceforth please to consider any question of my personal truth & sincerity as quite out of the province of your criticism.[140]

To the Committee of the Garrick Club, Thackeray wrote on the 19th of June: "Rather than have any further personal controversy with [Mr. Yates] I thought it best to submit our correspondence to you, with a copy of the newspaper which has been the cause of our difference. I think I may fairly appeal to the Club, to decide whether the complaints I have against Mr. Yates are not well-founded, and whether the practice of publishing such articles as that which I enclose will not be fatal to the comfort of the Club, and is not intolerable in a Society of Gentlemen"—an appeal which was reminiscent of Newman's publication of the correspondence that had passed between Kingsley and himself. The Committee took Thackeray's point and unanimously resolved that unless Yates apologized, "the Committee will consider it their duty to call a General Meeting of the Club to consider this subject."[141] Yates refused to apologize and the meeting was held. Before the meeting, Thackeray wrote to the Committee explaining that he had decided to make an issue out of Yates's slander for other club members as much as for himself. "I presume the effect of tomorrows meeting will be to confirm or to reverse that sentence. In the latter case, it may be that the next gentleman attacked will be more patient than I have been; and, for the sake of a quiet life, will suffer, without complaint or protest, indignities put upon him, hints thrown out against his honor and sincerity, & liberties taken with his name ..."[142] Moreover, Thackeray admitted, "more than one of my friends advised me to say nothing," just as many still imagine that Newman made too much of Kingsley's libel. However, Thackeray recognized that he could not leave the libel unanswered. "My duty, perhaps, my temper, caused me to follow a different course: but I shall grieve sincerely if my indignation at the injury wh I conceive has been done me shall have superadded any unnecessary annoyance to the doubt, distrust, division, recrimination, & heart burning, wh conduct like that of wh I complain, must bring upon our or any Society!"[143]

This solicitude for other club members in light of Yates's attack recalls Newman's solicitude for the Catholic priesthood and for Catholics in general in light of Kingsley's attack. As Newman told one correspondent, "I should not have singled out Mr Kingsley for public notice unless I thought it really worth while to deal a blow against a virulent blasphemer of the Catholic Church. Accordingly I say ... that his words are a great affront to myself and a worse insult to the Catholic priesthood ..."[144] Finally, the 140 Committee members gathered to decide whether Yates should indeed be required to apologize, and although Dickens, Wilkie Collins and the journalist Robert Bell all advocated leniency, the vote went against Yates 70:46. After he failed to respond to the secretary's letter requiring him to apologize, his name was removed from the club books. In the wake of the expulsion, Yates contemplated bringing a Chancery suit and even hiring Edwin James, the brilliant QC and redoubtable courtroom advocate (Dickens based Mr. Stryver on him in *A Tale of Two Cities*, describing him in one passage as an attorney whose object was "to smash his witness like a crockery vessel, and shiver his part of the case to useless lumber"), before realizing that he would have no case.[145]

Nearly a year after Yates's libelous article appeared, Thackeray wrote to none other than Charles Kingsley to defend his part in the Garrick Club affair. "I have no doubt in my own mind that I was right to be indignant in the matter, and to call the offender before the Club, wh is a social Institution quite unlike other clubs, and where men have been in the habit of talking quite freely to one another (in a room not 15 square feet) for this ¼ of a century or more. If this penny-a-liner is to come in to this sanctum, and publish his comments upon the conversation there held and the people he meets there, it is all over with the comfort and friendliness of our Society ... Scores of the pennyaline fraternity have written on his side, and a great number of them are agreed that it's the description of my nose wh makes me so furious—Not one of them seems to understand that to be accused of hypocrisy [and] base motives for public & private conduct ... are the points wh make me angry ..."[146]

In light of this defense of his actions, it seems likely that Thackeray would have seen the same point of honor at stake in Newman's defense of his actions. It also seems likely that he would have viewed Kingsley in the *Macmillan's Magazine* row in much the same light that he viewed Yates in the Garrick Club affair: as a bounder, whose transgression against the code of honor must be called to account. And with his interest in the autobiographical aspects of fiction, with which he played so ingeniously in *Pendennis*, it also seems likely that Thackeray would have admired the *Apologia*, which is infinitely more searching than anything his contemporaries managed in their autobiographies, whether Trollope, Ruskin, Pattison, Mill, Darwin, or Harriett Martineau.[147]

As to Kingsley's charge that Catholicism *ipso facto* required the Catholic faithful to be mendacious, Thackeray's correspondence suggests that he would have seen in this claim something of the same zealotry that he saw in his mother's Bible Christianity. While it is true that the skeptic in him was unpersuaded by the infallible claims of the Roman Church, Thackeray was entirely free of Kingsley's belligerent Protestantism. In 1846, Thackeray described an Anglican friend "in a glory of exultation at the newly erected Cheadle (Catholic) Church"—Pugin's masterpiece, which reminded Newman of the portals of heaven. "But I think Romanism begins to be drawn rather milder," Thackeray thought, "and the Poop of Room ... is not perwhirting so many as fommly."[148] There is a genial fun in this mockery that would have been inconceivable for Kingsley, for whom the sins of the "Poop of Room" were never a joking matter. Thackeray, on the other hand, tended to like the Catholics he met. In one letter to his mother chiding her for assuming that her Evangelical faith had a monopoly on Christian truth, he wrote: "As for Catholicism you may have your fling at it: but I am sure that the Xtian church has existed in it in all ages—it would be an insult to God to say it had not. Recollect that you are a woman with intense organs of love & respect born in Church-of-Englandism—do you think you would not have had the same love for Catholicism if you had been bred to it? Indeed you would, as I fancy, in any other creed."[149] Later, he returned to the same taunting hypothesis: "If you had been born a Catholic—you know what a good one you would have been: and then you would have been wretched if I had any doubts about the martyrdom of Polycarp or the Invention of the True Cross—and there are thousands of anxious mothers so deploring the errors of their skeptical children—But the Great Intelligence shines far far above all mothers and all sons—the Truth Absolute is God—And it seems to me hence almost blasphemous: that any blind prejudiced sinful mortal being should dare to be unhappy about the belief of another; should dare to say Lo I am right and my brothers must go to damnation—I Know God and my brother doesn't. And now I'll stop scolding my dearest old Mother about that favorite propensity of hers to be miserable. God bless us all."[150]

In his later years, Thackeray recalled the faith that a life-threatening illness gave him when he was a young man, which suggests that the deflationary skepticism that he first learned from Fitzgerald did not altogether take: "when I was going to die as I thought I was one night when I had my illness, I was as easy in mind and as trustful of God and as confident in his wisdom & mercy, as St. Augustin or St. Theresa or Lady Huntingdon or the Revd Cesar Malan. I mean any Church man high or low ..."[151] At the same time, he contrasted this sharply with his Mother's Evangelical faith, in a passage which suggests that one reason why he looked askance at religious certainty is that he associated it with fanaticism. "The very comforts you get from your religion the delights of rapturous faith with wh you receive and peruse the oracles of Heaven and wh you and all strong believers hold out as the blessed consequences of your belief ... the misery that those dear to you can't be brought to think like you, are cut off from inexpressible benefits or liable to awful penalties for rejecting the Truth—that is your Truth. You must be miserable. Your text-worship gives you vast advantages, refuges in sorrow, delights in contemplation, a communion with Heaven seeming to be actual & personal—but along with these pleasures a corresponding grief and gloom—or, according to the temperament of the believer, a righteous wrath against those who do not hold the faith. And you plead in tears and passion for the Unbeliever, or destroy his heresy by fire and sword according to your disposition or the age in wʰ you live. St. Theresa was as tender as you are but in her time the Church burned and racked heretics. How you would have gone off singing to be roasted!"[152] For someone who claimed to find so many aspects of Christianity, whether in its Evangelical or its Catholic guise, unsympathetic, it is remarkable how frequently he returned to the topic in his letters. One thing that might have kept him returning to the question of Christianity was the abiding guilt he felt over his wife's madness, which he might have had a hand in precipitating. In August 1840, when Thackeray decided to leave Isabella to holiday in Belgium, she was suffering from post-natal depression after the birth of her third child. Was it to see the young woman on whom he based Becky Sharp that he left his wife? And was this a lingering affair of which Isabella was aware? And did her awareness of the affair push her over the brink? These are questions that none of Thackeray's biographers have been able to answer conclusively. Nevertheless, it is clear that Thackeray was not only a haunted but a guilty man.[153] He certainly sought forgiveness in prayer, which was another aspect of the man that would have appealed to Newman, who knew that the Saints themselves, "whatever be their advance in the spiritual life … never rise from their knees … never cease to beat their breasts, as if sin could possibly be strange to them while … in the flesh." For Newman, "Such utter self-prostration was the very badge and token of the servant of Christ …"[154]

Yet what Newman could not have known was how hostile Thackeray was to the sacramental aspects of Catholicism—a hostility which the guilt he suffered may very well have exacerbated. From Munich, in 1852, he wrote of being in what he described as a "sham-antique church," where "at dusk he heard whisswhisswhisspiring in the confessional, and then hummummumbrum the Priest talking, and all this excited my awe and curiosity and I thought to myself perhaps there is some lovely creature on her knees to a venerable friar confessing some tremenjuous crime …" But when an old woman in a green shawl emerged, Thackeray was disappointed. As he confessed, "all the romance was gone at the sight of the queer little trot of a woman, who I am sure could have only had the most trumpery little Sins to chatter about and so I came out of the church not a bit better Catholic than I went in." Here one can see that Thackeray was more of a romantic than he cared to admit. "Don't you see if she had been a lovely Countess who had just killed her Grandmother or smothered her babby, I might have gone on being interested and awe stricken? but Polly the Cook maid who owns to having given a piece of pie to the Policeman, or melted the fat into the grease-pot I can't go for to waste my compassion and wonder upon her." In all events, the moral he drew did not argue any great insight into the needs of countesses or cook maids: "heres the mistake about these fine churches pictures music and splendid and gracious sights and sounds with wh. the Catholics entrap many people. Their senses are delighted and they fancy they are growing religious: it's a romantic wonder not a religious one. We must set to work to learn the Truth with all our hearts and Soul and Strength and take care not to be juggled by romanticalities and sentimentalities."[155] Here, again, Thackeray showed how susceptible he was to No Popery caricature. In seeming to deplore "romanticalities and sentimentalities," he perpetuated them.

And yet, for all his English antipathy to Roman Catholicism, his letters make clear that he yearned for a more definite faith, beyond caricature. Writing to his mother from Rome at the time that he was meeting with Pollen, he spoke of his three daughters, "who have been as happy as any women in Europe perhaps and so good and contented and obedient and eager to please me, that my heart is thankful to God for blessing me with them." Then he thought of his love for them in a wider context, of how they would have "this recollection when you & I are gone … So the generations of men pass away: and are called rank after rank by the Divine Goodness out of the reach of time and age and grief and struggle and parting—leaving these to their successors who go through their appointed world, work, and are resumed presently by the Awful Owner of us all—Whose Will is done on earth as it is in Heaven, and whose Kingdom and Glory are for ever and ever. Oh me! We all in our incomplete poor way adore and confess thee." That Rome should have inspired this impromptu prayer was fitting, but it was also the company he was keeping in Rome that inspired him. "I have been seeing something of some R. Catholic converts here, who have given up everything to follow the Truth as they best understand it. Their truth as it seems to me is a farrago of impossible follies, leading to inevitable farther falsehood deceit degradation and tyranny; but they give up rank ease and all worldly things for the sake of their convictions. They find consolations and delights and amendments even of life in their new creed. I am glad to have seen them, and to have been touched by their goodness piety and self-negation … My dearest old Mother. I think of these things and pray God to enlighten me and purify my life, and I love and worship my lord Jesus Christ—whose Divine Heart had pity for all errors, and will, I think & trust, compassionate mine …"[156]

Here was the admirable humility of the man, which Newman inferred from his published work, and Frederick Meyrick encountered face to face when the novelist was seeking to become M.P. for the city of Oxford. "As he was dining with me," Meyrick recalled, "after his first day's canvassing, I said to him: 'You must be in a different position from most men who canvas a strange constituency, as you must be known by fame to most of those whom you visit.' 'Now,' he said, laying down his knife and fork, and holding up a finger, 'there was one man among all that I went to see who heard my name before; and he was the circulating librarian. Such is mortal fame!'"[157]

CHAPTER 9

Newman and the Americans

In 1843, when John Henry Newman was living at Littlemore, the religious retreat he set up outside Oxford, he had an unexpected visitor: Jacob Abbott, a Congregationalist minister from Maine, whom Newman had taken to task for a book of his called *The Corner-Stone* (1834). There Newman detected the same tendency to deny the divinity of Christ that he saw in the liberal Broad Churchman R. D. Hampden, whose wildly unorthodox Bampton Lectures epitomized what Newman, even as an Anglican, saw as the undogmatical incoherence of the Established Church. Robert Wilberforce, one of the Great Liberator's sons, who would eventually follow Newman to Rome, fully agreed: "you have not overstated the falsehood and danger of them," he wrote to his friend. For Wilberforce, they exhibited a "marvelous fogginess."[1] In Tract 73, Newman complained that Abbott's book "savours unpleasantly of pantheism. It treats the Almighty, not as the great God, but as some vast physical and psychological phenomenon."[2] Moreover, he saw Abbott's misapprehensions as redolent of a much larger problem—a problem that is with us still. "There is a widely, though irregularly spread School of doctrine," Newman wrote, "within and without the Church" that "aims at and professes peculiar piety … I do not hesitate to assert that this doctrine is based upon error, that it is really a specious form of trusting man rather than God, that it is in its nature rationalistic, and that it tends to Socinianism." Newman regarded Socinianism as the besetting sin of American and indeed British religion. "To tell the truth," he wrote, "one special enemy to which the American Church, as well as our own … lies open is the influence of a refined and covert Socinianism."[3] Still, if Abbott's views were mistaken, the man himself was engaging. Before they parted, Newman noted, "We talked on various matters for an hour or so, and when he rose to go I offered him my *Church of the Fathers*—in which he made me put my name … I showed him on his way, accompanying him in the twilight through the village and across Mr. Allen's field into the road, and we parted with a good deal of warm feeling. He is a Congregationalist Minister—not much above 30, I should think—with somewhat of the New England twang, but very quiet in manner and unaffected. How dreadful it is that the sheep of Christ are scattered to and fro …"[4] This Anglo-American encounter shows how both countries, however dissimilar, were alike in their susceptibility to precisely that denial of the divinity of Christ, which, Newman recognized, even as early as the 1830s, was readying what he would later call the "plague of unbelief."[5] It also shows the personal interest that Newman took in Americans, which, by and large, Americans reciprocated. In 1851, for example, when Newman was sued for libel by Giovanni Achilli, an apostate Dominican, notorious for seducing scores of women, American Catholics helped cover his legal fees, which one historian estimates could have been as much as £100,000 in today's money, an outpouring of generosity for which Newman was deeply grateful.[6]

Since the topic of Newman and the Americans is an immense one, I shall limit myself in this chapter to a few themes. I shall compare the reception Tractarianism met with in England and America to show how it deepened Newman's understanding of that "temper of Socinianism," from which both countries suffered. I shall show how America demonstrated to Newman that if the laity were susceptible to this temper, they could also be made the means of combating it, as Newman himself combated it, especially in his role as Rector of the Catholic University in Dublin. Since Newman intended this center of Catholic learning—his Oxford on the Liffey—to benefit not only Ireland and England but also the United States, it is fitting that he first encountered examples of vibrant Catholic education in his study of a land otherwise rife with sectarianism. Accordingly, I shall also show how Newman's idea of Catholic education, far from being "narrow," "exaggerated" and "sterile," as the historian and former Warden of Merton, J. M. Roberts contended, was profoundly creative, though many of America's Catholic colleges have gone gravely astray.[7] And lastly I shall endeavor to show how the personal interest Newman took in America and Americans embodied his hopes for the future of Catholicism.

America always appealed to Newman's sense of awe. One suspects that he would have had no difficulty entering into that memorable passage in Scott Fitzgerald's *The Great Gatsby* where Nick Carraway imagines how "for a transitory enchanted moment man must have held his breath in the presence of this continent, compelled into an aesthetic contemplation he neither understood nor desired, face to face for the last time in history with something commensurate to his capacity for wonder."[8] In one of his sermons, Newman describes the sixteenth-century society which produced his patron saint, the Florentine Philip Neri, as one in which "America ... became known to Europe, and the extent of the earth was doubled ... The public mind was agitated by a thousand fancies; no one knew what was coming; anything might be expected; a new era had opened upon the world, and enormous changes, political and social, were in preparation. There was an upheaving of the gigantic intellect of man, and he found he had powers and resources which he was not conscious of before, and began in anticipation to idolize their triumphs."[9] Here was a Jazz Age with which Fitzgerald could identify. Certainly in those rueful essays of his that Edmund Wilson collected in *The Crack-Up* (1936), he wrote of idolatry's end with great cautionary conviction.

Newman also saw America as a means of showing how we arrive at certainty. In one letter, written a year after he composed that marvelous book, *A Grammar of Assent* (1870), Newman likened America to Heaven. "I believe absolutely that there is a North America, and that the United States is a Republic with a President – why then do I not absolutely believe, though I see it not, that there is a Heaven and that God is there? If you say that there is more evidence for the United States than for Heaven, that is intelligible – but it is not a question of more or less. Since the utmost evidence only leads to probability and yet you believe absolutely in the United States, it is no reason against believing in heaven absolutely, though you have not 'experience' of it."[10] Newman also liked to cite America to explode the branch theory for the catholicity of Anglicanism.[11] "The Church of England once was part of the Catholic Church, as the United States once were part of the Kingdom of England – but, as well might they at this day claim to have a pecuniary interest in our lands, in our rivers, in our harbour and docks, in our Cathedrals, in our public buildings, as the Anglican Church to have any part in the Sacraments and the spiritual privileges of the Catholic Church. Yet that does not hinder one's loving and interchanging good offices with members of the United States when one meets them, though we do not make them our Members of Parliament or our Ministers of State; and in like manner I will think all good of the Protestants I meet with, and rejoice in the fruits of grace I may discern in them, without owning them as members of the Catholic Church."[12] And finally in that rollicking send-up of English bigotry, *Lectures on the Present Position of Catholics in England* (1851), Newman likened the vastness of America to the vastness of Catholicism. Speaking of that contempt for the monastic that has held sway in England since at least Cromwell's visitations, Newman wrote: "It is familiar to an Englishman to wonder at and to pity the recluse and the devotee who surround themselves with a high enclosure, and shut out what is on the other side of it; but was there ever such an instance of self-sufficient, dense, and ridiculous bigotry, as that which rises up and walls in the minds of our fellow-countrymen from all knowledge of one of the most remarkable phenomena which the history of the world has seen? This broad fact of Catholicism—as real as the continent of America, or the Milky Way—which Englishmen cannot deny, they will not entertain; they shut their eyes, they thrust their heads into the sand, and try to get rid of a great vision, a great reality, under the name of Popery."[13]

Matthew Arnold articulated a common prejudice among the nineteenth-century English when he complained of how Americans "cover the defects in their civilization by boasting ... They do really hope to find in tall talk and inflated sentiment a substitute for that real sense of elevation which human nature ... instinctively craves. The thrill of awe, which Goethe pronounces to be the best thing humanity has, they would fain create by proclaiming themselves at the top of their voice to be 'the greatest nation upon earth.'"[14]

Newman would not have agreed with Arnold or with Goethe that the "thrill of awe" is "the best thing that humanity has" and he would never have begrudged Americans their delight in their own good fortune, for all their presumed "tall talk and inflated sentiment," though he could be sharply critical of Americans. In 1872, he wrote to his old friend Lord Blachford: "For these forty years the Yankees have in the eyes of the whole world been insulting us, and playing with us, and presuming on our tenderness for them, remorse at our past tyranny, and love of kindred. The more you grant, the more they ask – to be considerate is deemed cowardice ... it is the very worst policy to seem to be afraid of them." The relationship between the English and the Americans reminded Newman "of some of Punch's pictures, in which policemen are acting with great politeness towards thieves and vagabonds." Still, he was careful to qualify. "Don't suppose I so call the American people. I believe they have among them as great gentlemen as we have. I know many, whom I love and admire – but I have no affection for Grants and Fiskes ..."[15]

Something of Newman's interest in Americans and their country may have come initially from his father, a banker in the City of London, who, as Newman's brother Frank attested, was an admirer of Benjamin Franklin and Thomas Jefferson.[16] Like his father, Newman, for all his Englishness, saw the world in rather cosmopolitan terms, and his attitude to Americans, while not uncritical, was certainly never dismissive. The attitude of the Anglican churchman F. W. Hook, who was nearly sent down from Christ Church for devoting too much of his time to the novels of Walter Scott, was rather more typical. "It is obvious that surrounded as the Church there [in the United States] is by papists and fanatics, our grand hope, under God, must rest with a learned clergy ... Certainly the divinity of some of our transatlantic brethren (and fathers even) is somewhat crude ... We can purchase a complete set of the Fathers for (I should suppose) £350. Now why should not some two or three hundred of us subscribe this sum, and present these books to the Episcopal College of New York?"[17]

Hook is an instructive figure because as Vicar of Leeds he was presented with many of the same challenges that confronted Episcopal churchmen in America, most pressingly, how to integrate the Anglican Church into the new industrialized city and how to put Tractarian principles to work in the pastoral life of the Church. Hook was successful in negotiating the first challenge. Although Leeds was a Methodist stronghold, he doubled the number of Anglican churches from six to twenty-nine and increased the number of Anglican schools from six to thirty.[18] When it came to introducing Tractarian principles into his churches, however, he was less successful. When Edward Pusey came to him with the idea of building St. Saviour's as a model Tractarian church that would operate as a kind of Tractarian seminary, Hook offered his strong support, though he soon regretted it. He was particularly aghast when troops of Roman converts issued from the church.[19] In one letter to Pusey, Hook gave vent to understandable exasperation.

> I do not care for what men *say*: I look to what they *do*. What you have *done* is to send Romanizers here ... Undo what you have done, or at least attempt it. If you either cannot or will not, do not write any more. All you can say is that you think that they are not Romanizers—and all I can say is that, as I know them to be Romanizers, I shall warn all men of the danger of touching pitch.[20]

St. Saviour's was an incontestable case in point. When the Bishop of Ripon got wind of the Romanizing of the clergy at St. Saviour's, he wrote to his parishioners: "The nearer persons approach to the Roman system, the more will their powers of judgment be perverted, their moral sense blunted, and obliquity of moral vision superinduced, blinding them more and more to the simplicity of Christian truth, and estranging them more and more from the sincerity of Christian practice."[21] Hook was even more categorical. "It is not against *Romanists* but against *Romanizers* that we write; against those who are doing the work of the Church of Rome while eating the bread of the Church of England."[22]

When it came to integrating Tractarian principles into the American Episcopal Church, American clergymen encountered comparable problems. Apropos some of these, Newman wrote to Hook in 1835: "I feel quite what you say about the American Church ... . They have a great gift and do not know how to use it – Pusey tells me ... that there is great fear of their splitting in to two parties or rather Churches on the point of Baptismal Regeneration – the Western taking the ultra protestant view, the New York connexion the Catholic. Bishop Chase, now of Illinois, has lately been here ... He was very unsatisfactory altogether, and Pusey says he is one of the ultra protestants ... I have for some time thought that a greater service could not be done to the Church, than for two or three men who agree with us to go over to New York and make it their head quarters for several years. But where will you get men unemployed? One man, especially fitted for that work, and year by year more so, is in that precarious state that we do not know what to expect, – Froude."[23]

Here is wonderful fodder for counter-factual historians. Of course, one of the great 'what ifs' of Newman studies is what would have happened if Froude, the 'enfant terrible' of the Oxford Movement, as Ronald Knox called him, had not died young.[24] By all accounts, Froude was an extraordinary young man. Besides being Newman's dearest friend, he was handsome, brilliant, athletic, dashing and utterly original, a man with whom the Tractarian Isaac Williams dreaded being left alone for fear of what he might say. In addition to all his other distinctions, Froude was a confirmed celibate, which certainly set him apart in an English society that associated celibacy with what William Cobbett nicely called "monkish ignorance and superstition."[25] What Froude might have done, especially with respect to his religious development, had he not died of tuberculosis at the age of 33 in 1836 is a question that has always fascinated Newman scholars. Would he have joined Newman and converted to Rome? Or thrown in his lot with Pusey and Keble and the Anglo-Catholic party? Or, as Newman's letter to Hook suggests, gone to live in America? The idea of Froude working with the Episcopal Church in New York to Romanize the Yankees teems with speculative possibilities.

Throughout the 1830s and 40s, Newman would receive warm testimonials from Episcopal churchmen convinced that Tractarianism could help them strengthen the Church in North America. One bishop wrote to Newman, "The sound principles which your writings and those of your friends are disseminating in England are rapidly gaining ground in the United States ... Many of my clergy, who were rather low in their opinions on the Sacraments and sacred character of the Church are very much changed for the better." [26] Prominent American churchmen also praised Newman's *Parochial Sermons*. "For close pointed, and uncompromising presentation of the truths and duties of the Gospel," the Bishop of New York, Benjamin T. Onderdonk (1791–1861) attested, "I know not their superiors ..."[27] George Washington Doane (1799–1859), the Bishop of New Jersey, agreed: "While they are not above the level of the plainest readers, they will interest and satisfy the highest and most accomplished minds."[28] Apropos Doane, Newman told Pusey in 1840: "A friend of Bishop Doane has been here wishing to see you. He was in the woods of Transylvania before he set out, and being with a bedridden old woman told her he was going to England and among other places to Oxford— 'Ah' she said 'then you will see that wicked old man who writes Tracts.'"[29]

In 1843, the writer of these brilliant sermons responded by sharing with his American admirer how little his productions were appreciated by the Anglican Church, especially one, as he said, "about which there might be a difference of opinion."[30] Of course, Newman was alluding to Tract 90, in which he argued that the 39 Articles, to which all Anglican dons and clergymen were required to subscribe, might be accepted by those who were otherwise "catholic in heart and doctrine"—an argument which sharply delineated the battle-lines between those who considered the Anglican Church protestant and those who considered it catholic.[31] In seceding from the Established Church, Newman showed his English and indeed his American friends that, as far as he was concerned, the catholic claims of Anglicanism were unsustainable.

If Tract 90 precipitated the crisis of Tractarianism in England, the ordination of an extraordinary young man named Arthur Carey precipitated it in America. Carey was born in London in 1822 and moved with his family to America in 1830. After a brilliant undergraduate career at Columbia College, he formed a Tractarian group at the General Theological Seminary and in 1842 was ordained deacon.[32] In 1843, before his ordination as an Episcopalian priest, he was questioned by Dr. Hugh Smith, who was not prepared for the answers he received to his routine questions. Carey blithely admitted that he was "not prepared to pronounce the doctrine of transubstantiation an absurd or impossible doctrine;" he did "not object to the Romish doctrine of purgatory as defined by the Council of Trent;" he was "not prepared to consider the Church of Rome as no longer an integral or pure branch of the Church of Christ ... ;" and he believed that the Reformation was "an unjustifiable act, and followed by many grievous and lamentable results ..."[33] After receiving these startling answers, Smith refused to sign the required testimonial. Questioned further, Carey serenely informed his inquisitor that if he was refused ordination from the Episcopal, he would apply to the Catholic Church. Despite the controversy caused by the inquest, which divided High and Low Churchmen in the Episcopal Church for a generation, Carey was eventually ordained and became assistant to Samuel Seabury (1801–1872), Rector of New York's Church of the Annunciation. [34] In November 1843, Carey wrote Newman from New York asking him to pray for "a little band who are very lonely ... [and] exposed to the temptation of shrinking from points, which will make us suspected by the High Church party ..." And then he ended his brief, heartfelt letter by assuring his correspondent that "The call on your disciples to pray for their teacher has thrilled through our hearts, and made us feel more near to you, than we are to our friends in this country."[35] Newman does not appear to have replied, though it is clear that the letter made a strong impression on him.

To recuperate from overwork and poor health, Carey set sail for Cuba in 1844 but died en route. He was buried at sea on Good Friday. For Seabury, "Mr. Carey was, without exception, the ripest man of his age that I ever knew; and seldom have I conversed with one of any age whose conversation impressed me with a deeper sense, both intellectually and morally, of my own weakness ... On the abstruse subjects of metaphysics, on the profound dogmas of theology, he discoursed with the wisdom of a sage; bringing up from the deep of thought and placing in a clear and intelligible light, truths which the generality even of cultivated minds seldom approach without bewilderment or discuss without confusion: and this with the unconscious ease and simplicity of a child ..."[36] After Carey's death, a friend and fellow seminarian met with Newman and urged him to write the biography, an offer he turned down, convinced that the biography should be written by an American.[37]

Newman was profoundly affected by the news of Carey's death. Years afterwards, in 1866, he wrote to Carey's memoirist to tell him "how touching your Memoir of your dear friend is ..." For Newman, it had, as he wrote, "a special interest, over and above its own, from the circumstance that I have for so many years followed the history of the religious school in the United States, of which you tell us so much." Then, again, Carey reminded Newman of one of his dearest departed friends. "Perhaps it was from the likeness to Hurrell Froude," Newman wrote, "but I was much moved by what I heard of Arthur Carey ... every year since I have been a priest, up to this very morning, I have, before I began my Mass, mentioned his name with that of Hurrell Froude and of other Anglican friends, in my Preparation, recommending them to the mercy of God."[38] That both Froude and Carey died young, before they were able to fulfill their earthly roles in holy history, bound them together in Newman's mind. It is worth recalling, in this context, something Newman wrote to Froude two years before his death: "Methought, if your health would not let you come home, you ought to be a Bishop in India – there you might be a Catholic and no one would know the difference. It quite amused me for a while; and made me think how many posts there are in his Kingdom ... It is quite impossible that in some way or other you are not destined to be an instrument of God's purposes—Tho' I saw the earth cleave and you fall in, or heaven open and a chariot appear, I should say just the same—God has ten thousand posts of service, you might be of use in the central elemental fire, you might be of use in the depths of the sea."[39]

Later, in March 1883, Newman communicated with another priest in America who might have reminded him of Carey. William Stang, a German priest who became Rector of the Cathedral in Providence, Rhode Island, wrote in his simple, self-taught English: "I bought your works and ever since I am a faithful reader of them. Often when I am alone with your books, I feel a desire to express to the author my sincerest thanks and to tell him, how much I honor and love him." Stang also promised to remember Newman each day at Mass, just as Newman remembered Carey, and hoped God would preserve him "for the good and glory of his Church, of which you are so warm a defender."[40] Newman wrote back, "I am much touched by your letter and thank you for it with all my heart. It is a great consolation to me to know that in my declining strength, I have the spiritual aid of your prayers, and, though I should like to know you personally, still there is a special gratification in the circumstance that he who is so charitable to me, is, like the Good Samaritan in the Parable, a stranger to me."[41] Carey, if he had lived, might have said the same about Newman.

That Tractarianism inspired the same Protestant fears in America that it inspired in England is clear from a report of Carey's ordination written by perhaps the most articulate critic of the Oxford Movement in America, John Duer (1782–1858), a prominent Low Church Episcopalian, who studied law with Alexander Hamilton and eventually rose to become Chief Judge of the Superior Court of New York City, the state's commercial court. Indeed, commercial law was the judge's *métier*—a not insignificant detail in light of what Newman saw as the influence of commerce on the character of Anglo-American religion.

In his account of Carey's ordination, Duer claimed that Carey was only ordained as the result of Bishop Onderdonk acting as a sort of Roman mole, with the help of his crypto-Catholic accomplice, Seabury. Duer warned of the subversion that might result from such slack ordination procedures. "If the bishop, in deciding on the admission of candidates, is to act secretly, and, of course, irresponsibly; if suspected candidates are not to be subjected to a close and rigid examination ... if what occurs at such examinations is not to be carefully recorded, and the record carefully preserved, a bishop might pursue the treacherous course I have described for a series of years ... A Romanist bishop in a Protestant Church is no longer an improbable event."[42] Such fears were not those of an isolated alarmist. Catholics in America, even before the mass influx of Catholic immigrants in the 1840s, were deeply distrusted by their Protestant neighbors, as the English historian Paul Johnson relates:

> There were ... widespread fears of Catholic political and military conspiracy, fears which had existed ... since the 1630s, when they were associated with Charles I, and which had been resurrected and foisted on George III. In the 1830s, Lyman Beecher, so sensible and so rational in so many ways, included in his *Plea for the West* details of a Catholic plot to take over the entire Mississippi Valley, the chief conspirators being the pope and the Emperor of Austria. Samuel Morse, who was not particularly pro-Protestant but had been outraged when, during a visit to Rome, his hat had been knocked off by a papal guard when he failed to doff it as the pope passed, added plausibility to Beecher's theory by asserting that the reactionary kings and emperors of Europe were deliberately driving their Catholic subjects to America to promote the takeover.[43]

It is in light of these fears that Duer's fears should be seen. In his account of Carey's ordination, Duer asked: "Why is it that the minds of some of our clergy, and of a very large portion of our laity, are filled with suspicion and alarm? I shall answer these questions frankly and fully ... The doctrines of the Tractarian writers of Oxford have, in certain quarters, been openly embraced—have been propagated in the diocese with unusual diligence and zeal ..." And "the doctrines in question are neither warranted by Scripture nor reconcilable with our Articles ... On the contrary ... if adopted as the doctrines of the Church, they would gradually efface and abolish its true, distinctive, Protestant character."[44] For Duer, Tractarianism was crypto-Catholicism, which, if unstopped, would lead to Catholicism proper.

Another proof of how seriously the Episcopal Church took the threat of Tractarianism can be found in its vilification of the man most receptive to Tractarian principles. In 1844 Bishop Onderdonk was falsely accused of public drunkenness by an assembly of Low Churchmen who gave the condemned man no opportunity to defend himself. Ironically, the man who finally suspended Onderdonk from the Anglican priesthood was none other than Bishop Chase of Illinois, the ultra protestant whom Newman found so distasteful. Chase, according to one biographer, shared the battle cry of the Evangelical party, "No priest, no Altar, no Sacrifice"—not a cry likely to win much sympathy from John Henry Newman, who once observed, "If the word, Altar, Absolution, or Succession are not in Scripture ... neither is the word Trinity."[45]

The taint of Romanism was of particular concern to the American Episcopal Church because it was faced with such aggressive competition from other Protestant sects ready to poach disaffected members. In a review of a book on the Anglo-American Church by Henry Caswall, an Englishman who travelled to America as a young man, studied at Kenyon College, and was ordained Deacon by the Bishop of Ohio, Newman described some of the sects driving the great evangelical revival in Antebellum America.[46] "Besides the old Calvinistic Baptists," he wrote, "there are the Free-will, the Seventh-day, and the Six-principle Baptists; the Christian Baptists, who deny the proper Divinity of Christ; and the Campbellite Baptists .... Besides these there are the Seed and Snake Baptists, who, carrying out the Calvinistic system, divide mankind by a rigid line into the seed of the woman and the seed of the serpent; and lastly, the Dunkers, who are principally German Baptists ..." Newman described these last as wearing "a peculiar dress, a long robe with a girdle and hood." In addition, they "let their beards grow, feed on roots and vegetables, live men with men and women with women, not meeting even in their devotions, have each his own cell, a bench for a bed, a block of wood for a pillow, admit works of supererogation, and deny the eternity of future punishment. This strange mockery of Catholic Truth," Newman noted, "numbers as many as 30,000 adherents." He also marveled at the fact that various Calvinistic sects considered "the religious education of children as a sacrilegious inter-ference with the work of divine grace." Then, again, among the Methodists, he recognized "the same disorders ... which marked their first rise in England." And with regard to the Quakers, "one-third have lately declared themselves Unitarians." And besides these, there were "600,000 Universalists, who teach the annihilation of the wicked ..."[47]

Catholics listening to this catalogue might be inclined to snigger but they should recall what Newman said about the Catholic hierarchy after he worked so hard to make the Catholic University succeed, against immense apathy and opposition: "I cannot help feeling that, in high circles, the Church is sometimes looked upon as made up of the hierarchy and the poor, and that the educated portion, men and women, are viewed as a difficulty, an encumbrance, as the seat and source of heresy; as almost aliens to the Catholic body, whom it would be a great gain, if possible, to annihilate."[48] One result of Newman's study of the American Church was to convince him that the laity, however inclined to private judgment, could not be ignored, though he also recognized that the Church could not simply truckle to the prejudices of the laity, especially those of the educated laity. At the same time, by founding the Catholic University, Newman sought to form an educated laity expressly, as he wrote: "To provide a series of sound and philosophical Defences of Catholicity and Revelation, in answer to the infidel tenets and arguments, which threaten us at this time."[49]

In comparing the Episcopal Church to the various Protestant sects, Newman was happy to concur with Caswall that its very survival argued a certain staying power. "At the same time," as Caswall noted, "the wonderful progress and improvement of the American Church serve to confute the Romanist, who asserts, that the Church of England is sustained merely by the secular arm, and that in the event of losing that support, she must of necessity become extinct."[50] The Anglican Church, which first held services in America in Jamestown in 1607, and eventually became the Episcopal Church, with its own episcopate, in 1789, was disestablished after the American Revolution, which Lyman Beecher saw as a good thing. "They say ministers have lost their influence," he wrote, but "the fact is, they have gained. By voluntary efforts, societies, missions, and revivals, they exert a deeper influence than ever they could by queues, and shoe buckles, and cocked hats and gold-headed canes."[51] Newman would have entirely agreed. Nonetheless, he never lost sight of the fact that if the Episcopal Church was free of the American state, it was still liable to become thrall to the American laity. "Nothing is more Christian than that the people of the Church should 'willingly offer' for her support," he wrote; "nothing more unchristian than that individual clergyman should be at the mercy of the people, and be under the temptation of 'preaching smooth things' …"[52]

But what is also striking about this essay, from the standpoint of Newman's own religious development, is that it was written in September 1839, a month after he experienced his first serious doubts about the legitimacy of the Anglican Church while reading about the Monophysites.[53] Following what he described in the *Apologia* as "that great revolution of mind," he resolved to test his doubts before acting on them—a period which consumed six long years of his life and involved him in sedulous deliberation.[54] In his review of Caswall's book, we can see Newman extolling the putative vitality of the American church with strenuous resolve, even as he calls it sharply into question. Here is a passage in point.

> All systems, then, which live and are substantive, depend on some or other inward principle or doctrine, of which they are the development. They are not a fortuitous assemblage of atoms from without, but the expansion of a moral element from within … While their inward life remains, they repair

their losses; if existing portions are cut off, they put out fresh branches. But when that life goes, they are no more; they have no being, they dissolve .... Such a creature of time and chance many men have thought and think our own Church to be; and such she is proved not to be, as in ten thousand other ways ... by her vigorous offshoots growing up in the West. She scattered some of her seeds in the wilderness; and, while for a time they seemed to die, a spirit at length was found within them, which rose, throve, and at length took outward shape like her own. Thus she proved herself to be a living principle ...

Reading that last sentence, after the skeptical preamble, one wonders whether Newman truly believed what he was saying. Later, in July 1840, he would write to a Scotch Episcopalian, who eventually converted with his wife and children, that "A great experiment is going on, whether Anglocatholicism has a root, a foundation, a consistency, as well as Roman Catholicism, or whether (in the language of the day) it be 'a sham.' I hold it to be quite impossible, unless it be real, that it can maintain its ground—it must fall to pieces ... If it be a mere theory, it will not work ... The internal consistence of the whole is being severely tested. I securely leave it to this issue—I will not defend if it if will not stand it."[55]

Still, despite the sanguine assessment of the American Episcopal Church that he gave in his article for the *British Critic*, Newman was candid enough when it came to expressing his reservations about the corrupting influence that a proud, self-satisfied, commercial people naturally exerted on a church that could never afford to offend the popular pleasure. "Nor in this respect are we better circumstanced than they," he pointedly reminded his English readers; "we too in the time of the third William and the first Georges had certain impressions of the same kind made on us, which chilled, attenuated, and shrivelled up our faith and spirit. What, indeed, is that desire of Evidences, that delight in objection and spontaneous incredulity, that pursuit of secular comfort, that contentment with mere decency and morality, which in its degree exist still among us all, but remains of the Socinian temper inflicted on us during that calamitous period? Nor have those malign influences ceased. They have worked their way unseen ..."[56] In returning to this "Socinian temper," Newman got at a fundamental feature of the American Episcopal Church, and indeed of its parent church in England.

A trading country is the *habitat* of Socinianism ... Not to the poor, the forlorn, the dejected, the afflicted, can the Unitarian doctrine be alluring, but to those who are rich and have need of nothing, and know not that they are "miserable and blind and naked;"—to such men Unitarianism so-called is just fitted, suited to their need, fulfilling their anticipations of religion, counterpart to their inward temper and their modes of viewing things. Those who have nothing of this world to rely upon need a firm hold of the next, they need a deep religion; they are as if stripped of the body while here,—as if in the unseen state between death and judgment; and as they are even now in one sense what they then shall be, so they need to view God such as they then will view Him; they endure, or rather eagerly desire, the bare vision of Him stripped of disguise, as they are stripped of disguises too; they desire to know that He is eternal, since they feel that they are mortal.[57]

Notwithstanding Newman's deep sympathy with the immigrants whose material wants would soon transform America, he also recognized that the typical Episcopalian did not suffer these wants, and he asked himself how the comparative and the peculiar type of wealth enjoyed by the Episcopalian influenced his religion. The Episcopalian tended to be a self-made tradesman, without the responsibilities of the landed gentry, and this, as Newman recognized, colored his religion. "He has rank without tangible responsibilities; he has made himself what he is, and becomes self-dependent; he has laboured hard or gone through anxieties, and indulgence is his reward. In many cases he has had little leisure for cultivation of mind, accordingly luxury and splendour will be his *beau ideal* of refinement. If he thinks of religion at all, he will not like from being a great man to become a little one; he bargains for some or other compensation to his self-importance, some little power of judging or managing, some small permission to have his own way.

> Commerce is free as air; it knows no distinctions; mutual intercourse is its medium of operation. Exclusiveness, separations, rules of life, observance of days, nice scruples of conscience, are odious to it. We are speaking of the general character of a trading community, not of individuals; and, so speaking, we shall hardly be contradicted. A religion which neither irritates their reason nor interferes with their comfort, will be all in all in such a society. Severity whether of creed or precept, high mysteries, corrective practices, subjection of whatever kind, whether to a doctrine or to a priest, will be offensive to them. They need nothing to fill the heart, to feed upon, or to live in; they despise enthusiasm, they abhor fanaticism, they persecute bigotry. They want only so much religion as will satisfy their natural perception of the propriety of being religious. Reason teaches them that utter disregard of their Maker is unbecoming, and they determine to be religious, not from love and fear, but from good sense.[58]

No better description of nominal Christianity has ever been penned. And yet what is no less remarkable about this scathing critique of private judgment is that it was written by the son of a banker, who, by all accounts, eschewed religion for precisely the same prudential reasons as Newman's trader.[59] So there is something of an autobiographical cast to this passage. What is also striking about the passage is that, for Catholics in the twenty-first century, it captures the ethos not only of Protestant but Catholic Christianity. While it is true that America's immigrants were mostly poor Catholics, who had no difficulty recognizing that they were "blind and miserable and naked," their descendants put poverty behind them and now many are indistinguishable from their erstwhile Episcopalian betters. They, too, preen themselves on their private judgment and cleave to a worldly, self-congratulatory, nominal faith.

One notably heroic American who had the God-given grace to differentiate the true Faith from private judgment was Levi Silliman Ives, the only Episcopal bishop to convert to Catholicism, who visited Newman at the Oratory for a week after he converted. Before converting, Ives was the Episcopalian Bishop of North Carolina. In 1848, he formed the religious Brotherhood of the Holy Cross, the Tractarian character of which caused it to be shut down. In 1852 he resigned his see and submitted to Pope Pius IX at Rome. His wife, a daughter of Bishop Hobart, converted with her husband. Ives returned to the United States in 1854, where he became a Professor at St Joseph's Seminary and St John's College, Fordham. His secession from the Episcopal Church inspired jubilant crowing from the *Paris L'Univers*, which, after alluding to "the conversion of so considerable a personage," remarked: "now neither rage nor falsehood can lessen the effect of the blow which heresy has received from this brilliant defection."[60] The *New York Times* saw the conversion in a surprisingly sympathetic light. "Bishop Ives," the paper reported, "must not only relinquish his episcopal connection with old friends and a large diocese filled with those who have been taught to reverence him for the most amiable of personal traits; but he must abandon the clerical profession entirely, because he possesses that unlucky appendage, a wife." Still, the paper observed, "Temporal considerations were ineffectual to prevent what he was led to regard as an act of conscientious necessity and the vast sacrifice he has made, in consequence, attests his sincerity. There is no position in the Catholic Church prepared for him, half so gratifying to ambition as the one he has forsaken. Whatever pious or personal regrets we may entertain about it, it is impossible not to admire a man, thus true to his convictions. It is his honesty, and not his creed, that we applaud."[61] Here was a man who might have reminded Newman of John Keble, another Rome-leaning Anglican whose wife made conversion inexpedient.

Like Newman, Ives was finally converted by the early Church Fathers. Newman's letters are full of eloquent testimony to the impact that the Greek Fathers had on him. In one, he wrote William Joseph O'Neill Daunt (1807–94), an Irish convert from Tullamore, who was secretary to Daniel O'Connell, the author of a popular novel called *The Wife Hunter* (1838) and later Mayor of Dublin: "You speak of feeling drawn to the religion of Ireland by your love of Ireland; I felt something like this as regards the Fathers. After my conversion I had a sensible pleasure in taking down the Volumes of St Athanasius, St Ambrose etc in my Library—The words rose in my mind 'I am at one with you now.'"[62] Ives was similarly drawn to the Fathers. In his spiritual autobiography, *The Trials of a Mind in its Progress to Catholicism* (1853), he showed how the Fathers forcefully disabused him of the Protestant fallacy that there was something called the "Primitive Church" different from the Catholic Church. He brilliantly brought the witness of the Fathers to bear to reaffirm the early Church's subscription not only to transubstantiation and baptismal regeneration but to papal primacy, which Pusey could never bring himself to acknowledge. "In short," Ives concluded, "the first five centuries taught as distinctly, though not as formally as did the Fathers of the Council of Trent, the various dogmas set forth by that Council as necessary to the faith and practice of the Christian man."[63] Still another admirable aspect of Ives was his respect for the unprevaricating voice of conscience. In his autobiography, Ives recounts how, before finally converting, "I had actually flattered myself into the belief that my doubts had left me, and that I could henceforward act with a quiet conscience on Protestant ground. But, on recovering from the stupefaction of overmuch sorrow, I found myself fearfully deceived; found that what I had taken for permanent relief of mind was only the momentary insensibility of opiates or exhaustion. When I came again to myself, however, I was visited with reflections which no man need envy. The concessions I made, in good faith, at the time, for the peace of the Church, and, as I had falsely supposed, for my own peace, rose up before me as so many concessions, and cowardly ones too, *to the god of this world*. So that I can say with the deepest truth that the friendliness which greeted me on my subsequent visitation through my diocese was most unwelcome to my heart. Every kind word of those who had spoken against the truth seemed a rebuke to me, every warm shake of the hand to fall like ice upon my soul. I felt that I had shrunk publicly from the consequences of that truth which God had taught me—felt that I had denied that blessed Master who had grievously revealed Himself to me. But blessed be His name for that grace which moved me to 'weep bitterly.' Persecution for Christ's sake would have been balm to my wounded conscience ..."[64] Here was an affirmation of the primacy of conscience formed by the authority of what Newman called the "One True Fold."[65]

In speaking of the competition that the Episcopal Church faced from other denominations, Newman could not but acknowledge that "the Church of Rome ... by means of its numerous and well-conducted schools and colleges ... is daily acquiring a more powerful hold upon the public mind ..."[66] Alexis de Tocqueville, on his first visit to America in 1831, wrote a childhood friend back in Paris of the "prodigious" growth of Catholicism in America. "Forty years ago there were thirty Catholics in New York. The chapel of the Spanish consulate could accommodate all of them. Today there are thirty thousand, and they have built six churches at their own expense. The same is true in all the large cities, even Boston, the heartland of Puritanism, which has two Catholic churches and a convent ... We found it almost universal in Canada. Today there are seven or eight hundred thousand Catholics in the United States, ten seminaries and a great many establishments of various kinds."[67] The historian who had so brilliantly uncovered the causes of the French Revolution also wished to identify the causes of Catholicism's rapid rise. His analysis was highly Newmanian. Of course, immigration from Catholic Europe, particularly Ireland, France, and Germany was a significant factor. But there were other reasons. "It is said," De Tocqueville wrote, "that there are numerous conversions, especially in frontier settlements. I can't prove it, but I can easily believe it; Protestantism has always struck me as being to the Christian religion what the constitutional monarchy is to politics—a kind of compromise between opposite principles, a way station between two different states, a system, in short, unequal to its own consequences and unable completely to satisfy the human spirit. As you know, I've always believed that constitutional monarchies would end up as republics; and I am likewise convinced that Protestantism, once it has run its course, will become natural religion. What I am telling you here is very keenly felt by many religious souls; they recoil from the prospect of their doctrines having this outcome, and fly to Catholicism, whose principles may be highly debatable, but where everything coheres."[68] Antebellum America might have been rife with every conceivable species of dissident Protestantism but it was the rise of this robust Catholicism, as De Tocqueville saw, which was most characteristic of religion in the rapidly expanding new republic. And, again, as Tocqueville confirms, the Church of Rome could boast of the allegiance of more than Europe's struggling immigrants. Disaffected Episcopalians, Methodists, even Transcendentalists, made their way to what St. Jeremiah called its "ancient paths."

Orestes Brownson (1803–1876), an autodidact from Vermont who edited his own *Brownson's Quarterly Review*, came to those paths by a rather circuitous route. Before converting, he was not only a Transcendentalist but, by turns, a Presbyterian, an atheist, a Unitarian, and a Saint-Simonian. Newman first learned of this brash convert after Brownson attacked what he contrived to imagine the heterodoxy of Newman's *Essay on Development*, which prompted a memorable response from Newman: Brownson, he told his good friend Henry Wilberforce, "has acted like an uncharitable vulgar half converted Yankee ..."[69] Nevertheless, after Brownson admitted that he had misunderstood Newman's argument, Newman graciously offered him a teaching position with his newly established Catholic University, though he was careful to limit the offer to a position teaching geography. Newman would not let Brownson instruct his suggestible charges in theology.[70]

Another American who would have an indirect connection with Newman was James Aloysius McMaster (1820–1886), a fiery, impetuous, wayward man, who seems to have been something of an American William George Ward without the charm. The Catholic Encyclopedia summed him up nicely: "He spared no one, high or low, who differed from him, and his invective was as bitter as an unlimited vocabulary could make it." Coincidentally enough, he had been very close to Arthur Carey in the General Theological Seminary. Clarence Walworth, in his account of the Oxford Movement in America, recalled how Carey and McMaster "walked together, talked together, and read together, eagerly discussing every new publication that issued from Oxford ..."[71] At the Seminary, McMaster also became friendly with the eventual converts Isaac Hecker and Walworth himself. After becoming a Catholic in 1845, McMaster accompanied Hecker and Walworth to the Redemptorist novitiate at Louvain. On the way, they also called on Newman at Littlemore in August 1845, two months before his own conversion. The impetuous McMaster made a strong impression on Newman. Afterwards, whenever he spoke of Rome-leaning Americans, ready to convert, he called them "McMasters." When the friend of Faber and future Oratorian Thomas Francis Knox visited Newman in 1846, he noted in his journal, "Knox is here for the morning. He is not to join us, but to travel for 2 years in America. I hope he will convert all the Mac Masters."[72] After McMaster discovered that he had no vocation, he returned to New York and set himself up as a Catholic editor. In July 1848 he purchased Bishop

Hughes's share in the New York *Freeman's Journal* and *Catholic Register*, and became sole proprietor and editor. When Brownson attacked his theory of development, McMaster came to his defense: "I feel very sorry for the brutal attack of Brownson," he wrote Newman. "We had to join hands ... for a time and to work together, but he then said he would write no more on the development question ... I know that many of the most influential Bishops here are displeased at his uncalled for attack on you; and I have reason to think that very few approve of it."[73] In 1862 President Lincoln barred McMaster's paper from circulation, and for a brief period he was imprisoned. At the time of the First Vatican Council, he was extravagantly ultramontane and a great champion of Pius IX. Newman must have been at once amused and gratified to receive, after the appearance of his *Letter to the Duke of Norfolk* (1875), this warm letter from James Baptist Purcell, the Archbishop of Cincinnati:

'Cincinnati 5th Feb. 1875

Revd Dear Dr Newman

Thank you from my heart for all your admirable writings in defence of Catholic truth. Thank you for your most able, and, it ought to be most satisfactory reply to Mr Gladstone.

Our sense of its great merits is imperfectly expressed in this week's Catholic Telegraph. And now we are shocked by the tirade of a violent, half crazy, and it is said, drunkard's abuse of that noble Championship of our rightful allegiance to the Church and to the State, by McMaster of the New York Freeman's Journal. You disregard the persecution which foolish, or even wicked, men seek to make you suffer for your advocacy of justice and truth, but on earth as in Heaven your reward is great indeed. An humble individual who enjoyed your edifying supper at the Oratory in Birmingham and heard one of your pious instructions, should probably ask pardon for this intrusion on your precious moments; but he could not bear his own reproaches if he did not make this amende for an American journalist's violence.

Go on, Dear Dr. Newman, in the warfare until death, if necessary for the truth – In caelo quies.

Most respectfully Yours J. B. Purcell Abp. Cin.

Archbishop Purcell was eloquent proof of the crucial influence that Newman and his work were having on American churchmen. But he would also have an even greater influence on the "numerous and well-conducted schools and colleges" that the immigrant Catholic Church was erecting up and down the country, stemming as it did from the educational principles that he first articulated in his *Idea of a University* and put into practice in the Catholic University in Dublin, of which he was Rector from 1851 to 1858. That influence has always had to contend with precisely the forces of errant private judgment that Newman warned against so prophetically in 1839. Yet, at the time that he was laying the foundation for the Catholic University, Newman sensed that he was accomplishing something that would prove seminal. "We are getting on with the University," he told Mrs. Bowden in August of 1855. "It is swimming against the stream, to move at all—still we are in motion. The great thing is *to set up* things ... It will be years before the system takes root, but my work will be ended when I have made a beginning."[74] From that bold beginning, good things continue to flow. Now, more than ever, Newman's principles guide the authentic Catholic University. As he affirmed in his sermon preached in the University Church in Dublin in 1856, "A great University is a great power, and can do great things; but, unless it be something more than human, it is but foolishness and vanity ... It is really dead, though it seems to live, unless it be grafted upon the True Vine ..."[75]

Corroboration for Newman's influence on American Catholicism can be found in an article Evelyn Waugh wrote for *Life* magazine in 1949. Waugh was never an uncritical observer of the United States. To his friend, Graham Greene, he once wrote, "*Of course* the Americans are cowards. They are almost all the descendants of wretches who deserted their legitimate monarchs for fear of military service."[76] But Waugh also saw the good points of America, and especially of its Catholicism. Speaking particularly of the contribution that the Irish made to the American Church, Waugh noted: "The Irish with their truculence and practical good sense have built and paid for the churches, opening new parishes as fast as the population grew; they have staffed the active religious orders and have created a national system of Catholic education." Waugh does not say as much explicitly but it is clear that this system of education was, in character, largely Newmanian. If Newman's idea of Catholic education hardly prevailed in Dublin against the shilly-shally of the Irish hierarchy or the indifference of Irish and English Catholics, it found fertile ground in America. And this bore out Newman's recognition of the true meaning of failure, for as he told Lord Braye, an old Etonian with whom he was friendly in his dotage, "It is the rule of God's Providence that we should succeed by failure."[77] Certainly, Waugh's description of the highly successful American system of Catholic colleges shows its distinct affinity with objects that Newman identified for the otherwise abortive Catholic University.[78] "Without help from the state," Waugh wrote, "indeed, in direct competition with it—the poor of the nation have covered their land with schools, colleges and universities, boldly asserting the principle that nothing less than an entire Christian education is necessary to produce Christians. For the faith is not a mere matter of learning a few prayers and pious stories at home. It is a complete culture infusing all human knowledge ... Their object is to transform a proletariat into a bourgeoisie; to produce a faithful laity, qualified to take its part in the general life of the nation; and in this way they are manifestly successful. Their students are not, in the main, drawn from scholarly homes. Many of them handle the English language uneasily ... But, when all of this is said, the Englishman, who can boast no single institution of higher Catholic education and is obliged to frequent universities that are Anglican in formation and agnostic in temper, can only applaud what American Catholics have done in the last hundred years."[79]

The autonomy of this Catholic network of schools and universities, which Waugh justly singled out for praise, was something Newman also valued, though his understanding of self-reliance had nothing Emersonian about it.

In using the term, Newman was careful to distance himself from "every wild religionist who makes himself his own prophet and guide, and despises Holy Fathers and ecclesiastical rulers." Still, he confirmed that "One of the main secrets of success is self-reliance. This seems a strange sentiment for a Christian journalist to utter; but we speak of self in contrast, not with a higher power, but with our fellow-men. He, who leans on others, instead of confiding in his own right arm, will do nothing great."[80]

Newman's insistence on self-reliance can serve as a well-deserved rebuke to those American Catholics who have abdicated their self-reliance and made very dubious alliances indeed with a secular State and its agents that have nothing but contempt for the very idea of Catholic education—indeed, with Catholicism itself. Newman remarked how literary men, throughout history, often relinquished their self-reliance for the same reason as universities, because they were convinced that none could "possibly prosper without the sanction of the State and the favour of great personages." To prove the fallacy of this, Newman cited the example of the English universities: "They have been dragooned, indeed, by tyrannical despotism; they have had theories, or have felt the passion of loyalty; they all but worship the law as the first of all authorities in heaven or upon earth; but when the question is that of submitting to the Government of the day, or to persons in power, it requires but little knowledge of the history, for instance, of Oxford, to be aware that it has been its rule to rely upon itself—upon its prejudices, if we will, but still on what was its own." And here he cited the example of how Oxford had voted out Sir Robert Peel, "its favourite son, the Leader of the Commons," after he apostatized over Catholic Emancipation—an ousting in which Newman had played an ardent part. In conclusion, Newman wrote, "we hope that no Catholic University that is or that shall be, with its vantage-ground of higher principles, will ever show less self-respect, consistency, and manliness, than Protestant Oxford, in standing on its own sense of right and falling back upon its own resources."[81]

One American who agreed with Newman that Catholic education, in order to be authentically Catholic, must exercise Catholic self-reliance was a man named, oddly enough, Jenkins, a priest of the diocese of Louisville, who was also a passionate defender of Catholic schools.[82] Now with a surname like Jenkins this might strike my readers as rather improbable.[83] But, as a matter of fact, in 1882 Thomas Jefferson Jenkins wrote a book insisting on the indispensability of autonomous Catholic education. When Newman received his copy, he assured Jenkins that it was "as seasonable here and important as it is in America."[84]

Earlier, I had occasion to touch on the ill-fated Tractarianism of St. Saviour's, Leeds. Well, St. Saviour's had an interesting American connection. Bishop Doane of New Jersey, the leader of the High Church party in America, was invited to preach at the opening of St. Saviour's in 1845. Ten years later, Doane's son converted to Rome, to his father's profound chagrin. In 1856, when he was studying in Rome, George Hobart Doane met Newman. Later, he even considered joining the Oratory, but chose instead to return to the United States, where he became a well-known monsignor in the Newark diocese, founding many churches, hospitals, schools, orphanages and academies, as well as the

Catholic Young Men's Society, which, in 1880, sent Newman very handsome congratulations on his receiving the red hat from Leo XIII. In these American young men, Newman might have seen the antithesis of certain other young men he had known at Oxford, who were as contemptuous of religion as they were keen on getting on. In his sermon *God's Will the End of Life*, Newman addressed these would-be fashionable young men directly. "You my brethren have not been born splendidly; you have no high connections; you have not learned the manner or caught the tone of good society ... yet you ape the sins of Dives while you are strangers to his refinement ... you think it the sign of a gentleman to set yourself above religion ... to look at Catholic or Methodist with impartial contempt ... The Creator made you it seems ... for this office and work, to be a bad imitation of polished ungodliness."[85]

The American Catholics who wrote to congratulate Newman had in view another office and it was Newman who helped form them, who continues to form their counterparts today. When John D'Arcy, the Bishop of South Bend, described the events that led to President Obama being honored by Notre Dame, he gave his compatriots and indeed the world a useful lesson in the baleful moral consequences that follow from educated men delivering themselves up to the direction of "polished ungodliness." In his statement, Bishop Darcy wrote:

> President Obama has recently reaffirmed, and has now placed in public policy, his long-stated unwillingness to hold human life as sacred. While claiming to separate politics from science, he has in fact separated science from ethics and has brought the American government, for the first time in history, into supporting direct destruction of innocent human life. This will be the 25th Notre Dame graduation during my time as bishop. After much prayer, I have decided not to attend the graduation. I wish no disrespect to our president; I pray for him and wish him well. I have always revered the Office of the Presidency. But a bishop must teach the Catholic faith "in season and out of season," and he teaches not only by his words — but by his actions. My decision is not an attack on anyone, but is in defense of the truth about human life ... Even as I continue to ponder in prayer these events ... so must Notre Dame. Indeed, as a Catholic University, Notre Dame must ask itself, if by this decision it has chosen prestige over truth.[86]

As this clear rejection of our own followers of Dives shows, the promise that Newman saw in American Catholicism is alive and well, though the "Socinian temper" spreads apace.

One of the great "what ifs" of Newman's career is what might have resulted if he had traveled himself to America. In June 1854, Archbishop John Hughes of New York wrote to assure Newman that the money and students America could offer the University would be immense. He also invited Newman to cross the Atlantic to give what he was convinced would be a lucrative lecture tour.[87] Thackeray, after his 1852 tour, described it as including "plenty of good fellows, merry dinners, and pleasant cigars."[88] In the first six weeks alone, he earned £500—a tidy sum—especially since he put it into US railway stocks, which yielded a profit of 8 percent.[89] Newman might not have been interested in the cigars but he could have used the lecture fees. As it happened, Newman never made the crossing: he was duty bound to leave Dublin and return to his Oratory. So, willy-nilly, a huge opportunity for raising funds for the Catholic University was lost. Still, Newman would always be grateful to Americans for their generous support. He was keenly aware that the ties he was forging with the Catholics of America would bear long-lasting fruit. "This our first step," he told Archbishop Kenrick, "important as it is, will be by the Divine blessing, only the humblest in a long series (of successive movements) which are to follow; that, many as may be our difficulties, we shall, by the generous prayers and the persevering alms of the faithful, be carried over them; and, that an undertaking, founded in the union of Catholics so widely dispersed and so various by circumstances, will issue in more than corresponding benefits, external and temporal, to many countries and many generations."[90]

These "generous prayers and persevering alms" of American Catholics will always make conclusions about Newman and the Americans inadvisable: their heroic story remains unfinished. Nevertheless, some provisional conclusions can be made. While Tractarianism initially galvanized the Anglican Church on both sides of the pond, it never overcame its inherent contradictions. At the same time, the Tractarian movement embroiled Anglicanism in an identity crisis that, far from resolving its divisions, exacerbated them. What was perhaps most instructive about Tractarianism for Newman was that it corroborated something John Adams told Benjamin Rush in 1812: "No clear headed Man; no Man who sees all the consequences of a proposition can be an orthodox Church of England Man without being a Roman Catholic."[91] After Newman converted, despite his hopes for the revival of the English Catholic Church, which he expressed so unforgettably in "The Second Spring" (1852), it was in America, and, particularly in its network of schools and colleges, as Waugh intimated, that his vision for the future of Catholicism found its amplest embodiment.

In 1885, an anonymous friend of Newman's sent him a circular soliciting support for the nascent Catholic University of America. Newman wrote to James Gibbons, the Archbishop of Baltimore, welcoming "with the warmest interest the eloquent appeal of your University Board to the Catholics of the United States ... At a time when there is so much in this part of the world to depress and trouble us as to our religious prospects, the tidings which your Circular conveys of the actual commencement of so great an undertaking on the other side of the Ocean ... will rejoice the hearts of all educated Catholics in these Islands ..."[92] Gibbons assured Newman that: "though you have reached the evening of life, you are still regarded by us all as a tower of strength."[93] And so he remains. But the most eloquent testimony to Newman's influence on his American contemporaries came from the Rev. Clarence Walworth of St. Mary's Church, Albany, New York, who wrote to Newman in July 1866: "In truth, if you knew all the affectionate interest felt in all you do and say by so many converts in America whom your earlier writings have either led into the Church, or at least introduced to a knowledge of Catholic truth, you would feel that we have ... great claim on you in this country as children have upon a spiritual Father."[94]

CHAPTER 10

On the Track of Truth: Newman and Richard Holt Hutton

In the contemporary response to Newman and his work no figure stood out more than Richard Holt Hutton (1826–1897), the editor of the *Spectator*, who wrote over thirty essays on Newman, as well as a wonderfully incisive short biography. There is some irony in this, for Newman was continually misrepresented by journalists. "Of course there have been endless hits against me in Newspapers, Reviews, and Pamphlets," he told R. W. Church in 1864.[1] And although a crack journalist himself—his pieces in the *British Critic* and the *Rambler* show him to have been a well-informed, astute, lively judge of the passing scene—he tended to take a dim view of the public prints. Yet, as I shall show, he recognized their pivotal place in the formation of public opinion and was glad to have so independent-minded and capable a journalist as Hutton reviewing his books. Hutton, for his part, was equally critical of the periodical press, and in Newman's work he saw a bracing antidote to the influential fallacies of its approved sages. In placing Newman and his work squarely within his contemporary milieu, Hutton showed how they transcended that milieu. In this chapter, I shall revisit the correspondence and the work of the two men to show how they followed what Hutton called "the track of truth" in an age increasingly convinced that truth was unknowable.

The years directly prior to their correspondence were the years leading up to the writing of the *Apologia* (1864), when Newman was beset with troubles. He was worried that the Oratory School was losing its distinctly Catholic character. He was under a cloud at Rome for his article, "Consulting the Laity in Matters of Doctrine" (1859). He was accused of "moral dishonesty" by the Bishop of Oxford.[2] He was even rumored to be contemplating rejoining the Church of England. Such "gross misrepresentations," as he called them, were nothing new: he had been on the receiving end of malicious gossip for years.[3] Now, however, he had begun to find it especially wearying. "I have tried to do works for God year after year," he confessed, "and for thirty years ... they have all failed. My first sermon as an Anglican, was on the text 'Man goes forth to his work and to his labour until the evening;' and now the evening is come and I have done nothing ... it is most difficult to go on working in the face of thirty years disappointment ... every thing seems to crumble under my hands, as if one were making ropes of sand."[4] Yet Newman never lost sight of the sum of his trials. "I know I am deeply deficient in that higher life which lasts and grows in spite of the ills of mortality—but had I ever so much of supernatural love and devotion, I could not be in any different state from the Apostle, who in the most beautiful of his epistles speaks with such touching and consoling vividness of those troubles, in the midst of which these earthen vessels of ours hold the treasure of grace and truth."[5] When Charles Kingsley attacked his veracity in *Macmillan's Magazine* in January 1864, charging that "Father Newman informs us that truth for its own sake need not, and on the whole ought not to be, a virtue with the Roman clergy," Newman resolved to reacquaint himself with this "treasure of grace and truth."[6] But before he began writing the *Apologia*—the spiritual autobiography which he would compose in seven heroic weeks in what he told his friend Frederic Rogers was "the most arduous work ... I ever had in my life"—he received favorable notice from Hutton in a *Spectator* piece.[7] Of the initial correspondence between Kingsley and Newman, which Newman published in pamphlet form, Hutton observed: "Mr. Kingsley has just afforded, at his own expense, a genuine literary pleasure to all who can find intellectual pleasure in the play of great powers of sarcasm, by bringing Father Newman from his retirement, and showing not only one of the greatest of English writers, but, perhaps, the very greatest master of delicate and polished sarcasm in the English language ..."[8] After Newman thanked Hutton for the "flattering notice"[9] he had taken of him, Hutton thanked Newman for the great influence he had exerted on him:

> Your kind note gave me great pleasure though it was quite needless, as my article was a mere act of justice. It gives me however an opportunity which I have long wished for of expressing to you personally my profound admiration of your genius and my gratitude for the influence of your writings generally, which though they failed to persuade me of the truth of the Roman Catholic principles, have done more to enlarge and I believe also in many respects elevate my own faith than any other writer of the time when my mind was first turned to these subjects. Widely as of course I must differ from you, I trust I shall never forget the debt I owe you. 'Loss and Gain' was in some sense an era in my life, though it did not produce the only impression which you would say it ought to have produced.[10]

The passage from *Loss and Gain* (1847) that made such an indelible impression on Hutton was at the core of why Newman affected him so deeply and it would crop up in his correspondence and his reviews again and again. Speaking of the Mass, one of the book's characters says: "It is not a mere form of words,—it is a great action, the greatest action that can be on earth. It is, not the invocation merely, but, if I dare use the word, the evocation of the Eternal. He becomes present on the altar in flesh and blood, before whom angels bow and devils tremble. This is that awful event which is the scope, and is the interpretation, of every part of the solemnity. Words are necessary, but as means, not as ends; they are not mere addresses to the throne of grace, they are instruments of what is far higher, of consecration, of sacrifice."[11] This passage meant so much to Hutton because it touched on many of the themes that preoccupied him: not only faith, but the relationship between authority and personal belief; the reality of words; and the primacy of action in all religious endeavor. It also called into question the rationalism that Hutton had acquired as a Unitarian and never entirely abandoned.

Since I shall be looking at Newman's relationship with Hutton, in part, as a study in influence, it will be helpful to put that influence in some context. A number of nineteenth-century literary men would attest Newman's influence, especially those unpersuaded by "the truth of Roman Catholic principles." In 1871 Matthew Arnold wrote to Newman to say that "no words can be too strong to express the interest with which I used to hear you at Oxford, and the pleasure with which I continue to read your writings now. We are all of us carried in ways not of our own making or choosing, but nothing can ever do away the effect you have produced upon me, for it consists in a general disposition of mind rather than in a particular set of ideas. In all the conflicts I have with modern Liberalism and Dissent, and with their pretensions and shortcomings, I recognize your work; and I can truly say that no praise gives me so much pleasure as to be told (which sometimes happens) that a thing I have said reminds people, either in manner or matter, of you."[12] After Newman sent a letter to his old friend Mark Pattison, when the latter was sick and dying, the frustrated academic on whose intensely cerebral character George Eliot based Mr. Casaubon in *Middlemarch* (1871–1872), wrote back: "If I have not dared to approach you in any way of recent years, it has been only from the fear that you might be regarding me as coming to you under false colours. The veneration and affection which I felt for you at the time you left us, are in no way diminished and however remote my intellectual standpoint may now be from that which I may presume to be your own, I can still truly say that I have learnt more from you than from any one else with whom I have ever been in contact."[13] Even Walter Bagehot, the Unitarian founder of the *Economist*, and one of Hutton's best friends, had good things to say about Newman's influence: "Nothing but a very long illness could have prevented my acknowledging before the kind gift of your poems. I have known these in the Lyra by heart for many years, and am deeply gratified at being brought into personal communication with one whose writings – amid much difference of opinion – have fallen so deep into my mind. I should hold that some of the poems indeed have an intrinsic claim to a permanent place in English literature ... With the greatest respect of *very* many years standing, I am Yours sincerely Walter Bagehot."[14]

Pleased as he was with these warm testimonials, Newman recognized something different in Hutton's writings. They were the witness not merely of an admirer or even a critic but a man in search of the truth. Hutton read and wrote about Newman largely to prosper his own evolving faith. He was particularly interested in how Newman tackled the themes of skepticism and authority, since these were the matters that most troubled him in his struggles with his own Christian faith. As their correspondence proceeded, a true bond grew up between the two men. In one characteristic letter, Hutton confided to Newman: "It was a very real and deep satisfaction to me to know that you find a good deal in my essays that seems to you on the track of truth. If any thing you or any one else has written should strike you as likely to help me in any of my difficulties, I am sure I may trust you to point it out. I sometimes almost despair of gaining in this life the light I crave."[15] Here was a religious seriousness that deeply appealed to Newman. But what also appealed to him was Hutton's astute sympathy. In order to appreciate that sympathy, we should know something of Hutton's life.

Richard Holt Hutton, whom John Morley thought "the finest and bravest critic of his generation," was born in Leeds in 1826.[16] Both his father and grand-father—a lachrymose Dubliner—were Unitarian ministers. A short-sighted, diminutive, self-effacing man, Hutton was educated at University College, London, with the expectation that he would follow in his forebears' footsteps, but he chose instead to prepare himself for a career in the law. When the law proved unsuitable, he turned to journalism. It was at the "godless place in Gower Street" that Hutton first met Walter Bagehot, with whom he would become a close friend and colleague. "It is sometimes said," he wrote in a reminiscence of Bagehot, "that it needs the quiet of a country town remote from the capital, to foster the love of genuine study in young men. But of this, at least, I am sure, that Gower Street, and Oxford Street, and the New Road, and that dreary chain of squares from Euston to Bloomsbury, were the scenes of discussions as eager and as abstract as ever were the sedate cloisters or the flowery river-meadows of Cambridge or Oxford. Once I remember, in the vehemence of an argument as to whether the so-called logical principle of identity (A is A) were entitled to rank as 'a law of thought' or only as a postulate of language, Bagehot and I wandered up and down Regent Street for something like two hours in the vain attempt to find Oxford Street ..."[17]

After taking his M.A. in 1845 Hutton went on, first, to the University of Bonn, where he studied with Theodor Mommsen, the great historian of Rome, (whose disparagement of Cicero would not have met with Newman's approval) and, then, to the University of Heidelberg, where he studied under the Unitarian James Martineau's son Russell. On his return in 1847, Hutton briefly prepared for the Unitarian ministry at Manchester New College (where Newman's brother Frank taught classics after resigning his Balliol fellowship), before returning to Germany to study theology with the Martineaus *père et fils*. Matthew Arnold, who was in Europe at this same volatile time, came away enamored of what he regarded as the Continent's superior intellectual life. England, he told his sister in 1848, "is ... *far behind* the Continent. In conversation, in the newspapers, one is so struck with the fact of the utter insensibility ... of people to the number of ideas and schemes now ventilated on the Continent—not because they have judged them or seen beyond them, but from sheer habitual want of wide reading and thinking ... I am not sure but I agree in Lamartine's prophecy that 100 years hence the Continent will be a great united Federal Republic, and England, all her colonies gone, in a dull steady decay."[18] Although an admirer of European literature, Hutton was never uncritical of it, and as a result he was spared the grandiosity and the vagueness that often afflicted Arnold when he wrote of European authors. His fondness for Goethe and Heine, for example, bordered on hero-worship. As the bookman H.W. Garrod once observed, Arnold never dropped "the cosmopolitan pose, the affectation of being born on the Continent."[19] .

On his return from Germany, Hutton succeeded the poet Arthur Hugh Clough as Principal of University Hall, Gordon Square, which had been set up as a religious meeting place for Dissenters enrolled at University College, but he resigned after one year due to poor health. In 1851, his journalistic career began when he was invited to join the editorial staff of the weekly *Inquirer*, the Unitarian paper, which reunited him with Bagehot. At the same time, he married Anne Roscoe, the sister of his friend and fellow editor, William Roscoe. No sooner did he marry, however, than his health worsened. Ordered south by his doctor, Hutton and his wife succumbed to yellow fever in Barbados. In 1852, when he finally recovered from a week-long coma, he awoke to find his young wife dead, a shock which only deepened his interest in the world beyond the grave. Six years later, he married Elizabeth Roscoe, a first cousin of his first wife, to whom he was devoted. Like T. S. Eliot, another High Churchman cradled in Unitarianism, Hutton left instructions in his will that no biography should be written. Consequently, little is known about his domestic life—or, for that matter, his professional life. Although he held the professorship of Mathematics at Bedford College, London, he spent most of his time on his editorial and critical work. Over the course of his career, Hutton wrote over 7,000 articles and over 3,000 essays for various papers, including the *Inquirer*, the *National Review*, the *Economist*, the *North British Review*, the *Saturday Review*, the *Spectator* and the *Contemporary Review*. The only sure thing we know about his personal life is that, again like Eliot's, it was rife with misery. Elizabeth, after being knocked down by a horse and carriage in 1888, succumbed to deep depression and for the last nine years of her life declined to speak to her aggrieved husband. H. H. Asquith, whom Hutton hired to write leaders for the *Spectator*, observed how "His devotion to his poor mad wife makes an almost unique story."[20] Six months after his wife's death, on 9 September 1897, Hutton fell into a coma and died at his home at Crossdeep Lodge, Twickenham.

Another thing we know about Hutton is that he brought a keen sense of purpose to his professional life. Unlike many of his colleagues, he did not disdain reviewing or resort to it merely to take his mind off other business or to confound his enemies. For Hutton, the reviewer had an important job to perform, however lowly it might be in the larger scheme of literature. "No doubt it is a trial to men steeped in the culture of the noblest literature in the world, to appreciate fairly the ephemeral productions of a busy generation," he wrote. However, he was convinced that, "The more they trample it beneath them, the less are they competent to detect its higher tendencies. But still the critic who allows this feeling to grow upon him abdicates his true office. Unless he can enter into the wants of his generation, he has no business to pretend to direct its thoughts."[21]

In this, Newman would have entirely agreed. However critical he might have been of the biases of newspapers, magazines and periodicals, he recognized that they offered an important forum for the defense of truth. That he wrote one of his very best works of controversy, *The Tamworth Reading Room* (1841), as a series of letters to *The Times* was proof of his own readiness to enter that forum. For Newman, writing was a form of action, and the field in which that action was carried out was often London. As he pointed out in the *Rise and Progress of Universities*, "In every great country, the metropolis itself becomes a sort of necessary University, whether we will or no. As the chief city is the seat of the court, of high society, of politics, and of law, so as a matter of course is it the seat of letters also; and at this time, for a long term of years, London and Paris are in fact and in operation Universities, though in Paris its famous University is no more, and in London a University scarcely exists except as a board of administration." Hutton and Bagehot would certainly have objected to this Oxonian dismissal of University College London but not to what Newman had to say otherwise. In London, "The newspapers, magazines, reviews, journals, and periodicals of all kinds, the publishing trade, the libraries, museums, and academies there found, the learned and scientific societies, necessarily invest it with the functions of a University; and that atmosphere of intellect, which in a former age hung over Oxford or Bologna or Salamanca, has, with the change of times, moved away to the centre of civil government. Thither come up youths from all parts of the country, the students of law, medicine, and the fine arts, and the *employés* and *attachés* of literature. There they live, as chance determines; and they are satisfied with their temporary home, for they find in it all that was promised to them there … They have not learned any particular religion, but they have learned their own particular profession well. They have, moreover, become acquainted with the habits, manners, and opinions of their place of sojourn, and done their part in maintaining the tradition of them. We cannot then be without virtual Universities; a metropolis is such: the simple question is, whether the education sought and given should be based on principle, formed upon rule, directed to the highest ends, or left to the random succession of masters and schools, one after another, with a melancholy waste of thought and an extreme hazard of truth."[22]

Hutton took advantage of this "virtual University" by writing primarily about figures whose work was likely to endure, including Wordsworth, Carlyle, Browning, Clough, Arnold, George Eliot, Tennyson, Trollope, Thackeray and Newman.

Although he commanded a loyal readership, Hutton bristled at being thought overly intellectual. "I quite understand, my dear Richard, your mortification at being called too profound in your teaching," Martineau once commiserated with his friend after he was criticized for trying to explain Hegel to his readers, "I faithfully believe we must bear up against this reproach, and speak faithfully what is given us to say, without much regard to that standard of usage which regulates 'unintelligibilities.'"[23] That Hutton came in for such criticism is surprising; compared to our own academic reviewers, he is a model of clarity. Nevertheless, doubtless because of his serious moral interests, his Victorian contemporaries read him with avidity. Indeed, the *Spectator* was the most successful paper not only in England but throughout the British Empire. Even the *Spectator*'s chief competitor, the Tory *Speaker*, conceded that "bit by bit the conviction has been forced on us that if English journalism has a chief he is to be found in Mr. Hutton."[24]

Hutton's criticism is still undervalued. In addition to the 36 essays he wrote on Newman, principally for the *Spectator*, Hutton also wrote particularly insightful pieces about Bagehot, whom G. M. Young considered "the greatest Victorian." And consistently good pieces on Tennyson. In one, he observed "There is a not a single one of his greater poems which does not bear the signs of careful thought and meditation, not to say study. There is both care and ease in every line,—the care of delicate touches, the ease which hides the care. Tennyson is not a poet whose poetry bubbles up and flows on with the superfluous buoyancy and redundancy of a fountain or rapid. It is inlaid with conscious emotion, saturated with purpose and reflection. Its grace and ease—and it is almost always graceful and easy—are the grace and ease of vigilant attention. There is what theologians call 'recollection' in every line."[25] *Recollection*, in this sense, according to the *Oxford Dictionary of the Christian Church*, is "A term used by spiritual writers to denote the concentration of the soul on the presence of God. It involves the renunciation of all avoidable dissipations and its use is habitually recommended to all those who wish to lead an interior life. In a more restricted sense the word is applied to a certain stage of prayer, in which the memory, understanding, and will are held to be stilled by Divine action and the soul left in a state of peace in which grace can work without hindrance."[26] This opens a path to *In Memoriam* (1850), which has not yet been properly explored. About Newman's verse, Hutton recognized that it "engraves even more powerfully because with a greater reticence and severer reserve of manner, the scars and vestiges of a unique experience."[27] Towards the end of his career, Hutton even wrote a piece about the young Henry James, in which he observed: "The duty of lucid observation ... is almost the only duty which ... Mr. Henry James thoroughly and universally approves. A sadder remnant of the old Puritanism is not easy to conceive."[28] As these few examples show, Hutton's view of literature was robustly moral, even Johnsonian. Unsurprisingly, in the predominantly *l'art pour l'art* critical milieu of the twentieth century, Hutton's criticism fell out of favor and it has never regained its former vogue.

Nevertheless, it is precisely his moral approach to literature that makes him a reliable guide to Newman's literary achievement. Although he pays frequent tribute to Newman's mastery of English style, he is careful to specify the source of that mastery. "That [Newman] has the most musical and the most lustrous of English styles, would be nothing, if that style itself were not a living witness of the supernatural life in him which it expresses and reveals. For no one can love the style and not feel that its tenderness, and its severity, its keen thrusts and its noble simplicity, its flexibility of movement and its firm grasp, its ideal music, its iridescent lights, and its pathetic sweetness, could never have existed at all except as the echo of a great mind living under the immediate eye of God."[29] This understanding of the moral import of Newman's literary achievement enabled Hutton to rate Newman's work as a whole more accurately than most of his contemporaries, or indeed, most subsequent critics. In his biography of Newman, Hutton remarks in the opening of his chapter on "Newman as a Roman Catholic:" "I do not know that he ever again displayed quite the same intensity of restrained and subdued passion as found expression in many of his Oxford sermons. But in irony, in humour, in eloquence, in imaginative force, the writing of the later and, as we may call it, the emancipated portion of his career far surpass the writings of his theological apprenticeship."[30]

This refutes the undiscriminating claim that Newman, from a literary standpoint, never surpassed his Anglican writings, a view which James Joyce was fond of sharing with his European friends when he was living in Paris in the 1930s. "As usual I am in a minority of one," he wrote his patron, the long-suffering Englishwoman, Harriet Weaver. "If I tell people that no tenor voice like Sullivan's has been heard in the world for 50 years or that Zaporoyetz, the Russian basso, makes Chaliapin sound like a cheap whistle or that nobody has ever written English prose that can be compared with that of a tiresome footling little Anglican parson who afterwards became a prince of the only true church they listen in silence. These names mean nothing to them. And when I have stumbled out of the room no doubt they tap their foreheads and sigh."[31] Hutton argued that at least three of the Catholic works of this "prince of the only true church" were among his very best. Of *Loss and Gain* (1847), that charming, gentle, witty book, which is suffused with the playful spirit of the Florentine St. Philip Neri, the founder of the Oratory, whom Newman would take as his patron, Hutton confessed, "the book has been a great favourite with me, almost ever since its first publication, partly for the admirable fidelity with which it sketches young men's thought and difficulties, partly for its happy irony, partly for its perfect representation of the academical life and tone of Oxford."[32] In a prior chapter we have seen how much Hutton admired Newman's *Lectures on Anglican Difficulties* (1850). Indeed, for Hutton, "In matter and style alike, these lectures were marked by all the signs of his singular literary genius ... and more exquisite in form as well as more complete in substance than the *Essay on Development*, which was written under the heavy pressure of the dreaded and anticipated rupture between himself and the Church of his baptism."[33] Hutton was also one of the first critics to call attention to the brilliance of that exuberant book, *Lectures on the Present Position of Catholics in England* (1851), noting how, "There are passages in these lectures which pass the limits of irony and approach the region of something like controversial farce"—which was indeed how Newman chose to approach the ubiquitous bigotry that Catholics suffered in Protestant England.[34] Moreover, Hutton made a shrewd point about the equipoise that Newman maintains in his work: "His satire could not be as powerful as it is without his imaginative power of isolating what he wants to emphasize and contrasting it with its opposite. But it is when he exerts his flexible and vivid imagination in depicting the deepest religious passion that we are most carried away by him and feel his great genius most truly. Little as I am a Roman Catholic, I can never read without emotion, without a thrill of wonder at the power with which Dr. Newman describes what to Protestants seems most unlike the religion of Christ, his defence of the Mass in answer to the Protestant account of it as a mere muttered spell."[35]

Apropos his religious views, Hutton wrote Newman in September 1865: "Mr Martineau ... first made me see that the old Unitarianism was as weak as it was unsuccessful. Maurice first taught me that a belief in the Incarnation could be held on the Protestant basis, and all your books, Loss and Gain especially, have given me gleams of light which I have not found elsewhere. But since the last step I have stood still ..."[36] It was James Martineau (1805–1900), the intellectual leader of the new Unitarianism, whose "name was a word of fear in quiet households," who impressed upon Hutton that "Reason is the ultimate appeal, the supreme tribunal, to the test of which even Scripture must be brought."[37] As important as this principle became in Hutton's religious views, it was Maurice who finally extricated him from Unitarianism. In any discussion of Newman's influence on Hutton, it is essential to appreciate that it was always tempered by the influence of Maurice. In *F.D. Maurice and the Crisis of Christian Authority*, Jeremy Morris suggests what it was about Maurice's understanding of authority that appealed to Hutton. Maurice "upheld a 'High Church' conception of order and doctrine, insisting, for example, on episcopacy and on an ordered liturgical life as essential features of the universal Church, at the same time as attempting to prize apart these institutional aspects of the Church, or 'signs,' from particular theological lines of interpretation. In ... the 1830s, his blending of High Church doctrine and the 'Broad Church' principle of comprehensiveness came to fruition."[38] For Maurice, the Anglican Church was "most Catholic when most Protestant."[39] Here was the rather rarefied position that Hutton embraced himself, when, in 1862, he entered the Established Church, where he remained a High Churchman of the Mauricean cast for the remaining 35 years of his life.

Newman's view of Maurice was characteristically nuanced. As early as 1835, he wrote, "I am annoyed but not surprised about Maurice. He will hardly go the lengths you report. He has corresponded with Pusey, I believe. He is a Coleridgian and a Platonist, I believe – and so though not far from a Catholic, when contrasted with Rationalists, yet some way off too. He is of the Cambridge School – and from the little I have seen of those men, they seem to me never satisfied to take things as they find them, but to be always meddling and (as they think) improving truths which have been from the beginning – and to believe sacred doctrines, not because they have received them, but because they can prove them from philosophy. M. himself is an excellent and very deserving, as well as clever man, but I wish all those men would have something more of childlike faith."[40] Later, in 1863, after their differences had become patent, Newman wrote Maurice, "Of course we view the most important matters in very different lights; and there is no prospect, I fear, of this difference ceasing; but I ever shall rejoice at every soul whom you, or any one else who differs from me, saves from the abyss of infidelity or scepticism, and converts to a living faith in our Lord and Saviour."[41]

That Hutton's Mauricean Anglicanism had nothing to do with Tractarianism is clear from his acute criticism of that mandarin faith. "Puseyism," he wrote in one essay, "owns positively no living authority at all; it has no principle of development; it is averse to all principles of development; its desire is to live by the customs and observances of a past age. It talks, indeed, of the authority of the Church. But if you come to look into the meaning of what is said, you find it to mean only that clerical gentleman—especially bishops—are rather more likely to understand what was the ancient practice and the ancient creed than anyone else. But it is very far from recognising any practical and present dogmatic authority even in bishops or archbishops."[42] This shows how much Hutton agreed with the analysis of Puseyism that Newman mounted in his King William Street lectures. At the same time, Hutton's Protestantism was entirely free of that tribal hatred of Catholics, which defined so many nineteenth-century English Protestants. In one letter to Newman, for example, Hutton observed: "Protestant as I am,—thoroughly and cordially Protestant in principle,—my heart burns at the unfairness with which Protestants so often treat their Roman Catholic opponents."[43] Another proof of his independence of mind was his siding with the North during the American Civil War—he was a decided abolitionist—at a time when most of his English contemporaries were thoroughly in favor of the South.[44] But perhaps the best example of Hutton's evenhandedness can be found in his assessment of Newman's *Essay on the Development of Christian Doctrine*, in which he asks:

> ... who can fail to be grateful to the man who has insisted that a genuine "development" of revealed truth must preserve intact the original type, must keep continuously to the principles of the primitive doctrinal teaching, must show the power adequately to assimilate nutriment foreign yet subservient to it and to throw off alien material, must be able to show early indications that such a development would be likely, must be logically consistent with all that was originally taught, must be able to protect itself by "preservative additions" which secure the type instead of altering it, and, finally, must show tenacity of life? How far Dr. Newman's instances of those tests of development make good his own position is a very different question indeed —is, indeed, a question like that whether the House of Commons can be considered a "preservative addition" to the monarchy, or rather an addition which, while it has preserved it for centuries, is likely some day to supersede it. But what I hold to be the enormous value of Dr. Newman's essay is that it puts us on the way to a *true* investigation of the claims of our various churches to represent the primitive revelation of Christ. Do we or do we not preserve the original type? Do we or do we not show a continuity of principle with that primitive Christianity? Do we show any power of assimilating life from without, and imposing the structural law of Christian hearts upon that life from without? Can we show the power to reject as alien to us what is poisonous to Christian habits of life? Can we show early anticipations of our modern religious developments? Can we prove our logical continuity with the old teaching? Are our "preservative additions" monstrous innovations tending to the neglect of the deepest truths, or real provisions for the security of the Christian life? And is there true buoyancy and vital tenacity in our developments, or an ever-growing languor of life?

All these are questions which are no less relevant, and far more important, in regard to developments of revelation, than they are in biology in determining whether certain changes of structure cause an improvement or a marked degeneration of the stock which exhibits them. One of the great evidences of Cardinal Newman's genius is the proof that his mind was running on the tests of genuine developments and corruptions in doctrine, long years before the mind of the day had been awakened by Darwin and his contemporaries to the true touchstone of development or degeneration in biological forms.[45]

This independence of mind made Hutton an insightful judge of the pretensions of agnostics. If there is a common thread running through his criticism it is his impatience with the spurious authority that so many of the agnostics of his age were setting up in place of the authority of the Church. "Nothing is more surprising than the extravagance of Agnostics," he wrote in an essay entitled "Agnostic Dreamers" (1884). "After taking all the pains in the world to destroy the idols, as they think them, of Christian worship, after carefully demonstrating that a living God in the Christian sense of the term is a contradiction in terms, and that the life everlasting cannot rationally be attributed to beings deprived of their bodily existence ... they immediately proceed to substitute for these idols mere dolls of their own fashioning and dressing—dolls which they make no secret of having deliberately fashioned and dressed up for the occasion, and which, nevertheless, they dandle enthusiastically in their arms, and hold up as a sort of make-believe adoration, as the true and rational substitute for the old religions."[46] The agnostics of the age were convinced that the new dolls of skepticism were supplanting the old idols of religion "because," as Hutton wrote, they were convinced that "scientific wonder is deeper than ignorant wonder; because the geologist is capable of realising better how long it took to denude the rocks than any mere rustic, or traveller in search of the picturesque; because the astronomer who knows how big the spots on the sun are, can wonder at the energy of solar heat to better purpose than the Psalmist who talked of the heavens as declaring the glory of God and the firmament as showing His handiwork ..." But Hutton was unimpressed. Speaking specifically of what Herbert Spencer, the celebrated positivist called the "Infinite and Eternal Energy," Hutton observed: "Religion, to mean anything, must mean worship ... What is it to me, to be able to realise how many thousands of years the rocks were in getting themselves denuded; how many earths would go into one solar spot; how utterly insoluble the great enigma is? Even if I could realise these things better than any geologist alive, better than the most original of the astronomers, better than Mr. Spencer himself, I should be no nearer a religion. If the 'Infinite and Eternal Energy' is simply beyond the reach of either vision or thought, and can hope for no more living aid from it than from the unknown quantity of an insoluble equation, the 'sentiment' which it must excite in me cannot but be the most barren and empty in the world. It comes very much, so far as I can see, to the old Oriental notion of 'Om'—as absolute being and also absolute nothingness." Here one can hear the man who relished exposing not only the credulity but the nihilism of skepticism. "So far as religion is worth a farthing," he insisted, "it is founded on a real vision of what is far above us, and, nevertheless, more or less within our reach, and on an intense yearning to reach after it."[47] This was the conviction that made Hutton such a perceptive reader of Newman, whose own approach to the supernatural was equally practical.

With his interest in the real and the practical, it was understandable that Hutton should have paid so much critical attention to the materialism of Darwin, Spencer, Huxley, Mill, Clifford, and Tyndall. In a piece called "The Various Causes of Scepticism," he showed how skeptics could not escape the truth they denied.

God is not less behind the consciousness of men who have no glimpse of Him through their consciousness, than He is within the heart of those who worship Him; and the only real rejection of God is the resistance to His Word, whether it be felt as His Word, or only as a mysterious claim on the human will which it is impossible adequately to define. I hold that, in a sense, God is Himself, in all probability, no infrequent cause of the blindness of men to His presence. He retires behind the veil of sense when He wishes us to explore the boundaries of sense, and to become fully aware of a life beyond. The physicists of every school are doing this great work for us now. They are explaining, mapping all the currents of physical influence, and from time to time crying out, like Professor Huxley, for "the hen-coop" of which, like shipwrecked sailors, they see no sign; like Professor Tyndall, for the elevating idealism which is conspicuous by its absence in all their investigations; like Professor Clifford, for something to replace the theism of Kingsley and Martineau. To suppose that the men who are doing this great work—who are mapping for us the quicksands and sunken rocks of physical scepticism,—are necessarily deserted by God, because they do not see Him, is to be more truly atheists than any physicist. There is a scepticism which is of God's making, in order that we may see how many of the highest springs of human life are founded in trust,—how everything else fails, even in the highest minds, to produce order, peace, and clam. The physicists of to-day are suffering for us, as well as for themselves. It is their failure to find light, which will show where the light is not, and also where it is.[48]

This preoccupation with the mystery of skepticism never left Hutton. It was also what prompted him to become one of the founding members of the Metaphysical Society (1869–1880), which was established to give literary, clerical and scientific gentlemen an opportunity to discuss new developments in the continuing debate over faith and science. For Hutton, the purpose of the Society was to establish "some basis of metaphysical science on which all metaphysicians might agree."[49] The Society met once a month in Piccadilly in the Grosvenor Hotel to listen to a pre-distributed paper. Its members included A. P. Stanley, Henry Sidgwick, Cardinal Manning, Lord Selborne, the Duke of Argyll, Dean Church, J. A. Froude, W. G. Ward, Thomas Henry Huxley, Frederic Harrison, James Fitzjames Stephen, and John Dalgairns, who succeeded F. W.

Faber as Superior of the London Oratory—a rum lot, as Evelyn Waugh might have said.

At one of the first dinners, light skirmishing broke out between Ward and Huxley. Told that there could be no moral disparagement of any member's points of view, Ward responded that the Society could not expect that "Christian thinkers shall give no sign of the horror with which they would view the spread of such extreme opinions as those advocated by Mr. Huxley." To which Huxley replied, "As Dr. Ward has spoken I must in fairness say that it will be very difficult for me to conceal my feeling as to the intellectual degradation which would come of the general acceptance of such views as Dr. Ward holds."[50] Afterwards, both men contrived to keep their barbs to themselves, though Huxley once referred to the Society as "our galley—that singular rudderless ship, the stalwart oarsmen of which were mostly engaged in pulling as hard as they could against one another; and which consequently performed only circular voyages all the years it was in commission."[51] Hutton might have agreed and disagreed. While he recognized the inherent limitations of any society given over to merely speculative palaver, he also recognized that Ward often elevated its proceedings with his clarion Catholicism. "Mr. Ward had the opportunity of comparing his own deepest convictions with the convictions, or non-convictions of many of the ablest doubters of the age," Hutton recalled. "The clearness, force, and candour of his argument made his papers welcome to all," precisely because they stood out in a Society where "nebulousness was almost the rule, weakness chronic, and inability to understand an opponent's position, rather than want of candour, exceedingly common." Once Ward stopped attending, the Society "began to lose its interest, and to drop into decay. Such was the attractive power of at least one strong and definite philosophical creed."[52] It is helpful to bear this portrait in mind before looking at Hutton's essays on Newman, because although Newman and Ward had many significant differences, they both subscribed to the same "strong and definite philosophical creed," which Hutton always respected as a counterweight to the claims of the positivists. Moreover, one reason why Hutton wrote so perceptively about Ward is that he could enter into the bold evolution of his faith. If Ward found Catholicism after discovering the dead end of Liberalism, Hutton found High Church Anglicanism after similarly discovering the dead end of Unitarianism.

In February 1869, Newman declined Hutton's invitation to join the Metaphysical Society, writing his friend: "Of course I am greatly flattered by the invitation conveyed to me from such eminent men; but I have a bad conscience mixed with the gratification as I really have no pretensions to receive such an honour. It has been my misfortune through life to have dabbled in many things, and to have mastered nothing ..." Then, almost as an afterthought, he added: "As to metaphysics, though it is so wide and so deep a subject, I dare say if I published anything more ... it would be on some metaphysical point."[53] As good as his word, within a year, he published his *Grammar of Assent*, which mapped anew the topography of metaphysics. Nevertheless, Hutton was persistent. "Is it impossible you should reconsider your determination not to join our metaphysical society? Now and then we have papers and discussions of the first order of interest, and we really stand in the deepest need of a mind of your order of power on the positive side of metaphysical and ethical questions. The physicists are almost too many for us."[54] Newman, however, was not interested. Later, in 1876, he wrote to Dean Church apropos the Society: "I hear that you and the Archbishop of York (to say nothing of Cardinal Manning etc) are going to let Professor Huxley read in your presence an argument in refutation of our Lord's Resurrection. How can this possibly come under the scope of a Metaphysical Society. I thank my stars that, when asked to accept the honour of belonging to it, I declined."[55]

Hutton's interest in Newman, which spanned over forty years, began, as we have seen, when he read *Loss and Gain* (1847) in his youth. He first personally encountered Newman at his King William Street lectures, which would later be published as *Lectures on Certain Difficulties felt by Anglicans in submitting to the Catholic Church* (1850), about which he wrote:

> I shall never forget the impression which his voice and manner, which opened upon me for the first time in these lectures, made on me. Never did a voice seem better adapted to persuade without irritating ... its simplicity, and frankness, and freedom from half-smothered notes which express indirect purpose, was as remarkable as its sweetness, its freshness and its gentle distinctness.[56]

Throughout the letters that passed between Hutton and Newman from the 1860s to the 1880s there is a predominant note of mutual affection, but also of candid disagreement. In February 1864, after their initial exchange regarding Hutton's notice of the Kingsley–Newman correspondence, Newman wrote back, "Though I contrive to endure my chronic unpopularity, and though I believe it to be salutary yet it is a great relief to me to have from time to time such letters as yours, which serve to shew, that under the surface of things, there is a kinder feeling towards me than the surface presents."[57] Newman went on to say that when he initially responded to Hutton's notice, he had only seen an abstract of the article in a local Birmingham paper; when he saw the full article, he saw that Hutton had not been unqualifiedly favorable in his notice. Apropos Newman's response to Kingsley, Hutton observed how "Kingsley's little weaknesses, his inaccuracy of thought, his reluctance to admit that he had been guilty of making rather an important accusation on the strength of a very loose general impression, are all gauged, probed, and condemned by a mind perfectly imperturbable ... though vividly sensitive to the little superficial ripples of motive and emotion it scorns ..." In this, Hutton saw an "undue scorn" in Newman, "which the habit of his mind in judging all human weakness by inflexible dogma has made part of the very essence of his marvelous insight into human frailty." Elaborating on this, Hutton proceeded to note how "This little discussion brings clearly home to us that one of the greatest secrets of Dr. Newman's wonderful power is ... that peculiar hardness tending to cruelty which most easily allies itself with a keen intellectual sense of the supernatural. The finest balances ... are rested on a knife-edge, and so the finest intellectual sense of the valuelessness of things transient, often seems to be rested on a knife-edge so keen that it would cut through all human feelings, rather than on that charity which St. Paul says is the highest and rarest of supernatural gifts. Father Newman's views of life, with all their delicate insights, wonderful shading, and beautiful perspective, have veins of mockery running through them in every direction,—mockery such as a man who has conceived a view of life resting, as he thinks, on the Spiritual Rock, and who has learnt to triumph over the superficial softness of temporary phenomena, would, if more intellectual than sympathetic, be likely to cherish."[58] Newman's response showed that he had absorbed more of what St. Paul had to teach than Hutton may have imagined. "I thanked you for your Article, when I saw only part of it, on the ground of its being so much more generous, than the ordinary feeling of the day allows reviewers commonly to behave towards me. I thank you still more for it, as I now read it with its complement; first, because it is evidently written, not at random, but critically; and secondly it is evidently the expression of real, earnest, and personal feeling. How far what you say about me is correct can perhaps be determined neither by you nor by me, but by the Searcher of hearts alone; but, even where I cannot follow you in your criticism, I am sure to get a lesson from it for my serious consideration."[59]

Hutton's response was somewhat abashed. "I know I express myself badly, but, I should be sorry if my use of the word 'cruel' should be taken in any sense except that in which a very keen sense of the inflexible dogma of Christianity shivering to atoms all human entreaties or fears with which it may come into collision, would convey the same meaning." His letter also identified what would become a fundamental stumbling block to his entering the Roman Church, despite his considerable respect for it: "Underlying the wide and delicately sympathetic imagination which your writings show, there seems to me always to be a deep attachment to a dogmatic and systematic theological view of the universe, resting less on what I should call personal inspiration than on the connected view of a coherent body of theological truth."[60] Despite all of Newman's attempts to disabuse him of the notion, Hutton insisted on seeing the authority of the Church as hostile to personal belief.[61] At the root of the difference between the two men, according to Malcolm Woodfield, was "Hutton's defense of the authority of common men in opposition to Newman's reliance on an infallible ecclesiastical institution"—something Hutton may have felt but Newman would have rejected.[62] Certainly, in the passage from *Loss and Gain* of which Hutton was so fond, Newman exploded such false distinctions by describing the individual faithful at Mass: "Each in his place, with his own heart, with his own wants, with his own thoughts, with his own intention, with his own prayers, separate but concordant, watching what is going on, watching its progress, uniting in its consummation;—not painfully and hopelessly following a hard form of prayer from beginning to end, but, like a concert of musical instruments, each different, but concurring in a sweet harmony, we take our part with God's priest, supporting him, yet guided by him. There are little children there, and old men, and simple labourers, and students in seminaries, priests preparing for Mass, priests making their thanksgiving; there are innocent maidens, and there are penitent sinners; but out of these many minds rises one eucharistic hymn, and the great Action is the measure and scope of it."[63]

That Hutton never acknowledged how this passage addresses the relation between personal belief and authority seems puzzling, especially since he returned to the passage again and again. Perhaps he recognized what he could not fully articulate, or only recognized it dimly. Nevertheless, on the issue of religious certainty, he was fond of invoking Maurice—"the only other living theologian who has impressed me deeply," as he said, whose "deep and insulated insights into God's purposes ... he cares little to weave together and believes the human intellect ... unable to weave together."[64] And yet it is clear that he was ambivalent about Maurice's theological diffidence. To some extent, he recognized it as disabling. "The more Maurice believed in Christ, the less he confounded himself with the object of his belief, and the more pathetic was his distrust of his own power to see aright, or say aright what he saw."[65] Hutton could see this so clearly in Maurice because he suffered from the same distrust himself. One thing that drew him to Newman was precisely his confidence in the certainty of faith. And yet Hutton could never shake the suspicion that such certainty was unwarrantable. As far as he was concerned, Maurice was right: we could hunger for truth, but not know it, certainly not with the infallibility that the Roman Church claimed.

Newman could not have more pointedly disagreed: "I think, in answer to what you say, I may most confidently say, that I have never had a doubt, it has never occurred to me to have a doubt, I could not, without a cruel effort which would be as painful to me as a sin of impurity ... to get myself to doubt in the divinity of the Catholic Roman Church and the truth of its doctrines." In an interpolation, he clarified his thinking on this matter still more by saying, "it is difficult to analyse what I feel, but I mean something like Joseph's words 'how can I commit so great a wickedness and sin against God?'" Here one is given a glimpse into the devout character of Newman's sense of religious certainty, which one of his most spirited critics, A. M. Fairbairn failed to take into consideration.[66] For Newman, certainty inhered in practice, in devoutness, as much as in profession.

Then, again, in the *Apologia*, Newman addressed the beneficent tension between authority and private judgment in a passage that might have been expressly written with Hutton's objections in mind:

> ... on the part of the Catholic body, as far as I know it, it will at first sight be said that the restless intellect of our common humanity is utterly weighed down, to the repression of all independent effort and action whatever, so that, if this is to be the mode of bringing it into order, it is brought into order only to be destroyed. But this is far from the result, far from what I conceive to be the intention of that high Providence who has provided a great remedy for a great evil,—far from borne out by the history of the conflict between Infallibility and Reason in the past, and the prospect of it in the future. The energy of the human intellect "does from opposition grow;" it thrives and is joyous, with a tough elastic strength, under the

terrible blows of the divinely-fashioned weapon, and is never so much itself as when it has lately been overthrown. It is the custom with Protestant writers to consider that, whereas there are two great principles in action in the history of religion, Authority and Private Judgment, they have all the Private Judgment to themselves, and we have the full inheritance and the superincumbent oppression of Authority. But this is not so; it is the vast Catholic body itself, and it only, which affords an arena for both combatants in that awful, never-dying duel. It is necessary for the very life of religion, viewed in its large operations and its history, that the warfare should be incessantly carried on. Every exercise of Infallibility is brought out into act by an intense and varied operation of the Reason, both as its ally and as its opponent, and provokes again, when it has done its work, a re-action of Reason against it; and, as in a civil polity the State exists and endures by means of the rivalry and collision, the encroachments and defeats of its constituent parts, so in like manner Catholic Christendom is no simple exhibition of religious absolutism, but presents a continuous picture of Authority and Private Judgment alternately advancing and retreating as the ebb and flow of the tide;—it is a vast assemblage of human beings with wilful intellects and wild passions, brought together into one by the beauty and the Majesty of a Superhuman Power,—into what may be called a large reformatory or training-school, not as if into a hospital or into a prison, not in order to be sent to bed, not to be buried alive, but (if I may change my metaphor) brought together as if into some moral factory, for the melting, refining, and moulding, by an incessant, noisy process, of the raw material of human nature, so excellent, so dangerous, so capable of divine purposes.[67]

Notwithstanding this passage, Hutton never acknowledged Newman's appreciation of how the Catholic faith resolves the tensions between authority and private judgment.

Despite their differences, Newman recognized how fortunate he was to have someone as fair as Hutton reviewing his work: "I should be well off, if I never had a severer or more ill-natured critic ..." At the same time, he stressed that he welcomed candid, well-considered criticism. "Every reader has a right to his own impressions as to what I have written; and it would really be a kind act in any one, were he well disposed towards me or not, to bring against me formal charges, argued out fairly, about certain tendencies in my writings or about definite statements of mine which I had to defend, explain, or withdraw. If even a St Augustine published his Retractations, surely I could turn to good account an opportunity, if given me, of making mine ..."[68] Responding to a *Spectator* piece entitled "Roman Catholic Casuistry and Protestant Prejudice," which Newman rightly attributed to Hutton, he wrote: "I hope I shall be never slow to confess my faults, and if I have, while becoming a Catholic, palliated things really wrong among Catholics, in order to make my theory of religion and my consequent duty clearer, I am very sorry for it ... but Mr. Kingsley's charges are simply monstrous." By the same token, he appreciated Hutton's objective criticism: "You have uttered on the whole what I should say of myself

...">[69] In Newman Hutton saw an example of "that over-regulated mind which marshals every thought of his mind, every feeling of his heart, every word of his lips, in a definite place, to serve a definite end of life," which, as a critic in the *Saturday Review* noted, tended to "craftiness of statement." Nevertheless, for Hutton, "this very power of minute foresight makes [Newman] ... always candid to an opponent's real arguments, and induces him to state the case against himself with even unnecessary ability and strength." We saw this in the *Letter to Pusey*, where Newman mounted the case against the excesses of Roman devotion even more compellingly than Pusey. But in Kingsley, Hutton saw "a healthy and genuine scorn for intellectual *tactics*, a man who blurts out honestly enough the first thought of his heart, whether it be wise or unwise, but yet one who exhibits what we must call the grossest want of candour towards an opponent on the mere strength of his own personal impressions—one who does not deign to quote anything in support of his charges, and when attacked for such contemptuous indifference to his opponent's good name replies by a pamphlet which simply drags, from all possible sources, specimens of everything which Dr. Newman has ever said calculated to affect an English reading public unpleasantly; and, worse, still, conveys an impression that Dr. Newman always did despise truth, and does so now more than ever. We say this is unfair. Even if we ought not to take too much counsel about our ordinary words, yet when those words are challenged and cannot be sustained, Protestant candour would require a simple and hearty admission that there had been nothing to justify them ..."[70]

This concern for words was one of the best aspects of Hutton's own critical approach. Apropos this, Woodfield perceptively observes that "Hutton is deeply moved as a literary man by the notion of words which have the status of acts," and to exemplify his point he cites Hutton's great admiration for the passage in *Loss and Gain* on the Mass. Woodfield might also have cited an essay by Hutton on the nature of paradox, the force of which will strike anyone who admires Chesterton. Here, Hutton saw how it was the misuse of words that called out for startling correctives:

> The need for paradox is no doubt rooted deep in the very nature of the use that we make of language. Just as everything that we do habitually, we come to do automatically, without being in any real sense conscious of what we do, or even of the purpose in the execution of which we first did it, so language is no sooner employed habitually than it comes to be used as mere algebra—to the meaning of which we pay no more attention than we pay to the particular sounds that go to make up the ringing of a bell which reminds us that certain daily duties have to be done. And there is no harm in this when the only object of the language is to remind us of the mechanical duties which we have to discharge; but, unfortunately, there is harm in it, when the use to which we ought to turn our words is to remind us of the great realities of life, and when they fail to do so simply from the narcotic influence of habitual use. Then we need awakening anew to the old significance which lay beneath the words which have ceased to exert any magic

over us; and nothing awakens the true meaning of language like paradox, which, while it appears to contradict the superficial sense attaching to the formulas of our daily life, really points to the hidden depth beneath them and the unseen height above, and restores us to the freshness and the wonder of the thoughts which had shriveled with our constant manipulation of them till they seemed to have lost their sap. This function of paradox is the same which is ascribed to that divine life itself which makes all things new ...[71]

Not surprisingly, Hutton was a keen admirer of "Unreal Words" (1839), Newman's sermon describing the various ways profession can become an evasion not only of practice but of truth. In the sermon that Newman wrote just months before he would begin to have his serious doubts about the reality of the Church of England, he reminded his readers that "Words have a meaning, whether we mean that meaning or not; and they are imputed to us in their meaning, when our not meaning it is our own fault. He, who takes God's name in vain, is not counted guiltless because he means nothing by it,—he cannot frame a language for himself; and they who make professions, of whatever kind, are heard in the sense of those professions, and are not excused because they themselves attach no sense to them." He then enjoined his readers "to learn that new language which Christ has brought us. He has interpreted all things for us in a new way; He has brought us a religion which sheds a new light on all that happens. Try to learn this language. Do not get it by rote, or speak of it as a thing of course. Try to understand what you say. Time is short, eternity is long; God is great, man is weak; he stands between heaven and hell; Christ is his Saviour; Christ has suffered for him ..." Since these "solemn truths" required more practice than profession, Newman concluded by enjoining his auditors to act on them. "Let us guard against frivolity, love of display, love of being talked about, love of singularity, love of seeming original. Let us aim at what we say, and saying what we mean; let us aim at knowing when we understand a truth, and when we do not ... Let us receive the truth in reverence, and pray God to give us a good will, and divine light, and spiritual strength, that it may bear fruit within us."[72]

Hutton invoked Newman's sermon to argue that "the volume of unreal words talked in the present age against religion, by men of genius, has been indefinitely greater than the volume of unreal words talked by men of genius in its name." And to substantiate his point he cited some particularly notorious offenders. "Carlyle insisting on the Divine quality of reticence; Mr. Spencer preaching the awe with which we ought to regard "the Infinite and Eternal Energy from which all things proceed," and Mr. Frederic Harrison lecturing to the Positivist pilgrims on the grand continuity of the Comtist religion ... are all surely warnings which we cannot afford to ignore, against the unreality of the prophets of the age."[73] In a review of Matthew Arnold's lay sermons, he asked whether "Mr. Arnold lately read Dr. Newman's great Oxford sermon on 'Unreal Words,'" before concluding that in appropriating the words of faith Arnold was guilty of "a hardened indifference to the meaning of words ..." Indeed, for Hutton, "Mr. Arnold is really putting Literature—of which he is so great a master—to shame, when he travesties the language of the prophets, and the evangelists, and of our Lord Himself, by using it to express the dwarfed convictions and withered hopes of modern rationalists who love to repeat the great words of the Bible, after they have given up the strong meaning of them as fanatical superstitions."[74]

In his two-part review of the *Apologia*, Hutton revealed as much about his fascination with Newman as he did about the merits of the book itself. Speaking of Newman, Hutton wrote: "Far as we are severed from him in almost every principle of faith, and hope, and intellectual conviction, it would be mere dullness of nature not to recognize ... the noble truthfulness and almost childlike candour of the autobiographical sketch now before us. Dr. Newman admits freely how blindly he groped his way for many years in the Anglican Church, and how slowly his eyes were opened to his real destiny; how friends often surprised him into momentary admissions that were not really his own; how he himself laid down in perfect confidence at one period of his career apparently fixed principles which turned out at a later period to be mere straws at which he had, as it were, caught vainly, in order to arrest his onward path towards a goal from which he recoiled to the last." There is no suggestion here that Newman was a "confused schismatic," as a confused Yale professor has claimed. Nor that he was in any way double-dealing in his long-gestating conversion. "Nothing to us seems clearer," Hutton says, "than that all his premises of thought were Roman Catholic from the beginning, even at the very time when he was saying honestly the hardest things he ever said of the Roman Church. Even then he felt the current sucking him in, and it was this which made him protest so eagerly against the alleged Romanizing tendencies of his school of opinion."[75] Newman could not have had his self-portrait more fairly described, even if the image of the Church as a whirlpool sucking him into its irresistible current was more than a little outlandish.

Despite his praise for Newman, Hutton was careful to assure his readers, whom one wag described as "sheltered in leafy rectories and snug villas," that he was not entirely under the sway of the author for whom he otherwise had so much decided respect.[76] "To us, we confess, he does seem the preacher of a dream:—though we admire his genius, thoroughly believe in his sincerity, and go even so far with him that we could far more easily give up the belief in 'Liberalism' than the belief in God. Fortunately, we believe that the deepest Liberalism re-discovers that need for God's revelation which shallow Liberalism too often ignores."[77]

When the *Apologia* appeared, Hutton corresponded with Newman to tell him how deeply it appealed to him. "Your Apology has interested me very profoundly on its own account. I wish more than I can say that I could be nearer to you in faith for I feel the same fascination in all you write that I have always felt. I have struggled my way out of Unitarianism to a deep belief in the Incarnation, but not by the road of 'authority' which you teach as the only road to theological truth. Surely God can and does teach us His own truth without confiding it to any visible Church. I have never got so far as any really authoritative visible Church, I don't think the apostles had." Nonetheless, Hutton freely admitted, "I have always thought the Roman theology fuller of self-revealing truth than almost any other … but my stumbling block has always been that a true theology ought to be … self-revealing and does not need the organism of a visible institution to drive it home to the conscience and heart … . I am not denying that a Church grows naturally out of a Theology: what I cannot see is that a Theology should grow out of a Church."[78] Here was "the expression of real, earnest, and personal feeling," of which Newman had been so appreciative, on the part of a man grappling with the most pressing aspects of faith. "When I was eighteen," Hutton confided to Newman, "the passage in which Willis describes the mass in Loss and Gain very nearly made a Willis of me—a man I mean who dives experimentally into the Church in the hope of faith rather than one who goes into it because he sees it to be true. But since then I have got a growing conviction that faith however mysterious ought to prove itself to the mind …" As Hutton knew, Newman had insisted on similar proof himself before he converted. In his review of the *Apologia*, Hutton wrote, "In one remarkable passage of this apology Dr. Newman admits how little the reasoning by which he accounted for his changing intellectual positions may have really represented the influences at work within him."[79] It was only gradually that Newman came to realize that "Religious truths are reached, not by reasoning, but by an inward perception. Anyone can reason, only disciplined, educated, formal minds can perceive. Nothing, then, is more important … than habits of self-command."[80] Newman cited a maxim of St. Ambrose's to describe how, in his own case, not merely the intellect but the whole man converted: '*Non in dialectica complacuit Deo salvum facere populum suum*'—the same maxim that he would use as the epigraph for the *Grammar of Assent* (1870).[81] However unpersuaded by the claims of Rome, Hutton always confessed to a certain lingering ambivalence when it came to the Church about which Newman spoke with such powerful conviction. As he admitted to Newman, "that passage about the mass [in *Loss and Gain*] has a strange fascination for me which I cannot quite analyze. In this world I see no chance of ever following you. And yet there are passages in your teachings that cling to me still."[82]

Apropos those teachings, Newman was at pains to make Hutton recognize that he did not teach that "authority was the only road to truth in theology." Nor did he hold that authority, from whatever source, was somehow at odds with "self-revealing" faith. It might be true that "The Church is the ordinary, normal Oracle … the only visible authority to which we appeal, the only authority which signs and seals a doctrine as the common property of Christians or an Article of the Faith, but still to individuals accidentally there are various instruments or organs of that Divine Authority from whom … [supernatural] truth can primarily come, and the Scriptures constitute one of those channels – nay, I will say a Greek poem or philosophical treatise may be such – nay even the Koran. And thus, though I fully believe that certain theological truths, as a future retribution, can be proved independently of revelation, still I do not think any religion, as such, in the individual is without what may be called revelation – I mean that God reveals Himself to us directly, and we believe in 'Him' because He says 'I am He' to us, whether it be through our conscience, or through Scripture or in any other way … ." Having said this, Newman was careful to stress that "mere reasonings and inferences, however true, are philosophy, not religion." At the same time, "all religion is a revelation – an acceptance of truths conveyed to us from a Personal God …" From this it followed that "What you designate as 'self-revealing' is surely a truth which … commends itself intensely, manifoldly, intimately to our hearts." Nevertheless, one "should not consider such an internal acceptance or embrace of a doctrine a sine quâ non condition of its being a truth," and this because, "minds being very various, the subjective acquiescence in a doctrine cannot be the invariable measure and test of its objective reality or its truth." Newman made a similar point in his King William Street lectures, arguing that the Tractarians could not hold the via media true simply because it recommended itself to their affections.[83] "If then a Revelation is made, faith, that is, assent upon pure authority, will necessarily enter into the act of acceptance when the intellect has been awakened." But this did not diminish the vitality of the personal nature of faith, for Newman was "far from denying (just the contrary) that an externally-revealed truth may be in a certain sense, or to a certain point, self revealing …" Indeed, "an eager spontaneous appropriation of an object of faith may in some sense be called an act of love …"[84] Such extraordinary letters only reinforced Hutton's deep respect and affection for Newman, however much he failed to share his Catholic views. "The sight of your handwriting always gives me keen pleasure," he told his distinguished correspondent in December 1867, before relating to him that he had recently met Mr. Gladstone, with whom he had a "long chat … chiefly about your Apologia and poems. He expressed as warm an admiration for both as even I could feel, and was especially full of admiration for the Dream of Gerontius, the slight notice of which by the press filled him with amazement. Probably the subject is too theological and too full of Catholic theology to attract the notice which its imaginative power deserved in so keenly Protestant a country."[85] After Hutton's biography of Newman appeared, Gladstone told the author that he found the book not only "a most touching specimen of thoroughly disinterested admiration and affection" but "patient, conscientious, searching, delicate, and brilliant." At the same time, he disagreed with Hutton's estimate of Newman's Catholic writings. "My reliance here is on the Arians and the Parochial Sermons. Is it not the fact that these sermons are his largest gift to permanent, indestructible theology?" He also accused Newman of resorting to precisely the same private judgment that he criticized the Tractarians for crediting. "He was trained (as I was) in the Evangelical School, which is beyond all others—beyond … the English Nonconformists or Scotch Presbyterians—the school of private judgment." Moreover, Gladstone was convinced that Newman was "thoroughly unsound as a Butlerian," which was an interesting comment in light of Newman's correspondence with Keble, so much of which, as I show in my chapter on Keble, turned on their differences with respect to the import of Butler's work.[86]

In reply to Newman's letter on authority, Hutton admitted that "For many years I thought nothing short of an infallible Church could prove such a mystery [as the Incarnation] though my whole soul craved for it." Nevertheless, "the difficulty in reaching a human infallible authority was far greater to me than in receiving a great mystery, through human channels, on what I felt to be divine authority, because it laid such a hold of the whole conscience and nature." Hutton's resistance to the Church's claim of infallibility—and this was written six years before the First Vatican Council defined papal infallibility—was as strong as Newman doubtless suspected it would be. "I scarcely see the advantage of accepting [the truths of the Church] on external authority," Hutton wrote, "even if one could get over the enormous difficulty of satisfying oneself as to the actual gift of infallibility to any human organization." He gave rather short shrift to the section in the *Apologia* where Newman eloquently defended the infallible claims of the Church. "Your account of how sparingly the Church actually uses this formidable power is a testimony to her sagacity and wisdom, – not a help to conceding the power itself. The Liberalism you dreaded so much I should turn away from as heartily as you if I could think it led to atheism. It seems to me to lead to free subjection of the soul to divine truths one by one, just as they penetrate the heart by God's grace, and this I should feel higher than any formal grasp of even a larger area of truth."[87] Here, again, one can see the footprints of Maurice.

In a piece on Newman's *Plain and Parochial Sermons*, Hutton elaborated on why he could not follow Newman in his 'venture' of faith in the Church of Rome. "Dr. Newman seems to us to make obedience the root, not only of moral and religious action, but of moral and religious thought." And in order to do this, "he has to assume that we all have an intellectual authority over us as clear and articulate as the moral authority which speaks to our conscience." Indeed, Newman "identifies the submission to Church authority with the submission to God's voice …" And, of course, in this the good Protestant in Hutton refused to follow him. Obedience to a Church that claimed infallibility was the invariable sticking point. "All this network of assumption" struck Hutton "as having its root in the notion that obedience is *even more* the root of our intellectual than of our moral life …" While "Dr. Newman would not ask us to obey any moral command which does not appeal to our conscience," he had no qualms imposing "on our intellects a ready-made ecclesiastical system of the most complex kind, which it is quite impossible for any rational being to accept as a whole without knowing that he is going on a mere probability or possibility, —and, as it seems to us, on a strong improbability."[88] This was at the heart of why Hutton could not embrace Newman's Roman Catholicism, though Newman might have countered Hutton's objections with something he wrote in his *Apologia*: "I say, that a power, possessed of infallibility in religious teaching, is happily adapted to be a working instrument in the course of human affairs for smiting hard and throwing back the immense energy of the aggressive, capricious, untrustworthy intellect … ."[89]

In his correspondence with Hutton, Newman never explicitly responded to Hutton's objections to the obedience required of Roman Catholics. This might have been the result of his believing that he had already sufficiently addressed the matter in the *Apologia*. Nevertheless, in his *Letter to the Duke of Norfolk* he indirectly responded to Hutton by addressing the same objections to "the absolute and entire obedience" required of Catholics, to which Gladstone had objected, in a passage full of characteristic force.[90]

> Is there then such a duty at all as obedience to ecclesiastical authority now? or is it one of those obsolete ideas, which are swept away, as unsightly cobwebs, by the New Civilization? Scripture says, "Remember them which have the *rule* over you, who have spoken unto you the word of God, whose faith follow." And, "*Obey* them that have the *rule* over you, and *submit yourselves*; for they watch *for your souls*, as they that must give account, that they may do it with joy and not with grief; for that is unprofitable for you." The margin in the Protestant Version reads, "those who are your *guides*;" and the word may also be translated "leaders." Well, as rulers, or guides and leaders, whichever word be right, they are to be *obeyed*. Now Mr. Gladstone dislikes our way of fulfilling this precept, whether as regards our choice of ruler and leader, or our "Absolute Obedience" to him; but he does not give us his own. Is there any liberalistic reading of the Scripture passage? Or are the words only for the benefit of the poor and ignorant, not for the *Schola* (as it may be called) of political and periodical writers, not for individual members of Parliament, not for statesmen and Cabinet ministers, and people of Progress? Which party then is the more "Scriptural," those who recognize and carry out in their conduct texts like these, or those who don't? May not we Catholics claim some mercy from Mr. Gladstone, though we be faulty in the object and the manner of our obedience, since in a lawless day an object and a manner of obedience we have? Can we be blamed, if, arguing from those texts which say that ecclesiastical authority comes from above, we obey it in that one form in which alone we find it on earth, in that one person who, of all the notabilities of this nineteenth century into which we have been born, alone claims it of us? The Pope has no rival in his claim upon us; nor is it our doing that his claim has been made and allowed for centuries upon centuries, and that it was he who made the Vatican decrees, and not they him. If we give him up, to whom shall we go? Can we dress up any civil functionary in the vestments of divine authority? Can I, for instance, follow the faith, can I put my soul into the hands, of our gracious Sovereign? or of the Archbishop of Canterbury? or of the Bishop of Lincoln, albeit he is not broad and low, but high? Catholics have "done what they could,"—all that any one could: and it should be Mr. Gladstone's business, before telling us that we are slaves, because we obey the Pope, first of all to tear away those texts from the Bible.[91]

This was a witty way to confute Protestants who claimed to obey the obedience authorized by the Bible, but Newman went on to show that even if one took the Protestant objection to Roman obedience at its own estimation, it was still exaggerated. "So little does the Pope come into this whole system of moral theology by which (as by our conscience) our lives are regulated, that the weight of his hand upon us, as private men, is absolutely unappreciable. I have had a difficulty where to find a measure or gauge of his interposition. At length I have looked through Busenbaum's "Medulla," to ascertain what light such a book would throw upon the question. It is a book of casuistry for the use of Confessors, running to 700 pages, and is a large repository of answers made by various theologians on points of conscience, and generally of duty. It was first published in 1645—my own edition is of 1844—and in this latter are marked those propositions, bearing on subjects treated in it, which have been condemned by Popes in the intermediate 200 years. On turning over the pages I find they are in all between fifty and sixty. This list includes matters sacramental, ritual, ecclesiastical, monastic, and disciplinarian, as well as moral, relating to the duties of ecclesiastics and regulars, of parish priests, and of professional men, as well as of private Catholics. And these condemnations relate for the most part to mere occasional details of duty, and are in reprobation of the lax or wild notions of speculative casuists, so that they are rather restraints upon theologians than upon laymen."[92] Thus Newman exposed the misconceived notions that still misrepresent the nature and reach of papal authority.

His differences with Hutton notwithstanding, Newman continued to try to share with him the rational grounds for adherence to the Roman Church, though at the same time he was careful to stress that "I never shall wish you to become a Catholic, merely to get rid of your painful doubts. I don't believe that it is a sufficient motive—and I do see at least the danger of their reviving when you were in the Church, if you had not them die a natural death before you came into it." As had been the case when he was an Anglican, the Catholic Newman always dissuaded the impetuous from taking steps that they might later regret. Nevertheless, he was open enough with Hutton to share with him the news that "There is a report in this place among the Priests that 'a gentleman named Hutton connected with the Spectator, has been secretly received into the Catholic Church.' I mention this to put you on your guard, what you say and to whom."[93]

It was some mark of the high regard in which Newman held Hutton that he should have written to him the day after he completed his *Grammar of Assent* to apprise him of the long genesis of that brilliant book, a book which spoke directly to precisely the issue of authority and personal belief that Hutton had broached six years before. "For twenty years I have begun and left off an inquiry again and again, which yesterday I finished ... as far as I am able to carry it out. I began it in my Oxford University Sermons; I tried it in 1850 – and at several later dates, in 1859, in 1861, indeed I do not know when I have not wished to attempt it – but, though my fundamental ideas were ever the same, I could not carry them out. Now at last I have done all that I can do according to my measure ... Those who are told what pains it has cost me, will wonder, when they see it, that it is not worth more than they will find it to be – But I have said to myself, in such difficult subjects on which opinions vary so much ... the testimony of even one mind is worth something as a fact or phenomenon. I have said in one page of it, that on such subjects, egotism is the truest modesty, because it does not dogmatise – and though I do not rate my performance high I cannot be sorry that I committed myself to it."[94] Unfortunately, this crucial personal aspect of the book did not attract as much critical attention from

Hutton as it deserved. His long review focuses almost entirely on the argument from probability, which only exacerbated his resistance to the Church's claims of infallibility. "You remark in one place that a single clear instance of error disproves infallibility," Hutton wrote to Newman in April, 1870, less than a month after the book appeared, "as of course it does. But does not this render it all but impossible for any one who comes to the study of ecclesiastical history without the most absolute faith in a principle of human authority somewhere, ever to believe in what may be so easily disproved and what is so impossible to prove except a priori? ... The pain of uncertainty, terrible as it is, is no proof of the existence of a human source of certainty."[95] Although clearly unpersuaded by Newman's argument from probability, disputing whether "the outcome of combined probability is a real proof," Hutton praised the book's last chapter, in which Newman charted the rise of Christianity.

Newman graciously thanked Hutton for his review, going so far as to say that it was "a great pleasure to me to find how exactly you have translated me, in some places with a happiness of statement which I feel I had not hit myself," though, in the same letter, he also called attention to a number of Hutton's misstatements. Still, for Newman, these did not diminish the fact that Hutton had written one of the best contemporary responses to the book. "You have paid me the great compliment of reading it with attention, a compliment which I cannot expect ordinary reviewers to pay me, to whom, however, I am truly grateful for the good will and kindness they have shown to me, and for praise more than is my due, though it has been vague, not distinctive."[96]

Despite the relative substance of Hutton's review, it was only in the obituary he wrote on Newman for the *Spectator* that Hutton demonstrated that he had finally absorbed the true achievement of the *Grammar of Assent*. "There have been many more masterly thinkers of the kind which men call 'systematic,'" Hutton wrote. "But Newman perceived more vividly than any English thinker of our century the weakness of what is called systematic thought, and the faint influence exerted by any abstract system over the practical life of men." Then, again, together with Newman's distrust of abstraction, Hutton admired his insights into how the faithful actually perceive and practice their religious faith. "There is no religious thinker in our country ... of any century, who has apprehended more clearly how various and how mixed and unrecognised by men in general, are the elements of motive and perception which go to make up practical genius, the genius for *doing* successfully what most men only try to do and wish to do. The implicit reason by which those are practically guided who succeed in what they attempt, as distinguished from the explicit theoretic reason ... had never been analyzed by any English thinker as it was analyzed by Newman ... and this was the great source of his religious influence ... He could justify theoretically the potent implicit reason of man against the fruitless and formal explicit reason. He could show how much more powerful was the combination of humility, trust, imagination, feeling, perception, in apprehending the revealed mind and will of God, than the didactic and formal proofs to which the popular religious appeals of our day usually have recourse."[97]

Two years after his *Spectator* review of the *Grammar*, Hutton confessed to dissatisfaction with his own restless faith. If he could not agree with Newman on the certainties of the Catholic Church, neither could he deny that they had a definite allure in the burgeoning unbelief that was coming to characterize late nineteenth-century Britain. "The tendency of the religion of the day to dissipate itself in the vaguest sentiment and smoke oppresses me more and more, and often makes me turn to your Church with a vague passionate yearning that I feel to be dangerous and even distrustful of God, for surely the knowledge of the truth should not come from a mere repulsion against error, and if God could bring Christianity out of the society of the heathen world, He can much more teach us, after a very much longer period of incredulity and skepticism than we have yet gone through, what the divine truth is at which we find it so hard to get. I feel as if the tendencies of the day were all witnessing against the only truth I can firmly grasp, and telling me that that at least is not what the common sense of mankind will accept. But when I look more narrowly at your Church I see nothing but what daunts me still more on the other side, – an apparent utter disregard of evidence in fixing the Creed in the days when the Creed acquired its first hold on the mind. Can you doubt that the early Fathers and even the Evangelists themselves, like the Saints of all days, supplemented the deficiencies of their intellectual case for many of their facts from the depth of their devotional feeling, and did not even question the right of the religious spirit, to keep to its facts in this, as we know now, utterly misleading fashion? ... The duty of restraining one's belief within the limits of what is warranted by evidence seems to me to have been hardly at all understood in the first days of the Church, and though it is the most painful of duties surely it is a duty?"[98] Then Hutton invoked one of Newman's own most provocative statements to deplore the seemingly inexorable rise of apostasy.[99] "I feel heartily with you that I would prefer to see England bigoted, superstitious, gloomy, almost cruel, to seeing her without faith in the supernatural, but it is the most difficult of earthly problems to combine the religious spirit with the spirit of intellectual severity as to the objective conditions of belief." This returned Hutton to Newman's argument from probability in the *Grammar*. "The more I think of it the less can I understand how any accumulation of mere probabilities is to amount to mathematical certainty, or how moral certainty, short of mathematical, can be in the strictest sense certainly at all. If you put the letters of a line of Virgil into a box and after shaking them well up draw them out one by one, there is of course a mathematical possibility that you would draw them out in the old order; indeed there is just as much chance of that particular arrangement as of any other specified arrangement, and therefore there is of course a possibility. But no accumulation of practical probabilities such as you describe in the Grammar of Assent could come as near to certainty as the opinion of the man who expects that the letters will not be drawn out in that order, is, and yet his opinion is certainly not certain ..."[100] Here, one can see that it was less the Protestant than the student of Martineau in Hutton that refused to accede to the claims of the Church.

Nevertheless, Newman gamely set about fielding Hutton's objections. After admitting that "I cannot quite disguise from myself that it fatigues me to think accurately," Newman tried various other tacks with his scrupulous friend. As to Hutton's doubts about the accuracy of the Creed, Newman replied that he had "looked at St Francis's exposition of the Creed. That it is fresh, impressive, beautiful, suited to its hearers, I suppose will be generally allowed; but, as to the truth of every word of it, well, it seems to me a Meditation on the Creed, a quickening of it into substance and reality … St Francis impressed it as a living fact upon the hearts of his audience. It is in his hands reason elevated by imagination." If this explanation did not satisfy Hutton, Newman had another: "the living intelligence of the prudent man decides that a certain conclusion is trustworthy, or imposes on him the duty of believing it. He is not able, be he ever so logical, to express how much and what evidence in a logical shape is just sufficient, neither more or less, to impose a conclusion on his assent; he only sees that logically a certain modicum of evidence would be too little, and another modicum superfluously much, and that in this particular case it is his duty to himself to receive it as true on that particular evidence which he has, though he cannot compare it with other supposable evidence or assign precisely its logical value …" Moreover, Newman reminded Hutton, that it was "a fact of human nature" that "we all make acts of certitude without logical measurements … if on our best and most serious judgment we think a fact claims our assent, we give it, and feel ourselves bound to give it. Thus though I am not a physiologist, or a medical practioner, or an undertaker, I am downright certain … that I shall die, and should be a fool, if I were not."[101]

In January 1884, Hutton wrote Newman a letter demonstrating that if Hutton himself could not entirely enter into the Cardinal's point of view, there were others in London who could. "My dear Lord Cardinal," Hutton wrote, "I cannot resist the pleasure of telling you how warmly the working men received my lecture on you yesterday, and as the whole charm consisted in my quotations of your own words, of which I gave a long string threaded together by a very slender thread of narrative and criticism, you would have seen at once how heartily you are admired and loved and reverenced even among the Protestants of the working class. When I referred to the lines by which, among Protestants, you are best known, ('Lead kindly Light') there was a perfect thunder of applause, if so large a word be applicable at all to a meeting in which probably the total number was not 300, as the room would hardly hold more though it was full to overflowing. Knowing how sincerely you love your own countrymen, – especially I think those of the working class, – I think it would have been a great gratification to you if you could have been present without being seen last night. To me it was really a vivid delight to see how they entered into the beauty of every passage I read."[102] Newman's response was comically subdued: "I feel your great kindness in your late pains to introduce what I have written to a class of men to whom I am not known. The prejudice against Catholics is so great in England that to get thoughtful men to think well of an individual Catholic is to do a service to the Catholic Religion. But, apart from this, as I have felt pain at the false reports, which have been spread about concerning me, so I cannot but be relieved, when I am placed in a favourable light, and feel grateful to those who have so placed me." And with that modest expression of thanks, Newman signed off, only adding: "You will not refuse the only return I can make you, a Cardinal's blessing."[103] In May of that same year, Newman, who cherished so many anniversaries, wrote: "It is about 20 years since I wrote to thank you for your notice in the September of my Apologia on its first publication. I dare say it was against the etiquette of the literary world, for no one was kind enough to answer me but you. In consequence I called on you at your Office ..."[104] Newman visited Hutton in the *Spectator* offices on 10 May 1864, a visit which Hutton treasured "as one of the white days of my life."[105]

His most moving letter to Hutton, however, and the one that sums up the special regard he felt for his old defender, was the one he sent him on 29 December 1872.

> My dear Mr Hutton
>
> I have nothing to write to you about, but I am led at this season to send you the religious greetings and good wishes which it suggests, to assure you that, though I seem to be careless about those who desire to have more light than they have in regard to religious truths, yet I do really sympathise with them very much, and ever have them in mind.
>
> I know how honestly you try to approve yourself to God – and this is a claim on the reverence of any one who knows or reads you. There are many things as to which I most seriously differ from you but I believe you to be one of those to whom the angels on Christmas night sent greeting as 'hominibus bonæ voluntatis' and it is a pleasure and a duty for all who could be their companions hereafter to follow their pattern of comprehensive charity here. I cannot feel so hopefully and tenderly to many of those whom you defend or patronize as I do to you – and what you write perplexes me often – but when a man is really and truly seeking the Pearl of great price, how can one help joining oneself in heart and spirit with him?
>
> Most truly Yrs John H. Newman[106]

In conclusion, what bound Hutton and Newman together was their shared interest in the truth of religion at a time when unbelief was gaining enormous ground. The challenges to religion mounted by the age's various skeptics inspired in both men a critical interest in the grounds for faith, even though their approaches to those grounds often sharply differed. Moreover, Newman took particular interest in the editor of the *Spectator* not only because he showed such sympathetic insight into his work but because he encouraged Newman to hope that the faith of the English, which he had accounted so negligible in *Loss and Gain*, might yet revive. In a passage which made a deep impression on Hutton when he was a young man, Newman had one of his characters in the novel say: "Englishmen have many gifts, faith they have not. Other nations, inferior to them in many things, still have faith. Nothing will stand in place of it; not a sense of the beauty of Catholicism, or of its awfulness, or of its antiquity; not an appreciation of the sympathy which it shows towards sinners; not an admiration of the Martyrs and early Fathers, and a delight in their writings. Individuals may display a touching gentleness, or a conscientiousness which demands our reverence; still, till they have faith, they have not the foundation, and their superstructure will fall. They will not be blessed, they will effect nothing in religious matters, till they begin by an act of unreserved faith in the word of God, whatever it be; till they go out of themselves; till they cease to make something within them their standard; till they oblige their will to perfect what reason leaves sufficient, indeed, but incomplete. And when they shall recognise this defect in themselves, and try to remedy it, then they will recognise much more;—they will be on the road very shortly to be Catholics."[107] Once Hutton came into his ken, Newman began to hope that more English pilgrims might find this road.

Hutton, for his part, wrote a number of retrospective appraisals of Newman's career, which show that his difficulties with the authority of the Church were negligible compared to Newman's manifold achievement. In his *Spectator* obituary, he wrote that "We have lost ... our greatest Englishman in Cardinal Newman ... whose life has been more completely the outcome of consistent, deep, and coherent purpose, than that of any other man of genius whom this century of ours has seen. No where has there been a life so completely all of a piece, so patiently carved out of one pure block of purpose ..."[108] And in a long essay for the *Contemporary Review* written in 1884, he argued that there were three major aspects to this "consistent, deep, and coherent purpose." First, Newman remained faithful throughout his life to the "profound belief that Christianity is a religion of humility." For Newman, without humility, true faith was impossible. "When I see a person hasty and violent, harsh and high-minded, careless of what others feel, and disdainful of what they think," he wrote in one of his sermons, "when I see such a one proceeding to inquire into religious subjects, I am sure beforehand he cannot go right—he will not be led into all the truth—it is contrary to the nature of things and the experience of the world, that he should find what he is seeking. I should say the same were he seeking to find out what to believe or do in any other matter not religious,—but especially in any such important and solemn inquiry; for the *fear* of the Lord (humbleness, teachableness, reverence towards Him) is the very *beginning* of wisdom, as Solomon tells us; it leads us to think over things modestly and honestly, to examine patiently, to bear doubt and uncertainty, to wait perseveringly for an increase of light, to be slow to speak, and to be deliberate in deciding."[109] Here, Hutton saw the antithesis to that intellectual hubris, which animated so many of the positivists of his generation. Moreover, Hutton saw in Newman's great and consistent purpose an opposition to Liberalism. "The drift of Christian teaching seemed to him to involve not only great humility and teachableness, not only willingness to bear humiliation in seeking for guidance of revelation, but a revulsion against that glorification of good nature and of modern enlightenment, which was in those days so prevalent—as, for instance, amongst the Whig magnates ..." In this, Hutton had in mind principally Sir Robert Peel and Lord Brougham, the Liberal founders of the Tamworth Reading Room, which held up knowledge—and, pointedly, non-denominational knowledge—as the approved conqueror of "those two giants, the pride and the passion of man."[110] For Hutton, "Newman's whole nature protested against the doctrine that an amiable disposition and the desire for information are the secrets of human regeneration." And here Hutton quoted one of Newman's most provocative salvos: "I will not shrink from uttering my firm conviction, that it would be a gain to this country, were it vastly more superstitious, more bigoted, more gloomy, more fierce in its religion, than at present it shows itself to be. Not, of course, that I think the tempers of mind herein implied desirable, which would be an evident absurdity; but I think them infinitely more desirable and more promising than a heathen obduracy, and a cold, self-sufficient, self-wise tranquillity."[111] Hutton approved "Newman's belief that even the unenlightened and unregulated starts and terrors of conscience have in them far more of the kind of error which is akin to truth, than have the conceits and superstitious exaltations of the age of reason …"[112] This, again, showed the extent to which the lessons of the *Grammar of Assent*, which Hutton had initially questioned, informed his understanding of the character and scale of Newman's achievement. Hutton also recognized that "Newman had from the first the greatest horror of anything like worldly Christianity …" And here he quoted from a sermon that highlights another extraordinary aspect of Newman: his deep understanding of the world's worship of prestige, which was an essential feature of his understanding of the springs of skepticism. "I do not know any thing more dreadful than a state of mind which is, perhaps, the characteristic of this country, and which the prosperity of this country so miserably fosters. I mean that ambitious spirit, to use a great word, but I know no other word to express my meaning—that low ambition which sets every one on the look-out to succeed and to rise in life, to amass money, to gain power, to depress his rivals, to triumph over his hitherto superiors, to affect a consequence and a gentility which he had not before, to affect to have an opinion on high subjects, to pretend to form a judgment upon sacred things, to choose his religion, to approve and condemn according to his taste, to become a partizan in extensive measures for the supposed temporal benefit of the community, to indulge the vision of great things which are to come, great improvements, great wonders: all things vast, all things new,—this most fearfully earthly and grovelling spirit is likely, alas! to extend itself more and more among our countrymen,—an intense, sleepless, restless, never-wearied, never-satisfied, pursuit of Mammon in one shape or other, to the exclusion of all deep, all holy, all calm, all reverent thoughts."[113] For Hutton, this highlighted another of Newman's striking attributes: his ability to perceive and understand the very worldly vanities he renounced, which gave his life so much of its ungainsayable distinction. Not even those obituary writers most contemptuous of his Catholic faith could call into question his integrity. "In a century in which physical discovery and material well-being have usurped and almost absorbed the admiration of mankind," Hutton concluded in his biography, "such a life as that of Cardinal Newman stands out in strange and almost majestic … contrast to the eager and agitated turmoil of confused passions, hesitating ideals, tentative virtues, and groping philanthropies, amidst which it has been lived."[114] In the end, despite their unresolved differences, Hutton attested to the power of Newman's personal influence, which had been such a force in his own life. For Hutton, "the mere knowledge that he was living in the quiet Oratory at Edgbaston helped men to realise that the spiritual world is even more real than the material world, and that in that lonely, austere, and yet gracious figure, God had made a sign to Great Britain that the great purpose of life is a purpose to which this life hardly more than introduces us."[115]

CHAPTER 11

Culture and Hollowness: Newman and Matthew Arnold

"Your creeds are dead, your rites are dead,
  Your social order too!
Where tarries he, the Power who said:
  See I make all things new?"
                    Matthew Arnold, "Obermann Once More" (1867)

"I hold that unbelief is in some shape unavoidable in an age of intellect … considering that faith requires an act of will, and presupposes the due exercise of religious advantages."
                    J. H. Newman, *The Idea of a University* (1873)

"God keep us all from hollowness! I am sure I need this prayer for myself, as much as any one."
                    J. H. Newman to G. D. Ryder (7 January 1839)

Matthew Arnold and Arthur Hugh Clough will always be paired together, for all their differences, because they personify the doubts that riddled the Victorians. They were formed, in their separate ways, one as a neglected son and the other as an adopted son, by Thomas Arnold, the celebrated Headmaster of Rugby, with whose extravagant reputation Lytton Strachey had so much unfair fun. A. P. Stanley, Arnold's biographer, described Dr. Arnold in the pulpit of Rugby School Chapel, where, Sunday after Sunday, he could be seen and heard "combating face to face the evil with which, directly or indirectly, he was elsewhere perpetually struggling." For Stanley and for so many others, in addition to being a charismatic preacher, "He was still the scholar, the historian, and theologian, basing all that he said … on the deepest principles of the past and present. He was still the instructor and the schoolmaster, only teaching and educating with increased solemnity and energy. He was still the simple-hearted and earnest man, labouring to win others to share in his own personal feelings of disgust at sin, and love of goodness …"[1] The gist of Dr. Arnold's latitudinarian philosophy was that Christianity was moralism and it would prove of no

335

use whatever to either his son or his adopted son when they encountered what Bishop Ullathorne called "the subtle sophistries of unbelief."[2] There were other shared influences. Thomas Carlyle made a formidable impact on both men. In looking back at his undergraduate days at Balliol, Arnold recalled "the puissant voice of Carlyle; so sorely strained, over-used, and misused since, but then fresh, comparatively sound, and reaching our hearts with true, pathetic eloquence."[3] Clough referred to himself in a letter to a friend as a sort of Carlylean lieutenant, one who was "content to be an operative—to dress intellectual leather, cut it out to pattern and stitch and cobble it into boots and shoes for the benefit of the work that is being guided by wiser heads"—chief of whom was the author of *Chartism* and *Sartor Resartus*. Emerson was another strong influence. Arnold paid attention to him not because he thought him a good poet or even a good writer but because he held fast to "happiness and hope:" it was the hallmark of his "hopeful, serene, beautiful temper."[4] Clough saw Emerson as the epitome of a new American nobility. "He is very Yankee to look at, lank and sallow and not quite without the twang; but his look and voice are pleasing nevertheless and give you the impression of perfect intellectual cultivation as complete as would any great scientific man in England … One thing that struck everybody is that he is much less Emersonian than his Essays. There is no dogmatism … about him."[5] Few would have said that John Henry Newman lacked dogmatism and yet his was the influence over Arnold and Clough that was deepest precisely because he embodied the faith that neither could entirely reject nor accept. Arnold wrote a letter to Clough in which he bemoaned the discontents of the age, "these damned times," as he called them, in which "everything is against one—the height to which knowledge has come, the spread of luxury, our physical enervation, the absence of great *natures*, the unavoidable contact with millions of small ones, newspapers, cities, light profligate friends, moral desperadoes like Carlyle, our own selves, and the sickening consciousness of our own difficulties."[6] Newman, far from allowing himself to be made desperate by such difficulties, worked to resolve them, and although neither Arnold nor Clough adopted his Catholicism, they would always have their hands full trying to replace it. Arnold got at the very essence of the predicament that this put them into when he observed in *God and the Bible* (1875): "at the present moment two things about the Christian religion must be clear … One is that men cannot do without it; the other, that they cannot do with it as it is."[7] How Newman sheds light on the work of Arnold, especially in its religious aspects, will be the subject of this chapter. I shall look at Newman's influence on Clough in a separate chapter.

In 1880, in an essay entitled "The Study of Poetry," Matthew Arnold made a famous pronouncement: "The future of poetry is immense, because in poetry, where it is worthy of its high destinies, our race, as time goes on, will find an ever surer and surer stay. There is not a creed which is not shaken, not an accredited dogma which is not shown to be questionable, not a received tradition which does not threaten to dissolve. Our religion has materialised itself in the fact, in the supposed fact; it has attached its emotion to the fact, and now the fact is failing it. But for poetry the idea is everything; the rest is a world of illusion, of divine illusion. Poetry attaches its emotion to the idea; the idea *is* the fact. The strongest part of our religion to-day is its unconscious poetry."[8] Then, again, in the same essay, he was even more categorical. "More and more mankind will discover that we have to turn to poetry to interpret life for us, to console us, to sustain us. Without poetry, our science will appear incomplete; and most of what now passes for religion and philosophy will be replaced by poetry."[9] T. S. Eliot's response to this aspect of Arnold is worth quoting. "Nothing in this world or the next is a substitute for anything else," he told Harvard in 1933; "and if you find that you must do without something, such as religious faith or philosophic belief, then you must just do without it. I can persuade myself … that some of the things that I can hope to get are better worth having than some of the things I cannot get; or I may hope to alter myself so as to want different things; but I cannot persuade myself that it is the same desires that are satisfied, or that I have in effect the same thing under a different name."[10] This was to see the object as in itself it really is. Eliot was convinced that Arnold "comes to an opinion about poetry different from that of any of his predecessors. For Wordsworth and for Shelley poetry was a vehicle for one kind of philosophy or another, but the philosophy was something believed in. For Arnold the best poetry supersedes both religion and philosophy."[11] Arnold may have imagined that poetry was a substitute for religion but imagining such a thing and actually writing poetry in accordance with it are two different things. In his poetry, the personal God in whom he does not believe is his constant theme. Take that away and most of the poetry would be incomprehensible. So there is no sense in which his own poetry replaces religion: if anything, it shows that religion cannot be replaced. In his prose, he often expresses impatience with the practical, convinced that real discoveries in art and criticism can only be made in what he called "the order of ideas."[12] Yet since that "order" frequently landed him on "life's arid mount," where he could only attest the failure of ideas, his own preoccupation with the practical consequences of his ideas disproves them.[13] After all, what sharply differentiated Arnold from other English poets of the nineteenth century were not his ideas on religion or even his many critical and social interests but his despair. In trying to understand Arnold, therefore, it is best to pay attention to what he does rather than to what he claims he is doing. In all of his attempts to rub along without religion, one man came back to haunt him and that was Newman. But before I look at Newman's influence on Arnold, I should like to show how it was Newman, not Arnold, who first suggested that poetry might be a substitute for religion.

In *Lyra Innocentium*, the book of poems that John Keble published in 1846, the year after Newman's secession from the Church of England, Newman saw many contradictory impulses at play, which epitomized the incoherence of Keble's continuing adherence to an Anglo-Catholic faith that had more in common with Catholic Rome than Protestant Canterbury. At one level, he saw a kind of turning away from the world in Keble's poems: "Actual England is too sad to look upon. The Poet seems to turn away from the sight; else, in his own words, would it 'bruise too sore his tender heart;' and he takes refuge in the contemplation of that blessed time of life, in which alone the Church is what

God intended it, what Christ made it, the time of infancy and childhood. He strikes the Lyra Innocentium. He hangs over the first springs of divine grace, and fills his water-pots with joy 'ex fontibus Salvatoris,' before heresy, schism, ambition, worldliness, and cowardice have troubled the still depths."[14] Then, he saw the poems embodying Keble's devotion to the Blessed Virgin, which, for Newman, was proof of his yearning for genuine catholicity. "If the author is to sing of regenerate infants and their sinless blessedness, and is to view them in such lights as thence belong to them, to what is he necessarily brought back at once, but to the thought of our Lord in the first years of His earthly existence, when He was yet a little one in the arms and at the breast of His Blessed Mother? Hence the Virgin and Child is the special vision, as it may be called, which this truly evangelical poet has before him ..."[15] Bearing in mind their devotion to Mary, Newman saw Keble's verses tending to reinforce the Romish character of Anglo-Catholicism, even though their maker would not abandon the Church of England. Yet, despite the catholic tendencies of the verses, Newman saw in *Lyra Innocentium* evidence for what he saw in *The Christian Year* as well: Keble's readiness to use his verses to try to refurbish an otherwise dilapidated Anglicanism. "He did that for the Church of England which none but a poet could do: he made it poetical." In itemizing how Keble managed this, Newman brought to bear his own deep experience of "the huge ugly boxes of wood, sacred to preachers, frowning on the congregation in the place of the mysterious altar ..."

> Now the author of the Christian Year found the Anglican system all but destitute of this divine element, which is an essential property of Catholicism;—a ritual dashed upon the ground, trodden on, and broken piece-meal;—prayers, clipped, pieced, torn, shuffled about at pleasure, until the meaning of the composition perished, and offices which had been poetry were no longer even good prose;—antiphons, hymns, benedictions, invocations, shovelled away;—Scripture lessons turned into chapters;—heaviness, feebleness, unwieldiness, where the Catholic rites had had the lightness and airiness of a spirit;—vestments chucked off, lights quenched, jewels stolen, the pomp and circumstances of worship annihilated; a dreariness which could be felt, and which seemed the token of an incipient Socinianism, forcing itself upon the eye, the ear, the nostrils of the worshipper; a smell of dust and damp, not of incense; a sound of ministers preaching Catholic prayers, and parish clerks droning out Catholic canticles; the royal arms for the crucifix; huge ugly boxes of wood, sacred to preachers, frowning on the congregation in the place of the mysterious altar ... such was the religion of which this gifted author was,—not the judge and denouncer, (a deep spirit of reverence hindered it,)—but the renovator, as far as it has been renovated. Clear as was his perception of the degeneracy of his times, he attributed nothing of it to his Church, over which he threw the poetry of his own mind and the memory of better days.[16]

Here was how Keble's Marian, Anglo-Catholic poetry served as a substitute for an actual Anglican religion that was as little welcoming to Mary as it was void of true principles of catholicity. For Newman, this was a considerable achievement and he did not make light of it. "Such doctrine coming from one who had such claims on his readers from the weight of his name, the depth of his devotional and ethical tone, and the special gift of consolation, of which his poems themselves were the evidence, wrought a great work in the Establishment." For Newman, since it was clear that "the Anglican needs external assistance; [Keble's] poems became a sort of comment upon its formularies and ordinances, and almost elevated them into the dignity of a religious system. It kindled hearts towards his Church; it gave a something for the gentle and forlorn to cling to; and it raised up advocates for it among those, who otherwise, if God and their good Angel had suffered it, might have wandered away into some sort of philosophy, and acknowledged no Church at all. Such was the influence of his Christian Year; and doubtless his friends hail his Lyra Innocentium, as being likely to do a similar work in a more critical time."[17] Newman may have rejected the religion of art, towards which some of his contemporaries were beginning to incline, but he nevertheless showed that it was not an idea that Matthew Arnold had originated.

Arnold's version, however, was the one that became famous. It was also the one that inspired Walter Pater (1839–1894), the neurasthenic Fellow of Brasenose, whose overwrought essays had such an inordinate influence on Oscar Wilde and the aesthetes of the Nineties. "There are aspects of the religious character," Pater wrote in an early essay on Coleridge, "which have an artistic worth distinct from their religious import. Longing, a chastened temper, spiritual joy, are precious states of mind, not because they are part of a man's duty or because God has commanded them, still less because they are means of obtaining a reward, but because like culture itself they are remote, refined, intense, existing only by the triumph of a few over a dead world of routine in which there is no lifting of the soul at all." Art, in other words, could be a tenable substitute for religion, especially after the grounds of religion were shown to be untenable. "Religious belief, the craving for objects of belief, may be refined out of our hearts, but they must leave their sacred perfume, their spiritual sweetness behind." And to substantiate his point, he cited an unlikely authority. "This law of the highest intellectual life has sometimes seemed hard to understand. Those who maintain the claims of the older and narrower forms of religious life against the claims of culture are often embarrassed at finding the intellectual life heated through with the very graces to which they would sacrifice it. How often in the higher class of theological writings—writings which really spring from an original religious genius, such as those of Dr. Newman—does the modern aspirant to perfect culture seem to find the expression of the inmost delicacies of his own life, the same yet different!" Doubtless, Newman would have been surprised to see his theological writings cited to such confused purpose. Yet he could hardly have taken issue with Pater's confirming how the young were seeking in art what they could not obtain in Anglicanism; in this regard, Pater was only confirming what Newman had been saying since the 1840s. Protestantism could not satisfy the genuine religious impulse in men and women. Unlike Newman, however, Pater openly welcomed the exodus from Christianity. "The spiritualities of the Christian life have often drawn men on, little by little, into the broader spiritualities of systems opposed to it—pantheism, positivism, or a philosophy of indifference. Many in our own generation, through religion, have become dead to religion. How often do we look for some feature of the ancient religious life, not in a modern saint, but in a modern artist or philosopher! For those who have passed out of Christianity, perhaps its most precious souvenir is the ideal of a transcendental disinterestedness."[18] Michael Burleigh takes a different view in his brilliant book, *Earthy Powers*, which can be read as a comprehensive response to Matthew Arnold's claim that orthodox Christian faith became obsolete in the nineteenth century. "Art had replaced religion," Burleigh points out, "in the sense of giving higher meaning to a world that was increasingly disenchanted, temporarily giving striking form and purpose to mythic incarnations of the human self to audiences all too aware of the ambient chaos and meaninglessness of the Godless condition."[19]

One thing that makes Matthew Arnold (1822–1888) such an interesting figure is that he was never prepared for the full force of this "ambient chaos and meaninglessness" and when it gradually engulfed him it took him by a kind of tragic surprise. He was enamored of what he regarded as the "transcendental disinterestedness" of such figures as Sophocles and Goethe because he thought they might somehow sustain him in his own "Godless condition." *Culture and Anarchy* was written, in part, to suggest ways that this accelerating chaos could be negotiated. He sought out continental mentors largely because of his unhappy relationship with his father, who nicknamed him "Crab," after one of his legs was found to be deformed. When a doctor applied leg-irons to correct the problem, Arnold was left permanently maimed and always walked with a shambling gait. That he was a hobbled Pegasus even before he put pen to paper must have appealed to his sardonic sense of humor. If this deformity distanced him from his father, his temperament also set him apart. He had nothing of the earnestness or sanctimony that his father approved: he was too playful. Dr. Arnold's Christianity, with its emphasis on manliness, moralism and self-examination, alienated his more ironical son. When he was removed from Winchester and enrolled in Rugby, Arnold found himself competing for his father's affections with Clough, a devout and brilliant boy, four years his senior, who was the invariable apple of the famous Headmaster's eye. "I verily believe that my whole being is soaked through with the wishing and hoping and striving to do the school good," the insufferable golden boy in Clough wrote in 1836.[20] Arnold was the reverse of the golden boy, and this would always leave his father imagining him frivolous and unsound. Arnold initially took up writing poetry to escape the dreary loneliness he felt at Rugby. He certainly never attended to his studies with the diligence his father expected. Nevertheless, when it came time to sit his Balliol exam, the indifferent scholar suddenly buckled down. The exam itself was demanding: four days of written work followed by an extensive *viva voce*. More than 30 candidates competed for the two £30 per annum awards. In his incisive biography of Arnold, Ian Hamilton recounts the results.

When it was learned at Rugby that Matthew was one of the two winners, Dr. Arnold wrote: 'I had not the least expectation of his being successful ... The news actually filled me with astonishment.' For the headmaster, a Balliol scholarship meant Clough or—before him—Lake or A.P. Stanley, his own biographer-to-be. It meant surely a more strenuous Christian commitment than was evident so far in the always amiable Matthew. What did this triumph signify? A lowering of standards at Balliol? An error of judgment at Rugby? How was it that Matthew had managed to pretend to be his father's son? Had he been practicing in secret?[21]

At Oxford, where he arrived in October 1841, after the publication of Tract 90, Arnold refused to join either the Arnoldians or the followers of Newman. Nevertheless, he enjoyed hearing Newman preach, which was a fair testament to his independence, considering the "unmixed aversion" with which his father regarded Newman and his Tractarian views.[22] Still, however glowingly Matthew spoke of the man who had wondered aloud if his father was Christian, he always referred to Newman with an air of condescension. In this, he resembled Lord Acton, who referred to Newman in letters to his Liberal friends as "the venerable Noggs."[23] In 1881, Arnold wrote an account of what it was like to hear Newman's legendary sermons, in which he could not resist taking a swipe at the man, who, at other times, he was intent on claiming as one of his masters.

The name of Cardinal Newman is a great name to the imagination still; his genius and his style are still things of power. But he is over eighty years old; he is in the Oratory at Birmingham; he has adopted, for the doubts and difficulties which beset men's minds to-day, a solution which, to speak frankly, is impossible. Forty years ago he was in the very prime of life; he was close at hand to us at Oxford; he was preaching in St. Mary's pulpit every Sunday; he seemed about to transform and to renew what was for us the most national and natural institution in the world, the Church of England. Who could resist the charm of that spiritual apparition, gliding in the dim afternoon light through the aisles of St. Mary's, rising into the pulpit, and then, in the most entrancing of voices, breaking the silence with words and thoughts which were a religious music—subtle, sweet, mournful? I seem to hear him still, saying: 'After the fever of life, after weariness and sicknesses, fightings and despondings, languor and fretfulness, struggling and succeeding; after all the changes and chances of this troubled unhealthy state,—at length comes death, at length the white throne of God, at length the beatific vision.'[24]

Arnold was quoting here from "Peace in Believing," the sermon which Newman preached on Trinity Sunday in 1839, two years before Arnold came up to Oxford. In referring to the sermon as "religious music," Arnold was only the first of many who would effuse about Newman's style and ignore his content. The content of "Peace in Believing" could have been written expressly with the future poet in mind, who spent so many of his days chronicling unbelief's lack of peace. "The doctrine of the Blessed Trinity," Newman wrote, "has been made the subject of especial contention among the professed followers of Christ. It has brought a sword upon earth, but it was intended to bring peace. And it does bring peace to those who humbly receive it in faith. Let us beg of God ... that it may not be an occasion of strife, but worship; not of division, but of unity; not jealousy, but of love."[25] For Arnold to choose to quote this one sermon, out of the 1,270 Newman preached when he was an Anglican, showed a certain self-knowledge.[26] Here was the peace he elected to renounce.

Some of Arnold's most revelatory writing is contained in letters he wrote to Clough. "If one loved what was beautiful and interesting in itself passionately enough, one would produce what was excellent without troubling with religious dogmas at all," he explained to his friend in 1853. "As it is, we are *warm* only when dealing with these last—and what is frigid is always bad." However opposed he was to acknowledging that truth might have something to do with religion, he recognized why "most others stick to the old religious dogmas ... this *warmth* is the great blessing, and this frigidity is the great curse—and on the old religious road they have still the best chance of getting the one and avoiding the other."[27] Here, in a nutshell, was Arnold's peculiarly Anglican skepticism, in which he sought to retain the consolatory warmth after jettisoning the truth of Christianity. In this respect, he was reminiscent of another good English poet who made despair his specialty. "I'm an agnostic," Philip Larkin would tell anyone who asked, "but an Anglican agnostic of course."[28] For truth, Arnold would go not to religion but to culture, the consequences of which Eliot saw so clearly. "The total effect of Arnold's philosophy is to set up Culture in the place of Religion, and to leave Religion to be laid waste by the anarchy of feeling. And culture is a term which each man not only may interpret as he pleases, but must indeed interpret as he can. So the gospel of Pater follows naturally upon the prophecy of Arnold."[29]

After Newman's conversion, Arnold became a Fellow of Oriel, where Newman and his father had also been Fellows, and then, in 1851, an inspector of schools, a demanding post requiring much traveling up and down the country, which he held for 35 years. "I must go back to my charming occupation of hearing students give lessons," he wrote to one correspondent with an audible groan. "Here is my programme for this afternoon: Avalanches—the Steam Engine—The Thames—India Rubber—Bricks—The Battle of Poitiers—Subtraction—The Reindeer—The Gunpowder Plot—The Jordan. Alluring, is it not? Twenty minutes each, and the days of one's life are only threescore and ten."[30]

Thomas Arnold (1823–1900), Matthew's younger brother, was an inspector of schools in New Zealand and while posted in Hobart Town, he wrote to Newman to tell him how his writings had exercised "the greatest influence" over his mind. "You who have said that a man who has once comprehended and admitted the theological definition of God, cannot logically rest until he has admitted the whole system of Catholicism, will not wonder if after having admitted Christianity to be an assemblage of real indubitable historical facts, I gradually came to see that the foundation of the One-Catholic Church was one of those facts, and that She is the only safe and sufficient witness, across time and space, to the reality of those facts and to the mode of their occurrence."[31] Thomas converted in 1856, over the vehement objections of his wife. After lapsing from the Church in the 1860s and reconverting in 1876, his brother Matthew wrote him a revealing letter:

> As to Catholicism, that is a long story. Catholicism is most interesting, and were I born in a Roman Catholic country I should most certainly never leave the Catholic Church for a Protestant; but neither then or now could I imagine that the Catholic Church possessed 'the truth,' or anything like it, or that it *could* possess it.[32]

In 1857, Tom and Matthew dined with Clough at Verrey's Restaurant in Regent Street, and during dinner, Matthew warmly recommended some work of Voltaire. Clough took offense, objecting to its licentiousness. When Matthew brushed this aside, Clough replied, with some acerbity, "Well, you don't think any the better of yourself for that, do you?"[33] Had Newman been one of the diners that night (however difficult it is to imagine him dining in a London restaurant) he might have come to Matthew's defense. Newman always had a good word for Voltaire, despite his infidelity, asking *vis-à-vis* the authors of France, "who is there that holds a place among its writers so historical and important, who is so copious, so versatile, so brilliant, as that Voltaire, who is an open scoffer at everything sacred, venerable, or high-minded?"[34] At the same time, in Matthew's taunting Clough with his would-be infidelity, Newman might have seen a tell-tale diffidence. As he told Lady Herbert of Lea, "I think the great argument against this day's infidelity is, that it does not, cannot believe in itself. I do not deny, of course, that there are certain minds who have as little concern about their religious ignorance and [are] as well satisfied with themselves, as are Unitarians, or Wesleyans etc etc in their own form of faith; but in the majority of unbelievers there is a deep misgiving that they are wrong or probably wrong."[35] Whether Arnold was among these dubious doubters is questionable, but his poetry certainly suggests that he had trouble believing his own disbelief.

In 1851, Arnold married Fanny Wightman, whose delicacy put one observer in mind of a Dresden shepherdess.[36] Her husband made passing reference to her in his poem, "On the Rhine," where he speaks of "Eyes too expressive to be blue/Too lovely to be grey." The daughter of a prominent judge, Fanny had been brought up in the High Church and had strong Tractarian sympathies. In his vivid biography of Arnold, Park Honan gives a sympathetic portrait of this admirable woman, with whom Arnold had six children, three of whom predeceased him. Of all his friends and relations, Franny understood him best. Certainly, she recognized, for all his high spirits, the pain he suffered in measuring the confines of his willful skepticism.

Slowly she wore down his egocentricity. She was not swept off her feet by Rugby and the Dr. Arnold legend, or by Matthew's usually inchoate liberal views. She sensed in him, however, a paradoxical austerity, an inner area of mind that her love could not penetrate—and this made her curious about his verse. His poetry seemed rather gloomier by far than the delightful man who wrote it: 'From the austere tone of some of the poems,' she felt, nobody could imagine his 'lovable nature,' and that he, indeed, was 'Consoled by spirits gloriously gay!' This woman was his chief consoling spirit: 'beautiful & graceful as his prose is,' she wrote generously, 'he will be best remembered by his poetry.'[37]

Three years before marrying Franny, Arnold traveled to Thun, Switzerland, where he met "Marguerite," his elusive Alpine muse, in whose "frank eyes" he saw "an angelic gravity."[38] One of the reasons why Arnold went to Thun was to see the places where Etienne Senacour (1770–1846), the French litterateur, had set his epistolary novel *Obermann* (1804), the luxuriant melancholy of which had an enormous impact on French and English writers, including Arnold and Sainte-Beauve. Clough's decision to cast *Amours de Voyage* as a series of letters might have been a mocking response to *Obermann*. In any case, Arnold's "Marguerite" could have walked out of the pages of this paean to Romantic ennui. Although many biographers have set out to discover the real "Marguerite," none has ever succeeded, which leads one to suspect that she might have been imaginary. Nevertheless, the sense of solitude to which Arnold gave such moving expression in the "Marguerite" poems suggests the extent to which he felt cut off from his fellows:

> … in the sea of life enisled
> With echoing straits between us thrown
> Dotting the shoreless watery wild
> We mortals live *alone*.

Newman knew loneliness as well. After he survived his bout of fever in Sicily, he recalled how Gennaro, the faithful Neapolitan who had cared for him in his illness, hinted that he might like the blue cloak Newman had worn throughout the ordeal—"a little thing for him to set his services at," Newman admitted, though he himself was strangely attached to it. "It had nursed me all through my illness … I had nearly lost it at Corfu—it was stolen by a solider but recovered. I have it still. I have brought it up here to Littlemore, & on some cold nights I have had it on my bed. I have so few things to sympathize with me, that I take to clokes."[39] In January 1846, weeks before he left Littlemore, he wrote to his close friend Ambrose St. John, "You may think how lonely I am." Leaving Oxford and Littlemore was "like going on the open sea."[40] Arnold also invoked the sea to describe his loneliness.

> Who order'd, that their longing's fire
> Should be, as soon as kindled, cool'd?
> Who renders vain their deep desire?—

A God, a God their severance ruled!
And bade betwixt their shores to be
The unplumb'd, salt, estranging sea.

If Arnold's loneliness confirmed God's absence, Newman's reaffirmed His presence. Writing to his sister Jemima in June 1836, after the deaths of his mother and of his best friend, Hurrell Froude, Newman wrote: "I am not more lonely than I have been a long while. God intends me to be lonely. He has so framed my mind that I am in a great measure beyond the sympathies of other people, and thrown upon Himself ..."[41]

After writing the books of poetry on which his reputation rests, Arnold turned to criticism, in which he took up not only literature, society and education, but religion. *St. Paul and Protestantism* (1870), *Literature and Dogma* (1873), and *God and the Bible* (1875) attested to Arnold's growing interest in religious themes, though he would go to his grave convinced that, in the nineteenth century, God had somehow gone missing. A fair sampling of these books can be gleaned from *Literature and Dogma*, in which he dispenses with argument—never one of his strong suits—and simply records the trajectory of his own loss of faith. Thus, he says, "of the premature and false criticism to which we are accustomed, we drop evidently weak parts first; we retain the rest, to drop it gradually and piece by piece as it loosens and breaks up. But it is all of one order, and in time it will all go. Not the Athanasian Creed's damnatory clauses only, but the whole Creed; not this one Creed only, but the three Creeds ..."[42] Having unburdened himself of what he regarded as false credulity, Arnold could do as he liked, which was to treat the Bible as literature and, in the process, push aside the Fathers and Schoolmen and write his own theology. "The truth is," he writes in one inimitable passage, "one may have a great respect for Lord Shaftesbury," the Evangelical factory reformer, who gave England its first Lunacy Act (1845), "and yet be permitted ... to imagine something far beyond him. And this is the good of such an unpretending definition of God as ours: *the Eternal Power, not ourselves, that makes for righteousness;*—it leaves the infinite to the imagination and to the gradual efforts of countless ages of men, slowly feeling after more of it and finding it ..."[43] Here was the Arnoldian theory of development in all its bravura succinctness.

In the twenty-first century, a good deal of Arnold on religion calls to mind the relativism that has wrecked our own culture, which is the aspect of the man that makes him so appealing to Stefan Collini, one of the house intellectuals of *The London Review of Books*. "There is no surer proof of a narrow and ill-instructed mind," Arnold informs his readers in *Literature and Dogma*, "than to think and uphold that what a man takes to be the truth on religious matters is always to be proclaimed. Our truth on these matters, and likewise the error of others, is something so relative that the good or harm likely to be done by speaking ought to be taken into account."[44] Indeed, Arnold went further: "The man who believes that his truth on religious matters is so absolutely the truth ... is in our day almost always a man whose truth is half blunder, and wholly useless."[45] Newman must have marveled at how Dr. Arnold's son was following in his father's footsteps: the maker's mark was on the blade. And yet unlike his father, Arnold paid close attention to the toll of unbelief, what he called "this strange disease of modern life/With its sick hurry, its divided aims/Its heads o'er tax'd, its palsied hearts ..."[46]

> See! In the rocks of the world
> Marches the host of mankind,
> A feeble, wavering line,
> Where are they tending?—A God
> Marshall'd them, gave them their goal.
> Ah, but the way is so long!
> Years they have been in the wild!
> Sore thirst plagues them, the rocks,
> Rising all round, overawe;
> Factions divide them, their host
> Threatens to break, to dissolve ...[47]

In 1880, together with Lord and Lady Salisbury, the Bishop of London (John Jackson) and Dean Church, Arnold attended the reception at Norfolk House that the Duke of Norfolk held for Cardinal Newman because, as he said, "I wanted to have spoken once in my life to Newman." Arnold's description of the evening was characteristically mordant. "Newman was in costume—not full Cardinal's costume, but a sort of vest with gold about it and the red cap; he was in state at one end of the room, with the Duke of Norfolk at one side of him and a chaplain on the other, and people filed before him as before the Queen, dropping on their knees when they were presented and kissing his hand. It was the faithful who knelt in general, but then it was in general only the faithful who were presented. That old mountebank Lord Ripon dropped on his knees, however and mumbled the Cardinal's hand like a piece of cake. I only made a deferential bow, and Newman took my hand in both of his and was charming. He said, 'I ventured to tell the Duchess I should like to see you.'"[48]

In 1888, Arnold died of a heart attack at the age of 66—the same thing that killed his father at the same age. T. S. Eliot summed up his career by saying "He is the poet and critic of a period of false stability. All his writing in the kind of *Literature and Dogma* seems to me a valiant attempt to dodge the issue, to mediate between Newman and Huxley; but his poetry, the best of it, is too honest to employ any but his genuine feelings of unrest, loneliness and dissatisfaction."[49] Arnold himself would say as much himself in that wistful confection, "The Scholar-Gypsy:"

> Thou waitest for the spark from Heaven; and we,
> Light half-believers of our casual creeds,
>   Who never deeply felt, nor clearly will'd,
>   Whose insight never has borne fruit in deeds,
> Whose vague resolves never have been fulfill'd;
>   For whom each year we see

Breeds new beginning, disappointments new;
Who hesitate and falter life away,
And lose tomorrow the ground won to-day—
Ah! do not we, wanderer! await it too?[50]

To understand why poetry became such a necessary asylum for Arnold it is necessary to look at his prose. The work in which he gave his most sustained account of his cultural and social views is *Culture and Anarchy* (1869), in which he wrote: "The whole scope of the essay is to recommend culture as the great help out of our present difficulties; culture being a pursuit of our total perfection by means of getting to know, on all the matters which most concern us, the best which has been thought and said in the world, and, through this knowledge, turning a stream of fresh and free thought upon our stock notions and habits, which we now follow staunchly but mechanically, vainly imagining that there is a virtue in following them staunchly which makes up for the mischief of following them mechanically." Arnold only vaguely defined the culture for which he was advocating. "More and more he who examines himself will find the difference it makes to him, at the end of any given day, whether or no he has pursued his avocations throughout it without reading at all; and whether or no, having read something, he has read the newspapers only. This, however, is a matter for each man's private conscience and experience. If a man without books or reading, or reading nothing but his letters and the newspapers, gets nevertheless a fresh and free play of the best thoughts upon his stock notions and habits, he has got culture. He has got that for which we prize and recommend culture; he has got that which at the present moment we seek culture that it may give us. This inward operation is the very life and essence of culture, as we conceive it."[51] To claim that reading newspapers might become a matter for private conscience betrayed the ostentatious high-brow in Arnold, for whom newspapers were reprehensibly vulgar. Something of this occasionally amusing pose (which Oscar Wilde would later perfect) can be seen in his discussion of the English aristocracy. Apropos this passage, it is striking how many middle-class opponents of Disraeli's Tory democracy would complain about the political pact that Gladstone's great opponent forged between the working classes and the aristocracy. Yet Arnold knew English society well enough to recognize that this was a pact forged long before Disraeli arrived on the scene, though Arnold omits to mention the two passions that gave the pact its indissolubility: gambling and drink.

The Barbarians brought with them that staunch individualism, as the modern phrase is, and that passion for doing as one likes, for the assertion of personal liberty, which appears to Mr. Bright the central idea of English life, and of which we have, at any rate, a very rich supply. The stronghold and natural seat of this passion was in the nobles of whom our aristocratic class are the inheritors ; and this class, accordingly, have signally manifested it, and have done much by their example to recommend it to the body of the nation, who already, indeed, had it in their blood. The Barbarians, again, had the passion for field-sports; and they have handed it on to our aristocratic class, who of this passion too, as of the passion for asserting one's personal liberty, are the great natural stronghold. The care of the Barbarians for the body, and for all manly exercises; the vigour, good looks, and fine complexion which they acquired and perpetuated in their families by these means,—all this may be observed still in our aristocratic class. The chivalry of the Barbarians, with its characteristics of high spirit, choice manners, and distinguished bearing,—what is this but the attractive commencement of the politeness of our aristocratic class? In some Barbarian noble, no doubt, one would have admired, if one could have been then alive to see it, the rudiments of our politest peer. Only, all this culture (to call it by that name) of the Barbarians was an exterior culture mainly. It consisted principally in outward gifts and graces, in looks, manners, accomplishments, prowess. The chief inward gifts which had part in it were the most exterior, so to speak, of inward gifts, those which come nearest to outward ones; they were courage, a high spirit, self-confidence. Far within, and unawakened, lay a whole range of powers of thought and feeling, to which these interesting productions of nature had, from the circumstances of their life, no access. Making allowances for the difference of the times, surely we can observe precisely the same thing now in our aristocratic class.[52]

Max Beerbohm, a shrewd admirer of Arnold, got at something of his essence when he observed: "Surely it is because M.A. was so genuinely solemn (and even desperate) at heart that we love his outbursts of fun so much. Without the contrast of what underlies his writing, how much less delicious would be what suddenly now and again bubbles up!"[53] In the case of *Culture and Anarchy*, these "outbursts of fun" do save what would otherwise be an impossibly confused, vague, schoolmasterly performance.

After referring to his Barbarians, Philistines and Populace as a "humble attempt at a scientific nomenclature," he proceeds to describe how his various puppets confound license with liberty.

All of us, so far as we are Barbarians, Philistines, or Populace, imagine happiness to consist in doing what one's ordinary self likes. What one's ordinary self likes differs according to the class to which one belongs, and has its severer and its lighter side; always, however, remaining machinery, and nothing more. The graver self of the Barbarian likes honours and consideration; his more relaxed self, field-sports and pleasure. The graver self of one kind of Philistine likes fanaticism, business, and money-making; his more relaxed self, comfort and tea-meetings. Of another kind of Philistine, the graver self likes trade unions; the relaxed self, deputations, or hearing Mr. Odger speak. The sterner self of the Populace likes bawling, hustling, and smashing; the lighter self, beer. But in each class there are born a certain number of natures with a curiosity about their best self, with a bent for seeing things as they are, for disentangling themselves from machinery, for simply concerning themselves with reason and the will of

God, and doing their best to make these prevail;— for the pursuit, in a word, of perfection.[54]

Muddled as the conclusion of this might be, Arnold's insistence that "doing as one likes" is not the same thing as pursuing perfection is a theme to which Newman returned often as well. Some claim that Newman sanctions "doing as one likes" because he somehow shares the self-approving notion of conscience that *soi-disant* liberal Catholics prize. But Newman agreed with Arnold that "doing as one likes" is a recipe for anarchy. In his *Letter to the Duke of Norfolk*, Newman could not have been clearer that, for him, conscience could not warrant "doing as one likes."

> The rule and measure of duty is not utility, nor expedience, nor the happiness of the greatest number, nor State convenience, nor fitness, order and the *pulchrum*. Conscience is not a long-sighted selfishness, nor a desire to be consistent with oneself, but a messenger from Him who, both in nature and in grace, speaks to us behind a veil, and teaches and rules us by His representatives. Conscience is the aboriginal Vicar of Christ …[55]

Agreed though they might be on the dangers of self-will, Arnold and Newman profoundly disagreed on its remedy. For Arnold, culture was the solution; while for Newman it was obedience to conscience, formed not by "a desire to be consistent with oneself," but by the authority of the Magisterium.

Another striking aspect of *Culture and Anarchy* is Arnold's contention that his thoroughly materialist notion of culture—which he defined as "*a study of perfection*"—had something to do with the Oxford Movement. The very fact that he should invoke Newman and the Tractarians in this context reveals the supple confusions that beset him whenever he attempted to justify his skepticism.

> Oxford, the Oxford of the past, has many faults; and she has heavily paid for them in defeat, in isolation, in want of hold upon the modern world. Yet we in Oxford, brought up amidst the beauty and sweetness of that beautiful place, have not failed to seize one truth:—the truth that beauty and sweetness are essential characters of a complete human perfection. When I insist on this, I am all in the faith and tradition of Oxford. I say boldly that this our sentiment for beauty and sweetness, our sentiment against hideousness and rawness, has been at the bottom of our attachment to so many beaten causes, of our opposition to so many triumphant movements. And the sentiment is true, and has never been wholly defeated, and has shown its power even in its defeat. We have not won our political battles, we have not carried our main points, we have not stopped our adversaries' advance, we have not marched victoriously with the modern world; but we have told silently upon the mind of the country, we have prepared currents of feeling which sap our adversaries' position when it seems gained, we have kept up our own communications with the future. Look at the course

of the great movement which shook Oxford to its centre some thirty years ago! It was directed, as any one who reads Dr. Newman's *Apology* may see, against what in one word may be called "liberalism." Liberalism prevailed; it was the appointed force to do the work of the hour; it was necessary, it was inevitable that it should prevail. The Oxford movement was broken, it failed; our wrecks are scattered on every shore ...[56]

The reference here to "our wrecks" was revealing. However much the rhetorician in Arnold might wish to cover himself in the mantle of Tractarianism, he had nothing to do with the Oxford Movement, a fact which was made patent when he suggested that the Movement had been launched to gratify "the keen desire for beauty and sweetness" or "to know, on all the matters which most concern us, the best which has been thought and said in the world." Here was an interpretation of Tractarianism that would have richly appealed to Hurrell Froude's sense of the ridiculous. Arnold's characterization of what the Tractarians opposed and what opposed them was equally tell-tale. According to Arnold, the liberalism that the Tractarians opposed was "the great middle-class liberalism, which had for the cardinal points of its belief the Reform Bill of 1832, and local self-government, in politics; in the social sphere, free-trade, unrestricted competition, and the making of large industrial fortunes; in the religious sphere, the Dissidence of Dissent and the Protestantism of the Protestant religion."[57] This is so far off the mark it is funny. And by borrowing Edmund Burke's memorable phrase Arnold only called attention to the emptiness of his rhetoric, though no amount of rhetoric could conceal the fact that Arnold had no grounds for involving Newman or the Tractarians in his vague brief for the benefits of culture, especially a culture that should somehow spring from the grave of religion. In this regard, it is amusing that Newman should have instructed his publisher to send Arnold a copy of his *Discussions and Arguments on Various Subjects* (1872), which includes *The Tamworth Reading Room* (1841). If Arnold took the time to read this witty polemic, he might have paused over this sentence: "If we attempt to effect a moral improvement by means of poetry, we shall but mature into a mawkish, frivolous and fastidious sentimentalism."[58]

Even the Cambridge moralist Henry Sidgwick (1838–1900), who went from Rugby to Trinity College, Cambridge, where he taught ethics for many years, before succumbing to the table-tapping and hypnotism that attracted so many learned Anglicans, saw the absurdity of Arnold's trying to tout his own vague notions of culture by invoking Newman. Writing in response to Arnold's book in *Macmillan's Magazine*, Sidgwick argued that "Liberalism to Dr Newman may have meant something of all this; but what (as I infer from the *Apologia*) it more especially meant to him was a much more intelligent force than all these, which Mr. Arnold omits ... Liberalism, Dr. Newman thought ... wished to extend just the languid patronage to religion that Mr. Arnold does. What priesthoods were good for in the eyes of Liberalism were the functions, as I have said, of spiritual police; and that is all Mr. Arnold thinks they are good for at present; and even in the future (unless I misunderstand him), if we want more, he would have us come to culture. But Dr. Newman knew that even the existing religions, far as they fell below his ideal, were good for much more than this; this view of them seemed to him not only shallow and untrue, but perilous, deadly, soul-destroying; and inasmuch as it commended itself to intellectual men, and was an intelligent force, he fought against it, not, I think, with much sweetness or light, but with a blind, eager, glowing asperity which, tempered always by humility and candour, was and is very impressive. Dr. Newman fought for a point of view which it required culture to appreciate, and therefore he fought in some sense with culture; but he did not fight for culture, and to conceive him combating side by side with Mr. Matthew Arnold is almost comical."[59]

If there were comical elements in Arnold's analysis of the tensions within late Victorian society—his descriptions of his "Liberals", "Philistines" and "Barbarians" are always entertaining—there was also something distinctly authoritarian in his recommendation of the state as the repository of the culture he wished to see flourish. For Arnold, "a State in which law is authoritative and sovereign, a firm and settled course of public order, is requisite if man is to bring to maturity anything precious and lasting now, or to found anything precious and lasting for the future. Thus, in our eyes, the very framework and exterior order of the State, whoever may administer the State, is sacred; and culture is the most resolute enemy of anarchy, because of the great hopes and designs for the State which culture teaches us to nourish. But as, believing in right reason, and having faith in the progress of humanity towards perfection, and ever labouring for this end, we grow to have clearer sight of the ideas of right reason, and of the elements and helps of perfection, and come gradually to fill the framework of the State with them, to fashion its internal composition and all its laws and institutions conformably to them, and to make the State more and more the expression, as we say, of our best self, which is not manifold, and vulgar, and unstable, and contentious, and ever-varying, but one, and noble, and secure, and peaceful, and the same for all mankind,—with what aversion shall we not *then* regard anarchy, with what firmness shall we not check it, when there is so much that is so precious which it will endanger!"[60] The usefulness of such vague effusions for those advocating Marxist statism is obvious. Stefan Collini is surely right when he says in his entry on Arnold in the *Oxford Dictionary of National Biography* that "Politically, his leanings were always towards an enlarged liberalism ... Certainly, no writer who was as severe as Arnold was on the deforming power of inequality and who referred to the French Revolution as 'the greatest, the most animating event in history' could easily be accommodated in the ranks of conservatism."[61] Yet whenever Arnold attempted to define his understanding of the State, he only compounded this vagueness. In "Democracy" (1861), in answer to those who argued, as he says, that the State is little more than "a string of minister's names" and "their judgment on national affairs no "better than that of the rest of the world," Arnold replied that ministers "have two great advantages from their position: access to almost boundless means of information, and the enlargement of mind which the habit of dealing with great affairs tends to produce."[62] What is striking about this and indeed about *Culture and Anarchy* as a whole is how much of it recalls the belief in the moral force of knowledge that characterized Sir Robert Peel's Tamworth Reading Room, a belief which Newman had a good deal of fun lambasting in his 'Catholicus' letters to *The Times*.[63]

> It does not require many words, then, to determine that, taking human nature as it is actually found ... to say that it consists, or in any essential manner is placed, in the cultivation of Knowledge, that the mind is changed by a discovery, or saved by a diversion, and can thus be amused into immortality,—that grief, anger, cowardice, self-conceit, pride, or passion, can be subdued by an examination of shells or grasses, or inhaling of gases, or chipping of rocks, or calculating the longitude, is the veriest of pretences which sophist or mountebank ever professed to a gaping auditory. If virtue be a mastery over the mind, if its end be action, if its perfection be inward order, harmony, and peace, we must seek it in graver and holier places than in Libraries and Reading-rooms.[64]

These were sentiments later echoed by Tennyson, who wrote in *In Memoriam* of how he rediscovered God "...not in world or sun/Or eagle's wing, or insect's eye/Nor through the questions men may try/The petty cobwebs we have spun" but through a child's "doubt and fear ... a child that cries/But crying, knows his father's near."

If flippancy mars Arnold's prose, honesty distinguishes his best poetry. Indeed, the poetry repudiates the theoretical irresponsibility of his prose. In "The Function of Criticism at the Present Time" (1864), Arnold wrote that "Criticism must maintain its independence of the practical spirit and its aims. Even with well-meant efforts of the practical spirit it must express dissatisfaction, if in the sphere of the ideal they seem impoverishing and limiting."[65] For Arnold, in sharp contrast to Newman, the practical was tantamount to philistinism. This fondness for "the sphere of the ideal" led Arnold to question more than simply the "practical spirit." In "Civilization in the United States" (1888), he called for a re-translation of the text, "Except a man be born again he cannot see the kingdom of God," remarking "Instead of *again*, we ought to translate *from above*; and instead of taking the kingdom of God in the sense of a life in Heaven above, we ought to take it, as its speaker meant it, in the sense of the reign of saints, a renovated and perfected human society on earth, the ideal society of the future."[66] Here one can see why Arnold is often regarded as the Father of Modernism. In this regard, Arnold's boast that he "kept up communications with the future" is true enough.[67] By contrast, in his poem, "The Buried Life," the "ideal society of the future" might be a million years away. Instead, he turns his attention to something much more immediate, and infinitely more mysterious: the "unregarded river of our life." Here, the mountebank departs his platform and Arnold is only concerned that we should "seem to be/Eddying at large in blind uncertainty ..."—not the sort of admission that the witty lecturer permitted himself in his prose.

> But often, in the world's most crowded streets,
> But often, in the din of strife,
> There rises an unspeakable desire
> After the knowledge of our buried life;
>   A thirst to spend our fire and restless force
>   In tracking out our true, original course;
>   A longing to inquire
>   Into the mystery of this heart which beats
> So wild, so deep in us ...[68]

Speaking of his lost faith, Arnold invokes both his father and Newman, in "Stanzas from the Green Chartreuse" (1852), a poem which Eliot might have had in mind when he was composing "Little Gidding," with its introspective encounter with Eliot's dead master—"The eyes of a familiar compound ghost."

> For rigorous teachers seized my youth,
> And purged its faith, and trimmed its fire,
> Showed me the high, white star of Truth,
> These bade me gaze, and there aspire.
> Even now their whispers pierce the gloom:
> *What dost thou then in this living tomb?*
>
> Forgive me, masters of the mind!
> At whose behest I long ago
> So much unlearnt, so much resigned—
> I come not here to be your foe!
> I seek these anchorites, not in ruth,
> To curse and to deny your truth ...[69]

When Newman died, Richard Holt Hutton would write in the *Spectator*, "There are deaths yet to come which will agitate the English world more than Cardinal Newman's, but there has been none, so far as we know, that will leave the world that really knew him so keen a sense of deprivation, of a white star extinguished, of a sign vanished, of an age impoverished, of a grace withdrawn."[70] Since Arnold died two years before Newman, he could not have savored Hutton's allusion to his own poem. Still, as early as 1871, Arnold was writing Newman in an elegiac tone about what he saw as Newman's influence on him. "I cannot forbear adding, what I have often wished to tell you, that no words can be too strong to express the interest with which I used to hear you at Oxford, and the pleasure with which I continue to read your writings now. We are all of us carried in ways not of our own making or choosing, but nothing can ever do away the effect you have produced upon me, for it consists in a general disposition of mind rather than in a particular set of ideas. In all the conflicts I have with modern Liberalism and Dissent, and with their pretensions and shortcomings, I recognize your work; and I can truly say that no praise gives me so much pleasure as to be told (which sometimes happens) that a thing

I have said reminds people, either in manner or matter, of you."[71] Newman was doubtless startled to learn that anything Arnold had written could remind anyone of his own writings. Nevertheless, his response was at once tactful and candid. "I thank you sincerely for it," he wrote, "and with quite as intimate an interest have I read what you have lately written ... The more so, as regards your letters as well as your writings, for the very reason that I am so sensitively alive to the great differences of opinion which separate us. I wish with all my heart I could make them less; but there they are, and I can only resign myself to them, as best I may."[72]

These "great differences" notwithstanding, Arnold would always insist that Newman's influence on him had been equally great. After Newman sent him a volume of his verse, Arnold praised "their simple clear diction," which was refreshing "after the somewhat sophisticated and artificial poetical diction which Mr Tennyson's popularity has made prevalent." This "simple clear diction" often distinguishes Arnold's own best poetry, though Henry James complained that Arnold's style in this regard showed "a slight abuse of meagerness for distinction's sake."[73] Arnold also wished to thank Newman for "the more inward qualities and excellencies of the Poems," which reminded him of "how much I, like so many others, owe to your influence and writings; the impression of which is so profound, and so mixed up with all that is most essential in what I do and say, that I can never cease to be conscious of it and to have an inexpressible sense of gratitude and attachment to its Author; though I might easily, I fear, grow tedious and obtrusive in attempting to convey to him my acknowledgment of it in words."[74]

One aspect of Newman's influence on Arnold was to impress on him that renunciation of the Christian faith could not be undertaken lightly. Arnold's prose writings on religion might exhibit a tiresome glibness—the professional classes enjoyed reading about a faith to which they no longer subscribed and Arnold was always ready to exploit this demand by supplying what he called "recreative religion"—but his poetry shows that his inability to believe made for an anguish that he could never dispel.[75] So, in this regard, his poetry corroborates Newman's warnings about the true nature of unbelief—a subject on which Clough's poetry would also focus.

That so many of Arnold's poems are elegies is not accidental. For Arnold, the past had an enviable coherence that the faithless present lacked. In "Dover Beach," he acknowledged that it was the loss of faith that was at the center of his own vision of loss.

> The Sea of Faith
> Was once, too, at the full, and round earth's shore
> Lay like the folds of a bright girdle furl'd.
> But now I only hear
> Its melancholy, long, withdrawing roar,
> Retreating to the breath
> Of the night-wind, down the vast edges drear
> And naked shingles of the world.[76]

If such loss usurps the present and evacuates the future, it invests the past with an immemorial sadness, and here, in this unhappy context, in a poem called "Bacchanalia, or The New Age," Arnold once again invokes Newman and his father.

> Where many a splendour finds its tomb,
> Many spent fames and fallen mights—
> The one or two immortal lights
> Rise slowly up into the sky
> To shine there everlastingly,
> Like stars over the bounding hill,
> The epoch ends, the world is still.[77]

And in another sad, fragmentary poem, Arnold all but admits that he could only survive the heroic example of these masters as an exile from his own true feelings, which was one measure of the depth of his distress.

> Below the surface-stream, shallow and light,
> Of what we say we feel—below the stream,
> As light, of what we think we feel—there flows
> With noiseless current strong, obscure and deep,
> The central stream of what we feel indeed.[78]

In his correspondence with Newman, we can see Arnold trying to share at least some of these true feelings. Accordingly, he sent Newman his preface to a selection of passages from Isaiah for schools, in which he described his aim as that "of enabling English school-children to read as a connected whole the last twenty-seven chapters of Isaiah," which grew out of his "conviction of the immense importance in education of what is called letters; of the side which engages our feelings and imagination." Moreover, "If poetry, philosophy, and eloquence, if what we call in one word letters, are a power, and a beneficent wonder-working power, in education, through the Bible only have the people much chance of getting at poetry, philosophy, and eloquence."[79] Here was one argument for treating the Bible as literature, and in Newman's response we can see that he might have been reminded of Arnold's father, one of the great architects of liberal Anglicanism. In December 1841, Newman had written to Pusey, "I think you should lecture and publish on the latter chapters of Isaiah. It is said that Arnold will do harm just on this point—teach modern history without a church—considering Christianity a philosophy."[80] Now, he had an opportunity to tell the son something of what he might have wished to say to the father. "I have read with great interest the Preface of your 'Great Prophecy' etc …. doubtless the Old Testament is the only book, as you bring out so well in your Preface, which can serve as literary matter in popular schools. On the other hand, I should dread to view it as literature in the first place … ."[81] In principle, John Ruskin might very well have agreed with Newman, though in practice he always treated the Bible as a model for his own literary work. In his account of his early religious education in *Praeterita* (1899) he recalled: "My mother forced me, by steady daily toil, to learn long chapters of the Bible by heart; as well as to read it every syllable through, aloud, hard names and all, from Genesis to the Apocalypse once a year; and to that disci-pline—patient, accurate, and resolute—I owe, not only a knowledge of the book, which I find occasionally serviceable, but much of my general powers of taking pains, and the best part of my taste in literature ... . Once knowing the 32nd of Deuteronomy, the 119th Psalm, the 15th of 1st Corinthians, the Sermon on the Mount, and most of all the Apocalypse, every syllable by heart, and having always a way of thinking with myself what words meant, it was impossible for me, even in the foolishest times of youth, to write entirely superficial or formal English ..."[82] Newman's writings show that his familiarity with Scripture was comparable, though he always resisted the temptation of regarding the Bible as literature, about which T. S. Eliot was so witheringly critical: "I could fulminate against the men of letters who have gone into ecstasies over 'the Bible as literature,'" he wrote in 1935. "Those who talk of the Bible as a "monument of English prose' are merely admiring it as a monument over the grave of Christianity."[83] Newman's reasons for not treating Scripture as literature were rather different, though no less incisive.

> Literature is one thing, and ... Science is another ... Literature has to do with ideas, and Science with realities ... Literature is of a personal character ... Science treats of what is universal and eternal. In proportion, as Scripture excludes the personal colouring of its writers, and rises into the region of pure and mere inspiration when it ceases in any sense to be the writing of man, of St. Paul or St. John, of Moses or Isaias, then it comes to belong to Science, not Literature. Then it conveys the things of heaven, unseen verities, divine manifestations, and them alone—not the ideas, the feelings, the aspirations, of its human instruments ...[84]

In response to Newman's letter, Arnold wrote: "What you say about the reception of the prophetical Scriptures by the young has great weight ..." Still, he was convinced that it would be "better to give them the historical side plainly. But I did not mean to write of this; only to thank you ..." What inter-ested Arnold were not the details of their differences but what he imagined was the grander scheme of their affinities.

> There are four people, in especial, from whom I am conscious of having learnt – a very different thing from merely receiving a strong impression – learnt habits, methods, ruling ideas, which are constantly with me; and the four are – Goethe, Wordsworth, Sainte Beuve and yourself. You will smile and say I have made an odd mixture and that the result must be a jumble: however that may be as to the whole, I am sure in details you must recognise your own influence often, and perhaps this inclines you to indulgence.[85]

Newman usually dealt with those who disagreed with him with indulgence (always excepting Dr. Arnold's heretical friend, R. D. Hampden) but he might very well have goggled at seeing himself impressed into this odd pantheon.

When Arnold sent Newman another book he had written on education, Newman responded, "what specially interested and pleased me was your Preface, advocating the claims of the Irish Catholic University on State recognition. Your argument, as deduced from the Prussian policy and system, is clear and good, if it really be the fact, as I understand you to say, that Catholics have in Prussia two state-recognized Universities." He also clarified his views on the Catholic laity, which are as little understood in the twenty-first century as they were in the nineteenth. Specifically, he could not follow Arnold "in thinking that by 'the Church' ought to be meant 'the laity,' any more than the word is equivalent to 'the clergy.' I think the people are the matter, and the hierarchy the form, and that both together make up the Church. If you object that this virtually throws the initiative and the decision of questions into the hands of the clergy, this is but an internal peculiarity of the Catholic Religion. The Anglican Church is also made up of a like form and matter; though here, in consequence of the genius of Anglicanism, the power of the matter predominates. But if you attempt to destroy the existing relation between form and matter, whether in Anglicanism or Catholicism, you change the religion; it is more honest to refuse to recognize Catholicism, than to refuse to take it as it is." In this same letter, Newman wrote in passing, "By the bye, I don't acquiesce in your definition of a truism, which I conceive to be a truth too true for proof or for insistence. Triteness is at best an accident of it. If this be so, a falsism is a falsehood too false for refutation, not a trite falsehood"—a nice distinction. And then, in closing, Newman showed Arnold something of what one correspondent called his "captivating urbanity," when he wrote, "Now is it not ungracious in me to have said all this, when I am really grateful for your advocacy of us? As to your other Volume, your Edition of Isaiah, I will only say that it is a most attractive book – and your (excuse me) standing aloof from Revelation does not mar its beauty. It is that sympathy you have for what you do not believe, which so affects me about your future. It is one of my standing prayers that you and your brother may become good Catholics."[86]

Arnold's last years were so consumed with producing what Richard Holt Hutton called his "lay sermons" that he never got around to returning to poetry, which he had effectively stopped composing in 1869. As he told his mother in 1861, "I must finish off for the present my critical writings … and give the next ten years earnestly to poetry. It is my last chance. It is not a bad ten year of one's life for poetry if one resolutely uses it, but it is time in which, if one does not use it, one dries up and becomes prosaical altogether."[87] Still, in his last pieces, he did manage to write a few poems of an unsparing honesty—which were nearer to Clough's more prosaic poems than the academic elaborateness of his earlier verse. In "Growing Old," which he wrote in 1864 in response to Browning's "Rabbi Ben Ezra" with its famous summons, "Grow old along with me/The best is yet to be," Arnold anticipated Yeats and Eliot in their poems of disillusioned old age, but, alas, he wrote with far greater bitterness.

> What is it to grow old?
> Is it to lose the glory of the form,

> The lustre of the eye?
> Is it for beauty to forgo her wreath?
> —Yes, but not this alone.[88]

This was a dramatic renunciation of the passionate unbelief that had animated so many of his earlier poems. Instead of the roiling nihilism of "Empedocles on Aetna" (1852), where he had his defiant hero boasting, "I only/ Whose spring of hope is dried, whose spirit has fail'd ... I alone/Am dead to life and joy, therefore I read/In all things my own deadness," here an old man retails a life's disappointments in a thin, eviscerate, defeated voice.

> 'Tis not to see the world
> As from a height, with rapt prophetic eyes,
> And heart profoundly stirred;
> And weep and feel the fullness of the past,
> The years that are no more.[89]

This was senescence stripped of every consolation. Instead of what Eliot called "the evening with the photograph album," Arnold describes an old age in which past and future are obliterated and the only thing that survives is a sense of adding "month to month with weary pain," a sense of being "immured/ In the hot prison of the present ..." In his prime, the elegist in Arnold wrote to interrogate the past, to lament the evanescence of youth, promise, hope and glory. "Thyrsis," "Rugby Chapel," "Balder Dead," "Memorial Verses," "Heine's Grave," "Haworth Churchyard" are all threnodies. By contrast, in this most skeptical of stock takings, there are no backward glances. What is it to grow old? "It is to spend long days/And not once feel that we were ever young."

> It is to suffer this,
> And feel but half, and feebly, what we feel.
> Deep in our hidden heart
> Festers the dull remembrance of a change,
> But no emotion—none.[90]

Arnold had regarded emotion as the touchstone of reality because, for him, it was truer than the exploded dogmas of an exploded Christianity. "The true meaning of religion," he declared, improving on what his father had imagined, was "not simply *morality*, but *morality touched with emotion* ..."[91] Newman never confused moralism and religion, though he did recognize that emotion had an important, if subordinate role to play in religion.

> True it is, that all the passionate emotion, or fine sensibility, which ever man displayed, will never by itself make us change our ways, and do our duty. Impassioned thoughts, high aspirations, sublime imaginings, have no strength in them. They can no more make a man obey consistently, than they can move mountains ... Conscience, and Reason in subjection

to Conscience, *these* are those powerful instruments (under grace) which change a man. But you will observe, that though Conscience and Reason lead us to resolve on and to attempt a new life, they cannot at once make us *love* it. It is long practice and habit which make us love religion; and in the beginning, obedience, doubtless, is very grievous to habitual sinners. Here then is the use of those earnest, ardent feelings of which I just now spoke, and which attend on the first exercise of Conscience and Reason,—to take away from the *beginnings* of obedience its *grievousness*, to give us an impulse which may carry us over the first obstacles, and send us on our way rejoicing. Not as if all this excitement of mind were to last (which cannot be), but it will do its office in thus setting us off; and then will leave us to the more sober and higher comfort resulting from that real *love* for religion, which obedience itself will have by that time begun to form in us, and will gradually go on to perfect.[92]

The sort of emotion that Arnold had in mind might have been rather vague but it had nothing to do with obedience or conscience or reason. And when it disappeared, as emotions do, it left behind nothing but remorse. Growing old in the religion of art, in the religion of knowledge was no cakewalk.

> It is—last stage of all—
> When we are frozen up within, and quite
> The phantom of ourselves
> To hear the world applaud the hollow ghost
> Which blamed the living man.[93]

It is also to see the "order of ideas" collapse and something far grimmer emerge, something Jacques would find sans peace, sans faith, sans hope, sans everything ... But the poem also ends on a self-accusatory note. Why does the hollow ghost blame the living man? Perhaps Arnold regretted abandoning poetry to write those "lay sermons" of his, with all their witty evasions, which might have won the world's applause but left him "frozen up within."[94]

Of all Arnold's works, Newman might have admired this poem the most. It has nothing of the grace or finish of his more formal elegies. Its unadorned diction owes more to Clough than to Milton or Tennyson, the eulogists whom Arnold most admired. It is bitter and it is unrepentant. But it is true, and Newman would have recognized its truth because he knew something himself of "hollow ghosts." When he was near death with fever in Sicily, after he had left Hurrell Froude and his father, he recalled how "As I lay in bed the first day many thoughts came over me. I felt like God was fighting ag^st me—& felt at last I knew *why*—it was for self will. I felt I had been self willed—that the Froudes had been ag^st my coming ... Then I tried to fancy where the Froudes were, & how happy I should have been with them—in France, or perhaps in England. Yet I felt & kept saying to myself 'I have not sinned against light.' ... Next day the self reproaching feelings increased. I seemed to see more & more my utter hollowness. I began to think of all my professed principles, & felt they were mere intellectual deductions from one or two admitted truths. I compared myself to Keble, and felt that I was merely developing his, not my convictions." Then, revealingly, he switched to the present tense (he was writing a year after the events in Sicily). "Indeed, this is how I look on myself: very much ... as a pane of glass, which transmit[s] heat being cold itself. I have a vivid perception of the consequences of certain admitted principles, have a considerable intellectual capacity of drawing them out, have the refinement to admire them, & a rhetorical or histrionic power to represent them; and, having no great (i.e. no vivid) love of this world, whether riches, honors, or anything else, and some firmness and dignity of character, to take the profession of them upon me, as I might sing a tune which I liked—loving the Truth but not possessing it—for I believe myself at heart to be nearly hollow—i.e. with little love, little self-denial. I believe I have some faith, that is all—& as to my sins, they need my possessing no little amount of faith to set against them & gain remission."[95] Here, Newman saw his own hollowness with precisely the same uncompromising honesty that Arnold saw his.[96] Five years later, in 1850, when the reconstitution of the English hierarchy inspired so much anti-Catholic frenzy, Newman wrote a brilliant sermon called "Christ on the Waters," in which he demonstrated how his own weaknesses, his own susceptibility to hollowness, bound him to his contemporaries, both Catholic and Protestant: "No, I fear not, my Brethren, this momentary clamour of our foe: I fear not this great people, among whom we dwell, of whose blood we come, and who have still, under the habits of these later centuries, the rudiments of that faith by which, in the beginning, they were new-born to God: who still, despite the loss of heavenly gifts, retain the love of justice, manly bearing, and tenderness of heart, which Gregory saw in their very faces. I have no fear about our Holy Father, whose sincerity of affection towards His ancient flock, whose simplicity and truthfulness I know full well. I have no fear about the zeal of the college of our bishops, the sanctity of the body of our clergy, or the inward perfection of our Religious. One thing alone I fear. I fear the presence of sin in the midst of us. My Brethren, the success of the Church lies not with pope, or bishops, or priests, or monks; it rests with yourselves. If the present mercies of God come to nought, it will be because sin has undone them. The drunkard, the blasphemer, the unjust dealer, the profligate liver— these will be our ruin; the open scandal, the secret sin known only to God, these form the devil's real host. We can conquer every foe but these: corruption, hollowness, neglect of mercies, deadness of heart, worldliness—these will be too much for us."[97] Here was the light in which Newman saw culture and anarchy, a light which prompted him to speak not of Philistines and Barbarians but of "the wounds which one bears speechlessly, the dreadful secrets which are severed from the sympathy of others, the destruction of confidences, the sense of hollowness all around one, the expectation of calamity or scandal," which was the "portion of St Paul's trial, and of all ... who have to work for God in this world."[98]

CHAPTER 12

Newman and Arthur Hugh Clough

"Hope is the patient subdued tranquil cheerful thoughtful waiting for Christ."

John Henry Newman, "Sermon on the Liturgy" (March, 1830)

Francis Palgrave, the editor of the *Golden Treasury*, once remarked of his good friend Clough that "Many fragments of his verse show that whilst roused to a spirit of resolute self-reliance by what went on around him, he felt how much the war of conscience and conviction must be carried on within, until some clearer light should break upon the enquirer."[1] No nineteenth-century poet waited for that clearer light more agonizingly than Arthur Hugh Clough. Certainly, he was changed forever by "the war of conscience and conviction" that raged between Broad Church liberals and Tractarians in the 1830s and 40s when he was at Rugby, Balliol and Oriel. Of course, many were caught up in that war, but Clough had the singular distinction of being dragooned into it by two of its principal opponents, the latitudinarian Dr. Thomas Arnold and the dogmatical John Henry Newman. And yet, as Walter Bagehot showed, it was Arnold who prepared Clough for Newman's more abiding influence. Most public school boys, Bagehot pointed out, were content "to leave dilemmas unsolved, to forget difficulties … But it was this happy apathy, this common-place indifference, that [Dr. Arnold] prided himself on removing. He objected strenuously to Mr. Newman's creed, but he prepared anxiously the very soil in which that creed was sure to grow."[2] Clough's problem was that he recognized the power and indeed the appeal of Mr. Newman's creed, without ever being able to embrace it. This is why it was so apt of V. S. Pritchett to call Clough "the poet of dilemma."[3] In this chapter, I shall revisit Clough's life and work to show how in taking up questions of belief and unbelief, Clough confirmed Newman's influence, even though he failed to turn it to account.

Arthur Hugh Clough (1819–1861) was born in Rodney Street, Liverpool—often referred to as the Harley Street of the North—where Gladstone had been born nine years before. Clough's father, James Butler Clough (1784–1844), was a cotton merchant, who knew both boom and bust. If, as an exporter of cotton in America from 1806 to 1810, he had seen his cotton business end in bankruptcy, by 1819 he enjoyed something of the boom that followed the end of the Napoleonic Wars.[4] In 1822, when Arthur was three, he migrated with his family to Charleston, North Carolina, where the cotton trade was unpredictable, and he was reduced to taking on a ferry service from Charleston to Sullivan Island. From the few accounts that we have of his later career, he never regained his fleeting prosperity and much of his last years were blighted by debt. When the hapless trader died, his son wrote an epitaph for him that echoed Johnson's epitaph for his friend Robert Levet, "Thy busy toil thy soul had ne'er engrossed/And when thy griefs had purified thee most/Its chains, that kept thee painfully below/With a most gentle hand God loosed and let thee go." Clough might have been unconsciously emulating his father, as sons often do, when he followed up his early triumphs—the Rugby prizes, the Balliol scholarship, the Oriel fellowship—with a career of almost flamboyant failure.

If his father bequeathed Clough his sense of failure, his mother gave him his love of learning. Anne Perfect (d. 1860), the daughter of a Yorkshire banker, educated her son at home and it was while vacationing with him in upstate New York to escape the blistering southern summer that she taught him to read. Clough's sister Anne vividly recalled how central an influence their mother had on her brother:

> Arthur became my mother's constant companion. Though then only just seven, he was already considered as the genius of our family. He was a beautiful boy, with soft silky, almost black hair, and shining dark eyes, and a small delicate mouth, which our old nurse was so afraid of spoiling, when he was a baby, that she insisted on getting a tiny spoon for his special use. As I said, Arthur was constantly with my mother, and she poured out the fulness of her heart on him. They read much together, histories, ancient and modern, stories of the Greek heroes, parts of Pope's Odyssey and Iliad, and much out of Walter Scott's novels. She talked to him about England, and he learnt to be fond of his own country, and delighted to flourish about a little English flag he had possessed himself of. He also made good progress in French. He was sometimes passionate as a child, though not easily roused; and he was said to be very determined and obstinate. One trait I distinctly remember, that he would always do things from his own choice, and not merely copy what others were doing.[5]

This stubborn independence never left him. Although the Clough family resided in America until 1836, Clough returned to England in 1828 and attended school in Chester. In 1829, he entered Rugby School, where he became the famous headmaster's prize pupil and formed lasting friendships with his two eldest sons, Matthew and Thomas. He also distinguished himself in football, swimming and running, edited one of the school's papers, and even held office in the student government. How much of his boyhood successes blighted his later life is a nice question. Certainly there are aspects of Clough that put one in mind of Cyril Connolly's famous claim in *Enemies of Promise* (1938) that "the experiences undergone by boys at the great public schools, their glories and disappointments are so intense as to dominate their lives and to arrest their development. From this it results that the greater part of the ruling class remains adolescent, school-minded, self-conscious, cowardly, sentimental, and, in the last analysis, homosexual."[6] Although neither sentimental nor homosexual, Clough could be decidedly adolescent. For instance, he was convinced that since he had worked hard as a boy at Rugby he was entitled to be idle as an adult. To his future wife he wrote in 1852, when he was 33, "Certainly as a boy, I had less of boyish enjoyment of any kind whatever either at home or at school ... as a man I think I have earned myself some title to live for some little interval I do not say in enjoyment ... but without immediate devotion to particular objects or matter, as it were, of business ..."[7] What his fiancée made of this admission is anyone's guess.

In 1837, Clough won a scholarship to Balliol, which, after Oriel, was Oxford's most academically prestigious college. While Clough was in residence the college had some capable students, including A. P. Stanley, Benjamin Jowett, John Duke Coleridge and Frederick Temple. It also numbered A. C. Tait, Frederick Oakeley and W. G. Ward among its dons. Yet the most striking thing about Balliol when Clough entered in 1837 was how divided it was. Balliol's Master, Richard Jenkyns (1798–1854), a diminutive, pompous, resourceful High Churchman, "found himself with fellows who were either edging towards Roman Catholicism with the Tractarians or moving in the opposite direction with Thomas Arnold."[8] The Oxford Movement was deeply abhorrent to Jenkyns and he did not hesitate to stop Ward teaching mathematics when he became convinced that the tutor was infecting his pupils with subversively Romish doctrines. Here Jenkyns was guarding against the same Roman influence at Balliol that Hawkins guarded against at Oriel, when he stopped Newman, Froude and Robert Wilberforce from tutoring along the same pastoral lines. The Balliol senior common room was equally divided between "Taitians and Wardians." To make matters worse, A. W. N. Pugin's plans to rebuild the college in accordance with Gothic principles was another cause of heated division, though Jenkyns made sure that they were shelved. Clough's Balliol was thus an extension of his own inner divisions and aggravated his habit of seeing things in terms of irreconcilable opposites.

If Clough's interest in religion, which he had first acquired from his mother, intensified under Dr. Arnold at Rugby, it was brought to a boil by his Balliol tutor, William George Ward, the opera-loving Romanist who saturated Clough in theological debate. In the Epilogue to *Dipsychus*, Clough referred to "over-excitation of the religious sense, resulting in ... irrational, almost animal irritability of conscience," which sounds an accurate description of the effect Ward's febrile conversation must have had on him.[9] A. P. Stanley, noticing the two men walking down the street together, quipped, "There goes Ward, mystifying poor Clough, and persuading him that he must either believe *nothing* or accept the whole of Christian doctrine." Still, judging from Ward's correspondence, one can see that there were aspects of Ward's influence on Clough that made a very deep impression indeed, especially those tinged with what the dons of Balliol were fond of referring to as "Newmanism." In one letter of 1838, Ward wrote to Clough:

I had a long talk with Vaughan of Oriel last night who … says he is perfectly certain of this, that there is no mean between Newmanism on the one side and extremes far beyond anything of Arnold's on the other; that Arnold and all Anglican Protestants are in a false position: for his own part he trusts himself to the progress not knowing whither it will carry him, but not feeling confident that any part of Christianity will remain, except the truth of the main facts (miracles and Resurrection of our Lord) and those virtues (humility, forgiveness etc.) which though first brought to light by Christianity, carried their own evidence with them. Neither the canonicity nor authority of Scripture he thinks will remain: further he thinks Newman seems to see the real bottom of the question … and the way of thinking of infidels better than any Christian alive …[10]

From the first, with Ward's prodding, Clough was ready to look beyond the Arnoldian *Weltanschauung*. As soon as he was settled in his rooms, he recognized the power of Newman's work, asking one of his friends, "Have you ever read Newman's sermons? I hope you will soon if you have not, for they are very good and I should [think] especially useful to us."[11] Then, again, he wrote to his Cambridge friend, John Philip Gell: "I wish you would come, or rather that you were at Oxford. It is, I am sure, so much better a place than Cambridge and you would have the great advantage of a good chance of becoming a disciple of ὁ μέγας Νέανδρος [the great Newman], whom I like much better than I did and admire in many points exceedingly. Have you read Froude's Remains? If not, pray do." Clough thought it "one of the most instructive books I have ever read … in this [line]" and regretted that It was "sadly abused."[12] He had spent too much time trying to live the devout life himself to join Sir James Stephen and the *Edinburgh Review* in mocking Newman and Keble for publishing "contrite reminiscences of a desire for roast goose, and of an undue indulgence in buttered toast."[13]

In June 1838, Clough met Newman at a tea-supper at Oriel with other undergraduates, though he left no account of it. Anthony Kenny, Clough's most recent biographer, claims that Clough rejected Newman's sacramental system, but there is no proof of this in either his letters or his diaries.[14] Before Gell set out on his way to Tasmania, Clough gave him a copy of St. Augustine's *Confessions*. He had considered giving him something by Carlyle, despite his thinking him "somewhat heathenish," but he thought better of it. Nevertheless, Clough clearly recognized that "all literature, old and new, English and foreign, which is worth calling literature" has something "heathenish" about it.[15] Newman agreed, pointing out in *The Idea of a University* that "It is a contradiction in terms to attempt a sinless Literature of sinful man. You may gather together something very great and high, something higher than any Literature ever was; and when you have done so, you will find that it is not Literature at all. You will have simply left the delineation of man, as such, and have substituted for it … man, as he … might be …"[16] Newman and Clough were also alike in finding composition an ordeal. Clough wrote an amusing poem to confess his own struggles with the accustomed toil that he never found easy.

If to write, and write again
Bite now the lip and now the pen,
Gnash in a fury the teeth, and tear
Innocent paper or it may be hair
In endless chases to pursue
That swift escaping word that would do,
Inside and out turn a phrase, o'er and o'er,
Till all the little sense goes it had before,
If to be these things makes one a poet,
I am one—Come and all the world may know it.[17]

When Ward told Newman that he received "keen and constant pleasure" from writing, Newman was incredulous: "My own personal experience is the other way. It is one of my sayings (so continually do I feel it) that the composition of a volume is like gestation and childbirth. I do not think that I ever thought out a question or wrote my thoughts, without great pain, pain reaching to the body as well as the mind. It has made me practically feel that labour "in sudore vultûs ejus" is the lot of man; and that "ignorance" is truly one of his four wounds. It has been emphatically a *penance.*"[18]

By Clough's second year at Balliol, he was already beginning to appreciate that the *ethos* to which he had pledged allegiance at Rugby was destined for a shake-up, though he would always retain his respect for Dr. Arnold. After he got word that his former headmaster had persuaded "godless" London University to conduct examinations in the Gospels and Acts, he wrote to Gell:

It must have been a very grand thing to see him get up among all those people, and declare that they must do something to show that they were Christians, and that it was a Christian University. I do not know how we shall get on in Oxford against those very opposite sort of enemies—the Newmanists—they are very savage and determined, and such good and pious men to boot ... These people however have done a vast deal of good at Oxford, where anything so 'ungentlemanly' and 'coarse' and 'in such bad taste' as 'Evangelicalism' would never be able to make very much way. It seems just the sort of religious activity and zeal, which one would expect to develop ... in an age of activity and shaking-up ...[19]

Newman had equally kind things to say about the Arnoldians. Speaking of the Broad Church party at Oxford, in relation to the Tory party, he noted in his *Apologia*: "The Old Tory or Conservative party in Oxford had in it no principle or power of development, and that from its very nature and constitution: it was otherwise with the Liberals. They represented a new idea, which was but gradually learning to recognize itself, to ascertain its characteristics and external relations, and to exert an influence upon the University. The party grew, all the time that I was in Oxford, even in numbers, certainly in breadth and definiteness of doctrine, and in power. And, what was a far higher consideration, by the accession of Dr. Arnold's pupils, it was invested with an elevation of character which claimed the respect even of its opponents."[20] Clough's own settled estimate of Dr. Arnold was ambivalent. It is clear that Arnold made an ineradicable impression on him, though he could also see the liabilities of that impression. In the Epilogue to "Dipsychus," Clough records a dialogue between the presumed author of the poem and his uncle, in which the former explains how the poem is about "the conflict between the tender conscience and the world," but before he can elaborate, his uncle cuts him off, saying, "Oh for goodness's sake, my dear boy ... don't go into the theory of it ... I don't understand all those new words ... It's all Arnold's doing; he spoilt the public schools ... They're full of the notion of the world being so wicked, and of their taking a higher line, as they call it. I only fear they'll never take any at all.'" When the author pooh-poohs this, his uncle has his answer ready: "Put [a fourteen-year-old boy] through a course of confirmation and sacraments, backed up with sermons and private admonitions, and what is much the same as auricular confession, and, really, my dear nephew, I can't answer for it but he mayn't turn out as great a goose as you ..."[21]

After attending Newman's "Lectures on the Scripture Proof of the Doctrines of the Church," Clough wrote a friend how Newman had made his arguments in "a very fair and very candid manner," but he also followed this up by saying: "One thing is clear—that one must leave the discussion of Newmanist matters all snug and quiet for after one's degree ..."[22] In that same year, while reading Dickens' *Nicholas Nickleby*, he confessed, "I incline to think that I ought to give up seeking much about the great Newman questions: for I have little or no earnestness."[23] This recalls something Newman told his older brother Charles as far back as 1825, when Charles was first considering throwing over Christianity for Owenite atheism: "I consider the rejection of Christianity to arise from a fault of the *heart*, not of *the intellect* ..."[24] For Newman, atheism was not an alternative to belief but a failure of faith.

After taking a Second at Balliol, Clough took the train to Rugby to tell Dr. Arnold in person that his golden boy had failed. Tait attributed the poor result to Clough's examiners: "They had a man of genius before them and they were too stupid to see it."[25] Henceforth, Clough's worldly career unfolded in a series of missteps, though he always managed to make them serve his poetry. In 1842, he won a much-coveted fellowship to Oriel but resigned six years later after he realized that he could not subscribe to the 39 Articles. In 1850, he became Principal of University Hall, London, after Newman's brother Frank resigned the post but resigned himself when he found that he had no calling for guiding Unitarian youth. By the time he had left Oriel, Clough had apparently drifted far away from belief in Christianity—Kenny notes that he doubted the historicity of the Gospels—but his religious doubts were always accompanied with hankerings for faith, even though his faith was fitful and half-hearted.

One of the most striking things about Clough is how worldly adversity never rattled him. He was inured to failure because he was unimpressed with success. "He had a kind of proud simplicity about him," Richard Holt Hutton wrote of his friend after his death, "singularly attractive, and often singularly disappointing to those who longed to know him well. He had a fear, which many would think morbid, of leaning much on the approbation of the world; and there is one characteristic passage in his poems in which he intimates that men who lean on the good opinion of others might even be benefited by a *crime* which would rob them of that evil stimulant."[26]

> Why, so is good no longer good, but crime
> Our truest, best advantage, since it lifts us
> Out of the stifling gas of men's opinion
> Into the vital atmosphere of Truth,
> Where He again is visible, tho' in anger.

Here, in this acknowledgement of the reality of sin, Clough parted ways with his Pelagian contemporaries. And yet Newman insisted that it was the penitent who could best testify to the tenacity of sin. "We cannot rid ourselves of sin when we would," he wrote in "Sins of Infirmity" (1838), "though we repent, though God forgives us, yet it remains in its power over our souls, in our habits, and in our memories. It has given a colour to our thoughts, words, and works; and though, with many efforts, we would wash it out from us, yet this is not possible except gradually. Men have been slothful, or self-conceited, or self-willed, or impure, or worldly-minded in their youth, and afterwards they turn to God, and would fain be other than they have been, but their former self clings to them, as a poisoned garment, and eats into them ..." The only cure for this abiding poison, Newman insists, is penance, for, despite our infirmities, if "we can point to some occasions on which we have sacrificed anything for God's service, or to any habit of sin or evil tendency which we have more or less overcome, or to any habitual self-denial which we practice, or any work which we have accomplished to God's honour and glory; this perchance may fill us with the humble hope that God is working in us, and therefore is at peace with us."[27]

Despite his professional and personal setbacks, Clough was a disciplined, innovative, prolific poet. In 1848, he wrote *The Bothie of Tober-na-Vuolich*, a poem about an exuberant reading party in Scotland modeled after the parties Clough himself conducted when he was a don at Oriel. Into this sprightliest of poems, Clough poured his musings on love, life, nature, and philosophy in rollicking Homeric hexameters, which Arnold rightly praised for their "out-of-door freshness," "naturalness" and "buoyant rapidity."[28] Although a narrative poem with a hero and heroine and a finely observed Caledonian setting, the *Bothie* also has a marked autobiographical element, as here where Clough might almost be describing the faith—the "name of his home"—that he was continually in peril of losing.

> I was as one that sleeps on the railway; one, who dreaming
> Hears thro' his dream the name of his home shouted out; hears and hears not,—
> Faint, and louder again, and less loud, dying in distance;
> Dimly conscious, with something of inward debate and choice,—and

Sense of claim and reality present, anon relapses
Nevertheless, and continues the dream and fancy, while forward
Swiftly, remorseless, the car presses on, he knows not whither.[29]

In another passage, Clough echoes Thackeray's respect for what Joyce's Stephen Daedalus regarded as the one undeniable reality—*amor matris*—in lines that recall the propulsive rhythms of Gerard Manley Hopkins.

... There is a power upon earth, seen feebly in women and children,
Which can, laying one hand on the cover, read-off, unfaltering,
Leaf after leaf unlifted, the words of the closed book under,
Words which we are poring at, hammering at, stumbling at, spelling.[30]

Newman also saw a power in mother and children, the power of innocence, which, he recognized, too many of the educated scorned. "I suppose great numbers of men think that it is slavish and despicable to go on in that narrow way in which they are brought up as children, without experience of the world. It *is* the narrow way, and they call it narrow in contumely. They fret at the restraints of their father's roof, and wish to judge and act for themselves. They think it manly to taste the pleasures of sin; they think it manly to know what sin is before condemning it. They think they are then better judges, when they are not blindly led by others, but have taken upon them, by their own act, the yoke of evil. They think it a fine thing to curse and swear, and to revel, and to ridicule God's sacred truth, and to profess themselves the devil's scholars. They look down upon the innocent, upon women and children, and solitaries, and holy and humble men of heart, who, like the Cherubim, see God and worship, as unfit for the great business of life, and worthless in the real estimate of things."[31]

After finishing his bravura *jeu d'esprit*, Clough spent 1848 in Paris with his friend and confrere Emerson, witnessing the revolution that brought the world Louis Napoleon's Second Empire and Baron Hausmann's Paris. From Paris, he went to Rome, where he fell under the spell of Garibaldi, who, in the absence of Pius IX, briefly presided over the short-lived Roman republic. Out of this experience Clough wrote his masterpiece, *Amours de Voyage* (1848), an epistolary novel in verse (hexameters again), which is full of charm and élan, though he only managed to get it published ten years after he wrote it—proof of how little genius he had for practical affairs. In 1850, Clough went on to Venice, where he wrote *Dipsychus*, a dialogue, as he described it, "between the tender conscience and the world," which captures the double-mindedness with which he approached the crises of life. Clough always drew inspiration from being abroad—one reason why the equally itinerant Graham Greene found him so congenial. Greene certainly knew what Clough meant when he said that travel offered escape from "All the *assujettissement* of having been what one has been."[32] He also shared Clough's distrust of action—or perhaps one should say his fascination with its stakes. In *The Quiet American* (1955), Greene quoted these characteristic lines from Clough's *Amours de Voyage* (1849):

I do not like being moved: for the will is excited; and action
Is a most dangerous thing; I tremble for something factitious,
Some malpractice of heart and illegitimate process;
We are so prone to these things, with our terrible notions of duty.[33]

In taking up the theme of action, Clough entered ground Newman had made his own. In "The Danger of Accomplishments" (1831), he observed how "God has made us to feel in order that we may go on to act in consequence of feeling; if then we allow our feelings to be excited without acting upon them, we do mischief to the moral system within us, just as we might spoil a watch, or other piece of machinery, by playing with the wheels of it." In "Wisdom, as Contrasted with Faith and with Bigotry" (1841) from his *Oxford University Sermons* (1843), Newman reminded his readers that belief required the same faithful action that any great undertaking required. Here he might have had in mind William Froude's friend Brunel, the great engineer, so many of whose engineering projects required huge investments of faithful action. "There are men who, when in difficulties, by the force of genius, originate at the moment vast ideas or dazzling projects; who, under the impulse of excitement, are able to cast a light, almost as if from inspiration, on a subject or course of action which comes before them; who have a sudden presence of mind equal to any emergency, rising with the occasion, and an undaunted heroic bearing, and an energy and keenness, which is but sharpened by opposition. Faith is a gift analogous to this thus far, that it acts promptly and boldly on the occasion, on slender evidence, as if guessing and reaching forward to the truth, amid darkness or confusion …"[34] For Newman, in whatever one sets out to accomplish, "Premises imply conclusions; germs lead to developments; principles have issues; doctrines lead to action."[35] And, in any case, "The multitude have neither the time, the patience, nor the clearness and exactness of thought, for processes of investigation and deduction. Reason is slow and abstract, cold and speculative; but man is a being of feeling and action; he is not resolvable into … a series of hypotheticals, or a critical diatribe, or an algebraical equation."[36] In *The Tamworth Reading Room* (1841), Newman might have been addressing Clough directly when he observed how: "Few men have that power of mind which may hold fast and firmly a variety of thoughts. We ridicule 'men of one idea;' but a great many of us are born to be such, and we should be happier if we knew it. To most men argument makes the point in hand only more doubtful, and considerably less impressive. After all, man is *not* a reasoning animal; he is a seeing, feeling, contemplating, acting animal. He is influenced by what is direct and precise."[37] Since Clough also suffered from an abiding irresoluteness, Newman's passage was especially apposite. He could also have had Clough in mind when he declared: "Life is not long enough for a religion of inferences; we shall never have done beginning, if we determine to begin with proof. We shall ever be laying our foundations; we shall turn theology into evidences, and divines into textuaries. We shall never get at our first principles. Resolve to believe nothing, and you must prove your proofs and analyze your elements, sinking further and further, and finding 'in the lowest depth a lower deep,' till you come to the broad bosom of scepticism. I would rather be bound to defend the reasonableness of assuming that Christianity is true, than to demonstrate a moral governance from the physical world. Life is for action. If we insist on proofs for everything, we shall never come to action: to act you must assume, and that assumption is faith."[38] Once Newman converted and wrote that ebullient book *Loss and Gain* (1847), he recognized that another truth flowed from his understanding of the primacy of action. In the novel, Newman has Willis say to Bateman those words that so haunted Richard Holt Hutton: "'when the time comes, and come it will, for you, alien as you are now, to submit yourself to the gracious yoke of Christ, then, my dearest Bateman, it will be *faith* which will enable you to bear the ways and usages of Catholics, which else might perhaps startle you. Else, the habits of years, the associations in your mind of a certain outward behaviour with real inward acts of devotion, might embarrass you, when you had to conform yourself to other habits, and to create for yourself other associations. But this faith, of which I speak, the great gift of God, will enable you in that day to overcome yourself, and to submit, as your judgment, your will, your reason, your affections, so your tastes and likings, to the rule and usage of the Church. Ah, that faith should be necessary in such a matter, and that what is so natural and becoming under the circumstances, should have need of an explanation! I declare, to me,' he said, and he clasped his hands on his knees, and looked forward as if soliloquising,—'to me nothing is so consoling, so piercing, so thrilling, so overcoming, as the Mass, said as it is among us. I could attend Masses for ever and not be tired. It is not a mere form of words,—it is a great action, the greatest action that can be on earth. It is, not the invocation merely, but, if I dare use the word, the evocation of the Eternal ...'"[39]

In 1852, after becoming engaged to Blanche Mary Shore Smith (1828–1904) of Combe Hall, Surrey, a cousin of Florence Nightingale, Clough sailed with Thackeray to America, where he and Emerson spent nine months trying to find some suitable teaching post that would give him the wherewithal to marry. Florence was very fond of the penniless poet and instrumental in getting his improbable suit approved with Blanche's skeptical mother. Florence also helped Clough and Blanche with their precarious finances. As Florence's biographer points out, "She worked out detailed budgets showing what Clough and Blanche absolutely required to live on, including a scale of provision for children, basing her calculations on the frequency at which they would be likely to arrive at the average birth-rate ..."[40] Clough's letters to Blanche when they were courting are full of charm. "Here I am just back from Mazzini's lecture," he writes in one letter, "having deposited Mrs and two Misses Wedgwood (an old and a young) in one carriage and Mrs. Carlyle with a German Count and Baron in another. We dined with Mr. Darwin, which was pretty fair fun, with a spice of cynicism, champagne and moselle ..."[41] In another letter, he tells his intended, "Mr. Martineau's article in the Westminster is extremely ill written. A bad style is as bad as bad manners—and bad manners you do admit do mean something. Awkwardness is a defect; and other faults are *positive* faults morally. Things really ill-written it does one a little harm to read—would you forgive bad music because it was *well-meant?* "[42] Before departing for America, however, despite Florence's ministrations, Clough nearly scuttled his engagement when he wrote the woman he meant to make his wife: "Love is not everything, Blanche, don't believe it nor make me pretend to believe it. 'Service' is everything. Let us be fellow-servants."[43] Of course, he was telling a necessary truth but Blanche did not see it that way. For 15 months afterwards, she would not forgive him and ever afterwards referred to what she called "the terrible letter."[44] Although fiercely protective of her husband's reputation after his death, Blanche was highly critical of the living man. "Is it necessary for men to coarsen their imaginations," she asked him in one letter. "It is curious, how very seldom you read any poems—any book of any kind that does not in some degree offend."[45] Despite his fiancée's prenuptial pique, on returning to England, Clough finally found work as an examiner in the Education Office, and on 13 June 1854, the feast of Saint Anthony, the quizzical poet and his censorious bride were finally married.

That same year Clough began to help Florence Nightingale in her campaign to reform hospitals and even accompanied her to Calais on her first trip to the Crimea. Speculating on the relationship that developed between the unhappy poet and the reforming nurse, Lytton Strachey wrote: "Though the purpose of existence might be still uncertain ... here, at any rate, under the eye of this inspired woman, was something real ... his only doubt was—could he be of any use? Certainly he could. There were a great number of miscellaneous little jobs which there was not a body handy to do. For instance, when Miss Nightingale was travelling, there were the railway-tickets to be taken; and there were proof-sheets to be corrected; and then there were parcels to be done up in brown paper, and carried to the post. Certainly, he could be useful."[46] Strachey's heavy sarcasm notwithstanding, there was probably some truth to this picture. The Bloomsbury littérateur might have seen risible indignity in such tasks, but for Clough, who had known so much spiritual suffering in his life, there was nothing undignified about helping a woman reform hospitals, though such reforms could not cure his own ills. The only antidotes he found for himself were accidental and fleeting.

> Comfort has come to me here in the dreary streets of the city,
> Comfort—how do you think?—with a barrel-organ to bring it.
> Moping along the streets, and cursing my day as I wandered,
> All of a sudden my ear met the sound of an English psalm-tune,
> Comfort me it did, till indeed I was very near crying.
> Ah, there is some great truth, partial, very likely, but needful,
> Lodged, I am strangely sure, in the tones of the English psalm-tune.
> Comfort it was at least; and I must take without question
> Comfort, however it come, in the dreary streets of the city.[47]

That hymns were a significant part of Dr. Arnold's regimen at Rugby give this poem added poignancy. Later, in his last series of poems, entitled *Magno Mari* (1861), Clough took up the topic of marriage, specifically the difficulties that assail and dignify it, which shows that he did not entirely succumb to the permanent adolescence that might otherwise have been his fate if he had not met Blanche.[48]

> Of marriage long one night they held discourse,
> Regarding it in different ways, of course.
> Marriage is discipline, the wise had said,
> A needful human discipline to wed;
> Novels of course depict it final bliss,
> Say, had it ever really once been this?[49]

Sill, towards the end of his life, as Kenny observes, "Clough was finding even his most profound intellectual inquiries pointless."[50] To illustrate his own point, Kenny quotes these weary lines from *Dipsychus*.

> To spend uncounted years of pain,
> Again, again, and yet again,
> In working out in heart and brain
> The problem of our being here;
> To gather facts from far and near,
> Upon the mind to hold them clear,
> And knowing more may yet appear,
> Unto one's latest breath to fear
> The premature result to draw—
> Is this the object, end and law,
>   And purpose of our being here?[51]

In 1861, when he was only 42, after junkets to Greece, Constantinople and the Pyrenees, where he traveled with Tennyson and his family, Clough's ailing health broke down and he died on November 13th in Florence, where he was buried in the Protestant cemetery—a fitting final stop for the man whom one critic called "the poet of tourism."[52] Clough's career was nicely summed up by D. C. Somervell, whose abridgement of Arnold Toynbee's massive *A Study of History* (1934–1961) familiarized him with the often impracticable theories of men. "On the outermost frontiers of Broad Churchmanship may be placed those who had lost their faith, but could not be content to be without it; who retained, as it were, a fervent faith that faith was possible and necessary for men and might yet be possible for them. Of such was Arthur Hugh Clough, reputed the most brilliant of Arnold's Rugby pupils."[53]

Although much of Clough's poetry is fragmentary, there is one striking exception and that is his best-known poem, "Say not, the struggle nought availeth." Clough wrote it after the failure of the revolutions of 1848 to reaffirm not only the wisdom of hope but the folly of losing hope. It is one of those pellucid poems that balks commentary, a poem that Clough might have written to please the uncle in the Prologue to *Dipsychus*, who complains, "Nothing is more disagreeable than to say a line two, or, it may be three or four times, and at last not be sure that there are not three or four ways

of reading, each as good and as much intended as another."[54] Here there is
nothing "unmeaning, vague and involved," to borrow another stricture from
that sound avuncular critic.[55]

> Say not, the struggle nought availeth,
> The labor and the wounds are vain,
> The enemy faints not, nor faileth,
> And as things have been they remain.
>
> If hopes were dupes, fears may be liars;
> It may be, in yon smoke concealed,
> Your comrades chase e'en now the fliers,
> And, but for you, possess the field.
>
> For while the tired waves, vainly breaking,
> Seem here, no painful inch to gain,
> Far back, through creeks and inlets making,
> Comes silent, flooding in, the main.
>
> And not by eastern windows only,
> When daylight comes, comes in the light,
> In front, the sun climbs slow, how slowly,
> But westward, look, the land is bright.

Winston Churchill recited the poem on the radio in 1941 when he was trying
to cajole the Americans into joining the Allies in the fight against Nazism.[56]
One can easily see why that indomitable man thought so highly of the poem:
it is, after all, a poem about never losing heart, never despairing. Churchill
committed it to memory during the Great War when he was in the trenches of
France. Yet however distinct from Clough's other poems, it epitomizes the poet's
work as a whole by showing how his own faith and hope, though severely
tested, never entirely gave way. In "the war between conscience and conviction,"
Clough was always mindful that "If hopes were dupes, fears may be liars."

After Clough's death, Arnold mourned his friend in "Thyrsis," a highly
Miltonic eulogy, which Clough, in his modest way, might have found
overwrought. Walter Bagehot and Richard Holt Hutton also wrote reminiscences about the poet, in which they reiterated the common view that Clough's
career had been undone by religious mania, stirred up first by Dr. Arnold and
then compounded by Ward and Newman. In a long essay on Clough published
in 1897, the critic J. M. Robertson laid the blame for what he considered
Clough's personal and artistic failures squarely on what he called "the effem-
inate ecclesiastical atmosphere of the Oxford of the Newman epoch, when
currents of febrile mysticism and timorous scepticism drew young men this way
and that …" For Robertson, "not one in a hundred of those affected [were] able
to attain a stable and virile philosophy. Clough himself said afterwards that for
two years he had been 'like a straw drawn up the draught of a chimney' by the

Newman movement; and it would not be going too far to say that if he were not one of those 'wrecks' declared by Gladstone to have been strewn on every shore' by the academic tempest in question, he was at least left less seaworthy for life." This view proved remarkably tenacious, though Robertson himself called it into question when he observed that "it seems a trifle strange in these days that one such as Clough, having realised the force of the rational criticism of the popular creed, should be unable robustly to readjust his life to the sane theory of things."[57] Here Robertson was right: Clough never did manage to readjust his life to the "sane theory of things." His doubts may have tested but they never extinguished his faith. Clough's best poetry always pits the "sane view of things" against the "popular creed" and finds the former wanting. Here is a good example from *Dipsychus*:

> "THERE is no God," the wicked saith,
> "And truly it's a blessing,
>   For what He might have done with us
> It's better only guessing."

> "There is no God," a youngster thinks,
> "Or really, if there may be,
>   He surely did not mean a man
> Always to be a baby."

> "There is no God, or if there is,"
> The tradesman thinks, "'twere funny
>   If He should take it ill in me
> To make a little money."

These are the customary attitudes of unbelief, ingrained and unexamined, that define "the sane theory of things."

> But country folks who live beneath
> The shadow of the steeple;
>   The parson and the parson's wife,
> And mostly married people;

> Youths green and happy in first love,
> So thankful for illusion;
>   And men caught out in what the world
> Calls guilt, in first confusion;

> And almost everyone when age,
> Disease, or sorrows strike him,
>   Inclines to think there is a God,
> Or something very like Him.[58]

Clough returned to this pattern of denial and affirmation in a pair of poems that epitomizes his view of Christianity. "Easter Day" and "Easter Day II" were written after Clough left Oriel and before he sailed for America—that is to say, between 1848 and 1852. Katherine Chorley and Anthony Kenny discount "Easter II," insisting that only the first of the poems expresses Clough's settled view of Christian faith.[59] But this is to misread not only the individual poems but the way they complement and complete one another. In "Easter Day" the case for unbelief is mounted as Lucifer might mount it, in language borrowed from Scripture, which makes for an impious pastiche:

> And, oh, good men of ages yet to be,
> Who shall believe *because* ye did not see—
> > Oh, be ye warned, be wise!
> > No more with pleading eyes,
> > And sobs of strong desire,
> > Unto the empty vacant void aspire,
> Seeking another and impossible birth
> That is not of your own, and only mother earth.
> But if there is no other life for you,
> Sit down and be content, since this must even do:
> > He is not risen![60]

Kenny's gloss on this ode to negation makes Clough sound like a Labour politician: "What, then, should we do? Service to the dead Christ must be replaced by service to the living in the workaday world. The women disciples must give up the hope of laying up treasure in heaven, and the apostles must abandon their ambition to be fishers of men."[61] Is this what Clough is saying? Or is he defining the confines of unbelief to expose its desolation?

> Eat, drink, and die, for we are men deceived,
> Of all the creatures under heaven's wide cope
> We are most hopeless, who had once most hope
> We are most wretched that had most believed.
> > Christ is not risen.
>
> Eat, drink, and die, and think that this is bliss!
> > There is no Heaven but this!
> > There is no Hell;—
> Save Earth, which serves the purpose doubly well,
> > Seeing it visits still
> With equallest appointments of ill
> Both good and bad alike, and brings to one same dust
> > The unjust and the just
> > With Christ, who is not risen.

Rather than plead for unbelief, Clough descibes its condition, which gives his readers a chilling glimpse into what unbelief truly exacts.

> Weep not beside the tomb,
>   Ye women, unto whom
> He was great solace while ye tended Him;
>   Ye who with napkin o'er the head
> And folds of linen round each wounded limb
>   Laid out the Sacred Dead;
> And thou that bar'st Him in thy wondering womb;
> Yea, Daughters of Jerusalem, depart,
> Bind up as best ye may your own sad bleeding heart:
> Go to your homes, your living children tend,
>   Your earthly spouses love;
>   Set your affections *not* on things above,
> Which moth and rust corrupt, which quickliest come to end:
> Or pray, if pray ye must, and pray, if pray ye can,
> For death; since dead is He whom ye deemed more than man,
>   Who is not risen: no—
>   But lies and moulders low—
>   Who is not risen!

Newman was in the habit of saying that it was not so much the existence of God that was mysterious as the rejection of His existence.[62] In this poem, Clough showed how entirely he agreed. Indeed, "Easter Day" might have been written to illustrate what Newman had in mind when he referred to "the all-corroding, all-dissolving scepticism of the intellect in religious enquiries."[63] Neither man was unmindful of how anathema religion is to the natural man. Newman explains why this should be the case in the *Apologia*, in which he sheds a good deal of light on what Clough is doing in "Easter Day."

> I have no intention at all of denying, that truth is the real object of our reason, and that, if it does not attain to truth, either the premiss or the process is in fault; but I am not speaking here of right reason, but of reason as it acts in fact and concretely in fallen man. I know that even the unaided reason, when correctly exercised, leads to a belief in God, in the immortality of the soul, and in a future retribution; but I am considering the faculty of reason actually and historically; and in this point of view, I do not think I am wrong in saying that its tendency is towards a simple unbelief in matters of religion. No truth, however sacred, can stand against it, in the long run; and hence it is that in the pagan world, when our Lord came, the last traces of the religious knowledge of former times were all but disappearing from those portions of the world in which the intellect had been active and had had a career.[64]

If Newman himself chose faith over skepticism, it was not because he did not appreciate the allure of skepticism. For Newman, reason, unguided by faith, would always be inclined to deny God, to claim that He is unrisen. The implications of this were of pressing concern to Clough and indeed to Arnold, but they were even more so to Newman, who spoke of them with prophetic urgency.

> In these latter days ... outside the Catholic Church things are tending,— with far greater rapidity than in that old time ... to atheism in one shape or other ... . Lovers of their country and of their race, religious men, external to the Catholic Church, have attempted various expedients to arrest fierce wilful human nature in its onward course, and to bring it into subjection. The necessity of some form of religion for the interests of humanity, has been generally acknowledged: but where was the concrete representative of things invisible, which would have the force and the toughness necessary to be a breakwater against the deluge? Three centuries ago the establishment of religion, material, legal, and social, was generally adopted as the best expedient for the purpose, in those countries which separated from the Catholic Church; and for a long time it was successful; but now the crevices of those establishments are admitting the enemy.[65]

This is the backdrop of accelerating apostasy that gives so much of the poetry of Clough its point. Conversely, when Clough turns to affirming Christianity, he does so with marked astringency, as if to acknowledge that fallen human nature is necessarily reluctant to speak glibly of such terrible truths. As Samuel Johnson pointed out in his Life of Cowley, "Sacred history has been always read with submissive reverence, and an imagination over-awed and controlled. We have been accustomed to acquiesce in the nakedness and simplicity of the authentick narrative ... All amplification is frivolous and vain; all addition to that which is already sufficient for the purpose of religion, seems not only useless, but in some degree profane."[66] After briskly repudiating the disavowals of the earlier poem, Clough makes the case for belief in "Easter Day II" without elaboration—indeed with a kind of humility.

> So in the sinful streets, abstracted and alone,
> I with my secret self held communing of mine own.
>   So in the southern city spake the tongue
> Of one that somewhat overwildly sung,
> But in a later hour I sat and heard
> Another voice that spake—another graver word.
> Weep not, it bade, whatever hath been said,
> Though He be dead, He is not dead.
>   In the true creed
> He is yet risen indeed;
>   Christ is yet risen.

In *Amours de Voyage* (1848), Clough again returned to the question of faith in an epistolary novel set in Catholic Italy, which features a group of English Protestants, "Murray, in hand, as usual," trying to make sense of the ancient faith that their forbears renounced.[67] In the prologue to Canto II, Claude is in Rome and asks his friend Eustace a question that the poem as a whole will set out to answer.

> Is it illusion? or does there a spirit from perfecter ages,
>   Here, even yet, amid loss, change, and corruption abide?
> Does there a spirit we know not, though seek, though we find, comprehend
>   not,
>   Here to entice and confuse, tempt and evade us, abide?[68]

Newman began posing the same question on his first trip to Rome in March of 1833, when he asked: "How shall I name thee, Light of the wide west, or heinous error-seat?"[69] Ten years later, he would return to the question in his brilliant Oxford sermon, "The Theory of Developments in Religious Doctrine" (1843), which served as the prolegomena to his conversion. That Clough set his verse novel in Catholic Italy among English tourists was a stroke of genius. To dramatize how removed the nineteenth-century English were from the central reality of European civilization Clough had only to have his characters speak their minds. Here is Claude, the poem's hero:

> Rome disappoints me much; I hardly as yet understand it, but
> *Rubbishy* seems the word that most exactly would suit it.
> All the foolish destructions, and all the sillier savings,
> All the incongruous things of past incompatible ages,
> Seem to be treasured up here to make fools of present and future.
> Would to Heaven the old Goths had made a cleaner sweep of it!
> Would to Heaven some new ones would come and destroy these
>   churches![70]

As Kenny points out in his biography, some of these sentiments clearly were those of the poet.[71] In one letter written to his mother from Rome, he remarked: "St. Peter's disappoints me: the stone of which it is made is a poor plastery material. And indeed Rome in general might be called a *rubbishy* place …"[72] Still, in capturing his own aversion to Rome he captured that of an entire English civilization. After all, Clough was in no minority. Dean Church, visiting the immortal city for the first time in 1882, confessed to Newman's friend, Lord Blachford, "It is hopeless to talk of Rome … my feeling was one almost of hatred of the place. It seemed such a mixture of all incompatible things—ruins and magnificence, waste and civilization, tumbledown squalidness and untidiness, stateliness and grandeur … an anti-religious world and an ostentatiously religious world … I had the feeling that it is the one city in the world, besides Jerusalem, in which we *know* that God's eye is fixed, and that He has some purpose or other about it—one can hardly tell of good or evil."[73] Newman would have seen in Clough's epistolary hexameters echoes of the prejudices that he nicely enumerated in *The Idea of a University*, which he saw as stemming from what he called, "Intellectualism:"

> Catholicism, as it has come down to us from the first, seems to be mean and illiberal; it is a mere popular religion; it is the religion of illiterate ages or servile populations or barbarian warriors; it must be treated with discrimination and delicacy, corrected, softened, improved, if it is to satisfy an enlightened generation. It must be stereotyped as the patron of arts, or the pupil of speculation, or the protégé of science; it must play the literary academician, or the empirical philanthropist, or the political partisan; it must keep up with the age; some or other expedient it must devise, in order to explain away, or to hide, tenets under which the intellect labours and of which it is ashamed—its doctrine, for instance, of grace, its mystery of the Godhead, its preaching of the Cross, its devotion to the Queen of Saints, or its loyalty to the Apostolic See. Let this spirit be freely evolved out of that philosophical condition of mind ... and it is impossible but, first indifference, then laxity of belief, then even heresy will be the successive results.[74]

If Clough looked askance at the Catholicism of Rome, he was not comfortable with the sort of high-toned Socinianism that his character Claude approves.[75] When he was in America trying to find work, he wrote his wife apropos the Unitarians of Cambridge, "They are so awfully rococo in their religious notions that were I much in the way of hearing them expressed I should infallibly speak out and speak strongly."[76] But if we only see Claude as a stand-in for Clough, we lose half the satirical fun of the poem and all of its art. Asking himself what value the architecture of Rome has for him, Claude says:

> No one can cavil, I grant, at the size of the great Coliseum.
> Doubtless the notion of grand and capacious and massive amusement,
> This the old Romans had; but tell me, is this an idea?[77]

Matthew Arnold probably would not have thought so. But as this shows, the point of the novelistic form of the poem was to allow others to have their say. And here again Claude gives voice to four hundred years of Protestant prejudice.

> No, the Christian faith, as I, at least, understood it,
> Is not here, O Rome, in any of these thy churches;
> Is not here, but in Freiburg, or Rheims, or Westminster Abbey.
> What in thy Dome I find, in all thy recenter efforts,
> Is a something, I think, more *rational* far, more earthly,
> Actual, less ideal, devout not in scorn and refusal,
> But in a positive, calm, Stoic-Epicurean acceptance.[78]

This, one might say, is the "sane theory of things" *in excelsis*. After commending what he calls the "positive, calm, Stoic-Epicurean" strain in Protestantism—in itself a finely articulated absurdity—Claude shows what a good John Bull he is by traducing the Spanish contribution to the Counter Reformation in lines which recall the satirical exuberance of Newman's *Lectures on the Present Position of Catholics in England* (1851).[79]

> Luther, they say, was unwise; he didn't see how things were going;
> Luther was foolish,—but, O great God! what call you Ignatius?
> O my tolerant soul, be still! but you talk of barbarians,
> Alaric, Attila, Genseric;—why, they came, they killed, they
> Ravaged, and went on their way; but these vile, tyrannous Spaniards,
> These are here still,—how long, O ye heavens, in the country of Dante?
> These, that fanaticized Europe, which now can forget them, release not
> This, their choicest of prey, this Italy; here you see them,—
> Here, with emasculate pupils and gimcrack churches of Gesu,
> Pseudo-learning and lies, confessional-boxes and postures,—
> Here, with metallic beliefs and regimental devotions,—
> Here, overcrusting with slime, perverting, defacing, debasing,
> Michael Angelo's Dome, that had hung the Pantheon in heaven,
> Raphael's Joys and Graces, and thy clear stars, Galileo![80]

That the Spiritual Exercises of Ignatius helped convert Newman at a time when he, too, suffered from doubts is a striking irony, especially since the Exercises gave him the clarity of purpose without which he could not have acted on his hard-won convictions.[81] Clough, in his way, also dramatizes the need for moral action, though he does so by immersing his readers in the velleities of the tea table, where paltering Claude prefigures Prufrock.

> *Action will furnish belief,*—but will that belief be the true one?
> This is the point, you know. However, it doesn't much matter.
> What one wants, I suppose, is to predetermine the action
> So as to make it entail, not a chance belief, but the true one
> *Out of the question,* you say; *if a thing isn't wrong we may do it.*
> Ah! but this *wrong,* you see—but I do not know that it matters ...[82]

Of course, Clough also suffered from the inability to act. Indeed, his vacillations were representative of an entire age. In this regard, he was no different from many modern Hamlets whom Thomas Cook, the teetotal Baptist, sent moping about the Mediterranean on his inveterately popular Cook Tours. The cultural historian John Pemble, in his superb tour d'horizon, *The Mediterranean Passion: Victorians and Edwardians in the South* (1987) observes how "The intelligentsia were prone to fitful moods of revolt against the idea of reaching light through labyrinths of thought, and to sudden sharp awareness of needs unsatisfied in a life of introspection. It was this mood which drove George Meredith, Leslie Stephen, and Frederic Harrison to vigorous activity like club-swinging, hiking, and mountaineering, and which inspired Clough's yearning for action and Arnold's 'ineffable longing for the life of life.' 'Congestion of the brain is what we suffer from,' Arnold told Clough; 'I always feel it and say it and cry for air like my own Empedocles.'"[83] In *Dipsychus*, Clough gave the theme candid expression:

> 'Tis gone, the fierce inordinate desire,
> The burning thirst for Action utterly;
> Gone, like a ship that passes in the night
> On the high seas: gone, yet will come again
> Gone, yet expresses something that exists.
> Is it a thing ordained, then? is it a clue
> For my life's conduct? is it a law for me
> That opportunity shall breed distrust,
> Not passing until that pass? Chance and resolve,
> Like two loose comets wandering wide in space,
> Crossing each other's orbits time on time,
> Meet never. Void indifference and doubt
> Let through the present boon, which ne'er turns back
> To await the after sure-arriving wish.
> How shall I then explain it to myself,
> That in blank thought my purpose lives?[84]

Here, in the precinct of the labyrinth, Newman's work provides a clue that is proof against "void indifference and doubt." It can also help us to understand the fundamental predicament not only of Clough and Arnold but of most of their English contemporaries. In *The Tamworth Reading Room*, Newman wrote how "People say to me, that it is but a dream to suppose that Christianity should regain the organic power in human society which once it possessed. I cannot help that; I never said it could. I am not a politician; I am proposing no measures, but exposing a fallacy, and resisting a pretence. Let Benthamism reign, if men have no aspirations; but do ... not attempt by philosophy what once was done by religion. The ascendancy of Faith may be impracticable, but the reign of Knowledge is incomprehensible."[85] Yet, faced with the "problem of our being here," Clough has Claude at the end of *Amours de Voyage* reaffirm a trust in knowledge that is worthy of Arnold.

> Ere our death-day,
> Faith, I think, does pass, and Love; but Knowledge abideth.
> Let us seek Knowledge;—the rest may come and go as it happens.
> Knowledge is hard to seek, and harder yet to adhere to.
> Knowledge is painful often; and yet when we know we are happy.
> Seek it, and leave mere Faith and Love to come with the chances.
> As for Hope,—to-morrow I hope to be starting for Naples.
> Rome will not do, I see, for many very good reasons.
> Eastward, then, I suppose, with the coming of winter, to Egypt.[86]

Claude's trust in knowledge dramatizes Clough's Newmanian insight into how intellectual cultivation, if treated as an end in itself, betrays faith and love. Newman, for his part, always responded to the cult of knowledge by reaffirming the irreplaceability of faith. In one of his *Oxford University Sermons*, in which he differentiates between superstition and faith, he describes the latter as "a presumption, yet not a mere chance conjecture,—a reaching forward, yet not of excitement or of passion,—a moving forward in the twilight, yet not without clue or direction;—a movement from something known to something unknown, but kept in the narrow path of truth by the Law of dutifulness... ." Here, Newman might have been addressing Claude directly: faith, he wrote "is perfected, not by intellectual cultivation, but by obedience. It does not change its nature or its function, when thus perfected. It remains what it is in itself, an initial principle of action; but it becomes changed in its quality, as being made spiritual. It is as before a presumption, but the presumption of a serious, sober, thoughtful, pure, affectionate, and devout mind. It acts, because it is Faith; but the direction, firmness, consistency, and precision of its acts, it gains from Love."[87] This is why Newman was so adamant that "Devotion and self rule are worth all the intellectual cultivation in the world."[88] This is not the sort of definite statement of which Claude would approve but it is a useful corrective to what Arnold called the "light half-believers of our casual creeds."[89]

In reviewing Clough's first posthumous collection of verse, Walter Bagehot described the author as a man "who seemed about to do something, but who died before he did it."[90] Of course, he was speaking of what he regarded as Clough's unfulfilled literary promise. But if we look at Clough in Newmanian terms we can see that the "something" he did not live to do might have been more substantial than writing additional verses. The man who prized simplicity and hungered for reality and longed for peace might have fully reclaimed the faith he nearly lost in the "war of conscience and conviction." He might have joined those "uneducated persons, who have hitherto thought little of the unseen world," as Newman described them, who on "turning to God, looking into themselves, regulating their hearts, reforming their conduct, and meditating on death and judgement, heaven and hell ... seem to become, in point of intellect, different beings from what they were. Before they took things as they came, and thought no more of one thing than another. But now every event has a meaning; they have their own estimate of whatever happens to them; they are mindful of times and seasons, and compare the present with the past; and the world, no longer dull, monotonous, unprofitable, and hopeless, is a various and complicated drama, with parts and an object, and an awful moral."[91]

CHAPTER 13

Newman on Newman

"To make yourself an object external to yourself," Ronald Knox observed in his witty autobiography *A Spiritual Aeneid* (1918), "is to encourage in yourself habits of posing, of attitudinizing, of speculating over the figure you cut before the world; it may be of advantage in the literary profession to acquire such habits; in life it is a permanent nuisance. Children detected in the habit should certainly be smacked."[1] If this is true of self-absorbed authors and precocious children, it was not true of Blessed John Henry Cardinal Newman. No one can fairly say that he made his detached evaluations of himself and his work for purposes of "posing" or "attitudinizing." He made them to give himself and his readers some better understanding of his life and work. In this, he resembles Henry James, who was obliged to become his own best critic largely because there was too much of what he was trying to accomplish that his contemporaries could not fathom. The prefaces James wrote for the New York Edition of his works are a brilliant testimony to "the vigil of searching criticism" to which he subjected his novels.[2] Newman wrote some of his best books, his *Oxford University Sermons*, his *Essay on the Development of Christian Doctrine*, his *Idea of the University* and his *Grammar of Assent* in a similarly critical spirit to share with his contemporaries what he had in mind when he was coming to his various religious, educational and philosophical positions, most of which were fairly pioneering. If James wrote his prefaces and critical essays—especially those on Balzac, Maupassant, Hawthorne, George Eliot and Flaubert—to educate the taste by which he meant to be understood, Newman wrote his copious letters, in part, with the same purpose. After Frederic Rogers, Lord Blachford and Dean Church made him a gift of a violin, Newman wrote to Church: "I really think it will add to my power of working, and the length of my life. I never wrote more than when I played the fiddle. I always sleep better after music. There must be some electric current passing from the strings through the fingers into the brain and down the spinal marrow. Perhaps thought is music."[3] Here Newman captured the music that animates his own thought. This, in turn, recalled something he had said twenty years before in his great sermon, "The Theory of Developments in Religious Doctrine" (1843), which illuminates the attention he paid to underlying realities, to what one might call the music of the supernatural. Speaking of "musical sounds, as they are exhibited most perfectly in instrumental harmony," Newman wrote:

> There are seven notes in the scale; make them fourteen; yet what a slender outfit for so vast an enterprise! What science brings so much out of so little? Out of what poor elements does some great master in it create his new world! Shall we say that all this exuberant inventiveness is a mere ingenuity or trick of art, like some game or fashion of the day, without reality, without meaning? We may do so; and then, perhaps, we shall also account the science of theology to be a matter of words; yet, as there is a divinity in the theology of the Church, which those who feel cannot communicate, so is there also in the wonderful creation of sublimity and beauty of which I am speaking. To many men the very names which the science employs are utterly incomprehensible. To speak of an idea or a subject seems to be fanciful or trifling, to speak of the views which it opens upon us to be childish extravagance; yet is it possible that that inexhaustible evolution and disposition of notes, so rich yet so simple, so intricate yet so regulated, so various yet so majestic, should be a mere sound, which is gone and perishes? Can it be that those mysterious stirrings of heart, and keen emotions, and strange yearnings after we know not what, and awful impressions from we know not whence, should be wrought in us by what is unsubstantial, and comes and goes, and begins and ends in itself? It is not so; it cannot be. No; they have escaped from some higher sphere; they are the outpourings of eternal harmony in the medium of created sound; they are echoes from our Home; they are the voice of Angels, or the Magnificat of Saints, or the living laws of Divine Governance, or the Divine Attributes; something are they besides themselves, which we cannot compass, which we cannot utter,—though mortal man, and he perhaps not otherwise distinguished above his fellows, has the gift of eliciting them.[4]

The critic in Henry James had a good deal to say about content and form but nothing as brilliant as this. Still, James is a good figure to keep in mind when studying Newman because he recognized that heroes must not only be figures who experience great trials: they must be conscious of experiencing them. In his preface to *The Princess Casamassima* (1886), James observed how "the figures in any picture, the agents in any drama, are interesting only in proportion as they feel their respective situations; since the consciousness, on their part, of the complication exhibited forms for us their link of connexion with it. But there are degrees of feeling—the muffled, the faint, the just sufficient, the barely intelligent ... and the acute, the intense, the complete, in a word—the power to be finely aware and richly responsible. It is those moved in this latter fashion who 'get most' out of all that happens to them and who in so doing enable us, as readers of their record, as participants of their fond attention, also to get most. Their being finely aware—as Hamlet and Lear, say, are finely aware—*makes* absolutely the intensity of their adventure, gives the maximum of sense to what befalls them. We care, our curiosity and our sympathy care, comparatively little for what happens to the stupid, the coarse and the blind

..."[5] To revisit Newman's autobiographical writings, whether in his letters or his journals or his printed works is to recognize that he was precisely the sort of "finely aware and richly responsible" figure that James commends, though, of course, Newman's awareness was not the sort of awareness for the sake of awareness that figures so prominently in James's understanding of art and life. For example, it is not difficult to imagine what Newman would have made of James's advice to his friend Ivan Turgenev, the Russian novelist, who was struggling with depression:

> Life *is*, in fact, a battle. Evil is insolent and strong; beauty enchanting but rare; goodness very apt to be weak; folly very apt to be defiant; wickedness to carry the day; imbeciles to be in high places, people of sense in small, and mankind generally unhappy. But the world, as it stands, is no illusion, no phantasm, no evil dream of a night; we wake up to it again for ever and ever; we can neither forget it nor deny it nor dispense with it. We can welcome experience as it comes, and give it what it demands, in exchange for something which it is idle to pause to call much or little so long as it contributes to swell the volume of consciousness. In this there is mingled pain and delight, but over the mysterious mixture hovers a visible rule, that bids us learn to will and seek to understand.[6]

Recommending consciousness for the sake of consciousness to someone in the meshes of despair would not have struck Newman as the most useful counsel. Still, in his readiness to appreciate all sides of any given matter, and in his ability to express every nuance of every side, Newman could sound distinctly Jamesian. In this chapter I shall show how this attentiveness to his own fortunes was an important part of Newman's understanding of his vocation. Not only was he dedicated to living the devout life but he was dedicated to leaving behind a record of what that life had exacted in the way of trial and perseverance. In this he was emulating the early Fathers of the Church whose work revealed 'the daily life, the secret heart, of such ... servants of God, unveiled to their disciples in ... completeness and fidelity.' For Newman, "when a Saint is himself the speaker, he interprets his own action ... I want to hear a Saint converse; I am not content to look at him as a statue; his words are the index of his hidden life, as far as that life can be known to man, for 'out of the abundance of the heart the mouth speaketh.'"[7] What he sought to capture in his own letters and journals and in his other writings was precisely that "real, hidden but human, life," or, as he called it, the "*interior*."[8]

Something of Newman's *interior* can be found in the journal he kept periodically throughout his life. In 1869, he wrote:

> Another thought has come on me, that I have had three great illnesses in my life, and how have they turned out! The first keen, terrible one, when I was a boy of 15 and it made me a Christian—with experiences before and after, awful, and known only to God. My second, not painful, but tedious and shattering was that which I had in 1827 when I was one of the Examining

Masters, and it too broke me off from an incipient liberalism—and determined my religious course. The third was in 1833, when I was in Sicily, before the commencement of the Oxford Movement.

Here Newman showed the extent to which he saw trial as providing the defining structure of his life, and from this he concluded: "I suppose every one has a great deal to say about the Providence of God over him. Every one doubtless is so watched over and tended by Him that at the last day, whether he be saved or not, he will confess that nothing could have been done for him more than had been actually done—and every one will feel his own history as special & singular. Yet I cannot but repeat words which I think I used in a memorandum book of 1820, that among the ordinary mass of men, *no one* has been so mercifully treated, as I have; no one has such cause for humiliation, such cause for thanksgiving."[9]

The *Apologia* also furnishes insights into Newman's *interior*. When he was writing the book, sometimes for up to 16 hours a day, he wrote to James Hope-Scott, the parliamentary lawyer who made a fortune representing the railroads, "What good Angel has led you to write to me? It is a great charity. I never have been in such a stress of brain, and such pain of heart ... Say some good prayers for me ... I have been constantly in tears, and constantly crying out with distress – I am sure I never could say what I am saying in cool blood."[10] No work of autobiography ever revisited more harrowing ground.[11] And yet he also showed how the convictions that animated his life were with him even as a child. In the *Apologia* he recalled how his mind rested "in the thought of two and two only absolute and luminously self-evident beings, myself and my Creator."[12] He also quoted from a journal he wrote in 1820 to record how "I used to wish the Arabian Tales were true: my imagination ran on unknown influences, on magical powers, and talismans. I thought life might be a dream, or I an Angel, and all this world a deception, my fellow-angels by a playful device concealing themselves from me, and deceiving me with the semblance of a material world."[13] This readiness to see the world *sub specie aeternitatis* would never leave him. Those who imagine that Newman was somehow a crypto-skeptic must account for this most basal of his first principles. At the same time, Newman's deep-rooted faith never prevented him from entering into the psychology of skepticism, though understanding and subscribing to skepticism are two different things. The account he gives in the *Apologia* of his early reading attests to how attractive he found certain skeptical authors. "When I was fourteen, I read Paine's *Tracts against the Old Testament*, and found pleasure in thinking of the objections which were contained in them. Also, I read some of Hume's *Essays*; and perhaps that on *Miracles*. So at least I gave my father to understand; but perhaps it was a brag. Also, I recollect copying out some French verses, perhaps Voltaire's, in denial of the immortality of the soul, and saying to myself something like 'How dreadful, but how plausible!'"[14] Later, as I showed in an earlier chapter, Newman shared his doubts about his imminent conversion with John Keble in order to encourage his friend to try to resolve his own doubts. In the course of their correspondence, Newman confessed to Keble that "what quite pierces me" is "the disturbance of mind which a change on my part would cause to so many ... the temptation to which many would be exposed of scepticism, indifference, and even infidelity. These last considerations are so serious, in the standard of reason as well as in the way of inducement, that, if it were not for antagonist difficulties, I don't see how I could ever overcome them." Yet overcome them he did. Then, considering the Tractarians who would be left behind if he did convert, he predicted that, "The time may even come, when I shall beg them to join the Church of Rome and they will refuse"—a possibility which made him compunctious, since, when he was writing Keble, he had not made the move himself, which prompted him to admit: "Indeed I sometimes feel uncomfortable about myself—a sceptical, unrealizing temper is far from unnatural to me—and I may be suffered to relapse into it as a judgment."[15] As it happened, Newman did not succumb to this "skeptical, unrealizing temper," though the same cannot be said for Keble, whose decision to remain in the Church of England after Newman's secession caused him pitiable embarrassment. Speaking of "the position of English Churchmen," in his long sermon *Eucharistical Adoration* (1858), which gives the fullest expression we have of his Anglo-Catholic faith, Keble wrote: "it seems to be of the very last importance that we should keep in our own minds, and before all Christendom, the fact that we stand as orthodox Catholics upon a constant virtual appeal to the oecumenical voice of the Church ... The position may be called unreal or chimerical, but it is that which has been claimed for the Church of England by two great men [Thomas Cranmer and John Bramhall] ... And they were not either of them persons apt to take up with a chimerical, unreal view."[16] For the Anglo-Catholic in T. S. Eliot, the Anglican theology of John Bramhall (1594–1663) was "a perfect pursuit of the *via media*, and the *via media* is of all ways the most difficult to follow. It requires discipline and self-control, it requires both imagination and hold on reality."[17] As we have seen, no one knew the difficulties of the via media better than John Keble, or brought more discipline, self-control and imagination to its defense, though whether this brought him any closer to reality is questionable.

Newman, for his part, in leaving Oxford left all that was chimerical and unreal in his own life, though he accurately recognized that it was Oxford that had made him a Catholic. He also recognized something else: "I was undoing my own work, and leaving the field open, or rather infallibly surrendering it to those who would break down and crumble to powder all religion whatever."[18] The liberal dons Mark Pattison and Benjamin Jowett would see to that. Nevertheless, Newman's valedictory to Oxford is one of the glories of English prose.

> I left Oxford for good on Monday, February 23, 1846. On the Saturday and Sunday before, I was in my house at Littlemore simply by myself, as I had been for the first day or two when I had originally taken possession of it. I slept on Sunday night at my dear friend's, Mr. Johnson's, at the Observatory. Various friends came to see the last of me; Mr. Copeland, Mr. Church, Mr. Buckle, Mr. Pattison, and Mr. Lewis. Dr. Pusey too came up to take leave of me; and I called on Dr. Ogle, one of my very oldest friends, for he was my

private Tutor, when I was an Undergraduate. In him I took leave of my first College, Trinity, which was so dear to me, and which held on its foundation so many who had been kind to me both when I was a boy, and all through my Oxford life. Trinity had never been unkind to me. There used to be much snapdragon growing on the walls opposite my freshman's rooms there, and I had for years taken it as the emblem of my own perpetual residence even unto death in my University.

On the morning of the 23rd I left the Observatory. I have never seen Oxford since, excepting its spires, as they are seen from the railway [19]

Many years after leaving Oxford, and all the false theorizing of the via media, it was fitting that Newman should have left as his epitaph: "*Ex umbris et imaginibus in veritatem,*" which Ian Ker nicely translates: "Out of unreality into Reality."[20] If Newman gained from looking at himself from without, he also gained from looking at the Church of England from without—a fact which may not redound to his ecumenical credit but shows his readiness to see things objectively. In the *Apologia*, Newman spoke candidly of how his conversion had opened his eyes to aspects of the Established Church that he had only partially perceived before converting.

... unwilling as I am to give offence to religious Anglicans, I am bound to confess that I felt a great change in my view of the Church of England. I cannot tell how soon there came on me,—but very soon,—an extreme astonishment that I had ever imagined it to be a portion of the Catholic Church. For the first time, I looked at it from without, and (as I should myself say) saw it as it was. Forthwith I could not get myself to see in it any thing else, than what I had so long fearfully suspected, from as far back as 1836,—a mere national institution. As if my eyes were suddenly opened, so I saw it—spontaneously, apart from any definite act of reason or any argument; and so I have seen it ever since. I suppose, the main cause of this lay in the contrast which was presented to me by the Catholic Church. Then I recognized at once a reality which was quite a new thing with me. Then I was sensible that I was not making for myself a Church by an effort of thought; I needed not to make an act of faith in her; I had not painfully to force myself into a position, but my mind fell back upon itself in relaxation and in peace, and I gazed at her almost passively as a great objective fact. I looked at her;—at her rites, her ceremonial, and her precepts; and I said, "This *is* a religion;" and then, when I looked back upon the poor Anglican Church, for which I had laboured so hard, and upon all that appertained to it, and thought of our various attempts to dress it up doctrinally and esthetically, it seemed to me to be the veriest of nonentities.[21]

In the *Apologia*, Newman made another admission that revealed how fundamentally he differed from his latitudinarian contemporaries: "I was very superstitious, and for some time previous to my conversion used constantly to cross myself on going into the dark."[22] This was an important recollection because it showed how deep-seated his understanding of superstition was. In his *Oxford University Sermons* (1843), which, taken together, constitute "the intellectual and spiritual autobiography of a young teacher and pastor," Newman showed how superstition arises out of the sense of sin.[23]

> The world cannot bear up against the Truth, with all its boastings. It makes an open mock at sin, yet secretly attempts to secure an interest against its possible consequences in the world to come. Where has not the custom prevailed of propitiating, if possible, the unseen powers of heaven?—but why, unless man were universally conscious of his danger, and feared the punishment of sin, while he 'hated to be reformed'? ... Some have gone so far as to offer their sons and their daughters as a ransom for their own sin,—an abominable crime doubtless, and a sacrifice to devils, yet clearly witnessing man's instinctive judgment upon his own guilt, and his foreboding of punishment.[24]

The positivists of Newman's age unanimously claimed that natural knowledge, in freeing men from superstition, exculpated them from original sin. They were also convinced that it exploded the authority of the Church. "The improver of natural knowledge absolutely refuses to acknowledge authority," Thomas Huxley declared in 1866 at St. Martin's Hall in the Charing Cross Road.[25]

> For him, scepticism is the highest of duties; blind faith the one unpardonable sin. And it cannot be otherwise, for every great advance in natural knowledge has involved the absolute rejection of authority, the cherishing of the keenest scepticism, the annihilation of the spirit of blind faith; and the most ardent votary of science holds his firmest convictions, not because the men he most venerates hold them; not because their verity is testified by portents and wonders; but because his experience teaches him that whenever he chooses to bring these convictions into contact with their primary source, Nature — whenever he thinks fit to test them by appealing to experiment and to observation — Nature will confirm them. The man of science has learned to believe in justification, not by faith, but by verification.[26]

Throughout his long career, Newman always rejected the notion that science could moonlight as a kind of metaphysics. In *The Tamworth Reading Room*, he responded to the advocates of this overweening, false science by reminding his readers that, "Science gives us the grounds or premises from which religious truths are to be inferred; but it does not set about inferring them, much less does it reach the inference;—that is not its province. It brings before us phenomena, and it leaves us, if we will, to call them works of design, wisdom, or benevolence; and further still, if we will, to proceed to confess an Intelligent Creator. We have to take its facts, and to give them a meaning, and to draw our own conclusions from them."[27] What Newman took exception to was science arrogating to itself capabilities it did not possess—a theme which he would pursue in greater depth in *The Idea of a University* (1873). "First comes

Knowledge, then a view, then reasoning, and then belief. This is why Science
has so little of a religious tendency; deductions have no power of persuasion.
The heart is commonly reached, not through the reason, but through the imagination, by means of direct impressions, by the testimony of facts and events, by
history, by description. Persons influence us, voices melt us, looks subdue us,
deeds inflame us. Many a man will live and die upon a dogma: no man will be
a martyr for a conclusion."[28] Moreover, Newman saw that in congratulating
themselves on being free of superstition Huxley and the other advocates of
'natural knowledge' were losing sight of the moral and religious truths to which
superstition testified. Apropos the propitiatory sacrifices with which primitive
man sought to atone for sins, Newman observed: "Doubtless these desperate
and dark struggles are to be called superstition, when viewed by the side of true
religion; and it is easy enough to speak of them as superstition, when we have
been informed of the gracious and joyful result in which the scheme of Divine
Governance issues. But it is man's truest and best religion, *before* the Gospel
shines on him." Here Newman was trying to make his Pelagian contemporaries
see that from the oblations of primitive peoples they could learn something of
that holy fear which the civilization of intellect so dangerously counseled its
citizens to abandon.

> If our race *be* in a fallen and depraved state, what ought our religion to be
> but anxiety and remorse, till God comforts us? Surely, to be in gloom,—to
> view ourselves with horror,—to look about to the right hand and to the left
> for means of safety,—to catch at every thing, yet trust in nothing,—to do
> all we can, and try to do more than all,—and, after all, to wait in miserable
> suspense, naked and shivering, among the trees of the garden, for the
> hour of His coming, and meanwhile to fancy sounds of woe in every wind
> stirring the leaves about us,—in a word, to be superstitious,—is nature's best
> offering, her most acceptable service, her most mature and enlarged wisdom,
> in the presence of a holy and offended God. They who are not superstitious
> without the Gospel, will not be religious with it: and I would that even in
> us, who have the Gospel, there were more of superstition than there is; for
> much is it to be feared that our security about ourselves arises from defect
> in self-knowledge rather than in fulness of faith, and that we appropriate to
> ourselves promises which we cannot read."[29]

Apropos this sense of sin, which was so vital a part of Newman's understanding of the primacy of conscience, the poet Geoffrey Hill made an amusing
observation in a review of the second edition of the *Oxford English Dictionary*.

> Most of what one wants to know, including much that it hurts to know
> about the English language is held within these twenty volumes. To brood
> over them and in them is to be finally persuaded that sematology is a
> theological dimension: the use of language is inseparable from that 'terrible
> aboriginal calamity' in which, according to Newman, the human race
> is implicated. Murray, in 1884, missed the use of 'aboriginal:' it would

have added a distinctly separate signification to the recorded examples. In 1989 it remains unacknowledged. In what sense or senses is the computer acquainted with original sin?[30]

The issue of original sin may appear to have led us far afield but it was never far from Newman's inmost thoughts. That he so consistently acknowledged the effects of original sin in himself is what gives his autobiographical writings their appeal. "I know perfectly well, and thankfully confess to Thee, O my God," he wrote in a journal entry in 1859. "that thy wonderful grace turned me right round when I was more like a devil than a wicked boy, at the age of fifteen, and gave me what by thy continual aids I never lost. Thou didst change my heart, and in part my whole mental complexion at that time, and I never should have had the thought of such prayers, as those I have … but for that great work of thine in my boyhood …"[31]

Throughout his writings, even when he was not being explicitly autobiographical, Newman often shed light on the highly personal approach that he took to nearly every aspect of his life and work. Thus, we can glean something of the character of his faith from a sermon he delivered in 1849 on "The Glories of Mary for the Sake of her Son." Nothing shows the ardor of his faith better than his devotion to the Mother of God.

> … Mary is exalted for the sake of Jesus. It was fitting that she, as being a creature, though the first of creatures, should have an office of ministration. She, as others, came into the world to do a work, she had a mission to fulfil; her grace and her glory are not for her own sake, but for her Maker's; and to her is committed the custody of the Incarnation; this is her appointed office,—"A Virgin shall conceive, and bear a Son, and they shall call His Name Emmanuel". As she was once on earth, and was personally the guardian of her Divine Child, as she carried Him in her womb, folded Him in her embrace, and suckled Him at her breast, so now, and to the latest hour of the Church, do her glories and the devotion paid her proclaim and define the right faith concerning Him as God and man. Every church which is dedicated to her, every altar which is raised under her invocation, every image which represents her, every litany in her praise, every Hail Mary for her continual memory, does but remind us that there was One who, though He was all-blessed from all eternity, yet for the sake of sinners, "did not shrink from the Virgin's womb."[32]

And it followed from this, as he affirmed in "The Theory of Developments in Religious Doctrine," that "Mary is our pattern of Faith, both in the reception and in the study of Divine Truth. She does not think it enough to accept, she dwells upon it; not enough to possess, she uses it; not enough to assent, she develops it; not enough to submit the Reason, she reasons upon it; not indeed reasoning first, and believing afterwards, with Zacharias, yet first believing without reasoning, next from love and reverence, reasoning after believing. And thus she symbolizes to us, not only the faith of the unlearned, but of the doctors of the Church also, who have to investigate, and weigh, and define, as well as to profess the Gospel; to draw the line between truth and heresy; to anticipate or remedy the various aberrations of wrong reason; to combat pride and recklessness with their own arms; and thus to triumph over the sophist and the innovator."[33] In his immense correspondence with men and women from all walks of life from around the world which he conducted for over seventy years, Newman would follow the Blessed Virgin's pattern with a personal apostolate that was as untiring as it was wholehearted.

This attention to the personal is one aspect of Newman that endears him to Pope Benedict XVI.[34] If one's encounter with God is with a loving, merciful, personal God, one brings oneself to that encounter in a very direct, inimitable way, and no one urges readers to undertake that encounter more fully than Newman. Understanding how Newman saw himself also helps us to read Newman, for he meant his work to be read as personal testimony. Something of this can be seen in his discussion of literature in *The Idea of a University* (1873), where he says: "Literature is the personal use or exercise of language ... Language itself in its very origination would seem to be traceable to individuals. Their peculiarities have given it its character. We are often able in fact to trace particular phrases or idioms to individuals; we know the history of their rise. Slang surely, as it is called, comes of, and breathes of the personal."[35] In his own writing Newman often made brilliant use of slang. In one letter he vowed to be more faithful to St. Philip Neri, his patron saint, by becoming more self-effacing, because otherwise he could "fancy St Philip saying to me what a French conducteur once by gestures said, when I looked to see if he had put up all my luggage safely, 'Who are you? what's it to you? why do you put in your jaw? won't you be off? who, I say, are you? save your eyes, who are you? I say?' I fancy St Philip thus speaking to me ..."[36] Slang also appealed to Newman's dislike of side. When Henry Wilberforce was contemplating leaving his curacy at Bransgore for the more remunerative living of Walmer, Kent, Newman wrote to him: "I only hope that your new preferment will not make you a shovel hatted humbug. Beware of the Lambeth livery."[37]

For Newman, language was more than an opportunity for rhetorical swordplay: it was a way of being oneself. "The connection between the force of words in particular languages and the habits and sentiments of the nations speaking them has often been pointed out. And, while the many use language as they find it, the man of genius uses it indeed, but subjects it withal to his own purposes, and moulds it according to his own peculiarities. The throng and succession of ideas, thoughts, feelings, imaginations, aspirations, which pass within him, the abstractions, the juxtapositions, the comparisons, the discriminations, the conceptions, which are so original in him, his views of external things, his judgments upon life, manners, and history, the exercises of his wit, of his humour, of his depth, of his sagacity, all these innumerable and incessant creations, the very pulsation and throbbing of his intellect, does he image forth, to all does he give utterance, in a corresponding language, which is as multiform as this inward mental action itself and analogous to it, the faithful expression of his intense personality, attending on his own inward world of thought as its very shadow: so that we might as well say that one man's shadow is another's as that the style of a really gifted mind can belong to any but himself. It follows him about *as* a shadow. His thought and feeling are personal, and so his language is personal."[38]

Gerard Manley Hopkins recognized the personal stamp of Newman's prose when he observed: "Newman does not follow the common tradition—of writing. His tradition is that of cultured, the most highly educated, conversation; it is the flower of the best Oxford life. Perhaps this gives it a charm of unaffected and personal sincerity that nothing else could. Still, he shirks the technic of written prose and shuns the tradition of written English. He seems to be thinking 'Gibbon is the last great master of traditional English prose; he is its perfection: I do not propose to emulate him; I begin all over again from the language of conversation, of common life."[39] One can open Newman's collected works at random and find examples galore to illustrate the conversational force of his style. Here is one from *The Idea of a University* (1873). Apropos the many proposals for university reform that clamored for a hearing when he was setting up the Catholic University in the 1850s, Newman wrote:

> What would come … of the ideal systems of education which have fascinated the imagination of this age, could they ever take effect, and whether they would not produce a generation frivolous, narrow-minded, and resourceless, intellectually considered, is a fair subject for debate; but so far is certain, that the Universities and scholastic establishments, to which I refer [he is referring to Oxford and Cambridge] … these institutions, with miserable deformities on the side of morals, with a hollow profession of Christianity, and a heathen code of ethics,—I say, at least they can boast of a succession of heroes and statesmen, of literary men and philosophers, of men conspicuous for great natural virtues, for habits of business, for knowledge of life, for practical judgment, for cultivated tastes, for accomplishments, who have made England what it is,—able to subdue the earth, able to domineer over Catholics.[40]

However right Newman might have been about most proposals for educational reform, he could be patently wrong about himself. Four years after he converted, when he was 48, he remarked to his friend Henry Wilberforce, "It is an awful thing, beginning so new a life in the end of my days. How I wish I had in me the energy which I had when I began the Tracts for the Times! Now I am scarce more, to my own feelings, than an inutile lignum; so stiff so wooden. May you never have, dear Henry, the bitter reflection that you have left yourself but the dregs of life for God's service!"[41] In 1854, he wrote Henry's older brother Robert, "I am getting an old man now – and have too much to do, and it is telling on me …" In 1856, he wrote Lady Arundel, "Pray say a Hail Mary for me; tomorrow is my birthday, and I enter with thankfulness yet with fear into what the books call 'the period of old age.'"[42] A year later he wrote Viscount Fielding, "Pray, my dear Lord … don't forget me in your prayers, an old man with too much to do …"[43] In 1857, he wrote Mrs. Froude, "Thanks to you and Isy for not forgetting an old man."[44] In 1860, he wrote his sister Jemima, "All through last year I fell off in flesh, and suppose I shall ... never recover it ... My fingers are so thin that I can't get accustomed to the sight of them. My skin is getting to gleam like parchment, and I have had difficulty of lying at night from the prominency of my bones."[45] Why Newman persisted in imagining himself senescent when he was in the prime of life is hard to say. Evelyn Waugh saw something of the same thing in his father. "The illusion of old age was much enhanced by his own utterances," he wrote of Arthur Waugh. "Like his grandfather ... he often adverted to his imminent demise.... . He found great satisfaction in visiting the site of his grave in Hampstead parish churchyard ..." Arthur's make-believe old age was in complete contrast to the sprightliness he exuded. As his son confirmed, "Most of his acquaintances regarded him as exuberantly jovial." [46] Newman's friends similarly marveled at his energy, toughness and capacity for a level of work that most other men would have found unsustainable. Even by his own account, he was anything but the old man that he otherwise portrayed himself. In 1854, he wrote to Ambrose St. John from Harcourt Street in Dublin, where he was busy preparing for the launch of the Catholic University: "It blows a tempest, and rains furiously. I cannot think such weather will last. Next Sunday I am at Carlow – On Wednesday 22nd at Cork – Sunday 26th at Limerick – Ash Wednesday at Belfast. Sunday March 5, I trust in Birmingham. The first week I was here was simply lost, the Archbishop being away. Since then, I have engaged one Lecturer, and almost another – both distinguished persons here – I have laid the foundations of a quasi Oratory, with priests to confess the youths, ... set up a debating society ... and ... thrown lawyers, architects, painters, paperers, and upholsterers into the University house, with a view of preparing for our Autumn opening."[47] Here was proof of the wonderful vitality of the man that was not always on display in his more self-deprecatory letters.

Of course, Newman's prematurely aging himself might be seen as a consequence of his traumatic conversion. Seen thus, Newman could be said to have felt warrantably old: "wore aht," as Bill, the Cockney atheist tells Adolphus Cusins, the Professor of Greek in Shaw's *Major Barbara*. Newman appeared to support this view when he wrote in his journal in 1847 this lugubrious entry: "In a variety of ways I have fallen away from hope. In the Church of England I had many detractors; a mass of calumny was hurled at me ... I became an exile in solitude ... but not even in that retreat was I safe from those who pursued me with their curiosity ... And now the cheerfulness I used to have has almost vanished. And I feel acutely that I am no longer young, but that my best years are spent, and I am sad at the thought of the years that have gone by and I see myself as a useless log."[48] But even if we allow for the ordeal of his conversion, this screed is still distorting. Newman was never an "exile in solitude," he never fell away from hope, he never suffered his cheerfulness to vanish, and he was certainly never a *useless log*. Down in the dumps and alone with his journal, he could exaggerate his woes. Newman himself intimated as much when he was on his deathbed and turned to Father Neville and said, "You must not suppose that these little affairs of mine will be on the *tapis* in the courts of the next world."[49]

Still, the dismay that Newman suffered as a Catholic was real. In January 1863, he lamented what seemed to him the futility of his life as a Catholic: "it came upon me this morning as I lay in bed, What is the good of all this? what is to come of it? what am I living for? what am I doing for any religious end? Alas, it is my habitual thought, now for years, but circumstances have urged it on me at intervals more than usual of late, and something was told me yesterday which was a clincher."[50] Apparently, some busybody had told Ambrose St. John that Newman had not converted as many people as Faber and Manning, which prompted an Olympian grouse from Newman, though it has to be said that he had legitimate grievances with the short-sightedness and the unfair distrust of both the English Church and Propaganda. "Persons who would naturally look towards me, converts who would naturally consult me, are stopped by some light or unkind word said against me. I am passé, in decay; I am untrustworthy; I am strange, odd; I have my own ways & cannot get on with others; something or other is said in disparagement. I am put aside on the ground that I *ought* to be put aside ..."[51] In 1863, before the success of the *Apologia* relieved his sense of isolation in a country that did not always know what to make of him, he could be forgiven for looking back on his earlier Anglican career with occasional nostalgia. "O how forlorn & dreary has been my course since I have been a Catholic! here has been the contrast—as a Protestant, I felt my religion dreary, but not my life—but, as a Catholic, my life dreary, not my religion."[52] For Newman, the problem was that Propaganda expected him to make as many influential converts as he could in order to help convert the English *en masse*; and naturally Faber and Manning had a better opportunity to do this from London than he had from the Hagley Road. But even in his otherwise jaundiced account of his Catholic career, Newman made a number of shrewd observations. First, he differentiated his own mission from that of his London brethren: "I am altogether different—my objects, my theory of acting, my powers, go in a different direction, and one not understood or contemplated in Rome or elsewhere. I never courted men, but they have come to me ... And if they did not come to me, I did not gain them ... To me, conversions were not the first thing, but the edification of Catholics ... I am afraid to make hasty converts of educated men, lest they should not have counted the cost ... the Church must be prepared for converts, as well as converts prepared for the Church ... And Catholics in England, from their very blindness, cannot see that they are blind. To aim then at improving the condition, the status, of the Catholic body, by a careful survey of their argumentative basis, of their position relatively to the philosophy and character of the day, by giving them juster views, by enlarging & refining their minds, in one word, by education, is (in their view) more than a superfluity or a hobby, it is an insult. It implies that they are deficient ... Now from first to last, education, in this large sense of the word, has been my line," though he was convinced that his involvement with the *Rambler*, the liberal Catholic paper (which he attempted to steer clear of heterodoxy) and his establishment of his own Oratory School put him out of favor with the governing body of Catholics in England and in Rome. He was convinced that "so far from being thought engaged in any good work, I am simply discouraged and regarded suspiciously ... as doing actual harm."[53] Yet in his failure to endear himself to his superiors Newman saw a comical side. "I should be so out of my element if I were without that cold shade on the side of ecclesiastical authority, in which I have dwelt nearly all my life, my eyes would be so dazed and my limbs so relaxed, were I brought out to bask in the sun of ecclesiastical favor that I should not know how to act and should make a fool of myself."[54]

Despite his difficulties with his Catholic superiors, Newman never made the vulgar error of confusing the men who happened to figure in the Church's hierarchy with the Church herself. In 1868, Sir Frederic Rogers shared with Newman the letter of a man named Bartholomew who confessed to experiencing great anguish when Newman converted—anguish that was shared by many forlorn Tractarians. In his reply, Newman put the occasional asperities that he suffered from Catholic prelates in perspective: "To-day is the 20th anniversary of my setting up the Oratory in England, and every year I have more to thank God for, and more cause to rejoice that he helped me over so great a crisis ... there is a depth and a power in the Catholic religion, a fulness of satisfaction in its creed, its theology, its rites, its sacraments, its discipline, a freedom yet a support also, before which the neglect or the misapprehension about oneself on the part of individual living persons, however exalted, is as so much dust, when weighed in the balance. This is the true secret of the Church's strength, the principle of its indefectibility, and the bond of its indissoluble unity. It is the earnest and the beginning of the repose of Heaven."[55]

Newman's feelings of being passed over, distrusted, even scorned would dissipate after the warm reception of his *Apologia Pro Vita Sua* (1864), when the plain people of England first came round to recognizing what an extraordinary gaffer they had in their midst. But such feelings would never entirely leave him. He was, after all, surrounded by people who did not appreciate his gifts or who appreciated them but sought to thwart him from exercising them. One thinks of that wonderful aside in Max Beerbohm's *Zuleika Dobson*: "the dullard's envy of brilliant men is always assuaged by the suspicion that they will come to a bad end."[56] Many regarded Newman in a similarly envious light. Charles Golightly, who instigated the episcopal attacks on Tract 90, and George Talbot, who made continual trouble for Newman in Rome, were only the most notorious: there were many more.[57] Still, he took such buffetings in stride. In 1867, he wrote to his dear friend Catherine Anne Bathurst, a dedicated teacher who founded many schools and orphanages, first as a Sister of Charity and then as a Dominican Tertiary: "it has been for so many years my own case to be rudely treated, that (as far as I know myself) it does not distress me at all now – for it is the rule of my life; and I say deliberately, I do not wish it changed, for it is the lightest trial I could have – how much lighter than bad health, loss of friends, loss of faculties, poverty! Indeed the danger is, that, used as I am to be so treated, I could not bear any other lot – and should be as awkward and blundering if I had the sunshine on me, as prisoners who have for years been shut up in a dark dungeon."[58]

What makes Newman such an attractive figure is that, for all his greatness, he was never full of himself. "A Rector ought to be a more showy bustling man than I am," he told one of his friends about his role as Rector of the Catholic University, "in order to impress the world we are great people. I ought to dine out every day, and of course I don't dine out at all. I ought to mix in literary society and talk about new gasses and the price of labour—whereas I can't recollect what I once knew, much less get up a whole lot of new subjects – I ought to behave condescendingly to others, whereas they are condescending to me ..."[59] When his good friend and confidante, Sister Mary Gabriel Du Boulay, whom he received into the Church in 1850, asked if he would come and visit her, Newman wrote back: "Please God I will say Mass for you on the 11th. I am beginning a set of Masses for Revd Mother's intentions. Is not that more than coming to see you? And am I not wise, not to lessen the sort of imaginations you have of me – so kind, yet so unreal, by showing myself in propriâ personâ? I always feel like a hypocrite who can be detected by holy eyes, just as an accomplished thief or thimble rigger is at once recognized by a police officer. But at a distance I look like a great man, without any hang dog look which I can't throw off, do what I will, when I am in places where brass will not go for gold."[60]

Over the years, he became something of a connoisseur of what he called "the tin-kettle accounts of me which rattle to and fro in the world."[61] When he learned that someone was putting about the rumor that he had lost his mind, he nicely deplored the calumny as a "grave, sleek, imposing lie, which made one smile. People sucked it in greedily and smacked their lips."[62] He was particularly amused by the story a friend had heard in London that "I carried my austerity to such an extent that I would not let my wife wear anything but sad coloured ribbons in her bonnet."[63] In 1850, he wrote his fellow Oratorian Frederick Faber, "The report grows stronger and stronger here, that I am married, and have shut up my wife in a convent."[64]

In retrospect, we can see clues to the real character of this still widely misunderstood man in many of his writings. In "St Paul's Characteristic Gift" (1857), for instance, he divided saints into two kinds: those who "seem, even while ... in the flesh, to have no part in earth or in human nature ..." and those "in whom the supernatural combines with nature, instead of superseding it..." And in describing the latter category, in which he placed St. Paul, he described himself.

> They do not put away their natural endowments, but use them to the glory of the Giver; they do not act beside them, but through them; they do not eclipse them by the brightness of divine grace, but only transfigure them. They are versed in human knowledge; they are busy in human society; they understand the human heart; they can throw themselves into the minds of other men; and all this in consequence of natural gifts and secular education. While they themselves stand secure in the blessedness of purity and peace, they can follow in imagination the ten thousand aberrations of pride, passion, and remorse. The world is to them a book, to which they are drawn for its own sake, which they read fluently, which interests them naturally,— though, by the reason of the grace which dwells within them, they study it and hold converse with it for the glory of God and the salvation of souls.

Thus they have the thoughts, feelings, frames of mind, attractions, sympathies, antipathies of other men, so far as these are not sinful, only they have these properties of human nature purified, sanctified, and exalted; and they are only made more eloquent, more poetical, more profound, more intellectual, by reason of their being more holy.[65]

Holiness meant a good deal to Newman and it was therefore only natural that the aspect of himself about which he should be most perceptive was his celibacy. In one of his most powerful sermons, preached at the religious profession of Mary Anne Bowden (1831–1867), the eldest daughter of his good friend Mrs. J. W. Bowden, before she entered the Visitation Convent at Westbury in 1852, Newman pointed out that the "state of celibacy recommended by philosophers ... does but harden the heart," being "of that forlorn, haughty and repulsive nature," which "has been imaged and extolled in the pages of heathen writers or in the teaching of false religions ... To make a single life its own end, to adopt it simply and solely for its own sake, I do not know whether such a state of life is more melancholy or more unamiable, melancholy from its unrequited desolateness and unamiable from the pride and self-esteem on which it is based."

This is not the Virginity of the Gospel—it is not a state of independence or isolation, or dreary pride, or barren indolence, or crushed affections; man is made for sympathy, for the interchange of love, for self-denial for the sake of another dearer to him than himself. The Virginity of the Christian soul is a marriage with Christ.[66]

For Newman, as Ian Ker points out, "the essence of celibacy as a spiritual ideal as opposed to a pragmatic convenience, was not so much that it provides freedom from the ties of marriage and family for a fuller commitment to the work of a religious profession, but rather that the very pain of the lack of intimate human love is meant to impel the celibate to find affective fulfillment in the exclusive love of God."[67] Newman also saw the practical character of celibacy in the context of the sacrifices that all Christians are enjoined to make. "Since the coming of our Saviour on earth," he wrote in a public letter to the *Rambler* in 1859, "humiliation, suffering, and poverty are to be looked on as His livery; and His prophecies to His Church rather foretell thorns than roses, strife than peace, and humiliation than triumph. Of course, the lowly virtues of the New Testament are applicable to different states of life in different proportions; but there must be a recognition of them in the king as well as in the hermit. Heroic, by which I mean self-sacrificing, virtues are, as a general rule, less applicable to fathers of families, simply because all duties being relative, the duty of a man to his wife and children comes before a larger number of more distant duties. This it is which has led, in the Catholic Church, to the celibacy of the clergy; which is ... a mere consequence of what I may call the division of labour consequent on a more developed state of Christian civilisation. The attire of the glorified Church is to be wrought about with a variety of ornament."[68]

Newman's Protestant contemporaries saw the matter rather differently. Indeed, much of the hostility to Newman in his own day would always stem from the Protestant contempt for celibacy. The Anglican priest and poet, John Moultrie (1799–1874), who had been at Eton with Praed, wrote some verses to affirm this contempt.[69]

God give her wavering clergy back that honest heart and true
Which once was there ere Popish fraud its spell around them threw;
Nor let them barter wife and child, bright hearth and happy home
For the hectic bliss of the strumpet kiss of the Jezebel of Rome.[70]

Apropos Moultrie, one parishioner quipped: "They spoilt a jolly good navvy when they made that old cove a parson."[71] He was a muscular Christian in more ways than one.

Newman's response to muscular Christianity showed the bully boys of his age that he would not take their slurs lying down. "There have been Protestants whose idea of enlightened Christianity has been a strenuous antagonism to what they consider the unmanliness and unreasonableness of Catholic morality, an antipathy to the precepts of patience, meekness, forgiveness of injuries, and chastity. All this they have considered a woman's religion, the ornament of monks, of the sick, the feeble, and the old. Lust, revenge, ambition, courage, pride—these, they have fancied, made the man, and want of them the slave." Indeed, for Newman, it was only logical that "No one could fairly accuse such men of any great change of their convictions, if they were one day found to have taken up the profession of Islam." In all events, Newman was only too well aware of "men of the world who cannot enter into the very idea of devotion, and think, for instance, that, from the nature of the case, a life of religious seclusion must be either one of unutterable dreariness or abandoned sensuality, because they know of no exercise of the affections but what is merely human; and with others again, who, living in the home of their own selfishness, ridicule as something fanatical and pitiable the self-sacrifices of generous high-mindedness and chivalrous honour."[72]

In imagining that Newman's celibacy was an implicit criticism of the sexual love of marriage, the unbalanced Charles Kingsley followed the Rector of Rugby, though no one can read Newman's letters, especially to married friends and acquaintances, and credit such wild falsehood. In the sermon he preached for Mary Anne Bowden, Newman wrote of marriage:

Two mortal creatures of God, placed in this rough world, exposed to its many fortunes, destined to suffering and death, join hands, and give the faith to each other that each of them will love the other wholly until death. Henceforth, each is made for the other—each has possession of the affections of the other in a transcendent way; each is all in all to the other; each can confide in the other unreservedly, each is the other's irreversibly. There is but one mind, one aim, one course, one happiness, between two. Each is reflected in the other; each reads his own thought in the other's face; each feels for the other more than for himself. Such is the fountain head of human society and the continual provision of the human race: such is the beginning of civilization, the guardian of religion, the norm of philanthropy, and the sanctification of mankind. There is no such union elsewhere in the natural world ...[73]

For all of his gregariousness and, indeed, his genius for friendship, Newman was never spared loneliness. In 1836, in the wake of the death of his mother and Hurrell Froude, he wrote to his sister Jemima, "I am not more lonely than I have been a long while. God intends me to be lonely. He has so framed my mind that I am in a great measure beyond the sympathies of other people, and thrown upon Himself ..."[74] To his sister Harriet, he was even more revelatory: "Thank God, my spirits have not sunk, nor will they, I trust. I have been full of work, and that keeps me generally free from any dejection. If it ever comes, it is never of long continuance, and is even not unwelcome – I am speaking of dejection from solitude; I never feel so near heaven as then. Years ago, from 1822 to 1826, I used to be very much by myself; and in anxieties of various kinds, from money matters and other things, which were very harassing. I then on the whole had no friend near me – no one to whom I opened my mind fully or who could sympathize with me. I am but returning at worst to that state. Indeed, ever since that time I have learned to throw myself on myself. Therefore, please God, I trust I shall get on very well, and after all this life is very short, and it is a better thing to be pursuing what seems God's call, than to be looking after one's own comfort. I am learning more than hitherto to live in the presence of the dead – this is a gain which strange faces cannot take away."[75]

If there is one personal quality that comes out in Newman's self-portraits again and again it is his humility. "I have no tendency to be a saint," he told one correspondent in 1850. "Saints are not literary men, they do not love the classics, they do not write Tales. I may be well enough in my way, but it is not the 'high line.' People ought to feel this, most people do. But those who are at a distance have fee-fa-fum notions about one. It is enough for me to black the saints' shoes – if St Philip uses blacking, in heaven."[76] Newman's humility gave him not only self-knowledge but perseverance. Throughout his long career as the Father of the Birmingham Oratory, he would always be compared unfavorably to the Oratorians in London, who could seem, in worldly terms, more successful. In a letter to Ambrose St. John, Newman addressed the issue with characteristic candor. "I cannot conceal from myself that we are considered as slow, and humdrum, and twaddling, and unready, and incapable, and idle, and unfruitful, and unspiritual ... that we are a set of priests who do nothing equal to their number and their capabilities.

Well, my dear Fathers, if we are conscious to ourselves, if we have reason to suspect, that we are thus inferior to our vocation and our mission, then nothing is to be said for us; but if the case be otherwise, if we are really doing a work, or rather many works, and all that the complaint means is that we do not puff and advertise it to the four quarters of the earth, then I do but rejoice in it, as a mark, special and singular, of our being the children of St Philip. If there be one thing more than another, which is his gift and after his pattern, it is to live in the shade—if there is one thing that will specially interest him in us, it is that we are *despised*, and not only so, but that we despise being despised.[77]

This leads to another defining characteristic of Newman and that was his conviction that failure, far from being an unalloyed evil in his life, had always proved an agent of spiritual growth. Newman first became conscious of this conviction, which took shape gradually and over many years, in the wake of the collapse of his father's bank in 1816.[78] It was compounded by his father's bankruptcy in 1821. On 7 November 1821—six days after he learned the terrible news—Newman wrote to his Aunt Elizabeth: "I am convinced that nothing can be a greater snare and evil to a person than unalloyed prosperity. I cannot say how I should behave were the offer of possessing them made me but in my present state of mind there is nothing I would rather deprecate than wealth or fame or great influence."[79] In 1836, he wrote in response to those critical of the Tractarians, "Such is the law which God has annexed to the promulgation of the Truth: its preachers suffer, but its cause prevails."[80] In 1855, he was convinced that "all through life, when I have been despised most, I have succeeded most."[81] In 1858, he gave his long-held conviction fuller expression still: "from the first it has been my fortune to be ever failing, yet after all not to fail. From the first I have had bad strokes of fortune – yet on the whole I have made way. Hardly had I begun life, when misfortunes happened to my family – then I failed in the Schools; then I was put out of office at College; then came Number 90 – and later the Achilli matter. You talk of 'brilliant success' as not our portion – it is not, because you are all joined to me. When I was a boy, I was taken beyond any thing in Homer, with Ulysses seeming 'like a fool or an idiot,' when he began to speak – and yet somehow doing more than others, as St Paul with his weakness and foolishness. I think this was from some presentiment of what was to happen to me."[82]

To speak of how Newman accepted failure as a necessary condition for his spiritual development is a commonplace. Yet suffering failure was never easy for him. After all, he was highly talented and naturally eager to see his talents succeed. His own failures, when they came, were harrowing. It was only after the fact, sometimes years after the fact, that he could see the spiritual silver lining. "O Philip," he wrote in 1859 in one of his most moving journal entries, when he felt his Catholic career had been an irredeemable failure, "gain me some little portion of thy fervor. I live more and more in the past, and in hopes that the past may revive in the future. My God, when shall I learn that I have so parted with the world, that, though I may wish to make friends with it, it will not make friends with me?"[83] A year later, he was again pleading for the grace to endure failure, "O teach me … teach me how to employ myself most profitably, most to Thy glory, in such cases as remain to me; for my apparent illsuccess discourages me much. O my God, I seem to have wasted these years that I have been a Catholic. What I wrote as a Protestant has had far greater power, force, meaning, success, than my Catholic works—& this troubles me a great deal."[84] The failures Newman would suffer as a Catholic, including those associated with the Catholic University, his proposed translation of the Bible, his proposed Oxford Oratory, and his delation to Rome after the publication of his article on the laity were all attributable more to others than to himself. Nevertheless, Newman wrote his unhappy journal entries before he wrote some of his greatest Catholic works, including the *Apologia, The Dream of Gerontius, An Essay in Aid of a Grammar of Assent, The Idea of a University* and *A Letter to the Duke of Norfolk.* Moreover, even at his lowest ebb as a Catholic, he was still a most effective spiritual counselor for hundreds of individuals within and outside of the Church, as his letters attest. Still, the sense of failure he felt was lacerating. In April 1861, in what was something of an *annus horribilis*, he complained of how "every thing seems to crumble under my hands, as if one were making ropes of sand."[85] Yet towards the end of his life, he could look back and see how providential these terrible trials had been. In 1882, he responded to his friend Lord Braye, who had complained of personal setbacks:

> Now what can I say in answer to your letter? First, that your case is mine. It is for years beyond numbering – in one view of the matter for these 50 years – that I have been crying out 'I have laboured in vain, I have spent my strength without cause and in vain: wherefore my judgment is with the Lord, and my work with my God.' Now at the end of my days, when the next world is close upon me, I am recognized at last at Rome. Don't suppose I am dreaming of complaint – just the contrary. The Prophet's words, which expressed my keen pain, brought, because they were his words, my consolation. It is the rule of God's Providence that we should succeed by failure; and my moral is, as addressed to you, Doubt not that He will use you – be brave – have faith in His love for you – His everlasting love – and love Him from the certainty that He loves you."[86]

Newman's understanding of how failure brought him closer to God also figures in his prayers, where he is most himself. Apropos Newman's prayers, the Oratorian Father Henry Tristram wrote: "They are not the stiff, rather formal and stilted work of a man composing meditations for general use. Far from it, they are intensely personal, saturated through and through with Newman. It is he who is praying and none other; and as he prays, his mind is thronged with thoughts of his past sins and present needs, of the graces bestowed and of his failure to correspond, of the providence of God watching over him in his maturity, as in his boyhood and youth, of opportunities given and missed, but above all of God's infinite condescension, and unwearied love."[87] If this is hardly the stuff of panegyric, it is of the essence of hagiography. In acknowledging his own personal failures, and praying for the grace to overcome them, Newman was following the saints, whose own *interiors* he studied so closely, though his contemporaries could not have known the uncompromising honesty with which he undertook this most Christian of duties.

My most Holy Lord and Sanctifier, whatever there is of good in me is Thine. Without Thee, I should but get worse and worse as years went on, and should tend to be a devil. If I differ at all from the world, it is because Thou hast chosen me out of the world, and hast lit up the love of God in my heart. If I differ from Thy Saints, it is because I do not ask earnestly enough for Thy grace, and for enough of it, and because I do not diligently improve what Thou hast given me. Increase in me this grace of love, in spite of all my unworthiness. It is more precious than anything else in the world. I accept it in place of all the world can give me. O give it to me! It is my life.[88]

Here was Newman at his most "finely aware and richly responsible." When it came to understanding himself, he proved his own most insightful contemporary.

Bibliographical Note

The two biographers who have done the best work on John Henry Newman are Meriol Trevor and Ian Ker. Meriol Trevor's two-volume biography, which consists of *Newman: The Pillar of the Cloud* and *Newman: Light in Winter* (1962) is excellent on the personal aspects of Newman's life; it is also full of copious quotation from Newman's work, chosen by the great Oratorian, Father Charles Stephen Dessain, who was also the founding editor of Newman's 33-volume *Letters and Diaries*, which began appearing in 1961. Ian Ker's great intellectual life, *John Henry Newman* (1988), which OUP has published in a revised edition, remains the definitive life. It also includes a good epilogue on recent developments regarding the Cardinal.

Stephen Dessain wrote a good short biography of Newman, as did Richard Holt Hutton. Brian Martin also wrote a useful short biography, *John Henry Newman: His Life & Work* (1990), which is illustrated. Then, too, John Holloway has an excellent chapter on Newman in his book, *The Victorian Sage: Studies in Argument* (1953). Ronald Begley has an exhilaratingly good piece called "Metaphor in the *Apologia* and Newman's Conversion," in *Newman and Conversion*, edited by Ian Ker (1997). There are also good essays about Newman in *Newman after 100 Years* (1990), edited by Ian Ker and Alan Hill—especially one about Newman's preaching by the literary critic Eric Griffiths. There is also a good piece called "Newman the Writer" by Geoffrey Tillotson, in Geoffrey and Kathleen Tillotson's *Mid-Victorian Studies* (1965). Ian Ker wrote a good overview of Newman's career for the *Oxford Dictionary of National Biography*, and James Anthony Froude wrote a witty account of the Oxford Movement in *Short Studies on Great Subjects* called "The Oxford Counter-Reformation" (1882).

About the Oxford Movement, Newman's own *Apologia Pro Vita Sua* (1864) and Dean Church's *The Oxford Movement* (1890) are the best accounts. Peter Nockles' *The Oxford Movement in Context: Anglican High Churchmanship 1760–1857* (1994) is also worth looking at.

There are good books on special aspects regarding Newman, including Joyce Sugg's *Ever Yours Affly: John Henry Newman and his Female Circle* (1997), Ian Ker's *Newman and the Fullness of Christianity* (1993), Paul Shrimpton's *A Catholic Eton? Newman's Oratory School* (2005), Henry Tristram's *Newman and His Friends* (1933), Madeleine Beard's *Faith and Fortune* (1997), and *The Cambridge Companion to John Henry Newman* (2009) edited by Ian Ker and Terrence Merrigan. A good overview of Newman's work is provided in Ian Ker's *The Achievement of John Henry Newman* (1990).

For Newman's own writings, there are four good anthologies: *The Genius of John Henry Newman*, edited by Ian Ker (1989), which OUP is reissuing; *Newman: Prose and Poetry*, edited by Geoffrey Tillotson (1957) in the Reynard Library; *A Newman Anthology* edited by William Samuel Lilly (1949); and a superb little anthology edited by the Oratorian Henry Tristram called *The Living Thoughts of Cardinal Newman* (1948), which maps out some of the more combative aspects of Newman's thought. Readers might also like to hunt down *Letters of John Henry Newman* (1957) edited by Derek Stanford and Muriel Spark and *A Packet of Letters: A Selection of the Correspondence of John Henry Newman* (1983) edited by Joyce Sugg. For Newman's sermons, readers should also get hold of Ian Ker's *John Henry Newman: Selected Sermons* (1994), which has an excellent introduction and a characteristically pithy preface by Henry Chadwick.

Another little anthology worth buying is *Realizations: Newman's Selection of his Parochial and Plain Sermons* (1964), in the Foreword of which Muriel Spark brightly observes: "In [Newman's] own time his persuasive power was greatly feared. But what did it consist of? Simplicity of intellect and speech. Simplicity is the most suspect of qualities; it upsets people a great deal. I think it was this, more than his actual doctrine, that caused suspicion to gather round the Vicar of St. Mary's."

In addition to these anthologies, there are several good editions of Newman's separate works: Ignatius has a useful one-volume edition of his *Parochial and Plain Sermons*. Francis J. McGrath, F.S.M. has done a wonderful job finishing the editing of Newman's unpublished Anglican sermons, which OUP is publishing. Notre Dame launched a new edition of Newman's writings some time ago, but the volumes are overpriced, poorly produced and dully edited. Oxford recently published a good scholarly edition of Newman's *Fifteen Sermons Preached Before the University of Oxford* (2006) edited by Earnest and Tracey, though it is ruinously expensive. Ian Ker's editions of *The Idea of a University* (1976) and *An Essay in Aid of a Grammar of Assent* (1985) are worth looking at, as is Martin Svaglic's great edition of the *Apologia* (1967).

For the nineteenth-century context relevant to Newman, readers can consult any number of books. Elizabeth Longford's wonderful *Queen Victoria* (1964) gives a good general overview. Andrew Robert's biography of Lord Salisbury, *Victorian Titan* (1999) is masterly on the political and diplomatic history of the period, which Newman followed so closely. *The Oxford Book of Nineteenth Century English Verse* (1964) edited by Eliot's friend John Hayward exhibits the great poetic achievement of the period. Edward Norman's *The English Catholic Church in the Nineteenth Century* (1984) is still the best survey. Jonathan Clark's *English Society 1688–1832* (1985) and K. Theodore Hoppen's Oxford history, *The Mid-Victorian Generation 1846–1886* (1998), are both excellent for the political history. Everything on the nineteenth century by G. M. Young is worth reading, even though he did not understand Newman. Gertrude Himmelfarb is another historian who has written a number of consistently good books about the English nineteenth century; see especially *The Idea of Poverty: England in the Early Industrial Age* (1984). Michael Burleigh's *Earthy*

Powers: The Clash Between Religion and Politics from the French Revolution to the First World War (2005) is also worth reading. For Tractarian Oxford, Wilfrid Ward's books on William George Ward are still indispensable, as are William Tuckwell's *Reminiscences of Oxford* (1900) and the two nineteenth-century volumes in *The History of the University of Oxford* (1997), edited by Brock and Curthoys. Last but not least, for a good quick grasp of what Newman's contemporaries were writing when Newman was writing, readers might wish to pick up *The Spirit of the Age: Victorian Essays* (2007), edited by Gertrude Himmelfarb. Of course, there are many other worthwhile primary and secondary books that readers will want to dip into—I reference a good many in the notes to my individual chapters—but those listed here will give readers unfamiliar with the period a good start.

Select Biographical Index[1]

Abbott, Jacob, (1803–1879). A congregational minister from Maine, Abbott was also an educator. From 1825 to 1829 he was Professor of Mathematics and Natural Philosophy at Amherst College, and afterward he established the Mount Vernon School for Girls in Boston. He wrote over two hundred books, mostly for young people.

Achilli, Giovanni Giacinto (1802–1860?). Italian Dominican defrocked for seducing women. In 1850 he was brought over to England by the Evangelical Alliance to lecture Protestants on the evils of Catholicism. After Newman made reference to his notorious conduct in his *Lectures on the Present Position of Catholics in England* (1851), Achilli sued him for libel. After the presiding judge, Lord Campbell, refused to admit much of the evidence amassed by Newman's friends substantiating Achilli's seductions, the case went against Newman and he was fined £100. Achilli was last heard of in upstate New York in 1860, where he left behind a suicide note.

Acton, John Emerich Edward Dalberg, first Baron of (1834–1902). English historian and founder of the *Cambridge Modern History*, Acton was reputed to be very learned but spent most of his life making notes for books he never wrote. Educated partly in Germany under Dollinger and partly in Ireland under Wiseman, he was a liberal Catholic opposed to papal infallibility.

Allies, Thomas William (1813–1901). Educated at Eton and Wadham College, Allies converted in 1850, after which Newman appointed him Lecturer in History at the Catholic University. Known as the 'Bantam Cock' because of his small stature, dapper dress and combativeness, Allies corresponded with Newman throughout his life.

Arnold, Matthew (1822–1888). Poet, essayist and school inspector and first son of the famous Dr. Arnold of Rugby. His niece was Mrs. Humphry Ward, whose *Robert Elsmere* Oscar Wilde described as "simply Arnold's *Literature and Dogma* with the literature left out."

Arnold, Thomas Senior (1795–1842). Headmaster of Rugby, educated at Winchester and Oxford, whose personal influence held great sway over many

---

1 For information contained in this index, I am heavily indebted to the *Letters and Diaries of John Henry Newman* (London and Oxford, 1961–), the *DNB*, and the *ODNB*.

of his students, including Clough, Stanley, and Thomas Hughes, author of *Tom Brown's Schooldays* (1857). In "The Oxford Malignants," Arnold criticized Newman for his part in the controversy over R. D. Hampden's Bampton Lectures (1836). Afterwards, the Tractarians, as Dean Church recalled, were "the most unpopular and suspected body of men in the Church, whom everybody was at liberty to insult, both as dishonest and absurd, of whom nothing was too cruel to say, nothing too ridiculous to believe."

Arnold, Thomas Younger (1823–1900). Second son of Dr. Arnold, Thomas was an inspector of schools in New Zealand as a young man. Received into the Church in 1856 despite the passionate objections of his wife, Julia, he was good friends with Arthur Hugh Clough. By 1865, he had drifted away from the Church but returned to the fold in 1876. He was appointed Professor of English at UCD in 1882.

Badeley, Edward Lowth (1803–1868). Educated at Brasenose College, Oxford, Badeley met Newman in 1837, after which they became close friends. Badeley was called to the Bar, as a Member of the Inner Temple, in 1841, and became a leading Tractarian lawyer. Counsel for the Bishop of Exeter in the Gorham Case in 1850, he became a Catholic in 1852, and assisted Newman during the Achilli trial.

Bellasis, Edward (1800–1873). Educated at Christ's Hospital and the Inner Temple, Bellasis was called to the bar in 1824. After converting in 1850, he gave Newman inestimable support during the Achilli trial. His entire family was keenly fond of Newman and two of his sons joined the Oratory.

Blennerhassett, Sir Rowland, fourth Baronet (1839–1909). Succeeded his father in 1849, and after being at school first at Downside, then at Stonyhurst, went up to Christ Church, Oxford, in 1859, after which he studied at Louvain and at Munich. He was a friend of Döllinger and Sir John Acton, sharing their liberal Catholic views. Blennerhassett left behind some interesting reminiscences of Newman.

Bowden, Elizabeth (1805–1896). Wife of Newman's closest Oxford friend, John Bowden, who died young, Mrs. Bowden (née Swinburne) became one of Newman's closest and most trusted correspondents. An elegant, cultured woman, she was related to the poet Algernon Swinburne.

Bowden, Mary Anne (1831–1867). The eldest daughter of his good friends John and Elizabeth Bowden, Mary Anne entered the Visitation Convent at Westbury in 1852 and died young, like her father, of tuberculosis. "I baptized you with water in the name of the Three Divine Persons," Newman wrote her before her death, "and signed you with the sign of the cross ... I fully believe that from that moment you were rescued from the power of Satan, and made the subject of

God's supernatural promises and supernatural graces. From your very infancy then God has chosen you, and claimed you as his own."

Bowden, Marianne Frances (1839–1926). The eldest daughter of Henry and Marianne Catherine Bowden, Marianne Bowden became Catholic in 1852.

Bowles, Emily (1818–1904). Sister of Francis Bowles, who was received into the Church with Newman by the Passionist Father Barberi on 9 October 1845. Miss Bowles was converted in 1843 in Rome. Later, she served for a time as Dame of the Oratory School, while devoting most of her life to writing, translating and performing charity work in London. She was one of Newman's confidantes.

Brougham, Henry Peter, Baron Brougham and Vaux (1778–1868). Lawyer, politician and frequent contributor to the *Edinburgh Review*. In 1810 he entered the House of Commons, in 1830 he became Lord Chancellor, and in 1835 he was instrumental in seeing the Great Reform Bill passed. Brougham also represented Queen Caroline at her trial. However, his duplicity and increasing radicalism alienated his Whig friends and he spent his last years at Cannes in retirement, where Thackeray enjoyed drinking with him. In his letters to *The Times* under the pseudonym "Catholicus," which were later published as *The Tamworth Reading Room* (1841), Newman held Brougham and Sir Robert Peel up to scathing scrutiny for their part in the founding of a non-denominational library from which books of theology would be excluded.

Brownson, Orestes (1803–1876). New England intellectual, preacher, writer and Catholic convert.

Butler, Joseph (1692–1752). Bishop of Durham, he entered Oriel in 1714, after abandoning the Presbyterianism of his childhood. One of the ablest proponents of natural theology that England ever produced, Butler had a considerable influence on Newman and many others, including Keble. His *Analogy of Religion* (1736) was one of the sources on which Newman drew for his understanding of how probability relates to religious certainty. Newman also shared Butler's respect for the primacy of conscience.

Carey, Arthur (1822–1844). An Episcopal churchman who derived his Tractarian views from reading the various works of various members of the Oxford Movement. His ordination caused much rancorous controversy within the Episcopal Church in New York and around the country. Newman saw in him an American Hurrell Froude.

Carlyle, Thomas (1795–1881). Scottish historian, essayist and moralist. Although opposed to creeds, he held that "the Religious Principle lies unseen in the hearts of all good men."

Cecil, Robert Arthur Talbot Gascoyne, 3rd Marquess of Salisbury (1830–1903). English Conservative statesman, educated at Eton and Christ Church. Prime Minister from 1885–1886, 1886–1892 and 1895–1902.

Chatterton, Lady Henrietta Georgina Marcia Lascelles (1806–1876). The only child of Lascelles Iremonger, Prebendary of Winchester, and his second wife Harriett, youngest sister of Admiral Lord Gambier. In 1824 Henrietta Georgina married Sir William Abraham Chatterton (1794–1855), Baronet of Castle Mahon, County Cork, who lost his rents in the potato famine. Throughout her life, Lady Chatterton wrote popular travelogues, stories, verses and translations. In 1859 she married Edward Heneage Dering. She and her husband converted in 1865, though Lady Chatterton continued to suffer doubts about her faith until a year before her death.

Church, Richard William (1815–1890). Tractarian and Dean of St. Paul's, he was a lifelong admirer of Newman, though he considered his conversion a "catastrophe." His history of the Oxford Movement is still one of the best.

Clifford, William Joseph Hugh (1823–1893). Second son of the 7th Lord Clifford, he went to Prior Park before studying theology for 10 years at the *Academia dei Nobili Ecclesiastici*. He served Newman's first Mass in 1847 and was ordained himself in 1850, later being appointed Bishop of Clifton in 1857. An inopportunist and Scripture scholar, he preached Newman's funeral Mass.

Clough, Arthur Hugh (1819–1861). The son of a Liverpool cotton merchant, he became a poet and translator of Plutarch. Educated at Rugby, where he was Thomas Arnold's prize pupil, he won a scholarship to Balliol in 1837, and took his B.A. in 1841. Elected to an Oriel Fellowship in 1841, he was a college tutor from 1843–1848. Unable to subscribe to the 39 Articles, he left Oxford to spend a period travelling, principally in Italy. He was Principal of University Hall, London, from 1849–1852, after Francis Newman resigned the post. Much of his poetry remained unpublished until after his death.

Coleridge, Henry James (1822–1893). Second son of Sir John Taylor Coleridge. Educated at Eton and Trinity College, Oxford, Coleridge was elected a Fellow of Oriel in 1845 and later became curate at Alphington in Devon, near his family. In 1852 he converted to Rome. He studied in Rome, was ordained priest in 1856 and entered the Society of Jesus in 1857. In 1865 he was sent to Farm Street, where he edited *The Month* until 1881. He became a close friend and frequent correspondent of Newman's.

Comte, Auguste (1798–1857). Founder of Positivism and disciple of Saint-Simon, he sought to replace the worship of God with the worship of humanity. Acknowledging that the religious impulse was ineradicable, he drew up his godless philosophy by travestying Catholicism and even devised a 'Positivist Calendar' that would substitute scientists and positivists for the saints.

Copeland, William John (1804–1885). Fellow of Trinity, he became Newman's curate at Littlemore in 1840. In 1862 Newman's chance meeting with Copeland led to the reunion of Newman, Keble and Pusey at Keble's Hursley Vicarage.

Cullen, Paul (1803–1878). Archbishop of Dublin and first Irish Cardinal. A biblical scholar and linguist, Cullen worked with Newman on the founding of the Catholic University and drafted the definition for papal infallibility at the First Vatican Council. Apropos Cullen, Newman wrote: "It has lately been brought home to me that Dr Cullen has a sort of dicaphobia, or convulsive horror of the Law … He will not even accept a receipt for a sum of money given for a religious purpose."

Darwin, Charles (1809–1882). English naturalist whose epoch-making *The Origin of Species* (1859) and *The Descent of Man* (1859) set out the principles of natural selection and survival of the fittest. A graduate of Christ's College, Cambridge, Darwin was an agnostic, who yet respected religion, as did his granddaughter, Gwen Raverat, who recalls how her boarding school required the girls to sing "Onward Christian Soldiers" before their hockey matches, which "shocked and disgusted" her, because, as she said, "I was a very serious person then … and did not like seeing [religion] made ridiculous, even if I were not a believer myself."

De Lisle, Ambrose Phillipps (1809–1878). Convert and ecumenicist, De Lisle corresponded with Newman over many years about various ecumenical issues. In 1835 he gave 230 acres of Charnwood Forest to the Trappists to build the monastery of Mount St. Bernard. Of De Lisle, Newman wrote: "None can forget him or his great virtues or his claims on the gratitude of English Catholics … He has a place in our history, and place altogether special. Nor has he ceased to be our benefactor now that he has left us, but, as I believe most fully, we profit, and shall profit by his prayers."

De Vere, Aubrey (1814–1902). Anglo-Irish poet and convert who corresponded frequently with Newman over many years. He was educated at Trinity College and a friend of Tennyson and Browning. Newman made him Professor of Political Science at the Catholic University.

Disraeli, Benjamin (1804–1881). First Earl of Beaconsfield, he was Tory Prime Minister in 1868 and from 1874–1880.

Dodsworth, William (1798–1861). Educated at Trinity College, Cambridge, Dodsworth began his career as an Evangelical. In 1829 he took charge of Margaret Street Chapel, and in 1838 he was appointed Perpetual Curate of Christ Church, St Pancras. He became friendly with Newman at this time, and they corresponded frequently. He helped Pusey to found the first Anglican sisterhood in 1845, though he later rebuked him for acquiescing in the Gorham Judgment. A friend of Allies and Manning, he converted in 1850. After his conversion, he supported his large family by writing books of Catholic apologetics.

Döllinger, Johann Joseph Ignaz von (1799–1890). Liberal church historian and friend of Acton, Gladstone and Wiseman, he vehemently opposed papal infallibility.

Doyle, James Warren (1786–1834). Roman Catholic Bishop of Kildare and Leighlin and campaigner for Catholic Emancipation up to 1829, he was also an educator, church organizer and the builder of Carlow Cathedral. "When in 1822 the Protestant Archbishop Magee of Dublin said that 'the Catholics had a church without a religion and the dissenters a religion without a church', Bishop Doyle replied with a 'A Vindication of the Religious and Civil Principles of the Irish Catholics' (1824), and 'Letters on the State of Ireland' (1824–1825), which brought home the injustice with which Catholics were treated. In 1825 and again in 1830 Bishop Doyle was summoned to give evidence before parliamentary committees as to the state of Ireland. He was treated with much respect and the Duke of Wellington remarked that it was Bishop Doyle who examined the committees, rather than they who examined him ... Doyle was a model bishop, establishing confraternities and libraries, building churches and schools, conducting retreats, and bringing to an end many of the abuses that had survived from penal times. He also waged war unsparingly on secret societies." See LD, 27:445.

Du Boulay, Susan, Sister Mary Gabriel (1826–1906). Eldest daughter of James Du Boulay, Rector of Heddington, Wiltshire, Du Boulay was a frequent correspondent of Newman. She was living in Clifton with her aunt, Catherine Ward, when Newman received her into the Church at the Oratory in King William Street in 1850. After spending time in Italy, she entered Mother Margaret Hallahan's convent at Clifton. In 1853 Susan was professed in the newly opened convent at Stone.

Faber, Frederick William (1814–1863). An Oratorian of the Brompton Oratory with whom Newman had many exasperating dealings. His devotional writings, however, are still popular, which might not have surprised Newman.

Fairbairn, Andrew Martin (1838–1912). Scottish theologian and Congregationalist born in Perth, he was Principal of Mansfield College, Oxford, between 1888 and 1909. He is best known for his essays published in the *Contemporary Review*, and for his books, which include *Studies in the Philosophy of Religion and History* (1876) and *Christ in Modern Theology* (1894). His assaults on Newman are instructively misguided.

Froude, Catherine, née Holdsworth (1810–1878). Daughter of Arthur Holdsworth, M.P. for Dartmouth from 1802–1820, and Governor of Dartmouth Castle from 1807 until his death in 1860, she began corresponding with

Newman about religious matters in 1838, and they remained lifelong friends. She married William Froude in 1839, and became a Catholic in 1857, along with five of her six children.

Froude, Elizabeth Margaret (1840–1931). Always known as Isy, the eldest daughter of William Froude, she became a Catholic in 1859, and, in 1880, married Baron Anatole von Hügel, brother of Friedrich, who was later appointed Curator of the University Museum of Archaeology and Ethnology at Cambridge. She was greatly devoted to Newman, visiting him occasionally late in his life. She also gave readings from his works to students from Newnham College.

Froude, James Anthony (1818–1894). Younger brother of Hurrell and William Froude, historian of the English Reformation, and disciple of Carlyle, A. J. Froude wrote brilliantly, if sarcastically, about the Oxford Movement in a piece called "The Oxford Counter-Reformation" (1881). Educated at Oriel, Froude became a Fellow of Exeter College before writing *The Nemesis of Faith* (1849), an account of his religious doubts, which eventually led him to leave Oxford for a career as an independent historian. His Whig history is full of Whig bias but a model of brisk, witty narration.

Froude, Richard Hurrell (1803–36), Newman's dear friend and the true originator of the Oxford Movement, who had an enormous influence on Newman and Keble before dying of tuberbulosis at the age of 33. Froude entered Oriel in 1821, and was a Fellow from 1826–36, becoming a tutor with Newman in 1827. Charm, originality, wit and zest were his distinguishing characteristics, together with a deep longing for sanctity. In the *Apologia*, Newman remarked of his colleague: "… he had an intellect as critical and logical as it was speculative and bold. Dying prematurely … his religious views never reached their ultimate conclusion, by the very reason of their multitude and depth." Whether Froude would have converted if he had lived is a nice question. "The extracts from his Journal," Nicholas Wiseman observed, "present us a picture at once pleasing and distressing, of a mind yearning after interior perfection, yet at a loss about the means of attaining it; embarked on an ocean of good desires, without stars or compass by which to steer its course." Still, Wiseman was convinced that Froude was "another instance of the same mysterious Providence which guided a Grotius and a Leibniz to the threshold of Truth, but allowed them not the time to step within it, into the hallowed precincts of God's Visible Church." See Piers Brendon's brilliant biography of Froude—still one of the best books on the Oxford Movement.

Froude, William (1810–1879). Educated at Westminster School and Oriel College, William was the older brother of Newman's close friend Hurrell Froude and the historian James Anthony Froude. A railway engineer, he worked under Brunel. Later, he devoted himself to naval work, studying the effect of waves on ships. He became a celebrated naval engineer, for whom the Admiralty provided a large covered experimental tank at Torquay. A good friend of

Newman, William resigned himself to the conversion of his wife and children. Newman was drafting a long letter to him on assent and certitude, when he learned of William's death.

Fullerton, Lady Georgiana (1812–1885). Novelist and convert, her *Ellen Middleton* (1844) was both a commercial and critical success, as was *Grantley Manor* (1847). A later novel, *Mrs. Gerald's Niece* (1869) portrays marital divisions arising from the Oxford Movement. Dedicated to caring for the London poor, Lady Georgiana was a firm friend and admirer of Newman.

Giberne, Maria Rosina (1802–1885). A close friend of the Newman family, Miss Giberne was one of Newman's most faithful correspondents. After converting, she joined the Visitationists.

Gladstone, William Ewart (1809–1898). Liberal Prime Minister, Gladstone was educated at Christ Church and Lincoln's Inn. Conservative M.P. for Newark from 1832–1845, he eventually became Prime Minister of four Liberal governments (1868–1874, 1880–1885, February–July 1886 and 1892–1894). He also served as Chancellor of the Exchequer four times (1853–1855, 1859–1866, 1873–1874, and 1880–1882). His political career spanned over sixty years. A close friend of both Manning and Hope, he was devastated by their defection to Rome. He was at once a great admirer and continual detractor of Newman.

Golightly, Charles Portales (1807–1885). Entered Oriel in 1824 and received his B.A. in 1828. In 1836 Newman invited him to be his curate at Littlemore. He left after Pusey took exception to one of his sermons. Despite his earlier friendly relations with Newman, he became a fierce opponent of what he considered the Romanizing tendencies of Tractarianism. He stage-managed the condemnation that greeted Tract 90.

Grey, Charles, 2nd Earl Grey (1764–1845). British Whig statesman and Prime Minister from 1830 to 1834, he was one of the chief architects of the Great Reform Bill of 1832.

Hampden, Renn Dickson (1793–1868). Fellow of Oriel and friend of the Noetics, including Arnold and Whately, Hampden wrote his Bampton Lectures in 1832, which Newman, together with many Evangelicals and High Churchmen, regarded as heretical. When Melbourne was appointed Hampden Regius Professor of Divinity in 1836, the University voted to exclude him from the position. Principle, not bigotry, as Martin Svaglic notes, drove Newman's opposition to Hampden. See the *Apologia*, ed. Svaglic (Oxford, 1967), p. 519.

Hawkins, Edward (1789–1882). Educated at St John's College, Oxford, where he took a double first in 1811, Hawkins was elected a Fellow of Oriel in 1813. In May 1818 he preached his sermon on Tradition in St Mary's, Oxford, which greatly influenced Newman, and in 1828 he was elected Provost of Oriel, a position he held until his death. Newman said of Hawkins, "He was the first who taught me to weigh my words, and to be cautious in my statements. He led me to that mode of limiting and clearing my sense in discussion and in controversy, and of distinguishing between cognate ideas, and of obviating mistakes by anticipation, which to my surprise has been since considered, even in quarters friendly to me, to savour of the polemics of Rome."

Hegel, Georg Wilhelm Friedrich (1770–1831). German Idealist philosopher, one of whose philosophical contentions was that "the real is the rational and the rational is the real." Critical of the Romantics Schleiermacher and Schelling, Hegel succeeded Fichte as Professor of Philosophy at Berlin and based his elaborate thought on the idealism of Kant, whose confusion of moralism and religion still addles our threadbare metaphysics.

Herbert of Lea, Lady Mary (1822–1911). The wife of Sidney Herbert, Lady Herbert was a convert and friend of Newman, Manning and Vaughan. She corresponded with Newman about her frustrations concerning her apostate son, among other matters.

Holmes, Mary (1815–1878). Governess, who converted in 1842 and was a frequent correspondent of Newman, Trollope and Thackeray.

Hook, Walter Farquhar (1798–1875). English divine educated at Christ Church. In 1837 he was elected Vicar of Leeds and won the admiration of his parishioners for his pastoral care. See the *DNB*: "The secret of his immense personal influence consisted in his large-hearted sympathy, his enthusiastic zeal, his honesty, his high sense of justice and fair play, his shrewd common sense, and his inexhaustible fund of playful humour." Although a High Churchman, he had good relations with the Tractarians and, until Newman's conversion, showed him staunch support. In 1857 he was appointed Dean of Chichester.

Hope-Scott, James Robert (1812–1873). Entered Christ Church in 1828, awarded B.A. 1832. He was a Fellow of Merton from 1833–1847. He took up Tractarian views, and first met Newman in 1837. Called to the bar in 1838, he took a particular interest in ecclesiastical law. In 1847 he married Charlotte Lockhart, Sir Walter Scott's granddaughter, and through her he inherited Abbotsford. Hence, his later surname: Hope-Scott. He made a fortune as a parliamentary lawyer for the railway companies, and was munificent in his charities. The Gorham Judgment prompted his conversion to Catholicism in 1850. He helped support Newman through the ordeal of the Achilli trial, and suggested Newman as Rector for the Catholic University. He was a close and trusted friend of Newman's, who frequently turned to him for advice.

Hopkins, Gerard Manley (1844–1889). Poet, Jesuit, and Balliol Exhibitioner, Hopkins converted to Catholicism in 1866 and joined the Society of Jesus in 1868. A great admirer of Newman, he was also an avid Unionist who considered Gladstone unbalanced and treasonous.

Hügel, Friedrich Maria Aloys Franz Karl, Freiherr von (1852–1925). Born in Florence, Italy, the son of Charles von Hügel (Austrian ambassador to the Grand Duchy of Tuscany), and a Scottish mother, Elizabeth Farquharson (a Roman Catholic convert), von Hügel was educated privately, and moved with his family to England in 1867, where he remained for the rest of his life. Baron of the Holy Roman Empire, he was a frequent visitor to Rome. Although a biblical scholar and linguist, he never held any office in the Catholic Church or academe. He was deeply involved in the Modernist controversy. Apropos von Hügel, Cuthbert Butler described how he would appear in church, "the great deep eyes fixed on the Tabernacle, the whole being wrapt in an absorption of prayer, devotion, contemplation … Those who have not seen him so know only half the man."

Hutton, Richard Holt (1826–1897). Editor of the *Spectator* and frequent reviewer, Holt was Newman's most perspicacious critic, writing over thirty pieces about him in the pages of the *Spectator* and the *Contemporary Review* from the 1860s to the 1880s.

Huxley, Thomas (1825–1895). Biologist and popular lecturer.

Ives, Levi Silliman (1797–1867). Became Episcopalian Bishop of North Carolina in 1831. An admirer of the Oxford Movement, he set up the religious Brotherhood of the Holy Cross in 1847, but it was dissolved because of its Tractarian character. At Christmas 1852 he resigned his see and submitted to Pope Pius IX at Rome. His wife, a daughter of Bishop Hobart, became a Catholic at the same time. His *Trials of a Mind in its Progress towards Catholicism* (1853) confirms that it was his reading of the early Church Fathers that sealed his conversion. On returning to the United States in 1854, he became Professor at St Joseph's Seminary, New York, and St John's College, Fordham.

Jowett, Benjamin (1817–1893). Regis Professor of Greek and Master of Balliol whose Liberalism came to define late nineteenth-century Oxford.

Keble, John (1792–1866). Fellow and tutor of Oriel, Keble, whose assize sermon on National Apostasy (1833) helped launch the Oxford Movement, of which he was a leading figure, together with Newman, Hurrell Froude and Pusey. He became Vicar of Hursley in 1836. After Newman's secession in 1845, he remained an influential figure for Anglo-Catholics.

Kingsley, Charles (1819–1875). Novelist and Christian Socialist whose "gratuitous slander" prompted Newman to write his great autobiography, *Apologia Pro Vita Sua* (1864). For years after their controversy, Newman prayed for his accuser and was pleased when Kingsley publicly opposed the Church of England's dropping of the Athanasian Creed.

Lake, William Charles (1817–1897). After being at Rugby under Arnold, Lake entered Balliol College in 1835. A moderate High Churchman, he came under Newman's influence in his last year as an undergraduate. He became a Fellow of Balliol in 1838, and took orders in 1842. He played a part in university reform in the 1850s, and left Oxford in 1858 to become Rector of Huntspill, Somerset. In 1869 he was appointed Dean of Durham by Gladstone, and helped to found the College of Science at Newcastle. In his autobiography, Lake described Newman's abiding influence.

Leo XIII (1810–1903). Ruling the papacy with brilliant mastery for over twenty-five years, Leo expanded the Church outside Europe, encouraged Catholics to rediscover the work of St. Thomas Aquinas, reaffirmed the Church's role as the custodian of liberty, and enhanced the papacy's international stature. In 1879 he made Newman a Cardinal. Leo XIII exhibited special solicitude for the conversion of England in his letter *Ad Anglos* (1895). In 1896 he pronounced the invalidity of Anglican orders.

Liddon, Henry Parry (1829–1890). Pusey's disciple and biographer, with whom Newman corresponded about matters relating to Pusey and the High Church.

Lloyd, Charles (1784–1829). Regius Professor of Divinity and Bishop of Oxford. At Christ Church, Lloyd recommended that Pusey travel to Germany to report on the new biblical criticism being done there. His lectures on the apostolical roots of the Anglican Church inspired Newman, who later wrote of Lloyd: "He brought me forward, made me known, spoke well of me, and gave me confidence in myself."

Lockhart, William (1819–1892). After taking his B.A. at Exeter College, Lockhart joined Newman at Littlemore. In August 1843 he converted. Lockhart wrote vivid reminiscences of Newman in *Cardinal Newman: Reminiscences of Fifty Years* (1891).

Lothian, Machioness of (1808–1877). Before meeting Lady Lothian for the first time in 1851, Newman told a mutual friend: "I shall be truly honored by a visit from Lady Lothian – I am not so oppressed by this mountebank Achilli, as to be unfit for ordinary duties …" The only daughter of the 2nd Earl Talbot, in 1831 the marchioness married John William Kerr, 7th Marquis of Lothian, who died in 1841. She was received into the Church in 1851 by Father Brownbill at Farm Street. A woman of great generosity and faith, she was very fond of Newman, as he was of her.

Manning, Henry Edward (1808–1892). Convert and second Cardinal of Westminister, Manning went up to Balliol from Harrow in 1827. In 1832 he was elected Fellow of Merton and took orders. During the years leading up to his conversion, Newman often confided in Manning. Manning himself converted in 1851 after the Gorham Judgment. He was appointed Archbishop in 1865 and Cardinal in 1875. Although an Ultramontane, Manning had more in common with Newman than their personal antagonism might suggest.

Maurice, Frederick Denison (1805–1872). Church of England theologian and controversialist who wielded great influence over many within and outside the Broad Church. Educated at home in the Puritan tradition, he went on to Cambridge, where he was one of the founding members of the Apostles, with Alfred Tennyson, one of his lifelong friends. His view of Anglicanism was Gladstonian: he saw the Church of England as a Catholic Protestant Church, flexible enough to appeal to both Anglo-Catholics and Protestants, but pre-eminently an English nationalist Church. Speaking of Maurice and his many acolytes in 1838, Newman observed, "What a set they are! They cannot make religion a reality; nothing more than a literature." In 1863, Newman wrote to the editor of *The Times* to protest Maurice's claim that he interpreted the 39 Articles in Tract 90 in a "non-natural" way. "I would rather be judged by my own words than by Mr. Maurice's interpretation of them," Newman wrote. "I distinctly repudiate his accusation that I maintained, either in Tract 90 or elsewhere, the right of a man's subscribing the Thirty-nine Articles in a non-natural sense. Nor ought he to speak from mere memory, as he seems to confess he did, when making a serious charge against another. I maintained in Tract 90 that the Thirty-nine Articles ought to be subscribed in their 'literal and grammatical sense;' but I maintained also that they were so drawn up as to admit, in that grammatical sense, of subscription on the part of persons who differed very much from each other in the judgment which they formed of Catholic doctrine." Later, after Maurice apologized, Newman wrote him back: "It has before now surprised and pained me, that you have in print spoken of me in terms which jarred with my recollection of you. I have nothing but kind and pleasant thoughts, of the occasions, in times long past, which you have given me, of intercourse with you. Your letter of the 27th has put all right—it has destroyed that incongruity between the past and the present which was to me so unwelcome; and I thank you for it." Newman's final estimate of Maurice was generous. "That M. is a man of great powers as well as of great earnestness, is proved by what he has done since—but for myself I ever thought him hazy, and thus lost interest in his writings." Aubrey de Vere said that listening to Maurice was like trying to eat pea soup with a fork.

Meyrick, Frederick (1827–1906). Fellow, Bursar and Dean of Trinity College, Oxford. His brother was Meyrick, Thomas (1817–1903), who stayed briefly at Littlemore and converted in 1845. After joining the Jesuits, Thomas suffered bouts of violent insanity, which his brother vividly describes in his memoirs.

Monsell, William (1812–1894). Educated at Winchester and Oriel, Monsell married the sister of Lord Adare in 1836. He was M.P. for Limerick from 1837 until he was created Lord Emly in 1874. He held various offices in Gladstone's Liberal governments. While a member of the Church of Ireland, Monsell became influenced by the Oxford Movement, and in 1850 he converted to Rome. He was one of Newman's closest confidants.

Mozley, Mrs. John, Jemima Newman (1808–1879). Newman's second eldest sister and frequent correspondent.

Mozley, Thomas (1806–1893). English divine and journalist and wife of Newman's eldest sister Harriett.

Neri, Philip (1515–1595). Newman's patron saint and founder of the Oratory. Born in Florence, Philip learned the faith from the Dominican Fathers of St. Mark's and was known for his good-heartedness, good spirits and contempt for humbug. He was canonized in 1622. Of St. Philip, Newman wrote: "He would not permit any forms or observances to be the characteristics of his Congregation, besides mutual love and hard work. For the interior life he sent [his Oratorians] back, with especial earnestness to the Apostolic Fathers…"

Neville, William (1824–1905). Oratorian and Newman's literary executor.

Norfolk, Henry Fitzalan Howard, 15th Duke of (1847–1917). Succeeded his father in 1860, and was educated at the Oratory School, where he remained until July 1864. He was a model of the Christian gentleman, a generous supporter of Catholic schools and churches, and engaged in numerous public and political activities. Newman addressed his *A Letter to the Duke of Norfolk* (1875) to him. The Duke was also instrumental in securing Newman's cardinalate from Leo XIII.

Oakeley, Frederick (1802–1880). Educated at Christ Church, Oakeley became a Fellow of Balliol in 1827. After joining the Tractarians and befriending W. G. Ward, he converted in 1845. Once ordained, he became a priest at Islington, where he remained friendly with Newman for life.

Ogle, Octavius (1829–1894). Fourth son of James Adey Ogle, he was at Wadham College, Oxford, then Fellow of Lincoln from 1852–1859.

Palmerston, Henry John Temple, 3rd Viscount (1784–1865). English Whig statesman, Prime Minister from 1855–1858 and 1859–1865. When a deputation of Catholic Members of Parliament and of representatives of various corporate towns in Ireland called on Palmerston in 1862 to ask for a charter for the Catholic University, he declined on the ground that "the only possible system of education for Ireland was the mixed system." He added that with Trinity College and the Queen's Colleges there were "already in Ireland abundant facilities for the education of the sons of Catholic gentlemen." Disraeli also declined to grant the Catholic University a charter. In 1872, Newman summed up his view of the Prime Minister when he told Lord Blachford , "… little as I like Lord Palmerston, poor man, I think he with his coarse theatrical ways was the chap to deal with the Yankees."

Pattison, Mark (1813–1884). Tractarian and scholar, Pattison's life ambition was achieved when he became Rector of Lincoln College. An epitome of the disgruntled academic, Pattison wrote one of the greatest of Oxford memoirs, in which he fondly recalled the intellectual companionship that he enjoyed with his first cousin once removed, Philippa Meadows, an engaging autodidact, who had taught herself Greek and Latin. "We corresponded upon books, upon everything we thought or read, from as early a period as I remember, she taking the lead and I following." But then their intellectual bond unraveled. "We were beginning to resume our philosophical specula- tions together when the rising tide of Puseyism carried us both off—me first, and her through me ..." Pattison freely admitted the extent to which he subscribed to Tractarian principles before returning to his accustomed liber- alism; but his adherence was never as thoroughgoing as hers. As he admits, "When her Tractarianism grew to white heat it took the shape, not of a devotion to tenets promulgated in the Tracts, but of exaggerated antipathy to everything that savoured of Anglicanism. Her mother, a good and sensible woman, became alarmed, and thought to stop the mischief by removing from Yorkshire to some place where Anglican privileges could be enjoyed in their plenitude. No place could surely surpass Hursley in this respect; and to Hursley they went. But it was too late. The daughter had got the Roman fever in her veins; everything about the services at Hursley was contemptible, disgusting, odious, and Keble himself, far from being a saint, was discovered to be an addled-headed old hypocrite."

Peel, Sir Robert (1788–1850). Served twice as Prime Minister: from 10 December 1834 to 8 April 1835 and from 30 August 1841 to 29 June 1846. Educated at Harrow and Christ Church, Peel won a double first in Classics and Mathematics and Physics in 1808. In 1814 he was awarded his M.A. He entered Lincoln's Inn in 1809 and intended to pursue a law career, before his father bought him the seat of Cashel in Co. Tipperary with the help of the Duke of Wellington. In 1810 Peel began a parliamentary career that lasted until his death in 1850. Newman worked to unseat him as M.P. for Oxford when he reversed his position on Catholic Emancipation. He also attacked Peel for his Tamworth Reading Room scheme in 1841 through a series of letters to *The Times*, later published as *The Tamworth Reading Room*, one of Newman's greatest works of satire.

Pius IX (1792–1878). Enjoying the longest pontificate in history, Pius expanded the Church in England and America, carried out an unprecedented number of beatifications and canonizations, defined the Immaculate Conception of the BVM (1854) and consecrated the Catholic world to the Sacred Heart of Jesus (1875). With the publication of the *Syllabus of Errors* he disavowed the view that the pope "can or should reconcile himself to, or agree with, progress, liberalism, and modern civilization." During his pontificate, at the First Vatican Council (1870) the doctrine of papal infallibility was defined. Despite, or perhaps because of his Ultramontanism, 'Pio Nono' was immensely popular.

Pollen, John Hungerford (1820–1902). Great-great-nephew of Pepys and nephew of Sir John Walter Pollen, 2nd Baronet of Redenham, Hampshire, he was at Eton and Christ Church, then a Fellow of Merton from 1842–1852, where he came under the influence of the Tractarians. In 1844 he was curate at St. Peter-le-Bailey, Oxford, and from 1847 to 1851 he worked on the staff of St. Saviour's, Leeds. In 1850 he refused the living of Kibworth in Leicestershire, nearly £1,000 a year, because he was doubtful of Anglicanism. In 1852 he converted to Rome. Afterwards, he devoted himself to art and architecture. In 1855 he became Professor of Fine Arts for Newman's University Church, and built the University Church. Two years later he settled in London and became the first director of the South Kensington Museum from 1863 to 1867. He was also the private secretary to Lord Ripon. He married in 1855 and had a large family. Two of his sons became Jesuits and one joined Newman's Oratory. Pollen was one of Newman's most devoted, talented friends.

Pusey, Edward Bouverie (1800–1882). Canon of Christ Church and leader of the Oxford Movement, Pusey led the Tractarians after Newman's secession from the English Church in 1845. The historian Dr. Timothy Larsen describes him as a "Bible man who led an exegetical life."

Quin, Windham Thomas Wyndham, 4th Earl of Dunraven and Mount Earl (1841–1926). Tory politician and yachtsman, who competed for the America's cup in 1893 and 1894. Most of his wealth came from lands owned in New South Wales. Although Dunraven's staunch support of Lord Randolph Churchill scuttled his political career, he is principally known today for his lead role in drafting the Wyndham Land Act (1903), which revolutionized Irish land tenure by stipulating that Irish landlords should be bought out and the occupier become the owner. The DNB has a good entry on Dunraven, which concludes, "Few of his contemporaries touched life at more points, and although he experimented in many different directions, he dropped nothing that interested him … A large experiment in tobacco-growing at Adare was checked by the accidental burning of his factory in 1916; but even so he continued to grow as much Turkish leaf as would supply the cigarette factory that he had established."

Robinson, George Frederick Samuel Robinson, 1st Marquis of Ripon (1827–1909). Born at 10 Downing Street, when his father Viscount Goderich was briefly Prime Minister, his mother was Lady Sarah Hobart, daughter of the 4th Earl of Buckinghamshire. Despite being part of a wealthy Whig family, he was a descendant of Oliver Cromwell through his father and of John Hampden through his mother. In his youth, he became a radical and a democrat and approved the revolutions of 1848. For many years, he accounted himself a Christian Socialist. After spending six years in the House of Commons, he moved to the Lords. During the Crimean War he worked for Army reform; in the wake of the Indian Mutiny, he pressed for conciliation of India. As Under Secretary for War and Under Secretary for India, he advanced both policies. Thereafter he held various government posts. He also dealt adroitly in Washington with the aftermath of the American Civil War, and was rewarded in 1871 with a Marquisate. In 1874, after reading Newman's writings for many years, he converted to Catholicism.

Rogers, Frederic, later Baron Blachford (1811–1889). Permanent Under Secretary of State for the Colonies. He came to Oriel from Eton expressly to study under Newman, though he later broke off all relations with him after he converted. They were reconciled after 1863. Rogers was one of Newman's closest Oxford friends and their correspondence is full of interesting exchanges. In 1880 Lord Blachford wrote to Newman from Menton to reminiscence about the time he spent with Mrs. Newman and her daughters at Iffley in 1831: "I often think of those old Iffley days in which she [Jemima] added so much to the pleasure of all about her, and certainly – I am going to say not least – to mine. What a long time back it is – and how pleasant to remember. Before Germany or Italy or a Reformed Parliament – and when so many other things were so little what they are, and Froude used to say 'When will anything happen to disturb this stagnancy.'"

Rosebery, Archibald Philip Primrose, 5th Earl of (1847–1929). Scottish statesman educated at Eton and Christ Church. From 1874, he held various government posts. He was Prime Minister from 1894–1895. In addition to writing books on Pitt, Peel, Napoleon and Chatham, Rosebery was a fan of the turf, winning the Derby in 1894, 1895 and 1905. After his highly frustrating stint as Rector of the Catholic University in Dublin, Newman would have known what Rosebery was talking about when he said, "I have known the sweets of place with power, but of place with the minimum of power—that is a purgatory, and if not a purgagtory it is a hell."

Russell, Charles William (1812–1880). Irish Professor of Philosophy at Maynooth, Russell was critically sympathetic to Tractarianism and had a key exchange of letters with Newman before he converted.

Russell, John, 1st Earl Russell (1792–1878). British Whig statesman, Prime Minister 1846–1852 and 1865–1866. When Lord John Russell introduced the abortive Ecclesiastical Titles Bill (1851), which was framed to outlaw Wiseman's reconstitution of the English hierarchy, Ullathorne wrote to the editor of *The Times*: "Is it wise ... to put the religious teachers of a large body of her Majesty's subjects in conscientious opposition to the law ... ?"

Ryder, George Dudley (1810–1880). After studying with Newman at Oriel, Ryder converted with his wife and family in Rome in 1846. His eldest son, Henry Dudley Ryder, joined the Birmingham Oratory. His second son, George Lisle, became the Chairman of the Board of Customs.

St. John, Ambrose (1815–1875). One of Newman's best friends, St. John was educated at Christ Church and converted in 1843, after spending time at Littlemore. He studied for the priesthood with Newman in Rome.

Saint-Simon, Claude Henri de Rouvroy (1760–1825). Founder of French Socialism, he sought to reform religion by abandoning dogma and setting up in its place a new humanitarian lay religion.

Schleiermacher, Friedrich Daniel Ernest (1768–1834). German theologian influenced by Spinoza, Leibniz and Kant, he sought to revive religion by returning his contemporaries to "a sense and taste for the infinite." A great advocate of feeling as the basis of religion, he opposed at once German rationalism and dogmatic Christian orthodoxy.

Short, Thomas (1789–1879). Fellow of Trinity College from 1816 until his death, Short encouraged Newman to sit for the Oriel Fellowship. Legendary for his rigor and dry wit, he was one of Oxford's most famous Fellows. On returning to Trinity to receive his Honorary Fellowship in 1878, Newman visited Short in his old rooms. Years earlier, when Newman asked Short for a reference for Henry Wilberforce, Short replied that he would speak to someone at Durham University, though, as he said, "I should fear from the very miscellaneous religionists, by whom his father is perpetually besieged, and, as I suppose, duped, that his name will be the worst disadvantage which he will have to combat. But your account of the young man will go far to remove any unfavorable party impression."

Sibthorp, Richard Waldo (1792–1879). Fellow of Magdalen and incumbent of St. James, Ryde, Sibthorp converted briefly to Catholicism before returning to the Established Church. In *Oxford Memories: A Retrospect After 50 Years* (1886), James Pycroft dissented from the generally sardonic view of Sibthorpe by remembering him as "sincere but impressionable."

Simeon, Sir John (1815–1870). Succeeding his father as 3rd Baronet in 1854, Sir John Simeon was one of Newman's close friends. In 1851 he was received into the Catholic Church by Father Brownbill at Farm Street. He then resigned his seat in the House of Commons, where he had represented the Isle of Wight since 1847. He entered Parliament again in 1865. A proponent of improving Catholic higher education, he was a staunch supporter of Newman's plans to establish an Oxford Oratory.

Simeon, Louisa Edith (1843–1895). Sir John's daughter, and a friend of Emily Bowles, Louisa shared her difficulties concerning her Catholic faith with Newman in various letters. When she confessed that she often felt at a loss in the face of her Protestant friends' objections to Catholicism, Newman recommended that she read the *Plain and Parochial Sermons* that he had written as an Anglican, telling her: "I wonder how far you know what is called Tractarianism – and if you don't, whether a course of Tractarianism, so to say, would do you good."

Simpson, Richard (1820–1876). Liberal Catholic journalist, educated at Oriel, where he took a Second in Classics, Simpson was also a friend of Lord Acton.

His editorship of the *Rambler* caused Newman much annoyance. A keen Shakespearian scholar and gifted linguist, Simpson was one of the most talented of the converts of Newman's time. Newman was fond of him, despite or perhaps because of his provocations. "I DESPAIR of Simpson being other than he is," he wrote to one of his correspondents; "he will always be clever, amusing, brilliant, and suggestive. He will always be flicking his whip at Bishops, cutting them in tender places, throwing stones at sacred Congregations, and, as he rides along the high road, discharging pea shooters at Cardinals who happen by bad luck to look out of window."

Spencer, George (1799–1864). Educated at Eton and Cambridge, Spencer— the youngest son of the 2nd Earl Spencer— converted to Rome in 1830. In 1847 he joined the Passionists, taking the name of Ignatius. In 2007 Father Ignatius's cause for beatification was forwarded to Rome. Were Father Ingatius to be canonized, the British royal family would have its first saint, since Spencer is related to Princes William and Harry through their mother, Princess Diana of Wales. In the "hardships, mortifications, slights, insults, [and] disappointments" that Spencer endured to convert his countrymen, Newman saw a model of "persevering prayer."

Stanley, Arthur Penrhyn (1815–1881). Biographer of Dr. Arnold of Rugby.

Strauss, David Friedrich (1808–1874). German theologian, whose *Leben Jesu* (1835–1836), translated in England by George Eliot, saw the life of Christ in terms of unintended myth.

Talbot, George (1818–1886). Educated at Eton and St. Mary's Hall, Oxford, Talbot converted in 1843 and was ordained in 1846. He applied to Newman's Oratory in 1847 and was cordially rejected. Later, Wiseman appointed him Papal Chamberlain. An ecclesiastical trouble-maker *par excellence*, Talbot made much mischief for Newman. After he invited Newman to come to Rome to preach, Newman replied: "I have received your letter, inviting me to preach next Lent in your Church at Rome, to 'an audience of Protestants more educated than could ever be the case in England.' However, Birmingham people have souls; and I have neither taste nor talent for the sort of work you cut out for me; and I beg to decline your offer." In 1868 Talbot was put away in an asylum in Passy, France.

Tennyson, Alfred (1809–1892). Poet. For years, he tried to coax Newman to join him and Gladstone for breakfast, unsuccessfully. Tennyson was also friendly with Newman's dear friend Emily Bowles, who admired his poetry. Tennyson's son, Hallam, supported Miss Bowles's application to the Royal Literary Fund in her penurious old age.

Thackeray, William Makepeace (1811–1863). Novelist and essayist. His master-piece, *Vanity Fair* (1848), was published the same year as Newman founded the Birmingham Oratory. Max Beerbohm rightly considered the novel the greatest that England ever produced. Newman was an avid reader of Thackeray's things, although, like the literary critic John Carey, he detected a pattern of decline in his later work.

Tocqueville, Alexis Charles Henri Clerci de (1809–1859). French politician, historian and author of two of the most brilliant books of the nineteenth century: *De la Démocartie en Amerique* (1835) and *L'Ancien Regime et la Révolution* (1856). Tocqueville's insights into the emerging nature of religion in nineteenth-century America often tallied with those that Newman shared with readers in his long essay, "The Anglo-American Church" (1839).

Ullathorne, William Bernard (1806–1889). Heroic convert who, after organizing the Church in Australia, became Bishop of Birmingham. The correspondence between Ullathorne and Newman is revelatory of the great strengths of both men, though they were quite different in many ways. No two men ever had more mutual respect for one another. Ullathorne's autobiography, *The Devil is a Jackass*, is a good read.

Walsh, Walter (1847–1912), religious polemicist and author of several anti-Catholic books, including *The Secret History of the Oxford Movement* (1897), *The History of the Romeward Movement in the Church of England, 1833–1864* (1900) and *The Jesuits in Great Britain: an Historical Inquiry into their Political Influence* (1903). In the last he blamed the Society of Jesus for nearly everything that was wrong with nineteenth-century Britain. The political agent of the rabidly Protestant Charles Newdegate (1836–1887), Conservative MP for Nuneaton, Walsh also edited an anti-Catholic paper called the *Protestant Observer*. According to the ODNB, "Walsh was an example of a distinctive type of Victorian protestant: from humble origins [he was the son of a hotel porter] he undertook protestant apologetics in a professional capacity, and success in his work enabled him to enjoy a certain measure of upward social mobility."

Ward, William George (1842–82). Fellow of Balliol and ebullient controversialist, whose *Ideal of Christian Church* caused him to be degraded by Convocation in 1845, Ward married and converted in the same year and later became editor of the ultramontane *Dublin Review*. For years, he was also one of the founding members and chief attractions of the Metaphysical Society, which Newman declined to join. Despite their differences, Newman had great regard for Ward, which Ward entirely reciprocated.

Whately, Richard (1787–1863). Fellow of Oriel and Leader of the Noetics, Whately had a keen influence on Newman, though they never reconciled after parting ways. Whately was installed as Archbishop of Dublin in 1831. Newman often noted the fact that they crossed paths in Dublin in the 1850s without ever meeting. A droll man, Whately was fond of riddles. "What is the best female companion to the fish John Dory," he would ask his Dublin parishioners. "Ann Chovy!" In the *Apologia*, Newman paid his old colleague a handsome compliment, confirming how he "taught me to think and use my reason ..." Whately's anti-Erastian views particularly influenced Newman, who confessed of the logician whose liberalism he could not embrace, "I loved him too much to bid him farewell without pain."

White, Joseph Blanco (1775–1841) Apostate Catholic priest of Irish descent born in Seville. Settling in England in 1810, where he enjoyed the patronage of Lord Holland, he became an Anglican clergyman in 1825, and thereafter a member of the Oriel Common Room where he became good friends with Newman and the Noetics. "Blanco White has resided with us since October," Newman wrote a friend in 1827, "he is a man of considerable talent—well read, well informed, quick, lively, ingenious, sensible, modest, and of a most ardent and affectionate mind—there is a character! I wish you knew him—and the circumstances of his life invest him both with mystery and deep interest. I like him so ..." In 1832, White left Oxford to become Archbishop Whately's secretary in Dublin. In 1835, he moved yet again to Liverpool and adopted Unitarian views. He died, as Newman lamented, "almost a pantheist." When Whately learned of his Socinian views, he wrote his old friend, "Could you know the daily and nightly anguish we have suffered, or the half of it, and how much it has risen from sympathy with what you have suffered, and dread of the far greater evils anticipated to you, I am sure you would have no doubts of our affection." A crack violinist, White often played Beethoven with Newman, who praised his "exquisite ear."

Wilberforce, Henry (1807–1873). The Emancipator's youngest son and one of Newman's closest friends and favourite correspondents. Educated at Oriel College, he was Newman's pupil. Graduating with a First in Classics and a Second in Mathematics, he was ordained in 1834 and in the same year he married a daughter of Rev. John Sargent. In 1850 he and his wife converted with their children. After two years as secretary of the Catholic Defence Association in Dublin he became proprietor and editor of the *Catholic Standard*, which evolved into the *Weekly Register*. Newman preached at his funeral and wrote a short memoir of him. In a letter to Newman, written in 1835, Henry wrote: "I think the natural fault of my mind is that of thinking less than I ought of my absent friends; but I can truly say that you are an exception, for there has been, I think, hardly a day (indeed I think I might say not a day) since I saw you, in which I have not thought with grateful affection of your kindness to me, and the benefits which I hope I have received from it."

Wilberforce, Robert Isaac (1802–1857). Second son of the philanthropist, Wilberforce obtained a double-First at Oriel College in 1823, was elected a Fellow in 1826, and from 1828 was a tutor there with R. H. Froude and Newman. He moved to Burton Agnes in 1840, and in the following year was made Archdeacon of the West Riding. His *The Doctrine of the Incarnation* (1848) is one of the major works of Tractarian divinity. He became a Catholic in 1854 and travelled to Italy in the next year to study for the priesthood. A few weeks after being ordained, he died.

Williams, Isaac (1802–1865). Educated at Trinity College, Oxford, where he went on to become a Fellow, Williams was a poet and Tractarian, whose Tract 80, "On Reserve in communicating Religious Knowledge," caused much controversy. His being passed over for the Poetry Professorship after Keble's resignation in 1842 was a serious reversal for the Tractarians. He was Newman's curate at St Mary's and Littlemore. In his memoirs, Williams put about false reports concerning Newman's influence on Keble. After Newman converted, the two men corresponded rarely, though Newman paid Williams a farewell visit when he was dying. In 1840 he dedicated his *Church of the Fathers* to Williams thus: "To My Dear and Much Admired Isaac Williams … The Sight of Whom Carries Back His Friends to Ancient, Holy, and Happy Times."

Wiseman, Nicholas (1802–1865). Rector of the English College in Rome (1828–1840), Wiseman was also coadjutor to Bishop Walsh in the Midland district and President of Oscott College (1840–1847). Newman met with Wiseman in Rome in 1833, and in July 1841 Wiseman visited Newman at Oriel. Wiseman's article in the *Dublin.Review* on the Monophysites set Newman on the road to Rome. Wiseman followed the Oxford Movement closely, and welcomed the converts warmly, though Sibthorpe's defection was an embarrassment. In 1849 he succeeded Bishop Walsh, and was thus the last Vicar Apostolic of the London district. In the following year he was made the first Archbishop of Westminster and a Cardinal. Although frequently mocked by the Protestant English, Wiseman was a capable, astute, learned, good man.

Wood, Charlotte (1789–1873). The widow of William Wood (1768/9?–1841)—a student at Christ Church, Vicar of Fulham, and then a Canon of Canterbury— she was a catechumen of Newman. When she was about to become a Catholic in 1845, Archbishop Howley sent his chaplain to try to dissuade her, without success. She and her daughter were received together and settled in the Isle of Wight, where they remained close friends of Newman. Her son, Granville, a naval captain, became a Catholic in 1849 and a Jesuit. Miss Wood died in 1883.

Wood, Samuel Francis (1810–1843). Wood entered Oriel College in 1827 aged 17, taking a B.A. in 1831 and an M.A. in 1834. He was made a barrister-at-law, Inner Temple, in 1835, but died in 1843. Wood was one of Newman's closest Oxford friends.

Yates, Edmund (1831–1894). Born in Edinburgh of stage parents, he became a journalist and instigated the Garrick Club affair by libeling Thackeray. He was cremated at Woking.

Notes

References to Newman's works are usually to the uniform edition of 1868–81 (36 volumes), which was published by Longmans Green, and Co. of London until the stock was destroyed during the Second World War. Editions of posthumous works, (e.g. *Autobiographical Writings*) are noted in the references. Readers who do not have access to the physical uniform edition can find an electronic version of the same on *newmanreader.org*.

Preface

1   William Makepeace Thackeray, *Roundabout Papers: Little Travels and Roadside Sketches* (New York, 1904), p. 318.
2   John Hungerford Pollen, "Newman in Dublin," from *The Month* (September, 1906), pp. 318–20.

Introduction

1   See *Johnson: Prose and Poetry*, ed. Mona Wilson (London, 1950), p. 9.
2   *Apologia*, p. 4.
3   Frederick Meyrick, *Memories of Life at Oxford and Experiences in Italy, Greece, Turkey, Germany, Spain and Elsewhere* (London, 1905), p. 11.
4   J. C. Shairp, *Studies in Poetry and Philosophy* (Edinburgh, 1886), p. 247.
5   *The Letters and Diaries of John Henry Newman* (London and Oxford, 1961–), 10:303, JHN to Aunt Elizabeth Newman (25 July 1844). Hereinafter, I shall refer to the *Letters and Diaries* as LD.
6   *Lectures on Justification*, p. 337.
7   See *Positio for the Cause of the Canonization of John Henry Cardinal Newman* (Rome, 1989). The Reverend R. H. P. Lynch was the Superior of the Birmingham Oratory when the Cause for Newman's Canonization was first broached by Monsignor Davis in 1952, and when asked whether "canonizing someone was … alien to the British Catholic mentality," he responded, "Yes. As a matter of fact, I have heard it said that there are fifty or sixty persons in the diocese of Naples whose Causes are on the books! We have not the same idea of a Saint." See *Positio*, Vol. II, p. 67.

8   LD, 12:399, Appendix 5: Draft of a Preface for Faber's Lives of the Saints, probably written in the autumn of 1848.
9   *Meditations and Devotions*, p. 428.
10   Shairp, *Studies in Poetry and Philosophy*, p. 248.
11   See Eric Griffiths, "Newman: The Foolishness of Preaching," in *Newman After 100 Years*, ed. Ker and Hill (Oxford, 1990), p. 64. See also *John Henry Newman: Selected Sermons* ed. Ian Ker (New York, 1994).
12   LD, 3:288–89, JHN to Samuel Rickards (14 April 1833).
13   See *American Notes and Pictures from Italy in The New Oxford Illustrated Dickens* ed. Sacheverell Sitwell (London, 1957), pp. 368–70
14   LD, 3:267–68, JHN to Mrs. Jemima Newman (25 March 1833).
15   LD, 3:213, JHN to Harriett Newman (16 February 1833).
16   LD, 3:282, JHN to Jemima Newman (11 April 1833).
17   T. S. Eliot, "East Coker," from "Four Quartets", in *The Complete Poems and Plays* (New York, 1952), p. 127.
18   LD, 4:8, JHN to Henry Wilberforce (16 July 1833) and LD, 3:314, JHN to Frederic Rogers (5 June 1833).
19   *Historical Sketches*, Vol. II, p. 219.
20   D. C. Somervell, *English Thought in the Nineteenth Century* (London, 1929), p. 108.
21   Froude, quoted in Meriol Trevor, *Newman: The Pillar of the Cloud* (London, 1962), p. 149.
22   See *Vanity Fair*, "Men of the Day," No. 145 (20 January 1877).
23   In *The Secret History of the Oxford Movement* (1898), Walsh anticipated many of Turner's own No Popery obsessions.
24   See Frank Turner, "Introduction" to *Apologia Pro Vita Sua & Six Sermons* (New Haven, 2008), pp. 56–57.
25   *The Living Thoughts of Cardinal Newman*, ed. Henry Tristram (London, 1848), xii.
26   See Alfred North Whitehead, *Adventures of Ideas* (New York, 1933), pp. 161–62.
27   Turner, pp. 114–15.
28   LD, 27:161–62, JHN to Unknown Correspondent (27 November 1874).
29   This is from the famous speech Newman gave when he received the red hat, which is known as the 'Biglietto Speech' (1879). See *Addresses to Cardinal Newman*, Vol. 2, pp. 64–67. Also, see I. T. Ker, "Introduction to Newman's Biglietto Speech," in *Logos: A Journal of Catholic Thought and Culture*, Vol. 6, No. 4 (Fall 2003), pp. 164–69.
30   Wilfrid Ward, *The Life of John Henry Newman* (London, 1912), Vol. II, p. 464.
31   LD, 19:488, JHN to Malcolm Maccoll (24 March 1864).
32   "The Infidelity of the Future" (1873), in *Faith and Prejudice and other Sermons*, pp. 116–24.
33   See Edmund Adamus, in *Zenit* (23 August 2010). Adamus told the online news agency: "… whether we like it or not as British citizens and residents of this country – and whether we are even prepared as Catholics to accept

this reality and all it implies – the fact is that historically, and continuing right now, Britain, and in particular London, has been and is the geopolitical epicenter of the culture of death. Our laws and lawmakers for over 50 years or more have been the most permissively anti-life and progressively anti-family and marriage, in essence one of the most anti-Catholic landscapes culturally speaking than even those places where Catholics suffer open persecution. England itself nevertheless has a unique Christian heritage: St. Augustine, the apostle to the English appointed by Pope Gregory, defied the temptation to despair of ever converting the pagan Britons by reminding the degenerate race of the beauty, truth and dignity of marriage. St. Bede's chronicle of English Christianity recounts this strategy ... England is also the "Dowry of Mary," an ancient title going back to the 14th century and even further in the spiritual language of the people. This title signified the fact that from the earliest times English Catholic Christians revered the person of the Mother of Christ with such a singular and wholehearted devotion that the very nation itself was attributed with having a supernatural role ... in the 'marriage' between the Holy Spirit and his spouse – the Virgin of Nazareth. That is to say, English Christianity, in the plan of God, has a unique role to play in being a secure foundation (like a dowry in a marriage) to the work of redemption and salvation history globally."

34 LD, 30:319, JHN to St. George Jackson Mivart (6 March 1884).
35 *Apologia*, p. 78.
36 LD, 9:63, JHN to Maria Giberne (12 August 1842).
37 See E. I. Watkin. *Roman Catholicism in England: From the Reformation to 1950* (Oxford, 1958), pp. 186–7.
38 *The Present Position of Catholics in England*, pp. 61–62.
39 LD, 9:520.
40 *Apologia*, p. 245.
41 LD, 9:491, A Lady to Jemima Newman (30 August 1843).
42 See LD, 9: 336, note 1.
43 See LD, 9:560.
44 Meriol Trevor, *John Henry Newman: The Pillar of the Cloud* (London, 1962), pp. 358–59.
45 LD, 12:62, JHN to Dominic Barberi (14 March 1847).
46 Father Dominic quoted in Meriol Trevor, *Newman: The Pillar of the Cloud*, p. 360.
47 Frederick Maurice, *The Life of Frederick Denison Maurice* (London, 1885), Vol. 2, p. 476.
48 Thomas Huxley, *Science and Christian Tradition: Essays* (New York, 1897), Vol. 5, p. 343.
49 H. P. Liddon, *The Life of E.P. Pusey* (London, 1893), Vol. II, pp. 101–02.
50 In 1847, Bishop Phillpots of Exeter refused to install Charles Gorham to the living of Exeter because he would not accept the doctrine of baptismal regeneration. When Gorham appealed the ruling, the Judicial Committee of the Privy Council overruled the bishop, and Gorham was installed to

the living after all, which outraged High Churchmen and led to William Ewart Gladstone's two closest friends, Henry Edward Manning and James Hope, seceding to Rome. Although Gladstone deeply regretted these defections, he nonetheless recognized that the Judgment went "to the very root of all life and all teaching in the Church of England" by not only undermining the doctrine of baptismal regeneration but allowing the English State to overrule the Church on doctrinal matters.

51   *Memoirs of James Robert Hope-Scott of Abbotsford* (London, 1884), Vol. II, pp. 201–02.
52   See *Positio* for Newman's Canonization (Rome, 1989), p. 415.
53   Paraclita Reilly, *Aubrey de Vere: Victorian Observer* (Dublin, 1956), p. 91.
54   Aubrey de Vere, quoted in Reilly, p. 30.
55   Ibid., p. 92.
56   Ibid., p. 32.
57   See Robert Welch's entry on de Vere in the *Oxford Dictionary of National Biography*.
58   It is an amusing irony that the man whom the Republic of Ireland now regards as one of its cultural heroes never surrendered his British passport. Ibid., p. 30.
59   Ibid., p. 30.
60   *Further Letters of Gerard Manley Hopkins including his correspondence with Coventry Patmore*, ed. Claude Abbott (London, 1956), p. 58.
61   LD, 30:191, JHN to Gerard Manley Hopkins (27 February 1883).
62   LD, 9:212, JHN to E. B. Pusey (30 January 1843).
63   LD, 9:189, JHN to J. W. Bowden (29 December 1842).
64   See Wilfrid Ward, *The Life of John Henry Cardinal Newman* (London, 1912), p. 385.
65   See William Clifford, Bishop of Clifton, *Sermon preached at the funeral of His Eminence John Henry Newman Cardinal of the Holy Roman Church* (London, 1890), pp. 4, 13–14.
66   From *Cardinal Newman: Words spoken by the Cardinal Archbishop of Westminster at the Solemn Requiem at the Oratory, South Kensington August 20th, 1890* (London, 1890), pp. 5, 7–8.
67   LD, 9:270, JHN to Samuel Rickards (7 March 1843).
68   LD, 9:463, JHN to John Keble (20 August 1843).
69   LD, 9:344, JHN to Henry Wilberforce (11 May 1843).
70   LD, 11:294, JHN to Henry Wilberforce (13 December 1846).
71   *Memorials of Edward Burne-Jones*, ed. Lady Georgiana Burne-Jones (London, 1904), p. 59.
72   LD, 25:440, Matthew Arnold to JHN (29 November 1871).
73   Shairp, *Studies in Poetry and Philosophy*, p. 208.
74   Frederic Rogers, quoted in Robert Dudley Middleton, *Newman at Oxford* (Oxford, 1950), p. 98.
75   John Hungerford Pollen, quoted in Meriol Trevor, *Newman: Light in Winter* (London, 1962), p. 61.
76   Mark Pattison, *Memoirs of an Oxford Don* (London, 1885), pp. 100–01.
77   Mark Pattison, Review of Tom Mozley's *Reminiscences of Oriel College*

and the Oxford Movement, in *The Academy*, Issue 22 (July–December 1882).

78   LD, 10:207–08, John Bramston to JHN (10 April 1844).

79   LD, 10:208, JHN to John Bramston (12 April 1844).

80   William Lockhart, quoted in Vincent Ferrer Blehl, *Pilgrim Journey: John Henry Newman 1801–1945* (London, 2002), p. 201.

81   A. M. Fairbairn, *Catholicism Roman and Anglican* (London, 1899), p. 215.

82   Ibid., pp. 87–89.

83   LD, 7:66, JHN to Mrs. John Mozley (23 April 1839).

84   LD, 24:130, JHN to Henry Wilberforce (20 August 1868).

85   LD, 24:77, JHN to J. Walker of Scarborough (22 May 1868).

86   Fairbairn, *Catholicism Roman and Anglican*, pp. 92–93.

87   Noel Annan, *Our Age: English Intellectuals between the World Wars – A Group Portrait* (London, 1989), pp. 157–70.

88   Paul Johnson, *Intellectuals* (New York, 1988), p. 342.

89   To argue that Newman's work in the Oxford Movement was nothing more than an unconscious continuation of much that the eighteenth-century High Church had been doing requires one to imagine a very high level of unconsciousness in Newman, or ignorance. As it was, he was convinced that his purposes were otherwise, as he showed in a letter to Catherine Froude: "… the hollowness of High Churchism (or whatever it is called) is to me so very clear that it surprises me, (not that persons should not see it at once), but that any should not see it at last, and, alas, I must add that I do not think it safe for any one who does see it, not to act on his conviction of it *at once*." (LD, 12:223, JHN to Mrs. Froude (16 June 1848))

90   Frederick Meyrick, *Memories of Life at Oxford*, p. 27.

91   LD, 20:443, JHN to Mrs. John Mozley (18 May 1863).

92   LD, 31:125, A. M. Fairbairn to JHN (11 March 1886).

93   LD, 31:126, JHN to A. M. Fairbairn (15 March 1886).

94   See "Faith And Reason Contrasted its Habits of Mind" (1839) in *Oxford University Sermons* (1843), p. 201.

Chapter 1 John Keble and the Crisis of Tractarianism

1   The witty Oratorian Father Francis Bacchus quotes this observation of Charles Reading, the hero of *Loss and Gain* in his edition of Newman's letters to Keble. See *Correspondence of John Henry Newman with John Keble and others 1839–1845* (London, 1917), p. 359. I have used this edition of the Keble/Newman correspondence in certain cases because it includes letters from Keble to Newman that are not included in the *Letters and Diaries*. In addition, it is easier to see the drama of the correspondence when the Keble/Newman letters are presented separately. I have included dates of the letters for those who wish to locate the letters in the *Letters and Diaries*.

2   R. W. Church, *The Oxford Movement: Twelve Years 1833–1945* (Oxford, 1922), p. 385.
3   LD, 8:161, JHN to Dr. Wiseman (6 April 1841).
4   LD, 9:346–47, JHN to John Keble (18 May 1843).
5   LD, 28:373, 'Notice to Letters of 1843–1845' (19 June 1878).
6   *Lectures on Certain Difficulties felt by Anglicans in submitting to the Catholic Church* (1950), p. 3.
7   Thomas Mozley, *Reminiscences Chiefly of Oriel College and The Oxford Movement* (London, 1882), Vol. 1, p. 219.
8   Georgina Battiscombe, *John Keble: A Study in Limitations* (London, 1963), p. 6.
9   Ibid., p. 37.
10 Ibid., p. 11.
11 Ibid., p. 11.
12 John Keble, *Sermons Academical and Occasional* (Oxford, 1848), pp. i–ii.
13 R. W. Church, *The Oxford Movement*, p. 24.
14 Battiscombe, *John Keble*, p. 9.
15 Ibid., Vol. 1, p. 220.
16 A. J. Froude, "Oxford Counter Reformation," in *Short Studies on Great Subjects* (London, 1907), p. 193.
17 Owen Chadwick, *The Spirit of the Oxford Movement: Tractarian Essays* (Cambridge, 1990), p. 62.
18 Edward Pusey, quoted in Walter Lock, *John Keble* (London, 1895), p. 4.
19 Battiscombe, *John Keble*, p. 37.
20 R. W. Church, *The Oxford Movement*, p. 24.
21 John Taylor Coleridge, *A Memoir of the Rev. John Keble* (London, 1870), p. 70.
22 Thomas Mozley, *Reminiscences Chiefly of Oriel College and the Oxford Movement* (London, 1882), Vol. 1, p. 37.
23 See "Newman and Roman Catholicism," by Ronald Knox, in *Ideas and Beliefs of the Victorians: A Historic Revaluation of the Victorian Age* (New York, 1966), p. 127.
24 R. W. Church, *The Oxford Movement*, p. 51.
25 Keble, quoted in Piers Brendon, *Hurrell Froude and the Oxford Movement* (London, 1974), p. 47.
26 Ibid., p. 47.
27 Ibid., p. 56.
28 Ibid., p. 47.
29 *Apologia*, p. 34.
30 Froude quoted in Church, *The Oxford Movement*, p. 54.
31 *Remains*, Vol. 1, pp. 370–71.
32 Mark Pattison, *Memoirs of an Oxford Don* (London, 1885), pp. 53–54.
33 Piers Brendon, *Hurrell Froude and the Oxford Movement* (London, 1974), p. 82.
34 LD, 2:45 JHN to Pusey (29 June 1882). For Pusey, were "personal

excellence, high talents, a pure and beautiful mind, alone necessary," Keble might have been the better choice; but the Provostship demanded "a great knowledge of human nature, and a general practical turn of mind," which Keble did not possess. Later, in 1876, at the consecration of Keble College Chapel, Pusey regretted the choice, saying that "The whole of the later history of our Church might have been changed had we been wiser ... To us it became a sorrow of our lives" (Liddon, *Pusey*, Vol. I, pp. 136–37). Newman's assessment took in the longer view: "I recollect making Jenkyns laugh by saying in defence of my vote: 'You know we are not electing an Angel, but a Provost. If we were electing an Angel, I should, of course vote for Keble, but the case is different.' I voted, however, for Hawkins from my great affection for, and admiration of him. I have never ceased to love him to this day. I certainly was sorry I had helped in electing Hawkins – but I can't say I ever wished the election undone. Without it, there would have been no movement, no Tracts, no Library of the Fathers." – Letter of 29 June 1882 to Pusey; cf. letter of 9 August 1866 to Henry James Coleridge.

35 *Remains of the Late Reverend Richard Hurrell Froude: Fellow of Oriel College Oxford* (London, 1838), Vol. I, p. 438.
36 Battiscombe, *John Keble*, pp. 139–40.
37 T. S. Eliot, "Tradition and the Individual Talent," in *Selected Essays*, enlarged edition (London, 1951), p. 21.
38 Thomas Hardy paid close attention to Keble. Robert Gittings, Hardy's biographer, noted how "Hardy's debt to Keble in his own later poems is not only in verbal half-memories, like the 'bright hair flapping free' of his lyric to his first wife; it is also in his ceaseless lyric invention." See Robert Gittings, *Young Thomas Hardy* (London, 1975), p. 50.
39 See Anne Ridler's comments regarding her poem "Villanelle for the Middle Way," from *Collected Poems* (London, 1997) at http://www.poetryarchive. org/poetryarchive/singlePoem.do?poemId=1720.
40 Eliot, quoted in Lyndall Gordon, *T.S. Eliot: An Imperfect Life* (New York, 1998), p. 147. Eliot referred to *The Waste Land* as "the relief of a personal ... grouse against life."
41 Basil Willey, *Nineteenth Century Studies: Coleridge to Matthew Arnold* (London, 1949), p. 77.
42 Charlotte M. Yonge, *John Keble's Parishes: A History of Hursley and Otterbourne* (London, 1898), p. 75.
43 Battiscombe, *John Keble*, p. 55.
44 Ibid., p. 165.
45 Hurrell Froude to JHN (9 August 1835), in *John Henry Newman and Abbé Jager*, ed. Louis Allen (Oxford, 1975), p. 179.
46 Coleridge, Vol. 1, p. 271.
47 Battiscombe, *John Keble*, p. 165.
48 Ibid., p. 338.
49 *Edinburgh Review*, Vol. 63 (April–July 1836), p. 238.
50 Battiscombe, *John Keble*, p. 191.

51 Arthur Penryn Stanley, *Life of Thomas Arnold, D.D. Head-Master of Rugby* (London, 1904), p. 399.

52 *Letters of Frederic Lord Blachford*, ed. George Eden Marindin (London, 1896), p. 158.

53 LD, 5:251, JHN to Simeon Lloyd Pope (3 March 1836). For a less polemical view of Hampden, see Richard Brent's excellent article on him in the ODNB, Vol. 24, pp. 987–90.

54 Battiscombe, *John Keble*, p. 226.

55 About Peter Young's selflessness, Charlotte Keble once remarked: "he is the sort of person who must be made to think about himself or he would quite forget." See Battiscombe, *John Keble*, p. 223.

56 Church, *The Oxford Movement*, pp. 334–35.

57 LD, 9:375.

58 *Dictionary of National Biography*, Vol. X, p. 1180.

59 Ibid., p. 257.

60 See "Preface on the Present Position of English Churchmen," from John Keble, *Sermons Academical and Occasional* (London, 1848), pp. xxiv–xxv.

61 *Anglican Difficulties*, p. 72.

62 Ibid., pp. 47–48.

63 W. J. Copeland, quoted in Piers Brendon, *Hurrell Froude and the Oxford Movement* (London, 1974), p. 50.

64 *Apologia*, p. 28.

65 Wilfrid Ward, *William George Ward and the Oxford Movement* (London, 1889), p. 318.

66 *Apologia*, pp. 28–29.

67 Hurrell Froude, quoted in Brendon, p. 73.

68 Archdeacon Froude, quoted in Brendon, p. 84.

69 R. W. Church, *The Oxford Movement*, pp. 26–27.

70 Ibid., pp. 31–32.

71 *The Autobiography of Isaac Williams*, ed. George Prevost (London, 1893), p. 19.

72 Ibid., p. 19.

73 In 1830, Keble wrote Perceval, "the Press is the real mischief." See Battiscombe, *John Keble*, p. 136. Newman devoted as much time as he did to the *British Critic* and to the *Rambler* because he recognized that it was important to give first Tractarian and then Roman Catholic views some popular dissemination. Of course, there were many others who saw Newman's own periodical efforts—particularly with respect to the *Tracts of the Times*—as themselves mischievous. In May, 1838, Newman wrote Pusey: "Fausett to-day fired off a sermon against us, as leading to Popery ..." Godfrey Faussett, Lady Margaret Professor of Divinity, complained that, "when ... the marks of deliberation and design, the evidence of numbers and of combination ... find their way into the periodical and popular and most widely disseminated literature of the day; – when the wild and visionary sentiments of an enthusiastic mind, involving in their unguarded expression an undisguised preference for a portion at least of Papal

superstition, and occasionally even a wanton outrage on the cherished feelings of the sincere Protestant ... and this too under circumstances which imply the concurrence and approval, and responsibility too, of an indefinite and apparently numerous body of friends and correspondents and editors and reviewers; – who shall any longer deny the imperative necessity which exists for the most decisive language ..." *The Revival of Popery*, Oxford, 1838, pp. 13–15; see also LD, 6:247

74 *Apologia*, p. 200.
75 *Autobiographical Writings*, pp. 200–01.
76 Battiscombe, *John Keble*, p. 40.
77 LD:20:450, JHN to Mrs. Edward Bellasis (21 May 1863).
78 See Newman's sermon, "Obedience Without Love, As Instanced in the Character of Balaam," 2 April 1837.
79 See John Lock, *John Keble* (London, 1895), p. 15.
80 "Father Dominic the Passionist is passing this way, on his way from Aston in Staffordshire to Belgium ... He is to come to Littlemore for a night as a guest of one of us whom he has admitted at Aston. He does not know of my intentions, but I shall ask of him admission into the one true Fold of the Redeemer." See LD, 11:3, JHN to Henry Wilberforce (7 October 1845).
81 A. J. P. Taylor, *From Napoleon to the Second International: Essays on 19th Century Europe* (London, 1993), p. 122.
82 LD, 2:125, JHN to Mrs. Jemima Newman (1 March 1829).
83 LD, 2:119, JHN to Samuel Rickards (6 February 1829).
84 Lord Wellington, quoted in J. C. D. Clark, *English Society* 1688–1832 (London, 1985), p. 413.
85 Ibid., p. 413.
86 Lord Melbourne, quoted in David Cecil, *Melbourne* (London, 1955), p. 245.
87 LD, 2:130, JHN to Mrs. Jemima Newman (13 March 1829).
88 *Apologia*, pp. 257–58.
89 Keble to John Cornish, quoted in Battiscombe, *John Keble*, p. 130.
90 R. W. Church, *The Oxford Movement*, p. 26.
91 See Keble's assize sermon "On National Apostasy", in *Documents of the Christian Church*, ed. Henry Bettenson (London, 1967), p. 316.
92 LD, 8:118.
93 For more about the background of Tract 90, see LD, 8:xvi, on which my own précis is based.
94 In a letter to *The Times* (24 October 1863) F. D. Maurice wrote: "Dr. Newman distinctly maintained that the Protestant writers of the Articles had framed them so as to entrap 'the Catholics,' and that 'the Catholics' were at liberty to put a sense upon them which was different from that obviously intended by their Protestant writers. This seemed to the readers of the Tract a 'non-natural' sense." See LD, 20:414.
95 See VM, II, 347–48; also see Newman's Letter to the Editor of *The Times* (24 February 1863), LD, 20:413–15 in which he quotes this brilliant passage in a response to aforementioned Maurice's letter to *The Times*.

96   See Introduction to Tract 90, *Via Media*, 2, 271.

97   LD, 8:147, John Belaney to JHN.

98   John Keble, *On Tract 90* (London, 1841), p. 6.

99   R. W. Church, the first and in some respects the best historian of the Oxford Movement, qualified Pusey's support for Newman by telling Frederic Rogers in a long letter of 14 March 1841: "Pusey, I fear, has been much annoyed. He scarcely agrees with Newman's view, though he is very kind. A great difficulty with him and with the Bishop is that Newman has committed himself to leaving 'Ora pro nobis' an open question. The Moral Philosophy Professor [Sewell] has seized the opportunity to publish a letter, nominally to Pusey, but really to Messrs. Magee and the Irish Evangelicals in which he deeply laments the Tract as incautious, tending to unsettle and shake people's faith in the English Church, and leading men to receive 'paradoxes and therefore errors' ..." See LD, 8:111.

100 LD, 8:126, E. B. Pusey to Richard Bagot, Bishop of Oxford (26 March 1841).

101 Pusey to John Keble (21 October 1865) in H. P. Liddon, *Life of Pusey* (London, 1897), Vol. 4, p. 125.

102 Battiscombe, *John Keble*, p. 221.

103 R. W. Church, *The Oxford Movement*, p. 388.

104 The via media, broadly defined, was the theory that Newman cobbled together from the work of seventeenth-century Anglican divines to map out a 'middle way' between Catholicism and Protestantism.

105 LD, 8:181, Charles Russell to JHN (21 April 1841).

106 LD, 8:182, JHN to Charles Russell (26 April 1841).

107 *Apologia*, p. 99.

108 LD, 11:100, JHN to Henry Wilberforce (27 January 1846).

109 Ibid., p. 101.

110 *Discussion and Arguments*, p. 18.

111 William Tuckwell, *Reminiscences of Oxford* (London, 1900), p. 166.

112 LD, 6:7, JHN to Martin Routh (6 January 1837).

113 LD, 6:34, JHN to H. E. Manning (24 February 1837).

114 R. W. Church, *The Oxford Movement*, pp. 392–93.

115 Ibid., p. 296.

116 Ibid., p. 297.

117 Ibid., p. 302.

118 Ibid., p. 304.

119 Ibid., p. 305.

120 Ibid., p. 307.

121 Ibid., p. 308.

122 Ibid., p. 310.

123 Ibid., p. 311.

124 Ibid., p. 313.

125 Ibid., p. 316.

126 Ibid., p. 317.

127 Ibid., p. 318.

128 LD, 10:426, JHN to John Keble (21 November 1844).

129 LD, 8:120, JHN to John Keble (25 March 1841).

130 LD, 8:121, John Keble to JHN (26 March 1841).

131 LD, 8:178, E. B. Pusey to J. R. Hope (18 April 1841).

132 Newman had occasion to invoke the great saint in a letter to his good friend Maria Giberne, written in 1837 when the tide was turning against the Tractarians: "We have nothing to hope or fear from Whig or Conservative Governments – or from Bishops, or from Peers, or from Court, or from other visible power. We must trust our own ἦθος, (ethos) that is what is unseen, our unseen gifts and their unseen Author. I do hope we shall be strengthened to develop in new ways, since the ordinary ways are stopped up. Some of the Bishops, as Norwich, are driving fast at a denial of the Creed, which is heresy – and when a bishop is heretical, man, woman, or child has licence to oppose him. The faith is prior and dearer to us than the visible framework which is built upon it. And if we so account it, we shall perchance be blessed to preserve the framework too. It was a worse time after all, when Athanasius was against the whole world, and the whole world against Athanasius." (See LD, 6:174 (3 December 1837))

133 *Correspondence of John Henry Newman with John Keble and others 1839–1845* (London, 1917), p. 133.

134 LD, 8:286, JHN to John Keble (5 October 1841).

135 LD, 8:292, JHN to S. F. Wood (10 October 1841).

136 LD, 8:345, JHN to J. R. Hope (24 November 1841).

137 See Battiscombe, *John Keble*, p. 227.

138 Ibid., pp. 227–28.

139 LD, 9:279–81, JHN to John Keble (14 March 1843).

140 *Correspondence of John Henry Newman with John Keble and others 1839–1845* (London, 1917), p. 216, John Keble to JHN (3 May 1843).

141 Ibid., p. 221, Frederic Rogers to JHN (3 April 1843).

142 LD, 9:327, JHN to John Keble (4 May 1843).

143 LD, 9:328, JHN to John Keble (4 May 1843).

144 Battiscombe, *John Keble*, p. 240, and *Correspondence of John Henry Newman with John Keble and others 1839–1845* (London, 1917), p. 308.

145 *Correspondence of John Henry Newman with John Keble and others 1839–1845* (London, 1917), pp. 222–24, JHN to John Keble (14 May 1843).

146 See ODNB.

147 LD, 30:415, JHN to W. S. Lilly (15 October 1884).

148 *Apologia*, pp. 180–81.

149 *Correspondence of John Henry Newman with John Keble and others 1839–1845* (London, 1917), p. 224, John Keble to JHN (14 May 1843).

150 LD, 9:349, JHN to John Keble (18 May 1843).

151 LD, 9:349, JHN to John Keble (18 May 1843).

152 *Correspondence of John Henry Newman with John Keble and others 1839–1845* (London, 1917), p. 231, JHN to John Keble (30 May 1843).

153 Ibid., p. 231, JHN to John Keble (30 May 1843).

154 Ibid., p. 232, John Keble to JHN (30 May 1843).

155 Ibid., p. 243, John Keble to JHN (16 July 1843).

156 Ibid., p. 245, JHN to John Keble (20 August 1843).

157 *Apologia*, p. 157.

158 *Correspondence of John Henry Newman with John Keble and others 1839–1845* (London, 1917), pp. 255–56, John Keble to JHN (4 September 1843).

159 Ibid., p. 256, John Keble to JHN (4 September 1843).

160 Ibid., pp. 259–60, JHN to John Keble (6 September 1843).

161 Ibid., p. 261, John Keble to JHN (7 September 1843).

162 LD, 10:71 JHN to Henry Edward Manning (24 December 1843).

163 Ibid., pp. 296–97, John Keble to JHN (22 June 1843).

164 Ibid., p. 297, John Keble to JHN (22 January 1844).

165 LD, 10:4–5, JHN to James Hope (2 November 1843).

166 *Apologia*, p. 120. Speaking of the insight he had gained in 1839 after reading of the Monophysite heresy, Newman wrote: "my new historical fact had already to a certain point a logical force. Down had come the *Via Media* as a definite theory or scheme, under the blows of St. Leo. My *Prophetical Office* had come to pieces; not indeed as an argument against 'Roman errors,' nor as against Protestantism, but as in behalf of England. I had no longer a distinctive plea for Anglicanism, unless I would be a Monophysite. I had, most painfully, to fall back upon my three original points of belief, which I have spoken so much of in a former passage,— the principle of dogma, the sacramental system, and anti-Romanism. Of these three the first two were better secured in Rome than in the Anglican Church. The Apostolical Succession, the two prominent sacraments, and the primitive Creeds, belonged, indeed, to the latter; but there had been and was far less strictness on matters of dogma and ritual in the Anglican system than in the Roman: in consequence, my main argument for the Anglican claims lay in the positive and special charges, which I could bring against Rome. I had no positive Anglican theory. I was very nearly a pure Protestant. Lutherans had a sort of theology, so had Calvinists; I had none."

167 *Correspondence of John Henry Newman with John Keble and others 1839–1845* (London, 1917), p. 297, John Keble to JHN (22 January 1844).

168 Ronald Knox, *Let Dons Delight* (London, 1939), p. 183.

169 *Correspondence of John Henry Newman with John Keble and others 1839–1845* (London, 1917), p. 298, John Keble to JHN (22 January 1844).

170 LD, 10:422, John Keble to JHN (18 November 1844). Cf. *Antony and Cleopatra* Act II, Scene II, pp. 217–22:

> From the barge
> A strange invisible perfume hits the sense
> Of the adjacent wharfs. The city cast

Her people out upon her, and Antony,
Enthron'd i' the market-place, did sit alone
Whistling to the air; which, but for vacancy,
Had gone to gaze on Cleopatra too
And made a gap in nature.

171 LD, 10:102–03, JHN to John Keble (23 January 1844).
172 LD, 10:103, JHN to John Keble (23 January 1844).
173 LD, 10:260, JHN to John Keble (8 June 1844).
174 LD, 10:261, JHN to John Keble (8 June 1844).
175 LD: 10:260, JHN to John Keble (8 June 1844).
176 LD, 10:262, JHN to John Keble (8 June 1844).
177 LD, 10:262, JHN to John Keble (8 June 1844).
178 LD, 10:26:261, JHN to John Keble (8 June 1844).
179 LD, 10:268, John Keble to JHN (11 June 1844).
180 Battiscombe, *John Keble*, p. 234.
181 LD, 10:268, John Keble to JHN (11 June 1844).
182 LD, 10:269, John Keble to JHN (12 June 1844).
183 Apropos uncertainty, Archbishop Rowan Williams agrees with Keble, arguing in one of his many books that "church history suffers endemically from misplaced certainty." And to make his point, the Archbishop asks, "Why should not radical trust in the all-sufficiency of Christ's work coexist with mistaken, even gravely mistaken ideas about the specific content of Christian doctrine?" While conceding that the English Church's rejection of authority hampers Anglicans' attempts to resolve their differences, Williams calls on an authority of his own to argue that these differences may not require resolving. "The greatest of twentieth-century philosophers warned against having a concept of certainty that regarded it as a single and absolute quality of mind attainable by one set of clearly marked methods. Instead, he argued, we need to look at different sorts of uncertainty ... Wittgenstein's reflections on certainty ought to be (but are not all that often) a substantive aid for theologians. Before we ask how certainty is to be guaranteed, we should ask where and how the question, 'Am I sure?' posed itself. And rather than looking for one unshakeable foundation for one kind of certainty, we need to look at what in fact is done to answer the particular questions and doubts we face ..." Keble would probably be surprised to see his own uncertainty beneath this cascade of blather but it is there nonetheless. See Rowan Williams, *Why Study the Past? The Quest for the Historical Church* (London, 2005), pp. 88, 77, 90.
184 Tuckwell, *Reminiscences of Oxford*, p. 18.
185 LD, 10:639–40, JHN to Henry Wilberforce (27 April 1845).
186 See "Thoughts After Lambeth," in T. S. Eliot, *Selected Essays* (London, 1951), p. 369.
187 LD, 10:703, JHN to William Ewart Gladstone (12 June 1845).
188 LD, 10:271, JHN to John Keble (13 June 1844).

189 LD, 10:426, JHN to John Keble (21 November 1844).
190 LD, 10:427, JHN to John Keble (21 November 1844).
191 LD, 10:474, John Keble to JHN (27 December 1844).
192 On the tenth anniversary of the foiling of the Gunpowder Plot (5 November 1615), undertaken by recusants to blow up Parliament, Lancelot Andrewes preached a sermon referring to the plot as trampling on and tearing into pieces "all bands of birth, country, allegiance, nature, blood, humanity and Christianity …" See *The Folio Book of Historic Speeches*, ed. Ian Pindar (London, 2007), p. 56.
193 LD, 10:774, John Keble to JHN (3 October 1845).
194 J. C. Shairp, *John Keble* (Edinburgh, 1866), pp. 6–7.
195 See "Preface on the Present Position of English Churchmen" (1847), in John Keble, *Sermons, Academical and Occasional* (Oxford, 1848), pp. xxvi–xxvii.
196 LD, 28:418, JHN to Lord Coleridge (9 November 1878).
197 LD, 31:180, JHN to William Knight (7 January 1887).
198 Liddon, *Life of Pusey*, Vol. IV, p. 141.
199 LD, 10:774, John Keble to JHN (3 October 1845).
200 Battiscombe, *John Keble*, pp. 256–58.
201 *Correspondence of John Henry Newman with John Keble and others 1839–1845* (London, 1917), p. 386, John Keble to JHN (3 October 1845).
202 LD, 11:34, JHN to John Keble (14 November 1845).
203 LD, 2:289, JHN to Hurrell Froude (10 September 1830).

Chapter 2 Staying Put: John Keble After 1845

1   LD, 12:25, JHN to Mrs. John Mozley (26 January 1847).
2   LD, 11:74, JHN to Maria Giberne (21 December 1845).
3   *Essays Critical and Historical*, Vol. II, p. 451.
4   Ibid., pp. 452–53.
5   See *Life and Letters of Dean Church*, ed. Mary C. Church (London, 1897), pp. 387–88.
6   Ibid., p. 246.
7   LD, 21:121, JHN to Richard Holt Hutton (18 June 1864).
8   Rosemary Hill, *God's Architect: Pugin and the Building of Romantic Britain* (London, 2007), p. 449.
9   E. B. Pusey to J. Keble (1 October 1854), in Liddon, *Life of Pusey* (London, 1893), Vol. 3, pp. 428–29.
10 Ruskin to Henry Acland (May 1851), quoted in Robert Hewison, *Ruskin and Venice: Paradise of Cities* (New Haven, 2009), p. 201.
11 John Keble, "On Eucharistical Adoration," p. 174.
12 Keble, quoted in Georgina Battiscombe, *John Keble: A Study in Limitations* (London, 1963), p. 238.
13 LD, 30:74–75, JHN to Lord Blachford (4 April 1882).

14 LD, 11:227–28, JHN to T. F. Knox (20 August 1846).
15 Manning quoted Keble as saying this: see Battiscombe, *John Keble*, p. 303.
16 See *ODNB*, 22:314.
17 Battiscombe, *John Keble*, p. 278.
18 Ibid., p. 281.
19 Ibid., pp. 280–81.
20 Ibid., pp. 278–80.
21 LD, 11:60–61, JHN to A. J. Hanmer (11 December 1845).
22 John Coleridge, *Memoir of the late Rev. John Keble* (London, 1869), Vol. 2, p. 446.
23 Keble to Robert Wilberforce (19 August 1851), quoted in Battiscombe, *John Keble*, p. 306.
24 See David Newsome, *The Wilberforces and Henry Manning: The Parting of Friends* (London, 1966), p. 406.
25 LD, 17:537, Letter from Robert Wilberforce to JHN, quoted in JHN to The Editor of the *Weekly Register* (8 March 1857).
26 JK to J. T. Coleridge (25 October 1847) Bodleian Library MS Eng. lett. d. 135 f. 354.
27 LD, 13:295, JHN to A. J. Hanmer (18 November 1849).
28 *Apologia*, pp. 155–56.
29 John Coleridge, *Memoir of the late Rev. John Keble* (London, 1869), Vol. 2, p. 501.
30 LD, 20:501, John Keble to JHN (4 August 1863).
31 LD, 20:502–03, JHN to John Keble (15 August 1863).
32 Charles Kingsley, quoted in the Editor's Introduction to *Apologia*, pp. xix–xx.
33 See *Apologia*, p. 6
34 LD, 21:98, JHN to William Copeland (19 April 1864).
35 LD, 21:103, John Keble to JHN (25 April 1864).
36 LD, 21:103, JHN to John Keble (27 April 1864).
37 LD, 21:103–04, JHN to John Keble (27 April 1864).
38 LD, 21:143, John Keble to JHN (28 June 1864).
39 LD, 21:143, John Keble to JHN (28 June 1864).
40 LD, 22:67, JHN to John Keble (8 October 1865).
41 *Letter to Pusey*, p. 7.
42 LD, 22:51, JHN to Ambrose St. John (13 September 1865). The brackets in this quote mark later interpolations made by Newman to his original letter.
43 LD, 22:147, John Keble to JHN (3 February 1866).
44 LD, 22:148, JHN to John Keble (7 February 1866).
45 LD, 22:202, JHN to Henry James Coleridge (3 April 1866).
46 LD, 23:43, JHN to Pusey (31 January 1867).
47 LD, 26:376, JHN to H. A. Woodgate (18 October 1873).
48 LD, 22:208, JHN to Charlotte Wood (8 April 1866).
49 LD, 27:370–73, JHN to Maria Trench (29 October 1875).
50 LD, 28:358, John to Edward Stuart Keble (20 May 1878).

51 Williams, quoted in Battiscombe, *John Keble*, p. 275.

52 LD, 28:372–73, "Notice to Letters 1843–1845."

53 When Newman learned through his friend Lord Emly that Anthony Trollope was suffering from asthma, he sent him a specific of saltpetre. Trollope wrote back to Newman, thanking him and telling him "how great has been the pleasure which I have received from understanding that you have occasionally read and been amused by my novels. It is when I hear that such men as yourself have been gratified that I feel I have not worked in vain; but there is no man as to whom I can say that his good opinion would give me such intense gratification as your own." See LD, 29:155 Anthony Trollope to JHN (27 October 1882). On the same day, Trollope wrote to Emly: "I am infinitely obliged to Cardinal Newman for his kindness in regard to my asthma. I have ventured to write to tell him so. In regard to his specific, though it shall have full loyal attention from me, I fear that it will do but little for me; not because it is inoperative, but because I am not in want of it. I find all fumigatory receipts to be of no avail, because I have not fallen into the period which they affect. Great spasmodic want of breath is the evil which affects me, and which at night sometimes becomes very hard to bear. I am indeed obliged to sit upright so as to catch my breath or to remedy the disease by taking chloral. But my throat is never so affected as to be touched by any kind of smoking. As before said, however, I will try saltpetre in the form recommended by the Cardinal and you no doubt will hear the result. I can hardly tell you the amount of pleasure which I have received from the Cardinal's opinions of my novels." See *The Letters of Anthony Trollope*, ed. Bradford Allen Booth (Oxford, 1951), pp. 494–95.

54 LD, 22:234, JHN to Emily Bowles (15 May 1866).

55 LD, 28:158, Julia Arnold to JHN (5 November 1876). See also Bernard Bergonzi, *A Victorian Wanderer: The Life of Thomas Arnold the Younger* (Oxford, 2003), p. 189: "Julia was a good hater with an energetically vituperative style, but here, as on other occasions, she gives the impression of being, in Mary's words, 'not really in her right mind.' Newman commented dryly, 'It was fitting, by way of contrast, that so sweet and amiable a fellow as Arnold should have such a yoke fellow—but except as an aesthetic contrast, it is marvelous that such a pair should be.'" See LD, 28:157. Arnold must often have been consoled by those memorable lines from *The Winter's Tale*: "… Should all despair/That have revolted wives, the tenth of mankind/Would hang themselves." Act 1, Sc. 2, 1, 198.

56 LD, 22:208, JHN to Charlotte Wood (8 April 1866).

57 LD, 22:216, JHN to Emily Bowles (16 April 1866).

58 LD, 28:20, JHN to Ambrose Phillipps de Lisle (27 January 1876).

59 William Oddie, "Cardinal Hume's 'Moment of Grace' may have arrived," *Catholic Herald* (30 October 2009), p. 12.

60 LD, 26:365, JHN to Miss Rowe (16 September 1873).

61 LD, 26:379, JHN to Miss Rowe (23 October 1873).

62 LD, 11:198, JHN to Manuel Johnson (8 July 1846).

63 *Oxford Sermons*, p. 170.

64 LD, 21:129, JHN to Henry James Coleridge (24 June 1864).
65 *Correspondence of John Henry Newman with John Keble and others 1839–1845* (London, 1917), p. 297, Keble to JHN (22 January 1844).

Chapter 3 The Anglican Difficulties of Edward Pusey

1 LD, 20:459, JHN to Isaac Williams (7 June 1863).
2 LD, 12:59, JHN to Mrs. J. W. Bowden (7 March 1847).
3 *Apologia*, pp. 65–66.
4 H. P. Liddon, *Life of Pusey* (London, 1897), Vol. I, p. 3.
5 Ibid., p. 3.
6 Ibid., p. 7.
7 Ibid., p. 7.
8 LD, 28:352, JHN to Anne Mozley (28 April 1878).
9 Liddon, *Life of Pusey*, Vol. I, p. 5.
10 David Forrester, *Young Dr. Pusey: A Study in Development* (London, 1989), p. 5.
11 Lytton Strachey, *Eminent Victorians* (Modern Library, 1918), pp. 204–05.
12 Russell, quoted in Stuart J. Reid, *Lord John Russell* (London, 1895), pp. 185–86.
13 William Tuckwell, *Reminiscences of Oxford* (London, 1900), p. 139.
14 Mark Pattison, *Memoirs of an Oxford Don*, Cassell Biographies (London, 1988), p. 102.
15 Pattison, *Memoirs of an Oxford Don*, p. 185.
16 See B. A. Smith, *Dean Church: The Anglican Response to Newman* (Oxford, 1958), p. 198.
17 Liddon, *Life of Pusey*, Vol. 3, p. 297.
18 Pusey, quoted in Forrester, *Young Dr. Pusey*, p. 22.
19 Forrester, *Young Dr. Pusey*, p. 55.
20 See Joyce Sugg's excellent little biography of Newman, *Snapdragon in the Wall* (London, 1965), p. 39. "Newman was always interested in soldier's exploits. When the Duke of Wellington's dispatches were published he said it made him burn to be a soldier."
21 Forrester, *Young Dr. Pusey*, p. 56.
22 Liddon, *Life of Pusey*, Vol. I, p. 23.
23 LD. Whately, once asked by one of his English friends if Puseyism was prevalent in Ireland, responded, "Not so prevalent as in England; but it exists. I was told that we should escape it—that, as we have the real thing, we should not adopt the copy—but I was sure that it would come. Ireland catches every disease after it has passed over England. Cholera came to us after you had it, so did the potato rot, so did Puseyism." See *Life and Correspondence of Richard Whately, D.D. Late Archbishop of Dublin*, ed. Jane Whately (London, 1866), Vol. II, pp. 235–36.

24 Pusey, quoted by David Forrester in "Dr. Pusey's Marriage," in *Pusey Rediscovered*, ed. Perry Butler (London, 1983), p. 126.

25 Ibid., p. 126.

26 H. C. G. Matthew, "Edward Bouverie Pusey: From Scholar to Tractarian," in *The Journal of Theological Studies*," Volume XXXII (Oxford, 1981), p. 103.

27 In the *Apologia*, Newman remarks how "… a broad distinction had to be drawn between the actual state of belief and of usage in the countries which were in communion with the Roman Church, and her formal dogmas; the latter did not cover the former. Sensible pain, for instance, is not implied in the Tridentine decree upon Purgatory; but it was the tradition of the Latin Church, and I had seen the pictures of souls in flames in the streets of Naples. Bishop Lloyd had brought this distinction out strongly in an Article in the British Critic in 1825 …" (pp. 100–01) Lloyd's article was "View of the Roman Catholic Doctrines," in the October 1825 number of the *British Critic*. Martin Svaglic points out that "The distinction here made is prophetic of Tract 90 and Newman acknowledged the influence." See ibid., p. 538. See also, *Autobiography*, pp. 69–72, for Newman's estimate of the limitations of Lloyd's influence on him.

28 Letter of Frank William Newman to Moncure Daniel Conway, undated, in Moncure Daniel Conway, *Autobiography: Memories and Experiences*, 2 vols (Boston, 1904), Vol. I, pp. 443–44.

29 See William J. Baker, *Beyond Port and Prejudice: Charles Lloyd of Oxford 1784–1829* (Maine, 1981), p. 108.

30 Ibid., p. 109.

31 Ibid., p. 127.

32 Ibid.

33 Liddon, *Life of Pusey*, Vol. I, p. 154.

34 Ibid., pp. 164–65.

35 Ibid., p. 153.

36 Forrester, *Young Dr. Pusey*, p. 37.

37 Liddon, *Life of Pusey*, Vol. I, pp. 175–76.

38 Matthew, "Edward Bouverie Pusey: From Scholar to Tractarian," p. 112.

39 Liddon, *Life of Pusey*, Vol. I, p. 77.

40 Forrester, *Young Dr. Pusey*, p. 48.

41 Liddon, *Life of Pusey*, Vol. I, p. 207.

42 Timothy Larsen, "E.B. Pusey and Holy Scripture," in *The Journal of Theological Studies*, Vol. 60, Pt. 2 (October 2009), p. 513.

43 Ibid., p. 514.

44 See John Ruskin, *Praeterita*, introduced by Kenneth Clark (Oxford, 1978), p. 190.

45 LD, 3:114, JHN to EBP (12 November 1832).

46 Liddon, *Life of Pusey*, Vol. I, p. 225.

47 Forrester, *Young Dr. Pusey*, p. 60.

48 Ibid.

49 Liddon, *Life of Pusey*, Vol. I, p. 2.

50 Ibid., pp. 41–44.

51 Forrester, *Young Dr. Pusey*, p. 57.
52 Ibid., p. 57.
53 Ibid., pp. 57–58.
54 Ibid., pp. 59–60.
55 Liddon, *Life of Pusey*, Vol. I, p. 228.
56 LD, 3:127, JHN to EBP (5 December 1832).
57 *Apologia*, p. 257.
58 Forrester, *Young Dr. Pusey*, p. 62.
59 Liddon, *Life of Pusey*, Vol. I, p. 279.
60 See Tract 18.
61 Liddon, *Life of Pusey*, Vol. I, p. 280. Newman also met with criticism for his defense of baptismal regeneration. "Mr. McGhee came up here twice last Sunday—he heard me preach on baptismal regeneration—Accordingly he sent me a remonstrance of three large sheets full, ending with a challenge; 'to select whom I pleased, e.g. Dr Pusey, as a friend, he would come with a friend—' stenographists he must stipulate for; we were to expound St Paul's Epistle to the Romans alternately; they were to take it down verbatim; and it was to be published through the country. It was a piece of simplicity in the worthy man to propose a debate—I might as well propose a duet on the violin, for I am little able to controvert on a platform as, I suspect, he is to execute a concerto." See LD, 8:514, JHN to John Keble (29 April 1842).
62 *Apologia*, pp. 64–65.
63 See Forrester, *Young Dr. Pusey*, p. 88: "Unlike Newman, who had set about reading the Fathers systematically as early as 1828, and on whom such Fathers as Clement and Origen of the Church of Alexandria had made a profound impression, Pusey seems to have studied the Early Church very little before he joined the Oxford Movement."
64 Liddon, *Life of Pusey*, Vol. I, p. 283.
65 Ibid., pp. 282–83.
66 Forrester, *Young Dr. Pusey*, pp. 82–83.
67 *Apologia*, p. 29.
68 Liddon, *Life of Pusey*, Vol. I, p. 345.
69 Liddon, *Life of Pusey*, Vol. II, p. 122.
70 From Tract 69, quoted in Liddon, *Life of Pusey*, Vol. I, p. 347.
71 LD, 4:228, JHN to John W. Bowden (1 April 1834).
72 LD, 5:145, JHN to Samuel Rickards (14 September 1835).
73 See Newman's Advertisement to second volume of Tracts (1835), p. vi.
74 *The Life of Frederick Denison Maurice*, ed. Frederick Maurice (London, 1884), Vol. I, p. 186.
75 Tract 67, p. 12, quoted by Liddon, *Life of Pusey*, Vol. I, p. 349.
76 LD, 23:50, JHN to Unknown Correspondent (4 February 1867).
77 Peter Nockles, *The Oxford Movement in Context: Anglican High Churchmanship 1760–1857* (Cambridge, 1994), p. 230.
78 Owen Chadwick, *The Victorian Church* (Oxford, 1966), Vol. I, p. 265.
79 Liddon, *Life of Pusey*, Vol. III, pp. 240–41.
80 LD, 27:320, JHN to Lord Blachford (16 June 1875).

81 Liddon, *Life of Pusey*, Vol. I, p. 263.
82 Liddon, *Life of Pusey*, Vol. II, p. 311.
83 Ibid., p. 313.
84 Ibid., p. 312.
85 Ibid., p. 317.
86 Ibid., p. 324.
87 Ibid., p. 329.
88 Ibid., p. 328.
89 Ibid., p. 337.
90 Ibid., p. 347.
91 Ibid., p. 348.
92 Ibid., p. 363.
93 LD, 9:357–58, JHN to Mrs. John Mozley (24 May 1843).
94 LD, 9:385, JHN to Henry Wilberforce (9 June 1843).
95 LD, 9:391, JHN to EBP (14 June 1843).
96 LD, 6:283, JHN to EBP (13 August 1838).
97 LD, 7:78, JHN to EBP (19 May 1839).
98 Liddon, *Life of Pusey*, Vol. II, p. 97.
99 LD, 7:79, JHN to EBP (19 May 1839).
100 LD, 7:84, JHN to EBP (26 May 1839).
101 Liddon, *Life of Pusey*, Vol. II, p. 101.
102 Ibid., p. 101.
103 Nathaniel Hawthorne confirmed this melancholy quirk in Pusey, when he recalled how "Mr. Parker told us that Dr. Pusey … would soon probably make his appearance in the quadrangle, on his way to chapel; so we walked to and fro waiting an opportunity to see him. A gouty old dignitary, in a white surplice, came hobbling along from one extremity of the court; and by-and-by, from the opposite corner, appeared Dr. Pusey, also in a white surplice, and with a lady by his side. We met him, and I stared fixedly at him, as I well might; for he looked on the ground, as if conscious that he would be stared at … He was talking with the lady, and smiled, but not jollily." See Nathaniel Hawthorne. *Our Old Home and English Note-books in The Complete Works of Nathaniel Hawthorne* (Boston, 1884), V. 4, 352.
104 Liddon, *Life of Pusey*, Vol. II, p. 103.
105 B. A. Smith, *Dean Church: The Anglican Response to Newman* (Oxford, 1958), p. 75.
106 William Tuckwell, *Reminiscences of Oxford* (London, 1900), pp. 136–37.
107 LD, 22:153, JHN to T. W. Allies (19 February 1866).
108 *Pusey Rediscovered*, ed. Perry Butler (London, 1982), p. 235.
109 LD, 10:412, JHN to H. E. Manning (16 November 1844).
110 LD, 10:476, JHN to John Keble (29 December 1844).
111 LD, 9:307–08, JHN to John Keble (15 April 1843).
112 Liddon, *Life of Pusey*, Vol. II, p. 380.
113 LD, 10:126, JHN to EBP (19 February 1844).
114 LD, 10:135, EBP to JHN (23 February 1844).

115 LD, 10:136, JHN to EBP (23 February 1844).
116 Liddon, *Life of Pusey*, Vol. II, pp. 382–83.
117 Ibid., p. 383.
118 LD, 10:215, EBP to JHN (22 April 1844).
119 Liddon, *Life of Pusey*, Vol. II, p. 385.
120 Ibid., p. 385.
121 LD, 10:206, JHN to EBP (10 April 1844).
122 LD, 29:144, EBP to Father Belaney (20 May 1879).
123 Liddon, *Life of Pusey*, Vol. II, p. 403.
124 LD, 10:315–16, JHN to EBP (18 August 1844).
125 Liddon, *Life of Pusey*, Vol. II, p. 403.
126 Ibid., p. 406.
127 LD, 10:325, JHN to EBP (28 August 1844).
128 Liddon, *Life of Pusey*, Vol. II, p. 407.
129 LD, 10:528, JHN to EBP (6 February 1845).
130 Liddon, *Life of Pusey*, Vol. II, p. 430.
131 LD, 10:545, JHN to Charles Miller (11 February 1845).
132 LD, 10:623, JHN to Robert Francis Wilson (11 April 1845).
133 LD, 10:574, JHN to EBP (27 February 1845).
134 LD, 10:102, JHN to John Keble (23 January 1844).
135 Letter of Pusey dated 16 October 1845 from the *English Churchman*,
     quoted in Henry Parry Liddon, *Life of Edward Bouverie Pusey* (London,
     1893), Vol. 11, p. 460.
136 *Apologia*, pp. 201–02.
137 See Pusey, quoted in LD, 9:592, note 4.
138 Pusey could have seen convincing testimony to the Fathers' affirmation
     of papal primacy in the spiritual autobiography of Levi Silliman Ives, the
     Bishop of North Carolina who converted to Catholicism in 1852. In his
     autobiography, Ives confuted William Blackstone's flippant assertion that
     "the ancient British Church, by whomever planted, was a stranger to the
     Bishop of Rome and his pretended authority" by observing that the British
     historian St. Gildas (c. 493–570), although he described the Christians of
     Britain "as having become, in his time, sadly deteriorated both in faith
     and morals," still "he gave them credit … for orthodoxy in respect of the
     doctrine of the Trinity, the Incarnation of our Lord, and future rewards
     and punishments; and also stated that, among other Catholic truths and
     usages, they looked upon St. Peter as the Prince of the Apostles, and the
     source of all priestly authority in the Church." See Ives, *The Trials of a
     Mind in its Progress to Catholicism: A Letter to his Old Friends* (Boston,
     1854), pp. 215 and 221. For a more modern discussion of papal primacy
     in the Fathers, see Nicholas Afanassieff, "The Church which Presides
     in Love," in *The Primacy of Peter: Essays in Ecclesiology and the Early
     Church*, ed. John Meyendorf (New York, 1992), pp. 125–26. Apropos
     the patristic evidence for papal primacy, Afanassieff observes: "We find
     the first direct evidence about the priority of the Roman Church in the
     writings of Ignatius of Antioch. Speaking of the Church of Rome, Ignatius

uses the phrase 'which presides' in two passages … The Roman Church 'presides' in love, that is, in the concord based on love between all the local churches. The phrase 'which presides' needs no discussion; used in the masculine it means the bishop, for he, as head of the local church, sits in 'the first place' at the Eucharistic assembly, that is, in the central seat. He is truly the president of the church … Ignatius pictured the local churches grouped, as it were, in an Eucharistic assembly, with every church in its special place, and the church of Rome in the chair, sitting in the 'first place.' So, says Ignatius, the Church of Rome indeed has the priority in the whole company of churches united by concord … In his period no other church laid claim to the role, which belonged to the Church of Rome."

139 Liddon, *Life of Pusey*, Vol. II, p. 459.
140 LD, 11:9, JHN to Mrs. John Mozley (8 October 1845).
141 Liddon, *Life of Pusey*, Vol. II, p. 464.
142 LD, 11:124, JHN to EBP (21 February 1846).
143 LD, 11:127–28, JHN to EBP (26 February 1846).
144 LD, 11:128, JHN to EBP (February 1846?).
145 See *Mrs. Brookfield and her Circle*, ed. Charles and Frances Brookfield (London, 1906), p. 91.
146 LD, 11:203, JHN to Ambrose St. John (11 July 1846).
147 Liddon, *Life of Pusey*, Vol. II, p. 510.
148 *Apologia*, pp. 65–66.
149 *Anglican Difficulties*, p. 2.
150 Copleston, quoted in M. G. Brock, "The Oxford of Peel and Gladstone," in *The History of the University of Oxford: Nineteenth-Century Oxford*: ed. Brock and Curthoys (Oxford, 1997), Vol. 6, Part 1, p. 11.
151 See Owen Chadwick, *The Victorian Church* (Oxford, 1966), Vol. 1, p. 289 and John Griffin, "Newman's 'Difficulties Felt by Anglicans:' History or Propaganda?", in *The Catholic Historical Review*, Vol. 69, No. 3 (July 1983), pp. 371–83.
152 *Anglican Difficulties*, p. 105.
153 Richard H. Hutton, *Cardinal Newman* (London, 1891), p. 207.
154 LD, 13:468, JHN to F. W. Faber (28 April 1850).
155 Meriol Trevor, *Newman: The Pillar of the Crowd* (London, 1962), p. 519.
156 Hutton, *Cardinal Newman*, pp. 207–08.
157 *Anglican Difficulties*, p. 145.
158 Ibid., p. 148.
159 Ibid., p. 150.
160 Ibid., p. 151.
161 Ibid., p. 152.
162 Ibid., pp. 152–53.
163 Liddon, *Life of Pusey*, Vol. I, p. 420.
164 *Anglican Difficulties*, pp. 79–80.
165 Liddon, *Life of Pusey*, Vol. II, p. 460.
166 *Anglican Difficulties*, p. 79.
167 Ibid., pp. 79–80.

168 Ibid., p. 82.
169 Ibid., p. 88.
170 Ibid., p. 89.
171 Ibid., pp. 97–98.
172 Ibid., p. 96.
173 Ibid., pp. 97–98.
174 Ibid., p. 98.
175 Ibid., pp. 124–25. Apropos this matter, James Pereiro asks: "Did provi-
     dence intend to restore the Anglican Church to its lost perfection, or to
     direct people to Rome?" What "lost perfection" Pereiro had in mind is
     unclear. Surely, there was little perfection in the Act of Supremacy (1534).
     Nevertheless, Newman does not join Pereiro in raising the question only to
     shirk it. For Newman, Providence directed Anglicans to Rome so that they
     could free themselves of the grave imperfections of the Anglican Church.
     See Pereiro, *Ethos and the Oxford Movement* (Oxford, 2008), p. 237.
176 See David J. DeLaura, "'O Forgotten Voice:' The Memory of Newman
     in the Nineteenth Century," in *Sources for Reinterpretation: The Use of
     Nineteenth-Century Literary Documents: Essays in Honor of C.L. Cline*
     (Austin: University of Texas Press, 1975), pp. 23–25.
177 *Anglican Difficulties*, pp. 153–54.
178 For a succinct definition of the branch theory, see Colin Barr's *The
     European Culture Wars in Ireland: The Callan Schools Affair, 1868–81*
     (Dublin, 2010), pp. 127–28, where he remarks, "Gladstone's under-
     standing of the church was derived from E.B. Pusey's notion of branches:
     thus the Church of England, German's Old Catholics, Switzerland's
     Christian Catholics, the eastern Orthodox churches and the Roman
     Catholic Church itself were all members of the 'one holy catholic and
     apostolic Church' of the Anglican version of the Nicene creed."
179 The subtitle of Pusey's *Eirenicon* was "The Church of England a Portion
     of Christ's One Holy Catholic Church, and a Means of Restoring Visible
     Unity."
180 *Anglican Difficulties*, p. 170.
181 Ibid., p. 171.
182 Ibid., p. 175.
183 Ibid., pp. 211–12.
184 Ibid., p. 212.
185 Ibid., pp. 226–27.
186 LD, 11:9, JHN to EBP (8 October 1845).
187 *Anglican Difficulties*, p. 227.
188 Richard Holt Hutton, *Cardinal Newman* (London, 1891), p. 207.
189 *The Christian Reformer or Unitarian Magazine and Review* (London,
     January–December 1851), Vol. VII, p. 626.
190 *The British Quarterly Review* (London, August and November, 1850),
     Vol. XII, p. 218.
191 Ibid., p. 219.
192 Ibid., p. 225.

193 See G. K. Chesterton. "The Victorian Age in Literature" (1913) in *The Collected Works of G. K. Chesterton*, (San Francisco, 1989), Vol. 15, p. 441.

194 LD, 16:105–06, JHN to Mrs. William Froude (dated 1854/1855?).

195 LD, 20:417, JHN to Mrs. William Froude (3 March 1863).

196 LD, 21:303–04, JHN to EBP (22 November 1864).

197 LD, 21:304, EBP to JHN (24 November 1864).

198 LD, 20:428, JHN to Charles Crawley (9 April 1863).

199 *Letters of Matthew Arnold, 1848–88*, ed. G. W. E. Russell (London, 1895), Vol. 1, pp. 38–39.

200 LD, 21:143, John Keble to JHN (28 June 1864).

201 LD, 21:305, EBP to JHN (24 November 1864).

202 LD, 21:315, JHN to EBP (25 November 1864).

203 LD, 24:125, JHN to EBP (16 August 1868).

204 Henry Edward Manning, *The Workings of the Holy Spirit in the Church of England: A Letter to E.B. Pusey* (London, 1890), p. 11.

205 Manning, *The Workings of the Holy Spirit in the Church of England*, p. 33.

206 Ibid., p. 29.

207 *Apologia*, p. 342.

208 Manning, *The Workings of the Holy Spirit in the Church of England*, pp. 49–50.

209 Ibid., p. 50.

210 Ibid., pp. 41–42.

211 Liddon, *Life of Pusey*, Vol. IV, p. 99.

212 Ibid., p. 102.

213 See LD, 20:413, JHN to W. J. Copeland (23 February 1863): "It has sometimes struck me, though perhaps it would be impossible to do it, till every one was dead – whether a most interesting and authentic account of the movement could not be given, mainly by means of Letters; i.e. if Pusey, Keble, myself etc. etc. put into your hands any letters which they had, and they were published with the consent of all parties. You would edit and annotate. Froude's (in his remains) of course would come in. I think this idea would grow on you, if you read the collection of letters in my possession. As to propriety, one may consider transactions near 30 years old, historical; and it must be recollected that F. Trench, only the other day, published his letters."

214 Liddon, *Life of Pusey*, Vol. IV, p. 103.

215 LD, 21:370, JHN to EBP (4 January 1865).

216 Richard Church, *Occasional Papers* (London, 1897), Vol. I, p. 341.

217 Ibid., Vol. 1, p. 350.

218 LD, 22:90, JHN to EBP (31 October 1865). See also Roderick Strange, "Reflections on a Controversy: Newman and Pusey's 'Eirenicon'," in *Pusey Rediscovered*, ed. Perry Butler (London, 1982), p. 341.

219 Strange, "Reflections on a Controversy: Newman and Pusey's 'Eirenicon' in *Pusey Rediscovered*. Ed. Perry Butler (London, 1983)," p. 346.

220 *Letter to Pusey*, pp. 114–15.

221 Church, *Occasional Papers*, Vol. 2, p. 415.

222 LD, 22:67–69, JHN to John Keble (8 October 1865).

223 LD, 22:91, John Keble to JHN (8 October 1865).

224 LD, 22:306, JHN to Henry James Coleridge (24 October 1866).

225 Ibid.

226 LD, 28:380, JHN to Anne Mozley (6 July 1878).

227 Of course, Newman had not always shown such geniality. As a Tractarian, he brought a good deal of vitriol to his controversy with R. D. Hampden over his Bampton Lectures (1836). But when he became a Catholic, Newman mellowed. Then again, the older he became, the more experience showed him the accuracy of something he had said in his Oxford Sermon, "Faith and Reason Contrasted as a Habit of Mind" (1839): "When men understand what each other means, they see for the most part that controversy is either superfluous or hopeless." See *Oxford University Sermons* (1843), p. 201.

228 *The Idea of a University*, p. 210.

229 *Letter to Pusey*, p. 115. See also Ian Ker, *The Achievement of John Henry Newman* (Notre Dame, 1990), p. 137.

230 *Letter to Pusey*, p. 7.

231 Ibid., p. 79.

232 Church, *Occasional Papers*, Vol. 2, p. 437.

233 *Letter to Pusey*, pp. 80–81.

234 LD, 21:165, JHN to Ambrose St. John (25 July 1864).

235 Manning, quoted in *The Life and Times of Bishop Ullathorne 1806–1890* by Dom Cuthbert Butler (London, 1926), Vol. I, pp. 358–59. Certain exceptions notwithstanding, including, in our own day, Mary Kenny and Father Dermot Fenlon, England's Irishry have gravely disappointed Manning in this bold prediction. See also, Jerry White. *London in the 19th Century* (London, 2007), p. 139: "The 300,000 or so Londoners of Irish descent were more cockney than the cockneys—in speech, in locality, in the types of work they undertook, even in their abstention from religious services, as most London priests bemoaned. But their loyalty to 'Mother Church' continued to distinguish them from other sections of the London working class. And the Church, with its boys' and girls' clubs, its missions and loan societies, and above all its residual power over the imagination and susceptibilities of a community which believed its teachings to be in some magical sense 'true,' had a hold over the London Irish that was uniquely strong.'"

236 David Newsome, *The Convert Cardinals: Newman and Manning* (London, 1993), pp. 257–58.

237 LD, 22:197, Memorandum (11 May 1866).

238 LD, 21:361, JHN to EBP (28 December 1864).

239 LD, 21:401–02, JHN to EBP (3 February 1865).

240 LD, 23:294, JHN to EBP (12 August 1867).

241 LD, 25:20, JHN to Herbert Vaughan (28 January 1870).

242 See Ian Ker, *John Henry Newman: A Biography* (Oxford, 2009), pp. 651–93. Ker quotes Newman's amusing letter to Vaughan above referenced.

243 LD, 20:200, JHN to Miss Holmes (25 May 1862). See also Ker, p. 652.

244 Church, Vol. 2, pp. 364–65. Apropos these comments, it should be borne in mind that when Newman was given the red hat, it was Church, together with Gladstone, who scuttled the proposed congratulatory address that many Anglicans wished to make to the new Cardinal by refusing to participate in the address, which shows that Church might have preached magnanimity but he did not practice it. See LD, 29:xvi.

245 LD, 30:126, JHN to Lady A? (15 September 1882).

246 Church, quoted in Liddon, *Life of Pusey*, Vol. IV, p. 389.

247 Oliver Elton, *Frederick York Powell: A Life* (London, 1906), Vol. I, pp. 66–67.

248 See Thomas Huxley, "Agnosticism: A Rejoinder," in *The Nineteenth Century* (April 1889).

249 LD, 29:194–95, JHN to Octavius Ogle (5 November 1879).

250 LD, 29:195, Octavius Ogle to JHN (6 November 1879).

251 LD, 29:144, EBP to Father Belaney (20 May 1879).

252 LD, 29:349, JHN to Frederick George Lee (17 March 1881). See also *Anglican Difficulties*, Vol. I, p. 290: "Faith and love are separable."

253 *Anglican Difficulties*, p. 2.

254 LD, 22:302, T. W. Allies to JHN (19 October 1866).

Chapter 4 The Certainty of Vocation: Newman and the Froudes

1   *Discourses to Mixed Congregations*, p. 111.

2   LD, 11:78, JHN to Mrs. William Froude (24 December 1845).

3   LD, 10:51, Mrs. William Froude to JHN (1 November 1843).

4   Thomas Huxley, "On Improving Natural Knowledge," in *Lectures and Lay Sermons* (London, 1910), p. 53.

5   LD, 29:117, JHN to William Froude (29 April 1879).

6   LD, 21:245, William Froude to JHN (29 September 1864).

7   *Discourses to Mixed Congregations*, pp. 214–15.

8   Ian Ker, *The Achievement of John Henry Newman*, p. 71.

9   Sir Rowland Blennerhassett, "Some of My Recollections of Cardinal Newman," in *Cornhill Magazine*, Volume XI (July–December 1901), pp. 615–31.

10 LD, 26:213, JHN to Mrs. William Froude (21 May 1873). In December 1851, Richard Stanton wrote to Dalgairns: William Froude was in Malta and "He seems to have a great affection for him [Newman] and wishes to serve him—He proposes to go and see whether he can get anything out of the people at the protestant college [about Achilli]. He is most indignant at the account he has seen of the trial ..." See LD, 14:463.

11 Joyce Sugg, *Ever Yours Affly: John Henry Newman and his Female Circle* (London, 1996), pp. 105–06. Sugg also points out that "When all was over [with the Achilli trial] and Newman was low in health he bought port wine, ordered by the doctor, with money sent by Catherine Froude."

12 LD, 19:259, JHN to William Froude (24 December 1859).

13 Charles Stephen Dessain, *John Henry Newman* (London, 1966), p. xii.

14 LD, 29:116, JHN to William Froude (29 April 1879).

15 LD, 20:101, Mrs. William Froude to JHN (2 January 1862).

16 J. W. Burrow, *A Liberal Descent: Victorians Historians and the English Past* (Cambridge, 1981), p. 243.

17 Louise Imogen Guiney, *Hurrell Froude: Memoranda and Comments* (London, 1904), p. 216. As Newman pointed out, Hurrell came to his critical view of the Reformers only after making a careful study of them. "As to dear F., – he was a furious Church and King Man – I do believe reading mainly opened his eyes …" See LD, 3:304, JHN to Hugh James Rose (23 May 1836).

18 About Freeman, Froude complained: "He has described me as dishonest, careless of the truth, destitute of every reputable quality save facility in writing which I turn to a bad purpose." See Froude, quoted in Julia Markus, *J. Anthony Froude: The Undiscovered Great Victorian* (New York, 2005), p. 180.

19 Thomas Mozley, *Reminiscences of Oriel College and the Oxford Movement* (London, 1882), Vol. II, pp. 14–16.

20 Samuel Smiles, "Isambard Kingdom Brunel," in appendix of *Lives of the Engineers* (Folio Society, 2006), p. 360.

21 L. T. C. Rolt, *Isambard Kingdom Brunel* (London, 1957), p. 324.

22 Smiles, "Isambard Kingdom Brunel," p. 360.

23 LD, 16:103, William Froude to JHN (3 April 1854).

24 LD, 10:51, Mrs. William Froude to JHN (1 November 1843).

25 LD, 10:51–52, JHN to Mrs. William Froude (9 December 1843).

26 LD, 10:53, JHN to Mrs. William Froude (9 December 1843).

27 LD, 10:52–53, JHN to Mrs. William Froude (9 December 1843).

28 *Prophetical Office*, p. 331.

29 *Prophetical Office*, p. 355.

30 See G. K. Chesterton, *Tremendous Trifles* (London,1909), pp. 14, 134, 238.

31 Henry Chadwick, *Augustine of Hippo: A Life* (Oxford, 2009), p. 29.

32 LD, 10:53, JHN to Mrs. William Froude (9 December 1843).

33 LD, 11:7, JHN to Mrs. William Froude (8 October 1845).

34 LD, 11:113, JHN to Mrs. William Froude (15 February 1846).

35 LD, 12:223–24, JHN to Mrs. William Froude (16 June 1848).

36 James Bowell, *Life of Johnson*, ed. George Birkbeck Hill (London, 1934), Vol. IV, p. 289.

37 LD, 12:224–25, JHN to Mrs. William Froude (16 June 1848).

38 LD, 16:335, JHN to Mrs. Froude (26 December 1854).

39 See *The Collected Works of G. K. Chesterton.* (San Francisco, 1986), Vol, 1, p. 70.

40 LD, 16:66, JHN to Mrs. William Froude (2 March 1854).
41 LD, 16:108–09, JHN to Mrs. William Froude (1854/1855?).
42 LD, 17:544, JHN to Mrs. William Froude (19 March 1857).
43 LD, 10:209, JHN to Mrs. William Froude (12 April 1844).
44 LD, 12:228, JHN to Mrs. William Froude (27 June 1848).
45 LD, 14:399, JHN to Mrs. William Froude (20 October 1851).
46 LD, 17:544, JHN to Mrs. William Froude (21 March 1857).
47 "Faith and Doubt," in *Discourses to Mixed Congregations* (1849), pp. 214–37.
48 LD, 16:65, JHN to Mrs. William Froude (2 March 1854). Hurrell Froude died on 28 February 1836.
49 LD, 16:66, JHN to Mrs. William Froude (2 March 1854).
50 LD, 10:187, JHN to Mrs. William Froude (3 April 1844).
51 See Newman's Preface to Robert Nelson, *Life of George Bull D.D. Sometime Lord Bishop of St. David's* (London, 1840), p. iv.
52 LD, 10:192, JHN to Mrs. William Froude (4 April 1844). Barthold Georg Niebuhr (1776–1831), German historian of Rome born in Copehagen, about whom Magnus Magnusson wrote: "He possessed great intuitive sagacity in sifting true from false historic evidence; and though his scepticism as to the credibility of early history goes too far, the bulk of his contribution to history still stands substantially unshaken." His *Romanische Gesheschichte* is available in English translation.
53 See "Illuminating Grace," in *Discourses to Mixed Congregations*, pp. 189–90.
54 St. Augustine, *Confessions*, ed. Henry Chadwick (Oxford, 2008), p. 153.
55 LD, 12:382, JHN to Henry Wilberforce (9 December 1848).
56 Ian Ker, *John Henry Newman*, p. 342.
57 Richard Holt Hutton, *Cardinal Newman* (London, 1891), p. 197.
58 See "Faith and Private Judgment," in *Discourses to Mixed Congregations*, pp. 195–96.
59 See "Faith and Doubt," in *Discourses to Mixed Congregations*, pp. 216–17.
60 LD, 10:399, JHN to Mrs. William Froude (12 November 1844).
61 LD, 10:399–400, JHN to Mrs. William Froude (12 November 1844).
62 LD, 10:201, JHN to Mrs. William Froude (9 April 1844).
63 "Faith and Private Judgment," in *Discourses Addressed to Mixed Congregations* (1849), pp. 192–213.
64 LD, 12:227, JHN to Mrs. William Froude (27 June 1848).
65 LD, 15:307, JHN to Mrs. William Froude (23 February 1853).
66 See *The Tamworth Reading Room* (1841) in *Discussions and Arguments on Various Subjects* (1872), p. 295.
67 LD, 19:259 JHN to William Froude (24 December 1859).
68 LD, 19:268–70, William Froude to JHN (29 December 1859).
69 James Anthony Froude, "The Oxford Counter-Reformation," from *Short Studies of Great Subjects* (London, 1907), Vol. V, pp. 179–80.
70 Ibid., p. 180.

71   LD, 19:270, William Froude to JHN (29 December 1859).
72   LD, 19:270, William Froude to JHN (29 December 1859).
73   LD, 19:273, JHN to William Froude (2 January 1860).
74   LD, 19:284, William Froude to JHN (15 January 1860).
75   LD, 19:284–85, JHN to William Froude (18 January 1860).
76   LD, 27:230, JHN to Mrs. William Froude (22 February 1875).
77   LD, 25:34, JHN to Maria Giberne (18 February 1870).
78   LD, 24:184, JHN to James Hope-Scott (7 December 1868).
79   *Grammar of Assent* (New York, 1955), pp. 384–85.
80   LD, 6:198, JHN to Miss Catherine Holdsworth (6 February 1838).
81   Etienne Gilson, Introduction to *Grammar of Assent*, p. 16.
82   Ibid., p. 20.
83   *Grammar of Assent*, pp. 106–07.
84   Ibid., p. 108.
85   Ibid., p. 110
86   Sir Anthony Kenny, *Philosophy in the Modern World* (Oxford, 2007), p. 308.
87   *Grammar of Assent*, pp. 109–10.
88   Ibid., p. 396
89   See "Love the Safeguard of Faith against Superstition" (1839) in *Oxford University Sermons*, p. 171.
90   *Grammar of Assent*, pp. 397–98.
91   Ibid., p. 487
92   Ibid., p. 462: "And how is it possible to imagine with Gibbon that what he calls the 'sober and domestic virtues' of Christians, their 'aversion to the luxury of the age,' their 'chastity, temperance, and economy,' that these dull qualities were persuasives of a nature to win and melt the hard heathen heart, in spite too of the dreary prospect of the *barathrum*, the amphitheatre, and the stake? Did the Christian morality by its severe beauty make a convert of Gibbon himself? On the contrary, he bitterly says, 'It was not in this world that the primitive Christians were desirous of making themselves either agreeable or useful.' 'The virtue of the primitive Christians, like that of the first Romans, was very frequently guarded by poverty and ignorance.' 'Their gloomy and austere aspect, their abhorrence of the common business and pleasures of life, and their frequent predictions of impending calamities, inspired the Pagans with the apprehension of some danger which would arise from the new sect.' Here we have not only Gibbon hating the moral and social bearing, but his heathen also. How then were those heathen overcome by the amiableness of that which they viewed with such disgust? We have here plain proof that the Christian character repelled the heathen; where is the evidence that it converted them?" Besides being a deeply original theologian, Newman was an equally original historian, whose views of ancient, modern and contemporary history warrant closer study.
93   Ibid., p. 487
94   Ibid., p. 488

95   Ibid., pp. 487–88.
96   James Mozley, in *The Quarterly Review*, Vol. 129 (July and October 1879), p. 150.
97   F. D. Maurice, in the *Contemporary Review* (May 1870), p. 172.
98   See *ODNB*.
99   *Grammar of Assent*, pp. 256–57.
100   James Fitzjames Stephen, in *Fraser's Magazine* (May 1870), pp. 572–73.
101   Gilson, Introduction, p. 18.
102   Frederick Copleston, S.J., *A History of Philosophy* (London, 1967), Volume 8, Part II, p. 275 Copleston quotes from Oxford University Sermons, p. 230.
103   *Grammar of Assent*, pp. 198–200.
104   See David K. Brown. *The way of a ship in the midst of the sea: the life and work of William Froude.* (Penzance, 2006), p. i.
105   LD, 20:427–28, JHN to Sister Mary Gabriel Du Boulay (7 April 1863). The eldest girl, Elizabeth, "Isy," and the two eldest boys, Richard Hurrell and Arthur, had already become Catholics. The conversion of Robert Edmund, to which Newman refers in this letter, particularly dismayed William because he assumed that "Eddy" would become something of his protégé.
106   LD, 28:86, Mrs. William Froude to JHN (5 July 1876).
107   *Report and Transactions of the Devonshire Association for the Advancement of Science, Literature and Art* (July 1879), Vol. XI, p. 57.
108   LD, 21:175, Mrs. William Froude to JHN (30 July 1864).
109   LD, 29:120, JHN to William Froude (29 April 1879).
110   LD, 27:343–44, JHN to Edmond G. A. Holmes (13 August 1875).

Chapter 5 A Better Country: Newman's Idea of Public Life

1   Christopher Hibbert, *The Destruction of Lord Raglan: A Tragedy of the Crimean War* (London, 1963), p. 343.
2   LD, 16:340, JHN to Lord Blachford (23 May 1885).
3   "Who's to Blame?" (1855) in *Discussions and Arguments*, pp. 343–44.
4   LD, 31:35, JHN to Elizabeth Deane (27 February 1885).
5   *Selected Letters of Henry James*, ed. Edel (London, 1956), p. 112.
6   LD, 30:69, JHN to J. Walker of Scarborough (1 January 1855).
7   See the *Rambler* (September 1859), Letter to the Editor, "Napoleonism Not Impious."
8   Herbert Butterfield, *The Whig Interpretation of History* (London, 1931). Geoffrey Elton, *Policy and Police* (Cambridge, 1972). Eamon Duffy, *The Stripping of the Altars* (New Haven, 1992).
9   *Present Position of Catholics in England*, p. 63.
10   Robert Blake, *Disraeli* (London, 1967), p. 209.
11   Andrew Roberts, *Salisbury: A Victorian Titan* (London, 1999), p. 12,

12   Robert Rhodes James, *Rosebery* (London, 1963), p. 217.
13   Rosebery, quoted in Leo McKinstry, *Rosebery: Statesman in Turmoil* (London, 2005), p. 191.
14   LD, 28:351, note; see *The Times* (26 April 1878).
15   LD, 28:123, JHN to R. W. Church (15 October 1876).
16   LD, 2:125, JHN to Mrs. Elizabeth Newman (1 March 1829).
17   LD, 3:55, JHN to Charles Portales Golightly (10 June 1832).
18   LD, 3:242, JHN to Thomas Mozley (9 March 1833).
19   Lytton Strachey, *Eminent Victorians* (London, 1918), p. 121.
20   LD, 3:90, JHN to Samuel Francis Wood (4 September 1832).
21   Boswell, *Life of Johnson* (Oxford, 1934), Vol 2, p. 106.
22   "Wisdom and Innocence," (1843) in *Sermons on Subjects of the Day*, p. 300.
23   "Faith and the World," (1838) in *Sermons on Subjects of the Day*, Sermon 7, p. 91.
24   "Submission to Church Authority" (1836), in *Parochial Sermons*, Book 3, Sermon 14.
25   *Apologia*, p. 146.
26   Flannery O'Connor, *Mystery and Manners* (New York, 1969), p. 34.
27   "The Religion of the Day" (1832), in *Parochial Sermons*, Vol. I, p. 24.
28   *Anglican Difficulties*, p. 240.
29   "Conditions of the Members of the Christian Empire," (1840) in *Sermons on Subjects of the Day*, p. 274.
30   *Apologia*, p. 296.
31   *Tamworth Reading Room* (1841), in *Discussions and Arguments*, p. 268.
32   *The Idea of a University*, p. 121.
33   See Jenkins, in *Newman: A Man for Our Time*, ed. David Brown (Connecticut, 1990), p. 155.
34   *The Idea of a University*, p. 166.
35   *Letters of Sidney Smith*, ed. Nowel-Smith (Oxford, 1953), Vol. 2, p. 766.
36   Ian Ker, *Newman and the Fullness of Christianity* (Edinburgh, 1993), p. 81.
37   *Essay on the Development of Doctrine* (1845), pp. 357–58.
38   Edward Norman, *The English Catholic Church in the Nineteenth Century* (Oxford, 1984), p. 156.
39   "For The Dead," in *Verses on Various Occasions*, p. 315.
40   *The Rise and Progress of Universities*, pp. 130–32.
41   Theodore Hoppen, *The Mid-Victorian Generation: 1846–1886* (Oxford, 1998), p. 614.
42   LD, 26:55, JHN to Frederick George Lee (5 April 1872).
43   LD, 28:180, JHN to Lord Blachford (14 March 1877).
44   LD, 28:388, JHN to Lord Blachford (22 July 1878).
45   LD, 4:339–43 (October 1834).
46   "Profession without Ostentation," (1831) in *Parochial Sermons*, Vol. I, p. 14.
47   *Newman and Gladstone on the Vatican Decrees*, ed. Ryan (Notre Dame, 1962), p. 12.

48 William Ullathorne, *Mr.Gladstone's Expostulation Unravelled* (New York, 1875), pp. 19 and 37–38.
49 *Grammar of Assent*, p. 33.
50 *Apologia*, p. 340.
51 LD, 14:134, JHN to James Hope (20 November 1850).
52 From Matthew Arnold, "Dover Beach" (1851).
53 *Anglican Difficulties*, pp. 247–48.
54 "Preparation for the Judgment" (1848), in *Faith and Prejudice and Other Sermons*, p. 38.
55 LD, 8:415, JHN to John Keble (6 January 1842): "I do not agree with Gladstone ... Again his great object is the religionizing the State ..."
56 LD, 27:265, JHN to John Rickards Mozley (4 April 1875).
57 "The Danger of Riches," (1835) in *Parochial Sermons*, Book 2, Sermon 28, p. 353.
58 "The World Our Enemy," (1829) in *Parochial Sermons*, Book 7, Sermon 3, p. 33.
59 "The Danger of Accomplishments," (1831) in *Parochial Sermons*, Book 2, Sermon 30, p. 369.
60 *Letter to Pusey*, p. 89.
61 "In the World But Not Of The World," (1873) in *Sermons on Various Occasion*, *Sermon* 14, pp. 275–76.

Chapter 6 Newman and the Female Faithful

1   LD, 30:67, JHN to Geraldine Penrose Fitzgerald (17 March 1882). The Anglo-Irish Fitzgerald, who was as committed a Unionist as Gerard Manley Hopkins, must have bemused Newman when she reported to him in an undated letter: "I am at present engaged in writing a novel in which my design is to bring out the difference between the Irish and the English characters, the utter absence of all conception of truthfulness in the Irish brought into as sharp relief as I can place it with the sturdy unbending honesty of the English nature ..." See LD, 30:111, note 1.
2   Students of Tractarianism may recall Maria Giberne from Tom Mozley's *Reminiscences of Oriel and the Oxford Movement* (1882), where he describes her as "tall, strong of build, majestic, with aquiline nose, well-formed mouth, dark penetrating eyes, and a luxuriance of glossy black hair. She would command attention anywhere." Newman's brother Frank had an unrequited crush on her, which drove him to find solace in the wilds of Persia. See Mozley, Vol. II, p. 44.
3   LD, 1:151, JHN to Mrs. Jemima Newman (5 November 1822).
4   LD:13.239, JHN to Maria Giberne (23 July 1849):
5   *The Autobiography of Isaac Williams, B.D.*, ed. George Prevost (London, 1892), p. 61.
6   LD, 10:303, JHN to Aunt Elizabeth Newman (25 July 1844).

7   LD, 21:131, JHN to Sister Mary Gabriel du Boulay (25 June 1864).

8   See Charlotte Bronte. *Jane Eyre* (London, 1850), p. 186.

9   LD, 20:447, JHN to Emily Bowles (19 May 1863).

10   LD, 20:216, JHN to the Editor of the *Morning Advertiser* (29 June 1862).

11   LD, 20:453, JHN to Emily Bowles (29 May 1863).

12   LD, 20:454, JHN to Emily Bowles (29 May 1863).

13   LD, 24:280, Emily Bowles to JHN (3 June 1869). See note 3.

14   See Joseph Spence's excellent entry on Lecky in the new *ODNB*. As Spence notes, Lecky was "both the first national historian of Ireland and the first 'revisionist' of the nationalist idealization of Ireland," whose work on Ireland has been unjustly neglected. F. S. L. Lyons and J. J. Lee, modern Ireland's best historians, owed much to his pioneering example.

15   See *Alfred Lord Tennyson: The Major Works*, ed. Adam Roberts (Oxford, 2000), p. 527.

16   Emily Bowles, quoted in Meriol Trevor, *Newman: The Pillar of the Cloud* (London, 1962), p. 113.

17   Emily C. Agnew, *Geraldine: A Tale of Conscience*, single-volume edition (London, 1868), pp. 564–66. After reviewing the novel, which he considered a piece of straightforward, if bungling propaganda that sought to recommend the Church of Rome to English Protestants, Newman wrote to Catherine Holdsworth in April 1838, before she married William Froude: "… you could, I feel sure, be of use to the cause of Catholic Truth … Certainly we do want tales on our side very much – to take people's imagination – as such works as Geraldine on the one side and Father Clement [an anti-Catholic novel] on the other show – and I should much rejoice if persons such as yourself gave the composition of them a fair trial." See LD, 6:238, JHN to Catherine Holdsworth (27 April 1838). As it happened, Catherine was too busy bringing up her six children to undertake novel writing.

18   See Newman's review of *Geraldine* in *British Critic*, Vol. 24 (July 1838).

19   See the *British Critic*, Vol. 24 (July 1838).

20   See Matthew Arnold, "Emerson", from *Discourses in America* (New York, 1924), p. 141 and Emily Bowles, quoted in Trevor, *Newman: The Pillar of the Cloud*, p. 276.

21   Emily Bowles, quoted in Meriol Trevor, *Newman: Light in Winter* (London, 1962), p. 279.

22   Emily Bowles, quoted in Trevor, *Newman: The Pillar of the Cloud*, p. 320.

23   Sugg, *Ever Yours Affly*, pp. 65–67. Anyone familiar with this gem of a book will know that my indebtedness to it is immense. Also see *A Packet of Letters: A Selection from the Correspondence of John Henry Newman*, ed. Joyce Sugg (Oxford, 1983).

24   Trevor, *Newman: Light in Winter*, p. 391. Some complain that Trevor neglects Newman's writings and spends too much time defending him, especially with regard to his differences with the London Oratory. These are false complaints. Trevor brings out the Cardinal's vital personal qualities (without which his writings cannot be understood) and in

defending him shows how principle, not pique, animated his sometimes rocky relationship with the London Oratory.

25 Emily Bowles, quoted in Sugg, *Ever Yours Affly*, p. 71.

26 See *DNB*.

27 Thackeray met Lady Georgiana in London in 1852, when they discussed Miss Holmes, the governess, who at that time was without work, ·and the Achilli trial, about which he observed: "as the law is, the verdict was right—though I think the Judge's behaviour in the trial was most unfair and unworthy." Among several unfairnesses, Lord Campbell forbade Newman from delivering a speech he had prepared for his defense. See *The Letters and Private Papers of William Makepeace Thackeray*, ed. Gordon Ray (Harvard, 1946), Vol. III, p. 66.

28 Coincidentally enough, Father Brownbill lived in the Jesuit house at No. 15 Bolton Street, Piccadilly, at the same time that Henry James lived at No. 3.

29 LD, 15:236, JHN to Lady Georgiana Fullerton (1 January 1853).

30 William Gladstone, Review of *Ellen Middleton* in *The English Review*, Vol. 1 (April–July 1844), p. 337.

31 Ibid., p. 359.

32 LD, 10:295, JHN to Edward Bouverie Pusey (11 July 1844).

33 LD, 13:475, JHN to Mrs. Henry Wilberforce (27 May 1850).

34 LD, 9:523, JHN to Mrs. John Mozley (15 September 1843).

35 See David Bebbington, *The Mind of Gladstone: Religion, Homer and Politics* (Oxford, 2004), pp. 81–82: "Although Gladstone felt the characters in *Ellen Middleton* were unamiable, he judged Lady Georgiana Fullerton, its author, to be what was all too rare, 'the true preacher in the guise of a novelist …'"

36 William Gladstone, Review of *Ellen Middleton* in *The English Review*, Vol. 1 (April–July, 1844), p. 336.

37 See Article V, "Lady Georgina Fullerton," by Emily Bowles in *Dublin Review*, Vol. 20 (October–July 1888), p. 334.

38 Bessie Raynor Belloc, *In a Walled Garden* (London, 1895), p. 112.

39 *Tamworth Reading Room*, pp. 281–82.

40 Henry James, *Portraits of Places* (Boston and New York, 1883), pp. 190–97.

41 LD, 21:456, JHN to Emily Bowles (1 May 1865).

42 See Emily Bowles, *St. Martin's Home or Work for Women* (Dublin, 1864) and *The Inner Life of Lady Georgiana Fullerton* (London, 1899).

43 See Henry Mayhew, *London Characters and Crooks* (Folio Society, 1996), pp. 18–19.

44 See *The Month*, Vol. 1 (XX) (January–April 1874), p. 258.

45 See LD, 27:13, note 1.

46 H. H. Munro ('Saki'), *Reginald* (London, 1904), p. 13. Chartreuse is made by the monks of La Grande-Chartreuse (the head monastery of the Carthusians, near Grenoble) with aromatic herbs and brandy.

47 LD, 20:396 JHN to W. G. Ward (16 January 1863)
48 LD, 23: 324 JHN to Emily Bowles (27 August 1867).
49 LD, 24:341. Emily Bowles recounts this scene in her unpublished "Memorials of John Henry Newman."
50 LD, 23:365 JHN to Lady Simeon (10 November 1867).
51 Trevor, *Newman: Light in Winter*, p. 516.
52 LD, 27:204, Emily Bowles to JHN (27 January 1875).
53 See Wilfred Ward, *William George Ward and the Catholic Revival* (London 1893), p. 272.
54 Cuthbert Butler, *Life and Times of Bishop Ullathorne* (New York, 1926), p. 312.
55 LD, 23:16, JHN to Emily Bowles (8 January 1867).
56 LD, 20:446, JHN to Emily Bowles (19 May 1863).
57 LD, 28:13, JHN to Emily Bowles (15 January 1876).
58 Trevor, *Newman: Light in Winter*, p. 537.
59 LD, 32:428, JHN to Octavian Blewitt (8 May 1881).
60 See LD, 23:96, note 1. "*Pall Mall Gazette*, which was founded in London in 1865, took its name from a fictional paper that Thackeray described in *Pendennis*, the founder of which declares: We address ourselves to the higher circles of society: we care not to disown it—the Pall Mall Gazette is written by gentlemen for gentlemen; its conductors speak to the classes in which they live and were born. The field-preacher has his journal, the radical free-thinker has his journal: why should the Gentlemen of England be unrepresented in the Press?"
61 LD, 25:326–27, JHN to Emily Bowles (30 April 1871).
62 LD, 26:228, JHN to Canon Walker (5 January 1873).
63 Lady Georgiana's only son died of a brain tumor in 1854 when he was 21. Both she and her husband mourned him for the rest of their lives.
64 Belloc, *In A Walled Garden*, p. 108.
65 See Article V in *Dublin Review*, Third Series, Vol. 20, 1888, p. 328.
66 See the *ODNB* entry for Charles Worth.
67 Madeleine Beard, *Faith and Fortune* (London, 1997), p. 84.
68 See LD, 14:469, note 1 and *Cecil Marchioness of Lothian a Memoir*, ed. Cecil Kerr (London, n.d. [about 1920]), p. 111.
69 See LD, 5:263 JHN to Maria Giberne (20 March 1836).
70 LD, 16:365, JHN to Lady Lothian (26 January 1855).
71 LD, 26:309, JHN to Marchioness of Lothian (10 May 1873).
72 LD, 25:326–27, JHN to Emily Bowles (30 April 1871).
73 LD, 22:194, JHN to Lady Chatterton (Holy Thursday 1866).
74 LD, 29:181, JHN to Lady Herbert of Lea (6 October 1879).
75 LD, 22:194, JHN to Lady Chatterton (29 March 1866).
76 Edward Heneage Dering, *Memoirs of Georgiana, Lady Chatterton* (London and Leamington, 1901), p. 188. Apropos Ullathorne, Newman said after they had first crossed swords: "Just as gentlemen make acquaintance with bowing and civil speeches, so the way to be good friends with him is to begin with a boxing bout." After this initial skirmish, both formed a long

and deep respect for one another. Cf. LD, 12:337, JHN to J. M. Capes (19 November 1848).

77 Ibid., p. 217.
78 LD, 27:358, JHN to Lady Chatterton (20 September 1875).
79 Ullathorne, quoted in Judith Champ, *William Bernard Ullathorne: A Different Kind of Monk* (London, 2006), p. 412.
80 Dering, *Memoirs of Georgiana, Lady Chatterton*, p. 37.
81 Ibid., pp. 33–34.
82 Ibid., pp. 37–38.
83 Ibid., p. 61.
84 Ibid., pp. 63–64.
85 Sugg, *Ever Yours Affly*, p. 162.
86 Dering, *Memoirs of Georgiana, Lady Chatterton*, p. 171.
87 LD, 22:194 JHN to Lady Chatterton (Holy Thursday 1866).
88 Ibid., p. 195.
89 LD, 19:122, JHN to Isy Froude (8 May 1859).
90 LD, 24:248, JHN to Louisa Simeon (29 April 1869).
91 LD, 24:275, JHN to Louisa Simeon (25 June 1869).
92 After Julia's death, Arnold looked back on their stormy marriage and confessed to a friend who had advised against the marriage: "Your advice was quite sound, for in many ways we were quite unsuited to one another; and yet not only was it *impossible* for me to take it, for she had subjugated me by her beauty to that degree that I belonged much more to her than to myself—but now I thank God with all my heart for having given us to one another, and hope, and believe, that I shall see and know my darling again on the other side of the grave." See Bernard Bergonzi, *A Victorian Wanderer: A Life of Thomas Arnold the Younger* (Oxford, 2003), pp. 86 and 222.
93 LD, 24:34, JHN to Maria Giberne (11 February 1868).
94 LD, 28:19 JHN to Mrs. William Robinson Clark (27 January 1876).
95 LD, 28:115, JHN to William Robinson Clark (27 September 1876).
96 LD, 28:203, JHN to Vicar Clark (early in June 1877).
97 LD, 28:203, note 4.
98 The idea of conversion as delusion would give way in Ronald Knox's youth to conversion as bluff. In his autobiography, Knox observes how "… the *coterie* to which I belonged had a peculiar attitude towards conversion. It was thought of … as a kind of threat, useful for bargaining purposes; almost as a kind of blackmail. Very much as the representative of an Eastern European country will insist on having its own way at some conclave of the United Nations, making it clear that if he does not get his own way he will walk out, we thought and talked of submission to Rome as a useful weapon when we were trying to avert scandals in the Establishment. 'You mean to admit Nonconformists, publicly and officially to Communion? Very well then, I shall become a Roman Catholic.' When … your bluff was called, you would have to decide whether or not you really meant it. Thus we used to account for any defection from our own

ranks by the unsympathetic attitude of the Anglican authorities: 'He went over in the Brighton row,' was a typical epitaph." See Ronald Knox, *A Spiritual Aneid* (London, 1958), p. xvi.

99 LD, 11:18, JHN to Edward Badeley (19 October 1845).

100 LD, 11:62, note 2.

101 LD, 16:305, The Earl of Dunraven to JHN (30 November 1854)

102 LD, 28:329, JHN to Mrs. William Robinson Clark (14 March 1878).

103 Cf. Deuteronomy 30:10–14: "This commandment which I command you this day is not too hard for you, neither is it far off. It is not in heaven, that you should say, 'Who will go up for us to heaven, and bring it to us, that we may hear it and do it?' Neither is it beyond the sea, that you should say, 'Who will go over the sea for us, and bring it to us, that we may hear it and do it?' But the word is very near you; it is in your mouth and in your heart, so that you can do it."

104 I am using *perseverance* in the non-technical sense, which the OED defines thus: "The fact, process, condition, or quality of persevering; constant persistence in a course of action, purpose, or state; steadfast pursuit of an aim; tenacious assiduity of endeavour."

105 LD, 26:231, JHN to Miss M. R. Giberne (9 January 1873). In writing to Miss Giberne over the years (later Sister Pia), Newman was always full of good counsel: "I am grieved indeed at your illness, it arises from the damp. I wonder whether you have flannel next your skin. An old lady, a penitent of mine here, had rheumatism. I managed that she should get some woollen underclothing – and she has had no rheumatism since. It is only by constant vigilance that I keep rheumatism from me – and I doubt not if I did half the imprudent things you (I suppose) do every day, I should be laid up. I wish you had a good English doctor. Do you take quinine?"

106 LD, 14:29, JHN to Mary Holmes (31 July 1850).

107 *Autobiographical Writings* (15 December 1859), p. 251.

108 LD, 15:113–14, JHN to Sister Mary Agnes Philip (27 June 1852).

109 LD, 28:332, JHN to Stella Austin (21 March 1878).

110 LD, 14:292–93, JHN to Mrs. Lucy Agnes Vaughan Phillips (5 June 1851).

111 See LD, 17:272, note 3, "Obedience the Best Remedy for Religious Perplexity" (1830).

112 See "Obedience the Remedy for Religious Perplexity" (1830), p. 230 and 241; and Ian Ker's introduction to his *John Henry Newman: Selected Sermons* (1994).

113 LD, 25:68, JHN to Mary Holmes (26 March 1870).

114 LD, 21:182, JHN to Mary Holmes (3 August 1864). For such a literary governess as Miss Holmes, it was fitting that she should have been engaged by the Blounts, an old Catholic family, one of whose members was Martha Blount (1690–1763), who had a very rocky relationship with her fellow Catholic, Alexander Pope, whose *Epistle to a Lady on the Characters of Women* (1753) contains a long tribute to her. The poet was actually fond of both Martha and her sister Teresa, though as he wrote in a letter

addressed to both of them: "I have some times found myself inclined to be in love with you: [but] as I have reason to know from your Temper & Conduct how miserably I should be used in that circumstance, it is worth my while to avoid it." See ODNB entry for Martha Blount.

115 LD, 25:132, JHN to Mary Holmes (22 May 1870): "It amused me to find that Allies and Dalgairns found my book difficult. I don't say it is not – but I know that, among clever men, they are the least clearheaded that I know – and I have long thought so."

116 LD, 10:157, Miss Mary Homes to JHN (6 March 1844).

117 LD, 10:166, JHN to Miss Mary Holmes (15 March 1844).

118 LD, 9:184, JHN to Mary Holmes (27 January 1842).

119 *Anglican Difficulties*, p. 2.

120 LD, 12:267, Catherine Ward to JHN (22 September 1848). See also Ian Ker's wonderfully witty demolition of Owen Chadwick's claim that it was Newman, *pace* Catherine Ward, who was in search of an ideal church, which can be found in Ker, *Newman and the Fullness of Christianity*, pp. 103–22.

121 LD, 12:273, JHN to Catherine Ward (25 September 1848).

122 Henry Mayhew, *London Characters and Crooks* (Folio Society, 1998), p. 18.

123 What R. A. Soloway found in his study of the Anglican clergy and the poor still rings true: "More often [Anglican clergymen] distrusted the poor, feared them, and in some instances clearly loathed them. Since the lower orders could not be loved as they were, it was necessary that they be changed. It was necessary to strip them, scrub them, clean, and reclothe them in the reassuring and recognizable garments of middle-class virtue ..." One does not need to share Soloway's distaste for soap to agree that nineteenth-century Anglican clergymen found the poor's aversion to soap an often insuperable barrier to considering them fully Christian. See R. A. Soloway, *Prelates and People: Ecclesiastical Social Thought in England 1783–1852* (Oxford, 1969), p. 164.

124 LD, 12:273, JHN to Catherine Ward (25 September 1848).

125 See *Daily Mail* (13 August 1890).

126 LD, 12:274–75, JHN to Catherine Ward (25 September 1848).

127 LD, 12:291, JHN to Catherine Ward (12 October 1848).

128 LD, 12:334, JHN to Catherine Ward (18 November 1848).

129 LD, 12:335, JHN to Catherine Ward (18 November 1848).

130 LD, 12:354 JHN to Catherine Ward (30 November 1848).

131 See *Apologia*, p. 543 and *Essays*, Vol. I, p. 101.

132 LD, 12:354, JHN to Catherine Ward (30 November 1848).

133 LD, 12:378, JHN to Catherine Ward (19 December 1848).

134 LD, 12:335, JHN to Catherine Ward (18 November 1848).

135 LD, 24:275, JHN to Louisa Simeon (25 June 1869).

136 LD, 24:275–76, JHN to Louisa Simeon (25 June 1869).

137 See James Joyce, quoted in Richard Ellmann, *James Joyce*, revised edn (Oxford, 1982), p. 678. Joyce said this apropos his schizophrenic daughter, Lucia, in a letter to his old friend from university days, C. P. Curran: "It is terrible to think of a vessel of election as the prey of impulses beyond

its control and of natures beneath its comprehension and, fervently as I desire her cure, I ask myself what then will happen when and if she finally withdraws her regard from the lightning-lit revery of her clairvoyance and turns it upon that battered cabman's face, the world."

138 John Hungerford Pollen, "Newman in Dublin," in *The Month* (September 1906), pp. 318–20.
139 LD, 22:247–48, JHN to Marianne Frances Bowden (8 June 1866). This Marianne Bowden should not be confused with the Mary Anne Bowden (1831–1867), who was the oldest daughter of Elizabeth and W. J. Bowden and became Sr. Mary Frances Dominica, to whom Newman was very close and who died young, like her father, of tuberculosis. Newman regarded her as one of his most faithful friends. See Joyce Sugg, *Ever Yours Affly*, pp. 177–85.
140 William Ullathorne, *Patience and Humility: A Handbook for Christians* (Sophia Press, 1998), p. 5.
141 Cf. Christina Rossetti's poem, "Cardinal Newman," which opens with these lines, "O weary Champion of the Cross, lie still/Sleep thou at length the all-embracing sleep/Long was thy sowing day, rest now and reap/Thy fast was long, feast now thy spirit's fill." See *Complete Poems* (Penguin, 2001), p. 584.
142 See "Love, the One Thing Needful" (1839) in *Plain and Parochial Sermons*, Book 5, Sermon 23, pp. 339–40.
143 Ibid., p. 340.
144 Sugg, *Ever Yours Affly*, p. 5.
145 Ibid., p. 298.
146 LD, 13:419, JHN to Miss Munro (11 February 1850).

Chapter 7 Newman and Gladstone

1 Sir Robert Ensor, *England 1870–1914* (Oxford, 1936), p. 137.
2 According to one historian of bibliomania, "William Gladstone ... bought and sold whole libraries at a time; book dealers were often able to sell his own books back to him, and he didn't notice." See Julie Rugg. *Buried in Books: A Reader's Anthology* (London, 2010), p. 7. It was in 1840 that Newman began systematically putting together his wonderful library, which is preserved at the Birmingham Oratory. His account books show that he spent £858 on books during the course of this year alone. See *The Letters and Diaries of John Henry Newman*, Vol. 8, p. 34, n. 4; also Vol. 7, p. 231, n. 4. The *Letters and Diaries* are hereinafter cited as *LD*.
3 *Henry James: A Life in Letters*, ed. Horne (London, 1999), p. 80.
4 In August 1846, Newman attended the consecration of Cheadle Church with Lord Shrewsbury, the patron of Pugin and benefactor of the Catholic revival in the Midlands; later, Newman described the ordeal to St. John

Ambrose: "A house full of company and I looking like a fool ..." (LD, 11:241). As Meriol Trevor remarks, Newman "was never comfortable at parties in high society." (Trevor, *Newman: The Pillar of the Cloud.* p. 392.

5   E. F. Benson, *As We Were: A Victorian Peep Show* (London, 1930), p. 47.

6   T. B. Macaulay, *Prose and Poetry*, ed. Young (Harvard, 1970), p. 610: "Why go as deep into a question as Burke, only in order to be, like Burke, coughed down, or left speaking to green benches and red boxes." See also Michael Holroyd, *A Strange Eventful History: The Dramatic Lives of Ellen Terry and Henry Irving and Their Remarkable Families* (London, 2008), p. 259: "It has been suggested that Gladstone, who like Irving had been expected by his mother to be ordained into the Church, learnt some of his oratorical techniques from studying Irving's performances."

7   K. T. Hoppen, *The Mid-Victorian Generation 1846–1886* (Oxford, 1998), p. 688.

8   M. Ward, *Young Mr. Newman* (New York, 1948), p. 315.

9   Coleridge, quoted in LD, 15:284.

10   Guizot's *Lectures on European Civilization* also informed aspects of Newman's understanding of doctrinal development. See John Henry Newman, *An Essay on the Development of Christian Doctrine*, ed. J. M. Cameron (London, 1974). Newman quotes Guizot at length in Chapter 1, Section II. One of Guizot's observations tallies with a good deal of Newman's thinking on the relationship between faith and the doctrines that the Church has adopted to define it. "There are problems in human nature, in human destinies," Guizot wrote, "which cannot be solved in this life, which depend on an order of things unconnected with the visible world, but which unceasingly agitate the human mind with a desire to comprehend them. The solution of these problems is the origin of all religion; her primary object is to discover the creeds and doctrines which contain, or are supposed to contain it." (P. 112)

11   William Ewart Gladstone (WEG), quoted in Roy Jenkins, *Gladstone: A Biography* (New York, 1995), p. 281.

12   LD, 1:219, JHN to Charles Newman (24 March 1825).

13   John Henry Newman. *Rise and Progress of Universities and Benedictine Essays* (University of Notre Dame Press, 2001), p. 31: "There are those who, having felt the influence of this ancient School, and being smit with its splendour and its sweetness, ask wistfully, if never again it is to be Catholic, or whether at least some footing for Catholicity may not be found there. All honour and merit to the charitable and zealous hearts who so inquire!"

14   G. M. Young, "Mr. Gladstone," from *Today and Yesterday* (London, 1948), p. 18.

15   G. M. Young, "The Schoolman in Downing Street," from *Daylight and Champaign* (London, 1948), p. 56.

16   Gladstone quoted in H. C. G. Matthew. *Gladstone 1809–1898* (Oxford, 1997), p. 633.

17   LD, 11:7, JHN to F. W. Faber (8 October 1845).

18   LD, 22:241, JHN to W. J. Copeland (27 May 1866).

19   Wilfrid Ward, *The Life of John Henry Newman* (London, 1912), Vol. II, pp. 429–30. Edward White Benson (1829–1896) was also struck by the lines on Newman's face. In 1848, when he first heard him preach at St. Chad's, he told a correspondent: "His appearance was exceedingly interesting; he was very much emaciated, and when he began his voice was very feeble, and he spoke with great difficulty, nay sometimes he gasped for breath; but his voice was very sweet … But oh, Lightfoot, never you turn Romanist if you are to have a face like that—it was awful—the terrible lines deeply ploughed all over his face, and the craft that sat upon his retreating forehead and sunken eyes. He was a strange spectacle altogether …" See Trevor, *Newman: The Pillar of the Cloud*, pp. 431–32. Trevor's response to this is characteristically sensible: "Benson was perhaps too young to realize that other things besides craft may line a man's face" (p. 432). Benson was 19 and Newman 46 at the time.

20   Philip Magnus, *Gladstone* (London, 1954), p. 217.

21   Andrew Roberts, *Salisbury: Victorian Titan* (London, 1999), p. 366. It is interesting that this view of Gladstone should have passed from Salisbury to one of his sons, Lord Robert Cecil (1864–1958), the architect of the League of Nations. After hearing his brother Lord William Cecil (1863–1936) preach on England's duty to show moral leadership in the world, he wrote: "I have had a great feeling that I have been 'called' to preach the League spirit in public affairs and there seems so much in the Bible about that kind of thing … And yet there is the great danger of hypocrisy and self-deception as with Gladstone." See Kenneth Rose, *The Later Cecils* (London, 1975), pp. 159–60.

22   See William Allingham, *The Diaries*, ed. H. Allingham and D. Radford (Folio Society, 2007), p. 311.

23   D. C. Lathbury (ed.), *Correspondence on Church and Religion of W. E. Gladstone* (London, 1910), Vol. 1, pp. 248–49.

24   Ibid., p. 281, WEG to Manning (24 October 1843).

25   Lathbury, *Correspondence on Church and Religion of W. E. Gladstone* Vol. 1, p. 281.

26   LD, 9:585, JHN to Henry Edward Manning (25 October 1843).

27   Gladstone to Manning (28 October 1843), from Lathbury, Vol. 1, p. 283.

28   Gladstone to Manning (24 October 1843), from Lathbury, Vol. 1, p. 281.

29   Gladstone to Manning (30 October 1843), from Lathbury, Vol. 1, pp. 286–87.

30   Gladstone to Manning (28 October 1843), from Lathbury, Vol. 1, p. 283.

31   Gladstone to Manning (31 December 1843), from Lathbury, Vol. 1, p. 291.

32   LD, 10:165, JHN to James Hope (14 March 1844).

33   Gladstone to Manning (20 October 1845), from Lathbury, Vol. 1, p. 349.

34   Gladstone, Letter to *The Times* (31 January 1842), from Lathbury, Vol. 1, pp. 277–78.

35   LD, 4:67, John Bowden to JHN (28 October 1833).

36 See C. G. Checkland, *The Gladstones: A Family Biography 1764–1851* (Cambridge, 1971), p. 96.

37 See H. C. G. Matthew, *Gladstone 1809–1898* (Oxford, 1997), p. 317: The daily routine at Hawarden involved Gladstone in a good deal of exercise: "the early morning walk through the Park to the Church and back (along a specially built path to ensure privacy), walking in the surrounding countryside and, of course, silviculture, felling and planting trees. Gladstone always used an axe, and in these years many were presented to him. It became almost a totem among his admirers. Margaret de Lisle, daughter of the convert to Catholicism, always wore an axe to indicate loyalty to Gladstone, until Gordon's death in 1885, when she took it off."

38 See Checkland, *The Gladstones*, p. 96.

39 John Campbell, *F.E. Smith: First Earl of Birkenhead* (London, 1983), p. 73.

40 John Morley, *The Life of Gladstone* (London, 1903), Vol. I, p. 637.

41 Ibid., p. 640.

42 Ibid., p. 638.

43 Ibid., p. 43.

44 H. C. G. Matthew, *Gladstone: 1809–1898* (Oxford, 1997), p. 53.

45 Ibid., p. 94.

46 Benjamin Disraeli, in *The Times*, 29 July 1878.

47 Philip Magnus, *Gladstone* (London, 1954), p. 35.

48 The Jerusalem Bishopric, the brainchild of the Anglophile Baron Bunsen, was a joint bishopric established in 1841 to serve both Lutherans and Anglicans in Syria, Chaldaea, Egypt and Abyssinia. The scheme went kaput in 1886 after Lutherans decided that they had enough of episcopacy. Originally, many English Evangelicals supported it because it would 'uncatholicize' the Tractarians; some High Churchmen because it would extend the principle of episcopacy; and most liberals because they thought it would help realize their ideal of a non-dogmatic Church. In his protest to the Bishop of Oxford, Newman wrote: "I have now been for a long while assuring persons that the English Church was a branch of the Church Catholic. If then a measure is in progress which cuts from under me the very ground on which I have been writing and talking, and to prove that all I hold is a mere theory and illusion, a paper theology that facts contradict, who will not excuse it if I am deeply pained … ?" (JHN to J. R. Hope, 24 November 1841, LD, 8:345) Once the bishopric became reality, Newman predicted, "I shall not be able to keep a single man from Rome. They will be all trooping off …" (JHN to J. Bowden, 10 October 1841, LD 8:289). Four years later, he himself would be one of those troopers. Gladstone sensed as much himself and referred to the episode as "one of the saddest and most anxious" in which he had ever been engaged (P. Butler, *Gladstone: Church, State and Tractarianism* (Oxford, 1982), pp. 177–78.

49 In 1847, Bishop Phillpots of Exeter refused to install Charles Gorham

to the living of Exeter in 1847 because he would not accept the doctrine of baptismal regeneration. When Gorham appealed against the ruling, the Judicial Committee of the Privy Council overruled the Bishop, and Gorham was installed to the living after all, which outraged High Churchmen and led to William Ewart Gladstone's two closest friends, Henry Edward Manning and James Hope seceding to Rome. Although Gladstone deeply regretted these defections, he nonetheless recognized that the Judgment went "to the very root of all life and all teaching in the Church of England" by not only undermining the doctrine of baptismal regeneration but allowing the English state to overrule the Church on doctrinal matters.

50 Richard Shannon, *Gladstone: 1809–1865* (London, 1982), pp. 79 and 43–44.
51 LD, 7:8, JHN to Charles Marriott (8 January 1839).
52 For a spirited argument to the contrary, see David Bebbington, *The Mind of Gladstone* (Oxford, 2004), pp. 77–104.
53 Gladstone, quoted in *Fifteen Sermons Preached Before the University of Oxford*, ed. James David Earnest and Gerard Tracey (Oxford, 2006), p. xlv.
54 Ibid., p. 39.
55 Tracey Rowland, *Ratzinger's Faith: The Theology of Pope Benedict XVI* (Oxford, 2008), p. 66.
56 In his preface to the second volume of Newman's sermons collected by Vincent Blehl, the former archivist of the Birmingham Oratory, Gerard Tracey, wrote: "The reputation of John Henry Newman as a preacher is so long-standing and so widespread that it needs no comment." Well, my gentle reader being the general reader, I am assuming that he may not have encountered Church's lively eyewitness account of the sermons, or if he has, that he will not mind reading it again.
57 Church, quoted in Lathbury, Vol. 1, p. 262.
58 Lathbury, Vol. 1, p. 262.
59 Ibid., p. 265
60 Philip Magnus, *Gladstone* (London, 1954), pp. 98–99.
61 John Vincent, *Disraeli* (London, 1990), p. 48.
62 George Malcolm Young, "Mr. Gladstone," in *Today and Yesterday* (London, 1948), pp. 34–35.
63 David Bebbington, *The Mind of Gladstone* (Oxford, 2004), p. 302.
64 LD, 23:234: "What a sad thing this Gladstone controversy is … It is smelling out a Powder Plot."
65 *The Gladstone Diaries*, ed. H. C. G. Matthew, Vol. VIII, pp. 563 and 578.
66 Matthew, H. C. G., "Gladstone, Vaticanism and the Question of the East," in Derek Baker (ed.), *Studies in Church History* (Oxford, 1978), Vol. 15, p. 441.
67 F. D. Maurice, "Three Letters to the Rev. William Palmer" (1842), in *To Build Christ's Kingdom: F.D. Maurice and His Writings.*, ed. Jeremy Morris (London, 2007), p. 111. It was only after Newman's *via media* had

run its futile course that Newman could appreciate how incontrovertibly right Maurice was. The agents of the Reformation had done their work all too well and by the seventeenth century the English had indeed been transformed into a Protestant people.

68 Duff Cooper, *Old Men Forget* (London, 1953), p. 128.
69 H. C. G. Matthew, *Gladstone 1809–1898* (Oxford, 1997), p. 242.
70 *Disraeli, Derby and the Conservative Party: The Political Journals of Lord Stanley 1849–1869*, ed. John Vincent (New York, 1978), p. 346.
71 Ibid., p. 346.
72 Gladstone Diaries, VII, 28 October 1869, quoted in Richard Aldous, *The Lion and the Unicorn: Gladstone vs. Disraeli* (London, 2006), p. 209.
73 Gladstone Diaries, VIII, p. 563, quoted in Aldous, *The Lion and the Unicorn*, p. 209.
74 H. C. G. Matthew, *Gladstone: 1809–1898*, pp. 91–92.
75 Gladstone Diaries, VIII, p. 586, WEG to Laura Thistlethwayte (22 April 1870).
76 *Queen Victoria in her Letters and Journals*, ed. Christopher Hibbert (New York, 1985), p. 234.
77 William Hazlitt, "On Cant and Hypocrisy" (December 1828), in *Selected Essays of William Hazlitt 1778–1830*, ed. Geoffrey Keynes (London, 1930), p. 364.
78 LD, 9:175, JHN to John Keble (20 December 1842). See also an excellent essay by John Kirwan, "Father Newman at Confession," in *John Henry Newman in His Time*, ed. Philippe Lefebvre and Colin Mason (Family Publications, Oxford, 2007), pp. 209–22.
79 Ibid., pp. 567–68, WEG to Laura Thistlethwayte (22 October 1869).
80 *Political Correspondence of Mr. Gladstone and Lord Granville*, ed. Ramm, Vol. I (Oxford, 1952).
81 *Parochial Sermons*, Vol. II, p. 30.
82 *The Gladstone Diaries*, Vol. VI, p. 31 (December 1868).
83 J. Moody, *John Henry Newman* (New York, 1945), p. 236.
84 John Morley, *Life of Gladstone*, Vol. 1 (London, 1903), p. 381.
85 *Erastianism* refers to the doctrines of Thomas Erastus, the sixteenth-century Swiss theologian, who argued that in states professing one established religion, ecclesiastical must bow to secular power. In *Ecclesiastical Polity* (1594) Richard Hooker reaffirmed the idea of state supremacy that Henry VIII had made law in the Act of Supremacy (1534). In an attempt to furnish the English Church with some autonomy, the Tractarians sought to replace Erastianism with an acceptance of the doctrine of the Apostolic Succession.
86 Robert Gray, *Cardinal Manning: A Biography* (London, 1985), p. 133.
87 Ibid., p. 133.
88 John Morley, *Life of Gladstone*, p. 386.
89 See Michael Holroyd, *A Strange Eventful History: The Dramatic Lives of Ellen Terry, Henry Irving and Their Remarkable Families* (London, 2008), p. 41.
90 Gladstone to Manning (26 January 1851), in Lathbury, Vol. 1, p. 359.

91 G. M. Young, "Mr. Gladstone," in *Today and Yesterday* (London, 1948), p. 39.

92 M. Asquith, *More Memories* (London, 1933), p. 123.

93 Jenkins, *Gladstone*, pp. 281–82.

94 Vincent, *Disraeli*, p. 14.

95 LD, 30:9–10, JHN to John Rickards Mozley (20 October 1881).

96 LD, 29:336, JHN to Henry Bedford (6 February 1881).

97 John Hungerford Pollen, "Newman in Dublin," in *The Month* (September 1906), pp. 318–20.

98 LD, 31:195, JHN to GM Hopkins (3 March 1887).

99 R. F. Foster, *Modern Ireland 1600–1972* (London, 1988), p. 395.

100 AW, p. 333.

101 LD, 22:143, JHN to M. R. Giberne (29 January 1866).

102 LD, 24:187, JHN to Edward Heneage Dering (15 December 1868).

103 *Further Letters of Gerard Manley Hopkins*, ed. Abbott (Oxford, 1956), p. 293.

104 See Froude quoted in Waldo Hilary Dunn, *James Anthony Froude: A Biography*, (Oxford, 1963), Vol. 2, p. 368.

105 Ibid., p. 369.

106 See Roy Foster, *Modern Ireland 1600–1972* (London, 1988), p. 103.

107 William Allingham, *The Diaries*, ed. H. Allingham and D. Radford (Folio Society, 2007), p. 180.

108 *The Gladstone Diaries*, Vol. VIII, p. 216.

109 A. G. Gardiner, *The Life of William Harcourt*, (London, 1923), Vol. 1, p. 250.

110 F. S. L. Lyons, *Ireland Since the Famine* (London, 1971), p. 96.

111 Roy Jenkins, *Gladstone* (London, 1995), p. 363.

112 Ibid., p. 363.

113 Richard Shannon, *Gladstone: Heroic Minister, 1865–1898* (London, 1999), p. 123.

114 LD, 17:146, JHN to Finlayson (31 October 1874).

115 *The Gladstone Diaries*, Vol. VIII, p. 298.

116 LD, 26:279, JHN to Robert Ornsby (23 March 1873).

117 LD, 26:282, JHN to H. P. Liddon (27 March 1873).

118 K. Theodore Hoppen, *The Mid-Victorian Generation: 1846–1886* (Oxford, 1998), p. 606.

119 Ibid., p. 305.

120 Shannon, *Gladstone*, p. 125.

121 Ibid., p. 146.

122 Philip Magnus, *Gladstone* (London, 1954), p. 70. Disraeli had called WEG this in 1845 when he resigned over and subsequently voted for the Maynooth endowment.

123 Shannon, *Gladstone*, p. 147.

124 Ibid.

125 LD, 29:34, Lord Ripon to JHN (20 February 1879).

126 LD, 27:124, *Saturday Review* (12 September 1874), p. 328.

127 LD, 26:434, *The Times* (5 September 1874).

128 Piers Brendon, *The Decline and Fall of the British Empire* (London, 2007), p. 235. See also Roger Owen, *Lord Cromer: Victorian Imperialist, Edwardian Proconsul* (Oxford, 2004), pp. 141–79. Professor Owen makes some lively observations regarding the working relationship in India between Lord Ripon and Evelyn Baring, later Lord Cromer.

129 Anthony Read and David Fisher, *The Proudest Day: India's Long Road to Independence* (London, 1997), p. 70.

130 See *Apologia*, p. 18. Thomas Scott (1774–1821) was a Christian apologist and a crucial influence on Newman. In the *Apologia* he refers to him as "the writer who made a deeper impression on my mind than any other, and to whom (humanly speaking), I almost owe my soul."

131 See Edward Norman, *The Roman Catholic Church: An Illustrated History* (California, 2007), pp. 148–49: "Ultramontanism itself was not a 'movement,' any more than Liberal Catholicism was. It was a prevalent ethos, a practical summation of the centralizing tendencies of the nineteenth-century curia, a party label in the divergences of view over Catholic order throughout the world. The publication of Joseph de Maistre's *Du Pape* in 1819 provided an ideological pedigree, and had the effect of encouraging papal authority as a part of a revived emphasis on legitimacy which prevailed in the atmosphere of restoration following the fall of Napoleon … In the confrontation of Liberal Catholicism and Ultramontanism—in relation to social and political issues—the latter won the day in the Church, but in most countries most Catholics were probably untouched by the distinctions drawn by the literary combatants, and were loyal to the pope and hostile to the forces of the *Risorgimento* because that is what by instinct they knew to be right."

132 Shannon, *Gladstone*, p. 147.

133 Elizabeth Longford, *Queen Victoria* (Folio Society, 2007), p. 386.

134 Ibid., p. 386.

135 LD, 27:133–34, JHN to Lord Emly (9 October 1874).

136 Ibid., p. 133.

137 LD, 27:122–23, JHN to Lord Blachford (2 October 1874).

138 LD, 20:390–91, JHN to William Monsell (13 January 1863).

139 LD, 27:123. See note 4.

140 Lord Ripon also took Gladstone to task for his defamatory charges against English Catholics, forcing from him the admission "I do not think you 'likely to be wanting in civil loyalty and duty.'" See Lucien Wolf, *Life of the First Marquess of Ripon* (London, 1921), Vol. I, p. 309.

141 LD, 27:124, JHN to Lord Emly (2 October 1874).

142 LD, 27:152, JHN to Ambrose Phillipps de Lisle (6 November 1874).

143 *Newman and Gladstone: The Vatican Decrees*, ed. Ryan (Notre Dame, 1962), p. 78.

144 LD, 27:148, JHN to Lord Emly (4 November 1874).

145 Ibid.

146 In October 1876, Disraeli wrote to Lord Derby: "Posterity will do justice

to that unprincipled maniac Gladstone—extraordinary mixture of envy, vindictiveness, hypocrisy and superstition; and with one commanding characteristic—whether Prime Minister, or Leader of the Opposition, whether preaching, praying, speechifying or scribbling—never a gentleman." See Lord Blake's essay, "Disraeli and Gladstone," in *Victorian England* (Folio Society, 1999), p. 218.

147 John Henry Newman, *The Idea of a University*, ed. Martin Svaglic (Notre Dame, 1982), pp. 159–60.

148 LD, 27:148–49, JHN to Lord Emly (4 November 1874).

149 LD, 27:145.

150 LD, 27:183, JHN to Malcolm Maccoll (4 January 1875).

151 D. C. Lathbury (ed), *Correspondence on Church and Religion*, Vol. II, p. 378.

152 LD, 27:169–70, JHN to R. W. Church (10 December 1874).

153 LD, 27:183, JHN to Malcolm Maccoll (4 January 1875).

154 LD, 27:156, JHN to Lady Georgiana Fullerton (10 November 1874).

155 Sir Thomas Browne, *Religio Medici* (1643), from *Sir Thomas Browne: Selected Writings*, ed. Sir Geoffrey Keynes (Chicago, 1968), p. 11.

156 LD, 27:159, JHN to the Duke of Norfolk (22 November 1874).

157 LD, 27:159, JHN to Lord Emly (23 November 1874).

158 LD, 27:173, JHN to William Clifford, Bishop of Clifton (15 December 1874).

159 LD, 27:158, JHN to the Duke of Norfolk (22 November 1874).

160 LD, 8:23, JHN to Robert Belaney (25 January 1841).

161 Andrew Roberts, *Salisbury: Victorian Titan* (London, 1999), p. 760.

162 *DNB*, '1912–1921' (Oxford, 1927), p. 274.

163 LD, 27:198, JHN to Charles Russell (19 January 1875).

164 *Selected Writings of Lord Acton*, Vol. III, ed. Fears (Liberty Fund, Indianapolis), p. 350.

165 See *Positio* (Rome, 1989), p. 376.

166 LD, 27:202, Thomas Cookson to JHN (20 January 1875).

167 LD, 27:200, James Jones, S.J. to JHN (21 January 1875).

168 LD, 27:200–01, JHN to James Jones, S.J. (22 January 1875).

169 LD, 27:193, JHN to WEG (16 January 1875).

170 LD, 7:103, JHN to M. Giberne (11 July 1839).

171 LD 26: 282, JHN to H. P. Liddon (7 March 1873).

172 John Morley, *Life of Gladstone* (London, 1903), Vol. III, pp. 421–22.

173 *Correspondence on Church and State*, ed Lathbury, Vol. II, p. 88.

174 LD, 31:26.

175 LD, 28:199, JHN to Lord Blachford (25 May 1877). Leon Gambetta (1832–1882) was a French statesman and prime minister who, during the Franco-Prussian war, escaped to Tours by balloon during the siege of Paris and declared the French Republic (1870) after Napoleon III surrendered. A radical liberal, he was passionately anti-clerical. Recalling Gambetta's escape by balloon might have inspired Newman's own witty description of how he felt while writing *A Letter to the Duke of*

Norfolk (1875): "I felt as if up in a balloon and till I got safe down, I could not be easy. I might be turned upside down by a chimney pot, left atop a tree, or carried out to sea" (LD 27:215, JHN to Alexander Fullerton, 6 February 1875). Then again, balloons were common in the London of Newman's youth. His eldest sister Harriet wrote in 1824: "Mr. Graham ascended yesterday in his Balloon, we had a very good view of it; he alighted at Godstone, after having been an hour and a half surveying a splendid collection of clouds. I longed to be with him when I saw the Balloon ascending in such style, although I knew I have not courage, or according to myself *bravery* enough, for such an expedition." See *Newman Family Letters*, ed. Dorothy Mozley (London, 1962), pp. 6–7.

176 LD, 31:104, JHN to Bosworth Smith (22 December 1885).

177 LD, 30:169, William Ewart Gladstone to JHN (9 November 1882).

178 LD, 31:266, JHN to Gladstone to JHN (6 November 1888).

179 D. C. Lathbury (ed.), *Correspondence on Church and Religion of William Ewart Gladstone* (London, 1910), WEG to Lord Acton, 1 September 1890, Vol. I, pp. 404–05.

180 Lathbury, *Correspondence on Church and Religion of William Ewart Gladstone*, Vol. 1, p. 406, WEG to R. H. Hutton (6 October 1890), p. 406.

181 See Roland Hill, *Lord Acton* (New Haven, 2000), p. 271.

182 Lathbury, *Correspondence on Church and Religion of William Ewart Gladstone*, Vol. I, p. 406.

183 Huxley, quoted by David Bebbington, *The Mind of Gladstone* (Oxford, 2004), p. 3.

184 M. G. Brock, "The Oxford of Peel and Gladstone," in *The History of the University of Oxford*, ed. Brock and Curthoys, (Oxford, 1997), Vol. VI, Pt. 1 p. 69. Newman "had none of the cautious conformism of his seniors. Where his convictions pointed he followed; it was not in him to modify his message from prudence or alarm. He stands in the Oxford tradition of Wyclif and Wesley—inspired, disruptive and a stranger to moderation."

185 Frank Turner, *John Henry Newman and the Challenge of Evangelical Religion* (New Haven, 2002), p. 641.

186 LD, 27:24, JHN to Mrs. Margaret A. Wilson (23 February 1874).

187 Gladstone to Meyrick (26 April 1875), in Frederick Meyrick, *Memories of Life at Oxford and Experiences in Italy, Greece, Turkey, Germany, Spain, and Elsewhere* (New York, 1905), pp. 24–25.

188 See the excellent entry on Lord Westbury by R. C. J. Cocks in the *ODNB*.

189 See *ODNB*.

190 William Ewart Gladstone, *Gleanings of Past Years* (New York, 1897), Vol. 8, p. 309.

191 *Letter to the Duke of Norfolk*, p. 261.

192 *Newman and Gladstone: The Vatican Decrees*, ed. Alvan Ryan (South Bend, 1962), p. 132.

193 Ibid., p. 136.

194 See Rowland, *Ratzinger's Faith: The Theology of Pope Benedict XVI*, pp. 81–82.
195 LD, 28:351. This is from a moving speech that Gladstone gave at the opening of the hall and library of Keble College on 25 April 1878. After referring to the Oxford Movement, Keble and Pusey he told the audience: "But there is a name which, as an academical name, is greater than either of those – I mean the name of Dr. Newman (Cheers.) When the history of Oxford during that time comes to be written, the historian will have to record the extraordinary, the unexampled career of that distinguished man in the University. He will have to tell, as I believe, that Dr. Newman exercised for a period of about ten years after 1833 an amount of influence, of absorbing influence, over the highest intellects – over nearly the whole intellect, but certainly over the highest intellect of this University, for which perhaps, there is no parallel in the academical history of Europe, unless you go back to the twelfth century or to the University of Paris. We know how his influence was sustained by his extraordinary purity of character and the holiness of his life (Cheers.) We know also the catastrophe – I cannot call it less – which followed (Cheers.) We know that he who held the power in his hand found himself compelled by the action of conscience to carry his mind and gifts elsewhere ..." (*The Times*, 26 April 1878, p. 6)
196 *The Gladstone Diaries*, ed. Mathew, Vol. 3, p. xxix.
197 LD, 7:470, JHN to Frederic Rogers (26 December 1840).
198 J. H. Newman, "Wisdom and Innocence" (1843), *Sermons on the Subjects of the Day*, Sermon 20.
199 Philip Magnus, *Gladstone* (London, 1958), p. 236.
200 See David Bebbington *The Mind of Gladstone* (Oxford, 2004), pp. 310–11: "the master to whom Gladstone turned again and again ... was Bishop Butler ... whose doctrine of probability roused Gladstone decisively against Catholic teaching in the 1840s and it was Butler whose method seemed the ultimate remedy to Huxley's agnosticism four decades later."
201 Ibid., p. 177: "There can be no doubt that in *Studies of Homer* (1858) [Gladstone] was defending an essentially Tory Christian worldview"— which Bebbington sees as "the climax of his intellectual career as a Conservative." If this was the basis of Gladstone's conservatism, it is perhaps no wonder that his peculiar brand of liberalism continues to confound historians.
202 *The Prime Ministers' Papers: W.E. Gladstone 1: Autobiographica*, Royal Commission on Historical Manuscripts, p. 20.
203 Gladstone, quoted in Peter Stanksy, *Gladstone: A Progress in Politics* (Boston, 1979), p. 181.
204 In thanking Gladstone for sending a copy of his pamphlet *Vaticanism* (1875), Newman wrote: "Of course I ... quite understand how grievous it must be to you, that a person like me, who was doing his best to serve the Anglican Church, should have been led to throw off his allegiance to

it and to become its opponent. On the other hand stands the fact, that from the time I took that step, close on 30 years ago, I never have had a moment's misgiving about my conviction that the Catholic Roman Church comes from God, and that the Anglican is external to it ..." LD, 27:236, JHN to Gladstone (26 February 1875).

Chapter 8 Newman, Thackeray and *Vanity Fair*

1   Kingsley, quoted in *Apologia*, pp. 373–74. The quote from Newman is from *Anglican Difficulties*, Lecture 8, p. 207.
2   LD, 21:120, Charles Kingsley to Alexander Macmillan (8 June 1864). If Kingsley reviled Newman, he all but revered Thackeray. *Vanity Fair* was his favorite book. Whenever down in the dumps, he reread the book. Indeed, he confessed that he would have preferred drawing Rawdon Crawley "than all the folks I ever drew." See Susan Chitty, *The Beast and the Monk: A Life of Charles Kingsley* (London, 1974), p. 147.
3   *The Letters and Private Papers of William Makepeace Thackeray*, ed. Ray (Harvard, 1946), Vol. III, p. 66. In 1850, Giovanni Achilli, an apostate Dominican priest, was brought to England by the Evangelical Alliance to denounce the Catholic Church during the period known as the Papal Aggression, when Cardinal Wiseman was reconstituting the English hierarchy. After Newman called attention to charges brought against the defrocked priest for immorality, Achilli sued for libel. In the subsequent trial of 21–24 June 1852, Judge Lord Chief Justice Campbell would not admit evidence submitted by Newman and his lawyers, nor permit Newman to speak in his own defense, and as a result the jury found for Achilli and Newman was fined £100.
4   *The Letters and Private Papers of William Makepeace Thackeray*, Vol. II, pp. 676–77.
5   *The Letters and Private Papers of William Makepeace Thackeray*, Vol. I, p. cxxxiii.
6   Ibid., p. 140.
7   Gordon Ray, *Thackeray: The Use of Adversity, 1811–1846* (New York, 1955), p. 182.
8   D. J. Taylor, *Thackeray: The Life of a Literary Man* (London, 1999), p. 126.
9   See *Thackerayana: Notes and Anecdotes*. ed. Joseph Grego (New York, 1875), pp. 481–2
10 See William Makepeace Thackeray. *Vanity Fair*, (Everyman, 1991), Chapter XXVI, "Between London and Chatham," p. 269.
11 *The Letters and Private Papers of William Makepeace Thackeray*, Vol. I, p. 487.
12 *DNB*, 19:575.
13 Thackeray may have been a spendthrift but he was also a prodigiously

hard worker, whose toil eventually paid off: "Between 1837 and 1847 Thackeray contributed 450 articles to twenty-two periodicals; his first real book, *The Paris Sketch Book* (1840), earned him £50; in 1843, *The Irish Sketch Book* produced £385; he continued hand-to-mouth until *Vanity Fair* began to appear in 1847. Yet in the few years before his death in 1863 he was probably making £7,200 a year from literary activities (perhaps £350,000 in modern terms)—an extraordinary achievement after so grinding a start." See K. Theodore Hoppen's first-rate history, *The Mid-Victorian Generation: England 1846–1886* (Oxford, 1998), p. 377.

14 George Orwell, "Oysters and Brown Stout" (December 1944), in George Orwell, *Essays,* selected by John Carey (Everyman, 2002), pp. 794–95.

15 It is interesting to note, apropos *Vanity Fair*, that before Smith Elder finally decided to publish it, the book was turned down by five different publishers.

16 Since no one has yet to make a proper study of Newman's journalism, his stature as an historian continues to be underestimated. Nevertheless, like Thackeray, he was profoundly alive to contemporary history, which most professional historians either neglect or get wildly wrong.

17 See *Vanity Fair*, Chapter LXI, "In Which Two Lights Are Put Out," p. 660.

18 John Carey, *Thackeray: Prodigal Genius* (London, 1977), pp. 20 and 22.

19 In *The Newcomes*, Thackeray had Colonel Newcome reside at 120 Fitzroy Square, which he describes vividly: "The kitchens were gloomy. The stables were gloomy. Great black passages; cracked conservatory; dilapidated bathroom, with melancholy waters moaning and fizzing from the cistern; the great large blank stone staircase—were all so many melancholy features in the general countenance of the house ..." There, in 1873, the year that Newman published his *The Idea of a University*, Ford Madox Ford was born.

20 D. J. Taylor, *Thackeray: The Life of a Literary Man* (London, 1999), pp. 336 and 257. A good example of what Thackeray meant by his "uncouth raptures" can be found in a letter he wrote to Mrs. Brookfield on 19–22 December 1848: "About my future state I don't know. I leave it in the disposal of the Awful Father: but for today: I thank God that I can love you: and that you yonder ... are thinking of me with a tender regard; Hallelujah may be greater in degree than this, but not in kind: and countless ages of stars may be blazing infinitely: but you & I have a right to rejoice and believe in our little part, and to trust in to day as in tomorrow. God bless my Lady and her husband." See *The Letters and Private Papers of William Makepeace Thackeray*, Vol. II, p. 474.

21 See Thackeray's letter to Kate Perry of September, 1851: "I don't see how any woman should not love a man who had loved her as I did J.; I don't see how any man should not love a woman so beautiful, so unhappy, so tender ... I wish I had never loved her. I have been played with by a woman and flung over at a beck from the lord and master ..." See *The Letters and Private Papers of William Makepeace Thackeray*, Vol. IV, p. 431.

22 See *Vanity Fair*, Chapter LXVII, "Births, Marriages, and Deaths," p. 735, and Chapter LXVI, "Amantium Irae," p. 722.

23 William Allingham, *Diaries*, ed. Christopher Ricks (Folio Society, 2007), p. 79.

24 See *Vanity Fair*, Chapter XXXIV, "James Crawley's Pipe Is Put Out," p. 364.

25 See Francis W. Newman. *Contributions Chiefly to the Early History of the Late Cardinal Newman* (London, 1891), p. 112.

26 *The Letters and Private Papers of William Makepeace Thackeray*, Vol. II, p. 685.

27 See *The Tamworth Reading Room*, in J. H. Newman, *Discussions and Arguments on Various Subjects* (Notre Dame, 2004), p. 260.

28 See the essay "English Catholic Literature," in *The Idea of a University*, p. 235. In 1869, Newman told a correspondent that "the only master of style I ever had (which is strange considering the differences of language) is Cicero. I think I owe a great deal to him, and as far as I know to no one else. His great mastery of Latin is shown especially in his clearness." See LD, 24:241, JHN to John Hayes (13 April 1869).

29 *The Letters and Private Papers of William Makepeace Thackeray*, Vol. III, pp. 552–53.

30 LD, 20:302 JHN to William Neville (13 October 1862). Austin is Father Henry Austin Mills (1823–1903), one of the Oratorian fathers, whom Newman addressed at the end of the *Apologia*. "I have closed this history of myself with St. Philip's name upon St. Philip's feast-day; and, having done so, to whom can I more suitably offer it, as a memorial of affection and gratitude, than to St. Philip's sons, my dearest brothers of this House, the Priests of the Birmingham Oratory, Ambrose St. John, Henry Austin Mills, Henry Bittleston, Edward Caswall, William Paine Neville, and Henry Ignatius Dudley Ryder? who have been so faithful to me; who have been so sensitive of my needs; who have been so indulgent to my failings; who have carried me through so many trials; who have grudged no sacrifice, if I asked for it; who have been so cheerful under discouragements of my causing; who have done so many good works, and let me have the credit of them;—with whom I have lived so long, with whom I hope to die." See *Apologia*, pp. 371–72.

31 See Bradford Allen Booth, *The Letters of Anthony Trollope* (London, 1951), p. 403, and LD, 12:433.

32 LD, 20:566, JHN to Miss Holmes (27 December 1863).

33 Thackeray, "De Finibus," in *Roundabout Papers*, in *Works* (New York, 1904), Vol. 27, p. 307.

34 G. K. Chesterton, *Thackeray* (London, 1903), p. 7.

35 Ibid., pp. 7–8.

36 LD, 14:162, JHN to J. D. Dalgairns (8 December 1850).

37 LD, 17:49, JHN to Ambrose St. John (9 November 1855).

38 LD, 20:572, JHN to Mssrs. Macmillan and Co. (30 December 1863), and LD, 21:100, JHN to R. W. Church (23 April 1864).

39 *Apologia*, p. xiv.

40 LD, 21:81, JHN to Richard Gell Macmullen (16 March 1864).

41   LD, 27:207, JHN to Geraldine Penrose Fitzgerald (27 January 1875).

42   *The Letters and Private Papers of William Makepeace Thackeray*, Vol. II, p. 790.

43   See Carey, *Thackeray: Prodigal Genius*, p. 96: "The most prolific breeding ground for ... sham sentiment was, [Thackeray] believed, the social-conscience novel, as developed by Dickens. For one thing, he despised the bogus philanthropy that induced comfortably-off readers, who had every intention of remaining comfortably-off, to grow lachrymose over fictional accounts of workers' woes. For another, he felt that you could not have a political question fairly debated in a novel, in which the author was at liberty to invent characters and motives, in order to revile or revere them. The whole structure was rigged."

44   Delmore Schwartz (1913–1966) was a good friend of Robert Lowell and a good poet in his own right. The phrase "scrimmage of appetite" is from Schwartz's poem, "The Heavy Bear Who Goes with Me," which can be found in Richard Ellmann's *New Oxford Book of American Verse* (New York, 1976), p. 770.

45   *The Idea of a University*, p. 316.

46   W. M. Thackeray, *The Irish Sketch Book*, in *The Works of William Makepeace Thackeray*, New Century Library (London, 1900), Vol. V, p. 41.

47   LD, 16:110, JHN to Miss Mary Holmes (12 April 1854).

48   LD, 29:83, George Butler to JHN (20 March 1879).

49   One notable exception to this on Newman's part was his reaction to the monsignors he encountered in Rome in 1847: "As far as I can make out," he wrote to his sister Jemima, "the Roman Parochial clergy here are very exemplary, but Rome is a centre to which all persons come, and the foreign clergy are no ornament to the place. They have left their own neighbourhoods perhaps for no pleasant reason, and live here without public opinion upon them.... . But the worst set of all I suppose, (I speak of them as a body) are a number of fellows, part clergymen part laymen (but unluckily all in what to a foreigner the dress of clergymen), called Monsignors – They are often regularly bad fellows – and these are the persons whom the English generally come across, and from whom they take their ideas of a Roman priest. I hear a good account of the Cardinals – and certainly the few I know are pre-eminent instances of humility and sanctity." See LD, 12:27, JHN to Mrs. John Mozley (26 January 1847).

50   See *Vanity Fair*, Chapter LXIV, "A Vagabond Chapter," pp. 684–85.

51   D. J. Taylor, *Thackeray: The Life of a Literary Man* (London, 1999), pp. 33–34.

52   Ibid., p. 40.

53   William Makepeace Thackeray, *The Irish Sketch Book* (New York, 1848), p. 152.

54   William Makepeace Thackeray. *The Book of Snobs* (New York, 1848), p. 2.

55   *The Collected Works of Walter Bagehot*, ed. Norman St. John-Stevas (London, 1965), Vol. II, pp. 304–05.

56   *The Letters and Private Papers of William Makepeace Thackeray*, Vol. IV, p. 129.

57   See W. C. Roscoe, "Thackeray's Art and Morality," in the *National Review* (January 1856), in *Thackeray: The Critical Heritage*, ed. Geoffrey Tillotson (London, 1968), p. 277.

58   *Apologia*, p. 18.

59   Ibid., pp. 15, 17.

60   Ibid., p. 18.

61   Ibid., p. 16.

62   See Newman's profoundly moving sermon, "The Invisible World."

63   See *Vanity Fair*, Chapter LXI, "In Which Two Lights Are Put Out," pp. 651–52.

64   *Anglican Difficulties*, p. 250.

65   Ibid., p. 251.

66   See Herbert Butterfield, *The Whig Interpretation of History* (London, 1931), pp. 12–13.

67   Thomas Babington Macaulay, *The History of England from the Accession of James II* (Folio Society, 2009), Vol. I, p. 2.

68   See "Christ upon the Waters" (Part 1) (1850), in *Sermons Preached on Various Occasions*, p. 131.

69   Ibid., p. 132.

70   See *Vanity Fair*, Chapter XXXV, "Widow and Mother," p. 37.

71   See *Vanity Fair*, Chapter LI "In Which a Charade Is Acted Which May or May Not Puzzle the Reader." p. 543.

72   See *Vanity Fair*, Chapter XXXV, "Widow and Mother," pp. 379–80.

73   See *Vanity Fair*, Chapter XXXVII, "How To Live Well On Nothing A Year," p. 403.

74   Carey, *Thackeray: Prodigal Genius*, p. 180.

75   See Newman's sermon, "Religious Joy" (1825), in *Parochial and Plain Sermons*, Book 8, Sermon 17: "'The shepherds said one to another, Let us now go even unto Bethlehem, and see this thing which is come to pass, which the Lord hath made known to us.' Let us too go with them, to contemplate that second and greater miracle to which the Angel directed them, the Nativity of Christ. St. Luke says of the Blessed Virgin, 'She brought forth her first-born Son, and wrapped Him in swaddling clothes, and laid Him in a manger.' What a wonderful sign is this to all the world, and therefore the Angel repeated it to the shepherds: 'Ye shall find the babe wrapped in swaddling clothes, lying in a manger.' The God of heaven and earth, the Divine Word, who had been in glory with the Eternal Father from the beginning, He was at this time born into this world of sin as a little infant. He, as at this time, lay in His mother's arms, to all appearance helpless and powerless, and was wrapped by Mary in an infant's bands, and laid to sleep in a manger. The Son of God Most High, who created the worlds, became flesh, though remaining what He was before. He became

flesh as truly as if He had ceased to be what He was, and had actually been changed into flesh. He submitted to be the offspring of Mary, to be taken up in the hands of a mortal, to have a mother's eye fixed upon Him, and to be cherished at a mother's bosom. A daughter of man became the Mother of God—to her, indeed, an unspeakable gift of grace; but in Him what condescension! What an emptying of His glory to become man! and not only a helpless infant, though that were humiliation enough, but to inherit all the infirmities and imperfections of our nature which were possible to a sinless soul. What were His thoughts, if we may venture to use such language or admit such a reflection concerning the Infinite, when human feelings, human sorrows, human wants, first became His? What a mystery is there from first to last in the Son of God becoming man! Yet in proportion to the mystery is the grace and mercy of it; and as is the grace, so is the greatness of the fruit of it."

76 Anthony Trollope, *Autobiography*, The Oxford Illustrated Trollope (Oxford, 1950), p. 186.

77 See William Makepeace Thackeray. *Henry Esmond* ed. John Sutherland (Penguin, 1970), Part III, Chapter 5, "Mohun Appears For the Last Time in This History," p. 418.

78 *Anglican Difficulties*, pp. 4–5.

79 LD, 20:569, JHN to William Monsell (27 December 1863).

80 *Correspondence of Arthur Hugh Clough*, ed. Mulhauser (Oxford, 1950), Vol. I, pp. 247–48.

81 *The Letters and Private Papers of William Makepeace Thackeray*, Vol. II, p. 581.

82 *The Collected Works of Walter Bagehot*, Vol. II, p. 245.

83 See Clough's superb poem, "Easter Day, Naples, 1849," which Anthony Kenny unaccountably imagines a paean to atheism.

84 Carey, *Thackeray: Prodigal Genius*, p. 174. Leslie Stephen is nearer the mark when he refers to *The Roundabout Papers* as "models of the essay which, without aiming at profundity, give … the playful and tender conversation of a great writer" (*DNB*).

85 See "Small-Beer Chronicle," in W. M. Thackeray, *Roundabout Papers*, pp. 166–67.

86 *Present Position of Catholics in England* (London, 1851), pp. 180–81. It is interesting to note that one of Newman's childhood friends from Ealing School was the sculptor Richard Westmacott (1799–1872), who succeeded his father as Professor of Sculpture at the Royal Academy in 1857. His bust of Newman (1841), which adorns the recreation room of the Birmingham Oratory, is one of the best likenesses of Newman. That he and his father before him educated many of the sculptors who made the idolatrous monuments which Thackeray and Newman found outré gives Thackeray's piece added interest.

87 J. H. Newman, "The Religion of the Pharisee, the Religion of Mankind" (1856) in *Sermons Preached on Various Occasions*, ed. James Tolhurst (London, 2007), pp. 24–25.

88 *The Irish Sketch Book*, p. 16.
89 *The Letters and Private Papers of William Makepeace Thackeray*, Vol. II, pp. 675–76.
90 See *ODNB*.
91 *The Letters and Private Papers of William Makepeace Thackeray*, Vol. II, p. 705.
92 "The Religion of the Pharisee, the Religion of Mankind" (1856), in *Sermons Preached on Various Occasions*, p. 26.
93 *The Letters and Private Papers of William Makepeace Thackeray*, Vol. II, pp. 711–12.
94 Ibid., p. 616.
95 *The Letters and Private Papers of William Makepeace Thackeray*, Vol. III, p. 13.
96 For a good sense of Newman's idea of sanctity, see "A Short Road to Perfection:" "We must bear in mind what is meant by perfection. It does not mean any extraordinary service, anything out of the way, or especially heroic—not all have the opportunity of heroic acts, of sufferings ... By perfect we mean that which has no flaw in it, that which is complete, that which is consistent, that which is sound.... I insist on this because I think it will simplify our views, and fix our exertions on a definite aim. If you ask me what you are to do in order to be perfect, I say, first:—Do not lie in bed beyond the due time of rising; give your first thoughts to God; make a good visit to the Blessed Sacrament; say the Angelus devoutly; eat and drink to God's glory; say the Rosary well; be recollected; keep out bad thoughts; make your evening meditations well; examine yourself daily; go to bed in good time, and you are already perfect." (*Meditations and Devotions*, p. 209)
97 *The Letters and Private Papers of William Makepeace Thackeray*, Vol. II, pp. 423–24.
98 G. K. Chesterton, Introduction to the *Book of Snobs* (London, 1911), p. ix. See also Gordon Ray, *Thackeray: The Uses of Adversity* (London, 1955), p. 377.
99 T. S. Eliot to Eleanor Hinkley (1 April 1918), in *The Letters of T.S. Eliot*, Vol. I: 1898–1922, ed. Valerie Eliot (New York, 1988), p. 228.
100 Gordon Ray, *Thackeray: The Use of Adversity: 1811–1846*, p. 398.
101 See *Vanity Fair*, Chapter XXXVI, "How To Live On Nothing a Year," p. 388.
102 *The Idea of a University*, p. 121.
103 Ibid., p. 121.
104 See *Vanity Fair*, Chapter XXXV, "Widow and Mother," p. 371.
105 In 1854 Thomas Arnold wrote to his mother from Hobart Town, "I have just finished 'Pendennis', and found myself wishing at the end of it that it had been five times as long ..." See *The Letters of Thomas Arnold the Younger*, ed. James Bertram (Auckland and Oxford, 1980) p. 43.
106 Thackeray, *Pendennis* (Penguin, 1994), Chapter LXI, "The Way of the World," p. 801.

107 *The Letters and Private Papers of William Makepeace Thackeray*, Vol. II, p. 581.

108 *The Letters and Private Papers of William Makepeace Thackeray*, Vol. III, p. 439.

109 See *Pendennis*, Chapter LXI, "The Way of the World," p. 802.

110 See Samuel Wilberforce quoted in David Newsome, *The Parting of Friends* (London, 1966), p. 401.

111 See W. M. Thackeray, *The Newcomes*. (London, 1855), pp. 355–56. See also T. B. Macaulay. *Critical and Historical Essays* (Everyman's Library, 1937), Vol. 2, p. 39.

112 "The Adventures of Philip on his Way through the World," in *The Collected Works of Walter Bagehot*, Vol. II, p. 317.

113 See *Pendennis*, Chapter XVI, "More Storms in the Puddle," pp. 183–84.

114 LD, 19:415, JHN to Miss Holmes (4 November 1860).

115 Richard Doyle was the *Punch* illustrator who resigned his position to protest against what he felt were the paper's unacceptably anti-Catholic gibes during the period known as Papal Aggression in 1850; after Doyle departed, he was succeeded by John Tenniel, who would go on to illustrate Lewis Carroll's *Alice in Wonderland* (1865) and *Through the Looking Glass* (1871). When Thackeray supported Doyle, the false rumor went round that he himself might be moving towards Rome, which Newman seems to have credited. After Thackeray's death, he told Gladstone's political ally, the Catholic Irish Unionist William Monsell: "Thackeray's sudden death is very shocking, especially considering his utter contempt of Protestantism and his drawings to the Church." See LD, 20:569, JHN to William Monsell (27 December 1863).

116 *The Letters and Private Papers of William Makepeace Thackeray*, Vol. IV, p. 340.

117 See Rosemary Hill, *God's Architect: Pugin and the Building of Romantic Britain* (New Haven, 2007), p. 283.

118 Pollen wrote an indispensable account of St. Saviour's Leeds in *Narrative of Five Years at St. Saviours* (London, 1851).

119 LD, 23:42–3 JHN to Lady Shrewsbury (29 April 1848).

120 W. M. Thackeray, *The Paris Sketch Book*, in *The Works of William Makepeace Thackeray*, New Century Library (London, 1900), Vol. V, pp. 56–57.

121 LD 27:199, J. H. Pollen to Ambrose St. John (29 January 1874).

122 LD, 27:199, JHN to Unknown Correspondent (20 January 1875).

123 *Apologia*, p. xxiv.

124 Ibid., p. xxvi.

125 John Blackwood, quoted in Geoffrey Tillotson, *Thackeray the Novelist* (Cambridge, 1954), p. 227.

126 *The Letters and Private Papers of William Makepeace Thackeray*, Vol. III, p. 337.

127 In "Before the Curtain," *Vanity Fair*, Thackeray writes: "As the Manager of the Performance sits before the curtain on the boards, and looks into the Fair, a feeling of profound melancholy comes over him in his survey of

the bustling place. There is a great quantity of eating and drinking, making love and jilting, laughing and the contrary, smoking, cheating, fighting, dancing, and fiddling: there are bullies pushing about, bucks ogling the women, knaves picking pockets, policemen on the look-out, quacks (*other* quacks, plague take them!) bawling in front of their booths, and yokels looking up at the tinselled dancers and poor old rouged tumblers, while the light-fingered folk are operating upon their pockets behind."

128 Charlotte Bronte (17 June 1851), in *The Brontës: A Life in Letters*, ed. Juliet Barker (Folio Society, 2006), p. 345.
129 *The Letters and Private Papers of William Makepeace Thackeray*, Vol. III, p. 341.
130 Thackeray, quoted in Gordon N. Ray, *The Age of Wisdom: 1847–1863* (Oxford, 1958), p. 121.
131 For my understanding of the Garrick Club affair, I am heavily indebted to D. J. Taylor's excellent account of it in his *Thackeray: The Life of a Literary Man* (London, 1999), pp. 400–14.
132 Ibid., p. 402.
133 Ibid.
134 Michael Slater, *Charles Dickens* (New Haven, 2009), p. 522.
135 G. M. Young, "Thackeray," in *Today and Yesterday* (London, 1948), p. 247.
136 *The Letters and Private Papers of William Makepeace Thackeray*, Vol. IV, p. 337.
137 See John Gross, *The Rise and Fall of the Man of Letters* (London, 1969), pp. 94–96.
138 Taylor, *Thackeray: The Life of a Literary Man*, p. 408.
139 Michael Slater, *Charles Dickens* (New Haven, 2009), p. 458.
140 *The Letters and Private Papers of William Makepeace Thackeray*, Vol. IV, pp. 89–90.
141 Ibid., p. 97.
142 Ibid., p. 101.
143 Ibid., pp. 101–02.
144 LD, 21:82, JHN to Richard Gell Macmullen (16 March 1864).
145 See Charles Dickens, *A Tale of Two Cities*, Oxford Dickens (Oxford, 1949), p. 69.
146 *The Letters and Private Papers of William Makepeace Thackeray*, Vol. IV, pp. 133–34.
147 Thackeray would have been amused by the bravado of that section of Harriet Martineau's autobiography where the Unitarian mesmerist claims, "To think no more of death than is necessary for the winding up the business of life, and to dwell no more upon sickness than is necessary for its treatment, or to learn to prevent it, seems to me the simple wisdom of the case—totally opposite as this is to the sentiment and method of the religious world …" See Martineau, *Autobiography* (Boston, 1877), p. 440.
148 *The Letters and Private Papers of William Makepeace Thackeray*, Vol. II, p. 253.

149 *The Letters and Private Papers of William Makepeace Thackeray*, Vol. I, p. 466.

150 *The Letters and Private Papers of William Makepeace Thackeray*, Vol. II, pp. 206–07.

151 *The Letters and Private Papers of William Makepeace Thackeray*, Vol. III, p. 82. The Rev. Cesar Jean Salomon Malan (1812–1894), linguist, scholar, and critic of the "Higher Criticism," held the living of Broadwindsor in Dorset from 1845 to 1885. See Ray's note.

152 *The Letters and Private Papers of William Makepeace Thackeray*, Vol. III, p. 217.

153 See Taylor, *Thackeray: The Life of a Literary Man*, pp. 162–64. In addition, Carey's comments on this sad, murky matter are worth taking into consideration. "Isabella's loss helped to impress on Thackeray the terrible transience of love and beauty. It also occasioned qualms of conscience. Clearly he had been to blame: had he not deserted her and gone to Belgium, her post-natal depression might never have been developed into insanity. He began writing *Vanity Fair* in 1845, the year Isabella was finally shut away, and when in that novel George Osborne abandons his wife on the night before Waterloo and goes panting after Becky Sharp, Thackeray is near to self portraiture—very near, perhaps, for it is possible that the delights of his ill-timed continental holiday includes a reunion with the ex-governess Mlle Pauline, Becky's real life prototype." John Carey, *Thackeray: A Prodigal Genius* (London, 1977), pp. 17–18.

154 "The Religion of the Pharisee, the Religion of Mankind" (1856), in *Sermons Preached on Various Occasions*, pp. 16–17.

155 *The Letters and Private Papers of William Makepeace Thackeray*, Vol. III, pp. 50–51.

156 *The Letters and Private Papers of William Makepeace Thackeray*, Vol. III, pp. 347–48.

157 See Frederick Meyrick, *Memories of Life at Oxford and Experiences in Italy, Greece, Turkey, Germany, Spain and Elsewhere* (London, 1905), p. 213.

Chapter 9 Newman and the Americans

1 LD, 5:282, Robert Wilberforce to JHN (20 April 1836).

2 In *Discussions and Arguments*, Newman speaks of "the spread of a Pantheistic spirit, that is, the religion of beauty, imagination, and philosophy, without constraint moral or intellectual, a religion speculative and self-indulgent. Pantheism, indeed, is the great deceit which awaits the Age to come." The man most responsible for reviving pantheism in nineteenth-century Britain was Wordsworth. As a brilliant new intellectual history shows: "Wordworth's rhapsodies on the active powers immanent

in the fabric of nature troubled some commentators, because he could be understood to be expressing pantheism and seemed to disregard Christian doctrine." For the poet James Montgomery, "We do not mean to infer that Mr. Wordsworth excludes from his system the salvation of man, as revealed in the Scriptures, but it is evident that that he has not made 'Jesus Christ the corner-stone' of it." Coleridge was even more censorious, admitting that "the vague misty, rather than mystic, Confusion of God with the World & the accompanying Nature-worship ... is the trait in Wordsworth's poetic works that I most dislike." See P. M. Harman, *The Culture of Nature in Britain 1680–1860* (New Haven, 2009), p. 169. At the same time, Wordsworth can be seen as laying some of the groundwork for the Oxford Movement. As Juliet Barker writes in her biography of the poet, "In John Ruskin's beautiful phrase, William had taught [his admirers, including John Keble and John Henry Newman] that, 'A snowdrop was to me, as to Wordsworth, part of the Sermon on the mount.'" In the Latin oration, which Keble was required to deliver as Professor of Poetry at Oxford, he extolled this aspect in Wordsworth. "What Keble's oration also did was to claim William for the Oxford Movement, which sought to rise above doctrinal squabbles and regenerate the heart of the Anglican Church." Keble, Newman and Frederick Faber had been disciples of his poetry since youth, so that, in influencing them, he might even be said to have laid the foundations for the Oxford Movement. It was a debt which Newman himself identified, saying [Wordsworth] had been central to the "great progress of the religious mind of our Church to something deeper and truer than satisfied the last century." See Juliet Barker *Wordsworth: A Life* (London, 2000), p. 467.

3   Newman, "The Anglo-American Church" 1839, in *Essays Critical and Historical*, Vol. I, p. 347.

4   LD, 9:435, JHN to Mrs. John Mozley (22 July 1843).

5   LD, 27:102, JHN to Mrs. Wilson (3 August 1874): "I think our Lord's words are being fulfilled, 'When the Son of Man cometh shall He find faith upon earth?' The plague of unbelief is in every religious community, in the Unitarian, in the Kirk, in the Episcopalian, in the Church of England, as well as in the Catholic Church. What you want is faith, just as so many persons in other communions want faith. The broad section of the Church of England wants faith – you in the Catholic Church want faith. The disease is the same, though its manifestations are different."

6   See David K. Brown, R.C.N.C., *The Way of a Ship in the Middle of the Sea: The Life and Work of William Froude* (London, 2005), p. 34. Presumably Brown was given this figure by Gerard Tracey, the Oratory's archivist, who guided his research into the Newman/Froude friendship. I have rounded off the number.

7   See J. M. Robert, "The Idea of a University Revisited," in *Newman after 100 Years*, ed. Ker and Hill (Oxford, 1990), p. 219.

8   From *The Great Gatsby*, in F. Scott Fitzgerald, *The Bodley Head Scott Fitzgerald* (London, 1963), pp. 162–63.

9   "The Mission of St. Philip" (1850), in *Sermons Preached on Various Occasions*, p. 205.

10 LD, 25:324, JHN to William Robert Brownlow (29 April 1871).

11 William Palmer (1803–1885) of Worcester College, was one of the most learned of the Tractarians, and a champion of the 'Branch Theory' of the Church. In 1846 he published an answer to Newman's "Essay on Development" entitled "The Doctrine of Development and Conscience considered in relation to the Evidences of Christianity and of the Catholic System." He condemned Newman's understanding of development as rationalistic.

12 LD, 26:365, JHN to Miss Rowe (16 September 1873).

13 *Present Position of Catholics*, p. 43.

14 See Matthew Arnold, 'Civilization in the United States' (1888).

15 LD, 26:114, JHN to Lord Blachford (14 June 1872).

16 See Francis W. Newman, *Contributions chiefly to the early history of the late Cardinal Newman* (London, 1891), p. 6.

17 LD, 5:60, W. F. Hook to JHN (11 April 1835).

18 See the entry by George Herring for Hook in the *ODNB*.

19 One of the St. Saviour's converts was the gangling, indecisive, dutiful William Neville, who joined the Oratory in September 1851 and later became Newman's secretary. "William, William" were Newman's last recorded words. After his death, as literary executor, Neville diligently collected and copied Newman's letters and papers. See also Neville's comment in his preface to Newman's *Meditations and Devotions* (London, 1907), p. xi: "One name more there is to mention—and it belongs to America, where though our Cardinal had so many friends, one was pre-eminently such— that of Bishop James O'Connor, Bishop of Omaha, whose unaffected kindness was most grateful to our Cardinal, lasting as it did through all but the whole of his Catholic lifetime. For Bishop James O'Connor the Cardinal had a great affection, remembering always, with something of gratitude, the modesty and simplicity with which, as a youth, the future Bishop attached himself to him and to Father St. John when the three were at Propaganda together, thus forming a friendship which distance and years did not lessen, and which later on was enlivened by personal inter- course when the visits *ad limina Apostolorum* brought Bishop O'Connor through England."

20 See Henry Parry Liddon, *Life of Edward Bouverie Pusey* (London, 1898), Vol. III, p. 123.

21 John Hungerford Pollen, *Narrative of Five Years at St. Saviour's, Leeds* (Oxford, 1851), p. 166.

22 William Richard Wood Stephens, *Life and Letters of Dean Hook* (London, 1881), Vol. II, p. 279.

23 LD, 5:180, JHN to F. W. Hook (21 December 1835).

24 See Ronald Knox, "Newman and Roman Catholicism," in *Ideas and Beliefs of the Victorians* (New York, 1966), p. 127: "How Newman, an Evangelical at the roots of him and a Liberal by his early training, came

to throw in his lot with the party of reaction, is (humanly speaking) a mystery; not solved for us by the Apologia, or by Church's history of the Movement. Most probably it was due to the personal influence of Hurrell Froude, that infinitely attractive *enfant terrible* who so charmed and dazzled and shocked his contemporaries; the man whose early death sets one's mind aching with the problem, 'What line would he have taken in 1845?' "

25   William Cobbett, *A History of the Protestant Reformation in England and Ireland* (London, 1857), p. 14. Here Cobbett refers to what he calls: "Monkish ignorance and superstition." "*Monkish ignorance* and *superstition* is a phrase that you find in every Protestant historian, from the reign of the 'Virgin' Elizabeth to the present hour. It has, with time, become a sort of magpie-saying, like 'glorious revolution,' 'happy constitution,' 'good old king,' 'envy of surrounding nations,' and the like. But there has always, false as the notion will presently be proved to be, there has always been a very sufficient motive for inculcating it."

26   LD, 7:164, John Strachan to JHN (23 May 1840).

27   LD, 9:293, B. T. Onderdonk testimonial for *Parochial Sermons*.

28   LD, 9:293, G. W. Doane testimonial for *Parochial Sermons*.

29   LD, 7:366, JHN to E. B. Pusey (25 July 1840).

30   LD, 9:304, JHN to G. W. Doane (7 April 1843).

31   See Introduction to Tract 90 (1841).

32   One of Carey's closest associates at this time was James McMaster (1820–1886). In his account of the Oxford Movement in America, the convert Clarence Walworth recalled how "They walked together, talked together, and read together, eagerly discussing every new publication that issued from Oxford, and prospecting together over every storm that threatened their church and every opening in the clouds that gave hope of coming sunshine." See Clarence E. Walworth, *The Oxford Movement in America* (New York, 1895), pp. 59–60. At the General Theological Seminary, McMaster also became friendly with Isaac Hecker and Walworth himself. After becoming a Catholic in 1845, he accompanied them to Louvain, where they meant to prepare for becoming Redemptorists. They also called on Newman in August 1845, though McMaster discovered that he had no vocation and returned to New York. In July 1848 he bought Bishop Hughes's share in the New York *Freeman's Journal* and *Catholic Register*, and became sole owner and editor until his death. Taking Louis Veuillot as his model, he criticized the episcopate and was anti-Abolitionist. In 1861–1862 President Lincoln had his paper withheld from the mails, and he was for a short time imprisoned. At the time of the First Vatican Council, he was wildly Ultramontane. See the entry on McMaster in the old *Catholic Encyclopedia*.

33   See "The Ordination of Mr. Arthur Carey," in *The New Englander and Yale Review*, Vol. 1, Issue 4 (October 1843), pp. 586–96.

34   See Francis McGrath's biographical entry for Carey in LD, 9:785.

35   LD, 10:57, Arthur Carey to JHN (13 November 1843).

36 Samuel Seabury, *The Joy of the Saints: A Discourse on the Third Sunday After Easter A.D. MDCCCXLIV Being the First Sunday after the Intelligence of The Death of the Rev. Arthur Carey, A.M. An Assistant in the Church of the Annunciation, New York* (New York, 1844), p. 5.

37 Clarence Augustus Walworth, *The Oxford Movement in America* (New York, 1895), p. 34.

38 LD, 22:234–35, JHN to Augustine Francis Hewit (16 May 1866).

39 LD, 4:362, JHN to Richard Hurrell Froude (12 November 1834).

40 LD, 30:202, William Stang to JHN (23 March 1883).

41 LD, 30:202, JHN to William Stang (13 April 1883).

42 See Speech of Mr. John Duer, delivered in the Convention of the Protestant Episcopal Church of the Diocese of New York, on Friday, the 29th of September, IMA in Support of the Resolutions offered by Judge Oakley, New York, 1843, in *Christian's Monthy Magazine and Monthly Review* (London, 1844), pp. 447–49.

43 Paul Johnson, *A History of the American People* (London, 1997), p. 311. Lyman Beecher (1775–1863) was an eloquent Presbyterian preacher who worked to make Calvinism palatable to the young republic. The founder of the American Bible Society, he was also a fierce critic of Unitarianism, as well as of the rising presence of Catholicism in America, which he portrayed as foreign, authoritarian and power-hungry. When an anti-papist mob burned down the Ursuline convent in Charlestown, Massachusetts, in 1831, a series of anti-Catholic lectures that Beecher gave in Boston was held responsible. In the western territories, Beecher became an indefatigable missionary, after taking control of Lane Theological Seminary in Cincinnati, Ohio. He was also an attentive paterfamilias, whose seven sons and three daughters all led distinguished public lives. Harriet Beecher Stowe, the author of *Uncle Tom's Cabin* (1852) was one of his daughters. Samuel Morse (1791–1872), the inventor of the telegraph, was an anti-Catholic abolitionist who in 1836 ran unsuccessfully for mayor of New York on the Native-American ticket.

44 See Duer's speech in *Christian's Monthly Magazine and Monthly Review* (London, 1844), pp. 447–49.

45 From Tract 85, later published as "Difficulties in Scripture Proof of Doctrine," in John Henry Newman, *Discussions and Arguments on Various Subjects*, ed. James Tolhurst (South Bend, 2004), p. 123.

46 Henry Caswall (1810–1870) was the author of *America and the American Church* (1839) and studies of Joseph Smith and Mormonism. In 1843 he returned to England, and was Vicar of Figheldean, Wiltshire, from 1848–1870, and from 1860 a Prebendary of Salisbury.

47 J. H. Newman, "The Anglo-American Church" (1839), in *Essays Historical and Critical*, Vol. I, p. 326.

48 J. H. Newman, quoted from an unpublished manuscript in *The Living Thoughts of Cardinal Newman*, ed. Henry Tristram (London, 1946), p. 21.

49 See LD, 16:557–61.

50 Newman, *Essays Historical and Critical*, Vol. I, pp. 314–15.

51 Lyman Beecher, from his *Autobiography*, Vol. I, p. 253, quoted in Daniel Walker Howe, *What Hath God Wrought: The Transformation of America 1815–1848* (Oxford, 2007), p. 165.

52 *Essays Historical and Critical*, Vol. 1, p. 318.

53 See LD, 7:138, JHN to Mrs. John Mozley (8 September 1839): "I have no news to tell you. The thing uppermost in my mind of course is that B.C. Keble's Article on Gladstone is a very impressive one. I have written what I fear is a flippant one on the American Church, though I respect her members too much to mean to be so." The B.C. is the *British Critic*, which Newman edited from 1838 to 1840; hence his referring to himself in the article on the Anglo-American Church as a "Christian journalist."

54 John Henry Newman, *Apologia Pro Vita Sua: Being a History of His Religious Opinions*, ed. Martin J. Svaglic (Oxford, 1967), p. 90.

55 LD, 7:369, JHN to W. C. A. Maclaurin (26 July 1840). A clergyman at Elgin and later Dean of Moray and Ross, Maclaurin converted with his wife and family in 1850, after which he suffered great poverty. According to a biographical note in the *Letters and Diaries*, "In 1851 he hoped to become a professor at the Catholic University, and told Newman that he was about to spend his last five pound note. In 1854 he wrote from Yarmouth giving his name to the University, and still hoping for a professorship." See LD, 22:368.

56 J. H. Newman, "The Anglo-American Church," in *Essays Historical and Critical*, Vol. 1, 343.

57 *Essays Historical and Critical*, Vol. 1, p. 348.

58 Ibid., p. 349.

59 Newman was quite accurate about the role that rich traders played in the tone and spread of the American Episcopal Church. "Improved transportation on Hudson River sloops and barges," James Elliott Lindsley points out in his excellent history of the New York Episcopal Church, "encouraged the growth of small riverbank communities. Many of these hamlets had as seigneur an Episcopalian who had a summer house on the river and was glad to sponsor the beginning of an Episcopal Church for the handful of year-round residents." See James Elliott Lindsley, *This Planed Vine: A Narrative History of the Episcopal Diocese of New York* (New York, 1984), p. 156.

60 "Particulars of the Conversion of Bishop Ives," from the *Paris L'Univers*, in *The New York Times* (11 August 1854).

61 See "A Remarkable Conversion," in *The New York Times* (18 December 1852).

62 LD, 21:195 JHN to W. J. O'Neil Daunt (13 August 1864).

63 Levi Silliman Ives, *The Trials of a Mind in its Progress to Catholicism: A Letter to his Old Friends* (Boston, 1854), p. 229.

64 Ibid., pp. 230–31.

65 LD, 11:7, JHN to F. W. Faber (8 October 1845).

66 *Essays Historical and Critical*, Vol. I, p. 349.
67 *Letters from America: Alexis de Tocqueville*, ed., trans. and introduced by Frederick Brown (New Haven, 2010), pp. 223–24.
68 Ibid., p. 224.
69 LD, 13:79, JHN to Henry Wilberforce (7 March 1849).
70 Brownson dominates Patrick Allitt's brilliant study of Tractarianism in America in "Tractarians and Transcendentalists," in his *Catholic Converts: British and American Intellectuals Turn to Rome* (Ithaca, 1997), pp. 61–85.
71 Clarence Walworth, *The Oxford Movement in America or Glimpses of Life in an American Seminary* (New York, 1895), p. 59.
72 LD, 11:118, JHN to Ambrose St. John (17 February 1846).
73 See LD, 15:198, note 1.
74 LD, 16:535, JHN to Mrs. J. W. Bowden (31 August 1855).
75 "The Secret Power of Divine Grace" (1856), from John Henry Newman, *Sermons Preached on Various Occasions*, pp. 58–59.
76 See Waugh to Greene (27 February 1952), in *The Letters of Evelyn Waugh*, ed. Mark Amory (London, 1980), p. 370.
77 LD, 30:142, JHN to Lord Braye (29 October 1882).
78 Newman laid out these objects in a memorandum on the Catholic University in April 1854. See LD, 16:557–61.

    1. To provide means of finishing the education of young men of rank, fortune, or expectations, with a view of putting them on a level with Protestants of the same description.
    2. To provide a Professional education for students of law and medicine; and a liberal education for the mercantile class.
    3. To develop the talents of promising youths in the lower classes.
    4. To form a school of Theology and Canon Law, suited to the needs of a class of students, who may be required to carry on those sciences beyond the point of attainment sufficient for parochial duty.
    5. To provide a series of sound and philosophical Defences of Catholicity and Revelation, in answer to the infidel tenets and arguments, which threaten us at this time.
    6. To create a national Catholic Literature.
    7. To provide school books, and, generally, books of instruction, for the use of Catholics of the United Kingdom, the British Empire and the United States.
    8. To raise the standard, and to systematise the teaching, and to encourage the efforts, of the Schools, already so ably and zealously conducted throughout Ireland.
    9. To give a Catholic tone to Society in the great Towns.

79 Evelyn Waugh, "The American Epoch in the Catholic Church" (1949), from *The Essays, Articles, and Reviews of Evelyn Waugh*, ed. Donat Gallagher (New York, 1983), p. 385.

80 See LD, 18:580 (13 March 1858).

81 LD, 18:580, from the *Weekly Register* (13 March 1858). Speaking of his own independent role as Rector of the Catholic University, Newman wrote from Dublin: "What a great thing it is to be independent … good people here don't seem to have comprehended that nothing brought me here, nothing keeps me here, but the simple wish to do some service to Catholic Education. Even the Nation, in puffing me, talks of an honourable or natural ambition. Nor is the irksomeness of being here compensated by having every thing my own way – for the more autocratical I am, the more may fairly be expected of me – which is not pleasant." See LD, 18:45, JHN to Henry Wilberforce (20 May 1857).

82 See Thomas Jefferson Jenkins, *The Judges of Faith and Godless Schools. A compilation of evidence against secular schools the world over, especially against common state schools in the United States of America, wherever entirely withdrawn from the influence of the authority of the Catholic Church* (New York, 1882).

83 In March 2009, Father John Jenkins, C.S.C., President of Notre Dame, invited President Hussein Obama to Notre Dame to receive an honorary law degree and address the graduating class.

84 LD, 30:405, JHN to Thomas Jefferson Jenkins (3 October 1882).

85 John Henry Newman, "God's Will the End of Life," in *Discourses Addressed to Mixed Congregations*, ed. James Tolhurst (South Bend, 2002), pp. 113–14.

86 See *Catholic News Agency* story, "Bishop D'Arcy will not attend Notre Dame commencement featuring Obama" (24 March 2009).

87 See LD, 15:363, for reference to a meeting of the clergy and laity of New York, held on 14 March 1853: … in support of the exiled Archbishop of Bogotá and Newman. Archbishop Hughes spoke of how Newman, whom he called a "doctor of the Catholic Church," "might have looked forward to the highest honours of that high, wealthy and powerful religious community to which he belonged; but, weighing the things of time against those of eternity … he espoused the cause of that scattered and down trodden flock, the remnant of once Catholic England. Nor has he done this with impunity …" The Archbishop then described Newman's suffering during the Achilli trial, and appealed for a collection, "a purse for his private use." (The *Tablet*, XIV, 9 April 1853, p. 228, quoting the *New York Freeman's Journal*)

88 See D. J. Taylor, *Thackeray: The Life of a Literary Man* (London, 1999), p. 330.

89 Ibid., p. 332.

90 LD, 16:284–85, JHN to Francis Kenrick, Archbishop of Baltimore (November, 1854).

91 See John Adams to Benjamin Rush (17 August 1812), in *Old Family Letters*, ed. Alexander Biddle (Philadelphia, 1892), p. 420.

92 LD, 31:85–86, JHN to Cardinal Gibbons (10 October 1885).

93 LD, 31:86, Cardinal Gibbons to JHN (24 October 1885).

94   *Positio for the Cause of John Henry Newman's Canonization* (Rome, 1989), p. 432.

Chapter 10 On the Track of Truth: Newman and Richard Holt Hutton

1   LD, 21:100, JHN to R. W. Church (23 April 1864).
2   See LD, 20:29. In "Essays and Reviews London 1860," *The Quarterly Review*, Vol. CIX, p. 217 (January 1861), pp. 248–305, Samuel Wilberforce wrote: "Now we are not about to justify Number 90. So far from it, we consider it to be a singularly characteristic specimen of that unfortunate subtlety of mind which has since led its author into so many assertions and contradictions and acts, which with the largest judgment of charity a plain man must find it hard to justify from the charge of moral dishonesty, except upon what we believe to be in this case the true plea – to use the ugliest word which we can employ – that of intellectual eccentricity." Wilberforce went on to contrast "the amount of latitude conceded by these condemned views with those which are advocated in the Essays and Reviews," p. 279. See also Newman's letter of 5 December 1864 to Samuel Wilberforce, and notes there.
3   LD, 20:29, JHN to Sister Mary Gabriel Du Boulay (18 August 1861).
4   LD, 20:30, JHN to Sister Mary Gabriel Du Boulay (18 August 1861).
5   Ibid., p. 31.
6   LD, 20:571, JHN to Messrs. Macmillan & Co. (30 December 1863).
7   LD, 21:96, JHN to Sir Frederic Rogers (18 April 1864).
8   R. H. Hutton, "Father Newman's Sarcasm," in the *Spectator* (20 February 1864), p. 206.
9   LD, 21:55, JHN to RHH (22 February 1864).
10   LD, 21:60, RHH to JHN (25 February 1864).
11   *Loss and Gain* (London, 1847), pp. 327–29.
12   LD, 25:441, M. Arnold to JHN (29 November 1871).
13   LD, 30:284, Mark Pattison to JHN (28 December 1883).
14   Walter Bagehot to JHN (1 April 1868), in *The Collected Works of Walter Bagehot*, ed. Norman St. John-Stevas (London, 1986), Vol. 13, pp. 627–28.
15   LD, 25:303, RHH to JHN (21 March 1871).
16   Morley, quoted in Malcolm Woodfield, *R.H. Hutton: Critic and Theologian: The Writings of R.H. Hutton on Newman, Arnold, Tennyson, Wordsworth, and George Eliot* (Oxford, 1986), p. 1.
17   *The Collected Works of Walter Bagehot*, Vol. 15, p. 86.
18   Matthew Arnold to his Eldest Sister, afterwards Mrs. Forster (May 1848), in *Letters of Matthew Arnold 1848–1888*, ed. George W. E. Russell (London, 1895), Vol. 1, p. 10.
19   Garrod in *Arnold: Poetry and Prose* with an introduction and notes by E. K. Chambers (Oxford, 1939), p. xxxiv.
20   *ODNB*. See also Roy Jenkins, *Asquith* (London, 1964), p. 32: "Asquith's

Spectator period lasted ten years. It began, tentatively, even before his call to the bar, and it continued, perhaps with lessening intensity towards the end, until 1886, the year of the Home Rule split in the Liberal Party. Although Hutton had hitherto been a Gladstone man almost without reserve, the paper then took a firmly Unionist line against the Prime Minister, and Asquith thought that political divergence on an issue of such importance made it necessary for him to sever his connection."

21 Hutton, the *Spectator* (29 June 1861), p. 697, quoted in Woodfield, *R.H. Hutton: Critic and Theologian*, p. 18.

22 *Rise and Progress of Universities* (London, 1872), pp. 13–14.

23 James Martineau (November 1849), quoted in Woodfield, *R.H. Hutton: Critic and Theologian*, p. 6.

24 See Woodfield, *R.H. Hutton: Critic and Theologian*, pp. 12–13.

25 "The Genius of Tennyson," in *A Victorian Spectator: Uncollected Writings of R.H. Hutton*, ed. Tener and Woodfield (Bristol, 1989), p. 254.

26 See *The Oxford Dictionary of the Christian Church*, ed. F. L. Cross (Oxford, 1957), p. 1142.

27 R. H. Hutton, "Dr. Newman's Poems," *Spectator* (25 January 1868), p. 103.

28 "Thin Pessimism," in *A Victorian Spectator: Uncollected Writings of R.H. Hutton*, ed. Tener and Woodfield (Bristol, 1989), p. 242.

29 R. H. Hutton, "Cardinal Newman," *The Contemporary Review* (London, 1884), Volume 45, p. 665.

30 R. H. Hutton, *Cardinal Newman* (London, 1891), p. 190.

31 See James Joyce to Harriet Weaver (1 May 1935), in *Letters of James Joyce*, ed. Stuart Gilbert (New York, 1957), pp. 365–66. As Gilbert notes in his introduction, Joyce "had a habit of reciting [from the works of Newman] to his friends in the mellow after-dinner hour at Les Trianons or Fouquet's (his favorite Parisian restaurants) ..."

32 R. H. Hutton, *Cardinal Newman* (London, 1891), p. 194. As early as 1846, Newman wrote to Frederick Faber: "I have long felt special reverence and admiration for the character of St Ph. [Philip] Neri ..." (LD, 11:105, 1 February 1846).

33 Ibid., p. 207.

34 Ibid., p. 213.

35 R. H. Hutton, "Cardinal Newman," in the *Contemporary Review*, Vol. 45 (May, 1884), p. 660.

36 See Woodfield's entry on Hutton in the *ODNB*.

37 James Martineau, quoted in Malcolm Woodfield, *R.H. Hutton: Critic and Theologian*, p. 3. See also the old *DNB* Supplement, Vol. 22, p. 892.

38 Jeremy Morris, *F.D. Maurice and the Crisis of Christian Authority* (Oxford, 2005), p. 59.

39 F. D. Maurice, *Three Letters to the Rev. William Palmer* (London, 1842), p. 16, quoted in Morris, *F.D. Maurice and the Crisis of Christian Authority*, p. 95.

40 LD, 5:180, JHN to F. W. Hook (21 December 1835).

41 LD, 20:416, JHN to F. D. Maurice (1 March 1863).

42 "Romanism, Protestantism and Anglicanism," in R. H. Hutton, *Theological Essays* (London, 1902), p. 418.

43 LD, 21:95, RHH to JHN (29 March 1864).

44 Gladstone was representative of the pro-South sentiment of the English during the American Civil War. At Newcastle in October 1862, he declared: "Jefferson Davis and other leaders of the South have made an army; they are making, it appears, a navy; and they have made what is more than either, they have made a nation." See Gladstone, quoted in T. K. Hoppen, *The Mid-Victorian Generation: England 1846–1886* (Oxford, 1998), p. 230.

45 R. H. Hutton, *Essays on Some of the Modern Guides to English Thought in Matters of Faith* (London, 1891), pp. 92–93.

46 R. H. Hutton, *Aspects of Religious and Scientific Thought* (London, 1899), p. 337.

47 Ibid,, pp. 342–44.

48 R. H. Hutton, *Aspects of Religious and Scientific Thought*, pp. 15–16.

49 LD, 24:225, RHH to JHN (25 February 1869).

50 Wilfrid Ward, *William George Ward and the Catholic Revival* (London, 1893), pp. 309–10.

51 Ibid., p. 314.

52 R. H. Hutton, "William George Ward," in the *Spectator* (8 July 1882), p. 891.

53 LD, 24:226, JHN to RHH (27 February 1869).

54 LD, 25:303, RHH to JHN (27 February 1869).

55 LD, 28:11, JHN to R. W. Church (11 January 1876).

56 R. H. Hutton, *Cardinal Newman* (London, 1891), pp. 207–08.

57 LD, 21:60–61, JHN to RHH (24 February 1864).

58 "Father Newman's Sarcasm," in the *Spectator* (20 February 1864), p. 207.

59 LD, 21:60, JHN to RHH (26 February 1864).

60 LD, 21:67–68, RHH to JHN (28 February 1864). The article to which Hutton refers is "Father Newman's Sarcasm," in the *Spectator* (20 February 1864), pp. 206–08.

61 See Ian Ker, "The Personal Nature of Religious Belief," in *Healing the Wounds of Humanity: The Spirituality of John Henry Newman* (London, 1993), pp. 1–9.

62 Malcolm Woodfield, *R.H. Hutton: Critic and Theologian*, p. 47.

63 *Loss and Gain*, pp. 327–29.

64 LD, 21:68, RHH to JHN (28 February 1863).

65 R. H. Hutton, "Frederick Denison Maurice," in *Essays on Some of the Modern Guides to English Thought in Matters of Faith* (London, 1891), p. 318.

66 LD, 25:32, JHN to RHH (16 February 1870). See LD, 31:xiii: In the *Contemporary Review* for May 1885 there appeared an article by the Congregationalist A. M. Fairbairn, Principal of Airedale Theological

College, Bradford, which accused Newman of philosophical scepticism and of withdrawing the proofs of religion from the realm of reason into that of conscience and imagination. Hutton claimed the direct opposite: that Newman parried philosophical skepticism by showing how faith was corroborated by conscience and imagination.

67 *Apologia*, pp. 251–53.
68 LD, 21:68–9, JHN to RHH (3 March 1864).
69 LD, 21:90 JHN to RHH (27 March 1864).
70 R. H. Hutton, "Roman Catholic Casuistry and Protestant Prejudice," in the *Spectator* (26 March 1864), p. 358.
71 "The Use of Paradox," in R. H. Hutton, *Brief Literary Criticisms* (London, 1906), p. 40.
72 "Unreal Words" (1839), in *Parochial and Plain Sermons*, Book 5, Sermon 3.
73 R. H. Hutton, "'Unreal Words' in Religious Belief," in the *Spectator* (24 July 1886), p. 984.
74 "Mr Arnold's Lay Sermons," in R. H. Hutton, *Aspects of Religious and Scientific Thought* (London, 1899), pp. 322–29.
75 R. H. Hutton, "Dr. Newman's Apology," in the *Spectator* (4 June 1864), p. 655.
76 Malcolm Woodfield, "Victorian Weekly Reviews and Reviewing After 1860: R. H. Hutton and the *Spectator*," in *The Yearbook of English Studies*, Vol. 16, Literary Periodicals Special Number (1986), p. 79.
77 "Dr. Newman's Apology," in the *Spectator* (11 June 1864), p. 683.
78 LD, 21:120, RHH to JHN (15 June 1864).
79 "Dr. Newman's Apology" (4 June 1864), p. 655.
80 LD, 9:274 JHN to Mary Holmes (8 March 1843).
81 "It is not by logic that God has deemed to save his people." This is the epigraph from St. Ambrose's *De Fide ad Gratianum Augustum* that Newman used for his *Grammar of Assent*. In the *Apologia*, Newman admits, "I had a great dislike of paper-logic. For myself, it was not logic that carried me on; as well might one say that the quicksilver in the barometer changes the weather. It is the concrete being who reasons ..." (*Apologia*, p. 155).
82 LD, 21:121, RHH to JHN (15 June 1864).
83 *Anglican Difficulties*, p. 88: "If I let you plead the sensible effects of supernatural grace, as exemplified in yourselves, in proof that your religion is true, I must allow the plea to others to whom by your theory you are bound to deny it. Are you willing to place yourselves on the same footing with Wesleyans? yet what is the difference? or rather, have they not more remarkable phenomena in their history, symptomatic of the presence of grace among them, than you can show in yours? Which, then, is the right explanation of your feelings and your experience,—mine, which I have extracted from received Catholic teaching; or yours, which is an expedient for the occasion, and cannot be made to tell for your own Apostolical authority without telling for those who are rebels against it? Survey the

rise of Methodism, and say candidly, whether those who made light of your ordinances, abandoned them, or at least disbelieved their virtue, have not had among them evidences of that very same grace which you claim for yourselves, and which you consider a proof of your acceptance with God. Really I am obliged in candour to allow, whatever part the evil spirit had in the work, whatever gross admixture of earth polluted it, whatever extravagance there was to excite ridicule or disgust, whether it was Christian virtue or the excellence of unaided man, whatever was the spiritual state of the subjects of it, whatever their end and their final account, yet there were higher and nobler vestiges or semblances of grace and truth in Methodism than there have been among you."

84 LD, 21:121, JHN to RHH (18 June 1864).
85 LD, 23:385, RHH to JHN (21 December 1867).
86 Gladstone to RHH (6 October 1890), in *Correspondence on Church and Religion of William Ewart Gladstone*, ed. Lathbury (London, 1910), Vol. I, pp. 405–08.
87 LD, 21:123 RHH to JHN (28 June 1864).
88 See "Dr. Newman's Oxford Sermons," in *A Victorian Spectator: Uncollected Writings of R.H. Hutton*, ed. Tener and Woodfield (Bristol, 1989), p. 155.
89 *Apologia*, pp. 245–46.
90 W. E. Gladstone, *The Vatican Decrees in their Bearing on Civil Allegiance: An Expostulation* (London, 1874), p. 37.
91 *Letter to the Duke of Norfolk*, p. 225.
92 Ibid., pp. 229–30.
93 LD, 25:42, JHN to RHH (24 February 1870).
94 LD, 25:29, JHN to RHH (13 February 1870).
95 LD, 25:111, RHH to JHN (4 April 1870).
96 LD, 25:111, JHN to RHH (27 April 1870).
97 Hutton's *Spectator* obituary on Newman in LD, 32:630.
98 LD, 26:38, RHH to JHN (20 February 1872).
99 J. H. Newman, "The Religion of the Day" (1832), in *Plain and Parochial Sermons*, Book 1, Sermon 24.
100 LD, 26:39, RHH to JHN (20 February 1872).
101 LD, 26:39–41, JHN to RHH (1 March 1872).
102 LD, 30:294–95, RHH to JHN (13 January 1884).
103 LD, 30:295, JHN to RHH (14 January 1884).
104 LD, 30:356, JHN to RHH (6 May 1884).
105 LD, 30:356, RHH to JHN (10 May 1884). See also the *Contemporary Review*, Vol. 45 (May 1884), pp. 642–65.
106 LD, 26:223–24, JHN to RHH (29 December 1872).
107 *Loss and Gain*, pp. 385–86.
108 Hutton's *Spectator* obituary on Newman in LD, 32:631.
109 J. H. Newman, "Inward Witness to the Truth of the Gospel" (1825), in *Parochial and Plain Sermons*, Book 8, Sermon 8.
110 *The Idea of a University*, p. 121.

111 J. H. Newman, "The Religion of the Day," in *Parochial and Plain Sermons*, Book 1, Sermon 24.

112 Cf. *Grammar of Assent*, Ch. X, pp. 395–96. "It may at first sight seem strange, that, considering I have laid such stress upon the progressive nature of man, I should take my ideas of his religion from his initial, and not his final testimony about its doctrines; and it may be urged that the religion of civilized times is quite opposite in character to the rites and traditions of barbarians, and has nothing of that gloom and sternness, on which I have insisted as their characteristic. Thus the Greek Mythology was for the most part cheerful and graceful, and its new gods certainly more genial and indulgent than the old ones. And, in like manner, the religion of philosophy is more noble and more humane than those primitive conceptions which were sufficient for early kings and warriors. But my answer to this objection is obvious: the progress of which man's nature is capable is a development, not a destruction of its original state; it must subserve the elements from which it proceeds, in order to be a true development and not a perversion. And those popular rituals do in fact subserve and complete that nature with which man is born. It is otherwise with the religion of so-called civilization; such religion does but contradict the religion of barbarism; and since this civilization itself is not a development of man's whole nature, but mainly of the intellect, recognizing indeed the moral sense, but ignoring the conscience, no wonder that the religion in which it issues has no sympathy either with the hopes and fears of the awakened soul, or with those frightful presentiments which are expressed in the worship and traditions of the heathen. This artificial religion, then, has no place in the inquiry; first, because it comes of a one-sided progress of mind, and next, for the very reason that it contradicts informants which speak with greater authority than itself."

113 J. H. Newman, "Doing Glory to God in Pursuits of the World," in *Parochial and Plain Sermons*, Book 8, Sermon 11.

114 R. H. Hutton, *Cardinal Newman* (London, 1891), p. 251.

115 See LD, 23:629 for Hutton's *Spectator* obituary on Newman.

Chapter 11 Culture and Hollowness: Newman and Matthew Arnold

1 A. P. Stanley, *Life of Thomas Arnold* (London, 1904), pp. 156–57.

2 LD, 27:280, William Ullathorne to James Knowles (15 July 1877).

3 Matthew Arnold, "Emerson," from *Discourses in America* (New York, 1924), pp. 142–43.

4 Ibid., p. 195.

5 *Correspondence of Arthur Hugh Clough*, ed. Mulhauser (Oxford, 1957), p. 215.

6 See Letter of Matthew Arnold to Arthur Hugh Clough (23 September 1849) in *Letters of Matthew Arnold to Arthur Hugh Clough*, ed. Howard

Foster Lowry (Oxford, 1932), p.111. This is also quoted in Simon Heffer's lively biography, *Moral Desperado: A Life of Thomas Carlyle* (London, 1995), p. 274.

7   Matthew Arnold, *God and the Bible* (New York, 1883), p. xi.

8   Matthew Arnold, *Essays in Criticism: Second Series* (London, 1903), p. 2.

9 . Ibid., p. 2.

10   T. S. Eliot, "Matthew Arnold," in *The Use of Poetry and the Use of Criticism* (London, 1933), pp. 113–14.

11   Ibid., p. 113.

12   Matthew Arnold, "The Function of Criticism at the Present Time," in *Matthew Arnold: The Oxford Authors*, ed. Allott and Super (Oxford, 1986), p. 319.

13   See "The Progress of Poesy," p. 268: "Youth rambles on life's arid mount/ And strikes the rock, and finds the vein/And brings the water from the fount/The fount which shall not flow again."

14   *Essays Critical and Historical*, Vol. 2, p. 430.

15   Ibid., p. 436.

16   Ibid., p. 433.

17   Ibid., p. 445.

18   Water Pater, "Coleridge's Writings," in *Sketches and Reviews* (London, 1919), pp. 103–04.

19   Michael Burleigh, *Earthly Powers: The Clash of Religion and Politics from the French Revolution and the First World War* (New York, 2005), p. 273.

20   *The Poems and Prose Remains of A.H. Clough*, ed. Blanche (Smith) Clough (London, 1869), p. 68.

21   Ian Hamilton, *A Gift Imprisoned: The Poetic Life of Matthew Arnold* (London, 1998), p. 42.

22   Dr. Arnold, quoted in A. P. Stanley, *Life of Thomas Arnold*, p. 380.

23   See LD, 18:559, Lord Acton to Richard Simpson (1 January 1859): "I had a 3 hours' talk with the venerable Noggs who came out at last with his real sentiments to an extent which startled me, with respect both to things and persons, as H E [His Eminence], Ward, Dalgairns, etc., etc., natural inclination of men in power to tyrannise, ignorance and presumption of our would-be theologians, in short what you and I would comfortably say over a glass of whiskey. I did not think he could ever cast aside his diplomacy and buttonment so entirely, and was quite surprised at the intense interest he betrayed in the Rambler. He was quite miserable when I told him the news and moaned for a long time, rocking himself backwards and forward over the fire, like an old woman with the toothache ..." R. G. Collingwood said something in his autobiography about an Oxford philosophy don—John Cook Wilson (1849–1915)—which has always seemed to me the last word on Lord Acton: "There are two reasons why people refrain from writing books: either they are conscious that they have nothing to say, or they are conscious that they are unable to say it ... if they give any other reason than these it is to throw dust in other people's eyes or their own." See R. G. Collingwood, *An Autobiography* (Oxford,

1939), pp. 19–20. To be fair to Wilson, as the *ODNB* points out, if he produced no books, he was not idle: "Wilson was an energetic man who combined a passion for cycling with an interest in war games … During the last year of his life he was a regular writer in the correspondence columns of *The Times*, offering advice on military matters, including the establishment of an army cyclist corps to fight in Belgium."

24 Matthew Arnold, "Emerson," in *Discourses in America* (London, 1924), pp. 139–40.

25 "Peace in Believing" (1839), in *Parochial and Plain Sermons* (Ignatius Press, 1997), p. 1412.

26 See Gerard Tracey, Preface to *John Henry Newman: Sermons 1824–1843, Vol. 1: Sermons on the Liturgy and Sacraments and on Christ the Mediator*, ed. Placid Murray (Oxford, 1991), p. v.

27 Matthew Arnold to Arthur Hugh Clough (6 September 1853), in *The Letters of Matthew Arnold to Arthur Hugh Clough*, ed. Howard Foster Lowry (Oxford, 1968), p. 143.

28 Andrew Motion, *Philip Larkin: A Writer's Life* (New York, 1993), p. 485.

29 T. S. Eliot, "Arnold and Pater" (1930), in *Selected Essays* (London, 1951), p. 436.

30 Arnold, quoted in J. D. Jump, *Matthew Arnold* (London, 1955), p. 48.

31 *The Letters of Thomas Arnold the Younger*, ed. James Bertram (Auckland and Oxford, 1980), pp. 60–61. See *Discourses to Mixed Congregations*, pp. 260–61, for Arnold's reference to Newman's work.

32 Matthew Arnold, quoted in Bernard Bergonzi, *A Victorian Wanderer: The Life of Thomas Arnold the Younger* (Oxford, 2003), p. 189.

33 Ibid., p. 108. Verrey's Restaurant at 233 Regent Street was one of the most fashionable in Victorian London, its patrons including the Prince of Wales, Charles Dickens and Disraeli. Sherlock Holmes had sweet-meats delivered from the restaurant whenever he wanted a break from Mrs. Hudson's cooking. See *The London Encyclopedia*, ed. Weinreb and Hibbert (London, 1983), p. 912.

34 *The Idea of a University*, p. 315.

35 LD, 29:169, JHN to Lady Herbert of Lea (19 August 1879).

36 Park Honan, *Matthew Arnold: A Life* (Harvard, 1981), p. 187.

37 Ibid., p. 237.

38 See "To My Friends," and Hamilton, *A Gift Imprisoned*, p. 106.

39 *Autobiographical Writings* (25 March 1840), p. 138.

40 LD, 11:95, JHN to Ambrose St. John (20 January 1846).

41 LD, 5:313, JHN to Mrs. John Mozley (26 June 1836).

42 Matthew Arnold, *Literature and Dogma* (New York, 1903), p. 261.

43 See Matthew Arnold, *Literature and Dogma* (London, 1883), p. 315.

44 Ibid., p. v.

45 Ibid., pp. v–vi.

46 "The Scholar-Gypsy," lines 203–04.

47 "Rugby Chapel," lines 171–81.

48   The convert Lord Ripon (1827–1909), who was roundly abused in *The Times* for abandoning the Established Church and converting to Rome, had come to say goodbye to Newman before he departed for India to take up his duties as Viceroy.

49   "Matthew Arnold," in *The Use of Poetry and the Use of Criticism*, pp. 105–06.

50   "Scholar-Gipsy," pp. 171–80.

51   Matthew Arnold, *Culture and Anarchy* (New York, 1920), p. viii.

52   Ibid., pp. 63–64.

53   *Letters of Max Beerbohm 1892–1956*, ed. Rupert Hart-Davis (Oxford, 1989), pp. 139–40.

54   *Culture and Anarchy,* p. 10.

55   *Letter to the Duke of Norfolk*, ed. Alvan Ryan (Notre Dame, 1962), p. 129. See also Gerard J. Hughes, "Conscience," in *The Cambridge Companion to John Henry Newman*, ed. Ker and Merrigan (Cambridge, 2009).

56   Matthew Arnold, *Culture and Anarchy* (New York, 1920), p. 23.

57   Ibid., p. 23.

58   *See Tamworth Reading Room*, p. 275.

59   See Henry Sidgwick, "The Prophet of Culture," in *Macmillan's Magazine*, Vol. 16 (1867), pp. 271–80. Sidgwick's review is also included as an appendix to the Oxford World's Classics edition of Arnold's *Culture and Anarchy* edited by Jane Garnett (Oxford, 2006), where this quote appears on pages 166–67.

60   Matthew Arnold, "Democracy" (1851), in *Mixed Essays* (New York, 1903), p. 43.

61   Referring to the ideas of Lord Brougham, on which Peel relied for his Tamworth Reading Room, Newman recalled how Mr. Brougham talked much and eloquently of "the *sweetness* of knowledge," and "the *charms* of philosophy," of students "smitten with the love of knowledge," of "*wooing* truth with the unwearied ardour of a *lover*," of "keen and overpowering *emotion*, of *ecstasy*," of "the absorbing *passion* of knowledge," of "the *strength* of the passion, and the exquisite pleasure of its *gratification*"—all very Arnoldian terms. See *Tamworth Reading Room*, pp. 256–57.

62   *Tamworth Reading Room*, p. 268.

63   LD, 25:271–72, JHN to B. M. Pickering (21 January 1871).

64   *Tamworth Reading Room*, p. 275.

65   Matthew Arnold, "The Function of Criticism at the Present Time," in *Matthew Arnold: The Oxford Authors*, p. 335.

66   See "Civilization in the United States" (1888), in *Matthew Arnold: The Oxford Authors*, p. 504.

67   Matthew Arnold, *Culture and Anarchy*, p. 28.

68   "The Buried Life," lines 45–53.

69   "Stanzas from the Green Chartreuse," lines 67–78.

70   See Hutton, quoted in LD, 32:628.

71   LD, 25:440–41, Matthew Arnold to JHN (29 November 1871).

72 LD, 25:442, JHN to Matthew Arnold (3 December 1871).
73 *English Illustrated Magazine*, January 1884, quoted in *Matthew Arnold: The Oxford Authors*, p. 561.
74 LD, 25:442, Matthew Arnold to JHN (20 January 1868).
75 See Arnold, *Culture and Anarchy*, p. 3.
76 "Dover Beach," lines 1–14.
77 "Bacchanalia, or The New Age," lines 26–28.
78 "Below the Surface-Stream" (1869). Arnold wrote these lines around the same time that he composed *St. Paul and Protestantism* (1870).
79 See LD, 26:95, notes 1 and 2.
80 LD, 8:376, JHN to Edward Pusey (December 1841), p. 376.
81 LD, 26:95, JHN to Matthew Arnold (24 May 1872).
82 John Ruskin, *Praeterita* (Oxford, 1978), pp. 5–6.
83 T. S. Eliot, *Selected Essays* (London, 1951), p. 390.
84 *The Idea of a University*, p. 218.
85 LD, 26:96, Matthew Arnold to JHN (28 May 1872).
86 LD, 28:5–6, JHN to Matthew Arnold (3 January 1876).
87 Arnold, quoted in Hamilton, *A Gift Imprisoned*, p. 212.
88 "Growing Old," lines 1–5.
89 Ibid., lines 16–20.
90 Ibid., lines 21–25.
91 Matthew Arnold, *Literature and Dogma* (London, 1873), p. 46.
92 "The Religious Use of Excited Feelings" (1831), in *Parochial and Plain Sermons* (Ignatius Press, 1997), p. 76.
93 "Growing Old," lines 31–35.
94 Arnold was pleased with the essays contained in *Discourses in America* but was embarrassed by the success that met *Literature and Dogma*, which he regarded as a pot boiler. Still, it was his most critically acclaimed and commercially successful composition.
95 *Autobiographical Writings*, pp. 124–25.
96 For a lively critical analysis of Arnold's hollowness, see J. Matthew Hillis, "Matthew Arnold," in *Matthew Arnold: A Collection of Critical Essays*, ed. David J. DeLaura (New Jersey, 1973), pp. 24–45. Hillis is particularly astute about all of those catchphrases that Disraeli told Arnold made him a classic in his own lifetime. "Arnold's expressions of the truths which are the center of his own system are left deliberately vague," Hillis points out. They are scrupulously empty phrases. Their repetition empties them further of meaning … "make reason and the will of God prevail," "the best that has been thought and said in the world," "high seriousness," "the laws of poetic truth and poetic beauty," the "Eternal, not ourselves, that makes for righteousness," etc.… . See page 42. In this regard, no Victorian writer was guiltier of what Newman called 'unreal words' than Arnold.
97 "Christ on the Waters," pp. 161–62.
98 LD, 20:30, JHN to Sister Mary Gabriel Du Boulay (18 August 1861).

Chapter 12 Newman and Arthur Hugh Clough

1 Francis Turner Palgrave, "Memoir" to *The Poems of Arthur Hugh Clough* (1862), from *Arthur Hugh Clough: The Critical Heritage*, ed. Michael Thorpe (London, 1972), p. 110.

2 Walter Bagehot, "Mr. Clough's Poems," from *National Review* (October 1862), in *Arthur Hugh Clough: The Critical Heritage*, p. 168.

3 V. S. Pritchett, "The Poet of Tourism," in *Complete Collected Essays* (New York, 1991), p. 353.

4 Anthony Kenny, *Arthur Hugh Clough: A Poet's Life* (London, 2005), p. 1. Although I take issue with Sir Anthony in various ways, I am indebted to his lively biography for much of my own knowledge of Clough's life.

5 *The Poems and Prose Remains of A.H. Clough*, ed. Blanche (Smith) Clough (London, 1869), p. 4.

6 Cyril Connolly, *Enemies of Promise* (London, 1938), p. 271.

7 *Correspondence of Arthur Hugh Clough*, ed. Mulhauser (Oxford, 1957), p. 310.

8 John H. Jones, "Balliol: From Obscurity to Pre-Eminence," in *The History of the University of Oxford*, ed. Brock and Curthoys (Oxford, 1997), Vol. VI, Pt. 1, p. 180.

9 Epilogue, *Dipsychus*, line 84.

10 *Correspondence of Arthur Hugh Clough*, pp. 81–82.

11 Ibid., p. 66.

12 Ibid., pp. 68–69.

13 See Sir James Stephen, K.C.B., "The Lives of Whitfield and Froude: Oxford Catholicism," in *Edinburgh Review*, Vol. LXVII (July 1838), pp. 500–35.

14 See Anthony Kenny, *Arthur Hugh Clough: A Poet's Life* (London, 2005), p. 48, and *The Oxford Diaries of Arthur Hugh Clough*, ed. Anthony Kenny (Oxford, 1991), pp. xxv and 92–94.

15 *Correspondence of Arthur Hugh Clough*, p. 96.

16 *The Idea of a University*, p. 229.

17 *Poems of Arthur Hugh Clough*, p. 319.

18 LD, 20:169, JHN to W. G. Ward (15 March 1862).

19 *Correspondence of Arthur Hugh Clough*, p. 67.

20 *Apologia*, pp. 291–92.

21 Readers of Flann O'Brien's comic masterpiece *At-Swim-Two-Birds* (1939) will recognize that it was from Clough that O'Brien took the idea of unifying his narrative with conversations between a young author and his irascible uncle. It is also interesting that it was Graham Greene who accepted O'Brien's first novel for publication, when he was working as a publisher's reader for Longman. Doubtless, Green found O'Brien's debt to Clough endearing.

22 *Correspondence of Arthur Hugh Clough*, p. 71.

23 Kenny, *Arthur Hugh Clough: A Poet's Life*, p. 45.

24 LD, 1:219, JHN to Charles Newman (24 March 1825).
25 See Tait, quoted in Kenny, *Arthur Hugh Clough: A Poet's Life*, p. 60.
26 Richard Holt Hutton, "Arthur Hugh Clough," from *Essays Theological and Literary* (London, 1871), Vol. II, pp. 368–91.
27 See "Sins of Infirmity" in *Parochial and Plain Sermons*, pp. 212–13.
28 See *Clough: The Critical Heritage*, ed. Michael Thorpe (London, 1972), p. 107.
29 *The Bothie of Tober-Na-Vuolich*, Vol. VI, pp. 59–66.
30 Ibid., pp. 194–97.
31 "The State of Innocence," in *Parochial Sermons*, Book 5, Sermon 8, Page 10.
32 See *Amours de Voyage*, Canto I:

> It is a blessing, no doubt, to be rid, at least for a time, of
> All one's friends and relations,—yourself (forgive me!) included,—
> All the *assujettissment* of having been what one has been.

33 Ibid., Canto II, IX, lines 270–75.
34 *Oxford University Sermons*, p. 293.
35 *Essays Critical and Historical*, pp. 302–03.
36 Ibid., Vol. II, p. 353.
37 *Tamworth Reading Room*, in *Discussions and Arguments on Various Subjects*, p. 294.
38 Ibid., p. 295.
39 *Loss and Gain*, pp. 327–28.
40 Cecil Woodham-Smith, *Florence Nightingale 1820–1910* (London, 1950), p. 109.
41 *Correspondence of Arthur Hugh Clough*, pp. 305–06.
42 Ibid., p. 307.
43 Ibid., p. 300.
44 Kenny, *Arthur Hugh Clough: A Poet's Life*, p. 237.
45 Blanche Smith to Clough (4 March 1853), quoted in Robindra Kumar Biswas, *Arthur Hugh Clough* (Oxford, 1972), p. 418.
46 Lytton Strachey, *Eminent Victorians* (London, 1918), p. 170.
47 *Amours de Voyage*, Canto V, V, lines 86–94.
48 Kenny usefully points out that the title "bears a double meaning. *Mari Magno* is a natural title for a series of tales on seaboard; but it also echoes a famous passage of Lucretius, beginning 'Suave mari mango,' which describes the pleasure that watching ships battling with the elements can give to someone safe on shore. This suggests that the poem is meant to represent, from the standpoint of someone happily married, the various things that can go wrong on or after a wedding. Or the things that can go right as the result of storms survived." See Kenny, *Arthur Hugh Clough: A Poet's Life*, pp. 276–77.
49 *Poems of Arthur Hugh Clough*, p. 376.
50 Kenny, *Arthur Hugh Clough: A Poet's Life*, p. 213.

51   "To Spend Uncounted Years of Pain."

52   See V. S. Pritchett, "The Poet of Tourism."

53   D. C. Somervell, *English Thought in the Nineteenth Century* (London, 1929), p. 121.

54   Prologue, *Dipsychus*, line 3.

55   Epilogue, *Dipsychus*, line 4.

56   See Martin Gilbert, *Finest Hour: Winston S. Churchill 1939–1941* (London, 1983), pp. 1022 and 1070. Churchill learned Clough's poem by heart before World War I.

57   See J. M. Robertson, "Clough," from *New Essays Towards a Critical Method* (London, 1897) in *Clough: The Critical Heritage*, ed. Michael Thorpe (London, 1972), p. 363.

58   "There Is No God the Wicked Saith" often appears as a stand-alone poem in anthologies.

59   See Kenny, *Arthur Hugh Clough: A Poet's Life*, pp. 181–85, and Katherine Chorley, *Arthur Hugh Clough: The Uncommitted Mind* (Oxford, 1962), pp. 109–13.

60   "Easter Day, Naples, 1849."

61   Kenny, *Arthur Hugh Clough: A Poet's Life*, p. 184.

62   See H. Francis Davis, "The Catholicism of Cardinal Newman," in *Newman Centenary Essays*, ed. Henry Tristram (London, 1945), p. 36: "From the time that he began to think, it was inconceivable to [Newman] that God might have left mankind with no revelation of Himself and no guide for man's action. It almost seemed that for him God's ways were easier to understand than man's, and that the mystery of man's darkness was greater than the mystery of God's light."

63   *Apologia*, p. 243.

64   Ibid., p. 243.

65   Ibid., pp. 243–44.

66   See "Life of Cowley" in Samuel Johnson. *The Lives of the Poets* ed. Roger Lonsdale (Oxford, 2006),Vol. 1, p. 223.

67   *Amours de Voyage*, Canto II, V, line 98.

68   Ibid., Canto II, Prologue.

69   LD, 3:268, JHN to Mrs. Jemima Newman (25 March 1833).

70   *Amours de Voyage*, Canto I, V, lines 19–25.

71   There is one sense in which Claude is a reflection of Clough: as Paul Turner points out in an excellent overview of Clough's career, Claude "was Clough criticizing himself for constantly criticizing himself." See Paul Turner, *Victorian Poetry, Drama and Miscellaneous Prose 1832–1890* (Oxford, 1989), p. 69.

72   Clough, quoted in Kenny, *Arthur Hugh Clough: A Poet's Life*, p. 155.

73   See Church to Lord Blachford (27 April 1882), in *Life and Letters of Dean Church*, ed. Church (London, 1895), pp. 295–96.

74   *The Idea of a University*, p. 218.

75   Whatever his later views on Unitarianism were, earlier, in 1845, after reading Thom's biography of Blanco White, Clough confessed: "almost it persuaded

me to turn Unitarian—that is, for the moment ..." See *Correspondence of Arthur Hugh Clough*, ed. Mulhauser (Oxford, 1957), p. 155.

76 *Correspondence of Arthur Hugh Clough*, ed. Mulhauser (Oxford, 1957), p. 249.

77 *Amours de Voyage*, Canto I, II, lines 45–46.

78 Ibid., Canto I, IV, lines 70–77.

79 Of Loyola, Dr. Arnold wrote: "No man can doubt the piety of Loyola and many of his followers; yet, what Christian, in England at least, can doubt that, as Jesuitism, it was not of God; that it was grounded on falsehood and strove to propagate falsehood? So, again, the Puritans led to the Nonjurors; zealous, many of them, and pious, but narrow minded in the last degree, fierce and slanderous ..." See A. P. Stanley, *Life of Dr. Arnold* (London, 1904), p. 473.

80 *Amours de Voyage*, Canto I, IV, lines 101–14.

81 See LD, 9:307–08, JHN to John Keble (15 April 1843).

82 *Amours de Voyage*, Canto V, II, lines 20–26.

83 John Pemble, *The Mediterranean Passion: Victorians and Edwardians in the South* (Oxford, 1987).

84 *Dipsychus*, XI, lines 1–16.

85 *Tamworth Reading Room*, p. 292.

86 *Amours de Voyage*, Canto V, X, lines 197–205.

87 *Oxford Sermons*, "Love the Safeguard of Faith against Superstition" (1839), p. 172.

88 LD, 19:417, JHN to W. G. Ward (8 November 1860).

89 See Arnold's "The Scholar Gypsy" (1853), line 172.

90 Walter Bagehot, "Mr. Clough's Poems," in *National Review* (October 1862), Vol. XIII, p. 310.

91 *The Idea of a University*, p. 133.

Chapter 13 Newman on Newman

1 Ronald Knox, *A Spiritual Aeneid* (London, 1958), p. 11.

2 *The Art of Novel: Critical Prefaces by Henry James*, ed. R. P. Blackmur (New York, 1934), p. 57.

3 LD, 22:9, JHN to R. W. Church (11 July 1865).

4 "The Theory of Developments in Religious Doctrine" (1843), in *Oxford University Sermons*, pp. 346–47.

5 *The Art of Novel*, p. 62.

6 See Leon Edel, *Henry James: The Conquest of London* (London, 1962), pp. 168–69.

7 From "Last Years of John Chrysostom," in *Historical Sketches*, Vol. 2, pp. 218–20.

8 Ibid., p. 219.

9 *Autobiographical Writings*, p. 268.

10 LD, 21:107, JHN to James Hope-Scott (2 May 1864).

11 Newman's propensity to cry, whenever overwhelmed by strong feeling, put him in a great tradition. As Hilaire Belloc observes, "Cromwell was perpetually bursting into tears. He sniffed and rubbed his eyes to see Charles the king with his children. Tears rolled down his cheeks in prayer, and again in domestic bereavement. He was one of the great criers of history, an unfailing and repetitive, as it were, chainweeper. The second of the noble Hanoverians, whom I suppose I may call a Great Man, for he was of Nordic stock and reasonably rich, cried when his wife died; Dr. Johnson at the memory of his mother, Pitt the Younger upon the news of Austerlitz, and under the effect of port; Macaulay (I am told) at the discovery of a stumer cheque. Thiers wept when he signed the capitulation to Bismarck, and the Moltke of the last war when there reached him at head-quarters in Luxemburg the news of the Marne. Alfred, Lord Tennyson, Laureate, wept, or at least allowed the tears to gather to his eyes, at the prospect of the stubble of the English country-side. Carlyle wept when he thought of his wife after her death, and his wife when she thought of Carlyle before it ..." See "On the Tears of the Great," in Hilaire Belloc. *A Conversation with an Angel and Other Essays* (London, 1928), pp. 53–54.

12 *Apologia*, p. 4.

13 Ibid., p. 2.

14 Ibid., p. 3.

15 LD, 10:262, JHN to John Keble (8 June 1844).

16 John Keble, *On Eucharistical Adoration* (London, 1867), p. 177. John Bramhall (1594–1663) was Bishop of Derry under Charles I and Primate of Ireland under Charles II. A resourceful divine, he strengthened the Church of Ireland, defended episcopacy against the presbyterianism of the Puritans, attacked Hobbes's materialism, and reaffirmed the Anglican understanding of the Real Presence. See *Oxford Dictionary of the Christian Church*, ed. F. L. Cross (Oxford, 1957), p. 192. Thomas Cranmer (1489–1556) was made Archbishop of Canterbury in 1532 and advanced many of Henry VIII's anti-papal purposes. After Henry's death, he became one of Edward VI's counselors. In 1553, when Mary Tudor ascended the throne, he was accused of high treason and sentenced to death, but spared after he recanted his Protestantism. Charged subsequently with heresy, he recanted his recantation and died bravely at the stake an avowed Protestant on 21 March 1556. Hilaire Belloc had high praise for his literary achievement, writing of his translation of the Bible: "He could frame a sentence of rhythmical and exquisitely beautiful English as no man has ... before or since." But he thought rather less well of the churchman. "Cranmer was never more than an agent, though a willing agent—even in his heart of hearts an enthusiastic agent: a man who hated the Catholic Church and the Sacraments and in especial the Sacrament of the Altar and the Mass ..." See Hilaire Belloc, *Characters of the Reformation* (London, 1936), pp. 74–76.

17 T. S. Eliot, "John Bramhall," in *Selected Essays* (London, 1951), p. 351.

18 LD, 19:487, JHN to Malcolm Maccoll (24 March 1861).

19 *Apologia*, pp. 236–37.

20 Ian Ker, *John Henry Newman* (Oxford, 2009), p. 745.

21 *Apologia*, pp. 339–40.

22 Ibid., p. 2.

23 *Fifteen Sermons Preached Before the University of Oxford*, ed. Tracey and Earnest (Oxford, 2006), p. xiii.

24 See "Justice: Principle of Divine Governance" (1832), in *Fifteen Sermons Preached Before the University of Oxford*, pp. 115–16.

25 Matthew Arnold made reference to these lectures in the preface of *Culture and Anarchy* (1869). "At a moment when the Courts of Law have just taken off the embargo from the recreative religion furnished on Sundays by my gifted acquaintance and others, and when St. Martin's Hall and the Alhambra will soon be beginning again to resound with their pulpit eloquence, it distresses me to think that the new lights should not only have, in general, a very low opinion of the preachers of the old religion but that they should have it without knowing the best that these preachers can do." Arnold purveyed this same "recreative religion" in his own lay sermons.

26 Thomas Huxley, "On Improving Natural Knowledge," in *Lectures and Lay Sermons* (London, 1910), p. 53.

27 *Tamworth Reading Room*, in *Discussion and Arguments*, p. 293.

28 Ibid.

29 *Oxford Sermons*, pp. 117–18.

30 Geoffrey Hill, "Common Weal, Common Woe," in *Collected Critical Writings*, ed. Kenneth Haynes (New Haven, 2008), p. 279. See also "Scenes from Comus," in Hill's *Selected Poems* (2006), p. 255: "Nothing is unforgettable but guilt."

31 *Autobiographical Writings*, p. 250.

32 *Discourses to Mixed Congregations*, pp. 348–49.

33 *Oxford University Sermons*, p. 313.

34 See Tracey Rowland, *Ratzinger's Faith: The Theology of Pope Benedict XVI* (Oxford, 2008), p. 24: "Whereas Ratzinger has examined St. Augustine's contribution to the notion of the person and what in contemporary terms is called the self and its interiority, Wojityla developed Thomist philosophical anthropology in the direction of mid-twentieth-century French personalism. Again we can see in the works of the two pontiffs a dovetailing of two agendas: in general terms both were interested in Christian personalism, but Wojityla was working on the Aquinas-Mounier-Scheler line, and Ratzinger on the Augustine-Newman-Przywara-Guardini line."

35 *The Idea of a University*, p. 275.

36 LD, 28:376–77, JHN to Ambrose St. John (13 June 1858).

37 LD, 8:194, JHN to Henry Wilberforce (24 May 1841).

38 *The Idea of a University*, pp. 275–76.

39 *Further Letters of Gerard Manley Hopkins including his correspondence with Coventry Patmore*, ed. Claude Colleer Abbott (Oxford, 1938), p. 232.

40 *The Idea of a University*, pp. 145–46.

41 LD, 13:16, JHN to Henry Wilberforce (24 January 1849).

42 LD, 32:143 JHN to Lady Arundel (20 February 1856).

43 LD, 16:234, JHN to Robert Isaac Wilberforce (21 August 1854).

44 LD, 17:530, JHN to Mrs. Froude (24 February 1857).

45 LD, 19:310, JHN to Mrs. John Mozley (21 February 1860).

46 Evelyn Waugh, *A Little Learning: The First Volume of an Autobiography* (London, 1964), p. 64.

47 LD, 16:48, JHN to Ambrose St. John (17 February 1854).

48 *Autobiographical Writings*, pp. 247–8.

49 Newman quoted in *Letters of John Henry Newman*, ed. Derek Stanford and Muriel Spark (London, 1957), p. 160. I have pinched this from Muriel Spark's brilliant introduction to Newman's Catholic letters.

50 *Autobiographical Writings*, p. 254.

51 Ibid., p. 257.

52 Ibid., p. 254.

53 Ibid., pp. 258–59.

54 Ibid., p. 264.

55 LD, 24:24–25, JHN to Sir Frederic Rogers (2 February 1868).

56 Max Beerbohm, *Zuleika Dobson* (London, 1914), p. 29.

57 LD, 21:165, JHN to Ambrose St. John (25 July 1864). Edward Caswall (1814–1878), the great hymnologist, who gave Newman the necessary funds to purchase the Birmingham Oratory, called Talbot and his friends "those bumptious Romans."

58 LD, 23:394, JHN to Catherine Anne Bathurst (29 December 1867).

59 LD, 16:535, JHN to Mrs. J. W. Bowden (31 August 1855).

60 LD, 20:427, JHN to Sister Mary Gabriel du Boulay (7 April 1863).

61 LD, 7:183, JHN to Mrs. John Mozley (17 November 1839).

62 LD, 13:72, JHN to Henry Wilberforce (28 February 1849).

63 LD, 7:216, JHN to J. W. Bowden (17 January 1840).

64 LD, 14:163, JHN to F. W. Faber (8 December 1850).

65 See "St. Paul's Characteristic Gift" (1857), in *Sermons Preached on Various Occasions* (London, 1857), pp. 92–93.

66 See "Newman's Papers No 18," in *Newman the Oratorian*, ed. Placid Murray, O.S.B. (London, 1980), pp. 276–77.

67 See Ian Ker, *John Henry Newman* (Oxford, 2009), pp. 132–33.

68 See Newman's letter, "Temporal Prosperity, Whether a Note of the Church," from the *Rambler* (July 1859), in LD, 19:540.

69 ODNB.

70 See Battiscombe, *John Keble*, p. 312 and ODNB.

71 ODNB.

72 See *Grammar of Assent*, p. 241 and p. 27.

73 Ibid., p. 275.

74   LD, 5:313, JHN to Mrs. John Mozley (26 June 1836).
75   LD, 5:311–12, JHN to Harriett Newman (21 June 1836).
76   LD, 13:419, JHN to Miss Munro (11 February 1850).
77   LD, 17:49, JHN to Ambrose St John (9 November 1855).
78   John Newman's bank was Ramsbottom, Newman and Ramsbottom, 72 Lombard Street.
79   LD, 1:115 JNN to Elizabeth Newman (7 November 1821).
80   See "Christ upon the Waters" (1850), in *Sermons Preached on Various Occasions*, p. 160.
81   LD, 17:49, JHN to Ambrose St. John (9 November 1855).
82   LD, 27:271, JHN to John Stanislaus Flanagan (24 February 1858).
83   *Autobiographical Writings*, p. 249.
84   Ibid., p. 253.
85   LD, 20:30, JHN to Sister Mary Gabriel Du Boulay (18 August 1861).
86   LD, 30:141–2, JHN to Lord Braye (29 October 1882).
87   See Henry Tristram, Introduction to John Henry Newman, *Meditations and Devotions* (London, 1953), pp. xiv–xv.
88   *Meditations and Devotions*, pp. 403–04.

Index

The letter 'n.' indicates an endnote

512

on 'branch theory' 285
and *British Critic* 42, 181, 182, 303
and brother, Frank 89, 138, 208, 249, 268, 306
on George Bull 146
on Catholic Church
  and Anglican Church in England contrasted 41–2, 82, 206–7, 357
  baptism 92, 98, 207
  the Blessed Virgin 75, 125, 128, 130, 207, 391, 392
  Catholics
    devotion among 75, 128–9, 207, 320, 370, 382
    education among 169–70, 190–1, 193, 299–300, 395
    ignorance of before converting 11
  celibacy 398
  Communion of the Saints 67, 97, 143
  the Cross 46, 211
  infallibility of 19, 131, 162, 174, 319
  'invincible ignorance' 55, 61, 155
  Ireland, Catholic priests in 227, 253–4
  the Mass 4, 159, 192, 311, 317–18, 370
  notes of Catholic Church 203, 207–8
  the Rosary 483n. 96
  the Trinity 102, 291, 342
and indefectibility of the Catholic Faith 117, 396
and Catholic University, Dublin 6, 13, 204, 210, 227, 228, 254, 227, 284, 292, 297, 298–9, 302, 394
and Catholicism
  'foreignness' of for the English 61, 197
  as a "living" faith, 128, 131, 158–9
on centralization 173–4, 178
on certainty 113, 144, 154, 284–5, 318, 328

on the rise of Christianity and the "one deep wound of human nature" 158
and the Church Fathers 7, 295
on Cicero 479n. 28
on confession 39, 185, 224
on conscience 155–8, 209, 221, 240–1, 241–2, 333, 349, 358–9
and contemporaries
  Jacob Abbott 283
  Giovanni Achilli 202, 284
  T. W. Allies 103, 134
  Julia Arnold (née Sorrell) 80, 198–9
  Matthew Arnold 15, 53, 59, 305, 336, 337, 341–2, 346, 349, 350–1, 353–4, 355–7, 358–9
  Thomas Arnold (of Rugby) 361
  Thomas Arnold (the Younger) 198
  Lady Arundel 393
  Dominic Barberi 12, 217
  Sir Rowland Blennerhassett 137
  Elizabeth Bowden 82, 84, 110, 298–9
  Mary Anne Bowden 210, 399–400
  Emily Bowles 80, 178–80
  Lord Braye 299, 402
  Edward Burne-Jones 15
  Thomas Carlyle 18
  Lady Georgiana Chatterton 193, 194, 196, 197
  R. W. Church 303, 14, 167, 235, 316, 383
  Arthur Hugh Clough 15, 361, 364–5, 366, 369–70, 376, 377, 378–9, 382
  Auguste Comte 18
  Charles Darwin 18, 137
  Aubrey de Vere viii, 13
  Lord Derby 171
  Benjamin Disraeli 166, 172, 173, 227
  Mary Gabriel Du Boulay 162, 178, 397